Amos Bronson Alcott

Bronson Alcott. By permission of the Louisa May Alcott Memorial Association.

Amos Bronson Alcott

An Intellectual Biography

Frederick C. Dahlstrand

Rutherford • Madison • Teaneck
Fairleigh Dickinson University Press
London and Toronto: Associated University Presses

Associated University Presses, Inc.
4 Cornwall Drive
East Brunswick, N.J. 08816

Associated University Presses
27 Chancery Lane
London WC2A 1NF, England

Associated University Presses
Toronto M5E 1A7, Canada

92
AL19d

82102530

Library of Congress Cataloging in Publication Data

Dahlstrand, Frederick C., 1945–
    Amos Bronson Alcott, an intellectual biography.

    Bibliography: p.
    Includes index.
    1. Alcott, Amos Bronson, 1799–1888. 2. Philosophers—
United States—Biography. I. Title.
B908.A54D33   191 [B]   80-65282
ISBN 0-8386-3016-2   AACR2

Printed in the United States of America

To my mother
Virginia S. Dahlstrand
and in memory of my father
Alton F. Dahlstrand

Contents

Acknowledgments

The rights to quote from the various manuscripts used in this biography were obtained by permission of the Houghton Library, Harvard University; the Concord Free Public Library, Concord, Massachusetts; the Fruitlands Museums, Harvard, Massachusetts; the Massachusetts Historical Society, Boston, Massachusetts; and the Boston Public Library, Boston, Massachusetts. My thanks are here expressed not only for this permission but also for the kindnesses and courtesies extended to me by the staffs of these institutions during my year of research in the Boston area.

I owe a special word of thanks to Mrs. Frederic Wolsey Pratt of Concord, Massachusetts, the owner of the Alcott-Pratt manuscript collection at the Houghton Library. Not only did she grant me oral permission to quote from the manuscripts contingent upon the written permission of the Houghton Library, but she took time to speak with me at length about the manuscripts and about her late husband, the great-grandson of Bronson Alcott.

I also want to thank Professors Daniel H. Bays, Richard Jeske, John S. Macauley, Henry L. Snyder, and Lloyd Sponholtz for their patience in reading this lengthy manuscript and for their helpful suggestions. During the research and preparation of the manuscript I was aided especially by Marcia Moss of the Concord Free Public Library, Jayne Gordon of Orchard House, Joel Myerson of the University of South Carolina, William Henry Harrison, former director of the Fruitlands Museum, and John Chateauneuf, curator of the Concord School of Philosophy, who helped immeasurably with suggestions and with the gathering of illustrations.

This biography would not have been possible without the aid, encouragement, and suggestion of my adviser and dissertation director, Clifford S. Griffin. His wit, wisdom, and incisive intellect sustained both me and the project through two and one-half years of research and writing. No words can adequately express my gratitude to him.

Introduction

Amos Bronson Alcott, peripatetic philosopher and teacher, epitomized nineteenth-century American thought. Through his sometimes brilliant, sometimes erratic mind, amid his sometimes admirable, sometimes aggravating actions, and out of his always warm and sensitive heart, flowed every major intellectual current that shaped American ideas and culture. In a fascinating and captivating way these currents met in him, mingled, and clashed. Lockean sensationalism battled transcendental idealism, and both of these challenged and finally redefined orthodox Christianity. An optimism about the goodness of human nature and the inevitability of human progress struggled against a lurking suspicion that human failings were insurmountable. Grand visions of the potentiality of radicalism and reform alternately flashed and dimmed as they intermixed with peculiar forms of conservatism and reaction. Beautiful and lasting ideas lived amid superstitions, fads, cults, and manias. True to the essence of his epistemology, Alcott looked both within to the powers of his own mind and soul and without to the constantly changing environment to grasp and absorb all of the wonderful diversity and the perplexing paradoxes and contradictions of the nineteenth-century American mind.

One cynic has remarked that Alcott's only lasting contribution to humanity was his daughter Louisa. But that is not true. For in his projects for reform, his writings, his public conversations, his travels, and his family life he grappled with and endeavored to answer and relieve the vexing problems and tensions that have pervaded American life and thought. He attempted to resolve the conflict between religion and science, between human creativity and the shaping power of the environment, between free will and determinism, between freedom and authority, between individualism and the need for community, between the needs of this world and hopes for the next, and between what is lasting and what is constantly changing. The answers he provided were tentative and not wholly satisfactory. But the insight his lifelong search revealed about the nature of these problems and the means necessary for their solution is suggestive and stimulating even today. Out of the rich admixture of ideas, hopes, and feelings that swirled within him came something new and dynamic, which yet retained much that was old, long-revered, and unchanging.

Alcott participated in the nineteenth-century synthesis of evangelical religion with Enlightenment rationalism. At its core transcendentalism was the combination of a faith in the sovereign power of an immanent deity with the equally strong faith in the ability of human beings to manipulate their environment and to control their own destiny. For Alcott this synthesis meant that the human soul actively participated in the creative work of the Universal Spirit, that the human soul was itself divine and of unlimited potential. He spent a lifetime exploring the magnificent possibilities of that faith in human goodness and creativity. The results of his speculation, especially with regard to education, child rearing, and the expansion of human consciousness, are still challenging and exciting.

The broad synthesis of religion and rationalism was the central intellectual impulse to the multifarious reform movements of the mid-nineteenth century. That synthesis was created in the context of rapid social and economic change. Alcott witnessed change in microcosm with the social and economic dislocation experienced by his home town of Wolcott, Connecticut, in the first twenty years of the nineteenth century. His uplifting and sustaining belief in the possibility of reform justified by a religious faith in the power of the human soul for creation and regeneration, helped to explain change and to generate a hopeful assurance that human beings could control change for the betterment and progress of themselves and their world.

Trust in the power of reform led Alcott to accept the widespread nineteenth-century idea of progress. The idea of progress itself was a synthesis of traditional Christian teleological beliefs in God's providential plan for humanity, and the concept fostered by the Enlightenment that human beings had the power to be a part of that plan and to help effect a better world both in the here and now and in the hereafter. Faith in inevitable progress was tied closely to the concept, which Alcott shared, of the special mission and destiny of the United States as the ultimate example of the beneficial effects of human power. Faith in reform, progress, and human potential was naively optimistic, but it provided tremendous ferment and ceaseless activity. It helped undermine and bring down the centuries-old institution of slavery. It provided an intellectual defense of democracy and individual freedom. And as exemplified by Alcott, it was, and still is, a radical challenge to existing institutions and social orders.

Out of the synthesis of religion and rationalism came the most important philosophical question of the nineteenth century: to define the relationship between human beings and their environment, and thus to examine the consequences of human interaction with the forces of nature. This question was at the root of Alcott's intellectual exploration. The guiding impulse of his thought was to explain and defend human free will and human power, the underpinning of his faith in reform, in the face of the powerful molding force of the environment. At first he battled John Locke and the empiricists, who claimed that human knowledge and concomitant human action was the result of the impression of external objects on the mind. Alcott asserted the importance of innate human powers interacting with and manipulating external impressions, thus making human beings active, creative forces. In the same way he confronted the evolutionary naturalism and Darwinism of the late nineteenth century which, in Alcott's opinion, portrayed human beings helplessly caught up in the impersonal determinism of a constantly changing external environment. Fortified by Plato, he defended the power of innate ideas to alter, regulate, and transcend those natural forces. Yet he maintained his respect for scientific laws, for the influence of nature on human beings. Like Ralph Waldo Emerson, he believed that nature was a symbol of the spirit, which by interacting with innate human capabilities awakened spiritual consciousness, the mainspring of human power. His thought, like that of his transcendentalist contemporaries, was catalyzed by European philosophers who were dealing with the same fundamental question—among others, Immanuel Kant, Johann Fichte, and Samuel Taylor Coleridge. His ideas came to parallel Georg W. F. Hegel's belief that human identity was shaped in part by a continuous dialectical interaction with the external environment. Alcott anticipated the radical empiricism of William James, which became the superstructure of pragmatism. In his exploration of the dynamic mingling of innate human powers and the external environment, Alcott came close to James's fundamental perception that each person's concept of truth differs because each person's interaction with external things is unique.

Believers in progress, democracy, freedom, and human potential, like Alcott, also wished to preserve traditional moral and cultural values—the family, belief in God, sexual purity, clean living—in the face of rapid change. Thus they were not always willing to accept the logical consequences of their emotional and uplifting belief in human freedom. Alcott's attempt to reconcile the free individual with order and morality represented in microcosm a fundamental American problem. Democracy presented the same difficulty. Alcott celebrated human equality and human potential; he hated formal class structures. But he was still suspicious that the unenlightened masses were a danger to culture, morality, and true freedom. In his later years, as his faith in human goodness diminished, Alcott's reform impulse, reflecting that of many of the antebellum reformers, turned toward regulating morality rather than liberating human creativity and expression. Alcott's career as a reformer illustrated the virtues as well as the inconsistencies and failures of the broad tradition of American reform.

Alcott also directly confronted the conflict between the centrifugal force of American individualism, mobility, and free choice, and the social need for the bonds of community and family. Throughout his life he tried to balance the two. He strove to maintain the security, stability, and virtue of the cohesive community—a life he had known as a youth—and he developed a philosophy that celebrated the spiritual effects of interaction among human beings. He tried to formulate a spiritual community in his schools, at Fruitlands, in his public conversations, and in his chosen community of Concord. Yet at the same time he maintained a strong faith in individualism, free expression, and nonconformity. He both enjoyed and abhorred loneliness and solitude. A lifetime of wandering—first as a peddler in the South and then as an itinerant conversationalist—symbolized the tension he felt. He wanted the freedom and excitement of travel and exploration and resented leaving his home and family. His efforts to relieve this tension provide an invaluable look at the meaning of both freedom and community in American society.

Alcott was a perplexing but captivating man. He was an unschooled farmer whose innate intelligence and sensitivity drove him from manual labor to the world of books and academe, of the literati, of the genteel upper class. Yet he took part in intellectual developments without commitments to institutions and social classes. As a result his response to those developments differed considerably from that of his intellectual peers, who were in part defenders of such institutions and class structures. Thus he became more iconoclastic and extravagantly rebellious than most of his contemporaries, making his ideas singularly challenging and provocative. His life was a work of art, flawed but beautiful. He led a fascinating, a full, and a rich life. He could be exasperating, irritating, obnoxious, even silly. Truly Emerson's "tedious archangel," he could be both profound and nonsensical in the same breath. But on the whole his life was inspiring, exemplary, eminently successful, and lived unflinchingly in accordance with his ideals. He offered both hope for the future and reverence for the past. And he did so with a vision of the spiritual nature of human life that encompassed both change and the unchanging.

Amos Bronson Alcott

1

The Yankee Peddler, 1799–1825

DURING his first twenty-five years Bronson Alcott directly confronted the unsettling tensions that became the major themes of his life. Socially, he experienced both the desire for a stable community and family life and the captivating urge to travel, to explore and to break away from what was a stagnating and decaying small-town society. Intellectually, he fought the perplexing battle between the two great motive forces in American thought in the nineteenth century: an evangelical religion that stressed the belief in a transcendent and sovereign God who demanded unquestioning faith from human beings, and an Enlightenment rationalism that upheld the creative and manipulative power of human beings to order their own affairs both morally and intellectually. The social context and intellectual milieu in which Alcott grew up helped determine his singular responses to these problems. The Connecticut of Alcott's boyhood and youth was undergoing rapid and far-reaching social and economic change. This change disrupted farming communities such as Alcott's home town and forced a confrontation between mobility and stability and between adventure and security. Alcott's early years were also a time of religious revival in his home state, known as the Second Great Awakening. The resultant emotional energy and intellectual ferment demanded answers to the questions of the nature of God, the power of the human mind, the source of moral standards, and the value of ecclesiastical traditions and sectarian loyalties. Bronson Alcott was innately a genius with remarkable sensitivity and insight and great intellectual powers. Those internal qualities enabled him to respond to the social and intellectual currents surrounding him in a way that few of his contemporaries could.

Bronson Alcott was born on November 29, 1799, in Wolcott, Connecticut, a tiny farming community located twenty miles directly north of New Haven on the hills surrounding the valley of the Mad River. Alcott was proud of his hometown and of his English Puritan ancestors who helped settle it. The first American Alcott—the name was spelled Alcocke then—had accompanied John Winthrop from England in 1630. Thomas Alcocke had been a freeman and a landowner in the early Massachusetts Bay colony and a member of the covenant of the First Church in Boston. Some of Thomas Alcocke's descendants had migrated to Connecticut in the mid-seventeenth century, settling first at New Haven and then at Waterbury. The reasons for their departure are not clear. Like many colonists they may have been attracted by the chance for greater economic opportunities in the Connecticut Valley. Or like Thomas Hooker and his followers they may have been dissatisfied with religious and political conditions in Massachusetts Bay. Alcott's mother's ancestors, the Bronsons (or Brownsons), had come to the Connecticut Valley with Thomas Hooker's congregation in 1634.[1]

Alcott's great-grandfather, John Alcocke, had been a selectman and surveyor of highways for the town of Waterbury even after he and his family moved a few miles to the northeast in 1731 and settled the area that became the town of Wolcott. The constant threat of malarial fevers caused by the lowland dampness around Waterbury had forced John Alcocke and his contemporaries to the hills. In 1770 the scattered settlers who had followed Alcocke to his mountainous retreat came together on the authority of the colonial General Assembly and formed a congregation. They had first named their community Farmingbury, because they had largely come from Farmington and Waterbury. But in 1796 the Connecticut state government granted them the right of incorporation, and they changed their town's name to Wolcott in honor of the state's second governor, Oliver Wolcott.[2]

Alcott grew up in a happy, stable, close-knit family. His father, Joseph Chatfield Alcox, was a shy, quiet, mild-tempered, conscientious man. Alcott claimed that it was from his father that he inherited his mechanical ability, his love of order and neatness, his sense of justice, and his bashfulness. But his mother, Anna Bronson Alcox, had the greater influence on him. Her love had "christened his conscience," he believed, and her presence had brought quiet and order to the home and the neighborhood. Throughout his life Alcott maintained that there had been no stronger influence on him than his mother's piety and faith. "I know not," he said, "what felicity of humor, what strength of wit can add aught to the Faith my mother gave me, and question whether any shall take it away." Joseph and Anna Alcox had ten children, two of whom died shortly after birth. Of those who lived, Bronson was the oldest. He and his four sisters and three brothers enjoyed a loving and morally sure home life. His later views about education, child rearing, and the importance of parental and family influence in the development of moral culture grew out of his own family experiences.[3]

Like most of Connecticut in the early nineteenth century, Wolcott's economy was agricultural, although each family usully supplemented its income by engaging in various domestic handicrafts. Alcott's mother pulled flax, as did most other Wolcott women, and his father made plows, rakes, boxes, baskets, and brooms for local sale. The hill on which John Alcocke had settled and on which Bronson Alcott was born was called Spindle Hill because of the household crafts associated with it.[4]

Agriculture in Wolcott was typical of that of Connecticut in general. Farms were small. Farmers lacked knowledge of improvements in agricultural technique and efficiency. Their wooden plows barely scratched the surface of a rocky and already impoverished soil. Often they scattered their homegrown seeds over an unharrowed field. The Napoleonic Wars were creating a tremendous market for agricultural goods in Europe during the first decade of the nineteenth century, but Connecticut farmers were unable to produce enough to take advantage of it. The hilly terrain made the problems of the Wolcott farmers no easier. Muddy, rut-filled roads forbade significant extension of the local market. Joseph Alcox generally grew his crops for his own family's consumption and sold his wares to other farmers in Wolcott. Only on occasion would he risk taking a wagon load of grain or his hand-made farm implements to Waterbury or New Haven.[5]

Life for the twelve hundred residents of Wolcott during Alcott's boyhood was rugged and severe, a "steady toiling for bread." But such arduous labor produced a sympathy and a spirit of cooperation among the inhabitants. Similarity of economic position, as well as the ethnic and religious homogeneity of the population, helped preserve a stable, close-knit community life. The entire community attended services together at the meeting house on Sunday. All inhabitants observed the Sabbath strictly in their activities and behavior. All play was forbidden from sundown on Saturday until sundown on Sunday. On Sundays children struggled to memorize the text of the sermon of the day, while their parents were glued to their Bibles and catechisms. But on the other days of the week there were more light-hearted activities. Alcott fondly recalled community corn huskings, sleigh rides, dances, apple-gathering parties, and spelling bees. Each Saturday in the summer the young boys would gather at the stream by the mill for a swim before sundown. Alcott's earliest memory was of a quilting party with dancing led by a black fiddler and the serving of yellow custard, the delight of the five-year-old boy.[6]

Wolcott was an egalitarian community. Its homogeneity and general equality of economic position minimized any class or caste divisions. The only distinction in seating at the meeting house was by age. But with social democracy and equality came social conformity. Life in Wolcott was full of unwritten laws and unbending customs. It was no accident that everyone attended church on Sunday, and that all farmers painted their homes the standard red. Alcott later rebelled against the restraints of this traditional community, but his experience in it made him sensitive to a recurring problem in American society: the need to preserve a sense of community, with its stability, neighborly conviviality, spirit of cooperation, and secure value system, in the face of rapid social, economic, political, and intellectual change.[7]

Alcott's formal education was limited and sketchy. Class work was always secondary to his duties on the farm and in his father's workshop. From ages six to ten he attended the little Spindle Hill District School near his home. This school was no better or worse than most public schools in the state at the time. It was supported by the Connecticut School Fund, and it operated each year only as long as there was money in the Fund to keep it going. The school taught only reading, writing, and spelling, and it did so in a most uninviting atmosphere. The building was located near the junction of four roads, unprotected from the wind and the sun and the noise of passing carriages and wagons. The twenty-two-by-twenty-foot room was poorly ventilated and dirty. There were no decorations or pictures to please the eye. The rough-hewn, backless benches gave the pupils no comfort or rest. In the winter the room was heated by a large wood stove, which made it uncomfortably cold in the mornings and insufferably hot later in the day. Teachers, often only sixteen to eighteen years old, were underpaid and poorly trained. Discipline was their chief concern, and they were not hesitant to use the rod and the ferule to maintain it. Yet the community expected the school-masters to be of high moral character. They were to open each school day with a prayer and to read to the class from the New Testament and the catechism as frequently as possible. Besides the Bible, school books included Caleb Bingham's *American Preceptor*, Nathaniel Dwight's *Geography*, and the book common to all American primary education in the early nineteenth century, Noah Webster's *American Spelling Book*.[8]

At age thirteen Alcott went to nearby Cheshire, Connecticut, to work as an errand boy for his uncle, the Reverend Tillotson Bronson. He intended to supplement the family's income and at the same time to further his education by attending the district school in Cheshire. But the stuffy attitude of his fellow students in Cheshire oppressed him, and he was inconsolably homesick. He returned to Wolcott after only two months. Two years later he attended a school conducted by the Reverend John Keyes, the Congregationalist minister in Wolcott, but found little advantage in it and withdrew after a few months. Such was the extent of his formal education.[9]

Alcott's most significant education came through his own efforts. He was an intelligent and precocious individual who had a natural fascination with books and intellectual conversation. His youthful searching for knowledge was heroic enough to become part of the American myth of the self-made man. He borrowed books whenever he could. Since his family often had no money for paper, pen, and ink, he would trace out letters in the snow or write with chalk on his mother's well-scrubbed floor. When he did obtain paper he kept a diary and wrote notes in it from his reading in John Bunyan's *Pilgrim's Progress*, John Milton's *Paradise Lost*, James Hervey's *Meditations among the Tombs*, Daniel Defoe's *Robinson Crusoe*, and James Burgh's *Dignity of Human Nature*. He later claimed that his happiest experiences as a youth took place in the south room of the homestead, where he could retire to read and write.[10]

Few people in Wolcott read anything more than passages from the Bible and rarely wrote anything but their names. Most were too busy tilling the soil to spend time discussing philosophical questions. The town had no library, and good books were not easy to find. But Alcott was fortunate to find a kindred spirit in his second cousin, William Andrus Alcott. William Alcott was two years older than Bronson. His father, David Alcocke, was the brother of Bronson's grandfather. William also kept journals, borrowed books, and relished intellectual discussions. The two often studied together in the evenings and compared notes on the books they read. As teenagers they would walk two miles each weekend to the little crossroads called Woodtick to obtain New Haven newspapers. They corresponded with each other regularly, and together founded a small local library. "[William] was moderate, plain, punctual, a little superstitious and distrustful," Bronson later said, "while I was confident, sanguine, disposed to extravagance in action and ideas. If he restrained, I prompted, and we thus balanced and complemented each other."[11]

Both Alcotts were conscious of being different from the average Connecticut farmboy. When attending the district school Bronson took pride in classroom excellence. He was often the teacher's favorite and won prizes in penmanship, which gave him the preferred seat in the classroom. His only rival for academic honors was cousin William. One of them always won the town spelling bees.[12] In their teenage correspondence they attempted to avoid what considered the uncultivated colloquialisms of local speech by trying to copy the supposedly more elegant style they found in the newspapers. As a result their letters were pompous and stilted and revealed the arrogance and sense of superiority they felt in their relationships with their peers:

Wolcott, August 27th, Saturday, 1 PM 1814 Venerable Sir [William Alcott],
Improving the present variety in writing to you, with the greatest pleasure; hoping to receive the receipt of a letter from you before long, concerning our Libraric Institution. Perhaps it is best to appoint an attendance at some proper place to consult on the project; but, sir, your opinion of the matter would be Satisfactory to me. Why not as well improve our money in that way, as to spend it in going to Balls, or some useless, Nonsensical Object!...

I am Sir,
Sincerely Yours,
Amos B. Alcox[13]

Bronson and William often complained that money for books seemed much scarcer in Wolcott than money for the frivolous play and diversions of some of their friends. Their community had in large measure shaped their lives and determined their values and beliefs, yet they felt themselves to be above it, able to judge it and even to change it.[14]

Alcott's personal characteristics—his contemplative nature, his penchant for scholarly activity, even his quiet arrogance—helped dictate his response to the religious currents that confronted him as a youth. Religion formed a major part of his intellectual development, as it did of most Americans in the early nineteenth century. There were three main aspects to Alcott's early religious experience. First, and most important, was the personal piety and faith he gained through the example of his parents, particularly his mother. This sincere faith and its inspiration were complemented and solidified by his reading of John Bunyan's classic Puritan allegory, *Pilgrim's Progress*.[15]

Alcott had first read *Pilgrim's Progress* in 1811, having borrowed it from his cousin Riley Alcox. As a sensitive and impressionable reader, he readily identified with Christian and allowed the pilgrimage and the search to be motif for his own life experience, a symbolic vision of the relationship between God and humanity, between God and an individual. He later felt that the allegory had established the basis for his concept of himself. "More than any work of genius, more than all other books," he claimed, "the Dreamer's Dream brought me into living acquaintance with myself, my duties. . . ." He cared little about, nor did he fully understand, the theology of *Pilgrim's Progress*. True to John Calvin, it emphasized the sovereignty of God, regeneration by faith alone, and the powerlessness of human beings without God's guiding hand. But the attraction of the allegory for Alcott was its emotional power, its imagery, and the sense of meaning and purpose it gave to life. The counsel of "Mr. Worldly Wiseman" led Christian away from the "strait gate" to "Morality" and "Legality." But Christian, guided by faith alone, avoided this error and followed the path to righteousness and salvation. For Alcott this meant that personal faith and love superseded all structures of denomination or churchly tradition. Above all, Alcott's religious belief involved the heart, the inner consciousness. It was an intense relationship between an individual human being and God.[16]

The second aspect of Alcott's youthful religious experience was his interaction with the religious revival that was sweeping Connecticut during the first two decades of the nineteenth century. The Connecticut revival was part of the larger Second Great Awakening that was affecting all of American Protestantism. Initially, it was led in Connecticut by Congregationalist clergymen as a reaction to eighteenth-century rationalism, deism, and "irreligion." The ministers were making a concerted effort to instill a renewed fervor into the spiritual life of the state. In 1800 the *Connecticut Evangelical Magazine* was founded to encourage revivalism. And in 1801 Timothy Dwight, the grandson of the great leader of the first Awakening, Jonathan Edwards, converted one-third of the Yale College student body to the New Divinity. By 1810 revivals had become almost continuous on a local basis, and were to be characteristic of Congregational life in Connecticut for the next two or three generations.[17]

Although the Connecticut revivals were influenced to some extent by contemporary Western camp meetings, they were calm and sober in comparison. Evidence of God's grace came not by means of ecstatic outcries, bodily distortions, and general tumult, but rather through a renewed spiritual seriousness on the part of parishioners and through the reformation of public and private morals. A variety of religious and philanthropic societies sprang up in the state symbolizing and institutionalizing the zeal for goodness and spirituality. The Connecticut Bible Society sent Bibles to Western emigrants. The Connecticut Society for the Promotion of Good Morals labored furiously to prevent profanity, idleness, intemperance, and breaches of the Sabbath. And the Domestic Missionary Society of Connecticut aimed to save backsliders and to convert infidels in the Godless "waste places" of the state.[18]

Wolcott was certainly no "waste place." Bronson Alcott experienced his own personal revival through *Pilgrim's Progress* and the piety of his family. The Congregational ministers in Wolcott during his boyhood and youth, Israel Beard Woodward and John Keyes, brought with them the intensity of conviction encouraged by the New Divinity. And Lyman Beecher, the greatest leader of the revival in Connecticut, who came to the pulpit in nearby Litchfield in 1810, preached the ordination sermon for Keyes in Wolcott. His powerful presence in the pulpit left a lasting impression on young Alcott.[19]

The Congregational revival was important to Alcott not because of any conversion experience he received from it or for any specific theological mark it left on him. Rather, it was important because the leaders of Congregational theology were grappling with the very problems that Alcott found so troubling even in his youth: the connection between evangelical religion and Enlightenment rationalism. The leading theologians of the Congregational revival, Timothy Dwight, Nathaniel William Taylor, and Lyman Beecher, were attempting to synthesize those two great streams of American thought. Their theology affirmed the sovereignty of God, yet left plenty of room for the moral and intellectual agency of human beings in the work of salvation. In effect, the leaders of the revival believed that human beings could aid in their own regeneration by attending church, reading the Bible, praying regularly, and living a moral and upright life. The Calvinism that the New Divinity rebelled against had denied the efficacy of human participation in the work of salvation and had proclaimed redemption by God's grace alone. But Dwight, Taylor, and Beecher were children of the Enlightenment as well as heirs of Calvinist theology. Thus they asserted that human beings, as free, rational, and creative causes in the world, had the power to avoid sin and thereby facilitate the working of God's grace. The Congregational revival had effected a compromise with rationalism similar to that accomplished by Unitarianism in Massachusetts. In fact, the strength of Congregational leadership and the fervor of their New Divinity prevented substantial inroads by Unitarianism into the state. In the 1820s Samuel J. May's parish in Plymouth was the only Unitarian congregation in Connecticut.[20]

But the Congregational synthesis of religion and rationalism as he understood it was not satisfactory to Alcott. It was deficient in the same way that Alcott later found Massachusetts Unitarianism deficient. The New Divinity upheld the traditional Puritan emphasis on "God's moral government," with its adherence to social conformity, decorum, and law and order, at the expense of the emotional, mystical element of Puritanism that Alcott had found attractive about *Pilgrim's Progress* and his mother's personal piety. The effort to avoid sin and lead the righteous life through human agency, though it encouraged humanitarianism and reform, often led to a stifling moral legalism. It was Lyman Beecher who most effectively linked the evangelism of the revival with moral reform and social benevolence. And it was the same Lyman Beecher who led the crusade against Sabbath breaking, profanity, and intemperance. He was the man most responsible for the establishment of the Connecticut Society for the Promotion of Good Morals in 1813.[21]

Alcott's later career as an educational reformer found him in sympathy with many of the humanitarian reform efforts of the Congregational revival, such as the voluntary agencies serving the poor, the Hartford Retreat for the Insane, and the Reverend Thomas Gallaudet's Hartford Asylum for the Education of Deaf and Dumb. But even as a teenager he was repelled by the coldness, the harshness, and the legalism he found in the Congregational Church. The result was the third major aspect of Alcott's early religious experience: his participation in a broad movement of dissent from the established church in Connecticut.[22]

Congregationalism was the legally established church in Connecticut until 1818. Church membership and tithing were mandatory. Prospective office holders had to pass a test affirming their belief in the Westminster Confession. The Congregationalists controlled the religious content of education both at Yale College and in the public schools. There was a stong alliance between Congregational leaders and the Federalist Party in state and local government. Revivalism became political as it lashed out against the supposed infidelity of Thomas Jefferson and the Republicans in national office. But the revival spirit had also affected the dissenting churches, mainly the Episcopalians, Baptists, Methodists. Even by 1800, the numbers of dissenting congregations had increased sharply. A growing number of people not only lamented the prevailing irreligion but rebelled against the strictures of Calvinism.[23]

The most important dissent came from the Episcopal Church. From its reorganization in the 1790s to the War of 1812, its membership steadily increased, as did the number of its local churches. By 1812 the Connecticut Episcopalians had their own journal, the *Churchman's Monthly Magazine*, and a school, the Cheshire Academy. The latter was founded in 1801 to offset the Congregational bias at Yale. Often dissent arose from conflicts within local churches. Such a conflict began in Wolcott in the 1790s because of the reaction by some townspeople against the strict church discipline required by the Reverend Alexander Gillett. At length this led to a movement toward Episcopalianism in Alcott's hometown, which culminated in the formation of an Episcopal Society there in 1811.[24]

Alcott's immediate family was directly involved in the religious conflict in Wolcott. Anna Alcox had been reared an Episcopalian. Her brother, Tillotson Bronson, had been rector of St. John's Church in Waterbury from 1795 to 1805 and had subsequently become editor of the *Churchman's Magazine* and principal of the Cheshire Academy. Alcott's parents, despite his mother's Episcopal background, had attended Wolcott's Congregational Church and had dutifully introduced their eldest son to the Westminster Confession. But the "extreme Calvinism" of the Reverend Israel Beard Woodward drove them to the dissenters in 1808. Thereafter they attended Episcopal services in private homes, at the Spindle Hill school house, and occasionally at St. John's.[25]

Alcott did not follow his parents into Episcopalianism right away. They judiciously allowed their teenage son to choose his denomination and to fashion a religious faith of his own. Thus he continued to attend the Congregational Church, listened with awe to Lyman Beecher's ordination sermon for John Keyes, and chose to study under Keyes for a few months in 1814. By 1816, however, he had decided that Congregationalism no longer satisfied him. He and William, joining the "signers-off from Calvin's colder creed," became lay readers at the Episcopal services at the schoolhouse. On October 16, 1816, Bronson, William, and Joseph Chatfield Alcox all took the final step in becoming Episcopalians by undergoing confirmation at St. John's.[26]

The importance of Alcott's experience as a dissenter did not lie in his acceptance of any specific theological position. Clearly, his decision to leave Congregationalism resulted from his rejection of its cold legalism and his hope that the ritual and ceremony of Episcopalianism would be more emotionally and spiritually satisfying. But he quickly rejected Episcopalianism too. The freedom his parents had given him to choose among denominations, as well as their rejection of a legally established church body, called into question the validity of all sectarian distinctions. His sensitivity and perceptiveness led him to question whether a meaningful personal faith could depend on tradition or dogma or church structure. Denominational battles brought only rancor and bitterness. Piety and spirituality were matters of inward, personal experience. His dissent represented the beginning of a lifelong crusade against sectarianism and a search for spiritual awareness outside organized religion.

Along with his participation in the heightened religious awareness of revivalism, his personal exploration into the long tradition of Puritan piety, and his experience as a dissenter, the young Alcott became enthusiastically interested in Enlightenment rationalism. The Enlightenment, based on the physics of Isaac Newton and the epistemology of John Locke, had exalted the power of human reason to manipulate the environment, to order and regulate worldly institutions, and to explain the natural world in a systematic, verifiable way. It raised the troubling questions of the relationship between this human power and the power of God, and the extent of human free will. These were the questions that Jonathan Edwards had tried to answer in the mid-eighteenth century, and that his spiritual heirs, Dwight, Beecher, and Taylor, were still wrestling with. Alcott's first lengthy introduction to Enlightenment rationalism came with his reading of Englishman James Burgh's *Dignity of Human Nature* (1794). He first read the book in 1817, and he did so as avidly as he had read *Pilgrim's Progress*.[27]

Burgh believed that human beings had within them the power to become virtuous and happy by means of education and personal discipline. He assumed that there were definite moral laws of the universe that paralleled the physical laws described by Newton. If human beings would only make use of their God-given mental faculties to recognize and conform to these moral laws, Burgh said, they could make themselves a better life on earth and prepare the way for their own salvation. Like the New Divinity theologians, Burgh was attempting to integrate rationalism with traditional ideas of theology and morality. But in doing so he placed so much emphasis on human ability and the discipline of the rational human faculties that he obscured the place of God and the supernatural in the work of salvation. He defined salvation and regeneration in terms of secular pursuits and secular reformation. Human action and preparation superseded the work of supernatural agencies. Burgh presented Alcott with the burden, but also the exciting challenge, of self-improvement, even self-regeneration. More than any other this book gave Alcott the impetus to look to education and the development of the human mind as instruments for saving the world.[28]

His religious experiences and his interest in rationalism, as focused in his reading of Bunyan and Burgh, left Alcott with powerful and unavoidable tensions in his thought. The pietism of *Pilgrim's Progress* stressed an emotional reliance on the grace of God operating above any human power, a mystical faith in a sovereign deity. Yet Burgh left Alcott with an equally powerful faith in human ability, human freedom, and human creativity. It remained for him to try to reconcile and synthesize those faiths, to relate the power of God to the power of human beings in bringing about otherworldly salvation and this-worldly reformation. He lacked the guidance of a formal higher education. The best books were out of reach. There were few intelligent associates with whom he could discuss his philosophical and religious questions. He was not fully aware of the parallel intellectual synthesis being made by the New Divinity theologians. He rejected Congregational theology because of its coldness and its legalism, and as a result he failed to find help from it in his intellectual search. Unquestionably, he never appreciated its subtleties and its depth. Had he been able to fulfill his onetime dream of attending Yale, and had he then studied under Nathaniel William Taylor, he might well have discovered the spirituality he sought but missed in the preaching of Woodward and Keyes. Later in his life he rediscovered Congregational theology and recognized its affinity with his own transcendental synthesis of religion and rationalism. Taylor and the New Divinity at Yale produced Horace Bushnell, whose belief in the participation of human beings in supernatural life and the immanence of God in nature Alcott later welcomed and appreciated. However, as a youth, Alcott never had the opportunity to explore Congregational theology further. Thus his own intellectual synthesis took a different direction, with fascinating and far-reaching results.[29]

The intellectual questions Alcott confronted came in the context of social and economic change and disruption. Such change brought decay to his hometown community and dislocation to many young people such as Alcott. The result was exciting, challenging, and adventuresome. It led Alcott to a life of traveling and seeking new experiences and opportunities. But it was also troublesome. It brought personal rootlessness, insecurity, challenges to traditional values, uncertainty about vocation, and a desperate search to find meaning in life. For Alcott personal dislocation left him with a feeling of guilt at having fecklessly squandered his opportunities and disappointed his parents. But with the help of his developing ideas about religion and human nature, he finally managed to reconcile himself to change. He even came to celebrate change as a force for human progress. When he had accomplished this reconciliation and had transferred his personal guilt to the failures of society and its institutions, he became an iconoclast and a reformer.

The years of Alcott's boyhood were years of rapid economic change in Connecticut. The first quarter of the nineteenth century brought a steady rise in manufacturing and a concomitant decline in agriculture. Connecticut's poor soil, like that of New England generally, made the expansion of farming from subsistence to a commercial venture difficult. The more enterprising of Connecticut's citizens, anxious to take advantage of the growing national market system, and having access to increasing amounts of capital created by the shipping trade, began to turn to manufacturing. The disastrous effects of the Embargo and the War of 1812 on Connecticut shipping and on markets for agricultural products further hastened these developments. Early Connecticut factories produced textiles, leather goods, flaxseed oil, glassward, pottery, tinware, combs, suspenders, clocks, and other "Yankee notions" for which there was a nationwide as well as a local demand.[30]

The growth of manufacturing and factory production inevitably drew people, especially young people, from declining farm towns to cities or manufacturing towns. In the years between 1790 and 1820 the only Connecticut towns experiencing any population growth were those involved in manufacturing. Agricultural decline forced farmers either to move to the factories or to head west, where there was a promise of better farm land. Alcott's father had caught the westering fever in 1804, and attempted to move his family to upstate New York. But the land agents with whom he had dealt had sold him a false claim, and he had had to return to Wolcott. Many of Alcott's young contemporaries scurried out of Wolcott for opportunities in the factories, often leaving the management of the farms to the less capable and the less ambitious. At age fourteen Alcott went to work at Silas Hoadley's clock factory not far from Wolcott. Hoadley, along with Seth Thomas, was an associate of Connecticut-born Eli Terry, who was a pioneer in the mechanization of clock production. Alcott, however, was unimpressed by the wonders of factory technology, felt oppressed by factory labor, and left after only a few months.[31]

Many of those who did not head for the factories joined the growing numbers of Yankee peddlers who traveled throughout the West and the South selling the products of new England factories. By 1820 peddling had become a mania, a kind of gold fever. It provided a unique means of marketing manufactured goods as well as an outlet for discontented or venturesome youth. No less than ten young Wolcottians headed South during each of several seasons around 1820, selling pins, needles, hooks and eyes, scissors, razors, combs, buttons, tinware, books, and even clocks and chairs.[32]

Alcott later lamented the demise of his home community. "I survey the spot with sadness," he declared on a visit to Wolcott in 1873 as he viewed the barren fields, the broken fences, and the decay to which once-prosperous farms had fallen. He recalled how his own family had dispersed. His brothers and sisters had moved westward or to the cities, and his mother had abandoned the homestead to live with her daughter Betsey in Oriskany Falls, New York, after Alcott's father died in 1829. He felt that the crucial turning point for the town had been its failures to take advantage of a chance for a railroad and a chance to attract Seth Thomas's clock factory. But he failed to understand that a railroad and a clock factory would have created a very different community from the one he had known in his youth.[33]

It was the simple, hard working, neighborly farm community that Alcott later idealized and romanticized. His attempt to establish a New Eden at Fruitlands in 1843 and his lifelong concern about the need for community life in America reflected, in part, his desire to return to the lost Eden of his youth. His generation was among the earliest to experience the stirrings of industrialization and the attendant social upheaval. He and many of his contemporaries later lauded technological progress, improvements in communication and transportation, and the concomitant expansion of opportunities for knowledge and experience. Yet they mourned the loss of the security and stability of traditional community and family life, and they sought ways to preserve them as a part of the new order.[34]

Nevertheless, as a curious, intelligent, and adventurous youth, Alcott fully cooperated in destroying his boyhood community. He personified the tension in American culture between the desire for movement, expansion, growth, and adventure, and the equally strong need to preserve traditions and values. His thirst for new information and new experiences led him to condemn the artless and toilsome life in Wolcott. He sought out the *New Haven Register* and the *Hartford Courant* and read of the War of 1812, of battles with Indians on the frontier, of Jefferson, Madison, and Jackson. He and William tried to cast away the uncultivated speech of their family and neighbors by mimicking the supposed refinement they read about in other parts of the country. At fifteen he took up peddling and traveled into western Massachusetts with his cousin Thomas to sell small articles from door to door. The next year he ventured into western New York, hawking subscriptions to John Flavel's *Treatise on Keeping the Heart*, a sentimental religious tract.[35]

In October 1818 Alcott sailed from New Haven to Norfolk, Virginia, following the route of the Yankee peddlers. His original intention was not to peddle, but to teach. The district school committee in Wolcott, which accepted anyone who was literate, had examined and approved him as a teacher the previous year. But he had felt ill-prepared to teach in New England and thought it best to gain experience by enlightening Southerners, whom he supposed were generally more ignorant than people in the North. He arranged to meet a score of pupils in Kempsville, some twenty miles from Norfolk, but found to his mortification that Southerners were hostile to condescending

Yankees. No one in Kempsville would give him board or lodging. He then resorted to peddling to get the support and companionship of other Northern youths in the same business. Throughout the winter and spring of 1819 he sold small housewares around Norfolk, and then walked back to Connecticut, peddling along the way. He arrived in time to help his father with the spring planting. And he had made enough to buy a new suit of clothes and to contribute eighty dollars to the new house his father was building.[36]

The South had surprised Alcott. His peddling had taken him to several impressively elegant plantations near Norfolk. Instead of the expected ignorance, he found the kind of polish and sophistication that was lacking in Wolcott. And so in November 1819 he again sailed for Norfolk, this time accompanied by his younger brother Chatfield. His primary purpose was to raise money for the new house, but he also hoped to improve his knowledge of the world and humanity by "intercourse with the cultivated classes of the South." In January 1820 he reported to his parents of "fair success," but said that he felt self-conscious at being "a homespun Yankee without manners" amidst the aristocratic Virginia planters.[37]

Alcott was awed by the lifestyle on the plantations. He found on them a school of manners equal to any in Europe. And rude though he was, the planters welcomed him. "Hospitality is a distinguishing trait of the people, whether rich or poor," he wrote to cousin William, "and the graceful behavior, polished manner, suavity, and agreeable conversation ingratiate the traveller at once in their favor." He quickly began to contrast the exciting "prodigality and gaiety" of the South with the "sobriety and closeness" of the North. The impressionable young peddler confided to his journal his increasing dislike of Yankees and his growing enthusiasm for Virginians. Despite his admitted "diffidence"—he was so shy as a young boy that he would scarcely look anyone in the eye—he found conversing and socializing with the planters enjoyable. Some of them invited him into their libraries and plush reading rooms. It was in one of them in 1820 that he first read John Locke's *Essay Concerning Human Understanding*, which would have a great impact on him later in his career.[38]

Throughout his life Alcott remained fascinated by aristocracy, awed by nobility, and respectful of gentility. Yet at the same time he celebrated democracy, talked of social revolution, romanticized the homely village life, and lashed out against custom, creed, and usage. Though he accused the people of Wolcott of being rude, ignorant, and uncultivated, he praised them for being free of the "vices" of cultivated society. This tension in his thought reflected a similar tension in American culture generally. It was further evidence of the need to integrate secure and stable values with a world of rapid change.[39]

Alcott's trek through the Virginia plantations gave him a firsthand glimpse of slavery. It disturbed him, but he had not yet become an irreconcilable opponent of the slave system and was able to write about it with objectivity. He saw very little cruelty and even noticed a graceful, genial relationship between master and slave. The planters, he discovered, often denounced slavery themselves and claimed that it was as bad or worse of the whites as for the blacks. Yet one planter warned him that he should not talk too freely with the slaves, particularly about emancipation. He was often given sleeping quarters with the slaves, and found them civil toward him. He never saw one chained or tortured, although he knew they were subject to abuse, especially from the sometimes cruel overseers. In his abolitionist days he reflected that his worshipful attitude toward the planters may well have blinded him to the true enormities of slavery.[40]

He returned to Connecticut in June 1820, but in October he enthusiastically began a third Southern excursion. This time he sailed from New Haven to Charleston, South Carolina, hoping that he could avoid peddling there and find a teaching job. It was the prospect of teaching that enabled him to lure his studious and reserved cousin William out of Wolcott for the first time to accompany him. After enduring seasickness, poor food, a tyrannical captain, and the conversation of "blackguards and buffoons" on the voyage south, the cousins sent their trunks ahead by wagon and walked the one hundred eighty miles to Newbury, near Columbia, South Carolina, sleeping on beds of pine needles along the way. To their dismay, they found that school sessions had already begun and that they faced a two-month wait before any teaching positions would be available. They had no recourse but to peddle. Seeking a familiar area in which to buy and sell their wares, they walked to Norfolk, Virginia, some five hundred miles away, trudging through deep sand, fording rivers, traveling from dawn to dusk across the monotonous countryside for nearly three weeks. They had peddled in the Norfolk area for only a month or so when Bronson became dangerously ill with "typhus fever" (typhoid) as a result of drinking bad water. The faithful William gave up his own peddling to nurse Bronson back to health, risking his own life and limbs to keep bedridden his sometimes deliriously fitful cousin.[41]

After his recovery Bronson Alcott returned to peddling, but through "ill management and mischance," he overextended himself and fell heavily in debt to the Norfolk merchant from whom he bought his goods. Nevertheless, he arrived home in the summer of 1821 with an expensive broadcloth purchased in New York City in a fit of extravagance, and he "startled plain Wolcott" by flaunting his new garments at church. Unfortunately, these ventures forced Joseph Alcox to pledge his life savings to pay off his son's debt.[42]

With the hope of improving his financial condition, Alcott left with cousin Thomas and brother Chatfield for Richmond, Virginia, in October 1821. Finding little profit in peddling near Richmond, he agreed to teach penmanship to a dozen students in Warrenton, Virginia, during April and May 1822. Again his improvidence caught up with him. His school did not pay enough to meet the cost of the expensive inn where he was staying. To avoid his creditors, he stole away from Warrenton one night and fled—like a runaway slave, he later said—back to Wolcott.[43]

Still trying to straighten out his finances, he headed south again in October

1822. He and Thomas Alcott drove by horse and wagon to Chowan County, North Carolina, just south of Norfolk. Cousin William had written to him shortly before he left, criticizing him severely for his conduct, especially his thoughtlessness in burdening his parents with debt and disappointment. Alcott was filled with remorse. He penitently wrote to Chatfield that he had seen the folly of his past extravagances and hoped to make amends.[44]

During his peddling excursions early in 1823, Alcott came upon a community of Friends in Chowan and Perquimans Counties, North Carolina, near Albemarle Sound. He had become acquainted with these Quakers in 1821 during one of his jaunts out of Norfolk. They remembered him, welcomed him, and invited him to stay. Evidently they were attracted to a young peddler such as Alcott, who was more interested in talking about religion than selling them his wares. Alcott spent the winter and spring of 1823 with the Quakers. Through their influence he underwent a kind of religious awakening that helped him combat his guilt and his sense of personal rootlessness at lacking a concrete and permanent tie to a community or an established occupation. His extravagances and ill-starred adventures were the results of an aimless search for meaning in life, a life that thus far lacked any settled values or goals. His teaching efforts had been unsuccessful, and peddling seemed to lead to a dead end. He had no money to further his education. Factory labor was anathema to him. The homestead in Wolcott offered no future. But the Quakers introduced him to their religious literature: William Penn's *No Cross, No Crown*, George Fox's *Journal*, William Law's *Serious Call to a Devout and Holy Life*, John Woolman's *Journal*, Robert Barclay's *Apology*, and Thomas Clarkson's *Portrait of Quakerism*. These readings and conversation with the humble, "drab coated followers of the Inner Light," made Alcott aware of the personal satisfaction he could find in exercises of thought and devotion, and of the rewards that an ardent desire for purity and excellence could bring. Especially did he respect the Quakers for their sincerity, their esteem of silent worship rather than formality and convention, and their disregard for the clergy.[45]

In late March 1823 he wrote to William of his debt to his Quaker benefactors. "If religion was strange to me before I read these [books] and I knew these good people," he confessed, "I almost venture to say it is [no] longer so but an experience, deeply felt, and heartily expressed as never before." It was as though Providence had purposely sent him to the Quakers to save him. He was anxious to talk with William at length about the new light that had broken in upon his repentant soul.[46]

The winter with the Quakers caused Alcott to give up peddling. The "moral sentiment," he later said, had "clearly and finally" superseded the impulse to sell material goods.[47] He did not become a Quaker, but the experience touched the Puritan pietism, the personal and emotional element in his faith, the faith of *Pilgrim's Progress*. It was the first step in Alcott's lifelong search for a moral and spiritual purpose that would help him make sense out of the disorder of a changing environment and would enable him to turn change itself into an instrument for reform and this-worldly salvation. Now he knew that he need not seek life's meaning in the quantity or quality of material possessions—new clothes, elegant plantations—or in a vocation or occupation, or even in travel or worldly experience. Rather, that meaning resided in the moral and spiritual purpose that transcended worldly things and even transcended change itself.

As he began his search Alcott turned to the ideas that had interested him in his youth: the inspiration of *Pilgrim's Progress* and the optimistic rationalism of *The Dignity of Human Nature*. As the search continued he confronted more directly than ever before the need to synthesize the two sometimes clashing strains of thought. That effort became the focal point of his intellectual development, just as the search for meaning was the motive force. But initially he found his purpose in "doing good." And his prescription for that reads like a page from Burgh. He wrote to William that "whatever is calculated to win the esteem of our fellow men, and render our intercourse with them engaging, is agreeable to the God of Love himself; it is making a proper use of those faculties, with which his goodness has endowed us." He told Chatfield that life was not measured by the number of days but by the good accomplished.[48]

Burgh had suggested to Alcott the best means of doing good with his emphasis on education and the development of the human mind. Teaching, to which Alcott leaned anyway because of his scholarly interests, became the obvious means of accomplishing life's moral purpose, and of serving God's will in the world. When he returned home from North Carolina in the late spring of 1823, Alcott again underwent examination for teaching and took a ten-dollar-a-month job as master of the Fall Mountain District School in nearby Bristol, Connecticut. Cousin William taught a school in the adjoining district. In the spring of 1824, he walked to Chatfield's new home in Paris, New York, hoping to teach there, but illness drove him back to Wolcott. In November 1824 he agreed to another term at Bristol. Then in November 1825 he accepted the instructorship of the Centre District School in Cheshire, Connecticut, and moved there to live with his uncle Tillotson. It was in Cheshire that his enthusiasm for teaching truly began and where at last he could say that he had found the calling to which he was born.[49]

Notes

1. Samuel Orcutt, *History of the Town of Wolcott (Connecticut) from 1731 to 1874* (Waterbury, Conn.: American Printing Co., 1874), pp. 181-84; A. Bronson Alcott, *New Connecticut: An Autobiographical Poem* (Cambridge, Mass.: University Press, 1881), p. 10; A. Bronson Alcott, comp., "Genealogy of the Family of Alcocke," MS at Houghton Library, 59M-306 (19), pp. 19-21, 90-92, 189. The Alcocke name had evolved to Alcox by the time of Alcott's birth. In 1821 Alcott and his cousin William Andrus Alcott changed their names from Alcox to Alcott. Although there is no concrete evidence to suggest it, Bronson and William may have been the victims of lewd and silly puns, as Odell Shepard pointed out in *Pedlar's Progress* (Boston: Little, Brown and Co., 1937), p. 66. "Alcott" had a more dignified and polished ring to it, thought Bronson, than the crude "Alcox."

2. Alcott, "Genealogy," pp. 95, 109-13; Orcutt, *History of Wolcott*, pp. 1-4, 178, 231-32.

3. Alcott, *New Connecticut*, pp. 13, 22; A. Bronson Alcott, "Diary for 1873," vol. 48; p. 776. This volume and all of Alcott's manuscript journals, vols. 1-59 (except vols. 15-19), are owned by Mrs. Frederic Wolsey Pratt of Concord, Massachusetts, and are deposited at the Houghton Library, Harvard University, call numbers 59M-308 (1-61). Hereafter they are referred to as AJ, with volume, date, and page numbers. AJ, 38 (1863): 213, 215; A. Bronson Alcott to Betsey and Linus Pardee, August 6, 1863, in A. Bronson Alcott, comp., "Family Letters, 1859-1864," at Houghton Library, 59M-305 (28); AJ 39 (1864): 57; Alcott, "Genealogy," pp. 159-66. Many of Alcott's letters referred to in these notes as unpublished may be found in Frederick Wagner, "Eighty-Six Letters (1814-1882) of A. Bronson Alcott (Part One)," in Joel Myerson, ed., *Studies in the American Renaissance 1979* (Boston: Twayne, 1979), pp. 239-308. (Part Two will appear in the 1980 volume.)

4. Richard J. Purcell, *Connecticut in Transition, 1775-1818* (Washington D.C.: American Historical Association, 1918), p.3; Alcott, *New Connecticut*, pp. 12, 82-84; A. Bronson Alcott, comp., "Letters and Papers from 1814 to 1828," vol. 1, MS at Houghton Library, 59M-305 (1).

5. Purcell, *Connecticut in Transition*, pp. 159-60.

6. AJ 48 (1873): 383-88, 424-25, 427, 789, 976; A. Bronson Alcott, "Autobiographical Collections" (1818-1823), 2: 5, MS bound with "Autobiographical Collections," Vol. 1, at Houghton Library, 59M-307 (1); Alcott, *New Connecticut*, p. 121; AJ 50 (1874-75): 374.

7. AJ 48 (1873): 354, 385.

8. A. Bronson Alcott, "Autobiography," p. 10, in "Letters and Papers, 1814-28"; A. Bronson Alcott, "Autobiographical Index, 1800-1850," MS at Houghton Library, 59M-306 (21); Dorothy McCuskey, *Bronson Alcott: Teacher* (New York: Macmillan Co., 1940), pp. 7-10; [William A. Alcott], "History of a Common School from 1801 to 1831," *American Annals of Education and Instruction* 1 (October 1831): 468-72; Alcott to Samuel Orcutt, November 6, 1878, in A. Bronson Alcott, comp., "Letters for 1878," at Houghton Library, 59M-305 (18); Alcott, "Autobiographical Collections," 1:58; Russel B. Nye, *The Cultural Life of the New Nation, 1776-1830* (New York: Harper and Row, 1960), p. 158.

9. Alcott, "Autobiography," p. 11, in "Letters and Papers, 1814-28"; AJ 45 (1870): 41.

10. Alcott, *New Connecticut*, pp. 20-21; AJ 49 (1874): 878; AJ 43 (1868): 387; AJ 48 (1873): 379; Alcott, "Autobiography," pp. 10 ff., in "Letters and Papers, 1814-28."

11. Alcott, *New Connecticut*, pp. 36-37; AJ 48 (1873): 972; AJ 36 (1861): 145; Alcott, "Genealogy," pp. 104, 129; AJ 49 (1874): 655.

12. Alcott, *New Connecticut*, p. 25; AJ 48 (1873): 972; AJ 50 (1874-75): 374.

13. MS in Alcott, "Autobiographical Collections," 1:146.

14. [Alcott] to W. A. [Alcott], September 8, 1814, from a copy in Bronson Alcott's hand owned by the Fruitlands Museum, Harvard, Massachusetts. The names, of course, were still spelled "Alcox" in 1814.

15. Alcott to Mrs. Anna Alcott, March 18, 1839, in A. Bronson Alcott, comp., "Letters from 1836 to 1850," at Houghton Library, 59M-305(2); AJ 25 (March-December 1850): 86-87.

16. Alcott, "Autobiography," pp. 10 ff., in "Letters and Papers, 1814-28"; AJ 48 (1873): 351; Murray G. Murphey, "Amos Bronson Alcott: The Origin and Development of His Philosophy," BA honors thesis, Harvard University, 1949, p. 15; AJ 12 (January-July 1839): 67; Alcott, *New Connecticut*, pp. 143-44. John Bunyan, *Pilgrim's Progress* (Philadelphia: Presbyterian Board of Publication, 1844), pp. 87-89.

17. Charles Roy Keller, *Thé Second Great Awakening in Connecticut* (New Haven Conn.: Yale University Press, 1942), pp. 14 ff., 25; Sydney Ahlstrom, *A Religious History of the American People* (New Haven, Conn.: Yale University Press, 1972), p. 416.

18. Ahlstrom, *Religious History*, p. 417; Keller, *Second Great Awakening*, pp. 72, 144-45; Purcell, *Connecticut in Transition*, pp. 32-33.

19. Alcott, *New Connecticut*, pp. 125-26.

20. Ahlstrom, *Religious History*, pp. 418-20; Keller, *Second Great Awakening*, pp. 11, 33-34, 236.

21. Perry Miller, "From Edwards to Emerson" in *Errand into the Wilderness*, Cambridge,

Mass.: Harvard University Press, 1956), pp. 192, 196; Ahlstrom, *Religious History*, pp. 421-22, 426.

22. Ahlstrom, *Religious History*, p.427; Keller, *Second Great Awakening*, p. 33.

23. Purcell, *Connecticut in Transition*, pp. 2, 64, 94, 416-19; Keller, *Second Great Awakening*, pp. 10-11, 25, 188-93.

24. Purcell, *Connecticut in Transition*, pp. 47-60; Orcutt, *History of Wolcott*, p. 58; Murphey, "A. Bronson Alcott," p. 15.

25. Alcott, "Genealogy," p. 157; AJ 48 (1873): 725-26, 780; AJ 49 (1874): p. 409; Alcott, *New Connecticut*, p. 144.

26. Alcott, *New Connecticut*, pp. 52-53, 144-45; Alcott, "Autobiography," p. 13, in "Letters and Papers, 1814-28."

27. Ahlstrom, *Religious History*, pp. 306, 418-22; Miller, "From Edwards to Emerson," pp. 195-96; [Alcott] to W. A. [Alcott], May 27, 1817, from a copy in Bronson Alcott's hand owned by the Fruitlands Museum.

28. James Burgh, *The Dignity of Human Nature*, 1st American ed. (Boston: John W. Folsom, 1794), pp. 94-97, 164-65, 182-88, 199, 319-21, 411-15; Murphey, "A. Bronson Alcott," pp. 21-24; [Alcott] to W. A. [Alcott], May 29, 1817, from a copy in Bronson Alcott's hand in AJ 51 (May-December 1875): 263-64.

29. Ahlstrom, *Religious History*, pp. 610-13; AJ 34 (1859): 67, 162-63.

30. Purcell, *Connecticut in Transition*, pp. 116-19, 128-29; Clive Day, *The Rise of Manufacturing in Connecticut, 1820-1850* (New Haven, Conn.: Yale University Press, 1935).

31. Purcell, *Connecticut in Transition*, pp. 131, 140-44, 151; AJ 46 (1871): 420; AJ 48 (1873): 397; Alcott, "Autobiography," p.11, in "Letters and Papers, 1814-28"; Penrose R. Hoopes, *Early Clock-making in Connecticut* (New Haven, Conn.: Yale University Press, 1935).

32. Richardson Wright, *Hawkers and Walkers in Early America* (Philadelphia: J. B. Lippincott Co., 1927), pp. 18-21, 27; Father William [William Andrus Alcott], *Recollections of Rambles at the South* (New York: Carlton and Phillips, 1854), pp. 14-15; Alcott, *New Connecticut*, p.147.

33. AJ 48 (1873): 377-78, 960; Alcott, "Genealogy," pp. 159-67.

34. AJ 22 (1848), p. 79. George Ripley's effort to preserve a part of his boyhood community life at Brook Farm was another example of this phenomenon. Cf. Charles Crowe, *George Ripley* (Athens: University of Georgia Press, 1967), pp. 8 ff.

35. Alcott, "Autobiographical Collections," 2:5; Alcott, *New Connecticut*, pp. 122-23, 144; AJ 44 (1869): 661-63; Alcott, "Autobiography," p. 12, in "Letters and Papers, 1814-28."

36. Alcott, "Autobiography," pp. 12, 17, in "Letters and Papers, 1814-28"; Alcott, "Autobiographical Collections," 2:22; [Alcott] to Mr. and Mrs. Joseph C. Alcox, November 30, 1818, printed in A. Bronson Alcott, *New Connecticut*, 2d ed. (Boston: Roberts Brothers, 1887), p. 215.

37. Alcott, "Autobiography," pp. 17 ff., in "Letters and Papers, 1814-28"; A. Bronson and Chatfield [Alcott] to Mr. and Mrs. Joseph C. Alcox, January 24, 1820, from a copy in Bronson Alcott's hand owned by the Fruitlands Museum.

38. [Alcott] to W. A. [Alcott], March 19, 1820, from a copy in Bronson Alcott's hand owned by the Fruitlands Museum; Alcott, "Autobiographical Collections," 2:31, 34. The journal mentioned here, along with all of his journals from 1812 to 1825, was "consumed" in Philadelphia in 1833. It is not clear whether this was accidental or whether Alcott deliberately destroyed them. He later regretted their loss. *New Connecticut*, pp. 62-64; Alcott to Mrs. Anna Alcott, March 18, 1839.

39. AJ 9 (1836): 144.

40. Alcott, "Autobiographical Collections," 2:36-38; Alcott, *New Connecticut*, p. 157; [Alcott] to W. A. [Alcott], March 19, 1820, from a copy in Bronson Alcott's hand owned by the Fruitlands Museum.

41. [W. A. Alcott], *Rambles at the South*, pp. 28-29, 35, 50, 55, 73-74, 81-85, 166-69; Alcott, "Autobiography," p. 37, in "Letters and Papers, 1814-28"; Alcott, "Autobiographical Collections," 2:63.

42. Alcott, *New Connecticut*, 2d ed., pp. 88-92.

43. Ibid., pp. 97-98: Alcott to Chatfield Alcott, April 13, 1822, quoted in ibid., p. 95; Alcott, "Autobiography," p. 54, in "Letters and Papers, 1814-28."

44. Alcott to Chatfield Alcott, November 24, 1822, quoted in *New Connecticut*, 2d ed., pp. 238-39; Alcott, "Autobiographical Index."

45. Alcott, "Autobiography," p. 54, in "Letters and Papers 1814-28"; Alcott, *New Connecticut*, 2d ed., pp. 83-85: Alcott, "Autobiographical Collections," vol. 2.

46. Alcott to W. A. Alcott, March 30, 1823, from a copy in Bronson Alcott's hand owned by the Fruitlands Museum.

47. Alcott, "Autobiographical Index."

48. Alcott to W. A. Alcott, ca. 1824, and Alcott to Chatfield Alcott, June 15, 1825, in "Letters and Papers, 1814-28."

49. Alcott, "Autobiographical Index"; Alcott to W. A. Alcott, January 13, 1826, quoted in *New Connecticut*, 2d ed., p. 246.

2

The Teacher, 1825–28

IT was during his years as a schoolmaster in Cheshire and Bristol, Connecticut, that Alcott began to formulate a theory of education that would become a revolutionary challenge to the common school teaching of the day, and at the same time would give him a personal calling mingled with a strong sense of mission as a reformer. Having already cast aside formal religion as a hindrance to the true faith of the heart, he began to attack other traditions and mores that he considered to be an equal bother, especially those relating to education. His reading in philosophy and reformist literature accelerated these trends. It reinforced his striving toward a dynamic synthesis of Enlightenment rationalism, which emphasized the infinite capacity of the human mind, and of an emotional religion of the heart, which perceived the immanence of God in the world working for human regeneration and salvation. For the simple farmers of Cheshire and Bristol, the ideas of this zealot would be bewildering and frightening.

Cheshire, a small village located about ten miles southeast of Wolcott and fifteen miles directly north of New Haven, sent an average of forty-four of its children aged three to twelve to Alcott's Centre District School, which he taught for four successive five-month terms beginning in November 1825. He was paid $2.50 per student each term, which came to about $23 a month. In a good term he could make close to $135.[1] The common schools of Cheshire were much like others in Connecticut at the time and much like the one Alcott had known as a child in Wolcott. Students were forced to sit for hours on rough, backless benches. There was little variety in the classroom routine of rote learning, conducted by generally underpaid and ill-prepared instructors. Attendance was irregular because of the needs of the farm, the indifference of parents, and the student's dislike of the dullness of the classroom. Discipline was maintained by the threat of corporal punishment, undoubtedly another reason why children were hesitant to attend. Classroom equipment was scanty and textbooks few. Even worse, there was no clear philosophy or science of education to guide either students or teachers.[2]

It was a fertile field for the experiments of an enthusiastic and dedicated teacher, and Alcott slowly began to make alterations and improvements. Cousin William Alcott, still Alcott's respected confidant, provided a convenient sounding board for a consideration of these innovations. William had taught in the Connecticut common schools, primarily at Wolcott and Bristol, for several years and had a good reputation as an excellent teacher and a stern disciplinarian. In the winter of 1826 he was entering a new profession, having begun attending lectures in medicine at Yale College. Nevertheless, William was available through regular correspondence to give helpful advice and encouragement to his younger and sometimes irresponsible cousin.[3] With William's aid Alcott devised careful changes in the arrangement of his classroom. He built individual desks and seats for each of his pupils with the back of the seat attached to the desk behind it. The desks were lined up along the walls and windows of the classroom to allow space in the center for games and physical activities like dancing and marching. He hoped the interior of the classroom would lead his pupils to associate learning with a pleasant environment. Pictures, engravings, and decorations made of cyprus branches to suggest the beauty of nature softened the dullness and barrenness of the room, and Alcott permitted students to decorate their desks with flowers and ornaments.[4] "Every arrangement of exteriour objects under the immediate cognizance of the senses, has been made in relation to its probable effect upon the mind," Alcott recorded in his journal. He hoped to stimulate the imagination of and to suggest pleasant ideas to his young charges.[5]

Alcott was also aware of the need to alleviate the dullness of the common-school classroom routine. To accomplish this he introduced a variety of classroom materials designed to excite the students' interest. With his own money he purchased a juvenile library of over one hundred books for the use of his students, and he introduced the first slates to be used in a Connecticut public school for his students to write on. He also brought in writing books for exercises in composition and penmanship; blocks, cubes, and beans to aid in counting and arithmetic; and tangible letters to help younger students learn the alphabet. His classroom was to be lively, interesting, challenging, even entertaining, rather than dull, routine, and barren, and he knew that the key to this was variety in classroom activities. Thus, more traditional textbook exercises and recitations were interspersed with walks, games, physical exercises, storytelling, and directed conversation between Alcott and his students. These methods evidently succeeded in interesting and motivating the students, for they often came to visit Alcott in the evening to play games and to read with him.[6]

He knew that a child's memory could not be cultivated by mere rote repetition, that it depended on association, on cause-and-effect relationships, on analogy, and on the use of all the child's senses in the learning process. There was, Alcott believed, a science, a method to learning, and he felt that the best method was induction. That is, children learned simple and familiar things first and then built upon that knowledge to an understanding of complex and unfamiliar things. Reading, writing, and composition, for example, were to be cultivated first by learning letters, then words, then sentences describing simple objects. Every step in the learning process would build upon what was learned before it in a rational, orderly way. Mere rote

memorization would have no part in this process. The student had to understand clearly the concept behind each word or sentence and had to be able to
express it in his or her own words. "The parrot can utter words and sentences
but he is thinking no wiser than before," said Alcott. "So in reading, without
attending to the ideas of the composition, at the utterance of these sounds, we
only [do] like the parrot, without ourselves becoming wiser thereby."[7]

Composition was to be taught in a way that combined thought and
expression. In accordance with the inductive method, students would first
learn by example and comparison, by paraphrasing the writings of others, and
by hearing stories read or told by Alcott. Alcott would then ask the students to
formulate their own thoughts and to express them freely in individual journals
which Alcott provided, and orally in classroom conversation. Alcott had great
respect for the integrity, creativity, and potential of his students, and he hoped
his teaching would bring about an atmosphere that would enhance and
encourage them.[8]

Alcott believed that one great hindrance to learning was fear. The rod and
the ferule, the traditional wardens of the common school, did not provide the
pleasant associations that Alcott hoped to develop in his students. Not only
did they hinder creative thought and expression, Alcott felt, but they failed to
provide adequate discipline. "It [the rod] is, in the hands of the ignorant and
unthinking, one of the most dangerous enemies to the formation of juvenile
character, that has ever been invented. Its reign has been the reign of cruelty,
and terror," which has only impeded the "incipient energies" of humanity.
"Tyranny and oppression have marked the conduct of such as have taken
upon them the office of Instructor, and rendered the school room, in the
apprehension of the young, a place of suffering, confinement, and hatred."[9]
Alcott's policy was one of mildness and gentleness designed to cultivate the
students' "affections." Children most often learned behavior by example, he
thought, and therefore if the instructor was kind, considerate, and gentle, the
students would also develop those characteristics. He felt an instructor should
be just, should acknowledge faults, should be consistent and never capricious,
and should never make invidious comparisons among pupils nor allow
competition among them. The school should be governed by just a few clearly
defined and well-understood laws. Above all, the instructor should be sensitive
to the feelings of the children, and by his example should cultivate in them that
same sensitivity toward others. If reproach was necessary, Alcott felt it his
duty to make it clear to the child that he was punishing the offense, not the
individual.[10]

So confident was Alcott of the basic goodness of the children that he
developed a system of classroom democracy. He allowed the students to vote
on the rules under which the school would be conducted. A student
superintendent had charge of recording violations of class discipline, and
offenders were brought before a student court for trial and punishment,
although Alcott as judge reserved the right to reverse decisions. Experience
confirmed the students' competence for self-government. When Alcott was

absent one day, the students carried on by themselves.[11]

Alcott considered his school to be a community, and he sought to develop a community spirit among the children. By this he meant a concern by each student for the welfare, the moral and intellectual progress, of every other student. He wanted them to scrutinize one another and to hold each other up before the commonly agreed-upon set of rules established at the beginning of each term. Alcott thought that in a community each person should be willing to give and take advice, to practice mutual forbearance, and to stand up to "vice and iniquity" wherever they might appear. He had all students write in their journals the name of any student they felt had done something not in accordance with "moral rectitude." Each Saturday these names were read, the persons accused were tried and, if found guilty, had to make a public apology. This, Alcott thought, would make "improper conduct" unpopular and render corporal punishment unneccessary. Potentially, this kind of "mutual monitoring" could be nearly as dreadful and tyrannical as the rod. But Alcott largely avoided the possible crushing intolerance of class members toward one another by emphasizing the need for mutual support, kindness, concern, and sensitivity.[12]

Yet the Cheshire Centre District School was no "free school" in the modern sense. Despite his belief in the necessity of a positive joyful and attractive classroom atmosphere and his striving to allow self-expression on the part of the students, Alcott was a firm disciplinarian. Indeed, he believed a positive learning situation was impossible without discipline. Students were to be prompt, neat, attentive, silent in class unless called upon, and seated unless given permission to move about. They were to avoid interrupting the work of others, "idly lounging or gazing," or laughing at the instructor's remarks. Alcott believed that moral education was even more important than intellectual education, and that obedience was an essential element of moral education. Perhaps reflecting on his own earlier misdeeds, he told his students that disobedience to parents was the source of all mischief in society. Making children obey, he declared, would make them ready to obey God as adults.[13] Education, he believed, should provide students with an unquestioned value system and should prompt them to obey a moral law, God's law, good for all times and places, Obedience to the moral law was his prescription for causing students both to do good and to challenge existing institutions and customs:

> Rebel! Think for themselves! Let others grumble; dare to be singular. Let others direct; follow Reason. Let others dwell in the Land of Enchantments; be Men. Let others prattle; practise. Let others profess; do good. Let others define goodness; act. Let others sleep; whatever thy hand findeth to do, that do with all thy might, and let a gainsaying calumniating world speculate on your proceedings.[14]

He assumed that the moral law was absolutely true and transcended customs and creeds. It was the moral law that the rebellious individual had to obey.

Many of Alcott's ideas for reform in the classroom rose both from his own teaching experience and from a reaction against experiences he had had as a pupil in Wolcott. From these two sources came hs ideas for redesigning desks and seats, for rearranging the classroom, for avoiding harshness in classroom discipline, and especially for instilling in his students the moral values of his personal Christian faith. However, his philosophy of education, his theory of the development of the human mind, and his growing belief in the power of education as a means of reforming all of society came largely from his reading and the application of his reading to his own thoughts.

By the spring of 1826 Alcott had come across the *American Journal of Education*. The first number of this monthly had been issued in Boston in January 1826 by its publisher, the Scotland-born educator William Russell. The *Journal* was one of the first periodicals in the United States devoted entirely to educational reform and educational thought. It marked the beginning of an increased interest by Americans in pedagogical matters and in the ideas of European educators and reformers. The first issues of the *Journal* dealt with the importance of moral education, the value of schools for infants, the need for higher education for women, and the great potential for good in institutions to "improve" the deaf and dumb. Russell preached the gospel of education as the surest hope for humanity. In his "Closing Address" in the final number of volume 1, he wrote of all the hopeful signs that indicated an increased interest in education in the United States.[15] "It is gratifying," he said, "to observe education recognized as the surest and most successful instrument of effecting good, and as that which, though others may be more rapid and striking, seems to be the destined method of elevating the human race to a character generally if not universally—marked by whatever is pure, noble, amiable, or happy."[16]

Alcott wrote in his journal that he was greatly indebted to the *American Journal of Education* for his thoughts on education.[17] It had introduced him to the ideas of two Europeans who directly affected his methods and educational philosophy: a Swiss, Johann Pestalozzi, and an Englishman, Robert Owen. More important, it had given him a sense of being a part of a great movement for reform throughout the United States and the world. It helped legitimate his personal rebelliousness against established customs and traditions, and it enhanced the greater and greater importance he was attaching to his chosen profession.

By July 1826 Alcott was referring to his school as the "Cheshire Pestalozzian School." His acquaintance with Pestalozzi was only secondhand. He obtained it by reading the *Journal of Education*, the anonymously published English work *Hints to Parents*, and a recently published article by Owen's disciple William Maclure called "An Epitome of the Improved Pestalozzian System of Education."[18] The maxims for teaching that Alcott listed in his journal included basic Pestalozzian theories and methods: that teaching should be inductive, a gradual process by the shortest steps from the easy and known to the more difficult and unknown; that human nature should be allowed to develop in its own way; that rote learning should be avoided so that children might obtain a knowledge of things and ideas, not words and names; and that moral and sympathetic feelings and affections should be cultivated in the classroom.[19] Pestalozzi's methods impressed Alcott as being far more "philosophical" than the Lancastrian monitorial system, which the *Journal of Education* also described. The Lancastrian method was useful for teaching large numbers of students by mutual instruction. It was developed in England by Joseph Lancaster and Andrew Bell and was introduced to the United States as early as 1806. Alcott used monitoring to an extent in classroom discipline, but he preferred Pestalozzi's methods even if it meant that he had to restrict the size of his class.[20]

Especially attractive to Alcott was Pestalozzi's basic assumption that educators could reduce the process of learning and the development of each human mind to an exact science; that they could demonstrate step by step the acquisition of knowledge, the cultivation of the intellect, and even the development of morality. By mastering that natural process of human development, thought Pestalozzi, a teacher could help make people good, wise, and just. Pestalozzi believed that human nature was basically good. No original sin or innate human depravity stood in the way of that goodness; it was all a matter of proper education. Indeed, human beings had within them, he felt, a natural desire toward self-perfection. Just as human beings could develop their intellect by observation, they could perfect themselves by observing the perfection of God's nature as best revealed in a mother's love for her child, and in the heartfelt relationship between mother and child. Not only did human beings naturally seek their own perfection, said Pestalozzi, they also had a natural desire to foster perfection in others. Thus education, by properly guiding these natural tendencies, could be an instrument of regeneration—not just for individuals but for society in general.[21]

The heart of Pestalozzi's theory of education was in line with the epistemology of John Locke. Locke believed that learning proceeded as a result of impressions on the human senses from the external world, and that reflection built these sense impressions upon one another to form complex ideas. Pestalozzi attempted to bring order to this process of sense impression and reflection, so that the acquisition of knowledge and the development of ideas might take place in a natural, step-by-step manner. Alcott had read Locke's *Essay Concerning Human Understanding* in 1819, but in 1826 he was reading and referring to it again. He included it in his "Library for the Instructor's Use," and he found it congenial and helpful in developing his Pestalozzian school.[22]

Both Pestalozzi and Alcott stressed the power of education to develop moral character. In so doing they found themselves in line with the Scottish Common Sense school of philosophers who attempted to find a compromise between Enlightenment rationalism and traditional beliefs in an innate human capacity for religious faith. These philosophers, best represented by Thomas Reid and Dugald Stewart, accepted Locke's theory of sensation and reflection but added to this that human beings had certain innate ideas that did not come from sensation or reflection: ideas of God, of truth, of beauty, and of right and wrong. In this way they wanted to find an assurance of the validity of Christian morals and Christian principles that Locke's empiricism did not give. Locke had recognized an innate sense of God but had not satisfactorily explained or developed it.[23] Alcott's introduction to the Scottish philosophers came through his reading of Adam Smith's *Theory of Moral Sentiments* and Thomas Cogan's *Philosophical Treatise on the Passions*.[24]

Having digested the ideas of Pestalozzi and the Scottish philosophers, Alcott decided that the moral sense was indeed innately present in all persons but had to be developed, or called forth, by education. Pestalozzi had said that a mother's example could draw out the idea of God and thus the idea of perfectibility. Adam Smith had concluded that the moral sense could be cultivated by observation of the behavior of others, what Smith called "sympathy" or "fellow-feeling."[25] Thus Alcott believed that a teacher could bring out the moral and sympathetic feelings of his students by his own example. "In short," he said, "[the pupils] will be a counterpart of [the teacher]—a mirror reflecting his own image—light shining from the same sun."[26] Alcott expected his students to develop their moral sentiments in the same way that they developed their intellect—by observation. It was all very rational, all very scientific.[27]

Of hardly less influence on Alcott than Pestalozzi, Locke, and the Scottish philosophers, was the reformer Robert Owen. In December 1824, fresh from experiments in social reform in his native England, Owen had purchased New Harmony, Indiana, from a group of Rappites and had begun a utopian community there in May 1825. He had preceded the establishment of his community with a widespread publicity campaign that included a lecture at the Capitol in Washington and an audience with President-elect John Quincy Adams. He followed this in 1825 with the first American edition of his *New View of Society*, the basic statement of his reformist ideas. Owen believed that any evil that afflicted the human race could be removed by the manipulation of external conditions in accordance with the "laws of human nature."[28] As a result, he was very concerned with education as a means of properly relating the environment to the natural development of human beings. His schools at New Lanark in England had included many of the practices Alcott later found so important in Cheshire: variety in method; dancing, singing, and recreation as educative activities; teaching by conversation; and kindness in discipline. Owen took a broad view of education as instruction of any kind received from earliest infancy, and he believed that education was the primary source of all the good or evil, happiness or misery, that existed in the world. The schools established at New Harmony were Pestalozzian and were under the direction of Owen's associate William Maclure. Pestalozzi's appeal for Maclure and Owen was his rational ordering of the process of human development. Owen felt that the rational conduct of education in accordance with natural laws would bring the millennium.[29] Indeed, there was no stopping it, for how could a natural law be avoided? Owen believed that all opposition to his reforms was useless: "if, however, owing to the irrational principles by which the world has been hitherto governed, individuals, or sects, or parties, shall yet by their plans of exclusion attempt to retard the amelioration of society, and prevent the introduction into practice of that truly just spirit which knows no exclusion, such facts shall yet be brought forward as cannot fail to render all their efforts vain."[30]

Alcott included Owen's *New View* among the most important books in his "Instructor's Library," along with works by Locke, Pestalozzi, and Smith, the *American Journal of Education*, and the *Bible*. He was so intrigued by the news of the Pestalozzian school at New Harmony that he wrote to William Maclure asking for detailed information. Maclure responded in November 1826 with a description that so impressed Alcott that he referred to the New Harmony school as the best school in the United States. Alcott was sure that the "enemies of reformation" could never overcome Owen's great work. "Mental, moral, and physical man will be regenerated" at New Harmony, Alcott thought, because it was a practical experiment in the "true spirit of inductive philosophy." He predicted that Owen's theories would become popular and that a better world would result. He did not know when he wrote these words in October 1827 that New Harmony had already collapsed as a socialist community, and that Owen had left.[31]

The unexpected success and enjoyment Alcott found in his teaching convinced him that after several years of uncertainty and floundering he had truly found his calling and his personal mission in life. He told his parents: "How much reason have I to be thankful to the Creator for his goodness to me—Four years ago where was I?"[32] The identification he made of his work with the optimistic reform spirit of Owen and Pestalozzi and with the work of the *American Journal of Education* further elevated his calling from a vocation to a crusade. It was work that not only would give him personal satisfaction but could well lead to the improvement, even the regeneration, of society as a whole. "Education's All" became the motto for his journal. "Of all employments," he said, "that of an instructor, opens the most full and spacious channels of enjoyment." It mattered little if education were considered unimportant in the world's opinion, for it was infinitely important in the eyes of God. "On the character, and the energy of Instructors," he boasted, "the whole happiness of civil society depends." He was sure that all evil in the world resulted from the lack of proper education. Education was surely what Christ had in mind when he talked about being "born again"; education would be the agent that would regenerate the earth. Indeed, since children were born innocent, as Alcott believed, education could prevent the necessity of regeneration. "Education judiciously conducted'" he said, "preserves the human mind from depravity."[33]

The importance Alcott attached to education was based not only on his reading and his experiences in the classroom, but also on philosophical and religious ideas that had been fermenting in his mind for several years. He admitted to William Alcott that he sometimes feared that his "fondness for speculations'' might hamper his practical efforts as an instructor.[34] Nevertheless, this fear did not stop him from filling his journal with his developing ideas about religion, human nature, education, and reform as a supplement to the running account of the progress of the school. The problems he confronted in his thinking included the nature of the human mind, the relationship between the power of God and the power of human beings in regard to questions of sin and regeneration, and the potential of human beings to reform the institutions of this world.

Despite his growing faith in a rational approach to education, Alcott was plagued by the same unresolved philosophical questions evident in the ideas of the representatives of the Scottish Enlightenment that he had read: the uncertainty about the extent to which the human mind developed by the influence of external circumstances and the extent to which ideas innate in the human mind, such as ideas of God, truth, beauty, and right (the "moral sense"), helped in this development. In August 1826 Alcott claimed in his journal that the human heart, mind, and disposition were all formed by education and were not innate. Implicit in this was the idea that human beings at birth were a moral as well as an intellectual *tabula rasa*, and that external conditions determined whether a person became good or evil.[35] However, less than a month later he wrote that his study of the mind showed that all persons were not equally affected by the same external objects. "[I]t cannot be supposed," he reflected, "that the same mode of regeneration obtains on all persons. This varies according to the genius of the subject. . . ."[36] He went on to say that there were "native feelings and propensities" in the young mind that educators had to respect, encourage, and cultivate.[37]

Clearly, Alcott had come to believe that there was a creative power within human beings that somehow interacted with sense impressions received from external objects in the process of human development. The problem was how to define the limits of that human potential. He emphatically denied that human beings had the power to form their own character. If that were true, attempts at education would be fruitless. There would be no need for schools and churches, and children would just as well be allowed to do whatever was right in their own eyes. Yet he thought the powers of the children ought to be allowed to develop: "What we aim at is to make children understand what they are doing—to make them think—to reason—to invent. They are to a considerable extent their own instructors. They are told directly but little. What they learn is obtained by the regular and systematic application of their own powers."[38]

Alcott's struggle to define the extent of human freedom, choice, and creativity was based upon two major articles of faith that served as parameters of the problem. First, the concept that human beings were governed by natural laws, that external circumstances could determine human development in a rational, orderly way, was attractive to Alcott because it provided assurance that regeneration by education would indeed take place. "Like the great laws of nature, it [i.e., reform] knows no impediment," said Alcott.[39] However, this clashed with the second dictum, namely that human beings should be held responsible for moral decisions. How could human beings be held morally responsible if their lives were determined externally by natural laws? This would either make evil a part of natural law or raise the inexplicable possibility that a natural law might be broken, in which case the assurance of regeneration would slip away.

Alcott's solution to this dilemma was only tentative. With unwarranted assurance he said:

> It is now distinctly seen that the human character is, to a very considerable extent, under the control of man—that the character is formed by the influence of the peculiar circumstances with which man, during life, and especially during the period of infancy, childhood and youth, is surrounded —that he takes his sentiments, opinions, character, and disposition, from the sentiments, opinions, character, and disposition, of the persons with whom during this period he is concerned; and from the peculiar influence which these things have upon his mind and affections.[40]

Implicit in this was the idea that although circumstances determined character, human beings had the power to rise above and manipulate those circumstances, thus controlling the process of character development and directing it toward some innate concept of the good and true. Therefore human beings were the ultimate determining force. Human potential for good or evil, for creation or destruction was theoretically unlimited.

The problem of human nature and its potential was closely related to the problem of the relationship of human beings to God. Alcott had to integrate his theory of education with his theology. Early in 1826 Alcott displayed in his letters and in his journal the conventional, pietistic attitude of reliance on the hand of God to guide his actions. His maxims for teaching included "depending on Divine blessing for success." In January 1826 he wrote to William Alcott that "God in his goodness has thus far marked our course with his guidance, that, by experience, we might learn wisdom. Even from the commencement of our existence, his guiding and merciful hand appears." He was thankful that the "will of Providence" allowed him to become a teacher.[41] However, Alcott's growing enthusiasm for education began to temper his reliance on Providence. As he came to view education more and more as "the great engine of mental, and moral power," he began to relegate God to a minor role, or rather to the role of a distant prime mover. "Improvement is the great business of man," he was saying by August 1826; "creation is of God." Human beings, not God, were responsible for sin and evil in the world, and human beings were thus responsible for improving the world, for shaping human character. By March 1827 he was agreeing with Judson A. Root, a Yale Divinity School student and supply pastor at the Cheshire Congregational Church, that human beings were the authors of regeneration, that God had no part in it at all. At the same time human beings were, according to Alcott, the source of depravity. God made no one sinful; it was human choice, human free will, that led to sin and evil.[42]

In attempting to square his theology with his developing concepts of natural law, the human mind, the power of the environment, and education, Alcott was fighting the same battle that the theologians of the Second Great Awakening were fighting. They were looking for a compromise between the power of God and the Enlightenment emphasis on the power of human reason. At Yale this effort was being led by Divinity School professor Nathaniel William Taylor. Taylor believed that human beings, as free, rational, moral, and creative creatures, had the power through free will to sin or not to sin, contrary to the traditional Calvinist emphasis on original, unavoidable sin. Thus Alcott could find some reinforcement of his religious ideas in Yale theology students such as Root and Ira Talcott Bates, both of whom he had heard speak in Cheshire.[43] However, Alcott had no formal theological training and was not bound by the traditions, creeds, or doctrines of any sect. Therefore he could easily carry his ideas far beyond where most orthodox theologians could go or dared to go if they wished to stay in the good graces of their denomination. By June 1827 he was denying the divinity of Jesus. Jesus, Alcott thought, was a great and good man but limited a great deal by his time and its ignorance of "mental philosophy"; he was a man to be admired but not to be worshiped.[44] From that position Alcott came close to asserting the divinity of all human beings. He refused to accept the orthodox Congregational doctrine of the original depravity of human nature. Instead, he accepted the concept of the original goodness of human nature. "From Heaven the immortal spirit has just arrived," Alcott said of the newborn child. "This purity, divine and unsullied, can hold no affinity with ugliness and deformity."[45] He felt that children came from the Creator immaculate, but were led to evil by "circumstances," or rather the improper ordering of "circumstances."[46]

The idea that the environment caused evil led back to the problem of the extent of human power to avoid it. Alcott's answer was that God had created essentially good human beings with an inward spiritual power to rise above the dictates of the environment and to manipulate and control the environment for human benefit. This power permitted human beings to regenerate themselves voluntarily, or through education, to prevent the loss of original innocence in children, thus obviating the need for their regeneration. Having made a distinction between the internal aspect of human beings and the external environment, and having placed the essence of human goodness, of human power for self-regeneration, within this internal, spiritual aspect, Alcott even included the physical human body as a part of external "circumstances." Human power to rise above and overcome the power of the external environment included the power to overcome the defects of the physical body.[47] John Locke's empiricism had given Alcott a sense of the power of the exterior world to control human destiny, but Alcott's Puritan religiosity, the Quaker concept of the inner light, the Scottish belief in the moral sense, even the Enlightenment faith in human reason, had suggested to him the potential of human beings to control the natural laws of the exterior world. It was the power promised in the *New Testament*, he thought, the power to free human beings from the "sensible," the exterior, the material.[48] But the power Alcott saw in human beings went far beyond the free will the Great Awakening theologians talked about, or the indefinite moral sense of the Scottish philosophers, or even the inner light of the Quakers. It was the power of self-regeneration. Carried to its logical conclusion this meant that God had created "little gods," that human beings were divine.

This faith in human power opened up immense possibilities for reform and progress, even for the perfection of human beings and the world they lived in. It legitimized rebellion against the ignorance and intractability of established institutions and customs. "Reform must soon become the order of the day," he wrote confidently in August 1826, and he enjoined all people to begin a course of conduct that would hasten the approach of "that millennial day when peace and joy shall pervade the whole earth." This depended not on God but on human power and human conduct.[49] The slow pace of reform and the apparent inability of people to see the need for reform began to aggravate him. "Man still plods in his grovelling course," he complained in November 1826. "Mammon reigns. Oppression, war, and misery still grow in rank luxuriance. Virtue sleeps confined—benevolence is doomed a beggar—unclothed—unshod—without a friend—without a home."[50] His heroes were those who dared to defy tradition, "who have thrown off the shackles, and trammels of ancient monking, superstition, and authority, and are determined to think for themselves, to follow truth and reason, be the consequences what they may."[51] Among those intrepid few were Pestalozzi, Owen, Maclure, William Russell, and Alcott himself. He had identified the reforms he had made in his Cheshire school with the larger movement for reform in education and society. He had developed an emotional commitment to the idea of reform, improvement, progress, although he had defined these things only in a very general way. Of course, he knew what reform meant with regard to the classroom and to teaching methods. But in a larger sense he had no precise definition of reform; he placed no limits upon it. It could be a sweeping condemnation of anything he might choose to consider evil, or it could mean a specific program of change. What was important was not Alcott's definition of reform but his emotional attachment to the concept that reform was possible and that he was in the vanguard.

The more convinced Alcott became of his mission to reform the world, and the more innovations he introduced into his school, the more hostility to his ideas and to his school increased among the people of Cheshire. His problems began in the summer of 1826. "It is much to be regretted," he complained then, "that the state of things around us is, universally, so detrimental to the interests of the young. . . . Those who from affection to their offspring, one would suppose, would be compelled to cooperate with the instruction of their children. . . become opponents to their children & the instructor."[52] Rumblings of resentment turned to outright hostility in November 1826, when Alcott asked for an increase in salary, alterations in the classroom, and new class and library books to begin his third term. The town granted the salary and the alterations but refused to buy the new books. Alcott bought them at his own expense as the cries against "innovation" grew. By the beginning of the summer term of 1827 (April through September) Alcott had only thirteen pupils left, and his opponents were establishing a rival school with a female instructor whom they could pay less and who they supposed would be less of a troublemaker.[53]

As his difficulties increased Alcott became more and more embittered and self-righteous. He felt that the resentment toward him was caused only by his desire to separate truth from its "ancient shackles." The people of Cheshire further convinced him that most people inherited their opinions as they did their estates. "They believe," he said, "because their predecessors believed; they oppose anything new in opinion, because it is new, because the venerated association of age, is not connected with it."[54] One difficulty he perceived was that the villagers of Cheshire were not well enough acquainted with his school to make a fair judgment. But he added sarcastically that the reason for their ignorance was that they feared they might like what they saw and would be forced to doubt the correctness of "long received opinions." In despair he began to think of leaving Cheshire to find a place where "circumstances are favorable. . . . and where the publick sentiment is more correct." On June 14, 1827, he closed his school despite the efforts of a few townspeople, "certainly the most reflecting minds," to convince him that he should stay.[55]

Alcott could more easily bear his disappointment with the knowledge that his school had attracted the attention of leaders in educational reform in both Connecticut and New England in general. William Alcott had visited the school in February 1827, and had claimed that it was the best district school in the state. William Maclure of New Harmony had given encouragement, as had Pestalozzian educator John M. Keagy of Harrisburg, Pennsylvania. Alcott and Keagy had corresponded about a new "Primer" Keagy had written, and had commiserated about the loss of Pestalozzi, who had died in February 1827. More important, Alcott had aroused the interest of the newly formed Connecticut Society for the Improvement of Common Schools.[56]

This organization was a response to the increasing attention given to the need for school reform in New England in 1826 and 1827. The *American Journal of Education* helped generate the demand for improvements, as did articles by Thomas Gallaudet in the *Connecticut Observor* and James G. Carter in the *Boston Patriot*. In their annual messages, governors in each New England state called attention to the need for such reform. The main criticisms raised in this call for change were the inadequate training of teachers, the irresponsibility of committees charged with examining them, the wide variety in the level of instruction from district to district depending on the whim of local school committees and teachers, and the unevenness of school discipline, which ranged from apathetic to cruel depending on the locale and the teacher. There were ugly stories of teachers theatening to bleed or hang recalcitrant students. The low pay and poor conditions for teachers were scandalous, as were the indifference of local citizens to education and their failure to take advantage of improvements and ideas offered by European educators.[57]

In the spring of 1827 the school committee of Brooklyn, Connecticut, took the initiative and sent a circular letter to school committees and teachers in every town in the state. The letter asked towns to send delegates to a state convention and asked teachers to answer a list of questions prepared by Samuel Joseph May, the Unitarian minister in Brooklyn and a member of the school committee, in order to supply information on school conditions for the proposed convention. Upon receiving his copy of the circular Alcott rejoiced that at least one town was concerned with school reform, but he did not attend the convention, which met in Hartford in the middle of May. It was William Alcott's reply to the circular that directed the reformers' attention to Bronson Alcott's "remarkable" Cheshire school. May wrote to Alcott asking for a detailed report to be given to the Society for the Improvement of Common Schools formed in April, just prior to the convention. Alcott submitted his report on April 30, fearing that it was prepared in too great haste but hoping that it would make him better known and thus increase his ability to "improve mankind."[58]

The members of the Society were pleased with Alcott's description of his school, and they elected him a member. The *Boston Recorder and Telegraph* and the *Connecticut Observor* both carried articles reporting that "Mr. Alcott's School" was one of the best, if not the best, common school in the United States. Samuel May thought Alcott's account revealed a "deep insight" into human nature and a "true sympathy" with children. He felt that Alcott had to be a genius.[59]

In late June and early July 1827, after having closed his school in Cheshire, Alcott toured schools throughout the state surveying attendance, wages, books, public financing, periodicals taken, and the "intelligence of town inhabitants." He wrote to Chatfield that although his school was closed, he was flattered by the prospects and opportunities before him. In August he spent a week in Brooklyn, Connecticut, by invitation of Samuel May.[60] May was overwhelmed by Alcott. "I have never, but in one other instance," he said later, "been so immediately taken possession of by any man I have ever met in life. He seemed to me like a born sage and saint. He was radical in all matters of reform; went to the root of all things, especially the subjects of education, mental and moral culture."[61] May's sister, Abigail, was equally impressed, especially by Alcott's "earnest desire to promote better advantages for the young."[62]

Thomas Gallaudet and other leaders in the Society for the Improvement of Common Schools wanted Alcott to open an infant school in Hartford that fall. But Alcott told Samuel May that he looked rather to Boston, where he felt that the social and religious atmosphere for such a project would be more congenial. May replied that he looked forward with confident expectation to Alcott's settling in Boston, May's native city. May promised to write to friends and acquaintances there to aid the enterprise. In the meantime Alcott agreed to teach the West District School in Bristol, Connecticut.[63]

He began teaching in Bristol on November 6, 1827, and immediately ran into misunderstanding and prejudice against his methods and his "theological sentiments." Some parents were skeptical of his use of kindness as a means of discipline. Townspeople talked when his female students came to visit him in the evenings. Other parents judged Alcott's teaching only on the amount of material their children had memorized, and they did not understand when Alcott explained that words were just images of ideas and that there could be no learning without a comprehension of those ideas. By February 1828 an opposing school had been established. Alcott wrote to Abby May that while he was fighting the "impediments of custom and tradition" in Bristol, he hoped for a freer and larger field of action in the spring. Opposition really did not matter, for Alcott felt that his experiment had widespread importance and had the support of the intelligent part of the community. The "illiterate" could cause only temporary ferment. Besides, his school continued to attract visitors from all over the state, and he heard that three other schools had adopted his ideas into their course of instruction. On top of that, his account of the Cheshire school had appeared in the January 1828 issue of the *American Journal of Education*. He closed his school in Bristol on March 28, 1828, but felt that he had impressed enough influential people there that his work might be continued.[64]

On April 14 Samuel May wrote to Alcott that several Boston women were about to form an infant school, and that he had recommended Alcott to them as a teacher. Less than a week later Alcott, full of optimism and enthusiasm despite the lack of a firm offer, headed for Boston.[65]

Notes

1. AJ 1 (1826-27): 122.

2. McCuskey, *Bronson Alcott: Teacher*, pp. 25-28; Alcott to W. A. Alcott, January 1826, in "Letters and Papers from 1814 to 1828."

3. McCuskey, *Bronson Alcott: Teacher*, p. 20; Alcott to Chatfield Alcott, February 13, 1826, in "Letters and Papers from 1814 to 1828."

4. AJ 1 (1826-27): 100, 112; "School Journal number II," pp. 2, 8, in ibid. Volume 1 of Alcott's manuscript journals contains an introductory section and three school journals, each numbered separately but bound together.

5. "School Journal number II," p. 8.

6. [A. Bronson Alcott], "Primary Education: Account of the Method of Instruction in the Primary School No. 1, of Cheshire, Connecticut," *American Journal of Education* 3, no. 1 (January 1828): 26-31 and no. 2 (February 1828): 86-94; McCuskey, *Bronson Alcott: Teacher*, p. 26; "School Journal number II," pp. 41, 48.

7. [Alcott], "Primary Education," *American Journal of Education* 3, no. 2 (February 1828): 91-93; AJ 1(1826-27): 113-16; "School Journal number II," p. 31.

8. "School Journal number II," p. 38.

9. Ibid., p. 13; "School Journal number I," in AJ 1 (1826-27), p. 44.

10. AJ 1 (1826-27): 11, 98; "School Journal number I," p. 40; "School Journal number II," p. 34.

11. "School Journal number II," pp. 1-2, 4, 66.

12. Ibid., pp. 4, 38, 54.

13. AJ 1 (1826-27): 5; "School Journal number II," pp. 52, 84.

14. "School Journal number II," p. 28.

15. Alcott to W. A. Alcott, March 1826, in A. Bronson Alcott, "Autobiographical Collections," 3 (1823-1834): 42 located at Houghton Library, 59M-307 (2); "School Journal number II," p. 87; [William Russell], "Closing Address," *American Journal of Education* 1, no. 12 (December 1826): 1-9. Alcott pasted a copy of this address into his journal.

16. [Russell], "Closing Address," p. 8.

17. AJ 1 (1826-27), opposite p. 1.

18. Ibid., title page, p. 125; "School Journal number III," p. 89, in AJ 1 (1826-27); *Hints to Parents* (London, 1825-27); William Maclure, "An Epitome of the Improved Pestalozzian System of Education," *American Journal of Arts and Sciences* 10 (February 1826): 145-56.

19. AJ 1 (1826-27): 3-4, 104: J. A. Green, ed., *Pestalozzi's Educational Writings* (New York: Longman's Green and Co., 1912), pp. 87, 95, 101, 143.

20. "School Journal number III," p. 4; Frederick Mayer, *American Ideas and Education* (Columbus, Ohio: Charles E. Merrill, Inc. 1964), p. 230.

21. Green, ed., *Pestalozzi's Educational Writings*, pp. 87, 93, 104, 142, 151-53.

22. Ibid., p. 86; AJ 1 (1826-27): 125; "School Journal number III," p. 87.

23. Sydney Ahlstrom, "The Scottish Philosophy and American Theology," *Church History* 24 (September 1955): 257-72; Merle Curti, *The Growth of American Thought*, 3d ed. (New York: Harper and Row, 1964), p. 228.

24. " School Journal number III," p. 87.

25. Adam Smith, *The Theory of Moral Sentiments*, 2 vols. (New York: Evert Duyckinck, *et al.*, 1822), 1:1 ff.

26. AJ 1 (1826-27): 97; "School Journal number II," pp. 13-14.

27. AJ 1 (1826-27): 96.

28. J. F. C. Harrison, *Robert Owen and the Owenites in Britain and America* (London: Routledge and Kegan Paul, 1969), pp. 163-65: Arthur Bestor, *Backwoods Utopias*, 2d ed. (Philadelphia: University of Pennsylvania Press, 1970), pp. 104, 111-12; Robert Owen, *A New View of Society* (London: J. M. Dent and Sons, 1966), pp. 16-17.

29. Harrison, *Robert Owen*, pp. 140, 160, 36-39.

30. Owen, *A New View*, p. 19.

31. AJ 1 (1826-27): 125; "School Journal number II," pp. 4, 123-24; Harrison, *Robert Owen*, p. 165; William Maclure to Alcott, November 25, 1827, in "Autobiographical Collections," vol. 3.

32. Alcott to Joseph C. Alcox, December 15, 1825, in "Letters and Papers from 1814 to 1828."

33. "School Journal number I," pp. 31, 37, 43, 64, 73; "School Journal number II," pp. 4, 87.

34. Alcott to W. A. Alcott, January 1826, in "Letters and Papers from 1814 to 1828."

35. "School Journal number I," p. 70.

36. Ibid., p. 85.

37. Ibid., p. 88; "School Journal number II," p. 13.

38. "School Journal number II," pp. 12, 63.

39. Ibid., p. 78.

40. "School Journal number I," p. 68.

41. AJ 1 (1826-27): 3; Alcott to W. A. Alcott, January 1826, in "Letters and Papers from 1814 to 1828"; "School Journal number I," p. 34.

42. "School Journal number I," pp. 35, 51, 68; "School Journal number II," pp. 58, 79.

43. "School Journal number II," p. 79; Ahlstrom, *Religious History*, pp. 419-20.

44. "School Journal number III," pp. 61-62.

45. "School Journal number I," p. 37.

46. Ibid., p. 70; "School Journal number II," p. 79.

47. "School Journal number II," pp. 86-87, 79.

48. "School Journal number I," p. 79.

49. Ibid., pp. 51, 58.
50. "School Journal number II," p. 20.
51. "School Journal number III," p. 55.
52. "School Journal number I," p. 75.
53. [Alcott], "Primary Education," *American Journal of Education* 3, no. 1 (January 1828): 28-29; "School Journal number II," p. 48; "School Journal number III," pp. 4, 34.
54. "School Journal number III," p. 11.
55. Ibid., pp. 32, 55, 67.
56. "School Journal number II," p. 47; John M. Keagy to Alcott, April 27, 1827, in "Autobiographical Collections," 3:51.
57. Henry Barnard, "History of Common Schools in Connecticut," *American Journal of Education* (Barnard's) 5, no. 13 (June 1858): 128-29; Jarvis Means Morse, *A Neglected Period of Connecticut's History, 1818-1850* (New Haven, Conn.: Yale University Press, 1933), pp. 144-45; Samuel J. May, "The Revival of Education," an address to the Normal Association, Bridgewater, Mass., August 8, 1855, p. 17, from a printed cutting of this in A. Bronson Alcott, comp., "Autobiographical Collections" vol. 7, 1856-67, MS at Houghton Library, 59M-307 (6).
58. Thomas J. Mumford, ed., *Memoir of Samuel J. May* (Boston: Roberts Brothers, 1873), pp. 118-19, 121-22; "School Journal number II," p. 76; "School Journal number III," pp. 15-16.
59. "School Journal number III," pp. 26, 28, 30; *Connecticut Observor (May 7, 1827); Boston Recorder and Telegraph* (May 11, 1827); Mumford, ed., *Memoir of Samuel J. May*, p. 122.
60. "School Journal number III," pp. 79, 82, 107; Alcott to Chatfield Alcott, July 18, 1827, in "Letters and Papers from 1814 to 1828"; Mumford, ed., *Memoir of Samuel J. May*, pp. 122-23. It is not clear why Alcott did not attend the convention in Hartford himself.
61. Mumford, ed., *Memior of Samuel J. May*, p. 122. The "other instance" May referred to was probably his meeting William Lloyd Garrison.
62. Abby May Alcott, "Autobiography," p. 122, MS at Houghton Library, 59M-311 (3 and 4). This included pages torn from a notebook, fragments of the original autobiography.
63. Alcott to S. J. May, August 30, 1827, from a copy in Alcott's hand in A. Bronson Alcott, comp., "Autobiographical Materials," MS at Houghton Library, 59M-306 (24); S. J. May to Alcott, September 4, 1827, from a copy in Alcott's hand owned by the Fruitlands Museum.
64. AJ 2 (1827-28): 4-6, 9, 12, 15, 19, 21, 26; Alcott to Abby May [Alcott], January 21, 1828, from a copy in Alcott's hand in "Autobiographical Materials."
65. S. J. May to Alcott, April, 14, 1828, from a copy in Alcott's hand owned by the Fruitlands Museum.

3

The Reformer, 1828–30

ALCOTT found the exciting, bustling city of Boston considerably different from the environment he had known in Wolcott, Cheshire, and Bristol. When he arrived there in the spring of 1828, Boston was a hub of land transportation in the northeastern part of the United States. Indeed, by 1830 there were 250 daily stagecoach arrivals and departures. It was no less important in commercial shipping. Ranking third behind New York and New Orleans, it cleared 206,736 tons of vessels in 1830. Capital produced by Boston's commerce was a major factor in transforming New England from an economy based on farming and the production of raw materials to one based on manufacturing and the factory system. Such capital had allowed Francis Cabot Lowell and a group of fellow Boston merchants to organize in 1813 the cotton cloth factory in Waltham that would become the representative form of the factory system in the United States.[1]

Rapid economic transformation determined that the forces of social and cultural change that Alcott had experienced in microcosm in Wolcott would converge in Boston. The city's population, only 18,000 in 1790, was rapidly approaching 60,000 in 1828. It had increased by one-third just since 1820, making Boston the United States' fourth largest city behind New York, Philadelphia, and Baltimore. Already there were districts of the city inhabited by a class of urban poor, an ugly indication that the misery and abuses many Americans associated with Europe were finding their way to the United States. The threat to the social structure of the close-knit New England community and the threat to traditional religious and moral values were even clearer in Boston that in Connecticut. Alcott's confrontation with change would of necessity become even more dramatic and challenging.[2]

Yet Boston seemed to provide a large reservoir of answers to the problems created by rapid change, making the city as attractive as it was forbidding to the Connecticut farm boy. There were interesting people in Boston, people who were grappling with stimulating ideas, who readily gave a hearing to a multitude of humanitarian reforms, and who could help Alcott in his intellectual search for answers to the problems of human nature and human destiny. In addition, there were people who could reinforce his identity as a reformer, a rebel, an iconoclast. They could help promote his sense of certainty about the correctness of his views in the face of all odds, a certainty that hid much insecurity about himself and the world around him.

William Russell was in Boston in 1828, publishing his *American Journal of Education* and finding readers and supporters. Radical feminist Frances Wright flaunted all decorum and propriety by giving public lectures, and curious Bostonians assembled to listen. Some of these listeners gossiped and condemned, but others were receptive and would later subscribe to Wright's and Robert Dale Owen's irreverent periodical, the New York-based *Free Enquirer*. Josiah Holbrook would soon be laying the groundwork in Boston for the American Lyceum, and wealthy Maine merchant William Ladd, founder of the American Peace Society, would seek support for the abolition of war. William Lloyd Garrison would soon begin in Boston his most important work for the abolition of slavery. Such reforms added to and partly grew out of the religious ferment that had gripped Boston for more than a decade. Unitarianism, led by William Ellery Channing, was winning its lengthy battle with orthodox Congregationalism. Harvard College and the Boston Ministerial Association were Unitarian institutions by 1828. But the Unitarians did not dominate Boston. A religious seeker like Alcott could attend a Congregationalist service led by Nathaniel L. Frothingham, Henry Ware, or Lyman Beecher in the morning, and in the afternoon hear Channing or Ezra Stiles Gannett at the Unitarian Federal Street Church with plenty of time left for the Baptists, the Methodists, the Universalists, and even the Swedenborgians.[3]

No wonder Alcott felt that he had entered the center of "important operations." He encouraged his cousin William to join him in Boston in order to experience directly a society more "moral and intellectual" than that in Connecticut. Bostonians would surely place a greater value on their character and opinions than the people of Wolcott, Cheshire, or Bristol. There was no place in the country, Alcott fancied, where the means of intellectual and moral improvement were greater than in Boston.[4]

Soon after his arrival on April 24, 1828, Alcott sought the friendship and support of William Russell. He was overjoyed to find that Russell's ideas on education closely coincided with his own. Russell was a clear and forceful thinker with an unbounded enthusiasm for education that especially impressed Alcott. He found that Russell had been greatly influenced by the Scottish-English movement for popular education led by Henry Brougham and Thomas Campbell, whose "mechanics' institutes" were liberally advertised by Russell in his *American Journal of Education*. Russell, a Scottish immigrant, had taught in Savannah, Georgia, and in New Haven, Connecticut, before moving to Boston in the mid-1820s. "With no individual in B[oston] do I pass an hour, more to my inclination than with [Russell]," Alcott confided to his journal. "His mind is free from all those narrow prejudices, and arbitrary forms, which destroy the natural simplicity and frankness of the human heart."[5]

Russell acquainted Alcott with the "Infant School Society of Boston" that was to sponsor his school. On April 30 he met with this group to discuss plans and arrangements. The Society was made up of wealthy women from Boston's upper class who considered themselves "benevolent" and who wished to serve the poor by enabling poor mothers to work while their children were removed from the "everyday evils of want and vice." The infant school movement had begun in England under the influence of Robert Owen, who believed that education began at birth and required immediate guidance. The women of the Infant School Society, along with other philanthropists and educators in Boston, hoped to keep up with reformers in London, New York, and Philadelphia, were infant schools had already been established. The Boston school was to be a charity for poor children between the ages of eighteen months and four years. By paying annual subscriptions of two dollars, members of the Society shared the cost of teachers, school materials, and meals for the children. They expected parents of the pupils to pay a token six cents a week. The Society promised parents that there would be no corporal punishment in the school, but they demanded that parents make sure that their children attended every day and were "clean washed and dressed in whole and clean clothes." As advertised in the *American Journal of Education*, the school's purpose was to promote moral and religious improvement and to "prevent vice in the poorer classes."[6] Clearly, this was an attempt at enlightened social control. These scions of wealth and status combined a genuine concern for the poor with an effort to make sure that poverty and social dislocation in the rapidly changing city did not undermine their carefully guarded social position and value system.

Alcott agreed to be superintendent of the infant school and also agreed to visit other such schools in New York and Philadelphia while waiting for an appropriate classroom to become available in Boston. He was in those cities from May 15 to May 22, but was not impressed with the schools he found there. They were too "mechanical." They relied too much on memorization and on the mere repetition of the instructor's words. Though supported by sincere reformers like Philadelphia economist Matthew Carey and Swedenborgian minister Maskell M. Carll, these schools produced an unimaginative "sing song style of utterance." Like most American schools, Alcott felt, they were geared to inculcate orthodoxy, and were good for making only "fools and sectarians."[7]

On June 23, 1828, Alcott opened the Salem Street Infant School in Boston with eighteen students, "mostly foreigners." Undoubtedly, the growing numbers of urban poor resulted in part from immigration, although Alcott did not say which nationalities were represented in his school. By August 11 forty students attended regularly, and occasionally as many as sixty came. He was convinced that they were becoming "wiser, better and happier" under his guidance. Interested observers visited every day. Members of the Infant School Society were pleased, and Alcott actively sought their approbation.[8]

His teaching methods remained much as they had been at Cheshire and Bristol, although with younger children he could not expect to teach arithmetic and composition. But he conversed with the children, told them stories, led them in marching, and allowed them to write on slates and to pantomime pictures and stories. "We have attempted very little *formal instruction*," he wrote to William on August 4; "our chief design has been to *awaken* the *feelings*, and *faculties* of the children, by a course of kind, and affectionate treatment...." Alcott's methods and evident skill as a teacher impressed William Russell who wrote a letter to the editor of the *Christian Teacher's Manual* in November 1828, praising Alcott's success in bringing the goodness and happiness of the children into conscious exercise. Alcott used no force, said Russell; he simply led the students to be "free and voluntary agents in their own improvement."[9]

Encouraged by the initial success of the Salem Street School and Russell's acceptance of his ideas, Alcott began writing several articles on education and infant schools for volume three of the *American Journal of Education*, which appeared in the summer and fall of 1828. These didactic essays, including "Elementary Instruction," "The Education of Infant Children," "Maternal Instruction," and "The Infant School Society of Boston," were clear, concrete, well-organized, albeit dry and sermonlike. They reflected the originality and insight of his developing educational ideas and methods. They expressed ambitions by Alcott that went far beyond his daily work at Salem Street and the good women of the Infant School Society. He had grandiose plans to write articles and books on education, social morality, marriage, Christianity, "national equality in property," government, pacifism, and even human perfectibility. Teaching the infant school was but a lesser means to a greater end. "We are willing," he said, "to become 'hewers of wood and drawers of water,' to a thoughtless and thankless age, assured that our exertions will result in the improvement of our species. With the means of regenerating the world in our mind, we are willing to devote our time, our mind, and effort, to the instruction of children." He felt his efforts could save a "perverted world" from ignorance and misery and could substitute the "peaceful reign of Truth and Reason" for the "kingdom of Errour, Folly and Superstition."[10]

Alcott was prepared to give up everything for reform:

> Our life is to be devoted to the amelioration of our fellow beings.... We are aware that the projects which are contemplated are opposed to the ruling opinions, and prejudices of this age and that we shall render ourselves unpopular—and be deemed a visionary and an enthusiast. We care little about these things.[11]

In many ways martyrdom to the cause of reform would serve as penance for past sins yet unexculpated. His failures as a peddler, his thoughtless extravagance as a youth, the debt he had forced upon his father, all gnawed at his conscience. Unrelentingly, that conscience had saddled him with an awesome burden of self-doubt. But the elixir of reform, seemingly so abundant in Boston, had helped lift that burden. It enabled him to relieve his doubts by redirecting them to society and institutions. Personal guilt became society's guilt, and condemnation of society became self-justification. In a sense this was only fair, because the unasked-for social and economic changes that had disrupted society in rural Connecticut had caused the personal doubts about values and vocation in the first place. Reform was a freeing and regenerating force for Alcott. If it gave the power to condemn, it also bestowed the power to save. Since he had so closely interrelated his own guilt with the evils apparent in society, the power he had found to regenerate society also became the power to regenerate himself.

With such an important task before him, he could brook no obstacles. By early October 1828 he began to chafe under the direction of the Infant School Society. Some of the members had begun to complain about the lack of results at Salem Street. They were attempting to measure learning, Alcott believed, much as the people of Cheshire and Bristol tried to do, by the quantity of information the pupils could recite. He resented the implication that the children should be told what to say and how to say everything. His goal was to preserve the beauty and variety of God's purposes by preserving the individuality of each student. He could do this only by allowing the children room for self-direction, for individual creativity. "The business of an infant school," he declared, "is to make men—not parrots—active, independent, thinking men—not . . . obsequious, thoughtless machines."[12]

Samuel J. May, no doubt detecting an uncompromising attitude in his friend, warned Alcott to take all pains to make his ideas acceptable to the public. Alcott noted that this was good advice, but it did not make it any easier to bear what to him was the increasing nosiness and officiousness of the women of the Society. Even before he began teaching at Salem Street he planned to have a school of his own soon. By October this was imperative. He began to seek wealthy patrons who would sponsor a school under his sole control wherein he would have free rein to experiment. The Infant School Society had further added to his disenchantment by rejecting Abigail May as Alcott's assistant at the Salem Street School in favor of a forty-year-old matron by the name of Mrs. Brush. He was becoming increasingly attached to Abby May, and he hoped that she would assist him in his new school. On October 17 he left the Salem Street School in the care of Mrs. Brush, and three days later opened his own school on Common Street with six students aged three to seven, including the son of William Russell.[13]

The Common Street School proved to be moderately successful. By January 1, 1829, Alcott had seventeen students, sons and daughters of some of the most "worthy and intelligent" persons of the city. His patrons provided him a salary of five hundred dollars a year. He felt that his opportunities were greater than ever before. "I have the means of finding my own place among men," he exulted, "of obtaining a better knowledge of myself, and determining, with more certainty, the range of my future usefulness." Especially happy was his relationship with the May family, particularly Abby.[14]

Born October 8, 1800, Abby May was the youngest child of Colonel Joseph May, a prominent Boston merchant and a leading member of King's Chapel,

Boston's first Unitarian society. Joseph May was a man of connections. Thus Abby's family relations seemingly included everybody who was anybody in Boston: the Sewalls, the Quincys, the Frothinghams, the Greeles. Her great aunt, Dorothy Quincy Scott, had been John Hancock's wife. Alcott was understandably self-conscious in such company, a country boy amid the Brahmins. He feared his "manner and habit" often put people off, but he lashed back defensively with the observation that "what is deemed good manners, may often be but the varnishing of folly and ignorance." Upon meeting Madame Scott, an eccentric old woman who in Alcott's opinion flaunted her relationship with the Hancock name, he pointed out that she would provide moral philosophers with a perfect study of "the influence of station upon weak and ignorant minds."[15]

Whatever he may have thought of the Mays, they had the power to influence the very people who could best further his ambitions, and he knew it. But he was attracted to Abby not because of her social connections; rather he liked her vigorous, independent mind, her "moral excellence," and especially her interest in the "improvement of the human race." For her part, Abby found Alcott to be moderate, humble, prudent, tranquil, and firm, qualities that she felt balanced her emotional, impetuous, forward, and arbitrary nature. Her own impetuousness may well have hidden the fact that her "companion" was less moderate, humble, and prudent than she thought. Their courtship began soon after Alcott's arrival in Boston, but not until August 1828 did Alcott, being shy about such matters, finally admit to her that he was in love. And he did so indirectly by giving her his journal to read while she vacationed with friends in Hingham. The journal told all. The only disappointment in these months of courtship was Abby's decision not to be Alcott's assistant at the Common Street School. Samuel J. May had warned his sister that a "censorious world" would only ascribe selfish motives to such an arrangement, especially since the Mays were responsible for bringing Alcott to Boston. Abby wisely took the advice and declined Alcott's offer.[16]

Alcott found further happiness, as well as confirmation of his faith in the power of human beings to remake society, among the various reformers, radicals, and freethinkers who fluttered about Boston in the late 1820s. In July 1828 Josiah Holbrook became Alcott's roommate at Mrs. Newell's boarding house on Franklin Street. Like William Russell, Holbrook had become interested in the movement for popular education in England, particularly the mechanics' institutes. In October 1826 he had published an article in the *American Journal of Education* that became the manifesto of the American lyceum movement. He had proposed a Society for Mutual Education to provide economical and practical education for young people and to disseminate "useful information" throughout the community. A month later he had organized the first local lyceum in the United States—for the factory workers of Millbury, Massachusetts, near Worcester. After organizing several other local lyceums, including one for Worcester County, he had come to Boston to create similar societies in the city. Alcott and Holbrook quickly became friends and engaged in long conversations at Mrs. Newell's about the important of popular education. Holbrook visited Alcott's Salem Street School, and Alcott listened patiently to Holbrook's plan for an "American Lyceum," which was to be a National Society for the Dissemination of Useful Knowledge.[17]

On November 8, 1828, Alcott, who believed Holbrook's plan to be further evidence of the "spirit of improvement" pervading the nation in this "interesting age," attended a meeting at the Exchange Coffee House to organize a "National System for Popular Improvement." The new organization elected Daniel Webster president and George Barrell Emerson secretary. The members charged a committee, composed of Emerson, Holbrook, and William Russell, with the responsibility of promoting the lyceum idea. Alcott was enthusiastic. The lyceum would be another means of regenerating society. Branches of the National Lyceum in every American town could sponsor infant schools and education for women. They could improve the minds of the laboring classes and influence the tone of thought and feeling of town inhabitants. "A new vigor and energy may thus be thrown into the common mind," he concluded. "Improvement must be the consequence."[18]

However, there were many things about the lyceum movement fundamentally at odds with Alcott's theories of education and the development of human nature. To the leaders of the lyceum movement, education was a matter of imparting knowledge, disseminating information as though it could be poured into hungry and heretofore empty minds. There was little talk of studying the operations of the human mind, a study so essential to Alcott. Alcott believed that learning was a spontaneous process welling up from within according to the natural workings of the mind. Thus an educator, rather than pouring knowledge into students from without, had to call forth internal creative powers and allow plenty of liberty of action so that these creative energies could grow and expand. Also, the lyceum movement at bottom was patronizing in its attitude toward the lower classes. Although it fed upon democratic aspirations for equal opportunity and equal access to education for all, many of its leaders were concerned with disseminating only certain kinds of information, and with guiding the social and moral behavior of the lower classes. In a word, they wanted social control. Alcott was not averse to social control *per se*; in fact, he favored a supervision of the "amusements" and moral behavior of each community. But Alcott had no social position to defend against the encroachments of democracy, and his growing faith in the potential goodness of human beings tended to remove any need to control them. Indeed, he opposed coercive laws that limited human freedom, feeling that they were the result of that unenlightened theory of human depravity which was finally being challenged by more "liberal" views of human nature. He and Holbrook quarreled about religious beliefs in March of 1829, Holbrook taking the orthodox position that human nature was originally depraved. Alcott suggested that Holbrook, like most American educators, was "tainted with the poison of this doctrine."[19]

In the end, Alcott found the leaders of the lyceum movement much too limited in their vision. Although he approved their efforts, he felt that they could never effect the true regeneration. For lyceums were directed at adults, and adults were too far gone, Alcott believed, to be helped much. Perhaps that was the trouble with the forty-five-year-old Holbrook. Regeneration had to begin with the young, and it would be a long, slow process.[20]

As his dissatisfaction with Holbrook and the lyceum was growing, Alcott became attracted to the far more radical ideas of Frances Wright, feminist and advocate of the rights of the laboring classes. She and Robert Dale Owen had just established the *Free Enquirer* in New York City when in March 1829 Alcott sent for a subscription. He knew nothing about this magazine of "free thought" nor about the ideas of Wright and Owen except that they differed from the "general sentiment." But this was enough to make their opinions interesting, and Alcott decided he would read them with an open mind and judge for himself. Wright, influenced by Robert Owen's New Harmony experiment, had in 1825 established a community at Nashoba, near Memphis, Tennessee. This two-thousand-acre plantation was to have given slaves an opportunity to purchase their freedom through labor and to prepare themselves by means of an educational system modeled after that at New Harmony. The experiment had failed. Local citizens had objected to attempts by Nashoba residents to establish a racially integrated community, and talk of sexual relations between whites and blacks at Nashoba had earned it a local reputation as a brothel. Wright had then taken to the lecture platform, an action sure to offend a large majority of Americans who considered such public appearances inappropriate for women. She spoke of the need for educational reform, an end to capital punishment and imprisonment for debt, and the uplifting of oppressed workers and women. In the *Free Enquirer* she urged the abandonment of all authority based on "dubious" theological opinion and advocated instead a spirit of free inquiry and investigation by which all knowledge would be exact and verifiable.[21]

On July 16, 1829, Alcott heard Frances Wright speak at Boston's Tremont Theatre. Her lecture confirmed Alcott's own ideas about reform, that ignorance was the source of all evil in society and the education was the sure means to correct it. He met Wright briefly afterward and received a copy of the lecture from her. Although a little disturbed about her "masculine air," which seemed "a little unsuited to her sex," he praised her for her "good sense," her faith in education, and her spirit of free thinking. "Comparison of opinions on all subjects," he concluded, "is the only true method by which truth can be attained. We must view all sides of a question in an unprejudiced light. We must seek all the facts of the case: and having done this our opinion should then be [the] result of this comparison."[22]

Nevertheless, Alcott could not allow "free thought" to disturb his religious and moral convictions. The attacks on Christianity by the *Free Enquirer* and Robert Owen's *New Harmony Gazette* upset him, and he accused these proponents of free thought of not being free and liberal enough to treat all opinions with respect, even those of a religion with which they disagreed. In December 1829 a Boston society of "free enquirers" asked him to teach their children, but fearing that these people were too much a "party" and did not love virtue for its own sake, he refused. His major concern was that free-thought advocates, by denouncing Christianity, removed the chief support of moral behavior from "minds of little reflection." He was yet unwilling to place the grounds for defining good and evil solely on the power of the human mind. Although he questioned traditional Christianity as the best authority in these matters, he still felt the need for some authority greater than the individual to help define moral behavior. Wright and Owen, by challenging all authorities but the rational power of the human mind, were opening the door to a secular form of antinomianism; by condemning the authorities for virtue and good, they gave encouragement to sin.[23]

These reservations did not prevent Alcott from dabbling in other reformist and philanthropic activities or from engaging in what he considered to be "fearless free thinking." He read the literature of reform and benevolence as presented in the *American Journal of Education*, the *Christian Examiner*, the *North American Review*, and the *Unitarian Advocate*. Henry Brougham's *Views on Popular Education* gave him some insight into English reform thought. Benjamin Franklin's *Autobiography* impressed him because of Franklin's apparent ability to arrange all conditions and circumstances in a way that contributed to his "improvement." In the *Edinburgh Review* he ran across the ideas of Jeremy Bentham, and for a time he held the utilitarian view that the importance of philosophy was its adaptation to the promotion of human happiness. He read from the writings of Epictetus and Aristotle and concluded that ancient philosophy had much to offer modern society because it was written, he supposed, at a time of free inquiry into human nature and human character. The Massachusetts Peace Society attracted his attention, as did peace advocate William Ladd, with whom he spent an evening. Though sympathetic, Alcott was convinced that war could be ended only by drawing out the "pacific character" of children by means of infant schools and nurseries. He became more sensitive to the oppression of the poor and the working classes. Pestalozzi, he felt, had finally challenged the traditional idea that only the rich should be educated while the poor were relegated to menial labor. Education was a means of improving all human beings.[24]

Not surprisingly, Alcott's exploration of reform thought in Boston led him to a confrontation with the evil that seemed to him to overshadow all social evils of the time—slavery. He had directly observed slavery in his peddling trips to the South, yet he had never before given it thought as an object of reform. But by November 1828 he had begun attacking it. The slaveholders claimed that slaves had no desire for liberty, and Alcott argued that the fact that slavery had destroyed the slaves' love of liberty was the strongest reason for breaking the chains. On October 15 and 16, 1830, he heard William Lloyd Garrison speak on the abolition of slavery. Garrison, a native of nearby Newburyport, had been imprisoned in Baltimore the previous April for his scathing attacks on the barbarities of slavery. After his release he had come to Boston to organize an antislavery society with the aid of fellow propagandist Benjamin Lundy and wealthy New York merchant Arthur Tappan. No church would offer Garrison a meetinghouse, and he was forced to speak at Julien Hall under the good graces of Abner Kneeland's society of free thinkers, whom he considered to be infidels. Alcott found Garrison's diatribe against slaveholders and colonizers to be "full of truth and power," although he worried that Garrison attacked all slaveholders as unchristian without distinguishing those who kept slaves out of good motives. After the speech on October 15, Alcott, Samuel J. May, and lawyer Samuel Sewall introduced themselves to Garrison. Alcott invited them all to his home and they listened until midnight while Garrison discussed the need for immediate and unconditional emancipation of the slaves. May said later that his soul was baptized in Garrison's spirit that night. Alcott may not have been quite so enraptured as May, but he certainly was impressed. On November 8 Alcott attended a meeting of abolitionists to form a Boston antislavery society. Present that day at Sewall's office were Garrison, May, Baptist missionary and temperance advocate William Collier, and Isaac Knapp, who would become Garrison's partner in *The Liberator*. However, nothing permanent was accomplished, and when the antislavery society was finally formed in 1831, Alcott had left Boston.[25]

Antislavery would come to dominate reform in the United States, but to Alcott in 1830, it was just one of many movements demanding his attention. His was an uncertain quest amid a swirl of ideas. But underlying it all—his educational ideas, his reformist proclivities—was his ongoing need to find a personal religious faith and a theology that would make sense when united with his concern for a scientific study of the human mind and his belief in the ability of human nature and human society to regenerate and perfect itself. In his search, Alcott went from church to church, from denomination to denomination. He heard the leader of orthodox Congregationalism in Boston, Lyman Beecher. He made the rounds of the Unitarians: John Gorham Palfrey, John Pierpont, George Ripley, Ezra Stiles Gannett, and William F. P. Greenwood. But all of these and lesser figures paled in comparison to the powerful leader of Unitarianism, William Ellery Channing. Alcott perceived in Channing the "features of greatness." He was a man whose preaching filled his hearers with "energy and purpose," and made Alcott at least feel his own "value in the scale of being."[26]

Channing had been minister at the Federal Street Church since June 1, 1803. His 1819 sermon in Baltimore at the ordination of Jared Sparks entitled "Unitarian Christianity" had become the classic formulation of the Unitarian creed. He had been the acknowledged leader in the religious ferment that had caused about one-fourth of the Congregational churches in New England to become Unitarian. Central to Channing's theology was his high estimate of the spiritual nature of human beings. The elements of divinity, he believed, lay within each person, and the great work of religion was to unfold them. Human ability to know the attributes of God derived from those same attributes seen first in human nature then transferred to God. "We see God around us," said Channing, "because he dwells within us. It is by a kindred wisdom that we discern wisdom in his works." He cautioned that the "divine likeness" that he perceived in human nature did not mean extraordinary or extravagant powers, micraculous or supernatural gifts. The workings of divinity were mundane, resting in the essential faculties of human nature common to all human beings. "To resemble our Creator," he said, "we need not fly from society, and entrance ourselves in lonely contemplation and prayer. . . . Our proper work is to approach God by the free and natural unfolding of our highest powers—of understanding, conscience, love, and the moral will."[27]

Thus Channing and the Unitarians had been exploring the possibilities of the innate "moral sense," left so ill-defined by the Scottish philosophers, in the same way that Alcott had done in his reading and speculation while teaching in Connecticut. From the first time he heard Channing in April 1828, Alcott was impressed by and attracted to his positive view of human nature. It was a pleasant and hopeful contrast to Lyman Beecher, whose mind, Alcott felt, was full of "fear, depravity, doubt, and misery." Channing provided tentative answers to very troublesome questions for Alcott, especially to the question of the relationship between education, reform, mental development, and religious belief. He did this by directly relating the development of the human faculties to the development of spirituality. This was just what Alcott wanted to hear. It gave religious sanction to his idea that proper education could produce not just better people intellectually, but good people morally and spiritually as well.[28]

Alcott also liked Channing's de-emphasis of the role of the ordained clergy. In Channing's view, all individuals could be teachers, ministers, and priests, for salvation depended on the personal efforts of all people. Each individual had the power to make himself or herself virtuous by means of the "free, original, spontaneous exercise of the soul." Channing was certainly Boston's moral teacher, Alcott thought. He taught Christ's system, the system of redemption, of improvement, of happiness. "Future generations," Alcott concluded, "will hail Channing as a moral and intellectual benefactor."[29]

Channing was also a benefactor to Alcott's Common Street School. Such encouragement and support from this powerful and influential man were a key to the school's success. These alone would have been enough to convince Alcott of Channing's "liberality" and of his responsibility for giving Boston the means of intellectual and moral improvement greater than those of any other city in the country. Nevertheless, Alcott still refused to join a Unitarian congregation. He remained a religious rebel, unwilling to be a part of any denomination. Even the charisma of Channing could not get him to accede to an obnoxious sectarianism. Indeed, Alcott planned to write articles about the deleterious effects of battles among the various denominations. Truth, he felt, should not and could not be subjugated to sectarian forms and doctrines. He suspected that even Channing had a greater zeal for Unitarianism than he had for truth. Instead, Alcott sought a "true" theology and religion that would transcend sectarian bounds. He charged Unitarians with too great a concern with doctrinal matters and not enough with the practical. His faith would have relevance to daily life.[30]

> Religion, after all is not made a sufficiently *rational*, spontaneous, and social affair. Duty is too much involved in belief—in theory—in form— rather than in practice—in intelligent feeling and action. The morality of the pulpit is not sufficiently adapted to that of everyday life. Preaching is too much an affair of another life; to teach men how to die, rather than how to live, to present the felicities of another life as objects of attainment rather than those of the present. It takes the thoughts of men too far from themselves—to heaven, rather than to the concerns of the earth given us by our Great Employer.[31]

Alcott believed that he could find the true purposes of God only in the nature and purposes of human beings, not in the "dark labyrinth of antiquated theology." His would be a personal religion as he had always known it in the piety of his family on Spindle Hill and in the individual spiritual message he had found in the *Bible*, in *Pilgrim's Progress*, and in *Paradise Lost*. But it would also be a religion worked out not in lonely piety but through the demonstrable reform of this world. God's immanence would be proved in human action. Puritan pietism and Enlightenment rationalism had meshed in Bronson Alcott.[32]

The purpose of a minister, Alcott thought, was to acquaint human beings with themselves and to make them more "intelligently benevolent." Moral precepts were useless without practical illustrations of how to live the moral life in the present rather than in the future. "We want a Theology which is to teach us how to employ ourselves *here*—not how to employ ourselves hereafter." Alcott's reformist energies had led him to a firm belief in this-worldly salvation:

> Mankind have talked long enough of a *spiritual heaven*. It is time they began to talk of a *spiritual earth*. We have been seeking the nature of God, whom we have not seen, and remain ignorant of our fellow beings, who are ever before us, whom we clearly see. We have attempted to know God, without the knowledge of his works; whence we can only know him but through his works.[33]

Therefore Alcott thought it essential to combine religion with education. The cornerstone of education, he believed, was a knowledge of human nature, and this same knowledge was also the cornerstone of religious faith. "A knowledge of the principles of human nature and of the influences of society upon it, will, it seems to me, be an *adequate cause* to produce the *effects* ascribed to Christianity and its Author." Not surprisingly, Alcott considered his classroom to be a ministry and himself to be a minister as much as were Channing, Beecher, Gannett, Frothingham, and all the other respected divines of the city.[34]

To further his ambition to combine religion and education, Alcott agreed on September 7, 1828, to become superintendent of the Chauncy Place Sunday School—this in addition to his weekday work in the infant schools. Interdenominational and lay-controlled, this Sunday School was a local effort at religious benevolence in the manner of the national Sunday School movement sponsored by philanthropic organizations such as the American Bible Society, the American Tract Society, and the American Sunday School Union. Here Alcott could concentrate on applying his theory of proper moral instruction. He used stories and parables such as the biblical "good Samaritan" and Parson Weems's mythical tales of George Washington as practical illustrations of proper conduct. He vigorously opposed any attempt at indoctrination or forced memorization of abstract theological concepts. "Before they are taught to ask, they should be made to feel," he declared. "Before they are taught to pray, they should know to what, and to whom they are praying—to express their own feelings in their own way; and not in the ways of others, and thus raise a barrier against sincere and natural expression" He expected the children, as rational creatures, to be able to understand religious concepts fully by perceiving the relationship between cause and effect and applying this to everyday behavior. Thus he opposed telling the children stories of Jesus' miracles. Miracles would be "unreasonable" to them, impossible for them to understand, because the direct relationship between cause and effect in the miracles was obscure. The theology of the miracles was abstract and not immediately understood by the inductive method. Better to teach readily understandable concepts like the Golden Rule, which had obvious application in daily life.[35]

Alcott felt his method of religious instruction could instill morality and proper behavior in the children at Chauncy Place without injecting any "religious opinion" into them. Not only did this raise the thorny question of how to distinguish between truth and mere opinion, but it also antagonized those Sunday School teachers who thought it perfectly all right to mold the opinions of their charges. Some of the teachers accused him of heresy. Indeed, since Alcott's views were developed outside any structure, tradition, or authority, they could easily slip beyond the sanction of even the liberal-minded Unitarians.[36]

The Unitarians would agree to the great value Alcott placed upon human reason. They would support Alcott's belief that religion should be translated into benevolence, humanitarianism, good behavior, character, and the reform of obvious societal evils. The Unitarians believed as Alcott did that Jesus was a great and good man who set a high example of moral behavior. Channing and Alcott both agreed that human beings should love Jesus Christ for his moral goodness, and that they should imitate his practical virtues, not worship him for his supernatural powers. Channing and Alcott both felt that Christ defined moral laws in the same way that Locke, Newton, and Bacon described the physical laws of the universe. Though all Unitarians may not have accepted it, Channing agreed with Alcott that comparison of Christianity with other religions and beliefs in a rational and objective way was an important aid to the development of a reasonable faith. In faith, Channing felt that a closed-minded acceptance of Christian beliefs without comparison was far more dangerous to Christianity than opposition or infidelity. Above all, the Unitarians agreed with Alcott in his opposition to the orthodox Congregational belief in the original depravity of human nature. They believed that human beings were depraved, but not originally so. Depravity was the result of nothing innate. Unfavorable circumstances caused sin and evil, but human reason could alter these circumstances, allowing the original, innate goodness of human nature to come forth.[37]

As a result of this basic agreement Alcott decided that the Unitarians had a "more nearly correct" view of human nature than any other religious group. They addressed reason at every step; they presented a dignified idea of God, yet allowed imitation of God by human beings. Unitarianism essentially reinforced and solidified ideas he had already obtained from his reading of the Enlightenment empiricists and the Scottish philosophers and from his contacts with the Connecticut Awakening. Nevertheless, he soon ran into disagreement with the Unitarians over the problem of authority. He totally disregarded traditional authority and doctrine, rejecting such practices as the Eucharist because he felt that they subordinated truth to form and sectarian usage. His objection to teaching the miracles to his Sunday School class aroused the wrath of young Unitarian minister George Ripley. Ripley, who would later take the opposite position in the famous miracles controversy with Andrews Norton, now wanted the Chauncy Street children to be aware of the importance of this scriptural authority. It was a sensitive point, because the miracles provided for Unitarians the sole ground for the supernatural authority of the Christian scriptures, of Christianity itself. But Alcott cared nothing about such things. Human reason was fast becoming his only authority. He was coming to the same position that he had condemned in the free inquirers like Wright and Owen. He was close to making the awkward claim that his rational powers would lead him to the truth, whereas the rational powers of the free inquirers could lead to dangerous falsehoods.[38]

As the Unitarians became more and more suspicious of Alcott, his enchantment with them decreased. By 1830 he was accusing even the revered Channing, who in so many ways transcended his more truculent colleagues, of being enslaved to dogmatism. The major difficulty stemmed from the question of human nature and its potential. Not that the Unitarians disagreed about the existence of that potential; the question was the degree, the extent of it. The key to Alcott's intellectual development was his exploration of this human potential. It was the basis of his religious faith and his reformist impulse. He allowed no theological tradition nor philosophical position to hinder him. His growing discontent with the Unitarians resulted from the bounds they attempted to place on these explorations. Channing talked of cultivating the human mind, but he failed to consider the full ramifications of his position. Unitarianism was emotionally unsatisfying; it did not explore the full range of human faculties. "Theology is made a splendid assemblage of ideal Images," said Alcott of the Unitarians, "while the understanding, the affections, and the Conscience, are but too often left untouched."[39]

Alcott's exploration of the meaning of human potential meant a continuation of his attempt to reconcile human power with that of God and that of external circumstances or natural law. When he first arrived in Boston he was convinced of the awesome power of external circumstances in forming the mind, and his educational practices fitted that theory. "Man is, and owing to the very constitution of his nature, must be, to a very great extent, the creation of his surrounding circumstances," he said in May 1828. A year later he asserted that John Locke's belief that all ideas originated in sensations was the only safe foundation for educational theory. However, he continued to toy with the idea that there might be a reciprocal relationship between external circumstances and the power of the mind within. In October 1828 he said that "man is the author of his own condition—Society the author of the condition of its members. The providence of the Creator has nothing to do with it—unless we resolve this providence into the reciprocal influence of the circumstances in which its members are placed, and their influence upon the circumstances—modifying, and producing different conditions." Thus he identified God with the acting out of natural laws as seen in the interaction between the individual and the external environment. God's immanence, the ground of religious faith, was demonstrated, Alcott thought, in the mutual connection and dependence between the human mind and the material world surrounding it. The problem was to determine the precise nature of that connection and dependence, that reciprocal relationship.[40]

In early 1828 Alcott's definition of the inner capacity of the mind was as limited as that of the Scottish philosophers or the Utilitarians; that is, it amounted to the ability to perceive good and evil in the effects of things, and this because of the relative pleasure or pain involved in those effects. But by the end of 1828 his speculation and teaching, his growing faith in the ability of human beings to regenerate the earth, and the uplifting suggestions of Dr. Channing led him to give more range to the inner person. "There is a principle in human nature which earth cannot destroy," he said in December 1828 "there is a spirit in the human soul, which emanates not from the soil on which its natural body treads." It was shortly after this that Alcott lashed out against external authority of the kind that the Unitarians tried to establish with the evidence of the miracles. He began to perceive innate thoughts that could rise above these authorities or above external circumstances, thoughts born of God: "Our thoughts are the offspring of that divine power, which, when freed from the obstacles of human authority, and the influences of human circumstances, feels itself the agent of its own advancement, and the source of truth and virtue." Human beings were designed for progress, he confidently reported to William Alcott in January 1829, and the power of progress was within. The elements of future perfection were inborn. The soul had a redeeming power, and it was that principle, he felt, which constituted its "divine excellence" and rendered human beings worthy of the God who made them. Education had to form or reform this internal power of the soul.[41]

Whereas "circumstances" had long been for Alcott the determining force in human development, by June 1829 he had come to see them as a potential hindrance to the otherwise natural development of the divinity within. "The human mind," he said, "is too noble and divine a thing to be subjected to any influences, or to operate under any circumstances, which impair its beauty, or check its gradual and natural course toward perfection." This steadily growing acceptance of the idea of the innate potential of the human mind resulted from his increasing zeal for reform. Faith in the possibility of reform depended largely on the belief that human beings had the ability to manipulate the environment for good, to redeem society, and to redeem their own souls. He confessed to his cousin that he would despair if it were not for his faith in this redeeming power.[42]

The explanation for Alcott's driving need to believe in reform lay in the disruptive impact of social and economic change. Such change had formed a large part of his early life in the decay of the traditional structure of Wolcott and in the dramatic world of motion and excitement in Boston. At first it had brought him personal failure, insecurity, and guilt. Reform was his means of dealing with those feelings of inadequacy. He speculated about change after seeing the museum-preserved remains of a prehistoric animal in January 1830. This gigantic reminder of worlds gone by raised questions in Alcott's mind about the transient and permanent in the universe. He saw change, decay, innovation, life, and activity written on all living things. "About, within us, all is passing away, mingling with the material universe, and forming part of the great mechanism of nature. Truth and love are alone immutable and immortal; the unchanging elements of the divine economy." Only the mind, he continued, could perceive the celestial origins of unchanging truth and love. The human mind, divinely inspired and with access to the immutable, would be the instrument of human progress. The mind would be the agent of the soul's redeeming power. It could turn change into a force for good, for improvement, for reform, for progress. Change need not be feared; it could bring salvation both for society and for a guilt-ridden individual like Alcott.[43]

Alcott found time amid his teaching, his reform activities, and his speculation in theology and epistemology, to pursue his love affair with Abby May. The courtship lasted for nearly two years before Alcott finally called on Colonel May and asked for permission to marry Abby. Alcott found the Colonel uncongenial. He was a man who lived in the past and who dwelt on material things, in marked contrast, Alcott felt, to his own observing of moral and intellectual changes and his anticipating the future. Nevertheless, May did not stand in the way of the marriage and even promised a substantial dowry. Thus on May 23, 1830, the time having arrived that the proposed "connection" was "warranted by existing circumstances," Alcott and Abby May were married at King's Chapel by the Reverend Greenwood. "I enter upon it," Alcott said, "with confidence and hope—with fear and trembling."[44]

Despite the happiness of love and marriage, Alcott was becoming increasingly disillusioned with Boston. Though not failing, his school lacked the support he expected, especially given the high purpose and mission he had associated with it. In December 1829 he told William Alcott that the moral and intellectual character of Boston, which at first he had praised, was yet in an "imperfect state." Teaching was exhausting and city life did not entirely agree with him. He feared he would be an instant outcast were his religious and philosophical opinions more widely known. Therefore he was receptive when William Russell suggested that they jointly establish a school in Philadelphia "for the development of all the powers of human nature." Such a project was an exciting prospect. It offered the hope of a new start in a possibly more enlightened city, and a chance to work with a brilliant colleague. However, the means for such a venture were not immediately available, and Alcott despaired of ever seeing the school begin.[45]

In May 1830 Alcott entered a contest sponsored by Philadelphia's *United States Gazette*, the prize being one hundred dollars for the best essay on education. The essay turned into a twenty-seven-page pamphlet, *Observations on the Principles and Methods of Infant Instruction*, Alcott's first lengthy treatise on education. Its themes reflected Alcott's latest thoughts on purposes and methods. The purpose of education, he told his readers, was to be the improvement of human nature, the direction, expansion, and perfection of the child's faculties. Stories, familiar conversation, and the example of the teacher would develop the moral faculties. Variety in classroom technique would cultivate the intellect. All senses were to be trained by corresponding external stimuli: writing and drawing for the eye, music and marching for the ear. But of prime importance was the cultivation of conscience, the foundation of character. "The child becomes a law unto himself," Alcott declared, if only the teacher allows the goodness within each child to develop freely. Every incident, every object in the classroom had its moral lesson. These could be the teacher's instruments for drawing out the "moral habits" that were the result of an awakened conscience: truth, ingenuousness, obedience, confidence, forbearance, fortitude, justice, generosity. Of course, Alcott assumed that he knew, or could come to know, what was good and how best to arrange or use incidents and objects to effect this good. The children may have needed a heavy dose of those moral qualities in order to put up with Alcott's zealous concern for their welfare. For Alcott would not truckle to anything that stood in the way of "improvement." He went on in his essay to speak at length about freedom in the classroom, a concept bound to strike a harmonious chord with the growing democratic emphasis on individual liberty in the United States of the 1830s. But freedom for Alcott meant freedom to do good, or rather to engage in activities that in his opinion led to improvement. Freedom was not an end in itself, but a means to achieve moral goodness. This provided no difficulty for Alcott because of his belief in the inherent goodness of human nature. Restriction, arbitrary rewards and punishments, and elaborate rules only inhibited this goodness and produced evil, whereas freedom cultivated basic goodness. It was a circular argument: freedom generated goodness, and goodness determined the nature of freedom. But logic mattered very little. The idea that human beings could be both free and morally good was uplifting and exhilarating to Alcott and to many of his reform-minded contemporaries. It could be a radical challenge to traditions and institutions and yet uphold long-revered moral values.[46]

These heartening concepts, as well as Alcott's careful delineation of classroom procedures, attracted the attention of a circle of educational reformers in Philadelphia. He did not win the contest, but Roberts Vaux, the President of the Board of Controllers of the Philadelphia Public Schools and President of the Pennsylvania Society for the Promotion of Public Schools, wrote that Alcott's essay was more instructive than anything like it he had seen, and he urged its publication. This encouraging news came just as Alcott's personal financial condition was improving. Friends and relatives had provided him and Abby with a substantial sum of money after the wedding, and this had enabled him to pay off his seven years of accumulated debt. On October 3, 1830, he found to his great relief that he had a $1200 balance to his credit. Unfortunately, none of it had helped his long-suffering father. Joseph Chatfield Alcox had died in April 1829.[47]

As Alcott was pondering his present success but future insecurity—he feared that the income from his school would not be enough—he was visited by Reuben Haines, a wealthy Quaker philanthropist from Germantown, Pennsylvania, to whom William Russell had written for aid. Haines offered to provide the means for Alcott's and Russell's proposed school to be located in Germantown. Therefore, despite his being offered as a candidate for master of a public school for girls in Boston by a few friends including Dr. Channing, Alcott decided to leave Boston and accompany Russell to Philadelphia.[48]

He defended his decision to William Alcott by pointing to the "world of change" that surrounded them. Firm footing was difficult to find, and there was a danger of building one's edifice too quickly without a solid foundation. But change was a happy condition, he told William. Progress and happiness depended on it. By changing his residence he would be changing his opinions and his character. It could help him separate the "general and universal" from the "particular and individual." He was certain that "without [change] our opinions, our virtues, our very character would become local." On November 5, having rationalized a possibly reckless moved and having secure Abby's acquiescence, he closed his school in Boston. Five weeks later, fully as optimistic and enthusiastic as he had been when he left Connecticut for Boston, he and Abby left by stagecoach and steamboat for Philadelphia.[49]

Notes

1. Peter R. Knights, *The Plain People of Boston, 1830-1860* (New York: Oxford University Press, 1971), pp. 11, 20; George Rogers Taylor, *The Transportation Revolution, 1815-1860* (New York: Harper and Row, 1968 [1951]), pp. 229-31.
2. Knights, *Plain People*, pp. 11, 20; Charles N. Glaab and A. Theodore Brown, *A History of Urban America* (New York: The Macmillan Co., 1967), pp. 36, 84.
3. AJ 3 (1829): 84, 90-91, 168; AJ 2 (1827-28): 75, 94, 121-24; Ahlstrom, *Religious History*, pp. 393-99.
4. Alcott to W. A. Alcott, August 4, 1828, and October 18, 1829, in A. Bronson Alcott, comp., "Letters, 1828-1834," at Houghton Library, 59M-305 (34); AJ 3 (1829): 45.
5. AJ 2 (1827-28): 4, 28, 146; AJ 48 (1873): 618-22; Frank Thistlethwaite, *The Anglo-American Connection in the Early Nineteenth Century* (Philadelphia: University of Pennsylvania Press, 1959), pp. 136-38; Alcott to W. A. Alcott, August 20, 1829, in "Letters, 1828-34"; AJ 3 (1829): 166.
6. Thistlethwaite, *Anglo-American Connection*, pp. 141-42; AJ 2 (1827-28): 28-29; "Constitution and By-Laws of the Infant School Society," *American Journal of Education* 3, no. 9 (September 1828): 563-68.
7. "Constitution and By-Laws," *American Journal of Education*, 3:564; AJ 2 (1827-28) pp. 32-36, 42, 44.
8. Alcott, "Autobiographical Index"; AJ 2 (1827-28): 70, 110, 118, 137.
9. AJ 2 (1827-28): 175; Alcott to W. A. Alcott, August 4, 1828, in "Letters, 1828-34"; William Russell, "A Visit to the Salem Street Infant School in Boston in 1828," *Christian Teacher's Manual*, (November 1828), from a copy in Alcott's hand in "Autobiographical Materials."
10. AJ 3 (1829): 107; AJ 2 (1827-28): 61, 81, 82; Alcott to W. A. Alcott, December 21, 1829, in "Letters, 1828-34."
11. AJ 2 (1827-28): 61.
12. Ibid., p. 194.
13. Ibid., pp. 54, 197, 243, 245; Alcott to W. A. Alcott, August 4, 1828, in Letters, 1828-34."
14. AJ 3 (1829): 1-2.
15. AJ 2 (1827-28): 119, 257; A. Bronson Alcott, comp,, "Memoir of Abby May Alcott." This is a miscellaneous collection of letters and diary entries copied for publication by Alcott in 1878. The bound volume is located at Houghton Library, 59M-306 (28). AJ 4 (1830): 100-101.
16. AJ 2 (1827-28): 50, 96, 137, 223, 301; Alcott to W. A. Alcott, December 21, 1829, in "Letters, 1828-34"; Abby May [Alcott] to Lucretia May, January 3, 1829, from a copy in Alcott's hand in "Memoir of Abby May Alcott"; Abby May [Alcott] to S. J. May, August, 1828, in A. Bronson Alcott, comp., "Family Letters, 1828-1861," at Houghton Library, 59M-305 (25); Abby May [Alcott], "Diary," August 29, 1828, from a copy in Alcott's hand in "Autobiographical Materials"; S. J. May to Abby May [Alcott], July 21, 1828, from a copy in Alcott's hand in "Autobiographical Materials."
17. Alcott, "Autobiographical Index"; Carl Bode, *The American Lyceum* (New York: Oxford University Press, 1956), pp. 10-15; AJ 2 (1827-28): 72, 92, 94, 303.
18. AJ 2 (1827-28): 250, 274, 276, 282; Bode, *American Lyceum*, pp. 16-17.
19. AJ 2 (1827-28): 173, 276; AJ 3 (1829): 60-61, 70-73, 159; A. Bronson Alcott, "Elementary Instruction," *American Journal of Education* 3, no. 6 (June 1828): 369-70.
20. Alcott to W. A. Alcott, August 20, 1829, in "Letters, 1828-34."
21. AJ 3 (1829): 84; Frances Wright, *Views of Society and Manners in America*, ed. Paul R. Baker (Cambridge, Mass.: Harvard University Press, 1963), pp. 16-20; Harrison, *Robert Owen*, pp. 167-68.
22. AJ 3 (1829): 168-69, 202.
23. Ibid., pp. 120, 227; Alcott to W. A. Alcott, June 8, 1829, and July 8, 1829, in "Letters, 1828-34"; AJ 4 (1830): 91.
24. Alcott, "Autobiographical Index"; AJ 2 (1827-28): 88, 91, 292-93, 356; AJ 3 (1829): 79, 90-91, 121, 168, 169; AJ 4 (1830): 54; [A. Bronson Alcott], "Review of *Observations on the*

Establishment and Direction of Infant Schools by Reverend Charles Mayo (London, 1827),"
American Journal of Education 3 (October 1828): 612.

25. AJ 2 (1827-28): 293; AJ 4 (1830): 125; John L. Thomas, *The Liberator: William Lloyd Garrison* (Boston: Little, Brown, and Co., 1963), pp. 74, 108-13, 114, 124-27, 140; Mumford, ed., *Memoir of Samuel J. May*, pp. 140-42; AJ 54 (1878): 51.

26. AJ 2 (1827-28): 121-23.

27. Jack Mendelsohn, *Channing: The Reluctant Radical* (Boston: Little, Brown and Co., 1971), pp. 55, 168-69; Perry Miller, ed., *The Transcendentalists* (Cambridge, Mass.: Harvard University Press, 1950), p. 21; William Ellery Channing, *Works* (Boston, 1880), pp. 291-302.

28. AJ 2 (1827-28): 28, 124.

29. Ibid., pp. 219, 254; AJ 4 (1830): 67.

30. Alcott to W. A. Alcott, March 1, 1830, in "Letters, 1828-34"; AJ 3 (1829): 45, 114; AJ 2 (1827-28): 39, 61.

31. AJ 2 (1827-28): 199.

32. Ibid.

33. Ibid., pp. 201, 220, 240.

34. AJ 3 (1829): 187.

35. AJ 2 (1827-28): 143, 239, 265, 347, 351-52; Russel B. Nye, *Society and Culture in America, 1830-1860* (New York: Harper and Row, 1974), pp. 358-59.

36. AJ 3 (1829), pp. 127, 200; Alcott to W. A. Alcott, October 18, 1829, in "Letters, 1828-34."

37. AJ 2: (1827-28): 64, 183; AJ 3 (1829): 139, 202, 206; AJ 4 (1830): 140; Alcott to W. A. Alcott, March 1, 1830, in "Letters, 1828-34."

38. AJ 3 (1829): 72-73, 114; AJ 2 (1827-28): 351-55, Miller, ed., *The Transcendentalists*, pp. 157-59.

39. Alcott to W. A. Alcott, March 23, 1830, in "Letters, 1828-34."

40. AJ 2 (1827-28): 49, 200, 221; AJ 3 (1829): 163; AJ 4 (1830): 1.

41. AJ 2 (1827-28): 181-82, 200, 326; Alcott to W. A. Alcott, January 5, 1829, in "Letters, 1828-34."

42. Alcott to W. A. Alcott, January 5, 1829, and June 8, 1829, in "Letters, 1828-34."

43. AJ 4 (1830): 3.

44. AJ 3 (1829): 86; Joseph May to Abby May [Alcott], August 26, 1829, from a copy in Alcott's hand in "Memoir of Abby May Alcott"; AJ 4 (1830): 39, 97, 105.

45. Alcott to W. A. Alcott, December 21, 1829, and July 15, 1830, in "Letters, 1828-34"; AJ 3 (1829): 178.

46. AJ 4 (1830): 104; A. Bronson Alcott, *Observations on the Principles and Methods of Infant Instruction* (Boston: Carter and Hendee, 1830), pp. 4-5, 7-8, 9, 10, 12, 14, 16-17, 19-21, 22-23.

47. AJ 4 (1830): 110, 120; Roberts Vaux to Alcott, June 14, 1830, from a copy in Alcott's hand in "Autobiographical Materials"; AJ 3 (1829): 113.

48. AJ 4 (1830): 112, 121, 131, 136.

49. Alcott to W. A. Alcott, November 9, 1830, in "Autobiographical Collections," 3:194; AJ 4 (1830): 138, 149, 150.

4

Philadelphia and Germantown, 1831–34

THE three and one-half years spent in Philadelphia and Germantown were disappointing to Alcott the reformer. He did not attain the high goals he had set for his teaching. The people of Philadelphia were no more receptive, perhaps even less receptive, to his theories and methods than were the people of Boston. Nevertheless, these years, measured by intellectual growth and development, were the most fruitful of Alcott's long life. The lack of substantial success in his teaching ventures drove him to reading, speculation, and introspection. His own two children took the place of his pupils as objects of interest and affection as well as subjects for his experiments. He found time to explore fully the problem he had formulated: the nature of the interaction between the innate powers of the human mind and the power of the external environment in determining human development and human potential. He began to give a more precise meaning to his concept of the spiritual nature of human beings, that "divine excellence" which he perceived to be a part of the human soul. The intellectual synthesis that he made of this gave him a sense of satisfaction that his reform efforts failed to produce. If he could not redeem the world in the classroom, he could do so in the realm of ideas.

Alcott arrived in Philadelphia on December 18, 1830. Ten days later he and Russell visited Reuben Haines in Germantown, seven miles north of the city, to confer about the possibilities of establishing a school there. They were unimpressed. Germantown was a small, sleepy farming community that served as a vacation retreat for some of Philadelphia's wealthiest families. It did not promise to be a favorable place to begin such an important experiment as a school to cultivate all the powers of the human mind. So they rejected Haines's offer for the time being and turned instead to Philadelphia.[1]

For surely the City of Brotherly Love would be more receptive to reform than little Germantown. It was the second largest city in the country at the time, and like Boston was active, growing, and exciting. Alcott found Philadelphia to be more "practical" and less "speculative" than Boston, but it brimmed with philanthropic activities. Members of Philadelphia's upper class, those Alcott referred to as the "gentlemen of influence and intelligence," such as wealthy Quaker businessman Roberts Vaux and Harvard-trained Unitarian minister William H. Furness, had become the driving force behind educational reform in the city and in Pennsylvania generally. In the early 1820s they had brought English reformer Joseph Lancaster to the city to help develop a public school system in accordance with the monitorial plan. They had organized three infant school societies in 1827 and 1828. In 1827 they had organized the Pennsylvania Society for the Promotion of Public Schools to work for the establishment of universal, free public education. The president of this society, Roberts Vaux, had also been instrumental in establishing the Pennsylvania Institution for the Deaf and Dumb in 1820. The reform-minded Quakers, who formed a significant element of the city's elite, took the lead in helping to educate black people by organizing the Philadelphia Association of Friends for the Free Instruction of Adult Persons of Color. Philadelphia philanthropists also worked for the education of the blind, for the establishment of free libraries such as the Apprentice's Library formed in 1820, and for the development of schools to train treachers. All of this led Alcott and Russell to believe that patronage for their school would be easy to find in Philadelphia.[2]

One of the first of Philadelphia's philanthropic elite that Alcott met was Roberts Vaux. The forty-five-year-old Vaux had vowed to devote his life and wealth to charitable enterprises, reportedly as his personal memorial to his beloved sister who had died in 1812. He engaged in all kinds of reform —abolition, poor relief, penal reform, education, care of the insane—and he did so very effectively. He was president of numerous reform organizations. Support from such a prestigious and influential person would be of extreme value to Alcott and Russell, and they had good reason to believe that such support would be forthcoming. After all, Vaux had earlier been enthusiastic in his approval of Alcott's essay on education.[3]

Vaux was married to Margaret Wistar, daughter of Dr. Caspar Wistar, whose memory was revered by the intellectuals of Philadelphia. Wistar had succeeded Thomas Jefferson as president of the American Philosophical Society, and he had established weekly Saturday evening open houses for Society members that became institutionalized as the "Wistar parties." These events had become a focal point for the leading citizens of Philadelphia. There they met to discuss literary, scientific, theological, and philosophical topics. The parties gave a unity and a cohesiveness to the Philadelphia elite that were a valuable aid to philanthropic activities. It was common for members to invite notable visitors to the parties, and upon his arrival in Philadephia Alcott received one of these invitations. Vaux's interest in his ideas undoubtedly helped him win acceptance, as did a letter of introduction from Samuel J. May. The man responsible for formal invitations was John Vaughan, then president of the American Philosophical Society and a pillar of Philadelphia's only Unitarian church. Alcott had no sooner alighted from the steamboat on Saturday, December 18, 1830, when Vaughan appeared to conduct him to the party that evening.[4]

At his first Wistar party Alcott met a number of Philadelphia notables. Besides Roberts Vaux there were Dr. James Rush, son of the famous Revolutionary era physician Benjamin Rush; Dr. Franklin Bache, grandson of

Benjamin Franklin and professor of chemistry at the Franklin Institute and Jefferson Medical College; Walter Rogers Johnson, a leader in the establishment of lyceums and mechanics' institutes in Pennsylvania; Robert Walsh, editor of the *National Gazette* and the *American Quarterly Review*; and Nicholas Biddle, urbane and cultured president of the Bank of the United States, who combined interests in educational reform with high finance. Also present that evening were two former acquaintances of Alcott, Maskell M. Carll and John M. Keagy. Carll was a Swedenborgian minister who had helped found the first infant school in Philadelphia which Alcott had visited in 1828. Keagy had corresponded with Alcott in 1827 from Harrisburg, where he was publishing his *Pestalozzian Primer*. Alcott was very much taken by these influential proponents of culture and reform. Vaux impressed him with his "liberal mind," although Alcott noted that Vaux's efforts were mainly practical and popular rather than profound and speculative. He found Keagy to be a man of great intellectual powers and Carll to have attractive moral and philanthropic intentions.[5] The only man he disliked was Robert Walsh. Walsh, he felt, was too aristocratic:

> His whole mind seems identified with those forms of aristocratic procedure, which invests the rights of the many to the more aspiring and powerful few. Mr. Walsh seems to me, not at home in this republican country, where diffusion, as well as accumulation, is a popular maxim; and one in accordance with the genius and spirit of our government and character.[6]

Alcott was appalled by Walsh's belief that universal education would be detrimental to liberty. He also disliked Walsh's Irish Catholicism. He concluded that Walsh was a "small man" who possessed little intellectual power.[7]

As it turned out, all of the Philadelphia philanthropists might well have been considered as "small" as Walsh. Despite the high hopes that Alcott and Russell had of them, hopes that led them to reject the Germantown offer, they found little positive response. The reason is not clear, but no one in Philadelphia was willing to patronize their school, at least in January 1831. Fortunately, Reuben Haines's offer still held. Haines, President of the Geological Society of the United States, who also a member of the American Philosophical Society and a regular at the Wistar parties. He had investments in cattle and brewing, and was the owner of an extensive landed estate in Germantown. He was a busy man, Alcott noted, a man "designed for action rather than thought." But Haines had the money and the connections to give Alcott and Russell a start. He would provide the "action"; they would provide the thought. And it turned out that Germantown was not completely lacking in advantages. It was the location of several efforts at reform. There was a Manual Labor Academy, opened in 1829 and based on the ideas of Philipp Emmanuel von Fellenberg, whose school at Hofwyl, Switzerland, attempted to unite intellectual education with agricultural and technical training. There was also a nonprofit summer boarding school for infants begun in 1830, and there was the Germantown Academy, first opened in 1761, of which Reuben Haines was a trustee. Thus, after two months of frustration in Philadelphia, Alcott and Russell decided to accept Haines's patronage. On February 18, 1831, Alcott moved from Mrs. Austin's boarding house in Philadelphia to Mrs. Stuckart's on Main Street in Germantown. Abby and he expected their first child within a month.[8]

The initial plan was for Alcott and Russell to open a "female department" in the Germantown Academy. This department was to have no official connection with the all-male Academy; it would just make use of the Academy's facilities. They advertised the new school in the Philadelphia area, carefully noting the separation of the sexes and the emphasis the teachers proposed to place on the cultivation of character. They promised to develop the "filial and social affections," to avoid introducing any "controversial" moral or religious subject to their pupils, and to use the inductive and conversational methods that Alcott had employed in his earlier schools. By the time the school finally opened on May 2, 1831, Alcott and Russell had decided to accept both boys and girls into their school, probably to increase their enrollment. Alcott agreed to teach the younger pupils, ages three to nine, and Russell the older, ages ten to fourteen. Haines provided the Alcotts with a rent-free home, the Rooker Cottage on Main Street, and Alcott decided to hold his classes there. Russell held forth in another building. Every Saturday Alcott lectured Russell's older pupils on the "operations of the mind," a topic to which Alcott was giving greater and greater attention by the spring and summer of 1831.[9]

Meanwhile, Alcott wrote to cousin William and urged him to join the enterprise. Haines had offered to give William a job as his secretary and caretaker of his farm, and he further suggested that William might open an agricultural school with the Haines backing. William hesitated, fearing his Connecticut mannerisms would create prejudice against him. Alcott, who very much wanted to renew his ties with his long-time friend, assured him that the plain and simple folk of Germantown would never be that narrow. But Alcott's assurances and his optimistic forecasts of the success of the Germantown school were not enough to persuade William to come. As it turned out, William, ever more practical than his cousin, had made a wise decision.[10]

For Alcott had continuing doubts about Germantown. He still was not fully convinced that this little town was the appropriate place to open his school. He hoped that one day Philadelphia would open to him. Indeed, he and Russell maintained their interest in the activities of the Philadelphia reformers despite the coolness with which their project had been received. On February 11, just before moving to Germantown, Alcott and Russell had invited the teachers of Philadelphia, including M. M. Carll, John M. Keagy, and Walter R. Johnson, to meet at their boarding house to discuss plans for a journal of elementary education and for a society of teachers. This group had met again of February 17, and had taken the name of the "Philadelphia Association of Teachers."

They elected Alcott a member of the Board of Directors, and a member of the publishing committee. They asked him to lecture on the "principles of education." Alcott had often lamented that teachers were forced to work alone with no organization in which to exchange ideas, and he had further decried the lack of respect accorded the teaching profession. The new organization promised to correct both of these problems. There was even a possibility that the Association might sponsor a model elementary school as a means of experimenting on the human mind.[11]

Unfortunately, the Association did not attract the interest Alcott had hoped for. Few people gathered to hear his lecture at the Franklin Institute on April 27. The lecture was not well advertised and the weather was bad, but Alcott was wise enough to admit that his topic, the influence of early education on the formation of character, simply failed to arouse much interest. Undaunted, the Association in May 1831 sent circulars to friends and co-workers throughout the state in order to attract members and support. The circular declared that the Association's purpose was "to investigate those principles appertaining to the philosophy of mind, its faculties, their arrangement. . . . [and to] solicit a portion of that patronage and influence, which the subject so justly claims, and which is imperiously demanded by the spirit of the times." The Association also planned to issue a journal, but it ran into immediate opposition from William C. Woodbridge, the editor of the *American Annals of Education and Instruction*, who feared the competition. Woodbridge had taken over the *American Journal of Education* from Russell and had changed its name; now he evidently wished to prevent Russell from entering the field again. He visited Alcott and Russell in May 1831 and made his position clear, but Alcott and the Association felt that their new journal would complement, not injure, the *Annals*. Thus the Association went ahead with publication. In early 1832 the first issue of the *Journal of Instruction of the Philadelphia Association of Teachers* appeared.[12]

However, the circulars sent out by the Association attracted as meager a response as did Alcott's lecture. The new *Journal* found few readers and ended after only a few months. The Association lingered on through 1833 and sent delegates that year to the meeting of the American Lyceum in New York.[13] But Alcott attended Association meetings less and less. His interest in the organization waned as it failed to live up to its promise and potential. Undoubtedly, the major problem for the Association was the lack of solid financial backing. For although it attracted practicing educators such as Alcott, Russell, Keagy, and Carll, it did not win over the monied philan-thropists such as Roberts Vaux or Nicholas Biddle. The reason for this was the same as the reason for the continued lack of support for the Alcott-Russell proposal in Philadelphia. It amounted to a basic difference in theories of reform. It was a difference between the orthodox social reform promoted by Vaux, and the radical, holistic reform of individuals advocated by Alcott.

Roberts Vaux was a prime example of an orthodox social reformer. Although he wanted improvements in society and in people, and honestly desired to ameliorate the conditions of the poor and unfortunate, he wished to do so without threatening the basic structure of society and institutions. Thus he and most of the other Philadelphia philanthropists were chiefly concerned with increasing the size and numbers of educational institutions, with changing the organization of the Pennsylvania and Philadelphia school systems. To Vaux reform meant changing laws, raising money, and erecting buildings. The reports he submitted as president of several philanthropic organizations all dwelt on numbers—the number of books in the library, the number of hours devoted to education, the amount of money needed. Reform was a matter of structure and organization. Vaux had no time for reformers who believed that their pet project would save the world. When Frances Wright, Robert Dale Owen, and Anthony Morris proposed Fellenberg's manual labor schools as the basis for a universal system of education, Vaux denounced the idea as nonsense, an impossible panacea. He approved of manual labor schools as one method among many for improving education, but he felt that advancing them as the be-all and end-all was both impractical and dangerously radical. Manual labor schools on a large scale would require government direction, and indeed this was advocated by Wright's and Owen's Workingman's Party. Vaux feared that such extensive government control would be destructive of individual liberty. His cry that such ideas were impractical hid an unmentioned fear that they might not be.[14]

Vaux believed that any ill existing in society—poor prison conditions, intemperance, slavery, mistreatment of the Indians—could be treated successfully by the establishment of an organization. The organization could raise needed money, plan new institutions, and lobby for changes in the law.[15] But the organization could also be easily controlled by the upper classes. It could channel, direct, even co-opt reform energies to ensure that they would not become destructive of the social order. Thus Vaux was much less concerned with the substance of reform, the theory and the philosophy behind reform efforts. Here he differed radically from Alcott, Russell, Keagy, Carll, and the members of the Association of Teachers, who were less concerned with structure than with the goals and methods of education.

Alcott felt that educators had to know and obey the "laws of the human mind"; they had to strive to educate the *whole* person. He faulted present methods of education for lacking a sound philosophy, for being aimless and meaningless. The nature of the human mind had to be a subject of constant investigation. Without this, education could never serve its true purpose. It could never encourage original thought, moral purity, and the elevation of human purpose in life. It could lead only to routine, mindless memorization, and the sycophantic repetition of another's thoughts. A proper theory of education could bring freedom to pupils, an awakening of their own creative powers. "Education, rightly regarded," he said, "is not only an influence by which ideas are imparted, but an agency which calls them forth, in clear and palpable forms, from the sentient mind. It is a process of *expression* as well as *impression*."[16]

Alcott had elevated his view of the philosophy of education to the kind of world-saving panacea that Vaux so much disdained. By June 1831, soon after his school in Germantown opened, Alcott established a personal plan to read, study, and reflect for six or seven years on the subject of education, teaching all the while, and then to write an extensive course of lectures on human nature. He wanted to point out the total connection of human beings with nature, with society, and with each other, and to show how human faculties were developed by influences from within and without. Then he hoped to deliver these lectures in cities and towns across the United States. This would be the means of effecting true reform. It was a matter of raising people's awareness of their true potential.[17] Indeed, he believed that he, the educator, could more effectively lead true reform than ordained ministers or the existing reform bodies:

> The minister has long preached, but what has he accomplished? Ask our penitentiaries; our prisons; our jails, our alms houses; our domestic fire sides: —look into our civil, and political codes and institutions. . . count up the number of various societies, whose object is the suppression of some mighty vice, which is preying on the heart of society—our societies for the suppression of intemperance; of war; of slavery; of oppressive governments;—look into our individual life. . . view the low and debased forms of character which live, both in high and in humble life. . . then is the answer at hand, of what the minister, with all his. . . authority, has done. He has done little, because he has not known how.[18]

Early education was the redeeming force, he felt. Properly conceived, it could accomplish what ministers of the Gospel and reform organizations had failed to do and would always fail to do.[19]

This was a challenge to the more orthodox Philadelphia philanthropists. Alcott maintained that reform organizations, structures, laws, societies, were all useless without a well-developed philosophical base. An increase in the numbers of educational facilities availed nothing without a proper consideration of the principles and methods of education. And only in a model school—he hoped that the Germantown school would be just that—could these principles and methods get an adequate trial. This model school could best report its findings to the public for action. Vaux would have countered that principles, methods, and philosophies were useless without the structural means and the organization with which to effect them.

Of course, in the end both views were shortsighted. Alcott had no conception of the practical means, the organization, the money, the public support, needed to carry through reform. Vaux passed over the substance of reform for its outward structure, believing naively that once a reform organization was established, good would automatically and safely arise from it. Unfortunately for Alcott, the outward structure, the reform organization, attracted much more popular attention than did his experiments and theories. Societies to help the blind, or the insane, or the poor, or the drunk; increases in the numbers of public schools; political movements to establish free public education were all more easily understood than Alcott's ideas. They were obvious examples of progress. They were easily identifiable. They provided an immediate sense of accomplishment. The very existence of a reform organization was proof that the evil in question was being corrected and could be safely ignored. Such organizations found ready support among those who wanted outward evidence of reform but did not care to deal with the difficult problem of whether or not any meaningful change was taking place.

Oblivious to the difficulties he faced, Alcott blithely went on exploring the ideas he felt would lead to true reform, particularly ideas about the nature of the human mind. During the months of preparation for the Germantown school, the efforts to gain patronage, and the activities of the Teacher's Association, Alcott continued his reading. He kept up with current educational thought by reading Pestalozzi's *Letters on the Early Education of the Child* (1830); John Griscom's *Year in Europe* (1823), an American's report of European educational ideas and institutions; and Joseph Lancaster's *The Lancastrian System of Education, with Improvements, by Its Founder* (1821). He read them, he claimed, not so much to use their ideas but to "excite, and make creative, my own mind." Religion also remained a prime interest. The Quakers had been an early influence on Alcott; now he found renewed interest in Quaker literature with William Fisher's *Examination of Owen's New View of Society* and *Light of Truth in the Mind of Man*. Such works were inspiring and uplifting for Alcott as were *Thoughts on Religion and Other Subjects* (1670) by Blaise Pascal and *Review of the Progress of Religious Opinion* by Swiss revolutionary Jean-Charles-Leonard de Sismondi. Yet none of these altered the essential substance of Alcott's thought or changed its direction.[20].

Religious sectarianism remained a bugaboo. Philadelphia had the full run of denominations. Even the Quakers had factionalized. The Hicksite Quakers, unlike the Orthodox, based religious inspiration on the sole authority of the Inner Light rather than on Scripture.[21] Alcott denounced such sectarianism as a hindrance to reform:

> Humanity has suffered, not because there were none to advocate its rights, but because those few who were ready to do so, could not make themselves heard, amid the clamor and arrogance of sectarians. That expansive faith, which finds truth among all sects, and extends charity to all, can alone assist the true and permanent development of the mind, and subserve the cause of human happiness.[22]

Nevertheless, he occasionally attended Quaker services with Reuben Haines and found much beauty in their simple form of worship. The Unitarians also offered some reward for Alcott. He was impressed with the spirit of free thinking he found in their young minister, Harvard-educated William Henry Furness. Furness struck Alcott as a man of promise despite his quickness to defend Unitarian doctrines against the attacks of the other sects.[23]

Both of these interests—the religious and the educational—became absorbed and superseded in 1831 by Alcott's passion to study and understand the nature, development, and workings of the human mind. It was ever more clear to him that it was the mind that made humans creative intellectual and moral agents. "The mind is that which makes men valuable," he said. In the study of the mind he thought he could resolve the problem of the extent of human power and human free will.[24]

His initial interest in the workings of the mind derived, of course, from his reading of the works of John Locke and the Scottish philosophers. His faith in education as the most powerful instrument of reform posited the existence of a science of the mind. It rested on the ability of human beings to understand the laws of the mind and in turn to manipulate and shape them to work for human improvement. Especially useful to the educational reformer was the idea that the human mind consisted of several distinct faculties, such as will, memory, understanding, and the moral sense. All of these faculties related directly to separate aspects of human behavior. Educators could, by training each of the faculties, shape corresponding behavior.

As Alcott explored this science of the mind, he ran across the ideas of the phrenologists, phrenology literally meaning "science of the mind." The phrenologists were studying exactly what Alcott was interested in: the mechanism by which the inherent powers of the mind interacted with the external environment to produce mental activity. And, more important, they sought the means by which human beings could control this mechanism to produce beneficial results. The first phrenology Alcott read was George Combe's *Constitution of Man*. He had read it once in August 1829; in February 1831 he perused it again and called it the best essay on human nature he had ever seen.[25]

Combe, a Scot, had become a convert to phrenology after reading of the theories of Franz Joseph Gall and Johann Caspar Spurzheim in the *Edinburgh Review*. Spurzheim's defense of phrenology at Edinburgh University in 1815 further confirmed Combe's faith. Phrenology, as developed by Gall and Spurzheim in Vienna, assumed that all mental phenomena had natural causes, which human beings could determine through observation and study. It theorized that human anatomical and physiological characteristics had a direct bearing on mental behavior. As diagrammed by Gall, the human mind was made of thirty-seven independent, ascertainable faculties or propensities, each located in a different area of the brain, each related to some aspect of human behavior such as benevolence, hope, speech, and parental love. Education was the process by which each of these faculties might be developed and cultivated. Such development would lead to reform and human improvement. An educator, using phrenological charts and diagrams and studying anatomical features, could pinpoint those faculties needing further development and act accordingly.[26]

Gall, a physician, had been chiefly concerned with an objective study of the parts of the mind and how they worked. He cared little about the question of whether the mind was good or evil, although he admitted that some of the propensities he identified might be sources of evil. His student and disciple

Spurzheim, on the other hand, emphasized the philosophy of the mind. He believed that all the mind's propensities were good, and that evil resulted from the abuse of those propensities. His idea that the goodness within human beings, as identified in each of the faculties, might be preserved and cultivated, made phrenology attractive to reformers like George Combe. Combe was no physician; he was a popularizer, an advocate of reform. Such was the purpose of his *Constitution of Man*, published in 1828. Combe preached about the need for human beings to understand their own nature, to develop each of their propensities, and to work for harmony among the various propensities. By doing so, Combe felt, human beings could advance rapidly to happiness and goodness.[27]

These attractive ideas were receiving more and more attention in the United States in the 1820s and 1830s. Alcott was not alone in his buoyant faith that the development of the mind could lead to future perfection. Increasing numbers of Americans were reading the works of Spurzheim and Combe, all available in American editions. The "American Spurzheim," Dr. Charles Caldwell, had returned from Europe to popularize phrenology with his *Elements of Phrenology*, published in 1824. Phrenology fitted in nicely with an increasingly optimistic United States. It gave scientific sanction to the growing belief in the goodness of human nature and in the ability of human beings to reform themselves and their society. It accentuated each person's unique endowments and capacities, yet it taught the importance of obedience to the moral laws—sobriety, virtue, chastity, self-improvement—all of which were supposedly inherent in the mind's faculties. It neatly explained the inequities and inequalities of society as the fault of poorly developed faculties in unfortunate persons. The burden of reform, according to the phrenologists, was entirely the responsibility of each individual.[28]

Phrenology was quickly becoming a popular fad in the United States. The scientific integrity Franz Joseph Gall gave to it was lost in the demand for simplistic explanations of individual and social ills. Thousands flocked to hear Spurzheim lecture in New Haven, Hartford, and Boston in the summer and fall of 1832. When Spurzheim died in November 1832, exhausted from his whirlwind of lectures, thousands attended his funeral. The public watched as Dr. John C. Warren performed an autopsy on Spurzheim at Harvard. The ghoulish fascination of Americans would not let the Austrian physician rest in peace. Dr. William Grigg kept his brain in his office at the Boston Athenaeum.[29]

But it was not phrenology as fad that attracted Alcott. Combe gave Alcott a paradigm, a conceptual framework, from which he could begin his own investigation of the mind. Phrenology just confirmed many of Alcott's own ideas. He did not need to accept the details of the phrenological system; he could construct his own diagram of the interrelationship between human nature and surrounding circumstances.[30] "Circumstances around [a human being], give rise to thoughts within him," he said, and these thoughts create new circumstances in turn. The mind is related to everything around it; it is, further, related to itself: it is connected with other minds: it communes with itself by reflection; with others, by speech; with nature, by the common language of sensation.[31]

Phrenological diagrams of the human brain suggested to Alcott the possibility of making a philosophical map of human nature showing this intimate connection between human beings and the universe.[32]

Alcott became convinced that a history of one human mind from infancy could fully explain human nature. This would be of "more value to the world," he said, "than all the systems which philosophers have built concerning the mind, up to this day. It would be the history of human nature: a history which has never yet been written." This history would fill in the lines of his proposed map of human nature. The history and the map would be convenient guides to self-knowledge, and self-knowledge was the key to self-determination. He believed that with a proper understanding of the process of the development of human nature all persons could perfect themselves. He wanted to demonstrate this to the world: "I would prove that man may become good; that *moral* principle may become the guide of all minds."[33] This knowledge was exciting to him, yet he felt he was just a lonely wave washing against a tide of ignorance. He indicted the society he lived in for its shallowness and obtuseness, its inability to see the light that shone so clearly for him:

Our men of talent are chiefly occupied in objects of pecuniary advancement. There is little of profound research, and lofty speculation among us. We are improving our lands; inventing labour-saving machines; manufacturing improved fabricks; our citizens are crazy after associations for favorable investment. . . . but little is done to improve man.[34]

Conveniently, the Alcott's first child, Anna Bronson Alcott, named after Alcott's mother, was born on March 16, 1831. She became the subject of her father's history of a human mind. On March 25 he began his manuscript of "Observations of a Child During her First Year." The conditions were perfect. His investigation could begin right from birth. The child would not be encumbered by fixed habits as adults were. At birth the infant's nature was spotless. Alcott had believed this since his months of teaching and reading in Cheshire. He considered the idea of the depravity of human nature at birth to be impious. "Happy is it for the world," he said, "that the progress of our race, has outstripped this debasing doctrine; that nobler views are gaining currency." If only parents and educators accepted these nobler views and understood how to prevent this original goodness from being defiled, their children might grow up "comparatively pure and spotless; all [their] impulses might become principles of undeviating rectitude." It was the fault of human beings if their children's souls were debased: "Man, not his author, is the cause of crime. Evil enters the mind of a child through the vitiated nature transmitted to him by his parents, and the influences which continue to operate on him, after his introduction into being.''[35]

Now Alcott could start with an infant who was absolutely pure and untouched. Unlike the three- and four-year-olds he had taught in Boston and would be teaching in Germantown, Anna would be free of the burdens placed upon children by unenlightened parents. He planned to study carefully the laws of human development as they operated on Anna and to guide them in a way that would prevent debasement. If successful, his experiment would become an example for all the would. It would provide absolute proof that reform was possible, that human beings were perfectible. This meant an awesome burden for Alcott and his wife and daughter. They were to be nothing less that agents of universal reform. Yet they could remain independent of support from others, of institutions, of money, of politics and laws. Those things could only treat symptoms, not bring about a real cure, not bring about essential, radical reform. Alcott believed that he was digging at the very roots of the problems faced by human beings and by society. Proper child rearing, proper education, would make pure individuals; in turn these pure individuals would transform society and institutions. No evil need be accepted, for all evil was avoidable.[36]

Alcott's observations on his first child were to be objective, scientific, made in accordance with the inductive method. He was still convinced that the mind developed according to readily observable and understandable natural laws. Each day he planned to watch Anna carefully, writing down what he saw like a chemist watching an experiment. Accordingly, his comments for March 16, 1831, the day of Anna's birth, were clinical in tone:

> The subject of the following observations is a female. Respiration and crying, as usual, took place immediately after birth. The power of vision seemed active, the eyelids opening, and the eyes moving. . . . She partook of her natural aliment an hour after birth. The usual indications of health and vital energy followed her introduction into existence.[37]

Abby, meanwhile, was sympathetic, though bewildered by her husband's unceasing attention to little Anna. She noted that during the first ten days of Anna's life, Alcott did not leave the room except briefly. She was comforted by his presence but irked that he spent most of that time with his manuscripts and paid little attention to her.[38]

Alcott framed many of the questions he asked of his experiment in phrenological terms. He observed that his daughter was "obeying the great laws, by which nature is expanding her faculties, for her future use and happiness." After five months he discovered that the shape of her head indicated the growth of corresponding faculties: "The mind is modifying the head. The organs which indicate intellectual and moral attributes are protruding themselves; and making the mind, as it were, externally obvious." Reiterating Combe, he concluded that happiness was the result of the harmonious action of all the faculties, and that Anna seemed to be striving naturally for such harmony in her actions. As he observed and wrote, Alcott became ever more aware of the fabulous complexity of human nature. It was no wonder to him that humans remained so long under the care of others in comparison with other animals.[39]

Although Alcott tried to base his conclusions strictly on empirical observation, he easily succumbed to leaps of faith and prior assumptions. It had come to be an article of faith with him that children learned more from the example of others than from precept; his observations of Anna confirmed this. At five months he found that Anna's memory and power of association were developing quickly. His evidence was that she was anticipating the pleasure or discomfort of certain positions in which her parents placed her. And she was showing obvious affection for her parents. Pleasure or pain, he found, could induce or stop certain kinds of behavior. Experience taught her to keep away from the hot oil lamp. He believed that in the early days of infancy pleasure and pain were the sole motives for action, but he assumed that at some unspecified point a "moral life" began. From that point on, he supposed, motivation depended on choices between good and evil. The vigilance of the parents was the primary means of ensuring that such motivation remained pure, that pleasure and good remained synonymous as did pain and evil. Alcott diligently sought evidence of this incipient moral behavior and considered ways to influence and direct it. Parental example and the power of pleasure and pain could induce the moral behavior involved in love, pity, and the "affections." But the ultimate end was the awakening of the faculty of conscience, that innate sense of the good and the true upon which all moral choice should be based regardless of pleasure, pain, or parental example. Conscience was the motivating agent of the perfected human being. It was a divine principle; methods used by parents merely activated it, cultivated it.[40].

Since his major purpose was reform and purification, not experimentation, it followed that he would have preconceived notions about how infant development should proceed. He would not be content just to watch and see what happened. Every external incident or condition had its supposed effect on the growth of the child. Thus he and Abby had to be alert at all times to make sure that each of these incidents or conditions brought about a desirable effect. Of course, this presumed a knowledge of what was good and also an ability on the part of parents to determine how an external condition could produce something good. His experiment did not always provide this kind of knowledge. Therefore Alcott had to make judgments about how to proceed not always based on tangible evidence. Classroom experience had convinced him of the beneficial effects of variety as a stimulus to learning, so he decided that he should not allow Anna to be confined solely to nursery or a book. He wanted to introduce her to the multiformity of nature. Only diversity of experience, he thought, could develop all the mental faculties. Only variety could excite the imagination and gratify innate curiosity. Alcott could point to his classroom success to support this judgment. But other conclusions he made were based on support that was obscure at best. He deemed the motion of a rocking cradle to be injurious to the child's intellect, yet he built a swing for Anna in the parlor inexplicably believing that a back-and-forth motion was somehow less damaging than rocking. Since the child's mind had to be free to receive the flow of sensations from external objects, he sought to prevent loud noises and "incoherent prattle" from getting in the way. He demanded that Anna be restricted to breast feeding lest a meat diet be damaging to her. He asked Abby to design Anna's clothes to give her freedom of movement at all times. He allowed no covering for her head since that might restrict the flow of blood. The use of nurses was anathema to him. The mother's vigilant attention was necessary at all times. "Neither ignorant servants, nor silly visitors are allowed to exert their doubtful influence upon her," he claimed.[41]

Alcott's specific conclusions about child rearing were not so important as the fact that he made such as attempt to study it at all and with such high expectations. He was a pioneer in the fields of child psychology and child development. And the philosophical questions he asked were important too, especially his continued wrestling with the problem of freedom. Freedom had been his watchword in his Cheshire and Boston classrooms; now he applied it to the rearing of children. "Liberty is a primary right of all created natures," he said, "and the love of it inherent in all. The child has his rights, as well as the adult, and those rights should be respected by those to whom his early guidance is committed." He hoped to treat Anna as a "free, self-guiding, self-controlling being." The infant mind was greater than the authority of parents, he thought. It would be a great mistake for parents to impose their "narrow plans" on their child from without. But as was the case in his classroom, Alcott did not quite accept the logical consequences of his most attractive defense of freedom. Again, freedom to Alcott meant the freedom to be good, to be morally upright. No sooner had he finished extolling the virtues of the self-guiding, self-controlling child than he qualified his position. "The child should be free," he said, "so long as he uses his freedom for his own benefit and improvement." And it was clear that the child's benefit and improvement were things that Alcott, not the child, would define. As much as he wanted Anna to experience a variety of external stimuli, he also believed that such stimuli should excite only ideas of beauty, truth, and happiness. She would not be free to explore the ugly and the ordinary. "Improper objects" would be kept from her. Indeed, by giving such close attention to every detail, to every influence operating on Anna, Alcott came very close to tyranny. Clearly, Alcott's definition of true freedom did not include the freedom to do evil.[42]

Alcott viewed the problem of the relationship between freedom and virtue in terms larger than the home or the schoolroom. He saw the United States as an arena in which both human liberty and human virtue were to be tried and proved. True virtue, he exulted, could arise only from a condition of liberty. Then he said that whereas the United States had achieved liberty, it had not yet achieved virtue. But if liberty produced virtue why was there so much licentiousness and venality? It was a dilemma that Alcott could solve, as had many Christian theologians since St. John and St. Paul, only by equating true liberty with goodness. Thus he could say that by making Anna good he was also making her free. The crux of this combination of liberty and virtue was the faculty of conscience. Conscience was inherent. It permitted freedom of choice by the individual with a standard of goodness by which to make those choices. No person was truly free unless he or she obeyed the dictates of conscience. The job of parents and educators was to develop the conscience of the child, to call it forth and to guide it. Having made this assessment, Alcott could justify imposing his standards of virtue on his child. For to do so was to call forth that innate sense of virtue that already existed in a dormant state within the child:

It is by respecting the will [of the child], by kind and rational means of influencing it from the beginning, that the dawning conscience, is called forth, connected with parental desires, and becomes an agent in the work of progress.[43]

In attempting to explain the relationship between freedom and virtue by positing a connection between inherent goodness and external suggestion, Alcott was back at that unresolved epistemological problem he had been battling so long. He had to know the exact relationship between external circumstances and innate human powers in shaping human beings. To believe in freedom and the importance of human choice in the development of virtue, Alcott had to assume an innate goodness, an innate power, within human beings. For if external objects or external powers were solely responsible for human development, then the concept of freedom, of the ability of humans to reform themselves, would be meaningless. Yet his study of the human mind had taught him the overwhelming importance of the environment in shaping human behavior. He succinctly stated the problem he faced in the early pages of his manuscript of observations on Anna:

The connection between the mind and its object is so mysterious; there is such a union of both in the same process, that it is difficult to say when a sensation becomes an impression; an impression an idea, and an idea a defined thought.... Without the external impression there is no thought; without the thought there is no impression; mind and matter are merged into one. The nature of this union is only known to the Author of Mind itself.[44]

Despite the mystery, Alcott refused to let the problem rest in the hands of the "Author of Mind." He continued his search. Like Locke and the Scottish philosophers, the phrenologists offered no final answers for him. They too emphasized the power of external circumstances in the development of the human mind; yet at the same time they assumed an undefined human power, a moral sense that adjusted external circumstances to benefit and uplift humanity. In his confusion and groping, Alcott swung back and forth between the parameters of the dichotomy. In November 1831 he asserted that the mind was a mere passive receptacle for external impressions: "By its daily impression, the mind is taking its form, and shape. Like water, which is continually wearing away the hard stone upon which it falls, so circumstances are continually working their impress upon the mind." He further stated that infants needed external objects and persons to "build up from without, the mental edifice within." But nearly in the same breath he reiterated his belief that external influences alone would not suffice. There was an undefined "internal principle" that external influences only put into motion.[45]

He had returned to his religious faith in an innately good human soul, to his reformist faith in the ability of humans to perfect themselves. Surely the innately good soul would not remain passive in the face of external forces. As he observed Anna, he sought evidence of the soul within her. The two-month-old Anna's attraction to flowers convinced him that a "happy communion" existed between the infant soul and the beautiful in nature. He often used the "mind" and the "soul" interchangeably. His goal in child rearing and education was sometimes the development of the mind, sometimes the soul. This was a lack of precision in his own thinking. Clearly the soul, as he conceived it, included more than the mind, although the mind surely was the agent that gave the soul its importance. He could explain the mind in terms of faculties and natural laws, the soul in terms of innate goodness and character. How the two were related was the central philosophical question.[46]

God was responsible for the good within each human soul, Alcott felt. "Nature," he said, "has made provision for benevolent and beneficent activity in our constitution. The divine fire is planted within the soul, and man is to kindle it into flame. The parent is to light the torch in the infant mind, and it will burn, and continue to burn, after their efforts have ceased."[47] The soul was the key to human freedom and human virtue. It enabled persons such as Percy Bysshe Shelley, whose biography Alcott read in July 1831, to pursue high and noble aims in his writing despite personal vicissitude and doubt. "Though the body is imprisoned," Alcott concluded, "the soul is free: though virtue be contemned by their fellow-men; insulted and wronged, and doubted by others; they [the virtuous] still press her to their bosom, and in solitude, and slavery, and silence, find society, freedom & peace!"[48] Certainly he considered himself among the lonely and the virtuous.

The human body was to Alcott merely the interpreter, the instrument, of the soul. While the phrenologists looked for external bodily development as an indication of the relative development of faculties, Alcott sought external manifestations of the workings of the soul. He talked of the duty within each human being that superseded any external influence.[49] Echoing Channing, he said:

Thus man's duty is within him. It is his appreciation of his own nature, which gives him the idea of a divinity. It is his nobler part which he adores. The duty within him is more excellent than any which is revealed to him from without, for his senses having communion only with the external world, can never bring to him, those views of divine truth and beauty, which it is the peculiar province of the reflective powers to appreciate. Without is but the semblance of God, within he dwells and reveals himself.[50]

Further evidence of Alcott's growing awareness of the power of the soul within was a nasty conflict with his good friend and cousin William Alcott. Dr. Alcott had not accepted his cousin's offer to join him in Germantown, probably because of his growing reservations about Bronson's religious beliefs. Instead, he had gone to Hartford to join William Woodbridge in editing the *Annals of Education*. In August 1831 William wrote to Bronson warning him not to succumb to irreligion by denying the authority of the New Testament. Bronson Alcott responded that he did not reject the truths revealed in the New Testament but that his fundamental religious beliefs rested not on the historical proof of Scripture but on his own faith, the direct revelation of his own spiritual progress. There were two kinds of proof regarding moral subjects, he said; the first was internal existence, the second external manifestation. Alcott had come to believe that his own internal power to appreciate truth was what convinced him of the truth of Jesus' teaching, not vice versa. In December 1831 he accused William of being a slave to circumstances, a slave to his associates like Woodbridge, and of failing to be loyal to himself, to his individuality, to his inner powers.[51]

Clearly, Alcott had made the soul the foundation for human virtue, for human potential, for human individuality. The soul was itself divine and had powers to perceive moral truth over and above any external evidence. In saying this Alcott was in line with the antinomian strain of American Puritanism that harked back to the seventeenth century, to John Cotton and Anne Hutchinson. His definition of the moral sense went far beyond anything Locke, the Scottish philosophers, the phrenologists, or even Dr. Channing had to say about it. Yet he hung on to his belief that external circumstances played a large role in human development. Somehow he had to relate the two elements of the dichotomy. He had to account for the role of external conditions while maintaining his growing religious faith in the divinity of the soul within.

This left Alcott with two central problems. First, he had to explain the problem of evil. If the soul was divine and divinely created, how could sin and evil occur? Second, he had to define the specific relationship between soul and body, between mind and matter, between the spiritual world and the material world, between the inner power of the soul and the power of external circumstances.

He explained evil simply. The divinity, the goodness inherent in human beings, was merely potential. Parents and educators had to activate it. Failure to light this "divine fire" resulted in evil. Thus both previous ills and potential goodness were the responsibility of parents and educators. "The foundation is laid by the Supreme Builder," he said,

> the materials are furnished.... Ours is the humble task of assisting the Master Builder; of forming the materials into the pattern presented us; without altering of marring the Sublime Design! ... If we are true to our high trust, the edifice will be beautiful and perfect.... The infant body is committed to us. It contains within it, the germs of those powers, which, if

developed by our love, strengthened and supported by our wisdom, and directed by our purest view of Divine Truth, will bear fruit immortal and divine.[52]

The problem of the relationship between the soul and external circumstances was much more difficult. To solve it Alcott read and reread Locke's *Essay on Human Understanding*, Francis Bacon's *Novum Organum* and *Advancement of Learning*, Combe's *Constitution of Man*, and Aristotle's *Metaphysics* and *Ethics*. He spent endless hours discussing the problem with William Russell. The answer was missing. Then in December 1831, possibly at Russell's suggestion, he read two works that supplied the broad outline of an answer to his dilemma: an essay on Victor Cousin's philosophy in the December issue of the *American Quarterly Review*, and *Discourse on the Philosophy of Analogy* by Francis Wayland.[53]

Cousin, a forty-year-old French philosopher, was popularizing the idealism of German philosophers such as Immanuel Kant, Johann Gottlieb Fichte, and Friedrich Wilhelm Joseph von Schelling. In doing so he tried to synthesize these ideas with the sensationalism of Locke and the eighteenth-century Enlightenment. His hope was to draw upon the best of all philosophies to formulate an eclectic, universal philosophy. To Alcott the importance of the article on Cousin was not so much that it introduced him to Cousin's eclecticism as that it presented the terms of the philosophical controversy between idealism and sensationalism then going on in Europe. The article pointed out the general differences between the idealists and the sensationalists. Alcott recognized this as the same conflict he was having in his own thought. He saw that the ideas about which he was concerned were of international significance. The world's greatest thinkers were discussing them. He could now turn to German idealism for a counter to John Locke, whose ideas had largely determined his epistemology up to then.[54]

Francis Wayland was a former minister and a present professor of mathematics and natural philosophy at Union College. Later, he would become president of Brown University and a leader in the reform of higher education in the United States. His *Discourse on the Philosophy of Analogy*, published in 1831, claimed that objects and phenomena of the natural world were analogous to those of the spiritual world. Since God was an intelligent being, his creation would surely exemplify his character and qualities. A careful observer, said Wayland, could find traces of God in every created thing. This idea of analogy provided Alcott with the first step in finding a conceptual link between the material and spiritual realm. Soon after reading the *Discourse* he noted in his "Observations" that few thinkers had appreciated the influence of analogy on the human mind, that few thinkers had connected the outward world of things with the inward world of ideas. This failure, Alcott felt, had caused the philosophical debate that Cousin had described. One set of philosophers claimed that ideas were innate; another believed that ideas were drawn from external things. They could not agree because they had no way to relate the external with the internal, the material with the spiritual. But the ideas of analogy would provide the connecting medium; analogy would be the key that unlocked the inward gate. "Man and the universe," said Alcott, "have not been taken as forming a whole, mutually connected, existing as appulsive, and impulsive, influences upon each other, out of which human volition is born."[55]

In March 1832 Alcott read Cousin's *Introduction to the History of Philosophy*. He found it a beautiful book, full of truth, but the Platonism in it disturbed him. It had too little reference to the impact of experience, of external stimuli, on the formation of ideas. On the other hand, he found Combe's *Constitution of Man* and François Joseph Victor Broussais's *Principles of Physiological Medicine* too "material." The phrenologists and physiologists, he believed, extended "the material and organic theory as much beyond the line of experience on one side, as Cousin, and the Platonists, or spiritualists do on the other. Neither include the whole of humanity." The concept of analogy solved this problem by linking the material with the spiritual in human nature and by connecting both these elements to the surrounding environment, the universe: "Body and spirit are united in the human structure; and mutually cooperate in all human operations—the one now paramount and now the other. It belongs to a third element—the universe with which they are analogous—to touch the subtle springs of both."[56]

In order to explain the concept of analogy more concretely and to illustrate the actual mental operation that took place, Alcott applied his theory to the classroom. He had always emphasized the importance of the arrangement of external objects in the learning process; now he believed that such objects should be arranged to facilitate "analogous" experience. "When outward objects incite intellectual associations," he said, "observation and study become comparatively natural. The mind sympathizes with outward appearances, and truth flows into it with facility and inspires delight." Novelty, variety, and freedom in the classroom, Alcott thought, encouraged this stimulating interaction between the internal and the external:

> The analogy between the mind and the outward world is the parent of thought. Objects surrounding the child interest and influence him. They form the elements from which the intellectual fabrick is built up within him.... An early experience, fraught with the sympathetic and inspiring forms of nature, is the origin and spring of genius. What, indeed, are the artist, the poet, the philosopher, but children whose deep interest in nature, and trust in its teachings, have preserved their beings, in mature life, a faithful mirror of outward analogy. Their minds are pure and undefiled. Truth flows through them as from a sweet and lucid fountain. They behold in the vivid light of nature those deep truths, which by the perverted eye, are but dimly perceived.[57]

The medium of experience, communion with outward objects, could provide an intuitive knowledge of the attributes of the Creator: "Nature, and Providence, and experience, are full of analogies, by which the young mind may be led upward to the source of Creating Energy and Preserving Love."[58] Thus the spiritual powers of a human being could be awakened by the corresponding or analogous spiritual elements of the external world. This was the same process by which the physical elements of the external world developed, by sensation and reflection, the corresponding physical powers of human beings.

Alcott further attempted to explain the meaning of the process of analogy by relating it to the development of his infant daughter. In doing so he tried to synthesize and systematize his findings about human development, to analyze how the continuous influence of experience activated human powers and permitted growth. He listed five stages of infant development. The first stage was instinctive, the basic need for sustenance giving rise to human appetites and desires. The second stage, the affective, was the experience of pleasure or pain as induced by outward objects. This produced sensibility and sympathy in the child. The third stage, the intellectual, was the process by which a child experienced consecutive order in external objects and thus became aware of cause and effect. This gave rise to knowledge and truth. The fourth stage was moral. At this point the child became aware of of the consequences of an action by means of observation and reflection. The ideas of responsibility, conscience, and faith followed. The fifth and highest stage was the spiritual. Here the child's perception of the ideal and pure in outward things gave rise to analogous qualities within. This permitted the child to be conscious of inward merit and gave rise to self-approbation, wisdom, and piety.[59] Alcott based much of this analysis on assumption rather than observation. But it did represent his initial groping for a scientific explanation of how interaction with external circumstances developed both the physical and spiritual powers of human beings. He still believed he could control this process and thus mold his child in accordance with his view of the good and the true. However, his explanation of the process of analogy was vague and abstract; it was unsatisfactory even to him. He still had not explained clearly the difference between the spiritual and the physical powers within human beings and how these related to their analogous qualities in the external world. He had not explained the mechanism of analogy. His search would have to continue.

In the meantime tragedy struck. While Alcott was searching for a science of the mind, using his Germantown school as a "psychological observatory," and studying the growth of his infant daughter, the practical support for his school and his livelihood was destroyed. His wealthy patron and friend Reuben Haines died unexpectedly in October 1831. Abby wrote to her father describing Haines's death as a "paralyzing blow." Immediately the number of students in the school began to drop. Alcott managed to keep the school open through most of 1832, but with inadequate financial support. Once again he looked to Philadelphia for patronage, but without success. Angered and frustrated, he began to complain bitterly that the demands of daily living were interfering with his mission. He saw no reason why the "energies of first rate minds" should be "frittered away" by the problems of pecuniary support. He blamed the "public mind" for being unprepared to accept an experiment adequate to his desires and expectations.[60]

By the fall of 1832 Alcott was considering alternative means of spreading his message. He thought of writing original works on the mind to diffuse more widely a "purer" view of the philosophy of life and of education. Periodicals might convey his ideas in a series of articles. He even considered becoming an ordained minister.[61]

But despite the foundering of his school and his despair over financial support, Alcott did not go completely unrecognized and unreported. In December 1831 he completed his essay on the "Principles and Methods of Intellectual Instruction," which appeared in three segments in the *Annals of Education* during 1832 and early 1833. William Alcott, his religious conflict with Bronson notwithstanding, wrote a brief sketch of his cousin that told of the success of the Cheshire school. The *Annals* published it in May 1832. Then in June 1832 the American Institute of Instruction invited Alcott to read a paper on the early education of children at its meeting in Boston. Unfortunately, he was unable to attend because of the cholera epidemic then sweeping the entire eastern seaboard. Warnings that any change in daily habits could make a person more susceptible to the disease kept him in Germantown. He mailed the lecture to Boston and the Institute published it in its proceedings for 1832.[62]

Writing offered Alcott an outlet for his frustrations. Indeed, by mid-1832 he was becoming less interested in his school and more so in writing, reading, and speculating. His writing reflected the vagueness and uncertainty in his thought. His style was rarely attractive, and it became less so as his essays on education became increasingly abstract. These essays were unappealing to those interested in "practical," structural, educational reform. The essay he wrote for the Institute of Instruction, *On the Nature and Means of Early Intellectual Education*, was a prime example. It offered some excellent ideas, such as the need to develop spontaneity, free expression, and curiosity in the classroom and how to do it. It also chided the orthodox social reformers for not considering the principles of education:

> Intent on the improvement of methodical plans, we are in danger of treading principles under our feet.... Desirous chiefly, of effecting immediate results, we fail of establishing a sure foundation for theoretic and systematic practice.... Education should not be regarded as a process instituted on the human being, to fit him for a specific employment, by the instillation of a given amount of knowledge into his intellect; but *as the complete development of human nature, with a view to the habitual discharge of all its relations.*[63]

Yet the essay was filled with hazy references to analogy, to the idea that objects in the outward world were analogous to the child's mind. He did not carefully define in his essay, as he had not carefully defined it in his own mind, what he meant by analogy. The epistemological basis for his argument about the process of education was tentative and unclear. The lack of clarity in his theories and speculations made the market for them meager indeed. When he submitted for publication a summary of his observations on Anna, entitled "The History of an Infant," the *Annals of Education* refused it.[64]

Alcott's inability to write in a concrete and interesting way, and his failure to make his ideas attractive, obscured from his readers and the public in general the important questions he was asking about the process of human development. Even more tragically, it obscured his talent as a teacher, his ability to encourage, excite, and win the sympathy of his students. An excellent illustration of this ability was a series of letters to and from eight-year-old Elizabeth Lewis who boarded with the Alcotts in late 1832 and attended Alcott's school. Alcott often had his students correspond with him regularly in order to encourage self-expression. In this way he could criticize the writing and thinking of his pupils and give them an example to follow. He began this kind of correspondence with the precocious Elizabeth in October 1832.[65]

He told Elizabeth that she should write about subjects that interested her the most, and that writing should be spontaneous, natural, and simple. Elizabeth answered: "Do not let us confine our correspondence to any one thing; let it be many. One thing will lead to another, I dare say." Each letter to Elizabeth contained a word of encouragement and praise for her strengths. She asked questions about the Bible, about truth, about attending plays, about going to town for a day, about obeying her parents. Alcott praised her for being unafraid to ask questions. He always responded by discussing the topic of Elizabeth's letter; he did not coerce her into talking about the philosophical or religious theories in which he was interested at the time. If Alcott became too abstruse for her, especially on subjects such as truth or the Bible, Elizabeth would plead for him to use simpler language. He would then apologize and rephrase his explanation.[66]

In these letters Alcott demonstrated a sensitivity to young Elizabeth's needs and an ability to respond to them. Elizabeth obviously liked and respected Alcott. She worked hard to please him. He noted every gain she made in her ability to write and in her understanding of moral and intellectual questions. In each case he reinforced those gains with praise. His criticisms of her were pointed but gentle and always phrased in the context of encouragement. He was the model teacher. However, he could not resist telling her about his latest speculation concerning the mind and the soul, ideas sure to confuse her. For at the time of his correspondence with Elizabeth he was also reading that work which influenced his thought more than any other, Samuel Taylor Coleridge's *Aids to Reflection*.[67]

He first read *Aids to Reflection* in September 1832. The edition he used contained a helpful introductory essay by James Marsh, professor of philosophy at and president of the University of Vermont. This book, said Alcott, formed "a new era in my mental and psychological life."[68] Coleridge stated, and stated very well, what Alcott wanted to hear about the soul within each human being. "Life is the one universal soul," Coleridge said, which by virtue of the enlivening Breath, and the informing Word, all organized bodies have in common, each after its kind. But in addition to this, God transfused into man a higher gift, and especially imbreathed:— even a living (that is self-subsisting) soul, a soul having its life in itself.[69]

Coleridge was transmitting to English prose the idealism of the German philosophers that Cousin had written about. James Marsh remarked that Coleridge was another great force for idealism in its battle with John Locke and the sensationalists. Marsh felt that Locke's emphasis on the natural laws of sensation and reflection denied human free will and thus denied human morality and religion. Free will was the essence of Coleridge's self-subsisting soul. To Alcott Coleridge's great service was to make use of Locke's ideas in order to challenge Locke. Coming as he had from a Lockean background, Alcott was slow to shake off Locke's influence. His understanding of the workings of the mind was contingent on many of Locke's ideas, particularly on his concept of the faculties. To cast Locke away completely would mean a rebuilding of his own intellectual edifice from scratch. But Coleridge explained the higher spiritual powers of human beings, those powers which could transcend mere sensation and reflection, in terms of faculty theory. He said simply that all human faculties were not equal in kind, that some were spiritual, some mundane. He proposed a scale of faculties. The faculties of the "understanding" or the senses allowed knowing by means of inductive reasoning, Locke's natural laws of sensation and reflection. But the higher faculties, those of the "reason," allowed each person to communicate with the divine spirit. The reason was a higher spiritual power that allowed human free will and choice. It was the spirit of regeneration. It related to the spiritual world in the same way that the senses or the understanding related to the material world.[70]

This gave Alcott a means of conceptualizing the difference between the spiritual and the material within human beings just as the idea of analogy had permitted the same conceptualization of the external world. Thus he could integrate his belief in the soul, that creative power within human beings, with all he had learned and believed about the effects of external circumstances on the development of human faculties. He did not need to reject Locke and Bacon and all that they had had to say about the process of learning. Their ideas related to the power of understanding, the sense perception of the material world. But the spiritual faculty of reason gave additional powers to human beings, the power of choice, will, freedom, creativity. It allowed active participation by innate human powers in the acquisition of knowledge and truth. Alcott also did not need to reject the idea of natural law, that comforting theory that the universe operated in an understandable, orderly way. These Lockean natural laws accounted for the development of the understanding, while the higher reason developed in accordance with spiritual laws understandable only to reason itself.

Alcott joyously expressed these new-found concepts to Elizabeth Lewis when she asked about the nature of truth. He told her that there were three ways of arriving at truth: by means of the senses, the observation of outward things; by reflection on ideas obtained through sense impressions; and by intuition or faith. The bewildered Elizabeth asked her teacher to say it in simpler terms, but Alcott told her that that was impossible and apologized for taxing her powers too heavily.[71]

Success in his intellectual quest did not bring success to his school. By the end of 1832 the absence of Haines's patronage had brought continued "disheartening circumstances." Alcott began considering moving to Philadelphia and ending his association with William Russell. He hated to leave a man who he felt had been one of the greatest influences in his life to that time, but he still had hopes of joining Russell again later. He viewed himself as a prophet whose time had not yet come. His purpose was to enlighten the world about human nature amid prejudice and sectarianism. "Philosophy is unpopular," he said; "the age is wedded to matter, and afraid of spirit—man learns all things rather than himself; and he who penetrates the depths of human being and comes forth, making a true report of his discoveries, shocks and frightens the shallow and gaping multitude."[72]

With Haines gone, Germantown offered nothing. The people there seemed indifferent to education. Alcott felt isolated from intellectual society, and he sought a place more conducive to "pecuniary advancement and metal progress." Ultimately, he wanted to go back to Boston. Bostonians, he supposed, had a greater toleration of variant opinion. Indeed, he lamented his mistake in leaving Boston just as his experiment there was succeeding. Yet he still felt that a couple of years of experience in Philadelphia would be helpful. In January 1833 he wrote to William H. Furness, John Keagy, Maskell M. Carll, and Roberts Vaux asking for their help in establishing a school. He told them he wanted to teach twenty or thirty students, aged four to ten, for three hours a day.[73]

Furness responded that he had heard only good things about Alcott's teaching, and he assured Alcott that he could find a sizable number of patrons among the members of his church. But Alcott was cautious. "I have but limited faith," he said, "in the moral intelligence of Philadelphia as efficient patrons of early education." Only when twelve or fifteen pupils were guaranteed at twenty dollars per quarter would he take chance. Otherwise he resolved to go to Boston. Maskell Carll offered to permit him and Russell to join his school, but both Alcott and Russell hesitated to take on someone else's program for fear of losing their independence.[74]

Finally, Furness's efforts paid off. Sufficient patronage was guaranteed so that in March 1833 the Alcotts left Germantown, "with few regrets," and moved to Philadelphia. To defray expenses they sold the house in Germantown that Haines had given them and once again boarded at Mrs. Austin's. On April 22 Alcott opened his school on South Ninth Street with fifteen pupils. He and Abby had the additional care of a second daughter, Louisa May Alcott, born on November 29, 1832, Alcott's thirty-third birthday.[75]

For the first time in his teaching career, Alcott was unenthusiastic about the start of his new school. There were no grand statements about its ultimate mission or predictions of its success. His reading, his studies, the observation of his children were all of greater interest to him now. A good family friend, Mrs. Morrison of Germantown, had given him access to both the Philadelphia and the Loganian libraries. There he could lose himself in thought, and thought he now believed would do more good than teaching. The inward world could provide an escape from the awful depression brought about by the outward world's neglect of his ideas and his plans. Neglect could not enter his inward world. It was a world "where sympathy whispers her approval, and hope and faith ply their never-tiring pinions." He resigned himself to it. "There," he said, "let me dwell in Joy and Peace."[76]

He delved further into the works of Coleridge, reading *The Friend*, *Biographia Literaria*, and rereading *Aids to Reflection*. "No man since Jesus," Alcott thought," has perhaps penetrated deeper into the profound mysteries of the human spirit." By May 1833 he was reading the works of Plato, having found Thomas Taylor's translations of *Cratylus*, *Timaeus*, *Phaedo*, and *Parmenides* in the Philadelphia libraries. By the end of 1833 he had read the major works of George Berkeley, Thomas Carlyle, Johann Wolfgang von Goethe, Victor Cousin, Proclus, and Plotinus. Immanuel Kant's works were not available in translation, so he had to settle for a secondhand explanation of Kant's philosophy by F. A. Nitch. He began a commonplace book in which he copied from his reading and made extensive notes about his own ideas.[77]

The results of his reading he applied to his observations of his two young daughters. The record he made of Louisa's development became the chief subject of his speculation. He could observe her spiritual progress from birth and could directly apply to her his new theories of the spiritual nature of human beings.

His record of Louisa became a running commentary on his intellectual development as an idealist. He began it in December 1832, with the intention of considerng the effects of *all* outward circumstances and the manifestations of *all* innate qualities. He had even considered the well-being and mental state of his wife during pregnancy because, he said, education "commences with the period of conception, and all the influences operating upon the mother, whether from outward circumstances and persons or from her own state of mind and heart, should receive attention, in reference to their power of modifying the future being." Abby's good health, the company of Anna and Elizabeth Lewis, and his own efforts to raise the level of intellectual inquiry, all provided favorable circumstances, he thought, for the development of the child while in the womb.[78]

Unlike his notes about Anna's growth, Alcott's record of Louisa became less and less an account of observed behavior and more and more a catalogue of his own speculations about the relation of the inward spirit to the outward world. His description of this relationship corresponded to his reading and to his developing ideas. He assumed a divine purpose for the interaction of the spiritual within and external stimuli:

> Set down upon mundane things, to experience their qualities, and, by doing so, to attain self-consciousness, and self intelligence that might fit it for the visions of futurity, the soul is surrounded by celestial stimuli, supplied by Divine Providence, and designed to nurture and expand its energies into vigour and perfection of power.[79]

The "first truth" of psychological formation, he believed, was faith. Faith was a primal power given to each human being by God. Faith was an instinct for the divine. It could lead the soul to its "primal home." The child would first direct faith toward the mother, then to all the relations of life.[80]

For Alcott faith and intuition were among those higher spiritual faculties which corresponded to Coleridge's "reason." They helped explain the active role played by innate human power in the development of the mind. In his observations of Louisa, Alcott looked each day for evidence of those innate powers, those higher faculties, interacting with the outward world. The idea of analogy or correlation helped explain this interaction. Outward stimuli, analogous to the senses or the lower faculties, stimulated those lower faculties into action and thus developed them. For example, light and sound, being analogous to the senses of sight and hearing, awakened and activated those senses. In the same way the spiritual elements of the external world called forth the analogous spiritual faculties of the growing child. A mother's love could awaken the child's faith. Alcott believed that a clear view of this process was necessary for proper education to take place. "Education, when duly regarded," he said, "is the preservation of the relations of the human being to the universe. It is obedience to the correlations of the individual to the general—of the single to the universal—of the finite to the infinite."[81]

Alcott's explanation of this process left two questions unresolved. First, he had not yet fully described the nature of the spiritual element as he perceived it within the child. He said it included faith, conscience, will, and the ability to perceive truth, but he had placed no limits on it. Theoretically, he could have expanded his definition to include all the infinite powers of God. From Coleridge he learned that the human soul had had a primordial experience in the Infinite Spirit, that this soul had become temporarily embodied in the finite to be developed and would later return to that source of infinite energy whence it sprang. He was still exploring the full meaning of this concept of the nature of the soul.[82]

Second, he had not yet clearly decided whether the development of the spiritual aspect, the soul, depended upon external influence, upon some overriding spiritual law, or whether it depended upon the autonomous free will of that soul. His conception of the process of analogous influence implied that spiritual growth was contingent upon the action of external spiritual elements, that vital force of the spirit would lie dormant but for the presence of analogous external influences. In his comments on Coleridge early in 1833,

Alcott concluded that there were laws of nature and laws of spirit which acted upon a child, and to which the child passively submitted. Thus the child's will was free only to the extent that it obeyed the laws of nature and of spirit. But Alcott never fully accepted, nor consistently applied, the idea that an individual human being was a mere passive vessel for the spirit. He talked of the primal powers within, the primal creative powers of the soul. According to Coleridge these powers were the source of true genius. Alcott believed that they could be developed by education. In saying this he implied, but did not clearly state, that the individual soul had a creative life of its own and could act upon spirit and matter as well as be acted upon. It might even choose to disobey the laws of spirit or the laws of nature and thus cause evil. Or it might understand and manipulate natural or spiritual laws in order to perfect itself. The individual soul might be a God, a divine entity. He believed that Jesus' actions best illustrated the workings of the spirit, for Jesus and God were one. Jesus did nothing but by the inward working of the Eternal Spirit. However, Jesus acted in accordance with the Eternal Spirit because he was aware of the spirit and chose to follow it; the spirit did not lead him blindly and passively to predetermined ends. In the same way, thought Alcott, the child had to be aware of the divine spirit within before acting in accordance with it. This was the educator's responsibility; the educator had to ignite the hidden spark. So the individual soul was not a passive vessel of the spirit but rather separate from the spirit, needing an awareness of and an assent to spiritual laws in order to follow them.[83] Indeed, the very purpose of an individual life was to achieve a consciousness of its relation to the Eternal Spirit: "The organism, investing the innate spirit," said Alcott, "is projected into time and space to develope the Infinite on the forms of the Finite as the means of Revealing itself to itself."[84]

In struggling with these difficult matters Alcott was rehashing questions that Christian theologians had attempted to answer for centuries. These were questions of salvation and damnation. Salvation for Alcott was the awareness of the Eternal Spirit and the consequent obedience to spiritual laws. For orthodox Congregationalists salvation meant much the same thing, except that they believed that such awareness resulted from a conversion effected by the grace of God. Sin, evil, death, and destruction, according to the Congregationalists, resulted from the original depravity of human nature and the absence of God's grace. But Alcott had flatly rejected the concept of original depravity and also the idea that God was capricious in his distribution of grace. He believed instead that each person was a recipient of God's grace at birth, that each person was born good and pure, infused with the Eternal Spirit. This left him without an explanation for evil, for it was evident to him that God's grace, though bestowed at birth, did not mean certain salvation. Thus salvation could not be in the hands of God or in the hands of the Eternal Spirit. Instead, it had to depend on the use each person made of God's grace, the individual's awareness or consciousness of the spirit within. Since awareness of the spirit could not result from the grace of God—that had already been given—it had to be a matter of education, a matter of awakening innate powers by interaction with external forces.

The concept of the Eternal Spirit's presence in each human being explained for Alcott the infinite human potential for virtue and creativity, while the lack of awareness of that spirit explained evil. These ideas reaffirmed Alcott's faith in education by giving education the grand purpose of bringing about the consciousness of spirit. They made education a conversion experience. They combined Alcott's religious faith with his faith in the science of education and the science of human development. They explained the universe, God, the purpose of life, and they left plenty of room for a faith in growth and progress toward a better world on earth.

Alcott further developed these ideas upon reading Plato for the first time in May 1833. "Plato has cleared my vision," he said glowingly. Plato's ideas helped Alcott establish a definite relationship between spirit and matter. Now he saw spirit as the ultimate reality and matter as only the form and shadow of spirit. The individual soul was separate from the individual body, and the body was only a sepulchre of the soul. The soul was transcendent; it existed prior to the creation of the body. Material things, including the human body, were merely types or symbols of ideas. Ideas, like the soul or the spiritual aspect of the external world, originated in the infinite mind and existed without connection to material things. The universe was but an imperfect symbol of the spirit which pervaded it. Clearly matter was subordinate to spirit. Alcott had finally cast away Locke and the sensationalists. Their explanation of epistemology was totally inadequate. Outward sensation could not measure all things. Whereas his earlier definitions of education included the need to understand the influence of external circumstances on the mind, now Alcott emphasized the necessity of understanding the laws of the spirit. Education, he said, was "the science and art of educing the infinite from the surrounding encumbrances of the finite."[85]

In July 1833 Alcott found more support and illustration of his framework of idealism by reading F. A. Nitch's introduction to the ideas of Immanuel Kant. Alcott carefully recorded in his commonplace book Kant's distinctions between the faculties of the mind, that there was a receptivity in the mind that was totally passive but also an active faculty of the mind, a spontaneity about the mind. He noted Kant's belief in the existence of *a priori* ideas, those universal and necessary ideas like the concepts of space and time, which had objects within the mind and not objects distinct from the mind. *A priori* knowledge was pure knowledge as opposed to *a posteriori* knowledge gained from "experience" or by the influence of external objects. Alcott copied in detail the logical steps Kant used in arriving at his conclusions, and he evidently understood Kant as well as anyone could by reading in a secondary source. Kant's ideas reinforced and defined concepts Alcott had already accepted. He drew from Kant those ideas and definitions which best fitted his growing body of thoughts about the spiritual nature of the soul and of the universe. Kant's categories of *a priori* knowledge helped Alcott make explicit his belief in the infinite potential of the human mind as a partaker of the universal spirit.[86]

From Kant Alcott went on to the other bulwarks of German literature and philosophy. He read Goethe's *Wilhelm Meister* and Johann Gottfried von Herder's *Outlines of a Philosophy of the History of Man*. Again he found reinforcement. Goethe celebrated the power of human beings over their own destiny, the power to govern external circumstances rather than be govened by them. Alcott drew emotional sustenance from this idea in the face of difficulties that pressed him from every side, including financial problems and insecurity about vocation. Herder's *History of Man* dealt with the same questions about human nature that Alcott felt were so important and essential: the place of human beings in the universe, the nature of the human mind and faculties, and the spiritual powers of human beings. Herder wrote of human beings as the buds of future flowers, as having the godlike within, the potential to become nobler, freer creatures. He portrayed humanity as the connecting link between two worlds, the terrestrial and the heavenly, partaking of both. Within each human being, said Herder, was an infinite power that could develop and blossom if only the chains that bound it to terrestrial existence, the animal senses and passions, could be broken. Herder confirmed Alcott's opinion of the excellence of German philosophy. That philosophy had helped him "get some insight into the transcendental nature of man." Such reading, such thoughts, were emotionally uplifting. They confirmed his faith that the ugliness and ignorance of the world were but transitory, and that the true glory and perfection of human nature were within reach.[87]

They were within reach if only child rearing was accomplished with an understanding of the spirit:

> We shall never make our children what they were intended to be, portraitures and images of the Deity, in material colours and human shapes, till we awaken to the sense of our connexion with the infinite—our power to preserve this connexion—and our duty to understand, or at least, study this *connexion* of the *finite* and *infinite*.[88]

Consciousness of the spirit arose only by interaction between the spiritual and the material. The problem for Alcott was how to understand and control this interaction. "Psychology is yet in its infancy," he concluded, "and we have not the skill to unfold the hidden relations of matter and spirit—the play between the finite and the infinite." Ten-month-old Louisa was prone to tantrums, "paroxyms of rage," which her father had difficulty understanding. But he was sure that once she understood her own nature and became conscious of the spiritual powers within her, such troublesome behavior would stop. Rather than using severe punishment to stop the tantrums, he carefully tried to explain to her the problem, to make her aware of her power to do good. "There is in the deep mind of a child," he felt, "what the most sanguine enthusiast has never yet imagined, a power of virtue, which the influences of nature and providence have been as yet been fully allowed to develope and manifest.'' He viewed Louisa's curiosity about objects around her as the striving of the spirit to find outward types or symbols of its inward aspirations. Surely Louisa's evident love toward her sister and her parents was the work of the spirit. Love was the promise and symbol of immortality, and it had been awakened by the love of the mother toward the child. If only other appropriate symbols of the spirit could address the child's spirit, these would awaken the other "immortal senses," like the beautiful, the true, and the just.[89]

By the spring of 1834 Alcott felt that he had attained an intellectual synthesis. He believed that he had been led to the truth by a divine ray. His reading in German literature had saved him from the "thraldom of sense" into which he had been enticed by the "morbid food of English literature," meaning Locke and Bacon. Coleridge and the poet William Wordsworth had also helped him escape Aristotle, Locke, and Bacon, as had his own "innate tendency to pure ideality." Wordsworth's "Ode on Immortality" became the perfect poetic statement of Alcott's belief in a child's spiritual purity at birth. Children, Wordsworth said, came into the world "trailing clouds of glory." Coleridge had introduce him to German literature, which, he said, "has opened out to me a way of utterance for the conceptions which have so long been forming within me." Now he felt he lacked only an adequate means of expressing his ideas publicly in order to avoid the frequent charge that he was "mystical." He wanted to be able to make the "language of the heart" satisfy the practical mind.[90]

The epistemological problem he had wrestled with so long was solved. He now knew the relationship between the power of individual human beings and the power of surrounding circumstances. The spiritual principle, the spiritual element within human beings, gave them the ultimate power to transcend all external circumstances. This was genius. This was the "new life" stirring within, which could burst the bonds of the past and bring about new and improved people and institutions.[91] External circumstances were not only controlled by but were also the creation of the spirit:

> May we not believe that *thought* gives life and meaning to external nature—that what we see, hear, feel, taste, and experience around us, acquires these properties, by the self-investing power of our spirits.... The *reality* is in the *mind*, sense but gives us an outward type of it—an outward *shaping* to reduce it to the cognizance of the *understanding*; and in *space* and *time*, to *substantiate*, the indwelling forms, of our spirits. We throw ourselves outward upon nature, that we may the better look upon ourselves.[92]

Alcott's intellectual synthesis led him to a new direction in his educational theory. Now education was the process of making children aware of their inner spiritual nature. Since he believed that the external world was made of types or symbols of the spiritual world, he concluded that he could best awaken the spiritual element within a child by presenting to the child those external objects which most clearly typified or symbolized spiritual things. He felt that the best mode for this was the allegory, the fable, the emblem, or the parable. They best pointed out the symbolic nature of finite objects, he thought. He saw this clearly in reflecting upon his own experience reading the allegorical *Pilgrim's Progress*.[93]

In late July and early August 1833 he had visited Boston to attend the meeting of the American Institute of Instruction. At that time he had made arrangements with Wait, Lilly, Holden, and Company, publishers, to print an edition of children's fables and to reprint *Pilgrim's Progress*, Pestalozzi's *Leonard and Gertrude*, and stories by Mary Wollstonecraft. For the edition of children's stories he planned to draw upon fables by Northcote, Lessing, Krummacher, and Quarles. With them he had constructed in the fall of 1833 a book to be called "Pictures of Thought," in which he included an introduction explaining how emblems and allegories "supply the soul with that spiritual nurture which it requires while surrounded by the passing objects of sense." Unfortunately, the Boston publishers refused to accept the collection, adding to Alcott's disappointment over the fate of his practical reform efforts. When he learned this news in May 1834, he was already experiencing further failure with the decline of his Philadelphia school.[94]

By May 5, 1834, six pupils had withdrawn from his school, and he learned that several more were soon to follow. "This," he complained, "is, indeed, but the penalty I must pay for venturing to differ from the common modes of teaching." He called on all of the unappreciative parents and tried to convince them of the great evil they were doing to their children by removing them. Undoubtedly, this only reinforced the parents' decision. Some parents called Alcott "enthusiastic"; others thought him insane. One parent said he feared Alcott's stress on moral education would make his child unfit to deal with the practical world. One of his students, Charles Godfrey Leland, later wrote that Alcott was "the most eccentric man who ever took it on himself to train and form the youthful mind." Alcott suspected that his disgruntled parents objected to his keeping the children for only three hours a day. He noted that those teachers who kept the longest hours gained the most students. Either parents wanted their children out of the way, or they measured their children's learning by the number of hours spent in the classroom. Such long hours, Alcott felt, were injurious to a child's health and strength of mind. Three hours of confined study was long enough; the rest of the day ought to be free for play and exercise. Alcott may well have been right about the shallow motives of his patrons. But it was also true that he did not give the same intense effort and commitment to his Philadelphia school that he had given to his earlier ones. Reading and study took up most of his time, and his teaching became haphazard and disorganized. According to Leland, Alcott allowed his students to neglect subjects such as geography and arithmetic at their will. Such lack of structure and purpose was never true of his earlier schools, nor was it of his later ones.[95]

Whatever the reason, the school failed. Alcott resolved to seek "another sphere of labor," because he was unwilling to waste his time on so few pupils. Greater numbers, he felt, inspired greater powers in the teacher. He admitted that low attendance had diminished the pleasure of teaching. The consciousness of "benefitting the many" was far more exciting than the thought of teaching just a few. His discouragement and dissatisfaction were compounded by tension within his own family. Abby, who was pregnant and unwell, found the cramped quarters at Mrs. Eaton's boarding house, to which they had moved in May 1833, to be insufferable. Both Alcott and his wife feared that the city would be damaging to the health of their children. So in April 1834 Abby and the children moved back to Germantown under the good graces of Mrs. Morrison at Keppel Cottage. Alcott remained in an attic room at Mrs. Eaton's. He planned to visit the family on weekends, while staying close to his school and the libraries during the week. He thought he would enjoy the peace and quiet that the presence of small children had heretofore prevented, but he quickly found the isolation painful. The atmosphere of poverty and loneliness oppressed him as he stared out his fourth-floor window facing the library, his room furnished with only a trunk, two chairs, a washstand, his bed, and his books, "It matters little, after all, what surrounds us," he said, meaning just the opposite.[96]

He knew that his family suffered because of his reflective life. They had no money, no home of their own. But he felt that it was the only course he could pursue and still do justice to life. He would sacrifice, his family would sacrifice, in order to achieve a greater purpose. The trappings of wealth, the status and respectability it brought, meant nothing to him. Providence would provide enough for him and his family to eat. Abby, on the other hand, was less sanguine about the family's fortune and future. She argued that her husband's intellectual pursuits were endangering the family's welfare. He conceded that she had a point, but he continued to defend his motives and to explain why he would not "yield to the dictates of earthly prudence" and get a paying job.[97]

The family's condition reached its lowest point on May 27 when Abby gave birth prematurely and nearly died. Discouragement and despair mounted. In hopes of deliverance Alcott looked toward Boston. In late May William Russell went to Boston to speak with friends about a possible school for Alcott. He returned with a favorable report. From Alcott's perspective Boston looked like the Promised Land compared to Philadelphia. He would find support in Boston if nowhere else. Philadelphia, he thought, lagged fifty years behind Boston from a moral point of view. Reformers in Philadelphia concerned themselves with the evils of conditions rather than the evils of the mind. He was sure that in Boston his ideas would find adherents, and that his impact on public opinion would thus be greater than ever before. Boston reformers would respect those like himself with meditative and speculative tendencies, realizing that in the end it was thought, ideas, that led to all practical reform.[98]

Hope for a fresh start in Boston rested ultimately on the influence of William Ellery Channing. William Russell wrote to Channing on July 6, 1834, telling of Alcott's predicament in Philadelphia and assuring Channing of

Alcott's great talent for teaching. Alcott, Russell said, would surely introduce a "new era" in education. Channing answered that he was glad Alcott planned to return to Boston and that he would certainly aid the enterprise. With this assurance Alcott resolved to leave Philadelphia despite the prospect of twenty students enrolling in his school in September. A meeting with Channing at the latter's summer home in Newport, Rhode Island, in September added to his confidence. A new school was guaranteed. The intellectual isolation Alcott felt in Philadelphia would end. He had read of and heard of several people in the Boston area who seemed to have views in common with his own. Among them were Professor James Marsh of the University of Vermont; the Reverend Orville Dewey, formerly a colleague of Dr. Channing; the Reverend Frederic Henry Hedge, whose March 1833 article on Coleridge in the *Christian Examiner* had impressed Alcott; and Ralph Waldo Emerson. Alcott had good reason for his great expectations.[99]

Notes

1. AJ 4 (1830): 150, 152; AJ 5 (1831), part 1: 1, 24-25.

2. AJ 5 (1831), part 1: 3-15, 16; James Pyle Wickersham, *A History of Education in Pennsylvania* (Lancaster, Pa.: Inquirer Publishing Co., 1886), pp. 284-85, 288, 289, 296; Joseph J. McCadden, *Education in Pennsylvania, 1801-1835, and its Debt to Roberts Vaux* (Philadelphia: University of Pennsylvania Press, 1937), pp. 24, 26, 32-33.

3. AJ 4 (1830): 151-52; McCadden, *Education in Pennsylvania*, pp. 120-26, 145-47.

4. McCadden, *Education in Pennsylvania*, p. 121; F[rancis] R. P[ackerd], "Caspar Wistar," *Dictionary of American Biography* (New York: Charles Scribner's Sons, 1946), 19:433-34; Thomas P. Govan, *Nicholas Biddle* (Chicago: University of Chicago Press, 1959), pp. 73-74; Alcott to S. J. May, December 21, 1830, from a copy in Alcott's hand in "Autobiographical Materials."

5. AJ 4 (1830): 151-52; Alcott to S. J. May, December 21, 1830; McCadden, *Education in Pennsylvania*, pp. 19-20, 25, 57, 73; AJ 5 (1831), part 1: 3-14.

6. AJ 5 (1831), part 1: 9-10.

7. Ibid.

8. Ibid., pp. 23-26, 40, 44; Govan, *Nicholas Biddle*, p. 73; McCadden, *Education in Pennsylvania*, pp. 51, 58, 63-64; Wickersham, *History of Education in Pennsylvania*, p. 142; Alcott, "Autobiographical Index."

9. AJ 5 (1831), part 1: 36-39, 84-85; Alcott, "Autobiographical Collections," vol. 3 (1823-1834), clipping attached to p. 200; Alcott, "Autobiographical Materials"; Alcott, "Autobiographical Index"; AJ 5 (1831), part 2: 21-23.

10. AJ 2: (1831), part 1: 63; Alcott to W. A. Alcott, March 10, 1831, and May 26, 1831, in "Letters, 1828-34."

11. AJ 5 (1831), part 1: 41, 44, 45, 63-64. 69-70.

12. Ibid., pp. 82, 84, 87; McCadden, *Education in Pennsylvania*, p. 30-31.

13. McCadden, *Education in Pennsylvania*, pp. 30-31.

14. Ibid., pp. 134-35, 162-63. The background information used here is from McCadden.

15. McCadden, *Education in Pennsylvania*, pp. 141-44.

16. AJ 5 (1831), part 2: 4-5; [A. Bronson Alcott], "Principles and Methods of Intellectual Instruction Exhibited in the Exercises of Young Children," *American Annals of Education and Instruction* 2, no. 1 (January 1832): 52-54, and 3, no. 5 (May 1833): 219.

17. AJ 5 (1831), part 2: 14-15.

18. Ibid., p. 16.

19. Ibid., pp. 16-20.

20. AJ 5 (1831), part 1: 19, 55; Alcott, "Autobiographical Index."

21. Margaret Bacon, *The Quiet Rebels: The Story of the Quakers in America* (Philadelphia: University of Pennsylvania Press, 1937), p. 86.

22. AJ 5 (1831), part 1: 18.

23. Ibid., pp. 11, 73.

24. A. Bronson Alcott, "Observations on the Life of My First Child (Anna Bronson Alcott) During Her First Year, 1831," 1:142. MS located at Houghton Library, 59M-306 (1).

25. Alcott to W. A. Alcott, August 20, 1829, in "Letters, 1828-34"; AJ 5 (1831), part 1: 56-57.

26. Charles Gibbon, *The Life of George Combe*, 2 vols. (London: Macmillan and Co., 1878), 1:92-96; George Combe, *The Constitution of Man Considered in Relation to External Objects*, 8th American ed. (Boston: Marsh, Capen, Lyon and Webb, 1839), pp. 28, 88; John D. Davies, *Phrenology: Fad and Science* (New Haven, Conn.: Yale University Press, 1955), pp. 3-5.

27. Davies, *Phrenology*, pp. 8-11; Combe, *Constitution of Man*, pp. 102-13

28. Davies, *Phrenology*, pp. 12-14, 165-68.

29. Ibid., pp. 16-18.

30. AJ 5 (1831), part 2: 147.

31. Ibid., p. 1.

32. Ibid., p. 230.

33. Ibid., pp. iii, 9, 14-15.

34. Ibid., p. 5.

35. AJ 5 (1831), part 1: 20, 77; Alcott, "Observations on the Life of My First Child," 1:24, 40, 111-12.

36. An excellent study of Alcott's observations on his children is Charles Strickland, "A Transcendentalist Father: The Child Rearing Practices of Bronson Alcott," *Perspectives in American History* 3 (1969), pp. 5—73. However, Strickland does not deal sufficiently with the earlier background of Alcott's reform activities. Also useful in understanding Alcott's views on child rearing is Sherman Paul, "Alcott's Search for the Child," *Boston Public Library Quarterly* 4, no. 2 (April 1952): 88-96.

37. Alcott, "Observations on the Life of My First Child," 1: iv, 1.

38. Ibid., p. 3; Abby May Alcott to Samuel and Lucretia May, March 27, 1831, in "Family Letters, 1828-1861."

39. Alcott, "Observations on the Life on My First Child," 1:7, 109, 125, 151.

40. Ibid., pp. 44, 114-16, 258-59.

41. Ibid., pp. 36, 67, 70, 98, 170-71, 183, 218.

42. Ibid., pp. 17, 45-47, 117, 139.

43. Ibid., p. 198; AJ 5 (1831), part 2: 129-31.

44. Alcott, "Observations on the Life of My First Child," 1:28.

45. Ibid., pp. 146, 210, 250, 274.

46. Ibid., pp. 4-5, 10, 75.

47. Ibid., p. 108.

48. AJ 5 (1831), part 2:33-37.

49. Ibid., p. 170.

50. Ibid., p. 210.

51. Ibid., pp. 169-179; Alcott to W. A. Alcott, December 2, 1831, in "Letters, 1828-34."

52. Alcott, "Observations on the Life of My First Child," 1:108, 203.

53. Alcott, "Autobiographical Index"; AJ 5 (1831), part 2: 109, 121-24, 189, 252; AJ 6 (1832-33), part 1 ("Journal of Experience in 1832"): pp. 1-2.

54. Miller, ed., *The Transcendentalists*, p. 28; "Cousin's Philosophy," *American Quarterly Review* 10 (December 1831): 291-311.

55. Francis Wayland, *The Elements of Moral Science*, ed. Joseph Blau (Cambridge, Mass.: Harvard University Press, 1963), pp. ix, xxiii, xxvi; Alcott, "Observations on the Life of My First

Child," 1:277; AJ 6 (1832-33), part 1: 1-2.

56. AJ 6 (1832-33), part 1: 11, 14, 18-19.

57. A. Bronson Alcott, *On the Nature and Means of Early Intellectual Education as Deduced from Experience*, from American Institute of Instruction, *Lectures*, 1832-1833, pp. 132, 134, 136. This lecture was presented to the Institute in August 1832, and was also published separately as a pamphlet by Carter and Hendee in 1833.

58. Ibid., p. 153.

59. AJ 6 (1832-33), part 1: 5-7; ibid., part 2 ("Ideas and Paradigms or Ethical Memoranda for 1832"): 31-35.

60. AJ 6 (1832-33), part 1: 4, 21, 27, 32; AJ 6 (1831), part 2: 235, 255; Abby May Alcott to Joseph May, November 13, 1831, from a copy in Alcott's hand in "Autobiographical Materials."

61. AJ 6 (1832-33), part 1: 33-34.

62. Ibid., pp. 24, 30; AJ 5 (1831), part 2: 249; [William A. Alcott], "Biography of a Teacher," *American Annals of Education and Instruction* 2 (May 1832): 257-59; Solomon P. Miles to Alcott, June 19, 1832, in "Autobiographical Collections," vol. 3 (1823-34). Miles was the corresponding secretary of the American Institute of Instruction. Alcott to Mrs. Anna Alcott, August 20, 1832, from a copy in Alcott's hand in "Autobiographical Materials"; John Broderick, "Emerson, Alcott, and the American Institute of Instruction," *Emerson Society Quarterly* no. 13 (4 Quarter, 1958), pp. 27-29.

63. Alcott, *On the Nature and Means of Early Intellectual Education*, from American Institute of Instruction, *Lectures*, pp. 144-46, 161-62.

64. Ibid., pp. 130-31; A. Bronson Alcott, comp., "Memoir, 1878." This is a bound collection of copies of letters, diary entries, and notes dated 1834 to 1855, including the manuscript of "History of an Infant." The volume is located at Houghton Library, 59M-306 (23).

65. AJ 6 (1832-33), part 1: 41.

66. Alcott to Elizabeth Lewis, October 2, 19, 24, and 27, 1832; Elizabeth Lewis to Alcott, October 5, 18, 23, 31 and November 14, 1832. These are all bound together in A. Bronson Alcott, comp., "Letters, 1832 and 1834," MS located at Houghton Library, 59M-305 (33).

67. Elizabeth Lewis to Alcott, October 23, 1832, in "Letters, 1832 and 1834"; AJ 6 (1832-33): part 1: 35, 39-41.

68. AJ 6 (1832-33), part 1: 41.

69. Samuel Taylor Coleridge, *Aids to Reflection*, introductory essay by James Marsh (Burlington Vt.: Chauncey Goodrich, 1840), p. 70.

70. Ibid., pp. 31, 34, 37, 202, 208, 211-12, 216-17, 223, 233.

71. Alcott to Elizabeth Lewis, October 19 and 24, 1832; Elizabeth Lewis to Alcott, October 23, 1832, in "Letters, 1832 and 1834."

72. AJ 6 (1832-33), part 1: 66-68, 74-75; ibid., part 3 ("Journal of Experience, 1833"): 1-2.

73. AJ 6 (1832-33), part 3: 1-2, 4-5, 9-11; Alcott to Roberts Vaux, January 10, 1833, printed in Richard L. Herrnstadt, ed., *The Letters of A. Bronson Alcott* (Ames: Iowa State University Press, 1969), pp. 20-21.

74. William H. Furness to Alcott, January 29, 1833, from a copy in Alcott's hand in "Autobiographical Materials"; AJ 6 (1832-33), part 3: 15, 17-22.

75. AJ 6 (1832-33), part 1: 48; ibid., part 3: 31-33; Alcott, "Autobiographical Index"; Alcott, "Memoir, 1878."

76. AJ 6 (1832-33), part 3: 28, 36-37, 41.

77. Ibid., pp. 25-27, 43, 49, 52-53, 72, 76; Alcott, "Autobiographical Index"; A. Bronson Alcott, "Readings in 1833," MS at Houghton Library, 59M-306 (4).

78. A. Bronson Alcott, "Observations on the Life of My Second Child (Louisa May Alcott) during the First Year, 1832-33," pp. ii, 2, 3, 4, MS at Houghton Library, 59M-306 (3).

79. Ibid., p. 14.

80. Ibid., pp. 14-15, 58-61.

81. Ibid., pp. 20-23, 26-27, 55, 57-60, 75.

82. AJ 6 (1832-33), part 3: 24; Coleridge, *Aids to Reflection*, p. 76; Alcott to Elizabeth Palmer Peabody, May 7, 1833, from a copy in Alcott's hand in "Autobiographical Materials."

83. Alcott, "Observations on the Life of My Second Child, 1832-33," pp. 62, 76, 79-80, 107-8; Alcott, "Readings in 1833," pp. 19-20.

84. Alcott, "Observations on the Life of My Second Child, 1832-33," p. 119.

85. Ibid., pp. 157-58, 198, 218; AJ 6 (1832-33), part 3: 43-44; Alcott, "Readings in 1833," pp. 23-27, which includes quotations from Plato's *Cratylus*, *Phaedo*, *Parmenides*, and *Timaeus*, as well as Alcott's comments about them; A. Bronson Alcott, "Observations on the Life of a Child During the Third Year of its Existence," 3: 1833-34, p. 26, MS at Houghton Library, 59M-306 (2). This is bound with volume 2 of Alcott's observations on Anna.

86. AJ 6 (1832-33), part 3: 52-53; Alcott, "Readings in 1833," pp. 113-23.

87. Alcott, "Readings in 1833," pp. 160-164; AJ 6 (1832-33), part 3: 51-53; Johann Gottfried von Herder, *Outlines of a Philosophy of the History of Man* (New York: Bergman Publishers, 1966), pp. 119, 124-26, 127-31. This was first published in 1784 and translated into English in 1799.

88. Alcott, "Observations on the Life of My Second Child, 1832-33," p. 246.

89. Ibid., pp. 265-66, 267-70, 282, 284, 321; Alcott, "Observations on the Experience of a Child During the Third Year of its Existence," 3:52.

90. Alcott to W. A. Alcott, July 2, 1833, in "Letters, 1828-34"; AJ 7 (1834), part 2 ("Diary for 1834"): 14-19.

91. AJ 7 (1834), part 2: 34, 38-39.

92. Ibid., p. 350.

93. A. Bronson Alcott, comp., "Pictures of Thought comprising Fables, Emblems, Parables and Allegories Intended Principally to aid the Young in Self-Inspection and Self-Culture," 1834, MS at Houghton Library, 59M-306 (5); Alcott to Elizabeth Palmer Peabody, before September, 1834, in Herrnstadt, ed., *Letters*, pp. 22-23.

94. AJ 6 (1832-33), part 3: 55-60, 63-67; Alcott, "Pictures of Thought"; AJ 7 (1834), part 2: 196.

95. AJ 7 (1834), part 2: 154, 179, 227; Abby May Alcott to Joseph May, May 19, 1834, from a copy in Alcott's hand in "Autobiographical Materials"; Charles Godfrey Leland, *Memoirs* (New York: D. Appleton and Co., 1893), pp. 46-47; Charles Godfrey Leland, *Practical Education* (London: Whittaker and Co., 1888), p. 228.

96. AJ 7: (1834), part 2: 1-4, 43-44, 104, 178, 197, 295; Alcott, "Autobiographical Index"; AJ 7 (1834), part 1 ("Journal for 1834"): 13-14.

97. AJ 7 (1834), part 2: 97-100, 125, 129; Abby May Alcott, "Autobiography," a collection of fragments torn from a notebook located at Houghton Library, 59M-311 (3 and 4).

98. AJ 7 (1834), part 2: 237, 240, 275, 288-89, 370.

99. Ibid., pp. 151, 275; William Russell to William Ellery Channing, July 6, 1834, in Alcott, "Autobiographical Collections," 3: 281; William Ellery Channing to William Russell, August 8, 1834, in Alcott, "Autobiographical Collections," 3:282; Alcott to Abby May Alcott, September, 1834, from a copy in Alcott's hand in "Autobiographical Matherials."

5

The Temple School, 1834–36

BOSTON offered a new life for Alcott in the fall of 1834. With Dr. Channing's help Alcott won support for his proposed school from some of the city's wealthiest and most influential citizens. Lemuel Shaw, Chief Justice of the Commonwealth of Massachusetts, promised aid, as did Boston's mayor, Josiah Quincy. Educational reformer George Barrell Emerson, then tutor of geometry at Harvard, enthusiastically joined the list of patrons. Lawyers, successful merchants, and philanthropists such as Samuel Tuckerman, Nathan Rice, Patrick Jackson, Robert Bartlett, G. B. Cary, John Ware, and James Savage entrusted their sons and daughters to Alcott. All were from the upper middle class; all would otherwise have sent their children to private schools; all were attracted by Alcott's talk about superior methods of cultivating morality and intellect. Not all were Unitarians. Nearly every denomination in Boston was represented. There were orthodox Congregationalists, Baptists, Methodists, Episcopalians, Swedenborgians, Universalists, and Free Enquirers. Alcott hoped to add a Quaker and a Catholic or two. A major reason for the diversity was that respect for William Ellery Channing transcended denominational boundaries. When Channing spoke of Alcott's excellence as a teacher, few disputed the claim. Channing's Boston proved to Alcott's satisfaction its moral superiority over Philadelphia. For the next two years it gave him an arena for his experiments in human culture. It brought him success he had not known before and would not know again for many years.[1]

Alcott also found a willing assistant for his new school, thirty-year-old Elizabeth Palmer Peabody. She had been secretary for Dr. Channing, had tutored his daughter, and had operated a school of her own under Channing's sponsorship since 1826. When Alcott first met her in August 1828, she was helping William Russell edit the *American Journal of Education*. At that time he found her "interesting," but a little too "familiar" and "free" for a woman. But subsequent meetings convinced him that she had a superior and original mind. Most important, she held ideas on education similar to his own. He wrote to her several times during his Philadelphia years about his teaching and about his ideas. She was one of the few people with whom he felt it was profitable to correspond, and he sent her lengthy letters about his fascination with Coleridge. She was equally impressed with him. She had visited his earlier

Boston schools and early in 1829 had published a favorable account of those visits in the *American Journal of Education*. When Alcott suggested that she assist him in his proposed Boston school in 1834, she was delighted. Never known for understatement, reticence, or modesty, she told him that from the first time she saw him with a child she felt that he had "more genius for education than [she] ever saw or expected to see." He was the only person she knew that surpassed her own gifts as a teacher. She was effusive but effective. Her efforts in contacting patrons and making preliminary arrangements for the school were largely responsible for its initial success.[2]

On Monday, September 22, 1834, Alcott and Peabody opened their new school with thirty pupils, fifteen boys and fifteen girls aged three to twelve. They had rented five rooms at three hundred dollars a year on the top floor of the Masonic Temple on Tremont Street. Hoping to surround each child with appropriate symbols of the intellectual and spiritual life, Alcott tastefully furnished the rooms with paintings, busts, books, and comfortable furniture. All these emblems of the mind and spirit cost $317.41. They depicted many of Alcott's benefactors: Jesus, Plato, Socrates, and, most appropriately, Dr. Channing, whose portrait was prominently displayed. Alcott expected to receive at least $1,800 a year for his efforts, which would free him from debt. Teaching three to five hours a day would give him plenty of time for reading and contemplation. And he felt he could now do greater justice to his family. Abby, Anna, Louisa, and he were comfortably settled into three rooms at Mrs. Whitney's boarding house on Bedford Street, just a short walk from the Temple. He expected that they all would at last be free from the "constant scuffling with untoward circumstances."[3]

The Temple School promised to fulfill Alcott's sense of mission. He knew that only a few would appreciate it, but then, his mission was not to please people but to benefit them; he would not barter away his faith in the ideal for gold or popularity. Experience had convinced him of the rectitude of his actions. Though few seemed interested in human culture, in the study of the universal and the absolute, he would do his part to establish the truth that education was "the preservation of the Human Spirit, in its original divinity and glory." He would reveal to the world the spiritual agencies at work in childhood. His school would train children to be virtuous, to be excellent. It would draw out the spiritual goodness innate in the child, for childhood," he said, was the "Temple of the Holy Spirit." In his school he would have a priceless opportunity to observe children in action. Manifestations of the "unsoiled nature" of the children would be a revelation of the spirit to him. Such revelation would ensure his improvement as a teacher, for in the end a child learned and improved not because of the teacher but because of the action of his or her own inherent goodness working with the teacher. The best teachers acted merely as facilitators of that goodness.[4]

The teacher's main task, Alcott thought, was to make children conscious that they were spiritual beings, that their souls resided in God. This new consciousness would then liberate the child's spirit for goodness and virtue. It would release those "superhuman energies" struggling for utterance within each child's body.[5] Alcott did not explain, indeed he failed to ask the question, why a superhuman agency filled with spiritual goodness would become so trapped and restricted in the first place. His faith in human goodness was so important to him that his explanation and description of it far overshadowed his explanation of evil. Evil, he said, resulted from poor choices made by free, creative, and independent souls. But if these souls were born pure and unsoiled, as he believed they were, how could they make these poor choices? This problem haunted him in all his inward explorations, though he rarely faced it directly. He was more interested in creating beautiful visions of goodness and spirituality. The power, the attractive dynamism of his thought, rested on these assumptions about human goodness. Yet, without a convincing explanation of evil, all of this was airy rhetoric. He would have to confront the problem of evil again sooner or later.

Meanwhile he erected the theoretical superstructure of the Temple School on the belief that there was a vast potential, a boundless energy, within each child that the teacher could set free. There were no limits to what a child could learn or do. Alcott's purpose would not be restricted to the mere inculcation of knowledge. Rather, he expected to develop "genius," to give full play to the human soul. "He who kindles the fire of *genius* in the alter of the young heart," he said, "unites his own prayers for humanity, with every ascending flame that is emitted from it, through succeeding time."[6]

To implement the mission of the Temple School, Alcott set about "cutting the weeds" and "cultivating the soil" so that the soul of each child might be free to grow. He felt that the first element necessary for this was proper discipline. For if the soul was obedient, he thought, then all human faculties would be in harmony. Perfection would be the result. The standard of action that defined such obedience was the innate "idea of right," located in everyone's conscience. Obedience to it was the true end of human culture. But despite the conscience' being an instrument of moral law and innately good, it still needed guidance from the outside. That was the province of the teacher. The teacher had to discipline the child's soul and, by doing so, liberate it. As always, freedom for Alcott meant the freedom to obey moral laws.[7]

Alcott tried to make his pupils aware of the workings of conscience. But he was not concerned only with individual consciences. He believed that his group of students had a "common conscience" larger than the sum of all their consciences, which provided a standard by which all individual action could be measured. The common conscience in Alcott's philosophical scheme was an external emblem of each child's individual conscience. Thus it would serve to awaken each individual conscience and activate it. His faith in the innate goodness of children led him to believe that they could never defend wrong in the abstract, though they could do wrong things. If only they became conscious of the wrongness of their actions, that is, if they became aware of how their own consciences condemned such action, they would refrain from it. The common conscience could serve as a model of how their own consciences operated. Wrong actions would be measured by the standards of the common conscience. Accordingly, everyone would condemn them and they would be eliminated. In the same way each child supposedly would learn to judge each action himself by his own conscience.[8]

To facilitate his theory of discipline Alcott appointed, or sometimes allowed his students to elect, a student superintendent. This technique had worked successfully in his earlier schools. The superintendents were to police the conduct of the other students, maintaining proper attitude, attention, and appearance on the part of everyone. They were to call any offense to the attention of the class, to be judged by the common conscience. Every student had a chance to become superintendent. Even the worst-behaving students became scrupulously just, Alcott noted, when given that responsibility. Though skeptical at first, Elizabeth Peabody was completely won over by this disciplinary method and was amazed at its success. Alcott conversed at length with his students about discipline from the moment the school opened in order to cultivate the common conscience. He got them to agree that "right action" should be the primary goal of the school and that some form of punishment was necessary to ensure such right actions. He carefully illustrated the kinds of behavior that would require punishment and the types of punishment offenders might expect. Of course, Alcott imposed on his students his own preconception of what "right action" involved. In many ways this was extremely rigid: no talking or whispering among students, strict attention at all times. But he was careful to get the students to accept consciously the rules and the modes of punishment. Nothing would be arbitrary; the students themselves legitimated the mode of discipline.[9]

Punishment varied with the offense. Sometimes it involved a blow with the ferule on the palm of the hand. When Alcott did this he always took the victim outside the classroom to inflict the punishment and he carefully explained the reason for his action. He always got the offender to acknowledge the justice of the punishment. Twice Alcott had the guilty party strike him with the ferule. This caused the boys involved, who claimed to be unafraid of being hit themselves, to break into tears. For Alcott had successfully established himself as an object of admiration and respect, a paragon of "right action" with whom the students could compare their own behavior. Generally, Alcott attempted to avoid using corporal punishment. Instead, he would deny all his students a favorite activity or exercise. This would make the guilty one ashamed at having caused everyone's displeasure, at having offended the common conscience.[10]

After having established a mode of discipline, Alcott's next goal was to cultivate thought and expression. Freedom of thought and expression, he believed, would enable a child to manifest the spiritual good within. To accomplish this he further developed techniques he had used before. He had each student keep a journal, which he hoped would facilitate "self-analysis" as well as aid the students in composition. In it they were to express the "inner thoughts" of their souls. The children undoubtedly had trouble understanding what their teacher meant by that, but Alcott patiently worked with all children individually, reading their journals, criticizing them not for what they said, but only for what they did not say. He constantly encouraged them to express freely their thoughts and feelings. He avoided petty criticisms of spelling and grammar lest he discourage them.[11]

As in the past, conversation was a favorite technique used by Alcott in order to generate expression and thought. Alcott believed that the "spirit's workings" came out in conversation, so he spent a large amount of class time asking questions of his students and inviting their responses. The children talked with him freely about abstract topics such as the nature of the Bible, of freedom, of war, of love, of their own spiritual nature. He asked them about the spiritual aspects of birth, about what Wordsworth meant by "our birth is but a sleep and a forgetting." Of course, he looked for answers from the children that would give evidence of the spirit within them and thus confirm his theories. And the children soon learned the kinds of things they should say in order to please their teacher. Alcott claimed to be dispassionate, objective, and free of dogmatism in these discussions with his students. As Elizabeth Peabody explained it, he claimed nothing more than that "Spirit exists." But what an assumption! His overriding purpose in conversation was to point to what he believed were the workings of the spirit. He wanted his students to become aware of their spiritual nature. Only then, he thought, could the children be truly free to think and express themselves. He may have been right. The children's comments during conversation may have reflected the prompting of the spirit. But it was also true that he created a paradigm in accordance with which the students could always safely frame their answers and comments. They knew that if they referred to the spirit in some way, Alcott would be pleased. They also knew that if they did not show an awareness of the spirit, their teacher would be displeased. For he had said to them: "I believe that those who cannot conceive of Spirit without body, existing in God before it comes out upon earth, are the very ones who have required the most discipline and punishment, and have the least love of obedience." Clearly, this was indoctrination; it was passionate dogmatizing. The children were free to express their opinions, but only as long as they agreed with Alcott's basic assumptions. Nevertheless, Alcott did succeed in exercising the thought processes of his students in conversation. The children had to consider carefully each question within Alcott's paradigm of the spirit. They could not learn Alcott's stock answers by rote memorization. Rather, they were forced to use their own minds to synthesize their thoughts within the spiritual principle. Alcott gave them a general framework, but not a catechism.[12]

Alcott also sought to develop thought and expression by cultivating the imagination of his charges. He believed that the faculty of imagination was the shaping power of the soul. It was the instrument by which the spirit manifested itself. Thus it was the key to expression. However, the imagination needed proper guidance and cultivation, lest it come under the sway of the "senses" and the "passions" and cause evil. Here again Alcott's explanation of evil was weak, for why would an innately good faculty like the imagination become so easily tarnished? He might have said that the imagination was both innately good and innately weak. But as before, Alcott was more interested in demonstrating how to eliminate evil than in explaining its presence. To cultivate the imagination, that is to keep it unsoiled, he turned to his stock of fables, parables, allegories, and emblems. He read to his pupils from *Pilgrim's Progress*, the *New Testament*, Krummacher's *Parables*, Coleridge's "Rhyme of the Ancient Mariner," and a few allegories he had written himself. Two books, prepared by Alcott for the purpose, served as student readers. One was a pictorial "Biography of Jesus Christ." Another was F. W. Carové's emblematic *Story Without an End*, translated by Sarah Austin and edited with an introduction by Alcott. All of these were illustrations of the spirit, Alcott believed. They were external symbols corresponding to the spiritual elements within a child's soul. Just as the external common conscience awakened each child's individual conscience, so these symbolic stories of moral behavior would serve to awaken similar moral behavior in each child and facilitate the expression of it. They would stimulate the imagination, but also keep it an instrument for good.[13]

In encouraging expression by his pupils Alcott maintained a faith that all the outward expressions of a child would be good, true, and beautiful as long as they remained unhindered by moral evil. The job of the instructor was to strip away all such hindrances and to permit the inner goodness to flow forth. This was culture. Without it, expression would become evil. Uncultivated expression would result in distasteful activities such as land speculation or the "insane" pursuit of material goods. And expression meant more than just words spoken or written; it meant painting, sculpture, motions made by the body, moral behavior, for all of these were just different modes of externalizing ideas. Since Alcott assumed an unlimited potential for genius within each child, he wanted to prompt a wide range of creative expression by his students. In theory, any human expression could be the work of the spirit. Thus there was no limit to its possibilities. However, he assumed that a true expression of the spirit, one unhindered by evil, would be good, pure, and beautiful. He also assumed that there were absolute standards of what the good, pure, and beautiful would be. And he thought he knew what these standards were, though he did not specify them in detail. Given the logic of his belief in the spiritual goodness of children, it would not have been unreasonable for Alcott to have allowed the expressions of his students to define what was good, pure, and beautiful. But he was not about to do that. Rather, he used his preconceived standards to judge whether the expressions of the children were truly spiritual. This was directly at odds with his belief that children were closer to God, less debased, than were adults. Logically, the children, not he, should have been the judge.[14]

Not all of the school's time was used for discussion of abstract and weighty themes or for the pouring forth of inner thoughts. Alcott carefully planned the daily schedule to include time for the development of more mundane but necessary skills: reading, grammar, spelling, arithmetic, geography, and even Latin, taught by Elizabeth Peabody. He taught grammar as he had in the past, by conversing with the students about words and sentences, by breaking sentences down into their component parts and having the pupils study the function of each part. The students were not merely to memorize a word or sentence; they were to study it in relation to its meaning. Alcott asked them to be able to explain a word or sentence in conversation by the use of their own concrete examples. The stimulation of mental activity was always foremost; the acquisition of specific skills secondary. The ability to think, Alcott felt, would enable students to acquire any needed skill on their own. Thus he taught arithmetic and spelling by routine exercise, using Fowle's and Colburn's texts and Pike's speller. He had little interest in arithmetic, and so he taught it only out of duty and spent little time with it. The same was true of spelling, since he disliked making excessive criticisms of it for fear of discouraging expression. In fact, he often neglected to make sure that the words he asked his students to copy from Pike and define from *Johnson's Dictionary* had any relation to their ability, age, or experience. He forced ten-year-olds to struggle with mysterious words such as *vitreous, vassalage, expletive, derogate,* and *dissipate.*[15]

He taught geography more imaginatively. His pupils studied maps and listened to Alcott read stories of voyages and travels. Then he asked them to draw maps of their own and to write about what they drew. He asked them to describe mountains, lakes, and rivers by imagining that they were in a balloon looking down, or to picture the surface of the earth by imagining that they were the sun. Whatever the technique of instruction, Alcott ever remained conscious of the pupil's need for variety in the daily schedule as well as in the conduct of exercises, recitations, and conversations. There would be no dull, lifeless, grinding routine at the Temple School.[16]

The overriding mission of the school was moral and spiritual education, not the imparting of information or the development of skills. And Alcott wanted this moral and spiritual education to be a force for the reform of all of society, not just for the handful of youngsters at the Temple. The children were to become missionaries to their parents and friends, and the school itself was to be an example of true education and true reform for all the world to see. To further this end, Elizabeth Peabody began, on December 29, 1834, a daily account of the school's activities. In July 1835 this was published as *Record of a School*, with a preface and a general introduction also by Peabody.[17]

Upon its release to the public, the *Record* elicited comment, favorable and unfavorable, from several prominent people. It succeeded in publicizing Alcott's school, his disciplinary techniques, his conversations about the spirit, his ideas, and his mission, but not quite in the happy way he had hoped. William C. Woodbridge criticized the *Record* in his *Annals of Education*, calling it a "mingled mass of truth and error." He admired many of Alcott's principles and methods but feared that his "strained interpretation" of religion would lead his pupils astray. The pupils' minds, Woodbridge thought, could never fathom the depths of transcendental philosophy into which Alcott led them. "We esteem the author [meaning Alcott] highly," he said, "and hope reflection and experience will lead him to correct his views." Alcott shrugged Woodbridge off as a mind limited to popular, sectarian ideas, with no ability to apprehend the wants of the community. William Russell was far more encouraging than Woodbridge; he wrote from Philadelphia that he felt the *Record* to constitute an "eloquent testimony for humanity." And John Sullivan Dwight, a twenty-two-year-old divinity student at Harvard, flattered Alcott by inviting him to attend a meeting of the "Philanthropic Society" at the Divinity School on September 17, 1835. Dwight said that he planned to speak to the Society on education, using the *Record* as his text. Alcott attended the meeting, walking to Cambridge and back, and found much sympathy for his ideas among the theology students. Several of them visited the Temple School, and they invited him back later in the month.[18]

Most important, Dr. Channing was pleased with the *Record*. He thought Alcott's aim a true one, and he urged that the experiment go on. Nevertheless, he still had some doubts and reservations, especially about Alcott's claim that his conversations stirred the children's spiritual consciousness. Channing wanted proof that the children really acted on the subjects of the conversations and were not simply mouthing Alcott's ideas. He was also concerned that too much self-analysis by the children might be harmful to them. "The free development of the spiritual nature may be impeded by too much analysis of it," he said. "The soul is somewhat jealous of being watched, and it is no small part of wisdom to know when to leave it to its impulses, and when to restrain it. The strong passion of the young for the outward is an indication of Nature to be respected; spirituality may be too exclusive for its own good."[19]

On the whole, the reception of the *Record* was mixed. There was much less enthusiasm for it than Alcott had hoped. Yet he felt that "thinking people" generally accepted his ideas, and that the few new students who enrolled in September 1835 came as a result of the *Record*. It saddened him that his ideas did not find ready acceptance, but he was sure that the fruits of his work would ripen one day. "Such are the labours of all truly devoted to the human good," he said piously. "Life is a sacrifice to those who come after." There was some evidence, he thought, that his school was growing in popularity. Six hundred copies of the *Record* had been sold by mid-September 1835. Thirty pupils still greeted him at the Temple in October, after a decline during the summer when their wealthy parents took the children to summer retreats. In October Mary Peabody joined her sister on Alcott's staff to add French to the curriculum. His students liked and respected him; on November 28, 1835, they honored his thirty-sixth birthday by presenting him with a copy of *Paradise Lost*.[20]

Alcott was pleased with the success of his school. It was a feeling he had seldom experienced before. Finally, his mission was finding fulfillment. He perceived a "spiritual fire" beginning to enliven some of the "cold, drowsy natures" of his pupils. The "culture of the soul" was truly taking place, he thought, and his own capabilities were growing as a result. A fullness had come to his life after years of sterility. His coming to Boston was like a tree restored to its true soil. He could not measure his success financially, for his income did not fully meet his expenses. Yet after one year the school had produced $1,800, and though he had not even had enough to pay Elizabeth Peabody, his income matched his earlier expectations, and he felt good about it. At least it promised to provide future security and to relieve family tensions.[21]

Such relief was essential. Joseph May had written to his daughter in October 1834, complaining that the Alcott's "thoughtless expenditure" on impractical moves and impractical schools had caused unnecessary debt. Abby, a strong-willed and forthright person, lashed back at her father in defense of her husband, who was, she felt, a just and conscientious man who did not engage in thoughtless expenditure. Only "unfortunate contingencies," not extravagance, she said, had created the debt despite their constant striving for an honorable livelihood. When Abby asked her well-to-do father for a five-hundred-dollar loan to rent a house on Beech Street in September 1835, May refused. Only the good graces of friends enabled the Alcott's to rent the house and to cover Philadelphia debts.[22]

The Alcotts moved into the Beech Street house in mid-September and took in boarders to help defray costs. The new house gave Anna and Louisa a playroom of their own, relieving them from what Alcott deemed the far-too-cramped quarters of their succession of boarding houses on Bedford Street and Somerset Street. This would give them more scope for activity and expression, and in part compensate for the deleterious effects of the city's "impure air." Alcott feared that his school was depriving him of valuable time with his children, so he began washing and dressing Anna and Louisa in mornings and taking them to school with him. Abby needed the help, for on June 24, 1835, their third daughter, Elizabeth Sewall Alcott, was born, named after Elizabeth Peabody and Abby's deceased sister, Eliza.[23]

Relative success brought Alcott renewed enthusiasm for his observations on his children, which he had discontinued during the dark months of early 1834. In October 1834, with the Temple School well under way, he had returned to his manuscripts, feeling that during the preceding year he had been inexcusably negligent in the rearing of his children. He wanted to exercise a more direct influence over them than he had in the past, and he hoped his manuscript would reflect the beneficial results of his more careful attention to their development. Also, his earlier observations were deficient, he believed, because they did not sufficiently demonstrate the influence of innate ideas on the growth of the children's minds. His new record would reflect the change that his ideas had undergone. He had "inhaled a soul," and he now wanted to write a diary of the souls of his children. The whole truth about human nature was closer than ever to his grasp; the new observations would surely further that discovery.[24]

Alcott began his new record on October 27, 1834, calling it "Observations on the Spiritual Nurture of My Children.'' It would be an account of his "divine mission'' as a parent to supervise the development of the infinite spirit within each child:

> The glory of the Infinite radiates from the head of Infancy and Childhood. Clothed in raiment of flesh, the Divinity appears on earth, residing in the heart of the little child: here is *"God made manifest in the Flesh"*; and the incarnate one made to dwell among *men*.[25]

There were two larger purposes for the record. First, he wanted it to illustrate his noble experiment in freeing the infinite spirit from worldly debasement, thus bringing perfection. Second, he wanted to get glimpses, by watching the children's behavior and expressions carefully, of the nature of that spiritual element which he was sure resided within. In effect, it would be a religious exercise for him, a scripture, a sacrament.[26]

His contact with children, at home and in the Temple School, had refreshed and strengthened his faith and hope in himself and in humanity. "He who would retain his original freshness and vividness of being,'' he said, "who would look out upon life, with hope, and faith, and love, must commune often and daily, with the young, who are still in possession of the celestial radiance.'' Children became sources of inspiration, of revelation, for Alcott. Where the traditional authorities, Scripture and the Church, had failed, children would succeed. They were manifestations of God; they were mirrors into which parents could look to see themselves as God saw them. *"Infancy,"* he said, "is the *talisman* upon which we look, to reassure ourselves of our Celestial Lineage and Home!'' Indeed, children had been his one source of consolation in days of despair in Philadelphia; the children of the Temple School had given him success in Boston. It was reasonable, if exaggerated, that he should consider them an instrument of God, even prophets sent by God:

> Whoso would be a prophet, let him contemplate the spirit of Childhood—for here are all the Causes that effectuate the changes of the Future. Yes, every child is a Prophet, sent from God, and he bringeth tidings of gladness to all people.[27]

Much of Alcott's observations involved a search for the spiritual revelation he expected to get from his children. This caused him to see what he wanted to see in his daughters' actions and expressions, to focus on those things which would prove his theories. When Anna, in conversation with her father, said she felt that God was within her, Alcott was ecstatic. Surely this was the infinite spirit at work, for how else could she have got such an idea? The children's dreams were of special interest to him because he believed that they were efforts of the spirit to revive images of celestial life. He saw further evidence of the spirit when his children expressed affection for him in any way, and when Anna said, again in conversation, that she thought evil came from the body and good from the mind. Even the children's pencil scratches in his journals he thought might in some way signify the spirit.[28]

Alcott was so concerned about evidence of the spirit that he missed much that was important about the growth of his children. He confined much of what he did see to his preconceptions. Yet many of his observations and his approaches to child rearing reflected a sensitivity to the needs of children and a profound understanding of the process of child development. For example, he was conscious of pattern and sequence in the growth of a child. He still believed that the process of learning was inductive, a step-by-step development from the simple to the complex. To teach Anna and Louisa to read, he began by giving them picture books to familiarize them with the variety of forms. Next, he believed, the children would associate these pictures with the actual objects they represented. Then they would associate the objects with words written and spoken. This, he thought, was the best method to teach children to perceive ideas and to read. There would be no rote memorization of words without a prior understanding of the ideas they symbolized.[29]

As was his practice in the Temple School, Alcott provided the girls with a variety of children's stories, especially those telling of morality, such as the unfailing obedience of the little boy in Maria Edgeworth's "Frank." His purpose was to cultivate the imagination and encourage the moral behavior illustrated by the stories. He praised his young daughters for expressing themselves openly by dramatizing their favorite tales. Much to her father's amusement, two-year-old Louisa could impersonate the characters in the stories. He encouraged their theatrics by helping them dress up for their parts; he made hats and backpacks for them so that they could play soldier. Expression and creativity were the primary goals in the kinds of play that Alcott encouraged. Toys were not merely to entertain, but to permit the artist within each child to come out. Letters that the girls could arrange at will, or pins that they could make into shapes and designs, were the best toys, he felt. He even let them build towers with his books.[30]

Conversation was his favorite technique of child rearing. Talking with the children, he believed, was the best way to discipline them, to inculcate values. He thought that his prodding and his questioning would cause the ideal values of justice, truth, and beauty to come forth from the children spontaneously. But in practice, of course, he was merely reinforcing in Anna and Louisa his own value system. He always used conversation to explain punishment. As in the Temple School, he made sure that the children understood and accepted the justice of the punishment; never would it be arbitrary. The conversations became daily confessionals for Anna and Louisa, in which their father would ask them if they had been good that day and would give them a chance to admit their faults and misdeeds. There would be little doubt about right and wrong for the Alcott girls.[31]

Alcott was scrupulous about the kinds of punishment he used. He knew that excessive severity would cause his children to deceive him to avoid it, or it would cause them to obey for the wrong reason. To obey out of fear was not true obedience. Obedience had to be a matter of conscience; it had to result from a knowledge of principles, of absolute right and wrong. He thought if he addressed the children through love and careful attention to their needs and wants, he could awaken the spirit and develop this working conscience. His own behavior toward them would be the external symbol that would awaken similar behavior in them. Thus punishment usually involved the withholding of approval or of some favorite activity. Misbehavior could result in having to go to bed without a kiss or without a story; it could mean separation from the rest of the family for a short time. Sometimes physical punishment was necessary, more often for recalcitrant Louisa than for docile Anna. This always involved spanking by hand, never the rod. Generally, Alcott disliked any form of punishment. He preferred to encourage good behavior by positive reinforcement rather than to discourage the bad by punishment.[32]

For the most part, the kind of behavior Alcott hoped to encourage involved not petty things, but rather love, truth, and concern for the rights and needs of others. He imposed the same standards on himself, believing that parental example was the most important means of inculcating goodness. He tried to create in the children sympathy for other people. One cold September night in 1835, Abby, who spent an admirable lifetime in selfless service to others, gave one of Anna's nightgowns to a sick girl from a poor family nearby. Angered at the loss of her favorite nightgown, Anna was inconsolable. Finally, Alcott punished her for her selfishness by forcing her to climb into her cold bed without a nightgown. After Anna had become sufficiently uncomfortable, he explained to her that she was experiencing the same discomfort felt by the poor sick girl who had had no nightgown. The technique worked. Anna apologized and quickly offered to give the girl all of her clothes.[33]

Alcott was also sensitive to the differences between Anna and Louisa. He knew he could not always treat them alike. Louisa was obstinate where Anna was docile; Louisa was more active, forceful, and practical, while Anna was more sentimental and thoughtful. Anna never deliberately provoked Louisa, whereas Louisa would often aggressively attack Anna. Timid and delicate Anna needed careful, gentle treatment while Louisa sometimes required "authoritarian measures." Louisa's violence was alarming to her parents, causing Alcott to believe that Anna needed protection from her. Louisa was strangely moody, one day obstinate and violent, the next day sweet and tranquil. Alcott's explanation for the difference between his daughters was twofold. First, he believed that each person had unique innate endowments. Thus there was no reason to expect the children to be alike. The spirit manifested itself in different ways in different people. Second, he felt that Louisa's comparative nastiness resulted from her spiritual nature's being less awakened than Anna's. Why this should be so when he treated them alike he did not make fully clear. Age difference was one possible explanation, Abby's treatment of them another. Whatever the reason, he was sure that time would correct the problem. In the meantime, he sought to treat each of them differently so as to cultivate the unique characteristics of each. He admired Louisa's practical skill and her forceful personality; he liked Anna's delicacy and sentimentality. If he had to discipline Louisa for her excessive violence and obstinance, he had to correct Anna for her excessive timidity and obsequiousness.[34].

All aspects of child rearing were of concern to Alcott. He demanded that parents give careful consideration to every action, every angry look, every trifling disappointment, every severe voice. He wanted a complete philosophy of child rearing resting on a solid theoretical base. For it was in the home, in the relationship between parent and child, that true reform began. Even a model school like his at the Temple could not repair damages inflicted by the home environment. Again, the specific content of his theories was not so important as his belief that child rearing was in need of a philosophy, that such a thing might require searching examination. But the attractiveness of his ideas was marred by his sometimes obnoxious self-righteousness. Although he wanted the whole world to be aware of his discoveries, he also felt that he was the only person in the world who could do them justice. Even Abby was suspect. She did not understand the girls' dispositions, their tempers, their minds, as well as he did; proper development of his children, he thought, would simply not happen without him. He conceded that his wife's ill health and burdensome household chores were largely responsible for her failings, particularly her unwillingness to discipline Louisa properly. And he noted that at times her influence was beautiful, in keeping with that special gift, bestowed on mothers from above, which enabled them to instill love into their children. Unfortunately, Abby did not, in his opinion, always live up to that ideal.[35]

Unquestionably, Alcott placed a crushing burden on his wife and children by his expectation of perfection. Yet he did so in a spirit of love and understanding rather than harshness and intolerance. Never did he impatiently reject his family. On occasion he admitted his egotism, calling it a weakness to be overcome.[36] In the end he gave much more to his family than he took away. He encouraged expression and creativity that later bore fruit in all of his children. Above all, he gave them love and a secure value system, no mean accomplishment in an age of rapid change.

His observations of his children in 1834 and 1835 led him to a further consideration of the unresolved philosophical problem of evil. This involved two questions. First, he had to explain why evil occurred in the first place if human nature was inherently good. Second, he had to explain why the innate spirit of the child, which he believed was good and a part of the infinite spirit, could not produce that good unaided by external forces. That is, why did a teacher or a parent have to awaken the spirit in a child; why did it not work spontaneously? Indeed, it was a central element of his growing religious faith that children were instruments of God, that a child's spirit was an active, creative force for good that had an insatiable desire to make an impression on outward things. "Childhood ever riseth," he said; it was the great hope for humankind. In order to explain evil in this context, Alcott returned to his concept of the interplay between internal and external forces. There had to be forces at work in the world external to human beings, in both its material and spiritual aspects, that either limited the action of the spirit within an individual or enhanced that action. "Life external," he said, "is the nurse and feeder of the internal life; and if the spirit be fed on impure associations, on vicious indulgences, or deformed types in nature—then is its ideal perverted, and the whole soul is debauched." Thus nature, meaning here the material world external to human beings, was, for Alcott, potentially both good and evil. On the one hand, nature was a gift of God to the young spirit; it was the outward type or analogy of the spiritual world. Communion with it could feed the mind and awaken the spiritual aspect within. Nature was the language of the spirit; by studying it children could become conscious of their own spiritual being. On the other hand, nature could be deformed; it could symbolize evil. If this were so, it could mislead and pervert the child's soul. Alcott also considered the human body to be a part of nature, a part of the material world. As such, it had this dual characteristic of being both good and evil. It was the visible, tangible symbol of the soul's presence, yet it could be the source of the corruption of that soul, the source of debasing "animal appetites and passions." Alcott assumed that there was a constant battle raging between the spirit and the flesh. An untrained child, he said, was a mixed element in which the spirit and the flesh reigned by turns.[37]

His placing the source of evil in nature was merely an exploration of the problem of evil, not a conclusive or even a satisfactory explanation of it. He still had not said why an innately good soul could not transcend the evil in nature without help. Again, he was more concerned with preventing evil than explaining it. To prevent evil from debasing the child's soul, parents and teachers had to decide which external influences were producers of corruption and which were conducive to spiritual growth. It was a basic element of Alcott's faith that parents and teachers had this power. "The *Father* and the *Mother* are born out of God," he declared, "and in loving and obeying them, the child begins to love and obey God—they are the only true revealers to him of the divine nature." He did not say how parents managed to escape the evils of the flesh themselves in order to free their children.[38]

Alcott charged parents and teachers with the task of spiritual nurture. They had the responsibility, the awesome responsibility, of using external things to remind the child's spirit of its former life in the infinite spirit. They had to find in nature the most perfect symbols of the spiritual life, and they had to avoid symbols of evil.[39] This meant a further search by Alcott for a more complete definition of the spirit and how it worked. He wanted to discover all possible ways of shaping it for good, and he needed constant reassurance that his faith in the inherently good spiritual nature of human beings was well-founded.

To perfect his search for evidence of the spirit, Alcott decided to begin another manuscript on his children, this time centering on the life of his infant daughter, Elizabeth. "May I not look for a fuller *Revelation* of the *Divinity!*" he said. Full and perfect light would come to him in due time. This would be a complete history of a human mind. It would show how the Divinity, the spirit, revealed its attributes of goodness, truth, and beauty through the instrument of nature. He began the record on the day of Elizabeth's birth, June 24, 1835, and called it "Psyche," meaning soul or spirit. Upon witnessing the birth of his daughter he wrote: "The advent of a Spirit is a phenomenon that no words can body forth. We can find no types in external nature adequate to the purpose." But Alcott was rarely without words. Desperately seeking religious inspiration, he wanted to produce a scripture, a gospel of childhood, that would, when published, provide that inspiration for himself and all the world as well. He felt called to the task by God.[40]

Throughout "Psyche" Alcott described what he believed was the spirit in action: Elizabeth smiling when she saw flowers for the first time, Anna expressing sorrow and repentance for having done wrong. But generally the manuscript was an outpouring of speculation and imagery about the spirit. He described the spirit as the central force that flowed forth like a fountain through all of human nature. The actions of all human faculties, he believed, were signs and exponents of the working of the spirit. Change, whether in an individual human body or in the world, was evidence of the Spirit; it was the emblem of the spirit's universal presence. Growth was the spirit in the building process; decay was the spirit passing back into its primal elements, a constant process of synthesis and analysis.[41] "The elements of the Spirit are threefold," he said:

And the faculties which are put in motion, by these primal elements, are threefold also. *Beauty*, *Truth*, and *Good*, are the *Absolute Being of the Spirit*. These are opened out, and revealed to the Spirit's consciousness, through a series of influences, which are instituted at the moment of incarnation, and play their incessant agencies, from this moment, taking Nature as their instruments, on through every movement, till the structure wherein they hold their central and primal Force, is taken down, and returned again to the common elements from whence it was built up, by virtue of the absolute agency.[42]

This was Alcott's conception of God, the immanent, creative, dynamic force pervading the universe. As he proceeded in his description, his prose became increasingly prayerful, devotional. He worshiped, he praised, he apostrophized:

Mysterious Essence! All pervading—all-configuring-all-apprehending—all-meaning, principle! Life! Spirit!—or by what name soever, or under what form, thou art conceived, or presented,—who shall apprehend thee, as thou art in thyself—or find thee, as thou art found of these *Little Ones* who have not lost thee![43]

To supplement his speculative investigation of the Spirit, Alcott decided to add a further exercise in spiritual nurture to his curriculum at the Temple School. This would be a series of conversations on the life of Jesus. He decided that there was no better external symbol of the spirit at work than the life and teachings of Jesus. Surely a close study of the Gospels could help children and parents become more conscious of the spirit present in them. Conversation was the best means for this careful study since it was the teaching method used by Jesus himself. He also believed that by drawing out the children's spontaneous ideas about the Gospels, he would find confirmation of the truth of Scripture and further illustrate the workings of the spirit. After all, the children, being less debased than adults, had a greater innate knowledge of the spirit. Their insight would be priceless.[44]

The conversations began on Saturday, October 10, 1835, as a supplement to the regular course of instruction at the Temple. Elizabeth Peabody kept a transcript for possible publication. Intrigued by the idea, William Russell wrote to Alcott of his approval of the scheme and urged its continuance. He felt that, when published, the transcripts of the conversations would, as Alcott expected, give adults greater spiritual faith and a knowledge of the "celestial origins" of children. Russell hoped one day to assist Alcott in his noble enterprise.[45]

Alcott's role in these conversations on the Gospels was theoretically that of an enabler, desirous of calling forth the ideas of the children without imposing on them any opinions of his own. His only purpose in being there, he claimed, was to lead the children's thoughts in a "spiritual direction." He pledged to put no limits on the free expression of his pupils, for he had faith that any error, if expressed openly, would easily submit to the truth. Alcott began each session with a question and called on the children as they raised their hands. The children's answers, he was certain, provided "a testimony of unspoiled natures to the spiritual reality of Jesus. It is a revelation of Divinity in the soul of childhood."[46]

As much as he liked to think he was facilitating free expression and avoiding an imposition of his own opinions, Alcott still encased all discussions in his paradigm of the spirit. The idea of spirit was a given; no student dared question it. The first conversation was a general discussion of this idea of spirit. His first question to his young charges was: "Have you a clear feeling, idea, of something, which is not your body, which you never saw, but which is,—which loves, which thinks, which feels?" When all of the students gradually held up their hands in assent to this leading question, Alcott took it to mean that they had accepted his basic assumption that the spirit existed. He did not consider that they may have assented because they knew that was what he believed. Nevertheless, Alcott went ahead in the rest of the conversation, and indeed in all subsequent conversations, piling up evidence to support the initial assumption. He spread out before the children other terms of his paradigm: the idea that the body and the senses were just instruments of the spirit; the assumption that the spirit was always good, never a source of evil. One student suggested that the word "conscience" was better than "spirit." Alcott replied with an explanation of the relationship between human faculties and the spirit:

> *Conscience* is spirit acting on duty; *Mind* is spirit thinking; *Heart* is spirit loving; *Soul* is spirit feeling; *Sense* is spirit inquiring into the external world; *Body* is the instrument and organ of spirit.[47]

By his questions Alcott led his students to a belief in the immortality of spirit, in the perfection of spirit, and in the ability of spirit to measure all imperfection. He used the image of an acorn to illustrate for them his concept of spirit. With his illustration he included a tautological "proof" of the spirit's existence:

> All proof then is in God, spirit being its own proof, because there is more of God in it, than in anything outward. As an acorn reminds you of an oak, so does the spirit within remind you of God. Your spirits, like the acorn, (if you choose to carry on the figure) drop off from God, to plant themselves in Time. Once they were within the oak, but they came out individual acorns, the seeds of new oaks.... Spirits are born out of the Supreme Spirit, and by their power of reproducing spirit, constantly prove their own existence from his existence, and his existence from their own.[48]

But his "proof" evidently did not fully convince even him, for in all the conversations he kept searching for further evidence of the spirit and its actions in the life of Jesus.

The conversations touched on a wide variety of topics, all considered in relation to passages in the Gospels: birth, marriage, temperance, Scripture, heaven, hell, baptism, punishment, miracles, astronomy, human faculties, treatment of the poor, reformers, martyrdom.[49] The spiritual paradigm explained all of them. The children expressed their opinions in imagery that closely matched Alcott's imagery of the spirit. For example:

> Mr. Alcott. You may give some emblems of birth.
> Alexander. Birth is like the rain. It comes from heaven.
> Lucia. I think it is like a small stream coming from a great sea; and it runs back every night, and so becomes larger and larger every day, till at last it is large enough to send out other streams....[50]
> Mr. Alcott. Have any of you ever been in heaven?
> Two at once. Before I was born.
> George. I think we are always in heaven.
> Mr. Alcott. How so?
> George. Because heaven is spirit and that always exists.[51]

Alcott subtly made the students aware of the kind of answers he expected and favored. He made it clear that he wanted them to talk in terms of the spirit. When they did that, he took it as further evidence of the children's innate spirituality. Disagreement by a student over a fundamental element of Alcott's ideas brought denunciation upon the offender. Two of his students opposed his idea that human beings had the supernatural redemptive power of Christ. They felt that no human could ever be the equal of Christ. Alcott told them flatly that they did not have a sufficient faith in their own nature and therefore could never accomplish the moral good of the other students. He made clear to the students that those who understood spiritual things were the ones who were the most moral and good. His students actively strove to understand and use his paradigm of the spirit in order to win his approval. They even came to his defense when he was challenged. After several months of conversations a new student entered the class and promptly questioned the usefulness of studying the soul or the spirit. His classmates quickly corrected him by pointing out how the body was only an instrument of the spirit. They took Alcott's side when he asked the doubter if anything could be done without the aid of spirit.[52]

Alcott explained to his students that his goal was not to present his own views of truth but rather to call forth theirs, to make them conscious of their own powers to find truth. "Education, when rightly understood," he told them, "will be found to lie in the art of asking apt and fit questions, and in thus leading the mind by its own light to the perception of truth."[53] But clearly, he did present his own views of the truth. To a far greater extent than he realized, he channeled and formulated the students' ideas rather than permitting those ideas to develop spontaneously. Nevertheless, the conversations were not without merit. They did elicit some expression and creative thought. Daily procedure involved a reading of a brief Gospel passage by Alcott, then extensive discussion and explanation of the passage by the children. He encouraged them to explain the passage in their own words, using whatever imagery came to mind. When Alcott read the story of Jesus' birth (Luke 2:1-20), young Edward Bangs described what he heard and embellished it:

> I thought of the shepherds receiving the tidings, sitting on an eminence; and the flocks lying about on the ground, and the sky opened, and the light shone all around many miles, but not as far as Bethlehem. And an angel came down, not like the other angels that had come, but a smaller one, with a pink and white robe, and a plain gold girdle, and a gold band on his head. The other angels that came after, had no bodies, but only heads and wings—golden wings. And after they had told the shepherds, they went back and heaven closed. Then the shepherds went to Bethlehem; and angels followed, who were invisible to the people until they got into the barn, where they could be seen. And the people of the inn could not get near the barn, because there was an angelic influence that kept them away, for they were not worthy.[54]

Alcott wanted the children to do more than describe, though; he wanted them to interpret the passages they read,[55] not an easy task for six-to-ten-year-olds. But he provided them with a hermeneutical tool: the idea that external things and events were symbols or emblems of spiritual things. At first he led them to this by example:

> Mr. Alcott. Why should this star be in the East?
> Charles. Because the sun rises.
> Mr. Alcott. Why does the sun rise in the East?
> (no answer)
> Mr. Alcott. What is the sun rising an emblem of? What is that act called, which brings forth the spirit to the eyes?

Charles. Birth.
Mr. Alcott. What is the spirit born from?
Charles. From spirit, from God.
Mr. Alcott. Then is not the East the emblem of God? and where would Wise Men come from, if not from the East? Wisdom comes from the birth-place of light and life. The star was an emblem of Holiness. Some of the light came down and stood over the place where the child was. Is not the Soul a spiritual star which glitters out at the eyes?[56]

It was not long before the children were able to develop their own emblematic interpretations. In discussing the story of the baptism of Jesus (Matthew 3, Mark 1, Luke 3), the children variously interpreted the dove that appeared to Jesus as the symbol of innocence, of purity, of goodness, of peace. One child viewed the opening of heaven described in Mark 1:10 as a symbol of the opening of the spirit.[57] Thus Alcott's paradigm gave the children a means of exercising their minds. It served as a structure on which they could build ideas. In one sense the paradigm limited them, but in another important way it freed them—it freed them from the tyranny of disorganization. In time they could cast away the paradigm, but the thought processes it helped them develop could stay with them forever. Alcott may not have made his students more spiritual, nor awakened in them the truth of spiritual things, but he did make them think. Almost despite himself, his methods succeeded.

At the end of 1835, Alcott was full of hope. His school was going well. Enrollment remained constant at thirty to thirty-five students. Visitors were impressed. Dr. Nicolaus Heinrich Julius, a representative of the King of Prussia who traveled throughout the United States in 1835 collecting materials on education, honored Alcott with a visit. The *Record of a School* was doing well and Alcott was considering a new, improved edition. The conversations on the Gospels were a success. He felt that he had made steady progress in his intellectual and spiritual development. Now he was pursuing the "light of the spirit" both in theory and in practice. It remained only for him to find other minds who would share his excitement. Philadelphia had been a wasteland, he thought. But Boston promised to provide the intellectual and social communion he so much desired and needed.[58]

Notes

1. McCuskey, *Bronson Alcott: Teacher*, p. 84; A. Bronson Alcott, comp., "Letters from 1836-1850," MS at Houghton Library, 59M-305 (2).

2. Josephine E. Roberts, "Elizabeth Peabody and the Temple School," *New England Quarterly* 15, no. 3 (September 1942): 497-508; George Willis Cooke, *An Historical and Biographical Introduction to The Dial*, 2 vols. (Cleveland: Rowfant, 1902), 1:141-43; AJ, II, 1827-28, p. 107; AJ 3 (1829): 32-34; Alcott to Elizabeth Palmer Peabody, May 7, 1833, from a copy in Alcott's hand in "Autobiographical Materials"; AJ 5 (1831), part 2: 153; [Elizabeth Palmer Peabody], "Account of a Visit to an Elementary School," *American Journal of Education* 4, no. 1 (January and February 1829): 74-76; Elizabeth Palmer Peabody to Alcott, 1834, from a copy in Alcott's hand in "Autobiography, 1834," MS at Houghton Library, 59M-306 (22).

3. Alcott, "Autobiographical Index"; AJ 7 (1834), part 3 ("Diary beginning September 22 in Boston"): 1-8: AJ 8 (1835): 47-48; Elizabeth Palmer Peabody, ed., *Record of a School: Exemplifying the General Principles of Spiritual Culture*, 2d ed. (Boston: Russell, Shattuck and Co., 1836), pp. 1-2.

4. AJ 7 (1834), part 3: 66-68, 98, 130, 132-33: AJ 8 (1835): 235-36, 282; AJ 9 (1836): 87.

5. Elizabeth Palmer Peabody, ed., *Record of a School: Exemplifying the General Principles of Spiritual Culture*, 1st ed. (Boston: James Munroe and Co., 1835), p. iv; AJ 7 (1834), part 3:43, 46, 71-73, 108.

6. AJ 7 (1834), part 3: 168; AJ 8 (1835): 19.

7. AJ 7 (1834), part 3: 48, 50; AJ 8 (1835): 207, 209.

8. Peabody, ed., *Record of a School*, 2d ed., pp. xiv, xviii-xix.

9. Ibid., pp. xix, 2, 3, 7, 20-22.

10. Ibid., pp. 23-25.

11. Ibid., pp. xxvi, xxxviii-x1, 29, 95.

12. Ibid., pp. vi, 83-86, 105, 107-9, 110, 113, 114, 120-21, 123, 132.

13. Ibid., pp. x1i-x1ii, 9-13, 56, 154-55; AJ 7 (1834), part 3: 103, 167-68; A. Bronson Alcott, comp., "Biography of Jesus Christ," MS at Houghton Library, 59M-306 (7); F. W. Carové, *Story Without an End*, ed. A. Bronson Alcott, translated from the German by Sarah Austin (Boston: Joseph H. Francis, 1836); AJ 8 (1835): 443.

14. Peabody, ed., *Record of a School*, 2d ed., pp. x1-x1i, 8.

15. Ibid., pp. xxviii-xxxviii, 27; Martha Kuhn, "Diary, 1837," MS owned by the Fruitlands Museum. Martha Kuhn was a student at the Temple School.

16. Peabody, ed., *Record of a School*, 2d ed., pp. xxx-xxxiii, 86.

17. Ibid., p. 26; Peabody, ed., *Record of a School*, 1st ed., pp. iv-vi; AJ 8 (1835): 21-22, 159.

18. AJ 8 (1835): 249, 316-21, 347-48, 379-80; [William Woodbridge], "Record of a School, *"American Annals of Education and Instruction* 5 no. 10 (October 1835): 477-78; William Russell to Alcott, August 13, 1835, in A. Bronson Alcott, comp., "Autobiographical Collections," 4 (1834-1839): 22, MS at Houghton Library, 59M-307 (3); John Sullivan Dwight to Alcott, September 14, 1835, in "Autobiographical Collections," 4: 24; Cooke, *Historical and Biographical Introduction*, 2: 20-21.

19. William Ellery Channing to Elizabeth Palmer Peabody, August 24, 1835, in E. P. Peabody, ed., *Reminiscences of Rev. Wm. Ellery Channing* (Boston: Roberts Bros., 1880), pp. 356-57.

20. AJ 8 (1835): 289-90, 301, 346, 387-88, 473-74.

21. AJ 7 (1834), part 3: 105-6, 199; AJ 8 (1835): 29-30, 66, 278; Louise Hall Tharp, *The Peabody Sisters of Salem* (Boston: Little, Brown and Co., 1950), p. 109.

22. Joseph May to Abby May Alcott, October 1, 1834, Abby May Alcott to Joseph May, October 6, 1834, and September 3, 1835, and Abby May Alcott to Elizabeth Palmer Peabody, September 20, 1835, from copies in Alcott's hand in "Memoir, 1878"; AJ 8 (1835): 109.

23. AJ 8 (1835): 143, 162, 234, 300-303, 323-25, 331-32.

24. AJ 7 (1834), part 3: 181-93.

25. A. Bronson Alcott, "Observations on the Spiritual Nurture of My Children, 1834-1835," pp. 1-3, MS bound with "Researches on Childhood, 1835," and located at Houghton Library, 59M-306 (6).

26. Ibid., p. 4.

27. Ibid., p. 50; Alcott, "Researches on Childhood," pp. 20, 86, 206.

28. Alcott, "Observations on the Spiritual Nurture of My Children," pp. 92-93, 197-98; Alcott, "Researches on Childhood," pp. 121-22, 131; AJ 8 (1835): 20.

29. Alcott, "Observations on the Spiritual Nurture of My Children," pp. 17-18, 98-101.

30. Ibid., pp. 48, 65, 170-72, 178-80; Alcott, "Researches on Childhood," pp. 138-39, 191-92, 247.

31. Alcott, "Observations on the Spiritual Nurture of My Children," pp. 32, 77-78, 208-209.

32. Ibid., pp. 10, 59, 83, 96, 109-12, 158.

33. Ibid., p. 149; Alcott, "Researches on Childhood," pp. 176-78, 179, 200-202; A. Bronson Alcott, "Psyche or Breath of Childhood, 1835-36," pp. 139-43, MS at Houghton Library, 59M-306 (8).

34. Alcott, "Observations on the Spiritual Nurture of My Children," pp. 19-21, 22-23, 37-38, 210, 232-33; Alcott, "Researches on Childhood," pp. 81-82, 250-51; AJ 7 (1834), part 3: 222-24.

35. Alcott, "Observations on the Spiritual Nurture of My Children," pp. 110, 112, 137, 168, 203; Alcott, "Researches on Childhood," pp. 37-40, 44.

36. Alcott, "Psyche or Breath of Childhood," pp. 63-64.

37. Alcott, "Observations on the Spiritual Nurture of My Children," pp. 85-88, 158, 166, 214-15, 247; Alcott, "Researches on Childhood," pp. 91, 97, 147, 230, 258, 297-98.

38. Alcott, "Observations on the Spiritual Nurture of My Children," pp. 70-71.

39. Ibid., pp. 229-30, 252.

40. AJ 8 (1835): 114, 136, 143, 258, 447-48; Alcott, "Psyche or Breath of Childhood," pp. 10, 87-88.

41. Alcott, "Psyche or Breath of Childhood," pp. 100, 124, 204-7, 240, 295-96.

42. Ibid., pp. 435-36.

43. Ibid., p. 265.

44. AJ 8 (1835): 104, 111, 125, 150, 228, 260, 403-6, A. Bronson Alcott, ed., *Conversations with Children on the Gospels* (Boston: James Munroe and Co., 1836), 1: iv, v, xi-xiii; Alcott, "Psyche or Breath of Childhood," pp. 217-18; A. Bronson Alcott, *The Doctrine and Discipline of Human Culture* (Boston: James Munroe and Co., 1836), pp. 5, 8-10. This twenty-seven-page pamphlet was published separately and as an introduction to *Conversations on the Gospels*. It is the clearest statement of Alcott's transcendental theory of education.

45. AJ 8 (1835): 417; William Russell to Alcott, November 18, 1835, from a copy in Alcott's hand in "Autobiography, 1834."

46. Alcott, ed., *Conversations on the Gospels*, 1: v, vii, xiii, xiv.

47. Ibid., pp. 3, 6, 10.

48. Ibid., pp. 13-16.

49. Ibid., pp. 63 ff., 75 ff., 100, 246; A. Bronson Alcott, ed., *Conversations with Children on the Gospels* (Boston: James Munroe and Co., 1837), 2: 4-5, 8, 13, 15, 37-38, 109; Margaret Fuller, "Report of Mr. Alcott's Conversations with the Children," pp. 907, 911, 953-61, in "Works of Sarah Margaret Fuller Ossoli," vol. 2, MS at Houghton Library, fMS AM 1086 (2). This was intended by Alcott to be a third volume, but was never published.

50. Alcott ed., *Conversations on the Gospels*, 1: 63.

51. Fuller, "Report of Mr. Alcott's Conversations," p. 911.

52. Ibid, pp. 991, 993, 1019-27; Alcott, ed., *Conversations on the Gospels*, 2: 31-32.

53. Alcott, ed., *Conversations on the Gospels*, 2: 266.

54. Ibid., 1: 80.

55. Ibid., pp. 88-89.

56. Ibid., p. 246.

57. Ibid., pp. 150 ff.

58. AJ 8 (1835): 374, 389, 401, 451, 540; McCadden, *Education in Pennsylvania*, p. 175; Alcott, "Autobiographical Collections," vol. 4.

6
Transcendentalism, 1836–39

BEGINNING in 1835 Alcott found the intellectual intercommunication he sought so desperately. He found it among a diverse group of people who became known, derisively at first, as transcendentalists. They were, he said, the "thinking spirits of the time." Conversation with them gave Alcott both a means of spreading his own ideas and vision, and a source of stimulation and reinforcement.[1] But in the midst of joy and satisfaction came unexpected trouble. Publication of *Conversations with Children on the Gospels* brought not enlightenment and warm approval, but reproach and hostility. Enrollment in the Temple School fell and the school failed. He and his family were left penniless and desperate. Buoyant pride and confidence turned to bitterness and insecurity. By the fall of 1839 the hopeful words of December 1835 sounded distant and hollow.

In August 1835 Alcott made a list of those who he felt were in tune with the "spiritual philosophy," those interesting minds and "prophets of the present time." On the list, of course, were Dr. Channing, William Russell, Elizabeth Peabody, and William Henry Furness. He also included a few persons he had just recently contacted. Among them were artist Washington Allston, whom he and Elizabeth Peabody had visited in Cambridgeport in January 1835, and Robert C. Waterston, the enthusiastic leader of a group interested in "religious improvement." Also there was Frederic Henry Hedge, minister of the Independent Congregational Society in Bangor, Maine, who had studied German metaphysics in the original and had written several articles of a "spiritual" nature in the *Christian Examiner*. And finally there was Ralph Waldo Emerson, whose lecture on the character of Michelangelo at the Temple in February 1835 had convinced Alcott that he had a nobler view of the mission, powers, and destiny of human beings than anyone Alcott had ever known.[2]

Alcott first met Emerson in July 1835 at Alcott's boardinghouse at number three Somerset Court. Emerson, his brother Charles, Elizabeth Hoar of Concord, and Lydia Maria Child all visited that day, probably at the invitation of Elizabeth Peabody, who was then boarding with the Alcotts. Emerson had known of Alcott before this. George Partridge Bradford, a Harvard classmate of Emerson's, had become friends with Alcott and had told Emerson of Alcott's spiritual sympathies. Shortly after this first meeting, Emerson read and was delighted by *Record of a School.*[3]

Their first meeting convinced Alcott that Emerson was himself a "revelation of the divine spirit." On October 17, 1835, he eagerly took the three-hour trip with George Bradford to meet Emerson at his Concord home. The weekend in Concord confirmed his high opinion of Emerson, though he was concerned that Emerson's fine literary taste sometimes got in the way of his hearty acceptance of the spiritual. Alcott struck Emerson as "a wise man, simple, superior to display [who] drops the best things as quietly as the least." Emerson's indomitable aunt, Mary Moody Emerson, wrote to Alcott that her nephew had spoken of nothing but pleasure in talking with Alcott. She herself was "dazzled" by Alcott's ideas and wished him success.[4]

In late November Alcott again went to Concord to visit with Emerson and there met Frederic Henry Hedge for the first time. Emerson and Hedge, he felt, were the "most earnest spiritualists of the time." They were the leading figures in an intellectual ferment involving persons who were undergoing an inward search similar to his own. In general, these persons were Harvard-trained Unitarian ministers or former Unitarian ministers such as Emerson, Hedge, George Ripley, and James Freeman Clarke. Under the influence of Coleridge, Cousin, and German idealism, they had extended the Unitarian faith in the goodness of human nature to a consideration of how that goodness involved an unlimited range of spiritual insight. They revolted against "the corpse-cold Unitarianism of Brattle Street and Harvard College," as Emerson put it. They demanded a living religion that asked more of the human soul than social conformity and lip-service to an established creed. Like Alcott, they sought to combine the mystical, emotional element of the old Puritan faith with Enlightenment rationalism's celebration of human worth and dignity.[5]

Emerson had been dissatisfied with Unitarianism for several years, but his formal revolt began in September and October 1832, when he dramatically resigned from the pulpit of Second Church in Boston, stating that he could not accept the Church's view of the rite of the Lord's Supper. He felt that church dogma stood in the way of the self-evident truths of Christianity. Relying on churchly authorities for inspiration, he said, was like using a candle to see the sun rise. They obscured the godlike in each human being, which awaited an awakening. "Get the soul out of bed," he pleaded, "out of her deep habitual sleep, out into God's universe, to perception of its beauty, and hearing of its call, and your vulgar man, your prosy, selfish sensualist awakes, a god, and is conscious of a force to shake the world."[6]

Frederic Hedge, who had studied in Europe and had read Kant in the original German, began his attack with his article on Coleridge in the *Christian Examiner* of March 1833. He defended idealism against its critics. Those who denounced idealism, he said, simply lacked insight. They lacked the active, interior consciousness, the free intuition, which the German idealists celebrated. Then in March 1834, Hedge, in his article "The Progress of Society," told the readers of the *Examiner* that the "boundless resources of the human mind" were the keys to progress, liberty, and social improvement.[7]

James Freeman Clarke reacted against the philosophy of John Locke, then in vogue at Harvard and among Unitarians in general, while he was a student at Harvard Divinity School in the early 1830s. Like Alcott, he had read Coleridge's *Aids to Reflection* and James Marsh's "Preliminary Essay." These led him to believe that the innate power of the human soul to perceive truth, Coleridge's "reason," superseded knowledge obtained through sense experience, through the "understanding." Clarke had gone to Louisville, Kentucky, in 1833 to be minister of the Unitarian church there and had subsequently become the leading editor of the *Western Messenger*. The *Messenger* soon became a vehicle for transcendentalism. In September 1835 it published a favorable review of *Record of a School*.[8]

George Ripley, a graduate of Harvard Divinity School in 1826 and minister of Boston's Purchase Street Church, began his break with Unitarianism in 1832. Like Hedge, he used the *Christian Examiner* as a forum from which to defend German literature from the attack of Harvard Divinity School professors and from the conservative *North American Review*. He attacked Lockean empiricism as confining and cold, and praised the German idealists for infusing the spiritual into their writings. In May 1835 he published a laudatory article about Herder in the *Examiner*. He celebrated Herder's faith that human beings had within them the power to attain moral and spiritual progress as well as the intellectual power to gain worldly knowledge.[9]

For these ordained ministers, who were part of the Boston establishment, revolt against tradition and custom was a slow, tortuous process, full of painful decisions and much soul searching. Such rebellion meant for them a possible break from their chosen profession, a possible loss of the social prestige that was theirs by birthright or by the authority of a Harvard degree. But Bronson Alcott was not a part of the Boston establishment in any way. He had no prestigious profession to lose. For him revolt came much easier and without restraint. Thus Alcott's new-found intellectual compatriots, though they respected Alcott and generally agreed with him, retained a glimmer of suspicion of this unschooled farm boy turned philosopher. Alcott's idealism was an uncompromising challenge to religious traditions and social institutions. Most of the transcendentalist ministers, including Clark and Hedge, remained within the broad confines of church tradition and were unwilling to accept Alcott's extreme position. Even Ripley and Emerson, who left the church, stopped short of Alcott's unrestrained radicalism. Alcott served as both a stimulus and a warning to his idealistic friends. As an example of a practicing idealist, he urged and prodded them to carry their ideas to their logical extremes. Yet there was enough of the impractical, even the ridiculous, about Alcott to cause them to hesitate, to examine themselves and their ideas, lest they follow him to positions both dangerous and indefensible.

Few challenged church doctrine as completely as Alcott did. He felt that the sum of God's revelation to humanity was not sealed up forever in Scripture or in the traditions of the church. "The divinity has not yet completed the dispensation for the enlightenment of humanity," he claimed. "Revelations are yet to be made. The soul of man has not yet thrown open its celestial folds to the gaze of human eyes: the evil of the holy place has not yet been rent, and exposed to full view, the sacred emblem of the Divinity within.'' His worship of the spiritual, the divine ideal immanent in the world, meant perpetual revelation like the unceasing flow of a great fountain. "Should we regard the day of revelation passed—the communion of the human soul with the Divine, forever foreclosed; and man left to feed the infinite longings of his spirit on what has already been revealed! *I cannot thus believe.*'' Hence his faith that his study of his children and even his study of his own life as reflected in his journals were sources of divine revelation; hence his belief that the Divinity ceaselessly revealed its attributes of goodness, truth, and beauty through material things, that material things were symbols of spiritual things.[10] "*Every visible, conscious thing, is a revelation of the Invisible, Spiritual, Creator,*'' he said,

> *Matter is a revelation of mind.* . . . All growth, production, progress, are but stages of the spiritual being: they denote the spirit struggling to represent, reveal, shadow forth, itself to the *sense*, and *reason* of man; they are tests of his Faith in the infinite, invisible, spiritual life, that flows through, and quickens all *things* and *beings.*[11]

The transcendentalist ministers agreed with Alcott's concept of progressive revelation, for it did not necessarily reject the traditional authorities of the church. Rather, it supplemented them. But Alcott's position relected a strong anticlericalism. He rejected formal church attendance, believing that since he had the power to interpret the truths of the Bible for himself, he need not listen to the dictates of others. To attend church, he felt, would not result in his personal improvement; it would only be for show, and he disdained such hypocrisy. He preferred worshiping in the "Temple of Self.'' No one needed to go to church to find God:

> He that seeth God in every function of the human body, in every faculty of the human spirit; in the instincts of the animal kingdom; in the sublime laws that actuate the inanimate world; that display their forces in the elements of the material framework; he it is that hath apprehended God aright; he it is that is born out of the dim kingdom of Matter and Sense, into the blessed and clear vision of the kingdom of God.[12]

To Alcott revelation involved a sense of the beautiful, the good, and the true, which could come only through a spiritual act, through the influence of the divine spirit on the human spirit. No church, no creed, no minister could provide it.[13]

Alcott had also come to believe that human beings were divine, that the innate spiritual aspect of all people partook of the divine spirit. "We are all Christs,'' he said; "we came into the flesh—the divinity was clad in the robes of mortality of which we are alike the partakers, and we each have a mission to perform.'' The life of Jesus was an outward expression or symbol of that spirit which was potential in every human being. The Unitarians had pointed toward this idea in their celebration of the goodness of human nature. The beauty and attraction of Dr. Channing's sermons resulted from his expression of that idea of goodness. In their revolt, the transcendentalist ministers carried this view to its logical conclusion, elevating human power to the direct perception of supernatural truth and spiritual revelation. But none, not even Emerson, who had left the ministry, went as far as Alcott did in claiming divinity for humans, in claiming that humans were potentially equal to Christ as saviors of themselves and the world. Some barriers of tradition and dogma still remained for all but Alcott.[14]

Of course, all of the transcendentalist ministers agreed with Alcott's rejection of Lockean epistemology. To believe that the human mind was a passive recipient of external influences served to confine the "infinite capacities" of human nature to a study of only the outward world. It denied the spiritual nature of human beings, of which the senses and the intellect were but outward signs. Alcott believed that theological seminaries, specifically Harvard, wasted too much time on dogma, creed, formula, and convention, and neglected the great principles of human nature; by their adherence to John Locke, they neglected the power of the "divining heart." The rebellious graduates of these seminaries agreed.[15]

But few had the sense of mission that Alcott had. To him the "infinite capacities" of the spiritual nature of human beings made them potentially the "Sovereign of the Earth, fitted to subdue all things." The great purpose of each individual was to express his or her spiritual nature in outward actions and thereby become perfect. Only the lack of awareness or consciousness of that spiritual nature prevented progress toward perfection. "Few there are," he claimed, "that have retained the *perception* of their *original glory*: with the loss of the virtue that fed their flame of the spirit, has the spirit been dimmed, and all its primal glories lost, in the shades of the Senses!"[16] Thus his personal mission to children and to adults: to cultivate their awareness of their own potential. "Human culture," he explained, "is the art of revealing to a man the true Idea of his Being—his endowments—his possessions—and of fitting him to use these for the growth, renewal, and perfection of his Spirit. It is the art of completing a man."[17] "Completed" human beings would in turn regenerate philosophy, art, literature, society, and institutions. His mission, and the proper mission of the age as he perceived it, was to create "genius." Genius was human nature rising superior to things and events and transforming them into the image of its own spiritual ideal.[18]

Alcott embodied ideas that, though strictly his own, were the logical extreme of the Unitarian revolt. In rebelling against the Calvinistic doctrine of the basic evil of human nature, the Unitarians, especially Channing, had pointed to the almost infinite capacity of human beings for good. They had dramatically fought for free inquiry and free expression with full faith in the rational powers of human beings. But in the main the Unitarians, even Channing, were conservative. They were unwilling to test the limits of their faith in human goodness. They set limits to human ability to receive revelation of the supernatural, claiming for revelation only that set forth in Scripture. The Lockean limits of sense experience defined human reason for them. The transcendentalist ministers, inspired by the Unitarian message but frustrated by the limits placed on it, questioned these limits. They redefined reason in Coleridge's terms as the ability of humans to apprehend spiritual truths, to experience directly revelations from God.[19] Alcott, whose intellectual development paralleled and sometimes touched Unitarianism, believed all this and more. More than any other of the transcendentalists, he emphasized the mission to perfect all of humanity. While the others spoke of a living faith, of the potential for humans to create and express, Alcott nodded yes and then spoke of salvation, of the perfected world on earth.

Despite the potential differences that existed between himself and the transcendentalist ministers, even between himself and Emerson, Alcott exulted at having found other minds who thought much as he did. Their sympathy with his ideas reinforced the feeling he had in the spring and summer of 1836 that he was at the pinnacle of success. He bubbled with confidence and enthusiasm. Buoyed by favorable reviews of *Record of a School* by Clarke in the *Western Messenger* and by popular novelist Catherine Sedgwick in the February 1836 issue of *The Knickerbocker*, he prepared a second edition for publication. The work of a "praiseworthy reformer," as Sedgwick put it, had to be publicized. He was further elated by the interest taken in the Temple School and the conversations on the Gospels. Curious visitors came every day, including people of "sterling excellence." Even the distinguished English traveler Harriet Martineau had inquired about the school after getting word of it from William Furness in Philadelphia. She gathered gossip about it while socializing with Boston's elite, though she did not visit the school. Alcott met her at a party at Josiah Quincy's in January 1836 and tried to explain his ideas. But he had great difficulty forcing the spirit through the nearly deaf Miss Martineau's ear trumpet.[20]

One visitor who added greatly to Alcott's feeling of success in early 1836 was Hiram Fuller of Providence. Fuller was a young, enthusiastic teacher with a school of his own, who glowed with enthusiasm over *Record of a School*. After his visit to the Temple in June 1836, he told Alcott of his full sympathy with Alcott's methods and goals. He had used the *Record* as the basis of his curriculum and found that it impressed both his students and their parents. His enrollment had increased from twenty to sixty-five because of it. And Alcott found other admirers. Anna Thaxter, a young teacher whom he had met in Hingham in August 1834, wrote of her fascination with the *Record*. When she visited the school in February 1836, she was completely absorbed and delighted. Elizabeth Peabody's artistic sister, Sophia, who came to stay with the Alcotts in July 1836, was overwhelmed by Alcott's spiritual presence. She felt "elevated" and "enlarged" by him. "I cannot sufficiently thank my Heavenly Father," she beamed, "for the gift of Mr. Alcott as a friend."[21]

Such adulation increased Alcott's confidence and optimism. And added to that was his growing conviction that he was a part of a larger, immensely important, intellectual movement. In Perry Miller's words, the year 1836 was the "annus mirabilis" of transcendentalism. Nearly all of the major transcendentalists, including Alcott, published seminal works that year. Alcott, more than any of the others, viewed this as a single movement for social and intellectual transformation. He saw it not as a movement in the organized, cohesive sense, for he knew how diverse and lacking in agreement the leading figures were. But he saw it as a general feeling of enthusiasm and optimism, and a sense of "newness" that was imminently going to change the world. The most important outpouring of this "newness" was Emerson's *Nature*, published on September 9, 1836. "A beautiful idyll," Alcott called it. William H. Furness, Emerson's schoolmate and intimate friend, wrote to Alcott from Philadelphia that the essay was ringing in hs ear like the voice of an angel. In *Nature*, Emerson wrote in beautiful imagery of the correspondence between natural facts and spiritual truths, and of the spiritual laws that nature both obeyed and illustrated. To Alcott's great joy, the essay concurred with his belief that all things proceeded from the spiritual, that the spirit was immanent in all things. It reinforced his faith that nature could remind human beings of their spiritual potential, that nature was the language of the spirit. Indirectly, Emerson had also acknowledged Alcott's manuscript "Psyche," which he had given to Emerson for criticism, particularly in the idealism of the "orphic poet" in the last part of the essay.[22]

Emerson was soon joined in print by William H. Furness and George Ripley. Furness's *Remarks on the Four Gospels*, published late in 1836, asserted that the human mind had the power to intuit religious truths directly. It took issue with the Unitarian doctrine of the miracles, the belief that the scriptural account of Christ's miracles was the sole source of supernatural revelation. Furness claimed, as had Emerson and Alcott, that the divine, the spiritual, flowed through all of nature. Thus, he said, miracles were not an interruption of the natural order caused by God to confirm scriptural revelation. Rather, the miracles were just manifestations of the spiritual realm, of the "supreme spiritual force" that existed in all things. They were an example, but not the only possible case, of spiritual revelation. George Ripley picked up the attack on the doctrine of the miracles in the November 1836 issue of the *Christian Examiner* in reviewing Englishman James Martineau's *Rationale of Religious Inquiry*. In that article and in a subsequent pamphlet, *Discourses on the Philosophy of Religion*, Ripley declared that "the material universe is the expression of an Invisible Wisdom and Power." Human perception of that wisdom and power depended not on miracles, but on the state of each person's soul. Humans, he said, had the power to "reason" that gave them the immediate perception of truth; they needed no miracles to convince them of the supernatural.[23]

These apostles of the "newness" had been joined in the spring of 1836 by the blunt and caustic Orestes A. Brownson, a distance cousin of Alcott. Like Alcott, Brownson was a self-taught farm boy. His religious searching had taken him from Congregationalism to Presbyterianism to Universalism to

Unitarianism. He had been a one-time associate of Frances Wright and Robert Dale Owen in the Workingman's Party. With Ripley's support he left his Unitarian pulpit in Canton, Massachusetts, and came to Boston. Immediately, he began speaking against the coldness and sterility of the established churches and for what he perceived to be the vital aspirations of the day for reform. Alcott first heard Brownson on July 2, 1836, when the latter spoke about his "Society for Christian Union and Progress," the purpose of which was the reformation of humanity. Attracted by Brownson's reformist sympathies, Alcott joined the Society that day and pledged to attend his lectures regularly. Alcott believed that he and Brownson held the same basic principles, the same commitment to human culture. They just differed on the means of accomplishing their goals. In August 1836 Brownson moved in with the Alcott while continuing his lectures at the Temple. Alcott was entranced by the power and force of Brownson's ideas. He was convinced that Brownson would build a new church based on the spiritual idea, and that in doing so would draw upon the common people's festering dissatisfaction with established churches. In November 1836 Brownson added his *New Views of Christianity, Society, and the Church* to the transcendentalist ferment. In it he claimed that progress in the cultivation of the moral and spiritual in human beings would in turn bring progress in the perfecting of institutions, governments, and laws. Brownson was closer to Alcott than any of the other transcendentalists in demanding that ideas be translated into positive action for social reform.[24]

"It seems that the spiritualists are taking the field in force," said the scholarly Convers Francis, noting the burst of religious radicalism in 1836. Francis, Unitarian minister of the First Church in Watertown, Massachusetts, was sympathetic to the new ideas, though at forty-one he was older than the rest of the transcendentalists, who were in their twenties and thirties. Indeed, he contributed his own "spiritual" pamphlet that year, *Christianity as a Purely Internal System*. It seemed to Francis, as it did to the rest, that the general excitement ought to bring people with similar ideas together formally for discussion and exchange of views. Plans for these meetings began in the summer of 1836, even before the new ideas were available to the public in print.[25]

In June, Frederic Hedge, then in Bangor, Maine, contacted Emerson, Ripley, and fellow Unitarian minister George Putnam to propose a symposium to discuss the new ideas of the times. They met at Willard's Hotel in Cambridge on September 8, following the Harvard bicentennial celebration, and talked of ways of introducing "deeper and broader views" into theology and philosophy. Emerson had asked Hedge to allow Alcott to join the group even though Alcott was not ordained, for Emerson believed Alcott was "a God-made priest." Emerson invited Alcott to attend, but Alcott either decided not to go or failed to find the appointed meeting place. Anyway, he was not present at the meeting.[26]

The group met again on September 19 at Ripley's home. James Freeman

Clarke, Covers Francis, Orestes Brownson, and Alcott joined Ripley, Hedge, and Emerson. This became the first official meeting of the "Transcendental Club" or the "Symposeum" as Alcott preferred to call it. They agreed to create an atmosphere of free discussion; there would be only one rule for membership: that no one whose presence excluded any one topic from discussion would be admitted. For the next meeting they resolved to invite Dr. Channing; James Walker, editor of the *Christian Examiner*; conservative Unitarian Dr. Nathaniel Frothingham; aristocratic philanthropist Jonathan Phillips, a good friend of the May family; and three promising young ministers: Cyrus Bartol, John Sullivan Dwight, and Dr. Channing's nephew William Henry Channing. They planned to meet again on October 3 at Alcott's house on Beach Street.[27]

The representatives of the Unitarian establishment did not see fit to attend on the afternoon of October 3. Only Cyrus Bartol joined the others to discuss "American genius." But in the next four years the Club met thirty times and attracted a total of twenty-six people into close association, seventeen of them Unitarian ministers. Yet the members were never more in agreement than in the fall of 1836. That was the time of greatest enthusiasm and optimism. Alcott especially was filled with hope. "Reform is creeping into all things," he said in September 1836. "A voice has gone forth, uttering, in soft, yet earnest tones, '*All things shall be made new.*' The *past* shall be recast, into the mould of the Future."[28]

Alcott believed that the transcendentalists, as heralds of the "newness," would be the mainspring of reform. Indeed, their ideas opened the door to a faith that reform was possible. They called into question all elements of the established order—the church, the state, society. The values they attached to human potential made it theoretically possible for human beings to correct any abuse, to eliminate any evil. The transcendentalists participated in many of the specific reform efforts of the time, particularly educational reform and abolition. But generally they went beyond attempts to reform specific institutions or to eradicate specific evils. Instead, they talked of a new consciousness of the potential of human nature, the potential to commune with the divine, to experience directly religious truth. They pointed to a higher law, the spiritual law, by which all persons and institutions could be judged and measured. By it they challenged formal religion, demanding an experiential faith, a faith that grew by the direct experience of the human soul with the Divine. Such a faith, they felt, would add feeling and emotion to a cold, rational, and lifeless religion. They called for a fuller expression of the individual soul through art, literature, and conversation. This was Alcott's theme at the Temple School. He believed, as did his transcendentalist friends, that art was to the human soul what creation was to God. Drawing upon what was truly revolutionary about the Enlightenment and the American Revolution—that is, a commanding respect for human ability and potential—the transcendentalists celebrated the creative powers of the individual human being and each person's capacity for freedom and self-government. Theirs was a democratic faith; the spirit, the soul and its potential, was common to all persons regardless of station or class. They talked of alternatives for America, the land of hope and progress, the land with a special mission to the rest of the world: a new national literature, a richer culture, new life styles that rejected social conformity. Restraints, authorities, creeds, and established orders were all anathema. Transcendentalism, in the words of Perry Miller, "was the most energetic and extensive upsurge of the mind and spirit enacted in America until the intellectual crisis of the 1920s."[29]

But as much as transcendental ideas stimulated reform and provided emotional sustenance to committed reformers such as Alcott, the logic of those ideas made practical reform efforts difficult. The transcendentalists placed all authority for what was good, true, and beautiful in the individual soul. All authorities external to the individual, including other individuals, were held suspect. They defended themselves against the charge of solipsism by claiming that since the spirit, or the transcendental higher law, was absolute, it would be the same for all people, though they might perceive it in different ways. There was no danger that each person would define his or her own truth. Nevertheless, this position made concerted action for specific ends very difficult. Any organization with guidelines for action and declarations of principles would be at least a partial denial of individual freedom and choice. The Transcendental Club itself was an amorphous organization with few restraints or rules. Transcendental individualism inexorably led to positions exemplified by and beautifully expressed by Emerson and Henry Thoreau: self-reliance, self-cultivation, with little effort to reform society or the community in a cooperative way. Alcott was frustrated by this individualism. He had a vision of the cooperative society as exemplified by the common conscience he tried to create in his classroom. He also hoped to translate his faith into practical reform. But he found that few of his friends could go along with his version of the truth, any more than he could accept theirs. Cooperation among unrestrained individuals was next to impossible. By his own logic, the logic of the all-powerful individual, he was left standing alone, a prophet crying in the wilderness.

These difficulties were not apparent in the euphoria of late 1836. Caught up in the enthusiasm of the "newness," and fed by success and adulation, Alcott ventured to further his mission and to spread his ideas more widely. On December 27 his contribution to the "annus mirabilis" appeared in print: the first volume of the transcripts of his conversations on the Gospels. He was sure that *Conversations with Children on the Gospels* would increase public knowledge of his school and even bring light to parents and theologians. For here was the record of the simple but pure testimony of children to the truths of Scripture. Here was evidence that children indeed had special insight into the workings of the spirit. The *Conversations* would be a source of spiritual revelation for all to share. As an introduction to the *Conversations* he included the manifesto of his transcendentalism, *The Doctrine and Discipline of*

Human Culture, which had appeared as a pamphlet in August. It had received little attention except from Emerson, who found it "full of profound anticipations."[30]

Elizabeth Peabody, who had recorded all the conversations, had warned Alcott of possible trouble in the summer of 1836. She has suggested that before publication he excise a few of the more "questionable" and "superfluous" parts of the conversations, particularly those on birth and circumcision. She had not wanted her name associated with "unveiled physiological references," which a man could safely make but not a woman. With this, she had said that she was not returning to the Temple in the fall of 1836. Fear of censure was not the reason for her departure, she had explained. She had not planned to stay forever, and although she had said nothing about it, she had never been paid. Despite the warning and rumblings of discontent about the conversations, Alcott had serenely gone ahead placing the "superfluous" passages in the back of the volume as "notes," where they were likely to attract more attention than if they had been in the text. He had asked Hiram Fuller to come from Providence to replace Peabody as his assistant and recorder of conversations, but Fuller, busy with his own school, had refused. Then in Concord he had met a fervent admirer of Emerson, twenty-six-year-old Margaret Fuller—no relation to Hiram—who had come from Newburyport filled with a classical education administered stringently by her lawyer father. Alcott had asked this "lady of fine attainment" to record conversations and to teach Latin and French at the Temple School. She had accepted, telling him forthrightly that she could do as well as anyone in the job but warning that she had never been subordinate to anyone before. In late November, just about a month before the publication of volume one of the *Conversations*, this "worthy successor" to Elizabeth Peabody had begun recording the substance of what would become volume two and a proposed volume three.[31]

Alcott should have been more cautious about publishing the *Conversations*. Word of them had already caused increasing public distrust of his methods. Attendance in the fall of 1836 had dropped to twenty-five. Debt began to press upon the family once again. His more faithful patrons urged that he advertise by circular in the newspapers, but Alcott hesitated to use such "vulgar means." He wanted students who attended because of a "deeper sentiment" than that created by mere "advertisement." The *Conversations*, he thought, would serve to promote his school by awakening that "deeper sentiment" in parents and children. So would his newly instituted Friday evening conversations on the Gospels with Sunday School teachers, which he also hoped would prepare at least some adults to apprehend the published *Conversations* in the right spirit. Abby was less certain about the effects of the *Conversations*. She felt that publication would either build up the school or "pull it down forthwith." But she was sure that the *Conversations*, whatever its reception, would help form a new era in the literature of the country, and that history would recognize her husband as a benefactor to humanity.[32]

By late January 1837 three hundred copies of volume one had been sold. Volume two appeared in February. The word was out. Samuel J. May, then preaching in nearby South Scituate, Massachusetts, wrote that he intended to recommend the *Conversations* to his Sunday School teachers, but warned that most people would not accept it. The orthodox, he felt, would "scowl" because the *Conversations* did not square with their theory of human nature. The Unitarians would be afraid to praise it because "it expresses too plainly the result to which some of their prominent doctrines inevitably lead, and the public they will think are not yet prepared for such an exposure." May also predicted that "the worldly, the great, the wise, the prudent will sneer at it because its tendency is not to make good merchants, or lawyers, or civil engineers, or manufacturing agents." He was right. More and more patrons withdrew support, and the school began to languish. Alcott began the spring term in late February with only twenty pupils. Most of his remaining patrons agreed to an increase in tuition but warned that in the long run the increase would be detrimental. Chief Justice Lemuel Shaw, though he continued to patronize the school, told Alcott that he hoped he would introduce more of the "practical and accepted methods."[33]

Then the newspaper and periodical attack began. The *Conversations* and its editor were ridiculed and denounced. When the Reverend Chandler Robbins, the young, recently appointed editor of the Unitarian *Christian Register*, called for sensible criticism of the generally excellent work of a "pure-minded, industrious, and well-meaning man" like Alcott, he was, in his words, threatened with the Inquisition. Nathan Hale of the *Boston Daily Advertiser* was horrified that Alcott allowed children to express their "crude and undigested thoughts" on Holy Scripture. The questions raised by the *Conversations*, he said, were suitable only for "mature minds" and should not have been the subject of "flippant and off hand conversation." Hale, whose criticism Alcott felt was a "mere echo of the gossiping tribe among us," recommended that Alcott's experiment in spiritual culture come to an end. Joseph H. Buckingham of the *Boston Courier* was even more scathing. He said that the *Conversations* was "a more indecent and obscene book (we say nothing of its absurdity) than any other one we ever saw exposed to sale on a bookseller's counter." Buckingham agreed with Andrews Norton, the self-styled spokesman for the Unitarian establishment who had already attacked George Ripley for his position on the miracles, that Alcott's book was "one third absurd, one third blasphemous, and one third obscene." Another *Courier* article, signed "A parent," declared that the *Conversations* brought Scripture into contempt and threatened to sap the religious sentiment of the community. Buckingham added a postscript to this suggesting that Alcott had to be "insane of half-witted," and that his friends had better "take care of him without delay."[34]

With these scurrilous attacks by newspapers with the largest circulations in the Boston area—and he had confidently sent copies to each—Alcott saw the excitement over his book mount and the censure increase. There was a threat of a mob attack on his Friday evening conversations with Sunday School teachers, but it did not materialize. He feared that he would lose his expensive rooms at the Temple; he also doubted his ability to keep the school open.[35]

Alcott's transcendentalist friends rose to his defense. Emerson wrote to Hale and Buckingham asking them to print his reply to their attacks on Alcott. He criticized them for failing to give Alcott's experiment a fair chance, for taking passages of the *Conversations* out of context with the sole purpose of holding them up to ridicule, and for dealing unjustly with a man of "singular intellectual power." Buckingham printed the reply; Hale did not. Emerson told Alcott to ignore the criticism: "I hate to have all the little dogs barking at you; for you have something better to do than attend to them." But Emerson was concerned lest the bad publicity damage the Temple School. So was Elizabeth Peabody. She wrote an article for the *Christian Register* signed "A Frequent Spectator," in which she staunchly defended Alcott even though she disagreed with some of the details of his administration of the school. She lauded Alcott's ability to cultivate thought and develop the imagination of his pupils. "Will this generation be so unwise," she warned, "as not to avail itself of the peculiar genius of this singular enthusiast; who is also a pure-hearted and devout man;—because he has some errors in detail?" William H. Furness concurred. He wrote to Alcott that he should forget about the critics, for they had not the eyes to see. And James Freeman Clarke twice praised the *Conversations* in the *Western Messenger*, accusing Nathan Hale and his ilk of thoughtless criticism, and praising Alcott as a "prophet" sent by Providence to lift human beings to a higher ground in education.[36]

In early May Convers Francis called on Alcott to express his sympathy. He had read the *Conversations* with great pleasure and urged continuance of the school. He brought with him a sympathetic note from Alcott's admiring young friend Anna Thaxter. During that same week Alcott met George Ripley and discussed the situation with him at length. Ripley pointed to the crux of Alcott's problem. It was not so much the references to bodily functions —birth, circumcision—in the *Conversations*. They were guarded and delicately stated; they certainly were not obscene. Rather, Alcott's main offense was to consider matters of theology in the classroom, matters that the ministers felt were their purview alone. The ministers considered Alcott an interloper. According to Ripley, Alcott's predicament had given rise to a great deal of anguished discussion among the ministers about free discussion and free expression. As much as they valued it in theory, they felt bound to clamp down on the free expression of ideas as dangerous as those of Alcott.[37]

Alcott also found sympathy in other circles. William Andrus Alcott, though he strongly disagreed with his cousin's religious and philosophical opinions, wrote four separate articles during 1837 for the *Annals of Education*, which he now edited, praising his teaching methods. Even conservative James Walker of the *Christian Register* pointed out the worthiness of Alcott's methods of drawing out the inner thoughts and emotions of his pupils in a natural way. Walker agreed with the critics that the *Conversations* were open to serious challenge, but he praised Alcott anyway for his courage in publishing the book.[38]

But support from a few friends did not prevent the rapid decline of the Temple School. By the summer of 1837 only eleven pupils remained. Margaret Fuller left with Alcott's blessings to help Hiram Fuller in Providence. Alcott opened the summer session on May 22 in a smaller room of the Temple at one-third the rent. He had to sell his prized school library to help pay expenses. With no additional pupils promised for the fall, he doubted that he would be able to continue to teach. In mid-July he became seriously ill; his family and friends feared for his life. As a final blow Harriet Martineau's *Society in America* began to circulate, with its harsh criticism of the Temple School. "Such outrageous absurdities might be left to contempt, but for their consequences in practice," she declared without hesitation, despite having only secondhand knowledge of the school. On September 3 Alcott opened the fall session with only six students. "Quiddle, quiddle, on a half dozen souls, at No. 3 Temple—to this I am doomed," he said despairingly. He and his family survived only because of the food and clothing sent by friends. The city's intolerance had killed the school, as had the effects of the nationwide financial panic and depression, the country's worst yet, which began in 1837.[39]

Yet Alcott persisted. The school limped along through 1838 with between five and eight students. He pondered alternatives. A move to Concord offered many attractions. He thought he might be able to take in boarders as pupils there in order to make a living while being close to Emerson. Manual labor was another possibility, but he feared that this kind of work would give him too little time for thought and writing. Samuel J. May warned that such jobs were scarce anyway, especially during the current economic difficulties. He thought of becoming a traveling missionary to area towns and cities. With this in mind, he wrote to the Reverend Charles Brooks of Hingham, a sympathetic friend, explaining his plan to lecture, converse, and offer samples of instruction in "human culture" to all who would listen. Brooks responded with good wishes but warned that his community would pay money only for railroad and canal stock, banks, and real estate.[40]

In April 1838 Sarah Clarke, a close friend of the Peabodys and a one-time patron and drawing teacher at the Temple School, suggested that Alcott go to Louisville, Kentucky, as a "minister at large" to children and parents. She wrote to her brother, James Freeman Clarke, to urge him to further the plan. James Clarke responded that he could raise only four hundred dollars for the mission, but that he could assure eight or nine students for a part-time Alcott school. He promised that Louisville would provide Alcott with "good soil for his seeds." Elizabeth Peabody encouraged Alcott to go West. Surely Kentucky would be more accepting than Boston, which had proved to be "a lot less liberal" than she thought. But neither Alcott nor his wife wanted to leave Boston, despite their ill treatment and poverty. And Alcott told Sarah Clarke that he hesitated to take money subscribed by the American Unitarian Association, as was the case of the fund for the Louisville mission. He doubted that he could carry out its views.[41]

Whatever employment Alcott chose, it had to lead to a fulfillment of his grand sense of mission. The satisfying synthesis of ideas that he had found in the spiritual principle and his personal identity as a reformer, which his ideas had reinforced, caused his emotional commitment to his mission to intensify even amid turmoil, denunciation, and defeat. His ideas had a power over him that only served to justify for him his faith in that power. Public antagonism toward him brought out a tone of self-righteous martyrdom: "Destitution, debt—these are the terms that Society offers to those who would bless and save."[42] His formula for this-worldly salvation was sweeping:

I aim at reform—to unmake and reconstruct the consciousness of men—to gather all their intellectual conceptions around the august idea of spirit; using external nature as the element from which to shape their conceptions. For what is nature but the visible form of spirit? What its office but to form the associations of the intellect, and bind these by visible types to the Spirit.—Such a reform as this, aiming at the very seats of men's consciousness must provoke opposition. Men will not be taken to pieces without some outcry. They fear the loss of their identity, placing this, as they usually do, in forms: in the associations of their terrestrial experience; in the images which they have assumed upon their intellectual being. They fear that all is going. Hence distrust, fear, and all manner of misapprehensions and forebodings. But every reform implies all this. It is an experiment on the common consciousness of the time. It is a demolition of an old, traditionary, conventional form of consciousness, a substitution of a new, real, and true perception of things. It is a stripping off, from the intellects of men, of the outworn garb of associations and images in which they have been wrapt. It is taking all incumbrances from between their minds and things.[43]

He felt that his soul was "freed by living ideas." Despite the "tribes of timeservers" who cried out loudly against him, he had to speak, knowing full well that "often those truths which are best adapted to work out the regeneration of the age, are most offensive and provoke the greatest opposition." His ministry would be the foundation for a new and living culture. He vowed never to succumb to "tame and servile engagement" or to comply with the "vulgar aims and pursuits" of his age.[44]

But he found only further frustration and disappointment. In the midst of his own defeat he had hoped that Hiram Fuller's Greene Street School in Providence would carry on his ideals and be the firstfruits of his labors. In May 1837 Fuller had one hundred fifty students. He was paying high salaries to competent teachers, promising Margaret Fuller one thousand dollars a year. *Conversations on the Gospels* and *Record of a School* were basic elements of his curriculum. Great ceremony attended the opening of his new school building on June 10, 1837. Emerson gave the opening address in place of Alcott, who declined because of Abby's health and fear that his reputation would harm the school. However, in the end it was all show and no substance. At least that was what a disappointed Margaret Fuller reported. She found the gap between students and teachers intolerably wide. The school, she thought, buried the pupils' best powers rather than cultivated them. Her short-lived experience there helped her better appreciate Alcott and his methods. Then in November 1837 Emerson told Alcott of Hiram Fuller's plan to teach for five years and then go to Europe on the income. Alcott was horrified. "When I repeated all this to Alcott," Emerson said, "he expressed chagrin and contempt. For Alcott holds the school in so high regard that he would scorn to exchange it for the Presidency of the United States. The School is his Europe."[45]

Alcott hoped that writing would once again provide an outlet for his growing frustration. Self-expression, he believed, was the chief purpose of human life. If teaching could not be a channel for such expression, at least his pen could be. He wanted "Psyche or Breath of Childhood," his latest manuscript on his children and his scripture for childhood, to be the model for his personal mode of expression. In it he strove to lay before the public his central ideas in a transcendental style, which he felt best conveyed them. Again, failure dogged him.[46]

Greatly impressed with Emerson's genius in expression, Alcott gave him 'Psyche" on February 3, 1836, for his frank criticism. Emerson praised it for its earnestness, originality, vitality, and for its many beautiful passages. But he felt that it was a book of only one idea, deficient in variety of thought and illustration. Alcott simply lacked the power of imagery and description that might have made his single idea attractive. The manuscript was airy and verbose, full of the strained and affected use of archaic language like "saith" and "revealeth." Alcott evidently thought such biblical phraseology closer to spiritual language, but Emerson suggested that he eliminate it. Once trimmed and pared, Emerson said, the essay might be publishable. Alcott spent weeks revising, pruning, rethinking, troubled by the problem of what form was best for him. In August 1836 he gave it to Emerson again. In December Emerson returned it and urged its publication. Alcott thought of publishing it between volumes of the *Conversations*, but the public outcry against the *Conversations* and his own dissatisfaction with the manuscript scotched the plan.[47]

By June 1837 he was madly revising "Psyche" again. It truly became an outlet for his despair and frustration. He put so much time and effort into it that summer and fall that Abby feared that "in producing the life of Psyche he will produce also the death of his body." In November Emerson offered to publish it after his edition of Thomas Carlyle's *Sartor Resartus* was finished. Alcott could not afford to publish it at his own expense and he knew that his public reputation would scare away any commercial publishers. Yet he even hesitated to have Emerson publish it; he was not sure of its worth. The sad events of that year, and especially Emerson's just criticisms, had severely shaken his confidence in his ability to write.[48]

Alcott began another whirlwind of revisions and copying in April and May of 1838. He entitled his manuscript "Psyche an Evangele" which he believed better captured the spirit of the work. His finished product was radically

different from his earlier "Psyche or Breath of Childhood," not in substance
or ideas, but in tone and flavor. It dramatically reflected the bitterness and
resentment of a frustrated reformer. The prayerful optimism of the earlier
manuscript was dampened. There were more of the angry prophet, a Jeremiah
warning against the sins of humanity: "Hide thy face, close thine eyes: hold
thy tongue, shut this volume, reader; for thy face, thine eye, thy tongue shall
belie thee, if thou art unchaste or vulgar." It was as though Alcott needed to
describe sin in detail or order to explain for himself why the world had rejected
his ideas. He still celebrated childhood, the ability of children to reveal the
spiritual in human nature, and the divine responsibility of parents to cultivate
that childhood spirituality.[49] He still reverently described the spirit:

> The Soul is coeval with God. Its life is Spirit. And Spirit knoweth neither
> beginning nor end. It is prior to Time; Superior to Nature. Ever doth the
> instinct of perpetuity quicken its faculties, and demand of nature a history
> of its being.[50]

But he also lashed out angrily at society and institutions. The city became a
symbol, an emblem, of his discontent:

> The city is an offense unto me. It is feculent. It hath seventy plagues. Behold
> its markets, kitchens, distillers, sewers.... Do not these scent the air with
> nauseous odours. And then breath of men tainted with ravening beast;
> creatures human, canine, feline, huddled together, and pressing on the same
> common air, inpregnating [sic] it, in turn, with corrupting fluids.[51]

Ironically, Alcott was more pungent and forceful in describing evil than he was
in elucidating the realm of the spirit. "Psyche an Evangele," with all of its
anger and bitterness, was the most graphic and captivating expression of his
transcendentalism. Near the end of his three-hundred-fifty-page manuscript he
included a soliloquy of the suffering martyr, which pointed out the self-
assurance he so desperately sought in writing:

> Believe thou, O my Soul! that all needs, reverses, hindrance, misappre-
> hension, reviling, suffering, are blessed ministries, to unfold divinest
> faculties; disciplines for unfolding the noblest graces.... Take thy cross
> then, and follow after thy Duty; though thy reward shine upon thee,
> through the portals of the grave, and Death be the angel standing ready to
> conduct thee midst blood, flame, crucifixion, to courts of the blessed![52]

In early June Alcott submitted "Psyche an Evangele" to Emerson for
suggestions. Emerson found criticizing it an "irksome piece of work."
Though he claimed no jurisdiction over another's writing, he told Alcott that if
the manuscript were his he would not print it. It contained commanding ideas
and it inspired by its expression of faith, Emerson said, but it lacked unity and
cohesiveness. It vacillated in a perplexing way between prophecy and
philosophy. As prophecy it lacked simplicity, and as philosophy it lacked
systematic treatment. And it lack concreteness: "I thought as I read," said
Emerson,

of the Indian jungles, vast & flowering, where the sky & stars are visible alway, but no house, no mountain, no man, no definite objects whatever, & no change, or progress; & so, one acre in it is like another, & I can sleep in it for centuries. But mortal man must save his time, & see a new thing at every step.[53]

This latest criticism by Emerson made Alcott despair of ever writing anything worthwhile. He began to feel that he was too feeble an artist with the pen, that thoughts and deeds would have to serve as his creative instrument. He took Emerson's suggestion and did not attempt to publish "Psyche an Evangele." His months of effort had come to nothing.[54]

Adding further to Alcott's problems was the condition of his family "We are as poor as rats," Abby told her brother in the fall of 1837. The debt mounted to five thousand dollars by June 1838, while income diminished in turn. And Abby's health was not good. She suffered the physical and emotional trauma of miscarriages in the summer of 1837 and again in 1838. Her father and step-mother were no comfort. They disapproved of her marriage and her life-style, and she was never able to reconcile the differences fully. She grieved over the "cruel neglect" by her father and his family. Then, as the crowning sorrow, Abby, on April 6, 1839, gave birth to a boy, fully developed, but not living. They had lost four children in five years.[55]

Alcott finally closed his Temple School for good in June 1838. A few supporters, led by Dr. John Flint, had proposed that he teach in day school for the poor in Boston's South End, and he accepted. Samuel May had encouraged him to do so, suggesting that the people of the South End might respond to his ideas more readily than the "nabobs of Beacon Street." In September, the family moved to number six Beach Street where on October 14 Alcott opened his new school with fifteen pupils. In late October, William Russell moved in with the Alcotts and added his eldest son to Alcott's class, which now numbered twenty, mostly under age eight. By this time Dr. Flint and his fellow patrons, who evidently paid a flat rate for each student enrolled in the school, were upset that Alcott had included among his pupils a black girl, Susan Robinson. They demanded her immediate dismissal, but Alcott adamantly refused. Samuel May, who earlier had supported Prudence Crandall in Connecticut in her battle against the same injustice, praised Alcott's courage. "If suffering for righteousness sake (as I believe it is) is the method by which we are to be made perfect," he said," you and my sister, are in the way to that desirable end." The patrons did not remove their support precipitously, perhaps out of sympathy for Alcott, but the numbers of pupils steadily declined through the winter and spring of 1839. Alcott lost all interest in the school. By June 1839 he had only five students left, his three daughters, young William Russell, and Susan Robinson. On June 22 he closed his school, resolving to minister to adults. It was clear to him that his labors with children could not take root until adults were better informed about the importance of human culture.[56]

The crushing events of 1837 to 1839 made Alcott increasingly bitter and hostile. His journal and correspondence reflected his feeling of oppression and martyrdom. He felt that he was the victim of "vulgar prejudice" and "narrow sectarian opinion." Only the few understood and appreciated his great purpose, for the "multitude" cared little about the "mind." Those who rejected his plans simply did not know what was good for them: "Poor sick, infirm, lunatic Humanity. And these know nothing of the regimen that restores sanity and soundness."[57] When the news arrived that abolitionist newspaper editor Elijah Lovejoy had been killed by a mob in Alton, Illinois, in November 1837, Alcott immediately identified himself with the slain martyr. He saw the Apocalypse coming:

> Are there no signs of approaching dread. What say the times! Are not the men of the day lost to truth! Doth not wickedness reign in high places. Shall virtue, truth, wisdom, holiness, meet favour at its hand? The day of martyrdom hath already come. Even as I write, the land is bloody with the guilt of the slain, and slain for the defence of truth—for the rights of the Soul! . . . I expose the evils of the day. I call the age to account. Shall it bear it. Shall it not be provoked: and deal vengeance on my head?[58]

Even the once-revered Dr. Channing became the target of Alcott's rebuke. Channing had greeted Alcott's Friday-evening adult conversations with distrust and his *Conversations on the Gospel* with alarm. Alcott visited him twice in March 1837, at the height of the public outcry, but found little comfort. Channing expressed horror at Alcott's identifying the human soul with the divine, the more so, perhaps, because that was the logical outcome of his own ideas. Disappointed and disheartened, Alcott accused Channing of being a "disciple of the understanding" who lacked confidence in the "power of truth." Channing was "a pure and beautiful soul," Alcott concluded, but he was not original; he was not a man of vision. "His merit lies not in the utterance of new and quickening truths; but in a bolder and better utterance of those which are already accepted. His is the last, best word. Never is it the first." The "age," said Alcott, demanded "a wiser, nobler light" than what Channing provided.[59]

Alcott had a martyr's hope that the world would one day appreciate him and accept his views. "A wise man is not in haste to reap the fruits of his scattered wisdom," he told himself. "He waits patiently for it to take root, spring up, and ripen." He comforted himself with the resigned belief that the sower of the seeds of reform rarely lived to reap the harvest. Tribulation and suffering served to define the holiness of people like himself and Lovejoy. The world would one day see their lives as examples of "celestial radiance." "Men do not get mobbed for uttering nonsense or falsehood," he said, trying to squelch the nagging fear that maybe his ideas were as silly as the newspapers reported. "It is their sin to have spoken unsparingly of the time in which they lived. He who causes no stir among his fellows, does no good." He also found solace in the belief that he was living in a revolutionary time. Restlessness and revolt, emblems of the spirit, were evident everywhere, he thought. Life and light were indeed coming forth from the midst of death and darkness:[60]

> The day is not far distant when minds of creative genius—true lovers of humanity—shall associate for its regeneration. To this every sign of the Times now points. Men, intent on separate evils shall, at last, be led to the parent principle which is to kill every abuse and usage; and establish truth in the common mind.[61]

Nothing gave him greater comfort than his sense of participation in this upheaval.

The transcendentalists were prime evidence of the imminent revolution. Emerson's genius in particular was the "herald of a future time." That Emerson appreciated him when nearly everyone else scorned and mocked was proof to Alcott that "genius" always remained constant. It retained its full value in the midst of counterfeits and even when "fools and madmen" attempted to thrust it aside. Free from the slavery of the age, Emerson's mind would emancipate other minds from the traditions, usages, and conventions of the past. On July 15, 1838, this free genius outraged the Unitarian establishment by attacking the doctrine of miracles, exalting human reason, and preaching the divinity of human nature at the very stronghold of Unitarianism, Harvard College. The seven seniors at the Divinity School had provided him the forum by asking him to deliver their commencement address. Andrews Norton, horrified that men soon to occupy the pulpit should be exposed to such ideas, vociferously attacked Emerson's address as an insult to religion. The *Christian Examiner* urged the faculty at Harvard to exercise closer control over such events to avoid the dangers of "mysticism" in the future. John Gorham Palfrey, Dean of the Divinity School, accused Emerson of atheism. Alcott, who readily identified with Emerson's position, exulted at Emerson's courageous exploration of the soul and assault on the "dead letter of tradition." When the public attacks only served to increase interest in Emerson's lectures, Alcott took it as evidence that "the orb of light is rising and shall chase away the clouds of error, traditions, lies, that obscure the vision of the soul." Alcott's visits to Concord increased. He considered Emerson a brother, a confidant. Both were the "butt of sectarian scandal"; both were sources of "renovating ideas."[62]

The Transcendental Club also offered hope. The members took a "divine view of the soul" and were interested in "advancing humanity," although Alcott noted a timidity and a traditionalism among those members who remained within the church. Their writings, especially those of Emerson and Brownson, he found to be the firstfruits of a "new literature." He considered the *Western Messenger*, which demanded more "life, energy, soul, originality" in matters of religion, philosophy, and literature, to be the freest of all periodicals in America.[63] On July 19, 1839, Alcott attended the Harvard Divinity School address in which Andrews Norton called transcendentalism "the latest form of infidelity." In silent response, Alcott wrote in his journal a clear statement of the transcendentalists' opposition to Norton's Unitariansm:

He is quite unaware that the old theology, taught at the Cambridge School, and from Unitarian pulpits, has lost all hold on the hearts of men; having no vitality. What was it, indeed, but an attempt to make reason cover all the facts of the Godhead. It was the apotheosis of reason: It denied sentiment: It subordinated the moral to the intellectual attributes, and thus vitiated the faith of Conscience; making reason the oracle of revelation to the Soul, instead. Norton, Channing, have each misled the seekers after truth, by this subordination of Conscience; the one to the understanding, the other to the reason. They are fast losing their influence. "Rational Christianity" was a noble protest, in its day, against ecclesiastical domination; but it was merely a protest: it fixed on nothing stable, and, as such, could not endure. Now the soul protests alike against it, and will overthrow it.[64]

Norton "should have remained silent," thought Alcott. His address was the "popular argument" and therefore was "of no value." George Ripley publicly attacked Norton in his pamphlet *The Latest Form of Infidelity Examined*, which argued the "superiority of the testimony of the soul to the evidence of the external senses." To Alcott's satisfaction, anyway, Ripley had justly convicted Norton of ignorance and intolerance.[65]

In October 1838 Alcott made a list of rare "souls" who he felt were free and brave, who loved humanity, and who had faith in progress. He included himself, Emerson, Ripley, Hedge, Furness, Clarke, Francis, Dwight, William Henry Channing, who had publicly defended Emerson's 1837 Phi Beta Kappa address on the "American Scholar," and Theodore Parker, the scholarly and uncompromising minister from West Roxbury, who had attended the Club meetings several times but whose sharp attacks on the Unitarian establishment were yet to come. He also included Orestes Brownson, although by then Brownson had become a problem to him. He believed that Brownson had a mission of good, but that he put too much emphasis on collective change rather than individual change. Especially troubling was Brownson's article in the *Christian Examiner* of May 1837 in which he declared that he favored "spiritualism" but not the "transcendentalism" of Emerson, Alcott, Hedge, and Furness. Transcendentalism, he said, was fanciful, wild, and lacking in good sense. It was apparent that Brownson lacked the "deep enthusiasm" essential to a man of the spirit. Yet Alcott had high hopes for the *Boston Quarterly Review*, which Brownson edited and whose first issue appeared in January 1838 with a strong defense of Emerson. He felt that the *Review* could become an instrument for the expression of the "free mind of the nation," even though Brownson himself was a man of mere "talent," not "genius."[66]

In December 1838 Alcott met another herald of the coming age, the mysterious and ghostlike Jones Very. The Harvard faculty had just declared Very to be insane, causing him to leave his position there as tutor of Greek. He wrote and spoke in mystical phrases that bewildered even Alcott. In fact, Alcott had doubts about Very's sanity too, but amid the fog he detected "glimpses of genius." He found Very's essay on Shakespeare, later published by Emerson in *Essays and Poems* in 1839, to be better than any he had seen. Very struck Alcott as "a voice from the tomb," who "lingers yet a little while on the earth, but hastes to depart, and ascend again into heaven." In him, Alcott said, "the resurrection has become a fact, seen with the eyes." He was quite a contrast with the irascible and concrete Brownson. When both Very and Brownson chanced to visit on the same day in June 1839, Alcott was struck by the polarity between them: "They sat opposite each other at the table; but were sundered by spaces immeasurable. It was comic to behold them! They tried to speak, but Very was un-intelligible to the proud philistine."[67]

Religious, philosophical, and literary revolt was not Alcott's only evidence of the coming transformation. More than ever before, Boston of the late 1830s was seething with reform movements and reformers. The most obvious of these was abolitionism. Even when lost in thought during the Philadelphia years, Alcott had retained his concern with the antislavery movement. Samuel May and Samuel Sewall had kept him and Abby informed about antislavery activities in Boston in the early thirties, especially the establishment of William Lloyd Garrison's *Liberator* in January 1831. Abby had joined the Female Antislavery Society, formed in December 1833 by Lucretia Mott as a counterpart to the American Antislavery Society. Though family duties had kept her from full Society participation, Abby had made a special effort to meet and talk with Garrison when he visited Philadelphia in May 1834. Alcott's growing anti-organizational bias had prevented his joining the American Antislavery Society, but he had praised Garrison for his work in bringing the question into the open. It was a question that could not be hushed, he felt; it was intimately identified with the stability and perpetuity of the nation. Both he and Abby were opposed to the idea of colonization. That expedient, they felt, was only a dilatory method used to appease slaveholders. It made a business transaction out of a moral question. Garrison's demand for immediate emancipation, his unqualified condemnation of slavery in the light of "divine principles," proved that he too was a free, devout "soul" interested in the melioration of human woes. In Boston the Alcotts became caught up in the abolitionist crusade. In August 1835 Alcott attended the meeting at Julien Hall celebrating the end of slavery in the British colonies. He heard English abolitionist George Thompson's "phillipic" against slavery that day, and he witnessed the threat on Thompson's life by a proslavery mob. Two months later he and Abby visited Garrison at the Leverett Street jail after a mob had dragged him through the streets with a rope around his neck. That same day they spirited a portrait of George Thompson from the home of Maria Weston Chapman and hid it under their bed lest it cause trouble.[68]

Alcott was impressed with Garrison not only for his commitment to ending slavery, but also for his contemplation of more extensive reform—in the penal code, in religious rites and ceremonies, in the relations between the sexes. There were few people with whom Alcott had more sympathy than with Garrison. As Emerson was the leader in intellectual and philosophical change, so Garrison led in matters moral and social. "Garrison shall kill the hydras that lurk about the soul; Emerson [shall] reveal the angels that minister to its glory and its joy." Both were "heroic," he thought, and would "mould the age into their own image." Alcott found Garrison uncomfortably harsh and dogmatic at times, but he always respected him as a mightly "man of deeds," a "slayer of evils," and a "breaker of idols."[69]

Garrison's most splendid effort, Alcott believed, was the organization of the New England Non-Resistance Society. One hundred sixty delegates, including Alcott, Garrison, Samuel May, Henry C. Wright, and Wendell Phillips, attended the organizational meeting at Marlboro Chapel on September 18, 1838. Most were radical abolitionists concerned with the question of the relationship between aboliton and non-resistance raised by the Lovejoy affair. The "Declaration of Sentiments," written by Garrison, renounced the use of force for any purpose and renounced allegiance to any government. Most of the delegates were unwilling to go to that extreme; only twenty-five signed the document. Alcott, ever true to his firm belief that ideas and moral example, not violence, were the effective agents of reform, eagerly signed the Declaration, calling it a "herald of a new era." Both Alcott and Garrison saw the Declaration as a much needed commitment to moral principles. But Alcott, whose principles also forbade his joining any organization, refused to become a member of the society.[70]

Also of great interest to Alcott were the ideas of traveling lecturer Sylvester Graham. Graham promised his listeners salvation through a strict program of daily physical regimen: a vegetable and grain diet, bathing, exercise, sunlight, fresh air, and proper dress. Upon hearing him speak in February 1836, Alcott was enthralled. "I deem him the *prophet of temperance* to this age," he said, "his mission consisting of turning men to the knowledge and purification of their bodies, as the fit and appropriate baptism for the sanctifying influences of the spirit." Alcott was something of a convert to theories of diet and temperance even before hearing Graham. He had speculated about such things for several years. In August 1835 he had "instinctively" given up food produced by or from animals, believing that it somehow "clogged" the spirit in its function. Louisa's sometimes untoward behavior was the result, he thought, of too much "animal food." But Graham did reinforce Alcott's belief that some bodily preparation or purification was a prerequisite for the proper working of the spirit. He felt that Graham had provided him with physiological evidence that confirmed his own conclusions about the psychological nature of human beings. And Graham was a fellow martyr to narrowness and intolerance. Mobs threatened him and crowds jeered. He was worthy of attention and sympathy just for that.[71]

There were other intrepid zealots who fascinated Alcott. In July 1837 he heard thirty-two-year-old feminist and abolitionist Angelina Grimké speak in favor of the abolition of slavery in the District of Columbia. "One feels while hearing her speak, how ridiculous are all invidious distinctions of sex." He listened admiringly as she gave an unprecedented speech before the all-male state legislature. And there was Edward Palmer, a Boston printer who sought to overthrow "Mammon" by refusing to use money. He impressed Alcott as a "child of love," living from day to day by begging, sleeping in barns and outhouses, and eating from fields and orchards. He was indeed, as Alcott put it, "a contrast to the arrogant pretensions of the age."[72]

As much as he admired these reformers—Garrison, Graham, Palmer, Grimké—and saw them as prophets of a revolutionary epoch, Alcott felt that their pet reforms were too limited in scope. Attacks on specific evils, such as slavery or war, dealt only with symptoms, not root causes. Attempts to change institutions failed to get at the underpinning of all institutions, the individual human being. It was the character, the moral stance, of each person, he thought, that determined the nature and direction of institutions. Driven by the logic of this theory of reform, he became increasingly anti-institutional and individualistic. For in his opinion all institutions were corrupt unless the individuals in them were first purified. His disagreement with Orestes Brownson over means of reform reflected this individualism. "We can place little reliance on men acting in masses," he said, countering Brownson's faith in organization. "It is individual effort that is to reform abuses. Personal holiness in the only condition of general reformation. All change must be embodied in the life and being of the reformer, before he can hope for success. He must be the ideal man. Thus was Jesus, and hence the power and authority of his words." For Alcott, reform had overtones of a personal religious awakening, a sanctification, a regeneration. He hoped to make everyone a reformer, a sanctified person capable of creating sanctified institutions. In March 1837 he heard historian George Bancroft speak on the progress of humanity. Bancroft asserted that progress was an aggregate matter, that Society progressed, individuals did not. Alcott judged the speech a "second-rate performance." Individual progress was the condition and herald of social progress.[73]

The primary context of individual progress or regeneration, Alcott thought, was the family. The family was the only God-ordained institution. It was the key to human culture. Schools could not begin to repair the damage wrought by a bad family situation.[74] "Virtues and vices pre-exist in the Family," he claimed,

> Here all is simple. Here the intellect and morals of a nation are cradled and mannered. Society is the retribution, good or evil, of those traits and tendencies of the soul herein developed & fostered. Corruption is a private, before it becomes a public calamity. Violation of the sacred relations of family is treason to the state, and not until husbands, wives, parents, are faithful to the soul, shall governments, civil or ecclesiastical, have life or stability.[75]

He expected that the family would be the source of comfort, the source of inspiration, the source of moral and religious values for all people just as it had been for him in childhood and in marriage.

As his emphasis on individual reform increased, his interest in reform organizations diminished. In 1838 and 1839 he attended meetings of several of these organizations: the American Antislavery Society, the American Institute of Instruction, the American Peace Society, the New England Non-Resistance Society, the Massachusetts Temperance Union, and the Sunday School Society. He even attended the Boston Ministerial Conference and the Convention of Congregationalist Ministers. But he quickly became convinced that he had nothing in common with such "popular bodies." They all were limited in vision; the reform ideas expressed by them would die away as soon as the specific cause died away. They dealt with "forms" instead of "principles."[76]

His opinion of the work of Horace Mann further illustrated his concept of reform. In June 1837 Mann became Secretary of the Massachusetts Board of Education and began what he called a "holy and patriotic" crusade to reform the Massachusetts public school system. Alcott heard Mann speak at the Temple in March 1838, and Mann sent Alcott his school reports and his proposals for legislative changes. Mann's program struck Alcott as a much-needed "first step" that would prepare the way for radical improvement. But he was concerned that Mann had no gospel, no philosophy, no insight into the "principles of culture." The kind of reforms Mann asked for were structural; he wanted changes in methods, laws, organization. Thus, in Alcott's opinion, they could only be "preliminary"; they could not accomplish the "true work of improvement." He sympathized with Mann, though. As a "functionary of the State," he could do little that was radical.[77]

Alcott offered the challenge of a prophet, demanding that reformers transcend immediate goals and extend their vision in a radical way. But his perfectionism and unwillingness to compromise prevented his offering anything concrete to movements with which he sympathized. At best, he served as an inspiring example of selfless dedication to principles, but he did so only as long as people listened to him enough to take him seriously. His extreme individualism and anti-institutionalism brought him close to a snobbish asceticism, a withdrawal to a personal life that he considered sanctified or regenerated. Sometimes his sentiments reflected his desire to retreat to a lonely shell:

> It behooves a wise man, however, to move fearlessly and firmly onward, stopping not to confront evil or ignorant opposition, or befoul himself by entering the kennel with the ignoble and bestial calumniators. Slime clings not to him who frequents none but fair places.[78]

His spiritual epistemology also militated against his doing battle with evil. According to his plans for human culture, only communion with the pure and beautiful could awaken the spiritual element of the soul. The solitary genius, by withdrawing from all that was "disturbing and vulgar," could become eminently cheerful, loving, and pure. There was strength in independence; acting with the "rabble" brought only weakness.[79]

But Alcott's unremitting sense of mission prevented his complete withdrawal. Despite his growing dislike of the "rabble" and the "multitude," he felt duty bound to save them. Emerson suggested that Alcott "leave the impracticable world to wag its own way, and set apart and write oracles for its behalf."[80] Alcott rejected this idea as too limiting: "I desire to see my Idea not only a *written*, but a *spoken*—and an *acted* word—a *Word incarnate*." He berated Emerson for his lack of action, for holding things and people at a distance. He accused Emerson of seeking the beauty of truth rather than truth itself, for seeking to be more the "accomplished scholar" than the "perfect man." Emerson, said Alcott with some justice, was "an *eye*; more than a *heart*—an intellect, more than a soul." Alcott saw himself as an actor and a player more than a writer.[81]

Alcott wanted to act, but as an individual, not as a member of an organization. He wanted to confront evil while remaining unstained by it; he wanted to influence institutions while staying clear of their grasp. As the world of institutions and organizations increasingly mistreated him in the late 1830s, he reacted not by openly attacking his malefactors, but by rejecting institutions and accepted societal norms more strongly than ever before. The regenerated individual was the key to the "new age," he repeated, not organizations, customs, or creeds. "I belong to no sect," he said,

> I am connected with no association. I should belie my soul and cripple my action by such bonds. I prefer to act as an individual: Let my influence be that of my personal character alone. This is the only legitimate institution: it leaves all faculties free; it asks no pledges; it prescribes no creeds; it is above and sustains them all.[82]

By 1839, with the final collapse of his school, his individualism was vocal and bitterly antagonistic. In September 1839 he addressed the Non-Resistance Society and chided its members, many of whom had renounced allegiance to governments just as he had done, for paying too much attention to government. He told them to ignore government and worry only about the "theocracy of the human soul."[83] Neither Church nor State was worthy of the attention of the "best men," he declared. Each person had the prerogative of self-government, and he was assuming that prerogative. He was sure that Church and State were soon to crumble under the pressures of growing revolt, leaving only the individual soul to rule. Further, he advocated a more equal distribution of material goods, according to each person's "moral worth." Who or what would determine each person's "moral worth," he did not say. The accepted procedures for the distribution of goods disgusted him. Banks and marketplaces appalled him. The customs and conventions of society angered him. One day in February 1839 Abby sent him to buy meat. "A fool's errand," he remarked. He not only brought home the wrong piece of meat, to Abby's displeasure, but was sickened by the atmosphere at the meat market. "What have I to do with butchers? Am I to go smelling about markets? Both are an offense to me. Death yawns at me as I walk up and down in this abode of skulls." In April Emerson gave him a check to buy groceries, and he was forced to enter a bank, "Mammon's Temple," to cash it. Though he had to do it to feed his family, he felt "dishonored" to resort to these "haunts of idolaters," where "bevies of devoters were consulting on appropriate rites whereby to honour their divinity." Then in December George Bancroft asked him to dine along with Emerson, Margaret Fuller, and Nathaniel Frothingham. He refused. "Is it meet place for me at the tables of the fashionable, the voluptuous, the opulent!" he queried. He wanted no charity, no social standing, doled out by the "Sadducees."[84]

Even Alcott's good-hearted brother-in-law, Samuel J. May, became the target of his accusations. May had disappointed Alcott by remaining within the Unitarian Church, thus wrongly grounding his faith in "tradition" instead of the soul. "Religion," said Alcott, "is too vital and growing to be embodied in institutions." "Christianity has lost its significance," he declared. "Christendom is infidel. The Church is atheist. The Christian and the worldling are friends; and Christ and mammon are put on good terms with one another. The church has become the servile instrument of the state." But regeneration was coming. The immanent divine spirit within each human soul was Alcott's object of faith. The soul would transcend the institutionalized church and create a "new church." Traditions and forms would crumble before the living creed of the human soul.[85]

The method Alcott found for carrying out his mission of reform while maintaining his extreme individualism was conversation. Modeled after his classroom techniques, these conversations involved informal discussions with small groups of interested adults in the Boston area. Conversation was the most potent means of spreading his message, he believed, because it involved the interchange of ideas. Unlike the lecture or the sermon, a conversation drew upon the potential for good in each individual. He wanted to address the souls of his adult listeners much as he had the souls of the children in the Temple School. By unfolding the doctrine of the soul he expected to be able to release the divine spirit within the souls of each of his participants. This would be his means of human culture, his means of reform and regeneration.[86]

His first efforts as a traveling conversationalist and missionary of human culture came in September 1838. John Sullivan Dwight helped arrange a conversation with a group of people in Lexington, where Dwight preached on occasion. The session was successful, and the group invited Alcott back. Shortly afterward, Alcott began a series of conversations with a group in Hingham formed by Charles Brooks and Anna Thaxter. His second conversation in Lexington in early October attracted nearly fifty people, including Emerson, and between thirty and forty attended his second in Hingham. By December 1838 he had extended the series of weekly conversations to twelve. His faithful listeners heard and discussed his outpourings on the soul, on God, on the spirit, on revelation, on human culture. There was a glimmer of success. He was sure that he had awakened at least a few people to a reverence for their souls. In a burst of confidence he claimed the distinction of being one of the "Talkers of the age." "In this wise am I to teach," he exulted, "and my talking is to reach all classes and ages."[87]

Alcott also held a series of Monday evening conversations with parents of his pupils, beginning in mid-November, and Friday evening conversations with friends at his home in Boston. The latter sessions attracted his fellow transcendentalists and reformers, such as Garrison, Dwight, William Russell, Theodore Parker, and Edward Palmer. When his conversations in Lexington and Hingham ended in December, Alcott arranged another series to begin in January 1839 in Lynn, with the help of the Reverend Samuel Robbins. His "ministry of talking" was indeed becoming his means of "acting on the minds of men." And Emerson agreed: "Alcott is the only majestic converser I now meet. He gives me leave to be, more than all the others." Again, Alcott thought of publishing a book of transcripts of his conversations as a "living colloquy" speaking to the "needs of the people."[88]

There was vocal opposition. The Congregationalist minister in Lynn, the Reverend Parsons Cooke, lashed out against the "impiety" and "subversion" that Alcott's transcendentalism was bringing to the towns. He accused Alcott of obscenity, of using "filthy and godless jargon," and of blasphemy. But Alcott was sure that Cooke's polemic merely advertised the conversations and increased attendance. In April 1839 he closed his various conversations, having realized an income of one hundred fifty-five dollars. He hoped that future conversations at higher rates would support him and his family. He felt that he could now close his failing school and concentrate on his talking ministry.[89]

Unfortunately, his high hopes were not realized. In the fall of 1839 he met groups in Boston, Plymouth, and Concord, but without much success, certainly not enough to bring in a steady income. His family was still on the brink of starvation. By December 1839 he was again feeling like "an idler in the midst of an age which cheats itself of my gifts." Once again he turned to earlier modes of escape, to speculation and writing. He tried to find satisfaction amid discontent by continuing his search for a complete intellectual synthesis. Although it was not much help to his family, that search sustained him.[90]

Notes

1. AJ 8 (1835): 325-29, 490.

2. Ibid., pp. 33, 37, 65, 280-81; Cooke, *Historical and Biographical Introduction*, 2: 69 ff.; Miller, ed., *The Transcendentalists*, pp. 66 ff.

3. Alcott, "Autobiographical Index"; AJ 8 (1835): 137; Merton M. Sealts, Jr., ed., *The Journals and Miscellaneous Notebooks of Ralph Waldo Emerson*, vol. 5 (1835-1838) (Cambridge, Mass.: Harvard University Press, 1965), pp. 57, 63.

4. Sealts, ed., *Journals of Emerson*, 5: 98-99; AJ 8 (1835): 440-42; Mary Moody Emerson to Alcott, October 30, 1835, from a copy in Alcott's hand in "Autobiography, 1834."

5. Sealts, ed., *Journals of Emerson*, 5: 111; AJ 8 (1835): 477; William R. Hutchison, *The Transcendentalist Ministers* (New Haven, Conn.: Yale University Press, 1959), pp. 18-21; Miller, ed., *The Transcendentalists*, p. 8.

6. Ralph Rusk, *The Life of Ralph Waldo Emerson* (New York: Columbia University Press, 1949), pp. 163-65; Alfred R. Ferguson, ed., *The Journals and Miscellaneous Notebooks of Ralph Waldo Emerson*, vol. 4 (1832-1834) (Cambridge: Harvard University Press, 1964), pp. 45, 278.

7. Miller, ed., *The Transcendentalist*, pp. 66-67, 69, 72, 74.

8. James Freeman Clarke, *Autobiography, Diary and Correspondence* (New York: Negro Universities Press, 1969), pp. 38-40; Cooke, *Historical and Biographical Introduction*, 2: 63; AJ 8 (1835): 345.

9. Crowe, *George Ripley*, pp. 42, 56-65; Miller, ed., *The Transcendentalists*, pp. 59-62, 89-92.

10. AJ 7 (1834), part 3: 23, 27, 68, 114, 156, 189-92, 262-63; Alcott, "Researches on Childhood," pp. 18-20; Alcott, "Psyche or Breath of Childhood," p. 159.

11. AJ 8 (1835): 349.

12. Ibid., pp. 511, 515, 518.

13. Alcott, "Psyche or Breath of Childhood," pp. 97-99, 222.

14. Alcott, ed., *Conversations on the Gospels*, 2: 31; AJ 7 (1834), part 3: 28; AJ 8 (1835): 97-98, 225-226, 351.

15. AJ 7 (1834), part 3: 82-88, 152-53; AJ 8 (1835): 322.

16. Alcott, *The Doctrine and Discipline of Human Culture*, p. 3; AJ 8 (1835): 56, 86-87, 189.

17. Alcott, *The Doctrine and Discipline of Human Culture*, pp. 3-4.

18. Ibid., pp. 7, 13.

19. Hutchison, *Transcendentalist Ministers*, pp. 5, 12, 18-19; Paul F. Boller, Jr., *American Transcendentalism, 1830-1860: An Intellectual Inquiry* (New York: G. P. Putnam's Sons, 1974), pp. 44-54.

20. AJ 9 (1836): 8, 15-16, 21, 124, 134; C[atherine] S[edgwick], "Record of a School," *The Knickerbocker*, 7, no. 2 (February 1836): pp. 113-30; Anna Quincy Thaxter to Alcott, January 7, 1836, and Alcott to Anna Quincy Thaxter, January 31, 1836, from copies in Alcott's hand in "Memoir, 1878." Although references in these notes are to the manuscript, Alcott's "Journal for 1836" has been published by Joel Myerson in Myerson, ed., *Studies in the American Renaissance 1978* (Boston: Twayne, 1978), pp. 17-104.

21. AJ 9 (1836): 125, 128, 129, 180; Hiram Fuller to Alcott, June 17, 1836, from a copy in Alcott's hand in "Autobiography, 1834"; AJ 8 (1835): 222; Anna Quincy Thaxter to Abby May Alcott, October 1835, Sophia Peabody to Mrs. William Russell, July 25, 1836, from a copy in Alcott's hand in "Memoir, 1878."

22. Hutchison, *Transcendentalist Ministers*, p. 34; Miller, ed., *The Transcendentalists*, p. 107; Ralph Waldo Emerson, "Nature" in *Nature, Addresses and Lectures* (Boston: Houghton, Mifflin and Co., 1904), pp. 70-77; AJ 9 (1836): 188-90; A. Bronson Alcott, "The Transcendental Club and *The Dial*," *The Commonwealth*, 1, no. 34 (April 24, 1863); Alcott to Sophia Peabody, September 12, 1836, in Herrnstadt, ed., *Letters,* pp. 29-30; William H. Furness to Alcott, September 17, 1836, from a copy in Alcott's hand in "Autobiography, 1834"; Rusk, *Emerson*, pp. 241-42.

23. Hutchison, *Transcendentalist Ministers,* pp. 45-46; MIller, ed., *The Transcendentalists*, pp. 124-28, 129-40.

24. Miller, ed., *The Transcendentalists*, pp. 45, 114, 120, 123; Arthur M. Schlesinger, Jr., *A Pilgrim's Progress: Orestes A. Brownson* (Boston: Little, Brown and Co., 1939), p. 53; AJ 9 (1836): 133, 176, 192.

25. Miller, ed., *The Transcendentalists*, pp. 63, 107.

26. Cooke, *Historical and Biographical Introduction*, 1: 48; Joel Myerson, "A Calendar of Transcendental Club Meetings," *American Literature*, 4 (May, 1972): 198; Ralph Waldo Emerson to Frederic Henry Hedge, July 20, 1836, in Ralph Rusk, ed., *The Letters of Ralph Waldo Emerson*, 6 vols. (New York: Columbia University Press, 1939), 2: 29-30; AJ 9 (1836): p. 182; Ralph Waldo Emerson to Alcott, September 7, 1836, in "Autobiographical Collections," 4:82.

27. Myerson, "Calendar of Transcendental Club Meetings," pp. 199-200; Hutchison, *Transcendentalist Ministers*, p. 31; AJ 9 (1836): 203; Sealts, ed., *Journals of Emerson*, 5: 194-95.

28. Myerson, "Calendar of Transcendental Club Meetings," pp. 200 ff; Hutchison, *Transcendentalist Ministers*, pp. 31, 50-51; AJ 9 (1836): 190, 213; Sealts, ed., *Journals of*

Emerson, 5: 218.

29. AJ 7 (1834), part 3: 35; Miller, ed., *The Transcendentalists*, pp. 14-15. Among the best general treatments of transcendentalism are, besides Miller, Paul F. Boller, Jr., *American Transcendentalism, 1830-1860*; George Hochfield, "Introduction," in *Selected Writings of the American Transcendentalists* (New York: New American Library, 1966); and Octavius B. Frothingham's old but indispensable *Transcendentalism in New England* (New York: G. P. Putnam's Sons, 1876.)

30. AJ 9 (1836): 134, 178, 239; Sealts, ed., *Journals of Emerson*, 5: 248-49.

31. AJ 9 (1836): 139, 180, 230, 236; Tharp, *Peabody Sisters*, p. 109; Elizabeth Palmer Peabody to Alcott, August 7, 1836, from a copy in Alcott's hand in "Memoir, 1878"; Miller, ed., *The Transcendentalists*, p. 331; Rusk, *Emerson*, p. 234; Margaret Fuller to Alcott, August 23, 1836, from a copy in Alcott's hand in "Autobiography, 1834."

32. AJ 9 (1836): 214-15, 219, 228, 230, 232, 236; Abby May Alcott to Chatfield Alcott, November 20, 1836, and Abby May Alcott to Mrs. Anna Alcott, November 20, 1836, from copies in Alcott's hand in "Memoir, 1878."

33. AJ 10 (1837): 56, 92, 112, 121; Samuel J. May to Abby May Alcott, January 5, 1837, from a copy in Alcott's hand in "Autobiography, 1834"; Alcott to William Russell, January 12, 1837, from a copy in Alcott's hand in "Memoir, 1878"; Alcott to Lemuel Shaw, February 18, 1837, in Herrnstadt, ed., *Letters*, p. 31; Alcott, "Autobiographical Collections," vol 4; John Ware to Alcott, February 19, 1837, Nathan Rice to Alcott, February 20, 1837, James Savage to Alcott, February 20, 1837, G. B. Cary to Alcott, [February] 19, 1837, and Lemuel Shaw to Alcott, February 21, 1837, in A. Bronson Alcott, comp., "Letters from 1836 to 1850," MS at Houghton Library, 59M-305 (2).

34. AJ 10 (1837): 162, 198, 208, 214, 217; Hutchison, *Transcendentalist Ministers*, p. 72; [Chandler Robbins], "Conversations on the Gospels," *Christian Register* 16 (March 4, 1837): 34; [Chandler Robbins], "Mr. Alcott," *Christian Register* 16 (April 29, 1837): 66-67; [Nathan Hale], "Conversations with Children on the Gospels," *Boston Daily Advertiser and Patriot* 42 (March 21, 1837); Miller, ed., *The Transcendentalists*, pp. 157-59; [Joseph H. Buckingham], "Alcott's Conversations on the Gospels," *Boston Courier*, vol. 12 (March 29, 1837); A Parent, "To Fathers and Mothers," *Boston Courier*, vol. 12 (March 30, 1837). Alcott pasted clippings of most of the articles in his "Autobiographical Collections," vol. 4.

35. AJ 10 (1837): 214, 234-35, 269; Sealts, ed., *Journals of Emerson*, 5: 298; Alcott to Chatfield Alcott, May 7, 1837, from a copy in Alcott's hand in "Memoir, 1878."

36. AJ 10 (1837), pp. 181, 208-9; Ralph Waldo Emerson to Nathan Hale, March 24, 1837, in Rusk, ed., *Letters of Emerson* 2: 60-61 [Ralph Waldo Emerson], "To the Editor of the Courier," *Boston Courier*, vol. 12 (April 4, 1837); Ralph Waldo Emerson to Alcott, March 24, 1837, in Rusk, ed., *Letters of Emerson*, 2: 62, MS in Alcott, "Autobiographical Collections," vol. 4; A Frequent Spectator [Elizabeth Peabody], "Mr. Alcott's Book and School," *Christian Register*, 16 (April 29, 1837): 65; William H. Furness to Alcott, May 5, 1837, in "Autobiographical Collections," vol. 4; [James F. Clarke], "Religious Education of Children," *Western Messenger* 3 (March 1837): 540-45; [James F. Clarke], "Mr. Alcott's Book and the Objections made to it," *Western Messenger* 3 (May 1837): 678-83.

37. AJ 10 (1837): 327-29, 337-38.

38. William Alcott's four articles were "Record of Conversations on the Gospels" (March 1837), "Story Telling in the Schools" (May 1837), "School for Moral Culture" (May 1837), and "Moral Education and Instruction" (September 1837), all in volume 7 of the *American Annals of Education and Instruction*. [James Walker], "Conversations with Children on the Gospels," *Christian Examiner* 23 (November 1837): 252-61.

39. AJ 10 (1837): 294, 350, 375-76, 437, 440-41, 454; Alcott, "Autobiographical Collections," vol. 4; Sophia Peabody to Alcott, June 9, 1837, from a copy in Alcott's hand in "Autobiography, 1834"; Anna Quincy Thaxter to Abby May Alcott, July 19, 1837, from a copy in Alcott's hand in "Autobiography, 1834"; Abby May Alcott to Elizabeth Willis, July 2, 1837, from a copy in Alcott's hand in "Memoir, 1878"; Harriet Martineau, *Society in America*, 2 vols. (New York: Saunders and Otley, 1837), 2: 277.

40. Alcott, "Autobiographical Collections," vol. 4; AJ 11 (1838): 73, 127-30, 167-68, 287-89; Samuel J. May to Alcott, August 22, 1838, from a copy in Alcott's hand in "Autobiography, 1834"; AJ 10 (1836): 558-59; Sealts, ed., *Journals of Emerson*, 5: 328.

41. AJ 11 (1838): 260, 262; Joel Myerson, " 'A True & High Minded Person' Transcendentalist Sarah Clarke," *Southwest Review* (Spring 1974), pp. 163-65; Sarah Clarke to James Freeman Clarke, April 7, 1838, and August 20, 1838, from newspaper clippings in James F. Clarke, comp., "Letters of a Sister" located at Houghton Library, bMS AM 1569.3 (12); Sarah Clarke to Alcott, May 2, 1838, from a copy in Alcott's hand in "Autobiography, 1834"; Elizabeth Palmer Peabody to Abby May Alcott, May 7, 1838, and Abby May Alcott to Mrs. Anna Alcott, May 9, 1838, from copies in Alcott's hand in "Memoir, 1878."

42. AJ 10 (1837): 95, 224.

43. Ibid., pp. 251-52.

44. Ibid., pp. 309, 503, 556; AJ 11 (1838): 262.

45. AJ 10 (1837): 297, 385, 387-90, 419, 421; Hiram Fuller to Alcott, April 24, 1837, and Samuel J. May to Alcott, June 7, 1837, from copies in Alcott's hand in "Autobiography, 1834"; Alcott to Ralph Waldo Emerson, May 9, 1837, in Herrnstadt, ed., *Letters*, pp. 31-32; Margaret Fuller to Alcott, June 27, 1837, at Houghton Library, 59M-312 (122); William H. Channing, James F. Clarke, and Ralph Waldo Emerson, eds., *Memoirs of Margaret Fuller Ossoli*, 2 vols. (Boston: Phillips, Sampson & Co., 1852), 1: 175-77; AJ 11 (1838): 499-500; Sealts, ed., *Journals of Emerson*, 5: 419.

46. AJ 8 (1835): 187-90.

47. AJ 9 (1836): 21-22, 53-55, 92, 108, 141, 237-38; Ralph Waldo Emerson to Alcott, February 27, 1836, from a copy in Alcott's hand in "Autobiography, 1834"; AJ 10 (1837): 136.

48. AJ 10 (1837): 391-97, 499-500; Abby May Alcott to Samuel J. May, October 3, 1837, in "Family Letters, 1828-1861"; AJ 11 (1838): 7-8, 149-50.

49. AJ 11 (1838): 243-45, 247; Abby May Alcott to Samuel J. May April 22, 1838, in "Family Letters, 1828-1861"; A. Bronson Alcott, "Psyche an Evangele; in Four Books" (1838), pp. 16-17, 26, 57, MS at Houghton Library, 59M-306 (9).

50. Alcott, "Psyche an Evangele," p. 43.

51. Ibid., pp. 104-5.

52. Ibid., pp. 325, 327.

53. AJ 11 (1838): 259, 265-66; Ralph Waldo Emerson to Margaret Fuller, June 28, 1838, in Rusk, ed., *Letters of Emerson*, 2:142; Ralph Waldo Emerson to Alcott, June 28, 1838, in "Autobiographical Collections," vol. 4, and printed in Rusk, ed., *Letters of Emerson*, 2: 138-41.

54. AJ 12 (January-July 1839): 83-84, 195-96; AJ 13 (July-December 1839): 6.

55. Abby May Alcott to Samuel J. May, April 22, 1838, and October 3, 1837, in "Family Letters, 1828-1861"; Abby May Alcott, "Autobiography"; AJ 11 (1838): 270-71; AJ 12 (January-July 1839): p. 607; Abby May Alcott to Mrs. Joseph May, June 3, 1838, Abby May Alcott to Joseph May, June 3, 1838, and February 3, 1839, from copies in Alcott's hand in "Memoir, 1878."

56. Alcott, "Autobiographical Index"; AJ 11 (1838): 267, 288, 315, 323, 367; Samuel J. May to Alcott, August 22, 1838, and November 3, 1838, from copies in Alcott's hand in "Autobiography, 1834"; Alcott, "Autobiographical Collections," vol. 4; AJ 12 (January-July 1839): 501, 696, 911.

57 AJ 10 (1837): 100, 156, 209; AJ 12 (January-July 1839): 889, 918; Alcott to Ralph Waldo Emerson, June 6, 1837, in Herrnstadt, ed., *Letters,* pp. 33-34.

58. AJ 10 (1837): 541.

59. Ibid., pp. 133, 168-69, 192-95; AJ 11 (1838): 45-52.

60. AJ 10 (1837): 138-39, 229, 272, 378; AJ 11 (1838): 458; AJ 12 (January-July 1839): 838.

61. AJ 10 (1837): 463; AJ 12 (January-July 1839): 94, 828; AJ 13 (July-December 1839): 332.

62. AJ 10 (1837): 106-7, 267-68; AJ 11 (1838): 118, 300-302, 463-64; AJ 12 (January-July 1839): 514-15; Miller, ed., *The Transcendentalists*, pp. 192-98; Hutchison, *Transcendentalist Ministers*, pp. 64-70; Andrews Norton, "The New School in Literature and Religion," *Boston Daily Advertiser*, vol. 43 (August 27, 1838); "Emerson's Address," *Christian Examiner* 25 (November 1838): 266-68.

63. AJ 10 (1837): 381-82; AJ 11 (1838): 411-13; AJ 12 (1839) (January-July): 165-66, 609-11.

64. AJ 13 (July-December 1839): 53-55: Miller, ed., *The Transcendentalists*, p. 210.

65. AJ 13 (July-December 1839), pp. 54, 201, 276; Miller, ed., *The Transcendentalists*, pp. 213-15.

66. AJ 11 (1838): 356; Miller. ed. *The Transcendentalists*, pp. 180 ff., 186; Myerson, "Calendar of Transcendental Club Meetings"; AJ 10 (1837): 144, 315-18, 593-94, 598-600; AJ 12 (January-July 1839): pp. 101-2.

67. AJ 11 (1838): 439-40, 466, 498; Jones Very to Alcott, December 8, 1838, from a copy in Alcott's hand in ibid., pp. 441-46; Miller, ed., *The Transcendentalists*, pp. 344 ff; AJ 12 (January-July 1839): 207-9, 880.

68. Samuel E. Sewall to Alcott, April 13, 1831, in "Autobiographical Collections," 3: 208; Abby May Alcott to Samuel J. May, January 19, 1834, and March 11, 1834, from copies in Alcott's hand in "Autobiographical Materials"; AJ 7 (1834), part 2: 131-32, 157-59, 304; AJ 10 (1837): 462; AJ 8 (1835): 177-83, 442; Thomas, *The Liberator*, pp. 175 ff.; Bacon, *Quiet Rebels*, p. 105; AJ 54 (1878): 601-2.

69. AJ 11 (1838): 57-60, 505-6; AJ 12 (January-July 1839): 551.

70. Thomas, *The Liberator*, pp. 257-62; AJ 12 (January-July 1839): 551; AJ 11 (1838): 307-10; William Lloyd Garrison to Samuel J. May, September 24, 1838, in Louis Ruchames, ed., *The Letters of William Lloyd Garrison*, 2 (1836-40) (Cambridge, Mass.: Harvard University Press, 1971): 401-2.

71. Richard H. Shyrock, "Sylvester Graham and the Popular Health Movement," *Mississippi Valley Historical Review* 18 (September, 1931): 172-83; AJ 11 (1836): 45-46; Alcott, "Autobiographical Index"; AJ 10 (1837): 36-43, 158-61; AJ 11 (1838): 159-64; Alcott, "Observations on the Spiritual Nurture of My Children," pp. 25-26.

72. AJ 10 (1837): 434; AJ 11 (1838): 137, 141-44, 476-78; AJ 12 (January-July 1839): 840.

73. AJ 10 (1837): 143, 178-79; AJ 13 (July-December 1839): 317-19; AJ 11 (1838): 69-71.

74. AJ 10 (1837): 97; AJ 11 (1838), p. 86.

75. AJ 12 (January-July 1839): 357.

76. AJ 11 (1838): 91, 283-84; AJ 12 (January-July 1839): 825-30.

77. Jonathan Messerli, *Horace Mann* (New York: Alfred A. Knopf, 1972), pp. 247, 249; AJ 11 (1838): 179-80, 221-25; AJ 12 (January-July 1839): 444; AJ 13 (1839) (July-December): 462.

78. AJ 10 (1837): 10-11.

79. Ibid., p. 289; AJ 13 (July-December 1839): 169.

80. This is Alcott quoting Emerson in AJ 10 (1837): 355.

81. AJ 10 (1837): 356-57, 368-70; AJ 12 (January-July 1839): 763-65.

82. AJ 13 (July-December 1839): 139; AJ 12 (January-July 1839): 696.

83. From an unidentified newspaper clipping in AJ 13 (July-December 1839): 260-61.

84. AJ 13 (July-December 1839): 317-19, 489; AJ 12 (January-July 1839): 243-44, 675-77, 746.

85. AJ 13 (July-December 1839): 9, 144; AJ 10 (1837): 342; AJ 11 (1838): 66-68; 235-36; AJ 12 (January-July 1839): 928-32, 952.

86. AJ 11 (1838), pp. 20-27.

87. Ibid., pp. 303-5, 311, 331, 335, 369-71, 375, 379, 381, 387, 392, 437, 462, 468, 469, 483; Anna Quincy Thaxter to Alcott, September 23, 1838, from a copy in Alcott's hand in "Autobiography, 1834."

88. AJ 11 (1838): 368, 390, 401, 417, 433, 503; AJ 12 (January-July 1839): 174, 178-79; A. W. Plumstead and Harrison Hayford, eds., *The Journals and Miscellaneous Manuscripts of Ralph Waldo Emerson*, vol. 7 (1838-42) (Cambridge, Mass.: Harvard University Press, 1969), p. 177.

89. AJ 12 (January-July 1839), pp. 379-81, 625-26, 716; [Parsons Cooke], "Transcendentalism Translated," *Boston Recorder* (April 19, 1839). Alcott pasted a clipping of this into his "Autobiographical Collections," 4: 199-207.

90. AJ 13 (July-December 1839): pp. 89, 99, 257-59, 464; Alcott to Mrs. Anna Alcott, December 28, 1839, from a copy in Alcott's hand in ibid., pp. 503-8.

Abigail May Alcott. By permission of the Louisa May Alcott Memorial Association.

Anna Bronson Alcott Pratt. By permission of the Louisa May Alcott Memorial Association.

Louisa May Alcott. By permission of the Louisa May Alcott Memorial Association.

Elizabeth Sewall Alcott. By permission of the Louisa May Alcott Memorial Association.

May Alcott Nieriker. By permission of the Louisa May Alcott Memorial Association.

The farmhouse at Fruitlands as it looks today. Photograph by George M. Cushing. Courtesy of the Fruitlands Museums.

Orchard House as it looked in the 1860s, with Bronson Alcott's hand-hewn fence in the foreground. By permission of the Louisa May Alcott Memorial Association.

Bronson Alcott with his journals in his study at Orchard House. By permission of the Concord Free Public Library.

Bronson Alcott's Hillside Chapel, which housed the Concord School of Philosophy. By permission of the Louisa May Alcott Memorial Association.

An interior view of the Hillside Chapel. By permission of the Louisa May Alcott Memorial Association.

7
Fruitlands, 1840–45

As his personal crisis deepened in the late 1830s and early 1840s, Alcott turned more and more to his manuscript diaries for solace and comfort. The diaries ballooned in size during those years, from two hundred fifty pages in 1836, to six hundred in 1837, to five hundred in 1838, to thirteen hundred sixty pages in two volumes in 1839. In those pages, with their neatly arranged captions and margins and their careful handwriting, Alcott attempted to bring order to his thought, order that would vicariously compensate for the disorder and chaos in his personal life. He sought to explain the nature of the universe; the nature of God; the nature of human beings; the relationship between the universe, God, and human beings; the purpose of human existence; the presence of evil; and the means of human salvation or regeneration. He and his transcendentalist contemporaries had found the traditional answers to these questions, as provided by the Church and by Scripture, to be unsatisfactory in a world of rapid change. Alcott's nineteenth-century world was confronting ideas of change, movement, progress, evolution, organic growth, and decay. His philosophical system had to allow for these concepts of motion; it had to explain, even suggest means of controlling, the process of change, which had so affected him personally since his early days in Wolcott.

But the life of the mind could not completely satisfy Alcott. He still sought action, positive reform. With the encouragement of friends from England, he launched a new, even more dramatic reform effort: the establishment of an ideal community. This short-lived experiment of 1843 showed Alcott in his most exciting, interesting, and picturesque moments. It also showed him at his worst. His narrowness and intolerance helped bring his community to an end after only seven months. The two years that followed found him at the lowest points of his life, abashed and disconsolate.

Alcott and the transcendentalists participated in a "kinetic revolution." That is, they integrated into their world view an explanation of change and motion and the imagery that best expressed it: moving water, fountains, birth—symbols of the ceaseless activity of spirit.[1]They combined ideas of change and movement with traditional religious concepts of God, sin, salvation, grace, and the belief in a meaningful universe. With this they synthesized Enlightenment ideas about the potential of human nature, especially human rational powers, to understand and manipulate a mechanically ordered natural world and to bring goodness, truth, and harmony to it. Alcott's attempts to systematize his ideas reflected his effort to grasp what was a sweeping and complex intellectual transformation.

Central to Alcott's system, as he explained and defined it in the late 1830s, was his concept of the universe, a universe that he assumed to be good or benevolent. For Alcott, all parts, all aspects, of the universe, including human beings, were different manifestations of one spiritual essence. The spirit was a living, changing, creating, unifying agent. "Every man's life," he said, "is but a phase of the *One Divine Nature* that flows through all visible things, by whose subtle breath all are fed and sustained." The spirit had neither beginning nor end. It was present at all times; it was the one constant and predictable element amid flux. "It unites opposites. It demolishes all disturbing forces. It melts all solid and obstinate matters. It makes fluid of the material universe. It hopes even in despair—believes in the midst of doubts—apprehends stability and order, even in confusion and anarchy."[2]

God, then, was spirit. Or rather, the Godhead was spirit. Alcott believed that God, human beings, and the material world were three separate manifestations of the Godhead. Therefore, God was the unifying aspect of the Godhead, the synthesis, the identity, of everything in the universe, and this identity was hidden beneath the diverse manifestations of creation. In October 1838 Orestes Brownson wrote an excellent critique of Alcott's ideas of the Godhead in his *Boston Quarterly Review*. Brownson, who was reviewing *Conversations on the Gospels*, both praised Alcott for his courage and his pure motives and also carefully criticized and analyzed his ideas. He argued that Alcott had, in effect, identified the Creation with the Creator and thus had come perilously close to pantheism. Brownson believed that though God was immanent in his creation, He was also above and separate from it. In his conversations during late 1838 and 1839, Alcott faced constant clamor about the "pantheism" or "atheism" of his doctrine of the Godhead. Even members of the Transcendental Club disputed with Alcott and Emerson about the alleged pantheism of their ideas of God. The Godhead became a subject of heated debate by the Club in 1838 and 1839. George Ripley believed that Alcott denied the existence of any superior divinity by identifying the human soul with God. Convers Francis condemned Alcott's ideas of the Godhead as atheism. Alcott angrily denied the charges of atheism and pantheism. He had not denied a divinity superior to human beings, he said; the universal spirit was just such a superior divinity. And he had not precisely identified the creation with the Creator. The material world, though created by the spirit, was not divine itself; it merely symbolized or shadowed forth the divinity. Pantheism, he declared, was a convenient term of approbrium used to cast doubt on his ideas without allowing them an adequate hearing. Nevertheless, he did believe in the divinity of the human soul, something the ministers, even the transcendentalist ministers, could not accept.[3]

The material world in Alcott's scheme was that manifestation of the Godhead which represented the struggle of the spirit to present itself to the senses and reason of human beings. The spirit presented itself in the material world in the form of symbols, types, and emblems that were understandable to humans and thus able to shape the concept of the spirit in human consciousness. But the material world could never represent all of the spirit. The spirit was constantly in flux, in motion. It only seemed stable for a brief moment as represented by the material world. Thus, growth and decay, as evidenced in the material world, were also symbols of the spirit, representing the spirit in flux. Such was Alcott's "spiritual calculus." It corresponded to the epistemological calculus of Locke and Bacon, that process by which knowledge arose from an interaction between human beings and the external world.[4]

Human beings were also a manifestation of the spirit. Souls sprang from the Godhead wherein they preexisted and were thus divine. The true Christian, Alcott believed, was one who accepted the identity of his or her soul with God. A knowledge of one's soul and its potential was a knowledge of God. The soul was a divine revelation. "God is revealed to him [a human being], by the measure in which he apprehends the divinity of his own soul." Thus the spirit unfolded itself in the human soul. The soul, being divine, was superior to time, to sense, to the material world. There were no limits to the soul's potential.[5]

Alcott believed that the human body was a creation of the divine human soul. The body was just a temporary material form, he felt: "Enwombed in matter, incarnated in flesh, entombed in clay, it [the soul] dates itself in time, and marks its history in space; but passes on, in the cycle of its own eternity, no longer an embodied spirit." He took issue with the phrenologists, who, he believed, taught that the shape of bodily organs largely determined the nature of the soul. Alcott was sure that the soul determined the shape of bodily organs. Upon hearing George Combe lecture in October 1838, Alcott declared himself an unbeliever in these ideas that had once so fascinated him. The health, the growth, and the integrity of the body, he asserted, were directly related to the "free and full action of the soul." This was why he found Sylvester Graham so interesting. He preceived that Graham's crusade was an attempt to subordinate the body to the soul.[6]

It was Alcott's faith in the power of the divine soul that made his ideas such a radical challenge to existing institutions. For him the soul was the "measure of all things." By 1839 he was claiming that external material things, the facts of experience, were all a creation of each soul. No external object, no fact, was the same for two or more persons. The solidity of external objects was an illusion, for matter was constantly in flux. The vital action of souls determined the shape and character of external material things, including the human body. Alcott's extreme individualism of the late 1830s and 1840s led him to elaborate at great lengths on the sovereign power of the soul and the mode of its action. He borrowed the faculty theory of Locke and the empiricists, and built upon Coleridge's distinction between the "understanding" and the "reason," in order to construct his own theory of the soul's faculties. He distinguished between faculties of the soul that made use of or analyzed knowledge already obtainable in the external world and those which perceived truth directly. In the first category (which corresponded to Coleridge's understanding) he put sense perception, the intellect, and memory. In the latter category (which corresponded to Coleridge's reason) he put instinct, faith, hope, and conscience. The higher faculties of the soul had the power to perceive truth directly and immediately. They needed no associatons with external objects; they needed no steps of logic. They were instincts of the divine soul for good, truth, and beauty.[7]

The more Alcott elaborated on the divine power of the soul, the more he contradicted his earlier beliefs, especially his idea of the spiritual calculus, the process by which external symbols awakened the inner consciousness of the spirit. For if the individual soul created all external things, and these external things were different for each person, how could they serve as emblematic facilitators of the spirit? In his haste to defend the sovereignty of the soul, he was unknowingly destroying the superstructure of his carefully developed reform theories. Further, his paeans to the soul led him right back to the problem of evil, which he still had not sufficiently explained. He assumed that the universe was good, that the spirit was good, that the soul was good, but these assumptions left no account of evil. He had to explain how evil occurred, especially in his years of trial when there seemed to be an inordinate amount of evil around.

For a man who preferred to dwell on the positive, on visions of perfectibility, explaining evil was a tiresome and unpleasant task. But without such an explanation, his view of good would make no sense. He began with a concept of sin. Sin, he explained, resulted from the ability of the soul to alienate itself from God or the spirit. Sin was "analysis," that is, the breaking down of the oneness or unity of the spirit into parts. Sin caused the soul to "descend into matter," to lapse from original holiness. This "lapse" was not "original," predetermined, or necessay, but rather resulted from the choice of each individual soul. It was possible, he thought, for the soul to retain its original holiness, its perfection, and to avoid a lapse, a separation from the oneness of the spirit. But sin did occur, and its results were degeneration, degradation, suffering, cruelty, disease, war, and a multitude of other unpleasantnesses. Alcott attempted to explain how lapse occurred by using his concept of the faculties. He suggested that the lower faculties, those of the sense and the understanding, seduced or beguiled the higher faculties of faith, instinct, and conscience, thereby causing the soul to fall or lapse.[8]

But this concept of sin raised all sorts of logical difficulties within Alcott's philosophical system. If the soul was divine and had an instinct for the good, true, and beautiful, why should it sin or fall? How could a lower faculty beguile a higher one? The idea of lapse as a "descent into matter," as disunity and fragmentation, contradicted his ideas about the goodness of the process of creation. He had earlier explained the creation of souls by God as the expression of God's nature, that God or the spirit *was* creativity, *was* a continuing process of becoming.[9] Thus in one breath he said that the creation of the material world by the soul was an expression of the spirit's creativity and life, while in the next he said that the whole process was the result of sin. Alcott's idea of sin also contradicted his view of the child as the embodiment of innocence and purity. For, according to his theory of the lapse, an innocent and pure soul would not have taken the shape of a human body in the first place.

Thus, in explaining sin and evil Alcott developed a contradictory, dual view of the material world. On the one hand, he saw it as the spirit's creation, the symbol of the spirit at work, and an instrument by which humans became conscious of the spirit within. On the other hand, he saw it as the result of sin, the symbol of evil, even as the apalling excrement or defecation of the spirit.[10] The latter view—that matter was the result of sin—was a product of Alcott's years of despair, of his rejection of institutions and society, and hs withdrawal into extreme individualism. All external things—people, institutions, customs—smacked of evil. Instead of symbolizing the spirit, they had come to symbolize his powerlessness and his frustration. Yet he never rejected the more appealing, positive view of the material world. Without reconciling the two ideas, he could still appreciate the beauty and the spiritual symbolism of the material world, as did Emerson and Thoreau, while retaining his disturbing and unattractive explanation of evil.

Once he had explained sin, at least to his own satisfaction, he had to develop further his concept of salvation or regeneration. Since he believed in the divinity of the soul, it followed that he also believed that the soul had the means of its own salvation. All souls, he said, retained a lingering knowledge of their original divinity and perfectibility no matter how far they had lapsed because of sin. To avoid sin, and thereby to ascend back to purity and glory, the soul had to become aware of its true nature. Prior to 1837 Alcott's means of awakening, thus saving, souls was education. Although education was still important to him after 1837, he increasingly emphasized the inner action of the individual soul as the means of personal regeneration. His rejection of things external, his growing belief that they were manifestations of evil, caused him to back away from his once firm belief that salvation resulted from an interaction between humans and external things. Now salvation was more a matter of introspection, communion with one's own soul. It was as though his failures had made him uneasy and uncertain about his own standing in the eyes of God. He sought assurance that his soul would not lapse by exploring things he could do to restore his own primeval innocence. The means of salvation became a matter of personal discipline that would hopefully facilitate an intuitive communion with God. He talked of "living true to the Idea of the Perfect" and living in accordance with the "diviner faculties" of the soul, the instinct and conscience, rather than the lower faculties of sense perception.[11] The faculty of conscience was especially important:

Within Conscience, was the divine theocracy of the soul administered; which, like the agency of gravitation on the material world, reduces all the faculties and members of the soul to harmony and order. By conformity to its will, all are unfolded into the fullness of Beauty.[12]

This was regeneration through obedience to a spiritual law as revealed by the conscience. The shadow of Jonathan Edwards was looming larger than ever about Alcott. The exiting, hopeful talk of the early 1830s about free will and free expression was becoming lost amid Alcott's growing concern about the obligations laid on the soul by conscience. He spoke of the awful retributions of conscience and the "unerring justice" of their execution. Salvation was now a matter of religious inspiration, whereby the laws of the spirit were revealed through the conscience to those willing to obey. It was an idea harking back to the Great Awakening. Alcott had come to believe, as Edwards had, that the truly free will was one that obeyed the laws of God. Such an idea had been latent in his educational theories, but his hopefulness and faith in human goodness had meliorated the emphasis on obedience and discipline. Now in his years of despair, personal discipline and obedience gained a new importance for him.[13]

Alcott's idea of conscience was suspiciously like the Calvinistic idea of grace. And although he believed salvation possible for all persons, his concept of "genius" came uncomfortably close to the Calvinistic doctrine of election. His description of genius was the portrait of a person saved; it was a description of himself, or what he hoped to become. Genius, he said, was the herald of the inner life of the soul. He desperately tried to convince himself that he was saved, that he had genius, that he was among the elect:

> Amidst humblest, scantiest means, [genius] finds occasion for worthy labor. He draweth from these food for self-culture. He endows the emptiness of his lot with affluence of thought and nobleness of deed. Despair does not visit him. He yet feeds on Hope. He yet builds on faith. He finds his own gifts.[15]

But ideas about genius, about the workings of conscience, about communion with the divine, were too vague and uncertain to give Alcott full assurance of salvation. He sought actions and "works" that would convince him that he was indeed following the divine laws of conscience, and that all obstructions to that life of obedience were removed. First of all, he convinced himself that a purification process would enhance the soul's chances for regeneration. "Chaste souls possess clean bodies," he said. "Their members are unpolluted: their functions undefiled." Temperance in all things, he claimed, was the "herald of genius," the "preamble of holiness." Daily regimen in the style of Sylvester Graham could enhance the divine activity of the soul: early rising, walking, diligence in work; the avoidance of gluttony, drunkenness, sloth, "lusts," and excess of any kind. "Excess hath sickened, let abstinence restore the balance of thy nature." Self-denial prepared the soul for an awakening, a communion with the divine. "Subdue thyself," he declared, "and know the might that lies within thee."[16]

Another means of his attaining assurance of salvation was his effort to spread his message to others. "Thou wouldst be useful," he said. "It is an instinct of an unspoiled soul: a desire to actualize its ideal in other souls, by ministering to their well-being, and this is noble." It was evidence of the purity of a soul that it spoke out against the evils and evildoers of society even though such action was an "unspeakable offense to advocates of existing evils, opinions, usages, [and] institutions." Martyrdom to truth was a sure sign of the soul's return to purity and innocence.[17]

By 1840 Alcott had developed a philosophy, albeit filled with contradictions, that explained his suffering and failure, justified his life-style and goals, and reinforced his sense of mission to regenerate the age. But it also reflected a deep-seated insecurity that led in turn to a tyrannical asceticism. His efforts to convince himself of salvation through outward actions and daily habits caused him to impose rigorous behavioral standards on himself and those around him. His belief that antagonism to institutions and societal structures was further evidence of salvation led him to reject bitterly anything over which he had no control. Encouragement from abroad pushed him further down this road to ruin.

In October 1837 Alcott received a lengthy letter from James Pierrepont Greaves of London, England. Greaves, a former merchant, had lost his business during the wars with France because of Napoleon's economic blockades. Shortly thereafter, he reportedly had what by his own description was a "mystical" experience that drove him to Switzerland and to a four-year tutelage under Johann Pestalozzi at Yverdun. Filled with Pestalozzian ideas about education and child development, he had returned to England in 1825 an enthusiastic reformer, committed to the establishment of Pestalozzian infant schools and to popularizing Pestalozzian methods. Ironically, Greaves had heard of Alcott through Harriet Martineau, one of Alcott's harshest critics, who had given him a copy of *Record of a School*. Greaves was so impressed with the *Record* that he wanted to drop everything and sail to America to meet Alcott and visit his school. But first he sent Alcott a long list of questions about Alcott's methods and ideas, along with comments explaining his own practices.[18]

Alcott was gratified that a disciple of the great Pestalozzi had appreciated his efforts. However, he hesitated answering Greaves's letter because he feared further misapprehension. The public hostility engendered by *Conversations on the Gospels* in the spring of 1837 had caused him to doubt his ability to convey a full and true account of his ideas. And he hated to tell the admiring Greaves about the failure of his school. But Greaves pursued the matter and sent Alcott copies of his own pamphlets on education. His *Three Hundred Maxims for the Consideration of Parents* impressed Alcott by its strong assertion of the "sacredness of the soul." By June 1838 a fascinated Alcott had gathered several copies of both *Record of a School* and *Conversations on the Gospels* to send to his English counterpart. Greaves remained impressed; he thought *Conversations on the Gospels* was an "invaluable" work. Finally, in April 1839 Alcott wrote to Greaves telling of his troubles and hoping that he would hear more of Greaves's plans and the work of Greaves's small circle of reformist friends.[19]

Soon Alcott began receiving letters from Greaves's associates: J. Westland Marston, Richard Kennett, William Oldham, and Charles Lane. He became interested in the *New Monthly Magazine*, edited by Greaves's friend John Abraham Heraud, which was a vehicle for Greaves's reform theories. Alcott called it "the flower of current literature in Europe." Even more exciting to Alcott was Heraud's promise to publish and write an introduction to an English edition of *Conversations on the Gospels.*[20]

These English reformers said what Alcott wanted to hear in 1839. They talked about reforming individuals by first detaching them from Church and State. They confirmed and reinforced his growing emphasis on the solitary individual, his increasing desire to withdraw from institutions and social structures. Through Heraud's *Magazine* he heard of English reform movements, of the Chartists, and of communitarianism—especially Owenism. The *Magazine* induced him to read *Letters on Social Science* by William Hawkes Smith, a Birmingham reformer, Unitarian, and phrenologist, and a friend of Robert Owen. This book introduced him to the ideas of the French communitarians Charles Fourier and Claud Henri de Saint-Simon. It told of Owen's current efforts to establish communities in England, which recalled Alcott's former interest in Owen's American experiment at New Harmony. All of these things confirmed Alcott's belief that his was indeed an era of revolutionary change. The "newness" extended far beyond Boston and the United States. It was worldwide.[21]

Heraud's *New Monthly Magazine* also contained literary essays, poetry, and articles on German philosophy. Heraud himself was a poet and a student of German ideas. Alcott was able to interest some of his American friends in the *Magazine*. Emerson, Margaret Fuller, George Ripley, and John Dwight joined him in considering plans for a periodical that would serve as a vehicle for new ideas, for a new literature in America, just as Heraud's *Magazine* did in England. Heraud also acknowledged Alcott's contributions to education in book of essays called *The Educator*. He praised Alcott for putting into practice the sentiments of Wordsworth and Coleridge on childhood. Educators in England would do well, he declared, to adopt similar methods based on Alcott's "lofty ideas of man."[22]

Greaves, Heraud, and the other English reformers gave Alcott enough encouragement in the midst of doubt and despair to keep him at his "old trade of Hoping" as he told his mother. Abby was sure that one day he would go to England and find the recognition that America failed to provide. But hope could not always put food on the table. In January and February 1840 he received fifty-five dollars for conversations and twenty dollars for tutoring Susan Robinson. It was not enough. He began looking for an escape from the city which, as a symbol of his failure and his poverty, increasingly angered and disgusted him. "Bacchus holds court in the cities," he claimed. It was a seat of corruption. He sought the pure country air and the "poetry" of the work of the husbandman on the rural landscape. It was the country, he thought, that had preserved his purity as a child; it could now save him from the degradation and ugliness he found in Boston.[23]

Samuel J. May offered to find a home for the Alcotts in Scituate, near him, but Alcott preferred Concord, which he thought had better soil both for his crops and for his ideas. There he would be close to Emerson. He found a small cottage about a mile from Emerson's and a quarter mile from the center of the village. It had a large garden and an acre of land and rented for fifty dollars a year. He sold his schoolroom furniture to pay for garden tools and hay. During the first week of April 1840 the family left Boston for Concord. "I shake off the dust of my endeavors upon this city, wherein I have sought to demonstrate the True Culture. This people will not sustain me. My labors here have been coldly met by my townsmen." He had given everything to Boston, he thought: his time, his affection, his skill, and six thousand dollars of other people's money. It had given him nothing in return. Now he would give the toil of his own hands, and the soil would surely repay.[24]

The man Emerson had called the "highest genius of the time" was now a simple gardener and day laborer, planting his crops, mowing, and cradling grain for his neighbors.[25] Abby was pleased at the prospect of a steady source of food, although she too was embittered by the treatment her native city had given her husband. "It is a low state of moral discrimination," she said,

> which will give the man an honorable discharge who has been twenty years gambling in fancy stocks, but drives into the regions of starvation an exalted spirit whose desires and efforts for twenty of the best years of his life, has been to elevate and improve the moral and intellectual condition of mankind.[26]

Alcott was pleased with the chance for useful work and an income, meager as it was. Yet it bothered him that by working for a living he was also earning the favor of "merchants and brokers," a class of persons he did not wish to please.[27]

Alcott explained the family's situation plainly and patiently to his children. Nine-year-old Anna wrote in her diary:

> Father told us how people had treated him, and why we came to live at Concord, and how we must give up a good many things that we like. I know it will be hard, but I mean to do it. I fear I shall complain sometimes about it.

Anna soon began attending a school taught by Mr. Henry Thoreau, whose teaching methods, she thought, were very much like those of her father.[28]

Alcott's friend Anna Thaxter commended him for dignifying the manual occupations and the laboring classes by giving them the beauty of his "pure and holy life." Dr. Channing was pleased that Alcott was combining labor and culture, one of Channing's dearest ideas. Alcott tried to do just that by his daily routine at "Concordia," as he called his cottage. He spent mornings teaching his younger children, afternoons laboring outdoors, and evening with reading, with his friends, or with occasional conversations. He even retained hopes of teaching at one of Concord's district schools, but the town, at that time an agricultural community of 1,800 people, homogeneous, mostly of English descent, largely Unitarian, refused him the job. "I wish people thought half as much of a man's life and bearing to his neighbors as they do about some crinkle in his creed," Abby complained, "but it always has and always will be so." Despite the snub, the Alcotts were happy in their country home by the summer of 1840, and even happier with the birth of a fourth daughter, Abby May, born on July 24.[29]

The Transcendental Club continued to meet—five times in 1840, though Alcott attended only three of the sessions. And much excitement surrounded the founding of a new transcendental journal, the *Dial*. The members of the Club had first seriously discussed a journal to convey their ideas at a meeting at Cyrus Bartol's on September 18, 1839. There had been talk of such a journal earlier. In fact, Emerson once had asked Thomas Carlyle to come to America to take part in it. But the idea lay dormant until the appearance of Heraud's *New Monthly Magazine* in January 1839 caused renewed interest. There was also growing dissatisfaction with the narrow political perspective of Brownson's *Boston Quarterly Review*, which had served partially as a transcendental vehicle up to that time. Alcott suggested the name *Dial*. He had used the word to symbolize the soul as an index to the spirit. The soul, he said, was a dial by which the spirit marked its work just as the sundial marked the motion of the sun.[30]

Margaret Fuller agreed to edit the new journal. Emerson, Ripley, and Dwight promised to contribute to the first issue, and Fuller wrote to William H. Channing in Cincinnati and to Frederic Hedge in Bangor asking them to send something. The first issue appeared in July 1840. It was nobly advertised as a vehicle for "the freest expression of thought." It would "recognize every sincere production of genius" and would "reverently seek to discover the presence of God in nature, in history, and the soul of man."[31]

Alcott worked excitedly throughout the spring of 1840 on his contribution to the first issue of the *Dial*, which was to be a series of apothegms he called "Orphic Sayings." These sayings represented Alcott's latest attempt to find a suitable means of expression. His attempts at the prose essay, his "Psyche," had been a miserable failure. But apothegms, he thought, were like pulsations of the heart. They expressed to the reader the core, the essence, of an author's mind without "insignificant detail." Once again he laid bare his work for Emerson's critical eye. Once again he failed to impress. Emerson did not like the "Sayings." Though they contained some good things, he said, they also contained Alcott's "inveterate faults," meaning the same airiness, verbosity, and lack of concreteness that had plagued "Psyche." He informed Margaret Fuller and George Ripley, who was assisting her as editor, that they would not like the "Sayings" either, but that they ought to print them anyway. Those who knew Alcott, he said, would "have his voice in their ear as they read." He feared that Alcott would never write as well as he talked. After reading the "Sayings" Margaret Fuller agreed with Emerson. She found them "grand" but also often "grandiloquent." Yet she printed them. Fifty of the "Orphic Sayings" appeared in the July issue of the *Dial* and fifty more in the January 1841 issue. Despite his dislike of them, Emerson was glad the "Sayings" were a part of the *Dial's* first issue. All the other articles, he noted, could easily have appeared in other journals. The "Sayings" were at least unique and distinctive and helped set the *Dial* apart as a vehicle for the new and different.[32]

The "Sayings" began with an explanation of the dial image:

Thou art, my heart, a soul-flower, facing ever and following the motions of thy sun, opening thyself to her vivifying ray, and pleading thy affinity with celestial orbs. Thou dost "the livelong day Dial on time thine own eternity."

Those that followed were expressions of his favorite ideas: the spirit, the soul, the conscience, revelation, reform, genius. In the light of his philosophical system the "Sayings" made sense. For example, his glorification of the soul:

Every soul feels at times her own possibility of becoming a God; she cannot rest in the human, she aspires after the Godlike. This instinctive tendency is an authentic augury of its own fulfillment. Men shall become Gods. Every act of admiration, prayer, praise, worship, desire, hope implies and predicts the future apotheosis of the soul.

But to anyone unfamiliar with Alcott and the overall structure of his philosophy—and that was almost everyone—the "Sayings" were meaningless, even absurd. A few were mystifying even to those who understood Alcott's larger system:

The popular genesis is historical. It is written to sense not to the soul. Two principles, diverse and alien, interchange the Godhead and sway the world by turns. God is dual. Spirit is derivative. Identity halts in diversity. Unity is actual merely. The poles of things are not integrated: creation globed and orbed. Yet in the true genesis, nature is globed in the material, souls orbed in the spiritual firmament. Love globes, wisdom orbs, all things. As magnet the steel, so spirit attracts matter, which trembles to traverse the poles of diversity, and rests in the bosom of unity. All genesis is of love. Wisdom is her form: beauty her costume.

Like "Psyche an Evangele," his "Sayings" contained a confusing mixture of prophecy and philosophy, of prayerful apostrophe and didactic declaration. As philosophy they were useless because there was no thread tying them together in a system. As prophecy they were powerless because of their lack of concrete, captivating, or inspiring imagery. Margaret Fuller told Alcott that his ideas were magnificent but his expression of them was cold and unimpressive. "The break of your spirit in the crag of the actual," she said, "makes surf and foam but leaves no gem behind. Yet it is a great wave Mr. Alcott."[33]

The "Orphic Sayings" made the *Dial* a laughing stock. One unsympathetic newspaper referred to it as "the ravings of Alcott and his fellow zanies." Alcott, who unlike most of the other contributors blithely signed his "Sayings," once again became the subject of public ridicule. The *Knickerbocker* parodied Alcott with its "Gastric Sayings" of November 1840: "The popular cookery is dietetical. . . . Appetite is dual. Satiety is derivative. Simplicity halts in compounds. Mastication is actual merely. . . ." Even his transcendentalist friends snickered. Dr. Channing said he was amused rather than edified by the "Sayings." Supporters of the *Dial* were disappointed, believing the editors capable of better things. Orestes Brownson praised it for "rich thought" but attacked it for its "puerile and childish" expression. Alcott was not pleased either. He wrote to John Heraud to say that he liked the *New Monthly Magazine* better. The *Dial* was not venturesome enough for him. Like Emerson, he believed that there was little that was unique or distinctive. It was too "awed by the bearing of existing order," he judged, to be a truly revolutionary periodical.[34]

Alcott made just one other significant contribution to the pages of the *Dial*. He submitted some selections from his Diary for 1841, which appeared as "Days from a Diary" in the April 1842 issue. At that time he sent a letter to Margaret Fuller criticizing the *Dial* and his relationship to it. "The Dial prefers a style of thought and diction not mine," he told her, "nor can I add to its popularity with its chosen readers. A fit organ for such as myself is not yet, but is to be. The times require a free speech, a wise, humane, and brave sincerity, unlike all examples in literature, of which the *Dial* is but the precursor. A few years more will give us all we desire—the people all they ask." Margaret Fuller printed the letter in the April 1842 issue.[35]

Although the *Dial* and his public reception disappointed Alcott, there were several other transcendental activities that won his interest. Indeed, 1840 was a time of wonderful excitement, as Emerson told Carlyle:

> We are all a little wild here with numberless projects of social reform. Not a reading man but has a draft of a new Community in his waistcoat pocket. I am gently mad myself, and am resolved to live cleanly. George Ripley is talking up a colony of agriculturalists & scholars with whom he threatens to take the field & the book. One man renounces the use of animal food; & another of coin; & another of domestic hired service; & another of the state; and on the whole we have a commendable share of reason & hope.[36]

Alcott and Emerson talked of a "University" to be established in Concord to spread the "newness" to interested young people. Besides Alcott and Emerson the proposed faculty was to include Parker, Ripley, Hedge, George Bradford, and Margaret Fuller. In October 1840 Ripley proposed his community of the "friends of the new order," with labor and living in common. It was interesting, but Alcott and Emerson preferred a "simpler New Eden," Alcott wishing to preserve the sacredness of the individual and the family. When George and Sophia Ripley began Brook Farm in West Roxbury in April 1841,

Alcott and Emerson did not go along. Emerson did propose that the increasingly destitute Alcott family move in with his family in a plan of mutual cooperation. At the time Alcott was earning only seventy-five cents a day for cradling and mowing because his neighbors, according to Abby, thought him a "gentleman" who would only work at the tip ends of his fingers. Nevertheless, the Alcotts rejected Emerson's proposal mainly because Abby feared losing her independence by moving "into the orbit of another."[37]

The spirit of "newness" was also evident at the various religious and reform conventions held in the early 1840s, which lured Alcott away from "Concordia." In August 1840 he walked with Parker, Ripley, and Christopher Cranch to a meeting of the "friends of union" in Groton, Massachusetts, twenty miles northwest of Concord. Alcott found that most of those present were still "in bondage to sectarianism," but he was delighted with "a few free souls" like the "comeouters" who gathered in a Groton tavern to talk of "coming out" of the established churches and putting an end to all creeds, ceremonies, and clerical distinctions. Like the transcendentalists, they believed in the religion of the heart, in the immediate inspiration of the soul. Alcott was particularly impressed with young Benjamin Dyer, who talked as orphically as Alcott about the spiritualizing effect of knowing all truth.[38]

Alcott, Ripley, and Parker were convinced by what they had seen at Groton that there was a need for a convention to consider "universal reform." Alcott became part of a committee to issue a call for such a meeting. It met for three days in November 1840 at the Chardon Street Chapel in Boston. As Emerson described it, it was

> the most singular collection of strange specimens of humanity that was ever assembled. Madmen, madwomen, men with beards, Dunkers, Muggletonians, Come-outers, Groaners, Agrarians, Seventh-day Baptists, Quakers, Abolitionists, Calvinists, Unitarians and Philosophers—all came successively to the top, and seized the moment, if not their hour, wherein to chide, or pray, or preach or protest.

This was one meeting at which even William Lloyd Garrison found himself among the conservatives. There was little parliamentary order. The convention reached no conclusions. It passed no resolutions. Amid such a diverse gathering of zealots, each forwarding a singular plan to save the world, little agreement was possible. Emerson was impressed with the excitement, the life, and the love of religious liberty expressed at Chardon Street. He rejoiced at the scope given Alcott. But Alcott was less enthusiastic: "Not in conventions, amidst multitudes, but in small circles of men, am I to honor my thought and publish my doctrine." Despite the wild range of opinion present, he found that most were still tied to tradition and biblicism, unwilling to accept the divine inspiration of the soul.[39]

Members of the Chardon Street Convention proposed a further series of meetings to debate the reform of religious institutions. They met again in

March 1841 to discuss the Church; in October 1841 to decide the appropriateness of respecting the Sabbath; and again in March 1842 to question the authority of the Bible. His disdain for the multitude notwithstanding, Alcott attended all of these conventions to proclaim his doctrine of the divinity of human beings, to attack institutionalized religion, and to denounce those who claimed that "Scripture" was the sole property of Christians and did not contain the great thoughts of human beings worldwide.[40]

At these reform conventions Alcott expressed openly and without reservation ideas about reform that he had heretofore largely confined to his private journals. He evidenced his emotional commitment to the idea of reform, his heightened sense of mission, and his belief in the absolute necessity of personal sanctification prior to any structural or institutional reform. He preached the apotheosis of the soul. He put the individual soul above any institution, above all other people. To accomplish universal reform, he declared, the reformer had to lay the axe to the "root of evil in the private heart, and thus [fell] every abuse at once." In October 1840 William Henry Channing wrote to Alcott from Cincinnati and challenged the "peasant saint," as he called him, to act on his talk about universal reform. Channing agreed with Alcott that revolution was near, but he felt that the forces for change needed a builder, someone to put noble thoughts into action. He asked Alcott if he were "man enough" to undertake such a challenge. In response, Alcott talked only of his hope; he did not promise action. He prophesied regeneration but only after dissolution. The present time, he told Channing, was one of demolition. He heard around him the crash of falling timbers, not the sound of builders' tools. But such destruction was the herald of a new creation, which would come only with a "new faith" in the immortality of the soul.[41]

Alcott tried to act on his "new faith," and on Channing's challenge, by his "pilgrim's ministry" of 1841. He preached his message of the self-reliant soul to groups in Hingham, Scituate, Marshfield, Providence, Brook Farm, and to a congregation of "comeouters" in Haverhill. In June 1841 he lived for two weeks with Benjamin Dyer in Braintree, Vermont. He walked through the mountains with Dyer, preaching reform and distributing the *Dial*, health tracts, Emerson's essays, and copies of the recently issued reformist journal, the *Providence Plain Speaker*. At the Sabbath Convention of October 1841, he "took charge of the unrest," speaking freely and often against religious customs and traditions. On one occasion during the convention, an old gentleman rose behind Alcott as he spoke and suggested that Alcott ought to be crucified. Alcott replied that he was ready anytime. The gentleman then denounced Alcott as a blasphemer and an infidel. When the gentleman shouted that Alcott had no conscience, the convention fell into disarray until shouts for order brought it under control.[42]

In November 1841 he contributed several "Orphic Sayings" to the irreverent *Plain Speaker*, which was edited by two young and enthusiastic reformers, Christopher Greene and William Chace. Alcott had met Greene and Chace at the Chardon Street Convention of November 1840, and had been immediately impressed with their dedication to the "new faith." Greene had subsequently written to Alcott about his "beautiful visions" of the spiritual world, prompting Alcott to write him lengthy treatises about the nature of the soul. Both Greene and Chace visited Concord in September 1841, and impressed Abby with their "goodness." Their *Plain Speaker*, which first appeared in January 1841, was advertised as a paper dedicated to "truth not profit," which may have explained its brief existence. "We wish to inculcate the great ideas," the editors claimed, "that each individual of our race [i.e., the human race] should become a *true man*—not that we should be abolitionists or temperance men only, but that we should be *men*, standing on the broad platform of truth, ever ready to do battle for the right." They advocated "soul liberty," and demanded that the "light of truth" examine all institutions and opinions. But the iconoclastic antics of Greene and Chace sometimes embarrassed even Alcott. At the Sabbath Convention they cursed the name of Jesus Christ deliberately to shock and bait the members of the clergy and the "formalists" present. Then in Concord they climbed to the top of a hill on a Sunday morning and shouted blasphemies to unnerve and upset churchgoers.[43]

Alcott's reservations about Greene and Chace led him to reject their offer to welcome the Alcott family as members of their ideal community, Holly Home, in North Providence. When Thomas Davis, one of the founders of Holly Home, first made the formal offer in May 1841, the Alcotts seriously considered it. In fact, Abby stayed there for a few days to try it out. But in the end, especially after the shouting incident in Concord, they decided against it.[44]

To reject the offer from Holly Home was no light decision. For while Alcott was caught up in the swirl of reform in 1840 and 1841, his family's condition became worse and worse. His "pilgrim's ministry" came at the expense of his crops and his family's income. He remained $3,400 in debt despite the aid of a $3,100 legacy from Abby's father, Colonel May, who died in February 1841. Abby complained that the legacy was no more than a token remembrance by her wealthy father, who had never approved of her actions. She also complained that her husband's frequent absences in 1841 had caused all domestic chores to fall to her, and threatened to cost them their Concord cottage. Yet she maintained that she would rather live on acorns than compromise matters of principle, that no amount of money could divert them from their purpose.[45]

The family struggled through the winter of 1841-42 with the help of friends and with the small income Alcott got from chopping wood and what Abby and the girls could make sewing. They ate only two meals a day, commonly bread and water. Occasionally, they had fruit and vegetables, but no meat, butter, or cheese because Alcott forbade it. Despite their poverty, Alcott, whose generous spirit sometimes reached out desperately for expression and fulfillment, chopped wood for no pay to help a woman with four children whose drunken husband had disappeared.[46]

Alcott later referred to these months of late 1841 and early 1842 as his "winter of discontent." Abby was concerned for his survival that winter because his mood fluctuated dramatically from hope to despair. At times she was terror stricken by his "dreadful nervous excitations" when he would distort the simplest act into "the most complicated and adverse form." Alcott told his brother Junius that this winter had been the least hopeful of any period in his life, that every avenue of employment seemed closed to him. He admitted to Margaret Fuller that at times he had been on the "borders of frenzy."[47]

The one glimmer of hope that sustained Alcott in the winter of 1841-42 was provided by news of the activities of his English friends. In February 1840 Heraud's *New Monthly Magazine* had announced that Henry Gardner Wright, a friend of Greaves and director of Greaves's school at Ham Common, Surrey, was reopening the school under the name Alcott House. Wright had promised to teach in accordance with Pestalozzian principles as adapted by Alcott, to emphasize the "spontaneous development of the soul" rather than the mere acquisition of knowledge. The acknowledgment and encouragement these English reformers gave to Alcott, as well as their reform ideas, led Alcott to believe that they offered true reform, while their American counterparts had only a partial vision. He wanted to visit England to take advantage of their sympathy and their adulation.[48]

Emerson, who had already aided the Alcotts so much, gave reality to Alcott's hope of a voyage to England. In February 1842 he offered to raise the four to five hundred dollars necessary for the trip, telling Alcott that he needed the restorative stimulus and diversion that a total change of habits would bring. Alcott asked his brother Junius to stay with the family while he was away, and Junius agreed to come. Abby and the children dreaded the separation, but Abby was convinced that nothing should stand in the way of her husband's mission to "save mankind." She was certain that the friends in England would give more spiritual strength to Alcott in this "period of doubt" than anyone in America.[49]

Alcott left for England on board the "Rosalind" on May 8, 1842, armed with letters of introduction from Emerson and William Lloyd Garrison. Abby remained in Concord to confront anxious creditors, who demanded immediate payment when they heard that Alcott was leaving the country. Garrison told his friend John Bowring, M.P., that he was to meet in Alcott "a resolute and uncompromising foe of priestcraft, bigotry and sectarianism." Though he did not always agree with Alcott's radicalism, Garrison held him in high esteem for the "purity of his life" and for his "rare moral courage." Emerson asked Thomas Carlyle to forget anything he might have read by or about Alcott and to allow him to make a "new & primary impression." "You may love him or hate him, or apathetically pass him by, as your genius shall dictate," said Emerson. "Only I entreat this, that you do not let him go quite out of your reach until you are sure you have seen him & know for certain the nature of the man. And so I leave contentedly my pilgrim to his fate." Emerson also told

John Sterling not to fail to meet Alcott and to experience his unrivaled conversation, insight, and revolutionary impulse of thought.[50]

With these credentials Alcott arrived in London after a month of seasickness and endless conversation with the other passengers about reform. A few of the city's attractions caught his eye—London Bridge, St. Paul's Cathedral—but he was in no mood for sightseeing. On Tuesday, June 7, the day after his arrival, he called on Charles Lane, editor of the *Mercantile Price Current*, who had given up most of his London business connections in 1841 to help Henry Wright at Alcott House. Along with their teaching, Lane and Wright were then busily engaged in editing a monthly tract called the *Healthian*, which proclaimed the intimate connection between proper diet and spiritual renewal. Lane immediately took Alcott to Alcott House, about ten miles from the city. Alcott soon felt the sympathy he longed for. Although Greaves had died the previous March, he had left a "select and rare library," and his spirit had infected his circle of friends, particularly Lane and Wright. Alcott found Wright to be "a younger disciple of that Eternal Verity that I have loved and served so long." Lane was the "deepest, sharpest intellect" he had ever met. These men thought as he did. He had found fulfillment. "I now understand the instinct that sent me across the waves," he wrote to Abby; "it was to enjoy this spiritual communion, this concord of will and ideal—this concert of Thought and Act."[51]

He felt that he had found brothers at Alcott House. The school was "a happy and refreshing place." Wright, he thought, had "more genius for education" than any man he had ever met. No more than a month passed before he determined that he was bound to his English friends by ties that could never be sundered. Providence had surely directed him to England.[52]

Not long after his arrival Alcott was busy in London visiting reformers of various stripes and shades of opinion. There was Hugh Doherty, disciple of Fourier and editor of the *London Phalanx*; James J. Garth Wilkinson, scholar and disciple of Swedenborg; Francis Foster Barham, dramatic poet and one-time member of Greaves's Aesthetic Institution, or "Syncretics"; and John A. Heraud, so impressive in print and so unimpressive in person. He liked Doherty and talked with him at length about communites and about Emerson. He thought Wilkinson's explanation of Swedenborg fascinating. Barham and Heraud he found imitative and unoriginal.[53]

On June 25 Alcott rode to Chelsea to visit Thomas Carlyle. He was appalled. Carlyle was "impatient of all interruption: faithless quite in all social reforms." He was a dead man, Alcott thought, lacking in hope. As "Saul amongst the Prophets," he paid homage to the dead rather than the living. Carlyle liked Alcott for his natural intelligence and goodness, but he was also amused by him:

> The good Alcot, with his long lean face and figure, with his grey worn temples and mild radiant eyes; all bent on saving the world by a return to acorns and the golden age; he comes before one like a venerable Don Quixote, whom nobody can even laugh at without loving!

He was displeased with Alcott's singlemindedness and his attempts to "be something" rather than to "do something." Alcott's constant droning about vegetable diets bored him, and he longed to hear something useful from him, something about Emerson, or about literature in New England. It was clear to Carlyle that his "hopeless unbelief" pained Alcott no end.[54]

Other matters excited Alcott more than conversation with the cynical Carlyle. He attended anti-Corn Law conferences and Chartist meetings; he met with reformers George Thompson, John Minter Morgan, William J. Fox, and Robert Owen. John Goodwyn Barmby, a former Greaves associate, came to visit Alcott and to talk about French socialism. A visit to France in 1840 had converted him, and he had plans to establish his own community in England. Owenite Alexander Campbell also came to Alcott House to talk. Campbell had been a close friend of Greaves and later would edit and publish Greaves's papers.[55]

Alcott perceived much desperation and discontent in England. The time was ripe, it seemed to him, for effective reform. But, in general, the reformers he met offered no meaningful plan of action. Even the members of Greaves's group—J. Westland Marston, William Oldham, John Heraud—fell short of Greaves's ideal. Only Lane and Wright remained true; they talked of concrete action to accomplish universal reform. Their plan involved the establishment of a community, a "New Eden"—Lane called it a "true harmonic association"—wherein a combination of country living, labor on the land, and simplicity in diet and lifestyle would cultivate and harmonize all the intellectual, physical, and moral aspects of an individual. Like Alcott, Lane and Wright spoke of an "experiment in human culture."[56]

But Alcott felt, and Lane and Wright agreed, that England was a poor place to begin such an enterprise. As much as he resented his treatment in America and the half-measures of American reformers, Alcott believed that New England was destined to be the location of "God's garden." It had the resources; it was "free and fearless." Despite overwhelming evidence to the contrary in his own experience, Alcott still accepted the widespread American belief that theirs was a land of destiny. It only remained to bring "living minds" like Lane and Wright to the land of promise in order to begin the "new state of things." Lane and Wright were misplaced in England, he believed. England was hostile to human welfare and her institutions were averse to the "largest liberty of the soul." Alcott was disgusted and horrified by the "spectacle" and "masked show" of Westminster Abbey; by the celebration of nobility by the Royal Academy; by the Tower, that "relic of human barbarity," which "could have been designed and executed by the sanguinary Britons alone"; and by London, that "huge den ... wherein Beelzebub whelps."[57] America offered the only possible escape from such decadence:

Our freer, but yet far from free land, is the asylum, if asylum there be, for the hope of man: and there, if anywhere, is that Second Eden to be planted, in which the divine seed is to bruise the head of evil, and restore man to his rightful communion with God in the Paradise of Good, whereinto neither the knowledge of death nor sin shall enter but life and immortality shall then come to light: and man pluck wisdom from the tree of life alway.[58]

England was at the door of dissolution anyway. Its "cruelties and enormities," its "thrones and hierarchies," would soon, he thought, give way to a "nobler race of men." But he feared that pending revolution and the imminent downfall of the realm might endanger the new Eden. He sought the protection of stability and order in New England, forgetting that he had predicted a similar upheaval there. Ironically, as much as Alcott, Lane, and Wright disdained established institutions such as the State or the Church, they consciously depended on the stability of those institutions in order to begin their community.[59]

During the summer of 1842 Alcott House was alive with discussions, plans, meetings, and publications, all anticipating the new experiment in human culture. On July 6 Alcott and his enthusiastic friends hosted an open meeting of "disciples of the Newness." They aired all of England's current reform topics, including the corn laws, education, the established Church, and penal reform, but they concluded that "true" reform involved the regeneration of individuals. To that end they proposed an end to all property holding, the disavowal of all governments and creeds, and unqualified allegiance to the idea of "Universal Love." They urged the cultivation of a "fertile" mind and a chaste, healthful body as a means of removing all hindrances to the "influx of Deity." This purification, as well as close attention to proper marriage, proper relations to family, to neighborhood, and to God, would, they promised, ensure the development of a "new race of persons." Personal cleansing had its effect not only on the individual but also on his or her descendants.[60]

Alcott, Lane, and Wright advertised these ideas in various reform journals in order to attract participants to their new Eden. They promised to create circumstances in which the participants' relationship to God would return to what it supposedly was before the Fall, or, in Alcott's terminology, before the soul's lapse from original purity. They looked for a divine sanctification, a personal purification, and they were convinced that they knew how to bring it about. Universal love was the prime prerequisite for such sanctification and waves of rhetoric about it flowed out of Alcott House. But despite the emotionally uplifting aura about a concept like universal love, it was vague and ill-defined. Thus concrete programs of sanctification involved not love but diet, health, and regimen. Daily regimen was concrete and measurable. It was a definite and sure means of regeneration. Alcott, Lane, and Wright spent most of their time elucidating this outward means of gaining personal assurance of sanctification.[61]

Lane and Wright only reinforced Alcott's already well-defined ideas about health and diet. Such had been his faith in Sylvester Graham; such had been his gospel in "Psyche an Evangele." As early as July 1840 he had read Iamblichus's *Life of Pythagoras*, which told of the Greek sage's emphasis on personal purity among his group of followers at Croton. Pythagoras's ideas on health had confirmed his earlier speculation about the relation of the health of the body to the health of the soul.[62] In the summer and fall of 1842, Alcott contributed articles to the *Healthian* on Pythagoras and Pythagorean diet:

> [Pythagoras] not only admits the propriety of first well regulating the external nature before the more internal truth can be revealed, but enforces on his student a long and strict discipline as the only means of attaining an intuition of divine things.[63]

Health became an overwhelming concern to Alcott while in England. As soon as he arrived, he became a patron of the Physiological and Health Association. He heartily approved of the strict daily regimen demanded of the students at Alcott House. He found that the children who boarded there—some thirty of them, all under twelve—lived on plain bread with some vegetables and fruits, drank only water, bathed every morning, and engaged in a program of vigorous daily exercise. His last public meeting before leaving England for America was a September 19 gathering of the Health Association. He told the crowd assembled that all disease originated in the soul, that the body merely reported the state of the soul. By living a "pure life," he said, human beings were able to recover their "original pure constitution." To restore this original purity, temperance and moderation in all things were essential, as was a diet restricted to only "pure substances" such as fruits, grains grown on "unadulterated" soil, and water from a fountain. Though he believed that the body was merely the outward symbol of an internal spiritual condition, he also believed that by altering the symbol—that is, by purifying it—it would in turn purify the inner condition.[64]

Thomas Carlyle found Alcott's dietary ideas ridiculous. During Alcott's third visit they "quarreled outright" according to Alcott, who concluded that "greatness abides not here." Upon hearing Carlyle's report, Emerson was angered that Alcott dwelt on diet at the expense of his "proper topics," Emerson told Carlyle that

> [Alcott] is a great man & was made for what is greatest, but I now fear that he has touched what best he can, & through his more than a prophet's egotism, and the absence of all useful reconciling talents, will bring nothing to pass, & be but a voice in the wilderness. As you do not seem to have seen in him his pure & noble intellect, I fear that it lies under some new & denser clouds.

Carlyle agreed, and warned Emerson not to associate with the "bottomless imbeciles" who had become Alcott's English followers. He had known Greaves, and he told Emerson that "few greater blockheads (if 'blockhead' may mean 'exasperated imbecile' and the ninth part of a thinker) broke the world's bread in his day."[65]

But that "blockhead" Greaves had a tremendous influence over the plans to establish the new Eden. Alcott, Lane, and Wright looked upon him as an oracle, although for Alcott this was largely because Greaves confirmed much of what Alcott already believed. For example, Greaves believed, as had Alcott, that reform was an individual matter best facilitated in the family relationship. Reform for Greaves and Alcott was a matter of fostering a communion with the spirit, and the spiritual analogy of familial love, they believed, best accomplished that communion. But Greaves added one idea that caused a dilemma for Alcott: he believed that education could not correct the defects of birth. Improvement, he said, came only in subsequent generations through a "superior germination," resulting from a pure marriage relationship. The new Eden would involve an attempt to create such a relationship, and Alcott began thereafter to consider seriously the possibility that the irreparable consequences of inborn temperaments and characteristics might explain the existence of evil. Yet Alcott never fully gave up the idea that education and a close attention to life-style could regenerate individuals regardless of the effects of heredity. The problem became a moment of tension in his thought that he never reconciled.[66]

In early August Alcott wrote to Abby that his life's aim was about to be realized in the proposed community. He was ecstatic, admitting no possibility of failure. The plan was simple and inexpensive; it would secure an independence of the world yet provide the family with enough to live on. He suggested the need for a house with adequate land for a garden and an orchard. The community would begin with ten or twelve people and would expand when desirable. Possible participants included Lane, Wright, Thomas Davis, Christopher Greene, William Chace, Edward Palmer, and maybe even Emerson. "Henceforth I am no more alone," he exulted, "now cometh the spring and summer of Hope, and casteth the melancholy seasons behind."[67]

Abby was as interested and joyful as her husband, though somewhat skeptical. Immediately, she began seeking a location for the experiment. She looked at the Hosmer place in Stowe and the Codman farm in Lincoln, hoping to find a spot remote from neighbors yet near Boston. On October 21, Alcott and Wright, with Lane and his son William, arrived in Boston on board the "Leland," weighted down with one thousand volumes from Greaves's library. Alcott carried with him a letter of best wishes from Thomas Carlyle, who in the end thought more of Alcott than Alcott did of him. The reformers immediately began their ascetic life-style at Alcott's cottage in Concord and began giving lectures and conversations in Concord and Boston to advertise their proposed community. Emerson told Margaret Fuller that Alcott and his English friends "cannot chat, or so much as open the mouth on aught less than A new Solar System & the prospective Education in the Nebulae. All day and all night they hold perpetual Parliament." In November and December they conversed at Providence, Dedham, Lynn, Brook Farm, and in Boston where an angry mob, evidently upset at their hostility to church and state, drove them away from Marlboro Chapel to Ritchie Hall.[68]

On January 3, 1843, Henry Wright left Concord, disenchanted with the rigid life-style that Alcott and Lane had imposed. But Alcott and Lane went on undaunted. They talked openly of rejecting any governmental institution, and on January 17 Alcott was arrested for refusing to pay his poll tax. The tax was not particularly oppressive even for the impoverished Alcotts—a dollar and a half each year, assessed on every male over sixteen by the Commonwealth of Massachusetts for revenue purposes—but Alcott obviously wished to make his position a public issue. He had refused the same tax the year before but had not been arrested, presumably because no one enforced it. This time the constable came to the cottage with a general warrant and escorted the nonresisting Alcott to the jailhouse. The jailer's absence prevented his being locked up, and he waited patiently for two hours while the constable went off to find the jailer. By the time the jailer showed up, Judge Samuel Hoar, "the very personification of the state," had generously paid the tax and the costs, much to Alcott's dismay. "Thus," said Abby, "we were spared the affliction of his absence and he the triumph of suffering for his principles." However, Alcott and Lane did get the publicity they wanted. Lane wrote a dramatic article for the *Liberator* explaining this outrage against the sovereign individual. It was matter of individual judgment, Lane declared, whether or not a person should support the government.[69]

In the spring of 1843 Alcott and Lane began to search in earnest for a suitable location for their community. They looked at houses in Milton, Roxbury, Stowe, Southborough, Brookline, and Watertown. Finally, on May 20, they walked to Harvard, Massachusetts, a small village fifteen miles west of Concord, and purchased the Wyman Farm with ninety acres of land for $1,800. Alcott disliked it but gave in to Lane, who was supplying the money for the farm as well as one hundred seventy-five dollars to pay Alcott's Concord debts. William Oldham, who had faithfully remained in England to care for Alcott House, sent ten pounds to help with the costs.[70]

On June 1 the Alcotts and Lanes left Concord by horse and wagon for "Fruitlands." It was a beautiful location with a panoramic view of the mountains in the distance. Although they were in view of the Shaker families nearby, they felt protected from the invasion of the "rude secular world." There were fourteen acres of woods. The cleared land was satisfactory, but its hills and rocks would make farming difficult, as it was in all parts of New England. Alcott and Lane hoped to lay out gardens to replace the grazing land and to have fresh running water for each room of the farm house. On their eleven acres of arable land they planned to grow corn, rye, wheat, potatoes, oats, barley, beans, peas, melon, and squash, all without the use of animal manure as fertilizer, "as filthy a practice as an idea," they said. Most labor they expected to do by hand, although they had one yoke of oxen.[71]

It was clear that many more members would be necessary to ensure success because of the labor involved in clearing land, planting crops, and repairing buildings. Lane wrote to Henry Thoreau, who was then living on Staten Island, New York, urging him to join, and Alcott wrote to his brothers, Junius and Chatfield, for the same purpose. These persons did not come, nor did several others whom Alcott had counted on, such as Greene, Chace, Davis, and Edward Palmer. But the Alcotts and Lanes were soon joined by twenty-year-old Samuel Larned, former member of Brook Farm whom Alcott had met in Providence; by Abraham Everett, forty-two-year-old cooper, once imprisoned in a madhouse, and who called himself "Wood Abram"; and by Samuel Bower, a sometime nudist whom Lane had met in England. On July 11 Isaac Hecker arrived. Hecker was the twenty-three-year-old son of German immigrants. He had come from New York City to join Brook Farm in January 1843, and had heard of Fruitlands there through a good friend, Almira Barlow, to whom Alcott had written in February. In mid-July Ann Page of Providence joined the community, much to the relief of Abby, who had been saddled with all the household chores.[72] There was nothing radical about the role assigned to women at Fruitlands; on that both Abby and Ann Page agreed:

> Miss Page made a good remark and true as good; that a woman may live a whole life of sacrifice and at her death meekly says I die a *women*—a man pases [sic] a few years in experiments on self denial and simple life and he says "behold a *God*."[73]

The last to join was the eccentric Joseph Palmer, who arrived from Fitchburg in August with his ox and cow team, having endured years of persecution for wearing a beard. There were no more takers. Visitors came in droves, including Emerson, William Russell, Samuel J. May, Ellery Channing, Theodore Parker, and George and Sophia Ripley. Some came to scoff, some to get a taste of the discipline and quickly leave, but none to join. "The right people, with right motives, and holy purposes, do not come," said Abby, "and we are both wearing ourselves out in the service of transient visitors, and ungrateful participants. This is a Hotel, where man and beast are entertained without pay, and at great expense."[74] Emerson visited in early July and came away impressed but not fully convinced:

> The sun & the evening sky do not look calmer than Alcott & his family at Fruitlands ... I will not prejudge them successful. They look well in July. We will see them in December. I know they are better for themselves than as partners. One can easily see that they have yet to settle several things. Their saying that things are clear & they sane, does not make them so. If they will in very deed be lovers & not selfish; if they will serve the town of Harvard, & make their neighbors feel them as benefactors, wherever they touch them; they are safe as the sun.[75]

Alcott and Lane were prepared to take up Emerson's challenge, to put into practice the Fruitlands philosophy of universal love. The most concise statement of that philosophy was made by Alcott and Lane in a letter to Mr. A. Brooke of Oakland, Ohio, whom they were trying to persuade to join. The letter was published in the *Liberator* as "The Consociate Family Life" in September 1843. This article made clear Alcott's and Lane's prime assumption, that a reformation of individuals, not of conditions or circumstances, was the only means of true reform. Improved people, they said, created improved conditions and institutions. Simplicity in diet, in dress, in personal habits, and gentle behavior and serene minds were both evidence of and the means to achieve individual "goodness." The best context for achieving this goodness, they claimed, was the family:

> The family, in its highest divinest sense, is therefore our true position, our sacred earthly destiny. It comprehends every divine, every humane relation consistent with universal good, and all others it rejects, as it disdains all animal sensualities.

By *family* they did not mean a conjugal or nuclear family. Numbers or blood relationship did not define it. Rather, they defined it as consociate, as the union of members in the spirit. This did not mean complete rejection of conjugal ties, at least for the Alcotts. For as Alcott perceived it, the consociate family meant a union of likemindedness, a sharing of like conscience and consciousness, much like what he had tried to foster by his "common conscience" in the Temple School. By sharing ideas, life-style, moral values, and communion with the spirit, he thought, the members of the consociate family helped awaken the spirit in one another. By partaking of the spiritual within the consociate family, member conjugal families could generate goodness in their offspring. The consociate family was to be a union of sovereign individuals, which Alcott and Lane believed possible because of their faith that regenerated individuals, those with spiritual insight, would all arrive at the same conclusions about ideas, morality, and lifestyle.[76]

Thus there was a tension in the thought of the Fruitlanders as to whether the consociate family, once established, ought to impose rules and regulations on its members or allow complete freedom of choice. Alcott and Lane, respectful of the idea of freedom of choice, established no formal rules and procedures at Fruitlands. The spirit would guide all the members, they said. "Where the spirit of love and wisdom abounds, literal forms are needless, irksome, or hinderative: where the spirit is lacking, no preconceived rules can compensate." However, they had clear expectations about what spiritual behavior involved and what kinds of things were a hindrance to the influx or efflux of spirit and consequent goodness. The ownership of property, the rules of the marketplace, and the use of hired labor were all harmful to true spiritual union among humans, they believed. They opposed the use of animals for labor or for food. If grazing land was cultivated, they maintained, the world's population could eat from one fourth of the land then in use. "The divine man," said Alcott in Channing's *Present*,

> dwells amidst gardens and orchards, a grower of plants and fruits; a handler of spades and pruning knives; not a goader nor throttler of oxen, nor strippers of udders, nor scavenger of cattle, nor feeder of swine.... Husbandry, pasturage, trade and wages, are lapses from primeval innocency; the doom of expulsion from Paradise.

Alcott and Lane were also sure that the divine human being avoided certain foods like meat, eggs, butter, cheese—anything produced by or from animals—and tea, coffee, molasses, and rice, which were produced by slave labor. Pure humans drank only water and ate only native grains, fruits, herbs, and roots. "Outward abstinence is a sign of inward fulness," they said. Anyone who disagreed with their definition of the divine regimen they simply condemned as lacking in spiritual insight. So, despite the absence of formal rules and regulations, the unwritten ones made Fruitlands oppressive indeed.[77]

William Henry Channing called Alcott and Lane the "Essenes of New England."[78] And clearly they did hark back to the ancient ascetics who sought to attain spiritual renewal through physical purification. Fruitlands was a logical outcome of Alcott's belief in the perfectibility of human nature, his belief that humans could restore themselves to the state of purity or innocence that he believed existed before the lapse or the Fall. Asceticism was a means to that end. Fruitlands was also the most faithful attempt to carry into practice the ideal of the transcendent individual, the divine soul able to rise above any human institution, any temporary societal arrangement. Other communities of the time—Hopedale, Northhampton, even Brook Farm—were all attempts to realize a better life through some external arrangement of conditions, to make people better by first making their institutions better. Alcott vehemently opposed such efforts. "I have no belief," he said,

> in associations of human beings for the purpose of making themselves happy by means of improved outward arrangements alone, as the fountains of happiness are within, and are opened to us as we are preharmonized or consociated with the Universal Spirit. This is the one condition needful for happy association amongst men. And this condition is attained by the surrender of all individual or selfish gratification—a complete willingness to be moulded by the Divinity.[79]

But this called into question the necessity for a community such as Fruitlands. Emerson argued that a consociated family—a communion of transcendent souls—did not need to gather physically in one place. He believed that actual isolation, actual independence, best facilitated communion with the spirit and spiritual union among individuals. He even suggested prophetically that physical community was harmful to spiritual union.[80] The establishment of Fruitlands clearly revealed the differences between Alcott and Emerson. Alcott abhorred isolation. He thrived on intercommunication. He sought reassurance and confirmation of his own ideas in external things and people. Unlike Emerson, he could not be content to believe that spiritual union among transcendent souls existed without the physical symbol of that union there to remind him. More important, Fruitlands reflected a sense of mission in Alcott that was not present in Emerson. Alcott sought to reform others. The flurry of community building in the 1840s in Europe and in America suggested to him the ultimate means of carrying out his mission. Fruitlands was to be a latter-day "city on a hill," a seed that was to grow and spread. "We are not without hope," Alcott said, "that Providence will use us progressively for beneficial effects in the great work of human regeneration, and the restoration of the highest life on earth." The community would spread the word of reform faster than any individual could. Visitors would discuss it among friends and acquaintances; newspapers and journals would write about it. It would be outward evidence of the spirit at work, a symbol of accomplishment for Alcott and Lane, and a visible means of convincing others of the truth. Alcott was still the teacher, using external symbols of the spirit to awaken the spirit in others.[81]

In practice, Fruitlands was filled with contradictions. Lane and Alcott eschewed property holding, yet they had to buy property before beginning. They abhorred the state but depended on its stability for the existence of their community. They opposed the subjugation of animals but used oxen and horses to plow their fields. The most serious and disturbing contradiction was the escape from freedom evidence by their daily regimen. Alcott had always hated forms, customs, creeds, and usages. He and Lane talked at length about the free, divine soul's having a direct knowledge of the divine life once external obstructions were removed. But the impulse for conformity at Fruitlands was overwhelming. The outward evidence of spiritual communion became narrowly defined by Alcott and Lane. It was no wonder that few persons were interested. No one was willing to subject himself or herself to the rigid asceticism imposed by Alcott and Lane except social misfits such as Everett and Bower, who were themselves seeking refuge from worldly cares or an escape from freedom.

Alcott and Lane worried about the lack of participation. Although Lane bravely told William Oldham that the enterprise did not depend on numbers, he and Alcott set out in September and October to spread the news and to attract more people to Fruitlands. They visited Brook Farm and Adin Ballou's Hopedale. They held public conversations in New York where they saw William Henry Channing, William Emerson, Margaret Fuller, Edward Palmer, Horace Greeley, Parke Godwin, Albert Brisbane, and Lydia Maria Child. These people listened, but did not follow. In October Alcott and Lane made what Alcott called the "penniless pilgrimage." Wearing the marks of their self-denial—drab linens, straw hats, empty pockets—they visited Brook Farm again, saw Theodore Parker in Roxbury and Edmund Quincy in Dedham, and advocated the abolition of money among friends of Anna Thaxter's in Hingham. From Hingham they took a boat to Boston, offering their ideas and preaching repentance to pay their fare. In Boston they tried to buy a silver communion set for the Fruitlands family—they believed every meal to be sacramental because of the presence of the spirit among the consociate family—but the silversmith would not accept their doctrine as payment.[82]

None of their efforts succeeded in attracting more participants, and by October the original members had begun to drift away. Isaac Hecker had left on July 25, convinced that Fruitlands did not have what he wanted. Alcott's and Lane's devotion and spirituality impressed him but he found nothing unique about the community except the emphasis on self-denial. And Hecker felt he could practice self-denial anywhere. Samuel Bower and Abraham Everett were undependable. Alcott finally asked Ann Page to leave, reportedly because she had broken the strict rules of diet by eating fish.[83] The obvious lack of success created tremendous tension among the remaining members. Lane believed it was Alcott's rigidity that drove people away:

> Mr. Alcott makes such high requirements of all persons that few are likely to stay, even of his own family, unless he can become more tolerant of defect. He is an artist in human character requiring every painter to be a Michael Angelo.[84]

Lane blamed Abby for the dismissal of Ann Page, claiming that she was unwilling to accept a family larger than her own. She accused Lane of being moody, enigmatic, and generally disagreeable; he thought the same of her. Interpersonal hostility was compounded by the problems of day-to-day living. The absence of Lane and Alcott during the harvest season was almost disastrous for the crops. By November Fruitlands was beset by shortages of food and money as well as able bodies. Abby threatened to take the children away to ensure their survival. Lane tried to get Alcott to abandon his family, to join the community of "universal love" instead of the "selfish" conjugal relationship. Alcott talked of this with his family. Louisa and Anna cried and prayed that the family stay together. In the end Alcott decided to remain with his family and let Lane go separately to join the Shakers if he wished. On January 16, 1844, the Alcotts moved by sled from Fruitlands to take three rooms at neighbor Lovejoy's farmhouse. The experiment had come to an inglorious end.[85]

There have been various explanations for the failure of Fruitlands after only seven months: its impracticality and lack of organization, which made its members unable to sustain the community through the rigors of winter;[86] the personality conflict between Lane and Abby Alcott, which led Lane, the "hawk in Dove Cottage," to attempt to disrupt the Alcott family;[87] the clash between Lane's "socialism" and Alcott's "individualism";[88] Lane's alleged fanaticism, intolerance, and stupidity, which led the naive Alcott astray;[89] and Alcott's genteel faith in the conjugal family, which clashed with Lane's active reformism and his attempt to meld the conjugal family into the larger consociate family.[90] Alcott himself later looked on the scheme as impracticable under the existing circumstances. He viewed the difference in temperament between himself and Lane as contributing to failure, but he also felt that the experiment came too soon, that the "people" were not ready. His contemporaries, he felt, had failed to reap where he had sown.[91]

Thus Alcott pointed to the overriding reason for the failure of Fruitlands: it simply failed to attract any support. A life of rigid self-denial did not appeal to those who sought in community life a richer experience and a greater fulfillment. It lacked the leisurely union of labor and culture that attracted intellectuals and artists to Brook Farm. It lacked the well-organized communal sharing in work and profits of Hopedale or Oneida. It even lacked the carefully planned educational and vocational programs of an Owenite community like New Harmony. Unlike the Shakers, the Fruitlanders had no revered prophetic authority like Mother Ann Lee. As Hecker pointed out, Fruitlands offered nothing but a rigid asceticism. And even those like Hecker who were attracted to the ascetic life did not feel compelled to stay at Fruitlands to practice it. Fruitlands contradicted Alcott's uplifting message at the Temple School that human potential involved expression and creativity. He had taken the freedom offered by the transcendental vision of human potential—a vision he heartily accepted both before and after Fruitlands—and confined it to the rigidity of a daily regimen. As usual, Emerson stated the problem best:

> The philosophers at [Fruitlands] have such an image of virtue before their eyes, that the poetry of man & nature they never see; the poetry that is in man's life, the poorest pastoral clownish life; the light that shines on a man's hat, in a child's spoon, the sparkle on every wave & on every mote of dust, they see not.[92]

The failure to attract a sizable number of people to participate in the consociate family meant the failure of Fruitlands to regenerate the world, or at least to begin such regeneration. The "penniless pilgrimage" was the last straw. When the hoped-for droves of subscribers failed to materialize, both Alcott and Lane lost enthusiasm for their enterprise. Personality conflicts rose to the surface as zeal for the mission of Fruitlands, which had heretofore reconciled all differences, dissipated. Each blamed the other for the community's obvious failure. In the face of such disillusionment and disappointment, a group of saints doubtless could not have remained together long. Both Lane and Alcott realized, as had Hecker, that they could practice self-denial elsewhere.

Although Alcott and Lane certainly lacked organizational skills, the practicality of living simply off the not-so-prosperous New England soil was really not a problem. Alcott lived that way for several years both before and after Fruitlands. He was a good farmer, as evidenced by the lush gardens he maintained for twenty-five years after Fruitlands. Had the community attracted more members, presumably the daily problems of existence would have diminished. Greater numbers might well have provided the labor needed and whatever skills Alcott and Lane lacked. And the whole problem of definition of family was a later additon to the Fruitlanders' difficulties. Before coming to America Lane had accepted the nuclear family, as had his mentor Greaves. They only asked that the sanction for marriage be a divine rather than a civil matter. They did not wish to abolish the conjugal relationship but only to make sure that it was secondary to the spiritual union. Only in late 1843, probably influenced by the Shakers, whom they had visited several times, did Alcott and Lane begin to question the conjugal family. Only then did they begin to think of it as a selfish institution and a hindrance to a community based on universal love. And by then Alcott and Lane, faced with failure, were beginning to question everything, even each other, to help explain their plight. When the decision was forced, however, Alcott chose to stay with his family, which had been his bulwark, while Lane, once divorced, went away cursing the conjugal family.[93]

The Alcotts spent the winter of 1844 at the Lovejoys. Alcott spent day and night furiously writing an account of Fruitlands, eating only fruit and biscuits and drinking only water. For three days he went without food entirely. As a result of his regimen of self-deprivation he had what he later described as a "clairvoyant experience" while taking his cold water baths in the mornings. Louisa later described her father's condition as suicidal. Only the love of his family, she said, kept him alive.[94] Alcott described his struggle with despair in a short poem called "The Return":

As from himself he fled,
Outcast, insane,
Tormenting demons drove him from the gate.
Away he sped,
Casting his woes behind;
His joys to find—
His better mind.

Recovered
himself again
Over his threshold led.
Peace fills his breast,
He finds his rest;
Expecting angels his arrival wait.[95]

Meanwhile, his family had little to live on. Abby had to sell her few prized possessions—her cloak and a silver piece that had been a gift from Hannah Robie—in order to pay for food and the fifty cents a week that the Lovejoys charged. She wished her husband were more concerned about family support, though she knew that his dislike of working for gain was a matter of conscience. She visited Hopedale and Northhampton in hopes of finding a spot for her family in those communities. George Ripley invited them to be superintendents at Brook Farm. She rejected Ripley's offer because she preferred being a subordinate, and she felt, after Fruitlands, that her husband did not do well in positions of authority. None of the communities impressed her anyway. Northhampton life was "desultory and aimless," she felt, and Brook Farm was "no advance on the old world."[96]

They decided to "economize still further," and on April 24, 1844, they moved to Still River, Massachusetts, about a mile from Fruitlands, where they took four rooms and a garden for twenty-five dollars a year. In July Alcott, having partially recovered from the winter's doldrums, went with Anna to western New York to visit his mother, brother, and sister at Oriskany Falls and to visit the communities of Oneida, Marengo, and Skaneateles. They offered nothing. On the return trip a stagecoach drove away with two trunks full of his books and manuscripts. Among the lost items were his journals for 1842, 1843, and 1844, as well as his account of Fruitlands. It was just one more blow adding to his despair.[97] His poetry in the summer of 1844 reflected his loneliness and alienation:

> Lonely my dwelling here,
> Lonely the sphere,
> Weary the present, dark the future,
> Nor home have I, nor any Suitor;
> O when to me will come
> The long sought home,
> The friendly bosom;
> The tenement I covet
> Earth underneath and firmament above it,
> And tenures clear to prove it.
>
> Ah me
> Will this be
> Ere I die
> Life's mystic scroll
> And prophesy
> My destiny;
> A cheerless vagabond am I.[98]

His did not give up on the idea of community. In the fall of 1844 he sought participants for a new community in Boston and Concord. He thought he had Henry Thoreau talked into becoming a part of his family and a fieldmate. He wrote to his brother Junius asking him to join. The consociate family, the spiritual communion among families, was still important to him. "I cannot consent to live solely for one family," he told Junius,

> I would stand in neighborly relations to several and interpose an internal check to all selfish and narrow interests: institute a union and communion of families, instead of *drawing aside within the precincts of one's own acres and kindred by blood.*[99]

In mid-October the Alcotts left Still River for Concord, and temporarily occupied one half of Edmund Hosmer's home. With Hosmer's help they purchased the Cogswell property—"Hillside," Alcott called it—on the Lexington Road just east of Concord Center. Emerson paid five hundred dollars, and Samuel Sewall, agent of Joseph May's estate, paid eight hundred fifty from Abby's share. The property was held in trust on the advice of Samuel J. May. May felt that Alcott, who was never good at administering money or property, should not have direct control.[100]

The Alcotts considered Hillside to be the start of a domestic community founded on self-support, love, and labor. Alcott considered his new property to be "free soil" to which all interested parties could come to live "unmolested" by "tax-gatherers, usurers, and other oppressors of freemen." The family moved to Hillside on April 1, 1845, and Alcott immediately became immersed in repairs on the house and in planting his garden. Few people chose in join the proposed community. Thoreau did not come, nor did Junius Alcott. S. E. Jewitt from Haverhill talked of joining but never came. Sophia Ford came to help teach the children, and Charles Lane came to stay for several weeks, but this made no community. As was true at Fruitlands, no one wanted Alcott's "free soil." However, Alcott was more patient and resigned this time. "If a Holy Family is beyond us," he said, "we may at least exclude much that annoys and renders uncomely the Households on which we cast our eyes wheresoever we turn." He kept busy gardening, teaching his children, and conversing occasionally with Emerson. There were notes of encouragement. Young Emma Whiting wrote from Chicago that she had "found herself" by reading *Conversations on the Gospels* and wanted to meet Alcott. In October Robert Owen stopped to talk of communities and reform, but Alcott found greater satisfaction from harvesting his crops. "Planting and Building are the prime human creations," he told Samuel May. He was now prepared to plant and build gardens and houses rather than a new Eden.[101]

Notes

1. Catherine Albanese, "The Kinetic Revolution: Transformation in the Language of the Transcendentalists," *New England Quarterly* 48, no. 3 (September 1975): 319-40.

2. AJ 10 (1837): 3, 283; Alcott, "Psyche an Evangele," p. 43.

3. AJ 10 (1837): 202; AJ 11(1838): 233-42, 405-6, 427-28, 483-85; Orestes Brownson, "Alcott on Human Culture," *Boston Quarterly Review* 1, no. 4 (October 1838): 417-32; AJ 12 (January-July 1839): 803-6.

4. AJ 7 (1834), part 3: 148; AJ 8 (1835): 349; AJ 12 (January-July 1839): 433, 743-44.

5. Alcott, "Psyche an Evangele," pp. 43, 306-7, 310; AJ 10 (1837): 509-10; AJ 11 (1838): 103-4, 234-36; AJ 12 (January-July 1839): 393-94, 548.

6. AJ 11 (1838): 162-63, 330, 343-44, 394; AJ 12 (January-July 1839): 568, 571; AJ 10 (1837): 119.

7. AJ 12 (January-July 1839): 40, 99, 623-24, 669-70; AJ 11 (1838): 154-55; AJ 13 (July-December 1839): 30.

8. AJ 12 (January-July 1839): 44, 46, 218, 328, 478, 635-36; AJ 10 (1837): 572, 575; AJ 13 (July-December 1839): 154.

9. AJ 12 (January-July 1839): 194.

10. AJ 11 (1838): 256.

11. Ibid., pp. 239, 373; Alcott to Ralph Waldo Emerson, June 6, 1837, in Herrnstadt, ed., *Letters* pp. 33-34; AJ 12 (January-July 1839): 327-28; AJ 10 (1837): 261-62, 285-88.

12. AJ 11 (1838): 375-76.

13. AJ 12 (January-July 1839): 427; AJ 13 (July-December 1839): 483-84.

14. AJ 12 (January-July 1839): 296-99; AJ 13 (July-December 1839): 29.

15. Alcott, "Psyche an Evangele," p. 218.

16. Ibid., pp. 25, 90-92, 131, 148.

17. Ibid., pp. 213, 244-45, 325, 327.

18. James P. Greaves to Alcott, September 16, 1837, from a copy in Alcott's hand in AJ 10 (1837): 468-84; William Harry Harland, "Bronson Alcott's English Friends," typescript owned by the Fruitlands Museum, pp. 1-3. Harland's typescript has been published in Joel Myerson, "William Harry Harland's 'Bronson Alcott's English Friends,'" *Resources for American Literary*

Study 8 (Spring 1978): 24-60. Harrison, *Robert Owen*, pp. 127 ff.

19. AJ 10 (1837): 497 (this is the first of two pages numbered 497); Abby May Alcott to Mrs. Anna Alcott, October 29, 1837, from a copy in Alcott's hand in "Memoir 1878"; AJ 11 (1838): 119-20, 337-38; AJ 12 (January-July 1839): 521; Alcott to James P. Greaves, April 26, 1839, from a copy in Alcott's hand in AJ 12 (January-July 1839): 714-19; William Oldham to Alcott, June 18, 1838, from a copy in Alcott's hand in "Autobiography, 1834."

20. AJ 13 (July-December 1839): 93, 244, 309-10, 327; William Oldham to Alcott, June 18, 1838, from a copy in Alcott's hand in "Autobiography, 1834."

21. AJ 13 (July-December 1839): 316-19, 331-34; Harrison, *Robert Owen*, p. 74.

22. AJ 13 (July-December 1839): 264, 409, 412, 425, 468-74; Cooke, *Historical and Biographical Introduction*, 2: 149-50; John A. Heraud, "Expediency and Means of Elevating the Profession of the Educator in the Public Estimation," pp. 210-19, in *The Educator* (London: Taylor and Walton, 1839), pp. 133-260.

23. Alcott to Mrs. Anna Alcott, December 28, 1839, from a copy in Alcott's hand in AJ 13 (July-December 1839): 503-8; Alcott, "Autobiographical Index"; AJ 13 (July-December 1839): 19, 73-74, 143, 147; AJ 14 (1840): 55.

24. AJ 14 (1840): 55, 57-58; Abby May Alcott to Samuel J. May, March 13, 1840, from a copy in Alcott's hand in "Autobiography, 1834"; Alcott to Samuel J. May, April 6, 1840, in "Letters, 1836-1850"; Abby May Alcott, "Autobiography."

25. Sealts, ed., *Journals of Emerson*, 5: 328; Alcott, "Autobiographical Index."

26. Abby May Alcott to Samuel J. May, March 13, 1840, from a copy in Alcott's hand in "Autobiography, 1834."

27. Ralph Waldo Emerson to William Emerson, April 4, 1840, in Rusk, ed., *Letters of Emerson*, 2: 273.

28. Abby May Alcott to Samuel J. May, April 26, 1840, in "Family Letters, 1828-61"; Anna Alcott [Pratt], "Diary," MS in A. Bronson Alcott, comp., "Family Letters and Diaries, 1837-1850," at Houghton Library, 59M-305 (24).

29. AJ 14 (1840): 99; William Ellery Channing to Elizabeth Peabody, September 1840, in Peabody, ed., *Reminiscences of Dr. Channing*, p. 414; Anna Thaxter to Alcott, July 1840, from a copy in Alcott's hand in "Autobiography, 1834"; Alcott, "Autobiographical Index"; Alcott to Mrs. Anna Alcott, November 29, 1840, from a copy in Alcott's hand in "Memoir, 1878"; Alcott to Mrs. Anna Alcott, June 21, 1840, in "Letters, 1836-1850"; Abby May Alcott to Hannah Robie, September 13, 1840, from a copy in Alcott's hand in "Memoir of Abby May Alcott"; Franklin B. Sanborn and William Torrey Harris, *A. Bronson Alcott: His Life and Philosophy*, 2 vols. (Boston: Roberts Bros., 1893), 1: 303-6.

30. Myerson, "Calendar of Transcendental Club Meetings," pp. 205-6; AJ 13 (July-December 1839): p. 249; Cooke, *Historical and Biographical Introduction*, 1: 56-60; AJ 10 (1837): 403-5; Barbara Harrell Carson, "Proclus' Sunflower and The Dial," *English Language Notes* 11 no. 3 (March 1974): 200-202.

31. Cooke, *Historical and Biographical Introduction*, 1: 60-62, 68; Abby May Alcott to Hannah Robie, April 26, 1840, from a copy in Alcott's hand in "Memoir, 1878."

32. AJ 14 (1840): 65; Alcott, "Psyche an Evangele," pp. 199, 203; Ralph Waldo Emerson to Margaret Fuller, April 8, 1840, April 24, 1840, May 8, 1840, and July 8, 1840, in Rusk, ed., *Letters of Emerson*, 2: 276, 291, 294, 313; Margaret Fuller to Ralph Waldo Emerson, May 31, 1840, in Rusk, ed., *Letters of Emerson*, 2: 297n; A. Bronson Alcott, "Orphic Sayings," *The Dial* 1, no. 1 (July 1840): 85-98, and 1, no. 3 (January 1841): 351-61.

33. Alcott, "Orphic Sayings"; Margaret Fuller quoted by Alcott in AJ 14 (1840): 87.

34. AJ 14 (1840): 108, 110; unidentified news clipping in ibid., p. 108; Joel Myerson, " 'In the Transcendental Emporium': Bronson Alcott's 'Orphic Sayings' in the *Dial*," *English Language Notes* 10, no. 1 (September 1972): pp. 31-38; William Ellery Channing to Elizabeth Peabody, September 1840, in Peabody, ed., *Reminiscences of Dr. Channing*, p. 414; Cooke, *Historical and Biographical Introduction*, 1: 171-73; Alcott to John A. Heraud, September 1840, from a copy in Alcott's hand in AJ 14 (1840): 148-50.

35. A. Bronson Alcott, "Days From a Diary," *The Dial* 2, no. 4 (April 1842): 410-37; Alcott to

the Editor of *The Dial* [Margaret Fuller], December 6, 1841, printed in ibid., p. 409.

36. Ralph Waldo Emerson to Thomas Carlyle, October 30, 1840, in Joseph Slater, ed., *The Correspondence of Emerson and Carlyle* (New York: Columbia University Press, 1964), pp. 283-84.

37. Ralph Waldo Emerson to Margaret Fuller, August 16, 1840, in Rusk, ed., *Letters of Emerson*, 2: 323-24; Alcott, "Autobiographical Index"; AJ 14 (1840): 170, 199-200; Crowe, *George Ripley*, pp. 137-43; Rusk, *Emerson*, p. 289; Ralph Waldo Emerson to William Emerson, December 21, 1840, and March 30, 1841, in Rusk, ed., *Letters of Emerson*, 2: 371-72, 389; Abby May Alcott to Joseph May, August 4, 1840, and January 29, 1841, from copies in Alcott's hand in "Memoir, 1878."

38. Alcott, "Autobiographical Index"; Abby May Alcott to Joseph May, August 4, 1840, from a copy in Alcott's hand in "Memoir, 1878"; AJ 14 (1840): 131; Henry Steele Commager, *Theodore Parker*, 2d ed. (Boston: Beacon Press, 1947), pp. 47, 49; John Weiss, *The Life and Correspondence of Theodore Parker*, 2 vols. (New York: D. Appleton and Co., 1864), 1: 126 ff.

39. A. Bronson Alcott, comp., "Autobiographical Collections," 5 (1840-44): 21, 23, MS located at Houghton Library, 59M-307 (4); Alcott, "Autobiographical Index"; [Ralph Waldo Emerson], "Chardon Street and Bible Conventions," *The Dial* 3 (July 1842): 100-12; Commager, *Parker*, p. 50; Thomas, *The Liberator*, p. 302; AJ 14 (1840): 198.

40. [Emerson], "Chardon Street and Bible Conventions," pp. 102-3; Alcott, "Autobiographical Index"; Alcott, "Autobiographical Collections," 5: 75-95.

41. Alcott, "Orphic Sayings," *Dial* 1: 87; AJ 14 (1840): 22; Alcott to John A. Heraud, Septemebr 1840, from a copy in Alcott's hand in AJ 14 (1840): 148-49; William Henry Channing to Alcott, October 9, 1840, from a copy in Alcott's hand in AJ 14 (1840): 163-69. This letter was published in the *Providence Plain Speaker* in June 1841. Alcott to William Henry Channing, December 10, 1840, from a copy in Alcott's hand in AJ 14 (1840): 249-52.

42. Alcott, "Autobiographical Index"; *Boston Daily Advertiser*, October 27, 1841, from a copy of the article in Alcott's hand in "Various Papers, 1841-42," in Houghton Library, 59M-308 (14); George Thompson Scott to Maria Weston Chapman, November 29, 1841, owned by the Boston Public Library.

43. Alcott, "Autobiographical Index"; Alcott to Junius Alcott, September 28, 1841, from a copy in Alcott's hand in "Autobiography, 1834"; *Providence Plain Speaker* (January 30, 1841), from a clipping in "Autobiographical Collections," 5:53; Christopher Greene to Alcott, December 13, 1840, and Alcott to Christopher Greene, December 20, 1840, from copies in Alcott's hand in AJ 14 (1840): 256-60; Leo Stoller, "Christopher A. Greene: Rhode Island Transcendentalist," *Rhode Island History* 22, no. 4 (October 1963): 97-116. Additional information on Alcott's relations with Christopher Greene and the *Plain Speaker* can be found in Joel Myerson, "Additions to Bronson Alcott's Bibliography: Letters and 'Orphic Sayings' in the *Plain Speaker*," *New England Quarterly* 49 (June 1976): 283-92.

44. Stoller, "Christopher Greene," p. 103; Cooke, *Historical and Biographical Introduction*, 1: 168; Alcott to Junius Alcott, September 28, 1841; Abby May Alcott, "Diary," August, September, and October 1841, from copies in Alcott's hand in "Memoir, 1878."

45. Alcott, "Autobiographical Index"; Abby May Alcott, "Autobiography"; Abby May Alcott, "Diary," February, July, and August 1841, from copies in Alcott's hand in "Memoir, 1878"; Abby May Alcott to Mrs. Anna Alcott, October 3, 1841, from a copy in Alcott's hand in "Memoir 1878."

46. Abby May Alcott to Samuel J. May, November 24, 1841, and Hannah Robie to Mrs. Robie [Hannah Robie's sister-in-law], December 6, 1841, from copies in Alcott's hand in "Memoir, 1878."

47. Abby May Alcott to Samuel J. May, January 17, 1842, in "Family Letters, 1828-61"; Alcott to Junius Alcott, February 19, 1842, in "Letters, 1836-1850"; Margaret Fuller to Ralph Waldo Emerson, March 8, 1842, in Rusk, ed., *Letters of Emerson*, 3: 28-29.

48. Charles Lane to Alcott, March 16, 1840, from a copy in Alcott's hand in AJ 14 (1840): 88-90; Alcott's handwritten copy of the advertisement in the February 1840 issue of Heraud's *Monthly Magazine* is in "Autobiography, 1834"; Harland, "Alcott's English Friends," pp. 9-12;

Alcott to John A. Heraud [September, 1840] and Alcott to J. Westland Marston [September, 1840], from copies in AJ 14 (1840): 148-58.

49. Alcott to Junius Alcott, February 19, 1842; Ralph Waldo Emerson to Alcott, February 12, 1842, from a copy in Alcott's hand in "Letters, 1836-1850"; Abby May Alcott, "Diary for the Years 1841, '42, '43, and '44," MS at Houghton Library, 59M-311 (1); Abby May Alcott to Hannah Robie, May 1842, from a copy in Alcott's hand in "Memoir, 1878."

50. Alcott, "Autobiographical Index"; Abby May Alcott to Samuel J. May, May 15, 1842, from a copy in Alcott's hand in "Memoir, 1878"; Abby May Alcott, "Diary," May 6-June 1, 1842; William Lloyd Garrison to John Bowring, May 8, 1842, in "Letters, 1836-50"; Ralph Waldo Emerson to Thomas Carlyle, March 31, 1842, in Slater ed., *Correspondence of Emerson and Carlyle*, p. 320; Ralph Waldo Emerson to John Sterling, April 1, 1842, in Edward Waldo Emerson, ed., *A Correspondence between John Sterling and Ralph Waldo Emerson* (Boston: Houghton, Mifflin and Co., 1897), pp. 51-52.

51. Alcott, "Autobiographical Index"; AJ 51 (April-December 1875): 340; Alcott to Abby May Alcott, June 12, 1842, in "Letters, 1836-1850"; Harland, "Alcott's English Friends," pp. 16-17; [Ralph Waldo Emerson], "English Reformers," *The Dial* 3, no. 2 (October 1842): pp. 227-47.

52. Alcott to Abby May Alcott, June 12, 1842; Alcott to Abby May Alcott, June 17, 1842, in "Letters 1836-1850"; Alcott to William A. Alcott, June 30, 1842, in "Autobiographical Collections," vol. 5.

53. Alcott to Abby May Alcott, July 2, 1842, in "Letters, 1836-1850"; Emerson, "English Reformers," p. 233; Harland, "Alcott's English Friends," p. 4.

54. Alcott to Abby May Alcott, July 2, 1842; Thomas Carlyle to Ralph Waldo Emerson, July 19, 1842; in Slater, ed., *Correspondence of Emerson and Carlyle*, p. 320.

55. Alcott, "Autobiographical Index"; Harrison, *Robert Owen*, pp. 128-29.

56. Alcott, "Extracts from Diary" (AJ 16 [1842]), in "Autobiographical Collections," vol. 5. The Diary itself was among those papers lost by Alcott in 1844. Emerson, "English Reformers," p. 239; Alcott to Abby May Alcott, June 17, 1842, in "Letters, 1836-1850."

57. Alcott to Junius Alcott, June 30, 1842, in "Letters, 1836-1850"; Alcott to Abby May Alcott, July 2, 1842, and July 16, 1842, in "Letters, 1836-1850"; Alcott to William A. Alcott, June 30, 1842, in "Autobiographical Collections," vol. 5; Alcott, "Extracts from Diary."

58. Alcott to W. A. Alcott, June 30, 1842.

59. Ibid.; Alcott to Abby May Alcott, July 16, 1842.

60. Alcott to Abby May Alcott, July 16, 1842; a printed notice of the July 6, 1842, Convention at Alcott House in "Letters, 1836-1850."

61. Printed notice of Convention in "Letters, 1836-1850."

62. Alcott, "Autobiographical Index"; AJ 14 (1840): 217-18.

63. [A. Bronson Alcott], "The Pythagorean Life," *The Healthian* 1 no. 2 (October 1842): 81-83.

64. From a printed leaflet on the Physiological and Health Association in "Letters, 1836-1850"; Alcott to W. A. Alcott, June 30, 1842; "The Health Association," *The Healthian* 1, no. 2 (October 1842): 87-88.

65. Alcott to Abby May Alcott, August 2, 1842, in "Letters, 1836-1850"; Thomas Carlyle to Ralph Waldo Emerson, August 29, 1842, November 17, 1842, and March 11, 1843, and Ralph Waldo Emerson to Thomas Carlyle, October 15, 1842, in Slater, ed., *Correspondence of Emerson and Carlyle*, pp. 329-38.

66. James P. Greaves, *Letters and Extracts from the Manuscript Writings of James Pierrepont Greaves*, 2 vols. (Concordium, Ham Common, Surrey: 1843), 1: 3-13, 18-20; printed notice of Convention at Alcott House in "Letters from 1836-1850."

67. Alcott to Abby May Alcott, August 2, 1842, and August 16, 1842, in "Letters from 1836-1850."

68. Abby May Alcott, "Diary," August 22, September 8, and September 16, 1842; Alcott, "Autobiographical Index"; Ralph Waldo Emerson to William Emerson, October 26, 1842, in Rusk, ed., *Letters of Emerson*, 3: 93; Alcott, "Autobiographical Collections," 5: 216, 220, 224-25; Thomas Carlyle to Alcott, September 22, 1842, in "Autobiography, 1834"; Charles Lane

to Junius Alcott, December 26, 1842, owned by the Fruitlands Museum; Alcott to Edmund Quincy, December 24, 1842, owned by the Boston Public Library; Ralph Waldo Emerson to Margaret Fuller, November 16, 1842, in Rusk, ed., *Letters of Emerson*, 3: 96.

69. Alcott, "Autobiographical Index"; Charles Lane to the editor of *The Liberator*, January 16, 1843, in "Autobiographical Collections" 5: 256; Charles Lane, "Voluntary Political Government," *The Liberator*, February 21, 1843, from a clipping in "Autobiographical Collections," 5: 257-58; Charles Lane to William Oldham, December 31, 1842, quoted in Harland, "Alcott's English Friends," p. 13; Abby May Alcott, "Diary," January 17, 1843; John C. Broderick, "Thoreau, Alcott, and the Poll Tax," *Studies in Philology* 53, no. 4 (October 1956): pp. 612-26.

70. Alcott, "Autobiographical Index"; Charles Lane to William Oldham, May 31, 1843, quoted in Clara Endicott Sears, ed., *Bronson Alcott's Fruitlands* (Boston: Houghton Mifflin Co., 1915), pp. 14-15.

71. Abby May Alcott, "Diary," June 1, 1843; Alcott, "Autobiographical Index"; Alcott to Junius Alcott, June 18, 1843, owned by the Fruitlands Museum; Alcott to Chatfield Alcott, August 4, 1843, in "Letters, 1836-1850"; Louisa May Alcott, *Transcendental Wild Oats* (Concord, Mass: Thoreau Lyceum, 1974); Charles Lane to Henry Thoreau, June 7, 1843, quoted in Sears, ed., *Fruitlands*, pp. 22-23; Charles Lane to William Oldham, June 16, 1843, quoted in Sears, ed., *Fruitlands*, pp. 24-26.

72. Henry Seidel Canby, *Thoreau* (Boston: Houghton Mifflin Co., 1939), p. 147; Charles Lane to Henry Thoreau, June 7, 1843; Alcott to Junius Alcott, June 18, 1843; Alcott to Chatfield Alcott, August 4, 1843; Alcott, "Autobiographical Index"; Charles Lane to William Oldham, June 16, 1843; Lindsay Swift, *Brook Farm* (Secaucus, N.J.: Citadel Press, 1961), pp. 95-97, 125; AJ 24 (January-March 1850): 251; Vincent F. Holden, *The Yankee Paul: Isaac Thomas Hecker* (Milwaukee, Wis.: Bruce Publishing Co., 1958), p. 55.

73. Abby May Alcott, "Diary," August 1843.

74. Alcott, "Autobiographical Index"; Charles Lane to William Oldham, July 30, 1843, quoted in Sears, ed., *Fruitlands*, pp. 29-33; Abby May Alcott to Charles May, August 21 and November 6, 1843, from copies in Alcott's hand in "Memoir, 1878"; Abby May Alcott, "Diary," July 18, 1843.

75. William H. Gilman and J. E. Parsons, ed., *The Journals and Miscellaneous Notebooks of Ralph Waldo Emerson*, vol. 8 (1841-1843) (Cambridge: Harvard University Press, 1970), p. 433.

76. A. Bronson Alcott and Charles Lane, "The Consociate Family Life," *The Liberator* 3 (September 1843): 152; Alcott to [Almira Barlow], February 15, 1843, in Herrnstadt, ed., *Letters*, pp. 99-100.

77. Alcott and Lane, "The Consociate Family Life"; A. Bronson Alcott, "Sayings," *The Present* 1 (December 1843): 171.

78. [William Henry Channing], "Consociation, or the Family Life," *The Present* 1, no. 2 (October 15, 1843): 71-72.

79. Alcott to [Almira Barlow], February 15, 1843.

80. Gilman and Parsons, eds., *Journals of Emerson*, 8: 253-54, 305-6.

81. Alcott to [Almira Barlow], February 15, 1843; Charles Lane to William Oldham, July 30, 1843.

82. Charles Lane to William Oldham, July 30, 1843; Alcott, "Autobiographical Index"; Abby May Alcott, "Diary," September 17, 1843; Charles Lane to William Oldham, September 29, 1843, quoted in Harland, "Alcott's English Friends," pp. 35-38; Ralph H. Orth and Alfred R. Ferguson, eds., *The Journals and Miscellaneous Notebooks of Ralph Waldo Emerson*, vol. 9 (1843-1847) (Cambridge, Mass.: Harvard University Press, 1971), p. 26; AJ 31 (1856): 556-63.

83. Holden, *The Yankee Paul*, p. 60; Walter Elliott, *The Life of Father Hecker*, 2d ed., (New York: the Columbus Press, 1894), pp. 80-81; Isaac T. Hecker, *Questions of the Soul*, 10th ed. (New York: Catholic Book Exchange, 1899), pp. 73-82; Isaac Hecker, "Diary," quoted in Sears, ed., *Fruitlands*, pp. 76-82; Louisa May Alcott, *Transcendental Wild Oats*; Charles Lane to William Oldham, September 29, 1843.

84. Charles Lane to William Oldham, September 29, 1843.

85. Charles Lane to William Oldham, November 26, 1843, quoted in Sears, ed., *Fruitlands*, p. 123, and in Harland, "Alcott's English Friends," pp. 42-44; Louisa May Alcott, "Diary," September-December, 1843, quoted in Sears, ed., *Fruitlands*, pp. 107-11; Abby May Alcott, "Diary," December, 1843-January, 1844; Abby May Alcott to Samuel J. May, November 4, 1843, in "Family Letters, 1828-1861"; Abby May Alcott to Samuel J. May, January, 1844, from a copy in Alcott's hand in "Memoir, 1878"; Alcott, "Autobiographical Index."

86. Sanborn and Harris, *A. Bronson Alcott*, 1: 381; Aurele Durocher, "The Story of Fruitlands; Transcendental Wild Oats," *The Michigan Academician* 1 (Spring 1969): 37-45.

87. Victor F. Calverton, *Where Angels Dared to Tread* (Indianapolis, Ind.: Bobbs-Merrill Co., 1941), p. 251; Louisa May Alcott, *Transcendental Wild Oats*; Shepard, *Pedlar's Progress*, pp. 345-51.

88. David P. Edgell, "The New Eden: A Study of Bronson Alcott's Fruitlands," masters thesis, Wesleyan University (Middletown, Conn., 1939), pp. 28-29; Shepard, *Pedlar's Progress*, pp. 361-62.

89. Edgell, "The New Eden," p. 52; Franklin B. Sanborn, *Bronson Alcott at Alcott House, England, and Fruitlands, New England* (Cedar Rapids, Iowa: The Torch Press, 1908), pp. 74-76.

90. Richard Francis, "Circumstances and Salvation: The Ideology of the Fruitlands Utopia," *American Quarterly* 25 no. 2 (May 1973): 222-30.

91. AJ 21 (1847): 19; AJ 22 (1848): 373; AJ 45 (1870): 604.

92. Gilman and Parsons, eds., *Journals of Emerson*, 8: 356.

93. Printed Notice of Convention at Alcott House, in "Letters from 1836-1850"; Greaves, *Letters and Extracts*, 1: 6, 33; Ralph Waldo Emerson to Margaret Fuller, December 17, 1843, in Rusk, ed., *Letters of Emerson*, 3: 230.

94. Alcott, "Autobiographical Index"; Abby May Alcott to Samuel J. May, [between November 4, 1843 and April 9, 1844], and April 9, 1844, in "Family Letters, 1828-61"; AJ 21 (1847): 537-38: AJ 26 (1851): 303-6; Louisa May Alcott, *Transcendental Wild Oats*.

95. A. Bronson Alcott, "The Return," *The Commonwealth*, vol. 1, no. 36 (May 8, 1863). The poem was written in the spring of 1844.

96. Abby May Alcott, "Diary," January 16, January 28, and February 17, 1844; Abby May Alcott to Samuel J. May, January, 1844, from a copy in Alcott's hand in "Memoir, 1878."

97. Alcott, "Autobiographical Index"; Abby May Alcott, "Diary," April 24 and July 14, 1844; Abby May Alcott to Samuel J. May, August 11, 1844, from a copy in Alcott's hand in "Memoir, 1878"; Alcott to the Keeper of the Railroad House at Albany, New York, August 11, 1844, from a copy in Alcott's hand in "Autobiographical Collections," 5: 328. Alcott listed the lost items in "Letters, 1836-1850," p.111.

98. AJ 46 (1871): 514-15. The poem was written in July 1844.

99. Alcott to Junius Alcott, October 28, 1844, in "Letters, 1836-1850."

100. Alcott, "Autobiographical Index"; Alcott to Junius Alcott, January 2, 1845, in "Letters, 1836-1850"; Abby May Alcott, "Diary," November 12, 1844; Rusk, ed., *Letters of Emerson*, 3: 334n; Abby May Alcott, "Diary," January 1, 1845, from fragments of diaries at Houghton Library, 59M-311 (2).

101. Abby May Alcott, "Diary," January 1, 1845; Alcott, "Autobiographical Index"; Abby May Alcott to Samuel J. May, April 17, 1845, June 8, 1845, August 9, 1845, and December 10, 1845, in "Family Letters, 1828-1861"; Alcott to Samuel J. May, a note attached to Abby's letter of October 4, 1845, in "Family Letters, 1828-61"; Alcott to Junius Alcott, January 28, 1845, in "Letters, 1836-1850"; Alcott to Junius Alcott, July 27, 1845, in A. Bronson Alcott, comp., "Autobiographical Collections," vol. 6 (1845-1855), at Houghton Library, 59M-307 (5); Emma Whiting to Alcott, April 20, 1845, in "Letters, 1836-1850."

8

The Conversationalist, 1846–55

FOR nearly four years Alcott found vicarious satisfaction for his reform energies in his family, his garden, and his house at Hillside. He shaped the landscape instead of trying to shape society and institutions. His isolation became a kind of ongoing rebellion. By ignoring society he was also condemning it. Yet Alcott could not contain for long his desire to spread his ideas to other people. By 1848 his mood had changed from defiance to loneliness. He began to feel more and more useless and unwanted. For an answer to his dilemma he turned not to schools or communities but to that forum which he had tried with fair success in 1838 and 1839: the conversation. His message was less dramatic, less tinged with anger and rebellion, but his basic ideas remained the same. By the 1850s New England was more ready to listen to transcendentalist ideas, to take seriously talk about human culture. For a time Alcott made the conversation a recognized and valued cultural institution both in New England and in the West.

Alcott's retreat to home and garden in 1845 did not make him any less antagonistic toward the state. He believed that the "spark of freedom" was fast becoming extinct in America, and as a "protestant" and a reformer, it was his duty to fight to keep that spark alive. The "private persons" needed defenders to ward off encroachments by any power but conscience. Thus, in January 1846 he again refused to pay his poll tax. Again the authorities threatened him with imprisonment, but nothing came of it. Abby lamented that as the wife of a reformer she had to be willing to "die daily." Emerson complained that Alcott's attack on the state was narrow, that his true quarrel was with the "state of man," not with any single institution. "Why should [the scholar] poorly pound on some one string of discord," he said, "when all is jangle?" When Henry Thoreau went to jail for the same reasons in July 1846, Emerson thought it "mean and skulking"; Alcott thought it a "dignified non-compliance with the injunctions of civil powers."[1]

Alcott began to celebrate his isolation at Hillside as true freedom, the freedom of the sovereign individual. His retreat became a personal rebellion, a pinnacle from which he observed and freely judged the people and institutions around him. "Whoever needs the multitude, as the prop and surety of his greatness, and feeds on applause," he said defiantly, "forfeits his claim to enduring renown." To court the "democracy" was to impede genius, culture, virtue, and true freedom.[2] On the one hand he wanted to abolish the state:

> Why should I need a State to maintain me, and protect my rights? The man
> is all: let him husband himself[;] he needs no other servant. Self keeping is
> the best economy. That is a great age when the state is nothing, and men are
> all.[3]

Yet on the other hand he suspected that the state might be useful. The power
of government could preserve morality and prevent poverty and oppression.
He felt that governments should ensure that idlers, beggars, criminals,
oppressors, misers, and spendthrifts did not exist. A voluntary tax levied by
the government might maintain the ignorant and unfortunate. An equitable
distribution of earnings, he believed, would eliminate poverty; presumably the
state would have that responsibility. He wanted to compel parents either to
educate their children or to allow the state to do it. Alcott wished to avoid the
state, yet make use of its power. He lauded free-thinking, independent people,
but he expected those people to obey his moral absolutes.[4]

Alcott's isolation did not prevent his continued participation in the crusade
against slavery. Black emancipation, he felt, was a necessary prelude to
universal human freedom. The Alcotts continued to avoid using any article
produced by slave labor, especially things made of cotton. He believed that
civil strife, a war between freedom and slavery, was inevitable. In mid-
November 1846 he went to Providence to attend a three-day meeting of the
Rhode Island Abolition Society. In Boston he talked at length with the
abolitionist firebrands Garrison, Theodore Parker, Stephen Symonds Foster,
and Parker Pillsbury. Antislavery sentiment seemed to be spreading. He
became convinced that the abolitionists were finally stealing power from the
Whigs and the Democrats. And this was none too soon, he thought, for only the
abolitionists could save the nation from ruin. In January and February 1847
the Alcotts harbored a fugitive slave from Maryland and gave him provisions
for his flight to Canada. Alcott found the man sagacious, self-relying, and
possessed of "many of the elements of a hero." He believed the incident to be
a great lesson for his children, who he hoped would support the abolitionist
cause. The fugitive's stay at Hillside, thought Alcott, gave them all an image
and a name for the "dire entity" of slavery. No longer was it a mere
abstraction.[5]

Opposition to slavery caused Alcott to oppose vehemently the Mexican
War, which began in May 1846. The issue was clear to him. The war had
nothing to do with Mexican aggression or the threat of European intervention
in lands weakly administered by Mexico. It was blatant force by President
Polk and the United States government in the service of slavery. "The
Mexican War seems to have infatuated the country," he said.

> The love of conquest and glory leads numbers of young men, unfurnished
> with intelligence and moral principles, of which our country is all to[o] full,
> to enlist in this wanton strife for perpetuating the chains of slavery.
> Retribution must come at last.[6]

The war gave him greater distaste for the "multitude" that supported it and for the "seditious" United States Constitution that permitted such an inexcusable invasion of human liberties. "Are we a nation of Sharpers," he asked, "a people bent on conquest, on getting the golden treasures of Mexico into our hands, and of subjugating foreign peoples?"[7]

The Mexican War, the Irish potato famine, and the European revolutions of 1848 all combined to revive in Alcott the sense of impending cataclysm. He saw a great worldwide revolution in progress. "It is already 'too late' not only for kings, but for most else that now impedes man's steps to Imperial Self-Rule: the Imperial Man will arrive at last." He talked of organizing a "Freeman's League" to disseminate to the people of New England a knowledge of their rights. The League would sponsor clubs, lectures, tracts, and conventions, and would communicate with correspondents around the world. Members would practice abstention from church and state, nonvoting, nontaxpaying, and refusal of the products of wage or chattel slavery.[8]

But little came of Alcott's bitter and hostile rhetoric against the state. His Freeman's League did not materialize. The centrifugal force almost necessarily present among sovereign individuals made organizing them difficult if not impossible. Most of Alcott's energies at Hillside were directed to his house, his garden, his reading and writing. He conversed with neighborhood children and occasionally with adults. There were weekly discussions with Emerson about the state of literature in America, about reform and reformers, and about the personal needs of Alcott and his family. There were occasional excursions to Walden Pond to see Henry Thoreau, who had moved to his hermitage in the woods on July 4, 1845. Thoreau read to Alcott from his manuscript of *A Week on the Concord and Merrimack Rivers*, soon to be published, and from his essay on friendship. Alcott listened with admiration to Thoreau's Concord Lyceum address on civil disobedience in January 1848. He knew no other person besides himself who asserted absolute independence and individual self-rule as unreservedly as Thoreau did. Winter evenings with Emerson and Thoreau made real for Alcott his ideal conception of friendship. With them he felt that he was participating in ideas that would transform people and institutions. Yet he felt that Emerson limited his genius by taking refuge in the intellect, and that Thoreau limited his by taking refuge in nature. Complete genius, Alcott thought, encompassed intellect, nature, and society.[9]

Alcott carefully mapped out his daily winter regimen at Hillside. Order and routine were still means of purification for him. He arose at six and had breakfast at seven. The mornings he spent gathering firewood, reading, and writing; the afternoons, teaching his children. Supper was at six, then two more hours of reading and studying, then to bed promptly at nine. In the spring, summer, and fall, the routine still prevailed, but he spent most of each day outside with gardening, house repairs, and landscaping. He filled his journals with accounts of his daily labors—building his summer house, gathering his beans and turnips. His handwriting, normally neat and careful, became cramped and ragged from spending ten or twelve hours a day in hard, physical labor. He still abstained from eating meat, or drinking tea, coffee, or alcoholic beverages. He still took two cold showers a day, as had been his custom at Fruitlands.[10]

Gardening became a passion for Alcott. He wrote that he came to the earth with the same enthusiasm with which he had come to books in his younger days. His reformist tendencies had arisen from his desire to bring order to a changing world. Now his garden provided a vicarious sense of ordering and arranging that world. It was satisfying to improve barren ground. "External harmony of arrangement" brought a sense of order to his mind, he felt. "I am willing to convert this waste into a Paradise," he said after a long day's work one Saturday. The land proved much more malleable than other people, or institutions, or the world. He even passed up the Boston reform society anniversaries in May 1846, believing that his garden was his true province. The garden became a singular mode of therapy for a wounded and frustrated reformer.[11]

Landscaping became an art form for him, a mode of expression. If painting and writing were beyond his talent, he would draw his "picture" in the earth by completing the rough sketches that nature had made. Art, Alcott believed, was the combining of human creativity with the outlines, the designs, and the suggestions of nature. By improving the land at Hillside with gardens, orchards, and summer houses, he was applying his own creative genius to what nature had provided him. Nature was the "armory of genius," he said; it was the "Highest University and School of Eloquence." Yet Alcott did not celebrate nature for its own sake. Nature—meaning here the external material world—was passive, asleep, unless the "call of the spirit" aroused it. The dynamic interaction between human beings and nature was the important concept to Alcott, not nature itself. It reflected the synthesis he had made between Lockean empiricism and transcendental idealism. "All Nature," he said, "is replete with the tendencies to Beauty: and Genius alone knows how to combine these into elemental forms: Art is nature consummated."[12]

Alcott's renewed interest in nature reflected a more positive view of the external world than that he had known in his days of despair in the late 1830s and early 1840s. Then he had viewed it as the defecation of the spirit, the result of sin and evil. But in the years from 1845 to 1848, his conquest of nature in his garden was a salvation for him, and his friendship with the naturalist Thoreau was an inspiration to him. Thus he put a new emphasis on the potential of nature to stimulate genius and even to liberate a person from "demons." It was as though his interaction with nature had exorcised from his soul the evil that had overtaken him at Fruitlands.[13]

During the winter months at Hillside Alcott turned from his gardening and landscaping to find satisfaction in books. He read and reread from his favorite authors: Coleridge, Wordsworth, Milton, Spenser, Goethe, Plato, Pythagoras, even Thomas Carlyle. He read Emanuel Swedenborg's *Animal Kingdom*, a physiological study dealing with the relationship between the body and the soul. He delved into the *Epistles* of the sixteenth-century Protestant mystic

Jacob Boehme. The writings of Zoroaster, Saadi, Confucius, and especially the *Bhagavad Gita* suggested to him the need for a "Bible for Mankind," which would include the insight of Eastern scripture. He was charmed by Herman Melville's South Sea Island romance, *Typee*. Sophocles' *Antigone* justified civil disobedience for him. He studied ancient history, reading Tacitus's *Life of Agricola* and Connop Thirlwall's scholarly *History of Greece* as well as the letters of Pliny and Cicero. Reformist journals retained his interest, especially the *Herald of Freedom*, edited by abolitionist and nonresistant Nathaniel P. Rogers, who was a leader among the perfectionists and comeouters in New Hampshire in the 1840s. He also read regularly Brook Farm's *Harbinger*, the *Westminster Review* from London, and the *Liberator*.[14]

His reading was inspiring and reinforcing but it added little to the basic structure of his thought. He no longer found, as he once had, the satisfaction of shaping a new synthesis of ideas. The full pleasure of creating and building came through his landscaping and his summer houses. And Emerson and Thoreau both appreciated his work. Emerson was so impressed with the summer house that Alcott built behind Hillside that he asked Alcott to build him one. Alcott was eager to oblige. He began it in August 1847, with Thoreau assisting. His own summer house, made of hemlock and willow, was beautiful in its rustic simplicity. But for Emerson's he planned an elaborate "sylvan" style with odd curves and shapes. As it grew Emerson became more and more skeptical, calling it "Tumbledown Hall" in anticipation of its immediate collapse. He told Margaret Fuller that Alcott and Thoreau were building "a summer house of growing—alarming dimensions—peristyle gables, dormer windows, &c in the midst of my cornfield." Curious townspeople came every day to look, wonder, and laugh. Thoreau tried to convince Alcott that he should consider simple mathematics and geometry in designing the arbor, but Alcott would not hear of it. The witty Thoreau was amused, and Alcott, who was not easily amused, accused Thoreau of causing others to laugh at his masterpiece. He consoled himself with the belief that had Michelangelo placed his finest work in the "marketplace," the throngs would have scoffed at it too. Thoreau told Emerson, who had courageously left the unfinished summer house to its fate when he went to England in October 1847, that the arbor had "no disposition to be beautiful." Abby was appreciative, though. She called it "one of the most exquisite specimens of rustic architecture in the country."[15]

Alcott found time amid gardens, books, and summer houses to talk with Emerson, Thoreau, Ellery Channing, and a few members of the Transcendental Club about the need for a new journal and even a revival of club meetings. On April 14, 1847, Emerson hosted a group of interested literati to discuss a successor to the *Dial*. Alcott, Parker, Thoreau, William Henry Channing, Dwight, Caleb Stetson, James F. Clarke, James Elliot Cabot, Thomas T. Stone, John Weiss, and Charles Sumner attended; Emerson, Parker, and Sumner were appointed as a committee to find an editor and publisher. The result of these deliberations was the *Massachusetts Quarterly Review*, edited primarily by Parker. Alcott hoped it would be "a fair representation of the tendencies of the times," and "truly American in spirit and design." But he was disappointed. The first issue, in December 1847, contained "nothing of import," he felt. He believed that Emerson's beautiful opening remarks were "out of place" in comparison with the dull and uninspired material that followed. He was not the only one dissatisfied. In September 1848 Emerson, Thoreau, Ellery Channing, and Cabot met again to discuss another journal. They felt that the *Review* was too concerned with politics, economics, and the slavery question, thereby slighting the literary and philosophical issues it promised to convey as a successor to the *Dial*. It was no better than the *North American Review* or the *Christian Examiner*. Emerson told Parker that the *Review* could succeed only if the "idle lions" at Concord—Thoreau, Alcott, and Ellery Channing—were asked to contribute. Parker asked Emerson to see if "the aforesaid Lions would favor us with an occasional Roar, or at least a leonine whine." But the *Review* ended in September 1850, when the publishers failed. It received no help from the "Lions" or even from Emerson. Parker admitted that the *Review* never became what it was meant to be.[16]

As much as he wanted to see a fit medium for transcendentalism succeed, Alcott was more concerned about the survival of his family in 1847 and 1848. Life at Hillside was idyllic in many ways, but there was still too little income to provide an adequate livelihood. Abby felt especially oppressed by the constant debt, the sacrifice, and the continued begging from friends and relatives for help. Alcott hoped to take charge of a school to help increase the family's income. In August 1848 he applied once again to teach a district school in Concord, but the school committee rejected him in favor of "a child" because he refused to attend church. His political opinions were suspect, too. Horace Mann had refused to allow him to speak before the Massachusetts Teacher's Association in March 1847, lest his hostility to the state damage the cause of popular education.[17]

The life-style of the Alcott children was limited by poverty, but they were not unhappy. Their parents encouraged them to explore their interests and develop their talents. Anna studied French and German, the latter language taught by her father's friend George Bradford. Louisa was interested in writing, and Alcott noted that she seemed to have a genius for anything she chose to do. He felt, and undoubtedly hoped, that Elizabeth and young Abby were more scholarly and intellectual than the older girls. In November 1847 sixteen-year-old Anna left for Walpole, New Hampshire, to teach and help the family's income while living with Abby's cousin Elizabeth Wells. Alcott wrote to her several times with encouragement and advice about teaching. He told her that he could think of no greater pleasure than to have her choose teaching, that profession he considered second to none in the world.[18]

Poverty caused the Alcotts to seek alternatives. Emerson tried to get Alcott some land on the Sandwich Islands—his friend Giles Waldo was negotiating with the Islands' king—but Alcott was not interested. He felt he was "cured of seeking contentment in foreign parts." Abby's friends and benefactors did all

they could to help. In the fall of 1846 Hannah Robie had arranged for the
Alcotts to take as a boarder a mentally disturbed teenage girl, Eliza Stearns.
Eliza's father was about to put her in an asylum, but the ever-compassionate
Abby offered to do what she could to help Eliza for four dollars a week. Eliza
proved to be an enormous burden because she was in "a bad state of
imbecility," and the income neither justified the extra work nor solved the
family's financial problems. Friends suggested that the family move closer to
Boston and to a smaller house to help alleviate the misery. In April 1848 Abby
went to Portland, Maine, to see about a job as matron of James Farrar's
"Water Cure" in nearby Waterford. Farrar persuaded her to take the job, and
on May 11 she arrived in Waterford with little Abby and Eliza Stearns. She
hoped that the water cure, a daily regimen of baths and dieting, along with the
additional remedy of wrapping in wet sheets, would help Eliza. But Eliza did
not improve and Abby quickly became tired of the arduous routine of her
work as matron. Her income could not make up for the pain of separation
from her family. She returned to Concord on July 11.[19]

Abby continued to look for work. She applied as a matron at Samuel
Gridley Howe's new "Idiot Asylum" begun in South Boston in October 1848.
"Prejudice" against her husband, she said, denied her the job. She tried to
arrange for a school in Cambridge for Anna and Louisa to teach, but was told
that her husband's religious opinions were "repugnant to the Christian world
of Cambridge." By the summer of 1848 Alcott, too, was feeling the need for
action. Three years of relative seclusion and communion with nature had
restored his hope and his sense of mission. Once again he felt oppressed at
being unable to find an adequate means of carrying out that mission. He began
to consider seriously another round of conversations like those of 1838 and
1839 in Boston and neighboring communities. Again he thought of joining
Hopedale, and in late October he and Louisa looked for a house there, met
Adin Ballou, and conversed with members of the community. In the meantime
Abby's faithful friends—Samuel Sewall, Mrs. James Savage, Mrs. Lemuel
Shaw, Hannah Robie, Jonathan Phillips—each contributed thirty dollars a
month to pay her to visit the poor in Boston. So on November 17, 1848, after
"three years laborious struggle to get subsistence," the Alcotts moved from
Hillside to Dedham Street in Boston.[20]

Soon after arriving in the city Alcott arranged rooms and a prospectus for
his proposed conversations. He planned to hold seven weekly sessions on
"Man: His History, Resources, and Expectations," charging three dollars per
session for singles, five dollars for couples. Elizabeth Peabody sold the tickets
at her bookstore, and Alcott, having overcome his earlier reservations about
such expedients, advertised in the newspapers.[21]

The series began on Saturday, December 9, 1848, and ended successfully on
February 3, 1849. It became a prototype for eight highly successful series of
conversations that Alcott held in Boston between 1848 and 1853. They became
a recognized part of Boston's cultural life, and Alcott eagerly carried them to
other towns near and far: to Cambridge, Lynn, Haverhill, Hingham, Barre,

Plymouth, Salem, Abington, Millvale, Medford, Fall River, and Hopedale. To those who had heard him talk since the late 1830s, the message was familiar. He talked of the spiritual nature of the soul, the potential of human genius, and the means of human culture. He talked about the ancient writers: Socrates, Plato, Pythagoras, Confucius, Saadi, and Zoroaster. He discussed nature, childhood, diet and regimen, the family, the church, reform and reformers. In what was undoubtedly his best and most popular series, he characterized those whom he considered to be among the most important and influential people of the day: Webster, Garrison, Parker, Dr. Channing, William Henry Channing, Margaret Fuller, and Emerson. An average of fifty-seven people attended each of these sessions held in January and February 1851.[22]

For Alcott, conversation was both a means of reform and a form of art. It provided him both a means of carrying out his mission to humankind and a medium of expression. "Talking is the mightiest instrument which the soul can wield," he had said in 1839. "It is the Creative Word that works all changes in the world. This word is the revelation of the soul." Conversation would accomplish what his schools were meant to accomplish: the great work of human culture. It would draw out the innate goodness of the divine soul and provide it a means for its free expression. Conversation was no mere question-and-answer session for Alcott. It was a mood, an atmosphere; it was a work of art as surely as were paintings or symphonies. Alcott especially liked the analogy to a symphony. He believed that the ideal conversation developed a single theme and presented it in a variety of ways, providing the greatest scope and freedom for the genius of the participants. Each of the participants would contribute his or her ideas about the theme, thus presenting differing expressions of the theme like the various instruments in an orchestra. All would blend together in beautiful harmony as the session progressed. Noble thoughts were to him what beautiful melodies were to Haydn or Beethoven.[23]

Generally, Alcott opened his conversations with a short reading from one of his favorite authors, such as Plato, Pythagoras, or Coleridge. He would then make some introductory remarks about the theme chosen for the session and await comments from his audience. When beginning a session with an unfamiliar group, he would patiently explain the need to develop friendship and trust among the participants. The atmosphere for the free expression of thought needed careful cultivation, he said. He sincerely disliked monopolizing a conversation, although he often did just that, especially with a new group. Octavius B. Frothingham, later the historian of transcendentalism, criticized Alcott for talking too much. Frothingham called Alcott the "most adroit soliloquizer" he had ever heard, whose conversations were really "versations" without the "con." But conversations in which he had to do all the talking Alcott considered to be failures. His theory was that of the "true teacher," who "does not play the cook and spread the tables, but whets the curiosity to leap straightway forth upon the mountains and bring home the game which he has started and given the scent of."[24]

Alcott's conversations lacked strict method, systematic thought, or continuity. But Alcott cultivated that absence of order. "All the beauty & advantages of Conversation," he said,

is in its bold contrasts, & swift surprises; its large suggestiveness; its fine implications and unexpectedness. Its logic is swift & long, & it vaults over the passes, & is good as it is chasmic, & leaps into the dark, & across centuries & continents. . . . Prose and logic are out of place, where all is flowing, magical, & free.[25]

Therefore Alcott believed that conversations were the most difficult events to report in writing. No pen could capture the atmosphere, the spontaneity, the sparkle of magic that he felt he attained in his most successful sessions. With the exception of his introductory reading, he never used notes or a prepared outline. The art of conversation, he thought, was in liberating the mind from the fetters of form and tradition. Notes and texts just constrained the free flow of ideas. Conversation was the divine goodness of the transcendent soul freely expanding and exploring. "Conversation is best," he claimed, "when tentative, cumulative, & refuses the foreseen and determined passes, to have its own free and fearless way, opening out prospects which no foresight could command, & which are new and surprising." It was to be experiential in the same way that Alcott hoped religion would be. It was to be organic, developmental; if successful, the participants would have created a mood or an atmosphere greater than the sum of its parts, which itself would serve as a stimulus to each individual present.[26]

Anyone anxious to resolve some burning public issue or to engage in argument or debate was disappointed, even disgusted, at the lack of direction in an Alcott conversation. Alcott hated controversy and contention. An argumentative person such as William Lloyd Garrison was distinctly out of place in the parlor. Alcott appreciated Garrison's ability as an advocate in public conventions and in newspaper battles, but he recognized the limitations of such skills: "He [Garrison] must have an enemy, or he is no more than other men. And is never great except in controversy & argument, where he is eloquent and admirable." Such greatness as Garrison's, Alcott felt, added nothing to a conversation. Indeed, it often detracted from the mood Alcott tried to create.[27]

The success of an Alcott conversation depended largely on the group assembled. Alcott was not at his best unless he had a sympathetic audience. He needed reinforcement to draw out his best words. After several uncomfortable experiences with tireless debaters such as Garrison or the acidic Theodore Parker, Alcott concluded that there were social laws that strictly governed effective conversation. Harmony among personalities was essential to free-flowing talk. Unfortunately, some personalities attracted each other, some repelled. "I am distracted in some companies," he admitted,

mute in most; demented in some; quite social in others; and take these experiences as intimations of my standing with the parties I meet; and as renderings of the social laws for my benefit.[29]

A "select company" was best for conversation, he thought. Such a group included people with a certain "innocency" about them, who had an "openness of soul" and were willing to abandon themselves to ideas and sentiments. This required a diffidence and modesty about imposing one's own ideas on the group at the expense of harmonious discussion. It necessitated a willingness to listen, to help unfold the central idea, not dispute it.[30]

There was contradiction in Alcott's celebration of "free-flowing" conversation and his desire to create an aesthetic mood, an artistic work. Participants were free only to the extent that they contributed to that mood, to that flowing together of souls into a harmonious, magical unity. In effect, Alcott did not like to have people disagree with him.[31] He wanted his listeners to build upon what he said about the soul, or about human nature, or about proper diet; he wanted them to develop the idea with rich imagery and illustration in the same way that the elements of a painting or a symphony contributed to the wholeness of a work of art. Any challenge to his basic assumptions destroyed the atmosphere for him, ruined his work of art.

Despite the contradiction, Alcott's theory of the epistemological effects of conversation follow logically from his basic synthesis of Lockean empiricism with transcendental idealism. His theory implied a dynamic interaction of internal human powers with the external world. In conversation, other minds, other souls, served as external stimuli to him, and he to them. And all participants added to the overall mood and atmosphere and received stimulation from it. The atmosphere of a conversation, like the common conscience in the Temple School, was more than the sum of its parts and served as an external symbol of the spirit at work that called forth spiritual powers in each person present.

Attendance at Alcott's Boston conversations was generally good. A group of fifty or more was common. The conversations became a part of the city's cultural calendar along with series of lectures by Emerson, James Russell Lowell, James F. Clarke, and William H. Channing. They drew from Boston's intellectual elite. Transcendentalists, reformers, and literary figures came: Emerson, Thoreau, James Clarke, Sarah Clarke, William H. Channing, Elizabeth Peabody, Parker, Dwight, Bartol, Garrison, Lowell, and George B. Emerson. Among others in attendance were abolitionists Parker Pillsbury, Abby Kelly Foster, Thomas Wentworth Higginson, and Elizur Wright; women's rights advocates Dr. Harriot Hunt and Lucy Stone; German refugee writer and lecturer Emmanuel Scherb; critic Edwin Percy Whipple; former Temple School patrons Edward Bangs and Dr. John Flint; Abby's wealthy friend and benefactor, Hannah Robie; spiritualist Andrew Jackson Davis; former Temple School students Martha Kuhn and Lucia Peabody; Dr. Channing's brother, Walter Channing, and Dr. Channing's son, William Francis Channing; Emerson's friends Samuel Gray Ward and James Elliot

Cabot; wealthy lawyer and benefactor of the arts Horatio Woodman; and Swedish traveler and writer Fredrika Bremer.[32]

The conversations were successful enough to attract the attention and interest of those with the influence to open other doors for Alcott. Young Ednah Dow Littlehale, a devotee of Margaret Fuller, felt a "strengthening influence" from Alcott's "high ideal" upon first attending the conversations in 1848. She became a lifelong friend and supporter of Alcott and made transcripts of several of his conversations that he faithfully preserved in his journals. A leader and organizer, she arranged for Alcott a series of Platonic readings with a group of young women in the winter of 1849. Thomas T. Stone, Jones Very, and Nathaniel and Sophia Peabody Hawthorne helped arrange a series of conversations in Salem in the spring of 1849, and the influence of the Reverend Samuel Longfellow, brother of the poet Henry Wadsworth Longfellow, permitted a successful series in Fall River, Massachusetts, the following June. The Reverend John T. Sargent asked Alcott to lead Sunday evening meetings at his church in Boston's South End in the fall of 1849. In the spring of 1852 naturalist Benjamin Marston Watson sponsored Alcott conversations as a part of a Plymouth lecture series that also included Emerson, Thoreau, Henry James the Elder, Wendell Phillips, Adin Ballou, Edmund Quincy, Thomas W. Higginson, Jones Very, and Horace Greeley.[33]

By 1851 Alcott was experiencing a hint of success. He became more and more certain that the conversation was his best mode of interaction with society, his best reform instrument. He realized that talking was his best means of expression. He looked upon the conversations of 1848 and 1849 as having almost won the victory for him at a time when he came from Concord "gleaning and groping, here and there for some hint of what I wanted." Conversation, he believed, was the "natural gymnastic" for his talents. If writing failed to give him a way to serve human needs, he would speak his books. He theorized that his past failures had resulted from his lack of understanding of how to approach people. Conversation was the right approach, he thought. He would be a "spiritual pedlar." His "parlour teaching" would become a counterpart to the lyceum as an instrument for awakening the masses.[34] It would be a truly American institution:

Garrison made the *convention*. *Greeley* made the *newspaper*. *Emerson* made the *lecture*. And *Alcott* is making the *Conversation*. These are all purely American organs and institutions, which no country nor people besides ours can claim as we can.[35].

Emerson agreed that conversation was a "power" and ought to become an institution.[36]

That Alcott was not entirely wrong in believing that his calling was conversation was apparent in the comments of those who attended. Ednah Littlehale felt that his talks were "elevating" and "exhilarating," and that

Alcott's high aspiration and originality of thought were a great and helpful influence on young minds like hers. The Harvard students who invited him to converse several time at times at the Divinity School in the spring of 1853, most prominently Franklin Sanborn and Moncure Conway, confirmed their attraction to Alcott's idealism by frequent visits to Alcott's home. Alcott was honored. "I take these confidences of the young men as an evidence of the Private Professorship I am holding in these times," he said. Fredrika Bremer, the inquisitive Swede who was fascinated by Emerson and the transcendentalists, was both amused and excited by Alcott. She participated in several conversations in 1849 and 1850 and visited the Alcotts at home. "Alcott drank water, and we drank—fog," she concluded, after one session. Yet she was captivated by him, especially by his speaking for principles that were "neither salable nor yet transitory."[37] One attendant, M. D. Paine, was completely enraptured by Alcott's conversations:

> To say that I have been taught & cheered is not enough; you have made me dare to live, & feel, & exult. The earth I tread is not the same, the life I lead Transcends my former dream.[38]

Though not so extravagant in their praise as Paine, Emerson, and James Russell Lowell, both recognized Alcott's power in conversation. And they realized that he had no other means of expressing his ideas. Emerson believed Alcott was "a certain fluid in which men of a certain spirit can easily expand themselves and swim at large, they who elsewhere found themselves confined." But these people, thought Emerson—and he included himself among them—had no way to communicate their good opinion of Alcott to others because Alcott left no books, no doctrines, no sayings that might provide supporting evidence.[39] "Alcott is like a slate pencil which has a sponge tied to the other end," said Emerson,

> and, as the point of the pencil draws lines, the sponge follows as fast, and erases them. He talks high and wide, and expresses himself very happily, and forgets all he has said. If a skilful operator could introduce a lancet and sever the sponge, Alcott would be the prince of writers.[40]

Lowell agreed:

> While he talks he is great, but goes out like a taper, if you shut him up closely with pen, ink, and paper.[41]

As a part of his effort to promote conversations, Alcott prompted the organization of a new club, which he hoped would provide a forum for ideas, frequent discussion of the "great questions," and a meeting place for the "leading minds" of the time. In February 1849, with the end of his first successful series of Boston conversations, Alcott wrote and mailed a circular advertising a March 20 meeting to discuss the organization of the new club. A large number of Boston's intellectuals attended, including most of the original members of the Transcendental Club and many of the regular participants in Alcott's conversations. They agreed to occupy a club room near a café, to organize a library with subscriptions to the "best" European and American journals, and to hold regular meetings at which members would give lectures, readings, or conversations. A week later they met again and took the name "Town and Country Club."[42]

Alcott led the organizational drive, writing letters, talking to prospective members, looking for club rooms. By the end of April over one hundred persons had become members. Emerson, James Elliot Cabot, and James T. Fisher were elected as the executive committee. Alcott became the Corresponding Secretary and Librarian, responsible for maintaining the club room and notifying members of meetings. Unlike the Transcendental Club, the new club had formal rules for membership, a membership fee, a constitution, and a system for blackballing and exclusion. It included an enormous number of people covering an extremely broad range of interests. Though Alcott did not say so, he must have been concerned that a club of this size would fail to follow the social laws he thought necessary for the harmonious exchange of ideas. Indeed, dissension began quickly. At the May 2 election meeting William Lloyd Garrison and Thomas Wentworth Higginson objected to the exclusion of women from the club. The constitution read: "The Town and Country Club is formed to establish better acquaintance between men of scientific, literary and philanthropic pursuits." Consistent with his earlier defense of women's rights, particularly the right of women to speak publicly and to participate in reform organizations equally with men, Garrison demanded that the Town and Country Club's membership be "broad and universal" in this "age of progress and reform." He vehemently opposed any exclusion based on sex or race. Emerson opposed excluding blacks from the Club, but he also opposed making the club a "saloon for ladies." Garrison asked the reasons for excluding women, but the only response he received was that club members' smoking might bother the women, or that wives of members might object to their husbands' frequently meeting other women at the club rooms. The Club voted on whether to change the Constitution to read "men and women" or "persons" instead of "men," but those motions failed. The members finally agreed that "men" was a generic term and thus implied no official exclusion. But in fact the members asked no women to join.[43]

Even though the Club provided Alcott with a convenient room to hold his conversations in the fall and winter of 1849-50, he was disenchanted with it. He found that little was said at club meetings worth remembering despite addresses by Emerson, Parker, and Henry James. The energy and excitement of transcendentalism was dissipated in clouds of tobacco smoke as the Club devolved into an exclusive social organization for men. Alcott talked of forming another club with only the "flower" of the Town and Country Club. It had quickly become apparent that the diversity of membership did indeed constrain free discussion. By early 1850 the Club was in financial trouble. Its membership and attendance declined rapidly. Few came to the club rooms except for regular meetings. "Country" members, those living thirty miles or more from Boston, found it difficult to attend at all. Alcott noted an "indifference" creeping over Club members as discussion at meetings rarely became more profound than chatter about the reported sightings of sea serpents.[44]

By March 1850 Alcott was resigned to the imminent dissolution of the Club. Its size and diversity had caused major problems, as had its failure to include women. Women had always played key roles in his conversations, and he thought it folly not to admit them to the Club meetings. He took no active part in the debate over the admission of women, probably because of his distaste for contentious argument and his feeling that the question need never have been asked. His final pronouncement on the Club reflected his disgust: "The Club left out the feminine element, & is soon to be left out, in its turn." On May 2, 1850, the Club voted to sell its effects and dissolve. Alcott was given the records of the Club and the seventeen dollars fifty cents left over after the payment of debts.[45]

With all of Alcott's success in conversation in the late 1840s and early 1850s, the condition of his family improved very little. From 1848 to 1853 his conversations earned a total of only seven hundred fifty dollars. Alcott never measured success in financial terms. He lacked business sense and had no desire to make his conversations a business anyway. He charged very little and often allowed interested people to attend whether they paid or not. And one series of conversations a season was about all the market could bear. Thus the family depended upon the money Abby received for her missionary work to pay the greater share of daily expenses. She operated a relief room for collecting clothing, food, and household necessities, and distributing them to the poor. Her relief room was also an employment center, advertising the "best German, American, and well recommended Irish help procured at the shortest notice." She spent long, frustrating hours visiting the poor all over the city. Her supply of alms was never enough to meet the growing demand, especially by the increasing numbers of Irish immigrants who came in the aftermath of the potato famine. As her direct contact with poverty and misery increased—and her family was scarcely better off than her clients—she became more and more impatient with the clergy and the private agencies for poor relief, those traditional American instruments of dealing with ugly social problems. She accused the ministry of being nothing but a "sinecure," and the relief agencies of wasting time in laborious discussion of resolutions over toast and tea while the poor were starving. She called the state and municipal legislation on pauperism "shallow" and accused the "present social compact" of robbing the poor of their rights. She did her best to aid anyone who applied for help, even blacks, who were often excluded from relief help just as they were excluded from the public schools.[46]

Abby's work was exhausting and financially unrewarding. Her chief sponsor, the Huntington Society, was not so cooperative as she wished, so in

April 1850 she resigned as their agent. Six months later she opened her own "Ladies Help Exchange" at the Alcott home on High Street. She operated this private employment agency for two years until failing health forced her to stop in October 1852. The family struggled to survive on Abby's income of seventy-five cents to a dollar a day and with help from Samuel May and Hannah Robie, who contributed money for groceries and rent. The older girls also helped. Anna tutored the children of Abby's relatives, George and Louisa Bond, in Jamaica Plain, then opened a school of her own on Suffolk Street. In the summer of 1850 she went to Lenox in western Massachusetts to work as a "nursery girl" for Caroline Sturgis Tappan, leaving Louisa to teach the Suffolk Street School. Homesickness drove her back to Boston in July. Early in 1851 Anna took a job as governess for the George Minot family in Boston, while Louisa agreed to be a servant for a family in Dedham. Louisa found herself shoveling snow and splitting firewood. She hated every minute of it and quit after only a month. When Abby ended her mission work in October 1852, the family moved to Pinckney Street, where Anna and Louisa opened a school and Abby took in boarders. Elizabeth, who was left with the depressing burden of housework, planned to attend the Boston Normal School, but never did. Abby May, who was twelve in 1852, attended the Boston public schools.[47]

The annual return on Abby's inheritance, a little over one hundred dollars, as well as the pittance that Abby and the girls made at their various vocations, brought no substantial relief from the crunch of poverty in the early 1850s. The lowest point was in the spring of 1850 when, without visible means of support and help, the entire family contracted varioloid, a mild form of smallpox, probably from contact with an immigrant family that had come to Abby for relief. Alcott's illness proved to be confluent smallpox, which he battled for a month without the aid of physicians or medicine. His portrait, he said, was like that of "some grenadier of revolutionary cast, frightful to behold." In the meantime vicious gossip circulated that Alcott was indifferent to the welfare of his family, that he was thriftless, heartless, and incapable. But Alcott was not indifferent; he just felt unable to help them in the usual ways. He was a man of ideas, and ideas, he declared, could not be "borne about, like bales of merchandize, on the shoulder, and thrown down at rich-men's warehouses, as articles of commerce." He felt sure that if he could fight smallpox with his own resources, he could handle the gossip. His conscience assured him that his course was the right one; it mattered little what the world thought. Though he was poor of pocket, he felt that he was also the "richest of men."[48]

Friends and relatives such as Samuel J. May wondered, and rightly so, why Alcott could not find something to do that would add to his family's support. He did consider opening another school. In March 1851 John T. Sargent offered to sponsor six pupils. But Alcott hesitated, undoubtedly fearing further failure and censure, and wary lest he be restricted in practicing his ideal of human culture as he wished. Theodore Parker warned that there was no basis for a prosperous school for an idealist among the merchants and materialists of Boston. Alcott reluctantly considered opening an employment service for males corresponding to that of his wife's. Indeed, he occasionally helped Abby with her cases. But this plan came to nothing. He hesitated to work for money in any way that was unrelated to his ideals and principles. And he knew that his practical capabilities were few. He could not compete with the Irish in cradling grain; he had no training to be a clerk. So, aside from conversing, he passed the time reading, writing in his journals, walking on the Common, visiting Emerson in Concord, and receiving friends such as Thoreau, Sanborn, and Ellery Channing. There were very special, but high-minded, early morning walks on the Common with Ednah Littlehale, whose youthful energy and intelligence infatuated him. Sometimes he and Abby quarreled about his lack of productivity, but generally Abby defended him, aware that his talents were not marketable. Emerson, though at times he too became irritated at Alcott's lack of action, thought it a bitter satire on the social order that it could not support such an "advanced soul."[49]

The family's plight was eased a little in March 1852 with the sale of Hillside to Nathaniel Hawthorne for $1,550. The investment of one thousand of the amount brought in an additional seventy dollars each year. Louisa was now making a little extra money selling her short stories to magazines. By the spring of 1853 there was definite improvement. That winter had been one of Alcott's busiest in conversations, and his circle of Harvard students was sponsoring more conversations and coming to him for advice. In the summer of 1853 Emerson suggested that Alcott take his message to the canal and river towns of the West: Syracuse, Rochester, Buffalo, Cleveland, and Cincinnati. Edwin P. Whipple encouraged Alcott to do so and offered to contact friends in the West to help promote such a tour. Emerson did the same and paid the eighteen dollars for Alcott's train fare to Cincinnati.[50]

Alcott headed west on October 26, leaving Abby to wonder how it was that her husband was always provided for in some mysterious way. He stopped first in Oriskany Falls, New York, to visit his mother and brother Chatfield. It was a sad reunion. The previous year Alcott's dearest brother, Junius, who in between fits of insanity had dabbled in transcendentalism, mysticism, and spiritualism, had committed suicide by throwing himself into a machine. He left a wife and four children as well as a grieving eighty-year-old mother. From there Alcott went on to Syracuse to visit the Samuel Mays and Anna, who was staying with the May family. He conversed with some of May's parishioners before moving on to Rochester on November 1. In Rochester he met William Henry Channing, who was then serving the Unitarian church there. He and Channing visited a retreat for "juvenile offenders," and talked of reform. Channing promised to help Alcott arrange conversations for his return trip.[51]

After stopping briefly to visit his cousins, the Bronsons, in Medina, Ohio, just south of Cleveland, Alcott sped on to Cincinnati, where he arrived on November 8. In Cincinnati he met Ainsworth R. Spofford, a bookseller and organizer of literary clubs, whom Emerson had contacted to make arrangements for Alcott. With Spofford's aid Alcott held a series of five successful and well-attended conversations on "The Conduct of Life" at Cincinnati's Apollo Hotel between November 11 and November 23. He closed his stay on November 27 by meeting the Young Men's Literary Club. The Cincinnatians were receptive to his ideas on human culture, and rewarded him with $209 for the six evenings. He joyfully sent $150 to Abby, elated that fortune had finally found him. His success confirmed his belief that only by conversation could he win approval. He even hesitated to write to his family about his trip, knowing his lack of ability with the pen. "Poor philosopher all flowing at the lip," he said, "is so barren and disappointing in all ways else and writes with shame if he writes at all."[52]

On November 30 Alcott arrived in Cleveland and found that grocer H. M. Chapin had arranged a series of conversations to begin on December 7. This series of five, though well-attended, was not so successful, Alcott thought, because the participants said very little. But he collected another fifty dollars. He prospered under the management of businessmen like Spofford and Chapin. If Cincinnati impressed him by its readiness to converse, Cleveland impressed him by its similarity to cities in Connecticut. Much of its population consisted of emigrants from his home state. He spent an evening with United States Senator John A. Foote, whose brother, wife, and wife's sister had been Alcott's students in Cheshire.[53]

Alcott arrived in Syracuse on December 19 and sent twenty-five dollars to Abby and Christmas presents to the family. He held five conversations in Syracuse that were well received publicly, but he discovered that few people invited him to their homes for private conversation as had been the case in Cincinnati and Cleveland. Philosophers, he supposed, were "a class every where not a little dangerous if not embarrassing to encounter particularly in one's house, and at tea." The tour ended with his return to Boston on January 21, 1854. All in all it was a tremendous success despite his inability to arrange conversation in Buffalo and Rochester. As a result of his earnings, the financial condition of the family was better than it had been for many years. And the situation was further improved by a five hundred dollar bequest to Abby from the will of her Aunt May Davenport, and an investment by Emerson of the same amount in Alcott's behalf. Alcott planned to settle all debts; his daughters were able to buy new shoes, stockings, and frocks. The family was delighted with Alcott's contribution, although Abby was irritated at the obvious discrimination whereby her husband could get in six weeks what it took women six months to earn. Alcott was overjoyed at finally being able to contribute substantially to the family's aid and comfort. And his absence reawakened love and affection for him by his wife and daughters. "For the dear Sage has a precious corner in our heart of hearts," said Abby, "not always discernible to the naked eye, but very real to our happy existence and ease of life. His serene presence gives a dignity to poverty, and overshadows all duty with a rosy satisfaction."[54]

Throughout the years of conversing in the late 1840s and early 1850s, Alcott's ideas continued to evolve, so that by the mid-1850s his idealism differed significantly in detail and direction, though not in broad matters of substance, from what it had been in the mid-1840s. Especially was this true with regard to his idea of progress, his attempt to synthesize concepts of the physical and spiritual worlds, his continued speculation about human free will, and his concept of the nature of reform. As he had been doing since the 1820s and 1830s, Alcott took ideas that were flooding in from Europe or welling up from within America and filtered them through his own prisms to create a unique intellectual synthesis.

Progress was a central element of the transcendentalist faith. It followed directly from the belief that innately good human beings had the capability to improve themselves and the world around them. It was the teleological concept with which Alcott and the transcendentalists explained the process of change. The idea of progress—the hopeful, optimistic belief that the world was inexorably becoming better and better—was a comforting and reassuring explanation of what otherwise would have been an alarming sensation that all stability and order were crumbling in the rapidly changing America of the mid-nineteenth century. The transcendentalists always defined progress in spiritual and moral terms rather than as mere material progress wrought by human hands, although their vision of a better world included elements of material progress. Thus they synthesized the traditional Christian teleological explanation of the Universe—that the sovereign will of God was responsible for all change and movement in the world—and the secular faith that human abilities could make things bigger, better, and faster.

Alcott's concept of progress, like his concept of reform, had more emotion than substance to it. It was a hope, a vision, a faith; it was vast and open-ended. It included, once Alcott tried to define it specifically, visions of the future, relics of the past, things material and things spiritual, otherworldly hopes, and this-worldly plans, all together in a strange admixture.

At Fruitlands progress meant the attainment of a simple and pristine life-style, an Eden separated from the corruption of materialism and modern technology. It meant the liberation of individuals from all worldly restraints, a paradise on earth. But it also meant personal regeneration or sanctification in the more traditional Christian sense of looking toward an otherworldly salvation. Fruitlands looked to the past for a vision of the supposed goodness of Eden and projected that vision as a hope for the future.[55] In the years after Fruitlands, Alcott retained in his ideas of progress the tension between past and future, and the tension between his desire for a personal salvation transcending the social order and his desire to create an earthly paradise or a better world.

Especially in the face of his disillusionment over the failure of Fruitlands did Alcott seek a paradise within the mind rather than outside it. He believed that through thought he could be "born again," that ideas and speculation were means of grace. He sought separation from the world of material goods: "Emancipate the Soul from Things," he said, "and lo! a new Heaven and Earth springs into vision." He talked of allowing his mind to be "taken captive" by ideas, and of abandoning himself to the "enthusiasm" that those ideas inspired. His vision of the future had an eschatological aspect: "Nature, and man, his mind and being, are but means to a higher and final end, above and beyond, themselves." He listed sacraments by which human beings could rise into the spiritual life to become "celestial men" filled with divine enthusiasm. Among these sacraments he included baptism or purification by water, fasting or temperance, continence or chastity, prayer, and labor. It was an ascetic regimen such as that at Fruitlands. Though he would never have admitted it, his sacraments were a form of what the theologians have called works righteousness. He could never decide whether personal salvation was a matter of human attainment or the gift of a sovereign deity or spirit.[56]

Alcott could not for long limit his idea of progress to personal regeneration. It also meant a new order on earth. Here again he faced the problem of human responsibility. He could not decide whether worldly progress was a matter of human action or an inexorable process transcending human power. He talked of the day of judgment in tones of a Puritan jeremiad, implying that a superhuman, deterministic force would wreak awful retribution on a sinful world. "Clearly, the Supreme Power is taking all peoples by the ears," he declared, "and the battles are provoked already whose ends and issues are not seen or surmised by any of us." But he never fully gave up the idea that human beings had a major role to play in bringing about progress. He still believed that he was called by God to help effect the new order. Though for a while he escaped into his garden, his books, and his thoughts, he still desired to serve others, to improve humanity. The Transcendental Club, he believed, had been the "Court of the New Queen" and had worked for the "enthronement of Ideas." By the late 1840s the leading proponents of these "new ideas"—Emerson, Parker, Garrison, Wendell Phillips, Parker Pillsbury, William Henry Channing, George Ripley, even Alcott—were fast gaining recognition and rising to leadership in New England. Surely this was a sign of progress, he thought. And it was progress effected by human agency. Human beings were given the power and the duty to reform themselves and their society. "Man is born into institutions, as into his body," he said, "not to cherish and beautify its blemishes, but to lop them off and eradicate them as fast and as far as he can."[57]

The rapid development of technology in transportation and communications in the United States in the 1840s and 1850s—railroads, steamboats, telegraph lines, high-speed printing presses—added a new dimension to Alcott's idea of progress. In contrast to the simplicity he tried to encourage at Fruitlands, he began to see technology as a symbol not of evil materialism but of spiritual progress. In 1846 and 1847 he read with fascination in the *Westminster Review* about the work of Michael Faraday on the relationship between electricity and magnetism. He became interested in current research on the telescope and the microscope. The perfection of the telegraph evoked visions of the wonderful possibilities of electricity. If electricity could facilitate communication, he thought, why could it not print by fixing the motions of the air on some receptive substance. He predicted that some day electricity might record a "daguerreotype of thought" spoken in conversation, thus preserving his valuable but transient art form. The possibilities of rapid transportation and communication awakened visions of a new cosmopolitanism. It would mean the end of all sects, parties, and selfish private interests, he thought. "Neither *Slavery* nor *Ignorance* can much longer withstand the Power of those mighty *Potentates* Steam and Electricity," he declared. There was even evidence of the coming new order: the *Westminster Review* reported talk that all nations might become leagued together on a new basis of mutual assistance. The prospects were exciting to Alcott. He felt he was born a half century too soon.[58]

New ideas in technology and physics not only helped Alcott redefine his idea of progress, but also gave new substance to his concept of the relationship between spirit and matter. Especially did they add to his concept of how the spirit revealed itself through material things. His reading of Faraday led him to speculate that electricity, magnetism, and light were but three states of one substance; this substance was the mysterious nexus of spirit and matter, the immediate breath of life. He believed magnetism was the soul of the nervous system and thus that the ebb and flow of magnetic forces helped explain human nature. Magnetic laws, he thought, could even explain variations in personalities. The direction and degree of magnetic force could explain the iron will and power of a man such as Daniel Webster or the creative brilliance of Emerson. Magnetism explained all bodily energy and all changes in living things. Even sex was a magnetic phenomenon, Alcott thought. Magnetism accounted for the process of personal regeneration; it was the kind of force that caused the metamorphosis of a creature from a monad and embryo to a human to a demigod to a god.[59]

This idea that magnetism was the all-pervasive spiritual force animating the universe was a part of Alcott's exploration of natural philosophy begun in the summer of 1849. He worked day and night pouring his thoughts into a manuscript he called "Tablets" and nearly suffered a complete mental collapse. In "Tablets" he groped for a new synthesis of his concept of the spiritual nature of human beings with his reading in natural philosophy and with the currently popular theories of mesmerism and spiritualism. In March 1848 Theodore Parker had given him a copy of *The General Principles of the Philosophy of Nature* by German immigrant Johann B. Stallo, which introduced him to the natural philosophy of Hegel, Schelling, and Lorenz Oken. Meanwhile, he had been reading similar things in the works of Boehme, Swedenborg, and Goethe. Swedenborg reinforced Alcott's theory of magnetic forces with his own theory of the four atmospheres or elements which made up the cosmos: gravity, magnetism, "ether," and air. Goethe confirmed Alcott's theory that change and growth were the work of the spirit. But his reading gave him only stimulus and suggestion. He took from these authors only those ideas which supported, clarified, or illustrated his basic assumptions.[60]

Alcott's interest in the operation of magnetic forces in the body closely resembled the ideas of eighteenth-century Austrian physician F. A. Mesmer, who attempted to explain the connection between mind and body by electrical theory. But Alcott was more concerned with the theory, with explaining the relationship between spirit and matter, than with the popular practices of the mesmerists or hypnotists. He never attempted to manipulate the minds and bodies of others through hypnotism. Alcott also expressed initial sympathy with the ideas of Andrew Jackson Davis, the shoemaker's apprentice from Poughkeepsie, New York, who claimed that he could communicate with the spiritual world. Davis had been mesmerized in 1843 by James Stanley Grimes, a traveling popular lecturer on animal magnetism, and thereafter believed he had special powers as a medium. Alcott first met Davis in April 1849, and agreed, at least in theory, that since human beings were spirits in bodies, they could communicate with spirits in others people's bodies.[61]

But again Alcott was more interested in theories than in becoming a practicing medium, and he later denounced Davis's form of spiritualism as superstition. He wanted a broad, holistic theory of nature and of the relationship between human beings and the natural world. "Tablets" was his attempt to put together just such a theory. The result was reminiscent of the idea of the Great Chain of Being, which had been a part of Western culture for centuries. Nature, he said, meaning all of the physical world including the human body, was made up of a chain of ascending lives, with human beings, the "Coronation of Nature," at the top of the chain. The ascending chain represented the spirit's experiment at the complete realization of an ideal. Human beings were conductors of "heavenly forces"; they were instruments of the spirit.[62] The spirit worked through human beings by means of the faculties. "The brain," he said,

> is the Physical atlas of the Soul, the Pantheon of the Mind, wherein all the Gods and demigods, the talents, namely, and subtalents, abide as on the Spiritual Olympus [sic], and from thence descend, on the golden chain of the nerves, to animate and administer the Human Kingdom—talenting the blood, and ensouling the bodily organs throughout with vital personalities, and proper gifts of Being.[63]

The sole purpose of the earth, Alcott claimed, was to advance all creatures from inferior to superior states, to an apotheosis above nature's material elements. The spine represented the nucleus of all animals, the common symbol of life. The spine was symbolic of the means by which animals progressed from lower to higher forms. But apotheosis, he said, came only after a human being cast off the spine—the symbolic tie with lower forms of life—and commanded "celestial forces." Nature served then to educate human beings and thus to help deliver them from its own conditions. In the end nature had to transcended too.[64]

Total absorption in his work of synthesizing his ideas of nature, human beings, and the spirit led to a breakdown and the need for a two-week visit to Concord in the fall of 1849 to recuperate. He had had what he described as a "self-introversion." He could not describe it fully, but he was sure that he had experienced a revelation of the divinity, a period of clairvoyance. The most important idea he retained from this episode was a fully developed scale of seven faculties used by the spirit as instruments: instinct, memory, understanding, fancy [i.e., fantasy], reason, imagination, and conscience. The lowest forms of life on his scale of being were organisms of instinct alone. The highest forms of life were those with all seven active faculties. Those highest forms, having the highest faculty of conscience active, were perfected; they were "emancipated from mortality." This convenient scale of faculties not only explained for Alcott the differences among the various kinds of animal life, but also illustrated the means used by the spirit in the process of regeneration. He used this paradigm many times as the basis for conversations. It illustrated his belief in the constantly changing soul, which was either progressing upward toward perfection or lapsing downward toward lower forms of life.[65] The scale of faculties provided a neat explanation of how the spirit worked through the material world:

> All Revelations are infused, by the *Spirit*, through *Instinct* into *Memory* (whose seat is in the backhead) and flow forward into *Understanding* & upward through the facial talents of *Fancy* into *Reason* in the forehead, & through *Imagination*, to be coronated & completed in the verdicts of *Conscience* returning to their source & Head in the *Spirit* again.[66]

And magnetism helped explain the movement of spirit. The human brain, the seat of all the faculties, was an electrical machine, Alcott believed, and the spine a galvanic pile. "Creation is ablaze with Spirit," he said. "Orbed in Light, the brain diffuses its lustrous floods over the countenance."[67]

In his theories of the faculties and of the progression of species from lower to higher forms, Alcott had synthesized the action of spirit with material phenomena. This synthesis, albeit a vague and unsystematic one, gave him a philosophy of nature that assumed a unity of matter and spirit, a unity of human beings with nature. All change, whether material or spiritual, he concluded, was part of one organic whole. It was this organicism, this evolutionary idealism, that Goethe, Oken, and J. B. Stallo were talking about; it was a further elaboration of his own theories about the immanence of spirit in the world. Nature was not a final product, separate from God its creator, but rather it was constantly changing and becoming because of God's creative interaction with it. "Admit a present immanent deity," he said, "and all questions of History find an instant solution, in the immediate action of Spirit through Nature in man." The creative spirit worked through ideas and thoughts. Ideas created all things. Magnetism was an intermediary, a carrier of ideas.[68] "Call our thought the stream," he added, and

> its banks our mind, whose flow is the river's current. Thought —mind—motion—these the elements of the production, and metaphysical all and ideal. In essence, then and idea, mind and matter are one, indivisible and the same; divisible to the sense, only, and manifold.[69]

One further result of Alcott's linking the physical aspects of human nature with the spiritual was a new emphasis on the power of inborn physical characteristics to determine human life. As was the case with his idea of progress, Alcott toyed uncertainly with the dichotomy of determinism and free will.

In the spring of 1846, while reflecting on his past failure and the failures of other people to appreciate him, Alcott wrote that his once-unconquerable faith in education had diminished. He no longer felt that education could create or develop what was not inborn. Now he believed that character was more an innate nature than an acquirement. His speculation and reading about the philosophy of nature added further substance to this idea that inborn characteristics were a determinant of human behavior, which education could not always overcome. He began to believe that inborn dispositions and temperaments predetermined human callings, achievements, and destiny. "No art can do more, and impart," he said, "what nature reserves to herself. All is forecast in the temperament." And he added that "all powers of mind or of disposition are sown at birth, and mixed in the temperaments."[70]

Alcott was never fully clear about what he meant by temperament. He usually defined it in terms of personalities he knew such as Emerson, Garrison, or Daniel Webster. Some persons he labeled sentimental because in them an innate tendency to love predominated; others were forceful and active because the will was commanding; and others were thoughtful because of a dominant wisdom. he frequently referred to John of Milan's medieval classification of temperaments into sanguine, choleric, phlegmatic, and melancholic, but without precision and clarification. Generally, temperament was a convenient way for Alcott to categorize people and to explain their behavior, particularly if it differed markedly from his own.[71]

The emphasis James P. Greaves put on the influence of heredity had first caused Alcott to consider its impact, but he gave it even greater weight in the 1850s. "If we are not of royal extraction [i.e., born of good character]," he asserted, "it were better for us to have never been born; the stain and mark of inferiority will follow to defame us forever." Blood and heredity became of such concern to Alcott that he began an extensive search of his own ancestry. He pored over dusty records in Boston churches and court houses, and he asked his mother, brothers, and sisters to provide him with documents and family information. He began to paste together an enormous collection of autobiographical and genealogical material. In June and July 1852 he toured Connecticut for five weeks to sift through records of towns—Wolcott, Waterbury, New Haven, Hartford—which he thought might shed light on his ancestry. In September 1852 the New England Historical and Genealogical Society elected him a member. He later presided at some of the meetings of the Society. Thoreau thought it strange that Alcott should be so engrossed, "he whom only the genealogy of humanity, the descent of man from God, should concern!"[72]

But Alcott felt that blood was a history and that virtue and vice were passed down from generation to generation. He thought it was fortunate that he had inherited the fair complexion and the virtuous puritanism of his ancestors, John, Thomas, and George Alcocke. Good blood, he believed, was good the centuries through. To this belief in the importance of heredity he added a theory of race and complexion, believing that there was a clear connection between racial background and personality or character. He came to believe that one's complexion was an outward rendering of internal qualities, a visible type of the light or darkness of the soul within. Just as the phrenologists claimed that the outward appearance of the head revealed internal characteristics, so Alcott believed that outward color provided the same information.[73]

This theory of colors and complexions, of course, led directly to Alcott's ranking of various racial groups according to their spiritual qualities. Not surprisingly, since he was himself blond, he considered fair-skinned people to be the most spiritually advanced. The other races, as he categorized them, followed in rank order from higher to lower: yellow, olive, copper, and dark. Light colors were supernatural. Therefore human beings with light complexions were divine and had transcendent powers. Dark colors, and people of dark complexion, were preternatural, nocturnal, earthy, and slumberous.[74]

There was boundless potential for racism in Alcott's theory of complexions. His conclusions disturbed even some of his most faithful conversers. Ednah Littlehale Cheney reported that she once defended black people to Alcott during a conversation by alluding to Swedenborg's belief that blacks were the most beloved of all the races. Alcott, who always managed to slip away from potential debate, only replied: "that is very nice of Mr. Swedenborg." Emerson recorded a private conversation with Alcott in which Alcott suggested the need for a concerted effort to increase the white population even by means of polygamy, and to eliminate the black population by making eunuchs of all black males. Alcott never said anything like this in his own writings, but the logic of his ideas could lead directly to that end.[75]

Oddly enough, Alcott's racial theories did not diminish his opposition to slavery nor his desire to aid black people. He denounced discrimination and prejudice against minorities. He lauded the genius of American Indian George Copway, whom he heard speak on Indian life in the winter of 1851. Later he welcomed abolitionist and former slave William Wells Brown into his home. Practical experience provided him with overwhelming evidence that his theory of complexions was fallacious. He could never explain why Frederick Douglass, Sojourner Truth, and William Wells Brown, all of whom he respected highly for their character, were not fair-skinned. His wife and daughter Louisa, whom he loved and respected, were of darker complexion than his own. Yet he held on tenaciously to his theory and left the contradictions unresolved. Ideas of temperament and complexion played too great a part in filling out the details of his philosophic system to abandon lightly. And he was often more concerned with the neatness and completeness of his philosophic system than with its relationship to reality or its effects in practice. He always had difficulty translating his ideas into concrete action and, in this case at least, it was a good thing.[76]

The most difficult logical problem Alcott faced with all of his speculation about the effects of inborn characteristics was the constraints such ideas placed on human free will. Explaining behavior and character by innate characteristics left no room for the possibility of a human being transcending nature, of realizing perfection and divinity by an act of will. He wavered between ideas that paralleled a Calvinist doctrine of election and his long-held belief that all human beings were capable of salvation. At times he suggested that the transcendent genius, the perfected human being, was the result of an inborn gift of the spirit. Love and murder, he said, were inbred. Thus salvation was a matter of divine election. Yet he retained the faith that individuals could attain salvation by their own action. He still felt they had the power to act out of themselves and yet above themselves. "The victory of all victories is over one's self," he declared. Human beings had a spirit that by free choice could emancipate itself from every physical encumbrance. Thus, he said, humans had the freedom to build the houses they lived in, whether a "God's paradise" or a "devil's den."[77]

To reconcile his dichotomy, Alcott theorized that every person indeed had a free will but that it was limited in each case by inborn characteristics. "Personal freedom is a matter of degrees," he said, "originating in temperament and complexion." Temperaments were either divine or demonic and set limits to free will accordingly. But presumably all people, no matter how demonic their temperament, had the possibility of improvement.[78]

The tension between determinism and free will was further reflected in Alcott's theory of diet and regimen. Proper diet and clean living, like complexion, became for Alcott measures of a person's inner state. Preference for meats and strong drink, he said, indicated a demonic, barbaric nature. On the other hand, those who ate grains and fruits were divine, even "celestial." All this implied that one's diet was not a matter of free choice but was determined by innate characteristics. Yet here again Alcott retained his belief that proper diet and regimen were means of sanctification, a way by which humans could elevate themselves through free choice.[79]

Alcott's groping with the problem of free will and determinism in the late 1840s and early 1850s reflected his growing doubts about human nature. It had simply failed to live up to the strong faith he had placed in it in his early career. Ideas of temperament and complexion helped explain that failure and also reassured him that he possessed all the qualities of a sanctified soul—a proper complexion, a proper temperament, and a proper diet and life-style. Doubts about human nature also had a profound impact on his theory of reform. Although he continued to attend meetings of the New England Non-Resistance Society and antislavery conventions, and even spoke publicly against the mistreatment of criminals, his concern with reform dwindled in 1849 and 1850. "We cant take heaven by storm," he warned the abolitionists. He complacently mused that inevitable progress would eliminate evils without immediate action on his part.[80]

As Alcott's fervor for reform diminished, he criticized the relentless Garrison for his lack of kindness and clemency. "A poor creature," he said, reflecting on what he felt had been his own excesses as well as Garrison's,

> may be so overloaded with the sense of responsibleness, so frightfully executive, & instant & despotic in enforcing what he calls "his sense of duty" as to crucify the rest of himself in his endeavors to be faithful to himself & to others. For an overplus of Conscience is quite as disastrous & fatal, as a like excess of passion, or of Intellect, in our mixture.[81]

When Samuel Bower, the former nudist, visited him in February 1850, Alcott noted with a touch of amusement and even cynicism how every manner of zealot imaginable had sought his sympathy over the past ten years with their pictures of an ideal state and their "Vague longings" for a terrestrial Eden. Bower was considering quitting his job as a wood-comber at the Lowell textile mills and seeking another "Holy Land" on the western frontier. Alcott enjoyed reminiscing with Bower, but he felt removed and aloof from such efforts now. He saw that erstwhile radicals such as Emerson, Parker, William H. Channing, Phillips, Garrison, Pillsbury, and even Thoreau were frequently accepted at lyceums, lectures, and literary societies. Extremes, he thought, were becoming reconciled. It was a strong indication of an "improved order of things" that conservatives and reformers were coming closer together.[82]

But he was shaken out of his complacency in the spring of 1850 by the angry debates in Congress over the issue of slavery in the territories and the threat of Southern secession. He saw the forces marshalling North and South, personified by the intrepid Garrison and by John C. Calhoun, whom Alcott considered to be statesmanlike but morally perverse. In September 1850 the opposing forces reached a compromise, or rather a shaky armistice, which settled nothing of substance and only served to re-awaken passions among abolitionists such as Alcott. For the Compromise of 1850 included the odious Fugitive Slave Law, which made federal officials responsible for the capture of runaway slaves. It threatened to compel private citizens to join slave-hunting posses, and it left to suspected fugitives the burden of proving the charges against them false without benefit of jury trial or the right to testify in their own behalf.[83]

The Fugitive Slave Law outraged Alcott and drove him to a renewed commitment to the abolitionist cause. He heard impassioned speeches by Theodore Parker, Wendell Phillips, and Frederick Douglass on the fugitive slave question at Faneuil Hall on October 15 and began to meet frequently with firebrand abolitionists to talk of civil disobedience. He dwelt at length on the consequences of the Fugitive Slave Law in his January-February 1851 conversations on the New England reformers. No longer was he pleading with Garrison and Parker for moderation; he was heaping praise on them for their adamance. He lashed out at Daniel Webster for failing to live up to his greatness by his support for compromise and the Fugitive Slave Law. In January 1851 he attended with three hundred abolitonists the "soiree" held in honor of Garrison and the twentieth year of the *Liberator*. He applauded the bold rescue, on February 15, of Frederic Jenkins, or "Shadrach," the waiter at the Cornhill Coffee House accused of being a fugitive slave. When Elizur Wright went on trial accused on complicity in the Jenkins affair, Alcott attended the proceedings, became furious at the thought of Wright's facing possible punishment for an act of conscience, and once again filled his manuscripts with calls for blood as retribution. "The Republic is unsafe," he clamored, "union impossible; sedition and revolt inevitable, so long as slavery is in it, and good citizens are called to sanction and perpetuate the evil." He denounced the United States Constitution and claimed he would risk being shot to aid a fugitive slave.[84]

His words were reminiscent of the angry days of the late 1830s and early 1840s: "Consume us, O Justice! judge the guilty nation, the base multitude, the servile city. . . . Thy penalties must come. Swift and sure the vengeance." He condemned the North for bending to the will of the slave power. On April 3, 1851, Thomas Sims was arrested as a fugitive slave, and the court house was wrapped in chains and surrounded by armed police to prevent his rescue. The next day Alcott joined Boston's Vigilance Committee and helped patrol the streets to protect fugitives until midnight that night. He praised Parker for his valiant aid to fugitives William and Ellen Crafts, whom Parker married and provided with money and weapons. "No state enactment can contravene the statutes of the private heart," Alcott declared. Once again he saw in New England the stuff of which revolutions were made. Once again he talked of the sovereignty of individuals and the right of nonconformity. But he qualified his individualism. He now believed that few persons were capable of the self-control necessary for absolute liberty. He was no longer so naively confident of human nature as before.[85]

The Fugitive Slave Law provided abolitionists with an emotion-laden issue. The sight of a human being chased down like an animal and denied basic human rights, whether witnessed in the streets of Boston or dramatized in the pages of Harriet Beecher Stowe's hard-hitting *Uncle Tom's Cabin*, serialized in 1851 and 1852, took the evils of slavery out of the abstract and into people's hearts and homes. The possibilities of rescuing such fugitives gave the abolitionists a way to act upon their rhetoric. Rescues were not so important for the number of fugitives saved from the authorities as for their symbolic value as a means of propaganda. Twenty years of the *Liberator* could not elevate public passion like one dramatic rescue attempt. Whether successful or not, a rescue attempt illustrated vividly the helplessness of the slave and the cruelty and barbarity of the slaveholders and their accomplices.

The most dramatic rescue attempt engineered by the Boston abolitionists came in the spring of 1854. On May 24 Anthony Burns, a black clothing store employee, was arrested on a trumped-up charge of robbery and accused of being a fugitive slave. He confessed. The next day Alcott rode to Worcester to converse and told Thomas Wentworth Higginson, sponsor of the conversation, about Burns's capture. That night they plotted a rescue attempt and Alcott pledged to take an active part. On Friday May 26 he and Higginson met with the Boston Vigilance Committee, which originally had planned only a Faneuil Hall protest meeting. Higginson convinced them that they should use that meeting as the basis for a rescue.[86]

The plan was for Higginson and a few others to rush the Court House, where Burns was being held, and for the crowd at Faneuil Hall to follow and give support when told the attack was taking place. Accordingly, on the evening of the 26th Higginson and his men, armed with axes and meat cleavers, broke down the west door of the Court House with a wooden beam and stormed inside. They expected to whisk Burns away as easily as rescuers had freed Wilkins three years before. But instead they confronted the federal marshall and fifty armed men, who quickly drove them back outside. One of the marshall's men was killed in the melee, and Higginson was wounded on the chin. Meanwhile, the Faneuil Hall crowd, which had been listening to Wendell Phillips, failed to arrive at the Court House on time to intimidate the authorities and to provide Higginson with support. Alcott was with this crowd and upon arriving at the Court House he calmly walked alone up the steps leading to the west door and peered in, looking up the stairs to the room where Burns was held. When he saw no one but the marshall's men inside, he slowly walked down the steps to the square and asked the bleeding Higginson why they were not inside. Higginson replied angrily that no one would accompany them. By this time the police had arrived, and the crowd began to disperse. The rescue had failed.[87]

Alcott spent the next several days attending Burns's trial and meetings of the Vigilance Committee, plotting sedition. On June 2 Burns, having been convicted, was escorted to the Long Wharf and a waiting revenue cutter by a marshall's posse and a platoon of United States Marines. Rows of special police held back the fifty thousand spectators. Alcott had the urge to fling himself into the troops and either effect a rescue by mob action or die a martyr. He suppressed the impulse, but he felt ashamed to return to his home still breathing while Burns was headed to the South and to slavery. Higginson was indicted along with Parker and Phillips for complicity in the rescue attempt. Alcott fully expected to be arrested but was not. He offered to testify in Higginson's behalf, but Higginson felt that Alcott could not offer anything that would be helpful to his defense. The three were later exonerated.[88]

The excitement soon died away. Alcott spent the rest of 1854 and early 1855 seeking opportunities to converse and to keep his family out of poverty and despair. He fell back to his routine of writing, filling up his autobiographical and genealogical collections, and reading at the Athenaeum and at Harvard. There were frequent visits with Emerson, Thoreau, Ellery Channing, and Frank Sanborn. Thoreau gave him a copy of *Walden* on the day of its publication, August 9, 1854. Alcott read and reread it and predicted its fame. There were also occasional chats with James Russell Lowell and Convers

Francis. He attended several meetings of Horatio Woodman's newly formed Saturday Club. In September 1854 he spent a month at the extensive landed estate of Benjamin Marston Watson in Plymouth, enjoying peaceful reading and writing and an occasional conversation. Watson and Samuel Longfellow arranged a two-week visit to New York City for Alcott in October. There he met with the Sunday School teachers of Longfellows's church in Brooklyn and held a series of five conversations at the home of church musician I. N. Swasey. The conversations were not particularly successful, but Alcott enjoyed his chance to talk with Henry James about Swedenborg, to call on the popular minister Henry Ward Beecher, and to see George Ripley, who was then writing for the *New York Tribune*. He also met his old friend and supporter William Henry Furness, who promised to arrange some conversations in Philadelphia.[89]

Although the family's condition was improving, it remained precarious. Anna overcame her homesickness and went to Syracuse in June 1854 to teach the children of Samuel May's parishioner Charles Sedgwick. This added forty dollars to the family's income. Louisa continued to teach school at the Alcott home on Pinckney Street, but found more interest and greater success in writing. Her first book, *Flower Fables*, was published in December 1854. By Christmas twelve hundred copies had been sold, and it had received a favorable review in the *New York Tribune*.[90]

None of this brought stability and security to the family. Alcott's receipts for conversations in 1854 totaled only one hundred eighty dollars. They were forced to seek alternative living arrangements. Elizabeth Peabody wrote in her rambling but good-hearted way to suggest that Louisa become the assistant to the director of an "Idiot Asylum" in Germantown, where she had contacts. She also gratuitously warned Alcott that his faith in the West as a market for conversations was misplaced, and she offered the Alcotts a chance to join the Raritan Bay Association in Perth Amboy, New Jersey. Raritan Bay was an experimental community started by Theodore and Angelina Grimké Weld. The Alcotts considered it, but they did not go. Alcott wanted to return to Concord or even to Wolcott, but Abby, incensed by the opening of previously free territory to slavery by the Kansas-Nebraska Act, hoped to join the free state emigrants to Kansas.[91]

Opportunities for conversation were scarce in early 1855. Alcott's only invitation was from the Reverend David Wasson's church in Groveland, which paid him eleven dollars for preaching on April 8. By June 1855 he was desperate, and to add to the difficulty, their landlord on Pinckney Street wanted his house back, which would force a move by early July. Alcott considered gardening again and even taking a job in a Connecticut clock factory. He thought of another trip to England and asked his Providence friend Thomas Davis to help pay his passage. But Emerson was adamant that Alcott should not run off to England with no positive prospect but genealogical research while his family's fortunes were so low. Emerson offered to create a fund for Alcott's benefit and ask subscriptions to it from Alcott's

Providence and Boston friends. This would be added to the five hundred dollars already set aside for the purpose. Alcott relented. Emerson obtained contributions from Davis, Parker, Whipple, Lowell, Samuel Longfellow, Horatio Woodman, Frederick Beck, and Thomas Starr King, among others, and turned it all over to Samuel Gray Ward to be administered for the Alcotts. Alcott also agreed to his wife's plan to accept a rent-free house from her brother-in-law, Benjamin Willis, in Walpole, New Hampshire, a little village on the Connecticut River in the extreme southwest corner of the state. It promised a welcome escape from city rents, city taxes, and city social customs. The family moved there on July 10.

Notes

1. A. Bronson Alcott, "Leaves from Diary for January, 1846," MS at Houghton Library, 59M-308 (14); Abby May Alcott to Hannah Robie, January 1846, from a copy in Alcott's hand in "Memoir, 1878"; AJ 20 (1846), part 2 ("Idyllic Diary at Hillside from April to December, 1846"): 201; Edward Waldo Emerson and Waldo Emerson Forbes, eds., *Journals of Ralph Waldo Emerson*, 10 vols. (Cambridge: Riverside Press, 1909-1914), 7: 222-23.

2. AJ 21 (1847): 124, 141.

3. Ibid., p. 231.

4. AJ 22 (1848): 135, 137, 297-298, 384.

5. AJ 20 (1846), part 2: 50, 94, 158-59, 325-27; AJ 21 (1847): 175, 177, 215-16; AJ 22 (1848): 72-73; Abby May Alcott to Samuel J. May, January 13, 1847, in "Family Letters, 1828-1861."

6. AJ 20 (1846), part 2: 175.

7. AJ 21 (1847): 243; AJ 22 (1848): 216.

8. AJ 21 (1847): 417-18, 420; AJ 22 (1848): 53, 276-84, 385; Alcott to Thomas Davis, January 2, 1846, in "Letters, 1836-1850"; Alcott to Charles Lane, April 16, 1848, in "Letters, 1836-1850"; a printed notice of the Annual Meeting of the New England Non-Resistant Society, December 3-4, 1847, in "Letters, 1846-1850."

9. Alcott, "Leaves from Diary for January, 1846"; Alcott to Mrs. Anna Alcott, June 13, 1847, in "Letters, 1836-1850"; Canby, *Thoreau*, p. 217; AJ 20 (1846), part 1: 1, 28, 47-48; AJ 20 (1846), part 2: 11-19, 30, 150, 157, 165, 171, 190-91; AJ 22 (1848): 27, 37, 67, 220, 612; AJ 21 (1847): 131, 357, 378, 381, 382.

10. AJ 20 (1846), part 1: 1; AJ 20 (1846), part 2: 274; AJ 22 (1848): 421.

11. AJ 20 (1846), part 2: 29, 53, 84, 120; AJ 24 (January-March 1850): 412; AJ 26 (1851): 585; AJ 21 (1847): 666.

12. AJ 20 (1846), part 2: 136-37, 211; AJ 21 (1847): 95-97, 652; Alcott, "Leaves from Diary, January, 1846."

13. AJ 21 (1847): 207.

14. Alcott, "Letters, 1836-1850"; AJ 20 (1846), part 1: 66, 86, 338, 341, 350 ff.; AJ 21 (1847): 325, 345, 431, 439; AJ 21 (1847): pp. 279, 447, 687, 701, 707 ff.; Alcott to the Editor of the *Herald of Freedom*, March 16, 1847, from a copy in Alcott's hand in AJ 21 (1847): pp. 401-2; AJ 22 (1848): 11, 45, 53, 148, 149; Thomas, *The Liberator*, pp. 294-95.

15. AJ 20, part 2: 226, 238, 250, 252, 261-62; AJ 21 (1847): pp. 601, 603, 655-57, 678; Ralph Waldo Emerson to Lidian Emerson, August 23, 1847, and Ralph Waldo Emerson to Margaret Fuller, August 29, 1847, in Rusk, ed., *Letters of Emerson*, 3: 411, 413; Henry David Thoreau to Ralph Waldo Emerson, November 14, 1847, in Franklin B. Sanborn, ed., *Familiar Letters of Henry David Thoreau* (Boston: Houghton, Mifflin and Co., 1894), pp. 163-64; Abby May Alcott to Samuel J. May, October 22, 1847, in "Family Letters, 1828-1861."

16. AJ 21 (1847): pp. 499, 501, 503-5, 567-68; AJ 22 (1848): 3, 12, 537, 689; Ralph Waldo

Emerson to Margaret Fuller, April 30, 1847, Ralph Waldo Emerson to James Eliot Cabot, April 21, 1848, and Theodore Parker to Ralph Waldo Emerson, November 22, 1848, in Rusk, ed., *Letters of Emerson*, 3: 394, 4: 60, 123; Clarence Gohdes, *The Periodicals of American Transcendentalism* (Durham, N.C.: Duke University Press, 1931), pp. 160, 162, 166-70.

17. Abby May Alcott, "Diary," December 1846, and September 1848; AJ 20 (1847), part 2: 20; AJ 22 (1848): 581, 668; AJ 21 (1847): 413-15.

18. AJ 20 (1847), part 2: 24, 37; Alcott to Junius Alcott, June 22, 1846, from a copy in Alcott's hand in ibid., pp. 162-66; Abby May Alcott to Samuel J. May, January 10, 1848, February 13, 1848, and February 29, 1848, in "Family Letters, 1828-1861"; AJ 21 (1847): 654; Alcott to Anna Alcott, February, 1847, May 1, 1848, May 11, 1848, May 16, 1848, and June 6, 1848, in "Family Letters and Diaries, 1837-1850."

19. AJ 20 (1846), part 2: 101-2; AJ 21 (1847): 560, 600; Abby May Alcott to Samuel J. May, November 2, 1846, December 4, 1846, April 16, 1848, and June 14, 1848, in "Family Letters, 1828-1861"; Abby May Alcott to Samuel J. May, September 17, 1848, and Abby May Alcott to Alcott, May 20, 1848, and June, 1848, from copies in Alcott's hand in "Memoir, 1878"; Abby May Alcott, "Diary," May 1848; AJ 22 (1848): 497, 503.

20. AJ 22 (1848): 378, 538, 582, 720, 759, 770, 779; Abby May Alcott, "Autobiography"; Abby May Alcott, "Diary," September-October, 1848; Abby May Alcott to Samuel J. May, September 17, 1848, from a copy in Alcott's hand in "Memoir, 1878"; Harold Schwartz, *Samuel Gridley Howe: Social Reformer* (Cambridge, Mass.: Harvard University Press, 1956), pp. 142-43.

21. AJ 22 (1848): 779-86, 788.

22. Ibid., p. 798; AJ 23 (1849): 67; AJ 26 (1851): 353.

23. AJ 12 (January-July 1839): 480, 865-67.

24. Adolph B. Benson, ed., *America of the Fifties: Letters of Fredrika Bremer* (New York: The American-Scandinavian Foundation, 1924), p. 58; Ednah D. Cheney, "Reminiscences of Mr. Alcott's Conversations," *The Open Court* 2 (August 2, 1888): 1131-33; Ednah D. Littlehale [Cheney], transcriber, "Conversation of Self-Knowledge, Boston, 1848," pp. 45-49, in "Notes of Conversations," MS owned by the Concord Free Public Library; Octavius Brooks Frothingham, *Recollections and Impressions, 1822-1890* (New York: G. P. Putnam's Sons, 1891), pp. 51-52; AJ 24 (January-March 1850): 135-36.

25. AJ 24 (January-March 1850): 207-8.

26. AJ 24 (January-March 1850): 208, 294-95; AJ 32 (1857): 276. The best brief study of the transcendentalist theory of conversation, mainly that of Alcott, is Lawrence Buell, *Literary Transcendentalism: Style and Vision in the American Renaissance* (Ithaca, N.Y.: Cornell University Press, 1973), pp. 77-101.

27. AJ 24 (January-March 1850): 467-69; AJ 26 (1851): 721-22; AJ 22 (1857): 825.

28. Sanborn and Harris, *A. Bronson Alcott*, 1: 421.

29. AJ 26 (1851): 721-22.

30. Ibid., pp. 13-15, 1291; AJ 32 (1857): 263.

31. Ednah D. Cheney, "Reminiscences of Mr. Alcotts's Conversations," *The Open Court* 2 (August 2, 1888): 1131-33 and (August 9, 1888): 1142-44.

32. AJ 22 (1848): 798; AJ 23 (1849): 6, 29, 40, 403, 404; AJ 24 (January-March 1850): 386-88.

33. Ednah D. Littlehale to Alcott, July 19, [1849], owned by the Fruitlands Museum; AJ 23 (1849): 77, 80, 100 ff., 185, 192 ff., 362 ff., Benjamin Marston Watson to Alcott, January 15, 1852, in "Atuobiographical Collections" vol. 6; L. D. Geller, *Between Concord and Plymouth: The Transcendentalists and the Watsons* (Concord, Mass.: Thoreau Foundation, Inc., and Plymouth: Pilgrim Society, 1973), pp. 1-2; AJ 27 (1852): 64, 71, 138, 171, 225.

34. AJ 26 (1851): 10-12, 61, 463, 778, 825; AJ 27 (1852), pp. 21-22; AJ 31 (1856): 119-20, 669.

35. AJ 31 (1856): 310.

36. AJ 31 (1856): p. 372.

37. Cheney, "Reminiscences of Alcott's Conversations"; Ednah D. Cheney, *Louisa May Alcott: Her Life, Letters and Journals* (Boston: Little, Brown and Co., 1889), p. 41; AJ 28 (1853): 284, 291, 297, 325; Sanborn and Harris, *A. Bronson Alcott*, 1: 474, 477; AJ 23 (1849): 384; AJ 24 (January-March 1850): 279-81; Benson, ed., *America of the Fifties*, pp. 58-59, 64-66; Fredrika

Bremer, *The Homes of the New World: Impressions of America*, 2 vols. (New York: Harper and Brothers, 1868), 1: 174-76.

38. M. D. Paine to Alcott, March 26, 1849, in "Letters, 1836-1850."

39. Emerson and Forbes, eds., *Journals of Emerson*, 7: 524.

40. Ibid., 8: 70.

41. James Russell Lowell, "A Fable For Critics," in *The Complete Poetical Works of James Russell Lowell* (Boston: Houghton Mifflin Co., 1897), p. 128.

42. AJ 22 (1848): 537; Alcott to Mrs. Anna Alcott, April 22, 1849, in "Letters, 1836-1850"; AJ 23 (1849): 83-84, 87, 131-34, 140.

43. AJ 23 (1849): 163, 169-70, 241-42; A. Bronson Alcott, comp., "Records of the Town and Country Club," MS at Houghton Library, 59M-306 (12). This includes the Constitution and By-Laws, lists of members, and minutes of the meetings. Thomas, *The Liberator*, pp. 242 ff.

44. Alcott, comp., "Records of the Town and Country Club"; AJ 23 (1849): 279-80, 260-61, 365, 367; AJ 24 (January-March 1850): 22-23; John Weiss to Alcott, January 3, 1850, from a copy in Alcott's hand in AJ 24 (January-March 1850): 24-26; Samuel Longfellow to Alcott, October 30, 1849, in "Letters, 1836-1850."

45. AJ 24 (January-March 1850): 346-48; AJ 25 (March-December 1850): 23; Alcott, comp., "Records of the Town and Country Club."

46. AJ 23 (1849): 237; AJ 24 (January-March 1850): 391; AJ 26 (1851): 353; AJ 27 (1852): 117; AJ 28 (1853): 309; Cheney, "Reminiscences of Mr. Alcott's Conversations"; a printed notice of Abby May Alcott's relief room is pasted into AJ 23 (1849): 345; Abby May Alcott, "Autobiography"; Abby May Alcott, "Diary," January-February, 1849; Abby May Alcott to Samuel J. May, January 29, 1849, February 28, 1851, and April 28, 1851, in "Family Letters, 1828-1861."

47 Abby May Alcott, "Autobiography,"; Abby May Alcott, "Diary," April, 1850; AJ 24 (January-March 1850): 413, 480; AJ 23 (1849): 89, 99; Caroline Sturgis Tappan to Abby May Alcott, June 3, 1850, June 8, 1850, and July 25, 1850, in "Family Letters, 1850-1855"; Abby May Alcott, "Diary," July 14, 1850, from a copy in Alcott's hand in "Memoir, 1878"; AJ 26 (1851): 69; Louisa May Alcott, "Diary," 1850-1885, MS at Houghton Library, 59M-309 (8); Abby May Alcott to Samuel J. May, November 2, 1852, and December 19, 1852, in "Family Letters, 1828-1861"; AJ 27 (1852): 285.

48. Louisa May Alcott, "Diary," 1850-1885; AJ 25 (March-December 1850): 47, 51-54, 64, 67-68, 74-75, 77-78; Samuel J. May to Abby May Alcott, July 16, 1850, in "Family Letters, 1850-1855"; Abby May Alcott, "Diary," May 29, 1850, from a copy in Alcott's hand and with Louisa's explanatory note in "Memoir, 1878."

49. Samuel J. May to Abby May Alcott, September 23, 1850, in "Family Letters, 1850-1855"; Abby May Alcott, "Diary," July 14, 1850, from a copy in Alcott's hand in "Memoir, 1878"; Abby May Alcott to Samuel J. May, January 29, 1854, from a copy in Alcott's hand in "Memoir, 1878"; Abby May Alcott to Samuel J. May, September 1, 1851, in "Family Letters, 1828-1861"; AJ 25 (March-December 1850): 174-75; AJ 26 (1851): 81, 246-50, 485-86, 651, 743-49, 1143; Bradford Torrey, ed., *The Writings of Henry David Thoreau*, 20 vols. (Boston: Houghton Mifflin Co., 1906), 5: 365; Emerson and Forbes, eds., *Journals of Emerson*, 8: 363.

50. Louisa May Alcott, "Diary," 1850-1885; AJ 27 (1852): 109; Samuel J. May to Abby May Alcott, March 12, 1852, in A. Bronson Alcott, comp., "Letters for 1850, '51, '52, '53, and '54," vol. 5 at Houghton Library, 59M-305 (3); Abby May Alcott to Samuel J. May, April 12, 1853, in "Family Letters, 1828-1861"; AJ 28 (1853): 357-58, 363, 385; Elizabeth Sewall Alcott to Abby May Alcott [August, 1853], in "Family Letters, 1850-1855"; Alcott to Abby May Alcott, August 10, 1853, in "Family Letters, 1850-1855"; Ralph Waldo Emerson to Emily Mervine Drury, October 24, 1853, and November 23, 1853, in Rusk, ed., *Letters of Emerson*, 4: 391-92, 406.

51. AJ 28 (1853): 399-404; Abby May Alcott to Anna Bronson Alcott, October 9, 1853, from a copy in Alcott's hand in "Memoir, 1878"; AJ 26 (1852): 158; Cooke, *Historical and Biographical Introduction*, 2: 26-27.

52. AJ 28 (1853): 404-34; Alcott to Abby May Alcott, November 12, 1853, November 29, 1853, and Alcott to Anna Bronson Alcott, November 16, 1853, and November 22, 1853, in "Family

Letters, 1850-1855"; Alcott to Abby May Alcott, November 23, 1853, in "Letters, 1850-1854";
David Mead, "Some Ohio Conversations of Amos Bronson Alcott," *New England Quarterly* 22
(September 1949): 358-72; C. Carroll Hollis, "A New England Outpost," *New England Quarterly*
38 (March 1965): 65-85; Abby May Alcott to Alcott, December 4, 1853, in "Family Letters,
1850-1855."

53. AJ 28 (1853): 435-43; Mead, "Some Ohio Conversations"; Alcott to Abby May Alcott,
December 11, 1853, in "Family Letters, 1850-1855," and December 15, 1853, in "Letters,
1850-1854."

54. AJ 28 (1853): 443-49, AJ 29 (1854): 1-5; Alcott to Abby May Alcott, December 22, 1853,
December 26, 1853, and January 15, 1854, in "Family Letters, 1850-1855"; Abby May Alcott to
Alcott, December 28, 1853, and Thomas Wigglesworth, Jr. to Abby May Alcott, January 7, 1854,
in "Family Letters, 1850-1855," and to Benjamin Willis, January 9, 1854, in "Family Letters,
1828-1861"; Abby May Alcott to Benjamin Willis, January 9, 1854 etc; Abby May Alcott to
Samuel J. May, January 29, 1854, from a copy in Alcott's hand in "Memoir, 1878."

55. AJ 22 (1848): 777; Ednah D. Littlehale [Cheney], transcriber, "Report of Conversation,
January 6, 1849," from a copy in Alcott's hand in AJ 25 (March-December 1850): 300-302.

56. AJ 20 (1846), part 1: 23; AJ 20 (1846), part 2: 133, 158 175, 219; AJ 21 (1847), pp. 363, 473;
AJ 22 (1848): 433; AJ 24 (January-March 1850): 188, 376-77; Ednah D. Littlehale [Cheney],
transcriber, "Report of Conversation, December 31, 1849," from a copy in Alcott's hand in AJ 24
(January-March 1850): 12-14.

57. AJ 20 (1846), part 2: 338; AJ 21 (1847): 3, 393-96; AJ 22 (1848): 464; AJ 28 (1853): 111; AJ
26 (1851): 356; AJ 29 (1854): 229.

58. AJ 20 (1846), part 1: 335; AJ 21 (1847): 687-90; AJ 22, (1848): 79-80, 177-80, 251-53; AJ 26
(1851) 85, 919-21.

59. Alcott, "Leaves from Diary for January, 1846"; AJ 20 (1846), part 2: 335; AJ 21 (1847):
205, 687-90; AJ 23 (1849): 8, 11, 12-13, 15; A. Bronson Alcott, "Tablets in Colours disposed on
Twelve Tables" (1849), pp. 667-69, MS at Houghton Library, 59M-306 (11).

60. AJ 22 (1848): 8, 340; AJ 23 (1849): 225, 233; Signe Toksvig, *Emanuel Swedenborg* (New
Haven, Conn.: Yale University Press, 1948), p. 73; Emanuel Swedenborg, *Principia Rerum
Naturalium* (London: Swedenborg Society, 1912); Lloyd D. Easton, *Hegel's First American
Followers* (Athens, Ohio: Ohio University Press, 1966), pp. 32-33; AJ 24 (January-March 1850):
63.

61. I. Woodbridge Riley, *American Thought from Puritanism to Pragmatism* (New York: Peter
Smith, 1941), pp. 114-16; AJ 24 (January-March 1850): 101; Alice Felt Tyler, *Freedom's Ferment*
(New York: Harper and Row, 1962), pp. 80-81; AJ 23 (1849): 163; Alcott to Mrs. Anna Alcott,
April 22, 1849, in "Letters, 1836-1850."

62 Alcott, "Tablets, 1849," pp. 27, 31, 39. For the Great Chain of Being idea see A. O.
Lovejoy, *The Great Chain of Being* (Cambridge, Mass.: Harvard University Press 1957).

63. AJ 23 (1849): 249.

64. Ibid., pp. 267-69; Alcott, "Tablets, 1849," pp. 685, 689-91, 717.

65. AJ 23 (1849): 259, 280, 311-38, 391; Alcott to Abby May Alcott, September 17, 1849, in
"Letters, 1836-1850"; AJ 24 (January-March 1850): 164-66, 395-97; AJ 26 (1851), pp. 787-88; AJ
24 (January-March 1850): 62; Ednah D. Littlehale [Cheney], "Report of Conversation, December
16, 1848," from a copy in Alcott's hand in AJ 24 (January-March 1850): 264-68; AJ 26 (1851):
551; AJ 28 (1853): 33-34.

66. AJ 26 (1851): 32.

67. Ibid., pp. 137-38.

68. Easton, *Hegel's First American Followers*, p. 34; AJ 22 (1848): 735; Alcott, "Tablets,
1849," p. 669.

69. AJ 28 (1853): 130.

70. AJ 20 (1846), part 1: 31; AJ 24 (January-March 1850): 65, 415; AJ 27 (1852): 74.

71. AJ 26 (1851): 65-66, 131; Alcott, "Tablets, 1849," p. 355.

72. Alcott, "Tablets, 1849," p. 354; AJ 25 (March-December 1850): 10; Alcott to Mrs. Anna
Alcott, April 28, 1850, in "Family Letters 1850-1855"; AJ 27 (1852): 176-79, 189-222, 238,

245-48; AJ 28 (1853): 291, 294, 298-99; Torrey, ed., *Writings of Thoreau*, 4: 292.

73. AJ 28 (1853): 39-41, 59-64, 201; AJ 26 (1851): 27-29, 1072-73.

74. AJ 27 (1852): 88; AJ 28 (1853): 39-41, 169-71.

75. Ednah D. Cheney, "Reminiscences of Mr. Alcott's Conversations"; Ralph Waldo Emerson, "Journal HO," 1853-54, p. 276, from a typescript owned by the Concord Free Public Library. Ednah Littlehale married artist Seth Cheney on May 19, 1853.

76. AJ 26 (1851): 207-8; AJ 30 (1855): 460, 463.

77. AJ 24 (1850) (January-March): 27; AJ 26 (1851), pp. 89-90, 360, 808; AJ 22 (1848): 397, 659; AJ (1849): 130; AJ 27 (1852): 316, 344-45.

78. AJ 23 (1849): 264; AJ 24 (January-March 1850): 494; AJ 26 (1851): 89-90.

79. AJ 26 (1851): 143-45, 1070-72; AJ (1852): 79-80; AJ 28 (1853): 119-20.

80. AJ 23 (1849): 372; AJ 24 (January-March 1850): 178-80, 201-2, 471-72; AJ 25 (March-December 1850): 55.

81. AJ 24 (January-March 1850): 237.

82. Ibid., pp. 251-52, 321; AJ 27 (1852): 107-8.

83. AJ 24 (January-March 1850): 349-56; David Potter, *The Impending Crisis, 1848-1861* (New York: Harper and Row, 1976), p. 113; Thomas, *The Liberator*, pp. 368-69.

84. AJ 25 (March-December 1850): 174, 194, 206; Ednah D. Littlehale [Cheney], transcriber, "Report of Conversation on Daniel Webster, January 6, 1851," from a copy in Alcott's hand in AJ 26 (1851): 49-59, and "Conversation on Garrison, January 13, 1851," in ibid., pp. 110-22; AJ 26 (1851): 155-58, 193, 355-57, 361-64; Thomas, *The Liberator*, p. 378.

85. Thomas, *The Liberator*, pp. 376, 380; AJ 16 (1851): 472-73, 515-19, 563-64, 739-40; AJ 28 (1853): 111, 211.

86. Thomas, *The Liberator*, 384-87; AJ 29 (1854): 47-48; Thomas Wentworth Higginson to Alcott, April 11, 1854, in "Letters, 1850-54."

87. Thomas, *The Liberator*, p. 385; AJ 29 (1854): 48; Thomas Wentworth Higginson, *Contemporaries* (Boston: Houghton Mifflin and Co., 1900), p. 194; Thomas Wentworth Higginson, *Carlyle's Laugh and Other Surprises* (Boston: Houghton Mifflin Co., 1909), p. 90; Edith Willis Linn and Henri Bazin, eds., *Alcott Memoirs Posthumously from Papers Journals and Memoranda of the Late Dr. Frederick L. H. Willis* (Boston: Richard G. Badger, 1915), pp. 72-75; AJ 48 (1874): 171 ff.

88. AJ 29 (1854): 55-56, 61-62; AJ 49 (1874): 171 ff; Thomas Wentworth Higginson to Alcott, July 11, 1854, in "Letters, 1850-54"; Thomas, *The Liberator*, p. 386.

89. AJ 29 (1854): 84, 98, 120, 127, 138-71, 173, 175, 183-208, 368-69, 374; Benjamin Marston Watson to Alcott, September 8, 1854, Samuel Longfellow to Benjamin Marston Watson, October [6?], 1854, and Horatio Woodman to Alcott, October 8, 1854, in "Letters, 1850-54"; Edward W. Emerson, *The Early Years of the Saturday Club, 1855-1870* (Boston: Houghton Mifflin Co., 1918), pp. 11-12.

90. AJ 29 (1854): 229, 306, 308; Abby May Alcott, "Diary," June 14, 1854, from a copy in Alcott's hand in "Memoir, 1878"; Abby May Alcott to Anna Alcott, December 28, 1854, from a copy in Alcott's hand in "Memoir, 1878"; Louisa May Alcott, "Diary, 1850-1885."

91. Elizabeth Peabody to Abby May Alcott, March 10, 1854, Abby May Alcott to Alcott, September 22, 1854, in "Family Letters, 1850-1855"; AJ 29 (1854): 123; Ralph Waldo Emerson to George P. Bradford, August 28 and 30, 1854, in Rusk, ed., *Letters of Emerson*, vol. 4, p.460; AJ 30 (1855): 212, 215, 227.

92. AJ 30 (1855): 119-20, 143-44, 155, 163-64, 240, 251, 262, 270-71; Ralph Waldo Emerson to Frederick Beck, June 29, 1855, in Rusk, ed., *Letters of Emerson*, 5: 16; Abby May Alcott, "Diary," April 12, 1855, and June 2, 1855, from copies in Alcott's hand in "Memoir, 1878"; Abby May Alcott to Benjamin Willis, January 9, 1854, and Abby May Alcott to Samuel J. May, February 24, 1855, in "Family Letters, 1828-1861."

9

The Superintendent of Schools, 1855–65

ALCOTT'S little farmhouse in Walpole was a far cry from the bustle and variety of Boston. He was cut off from his friends, from the bookstores, from lectures and reform meetings. No longer could he take those crisp, early-morning walks on the Common. Nothing in Walpole could replace the Boston Athenaeum or the Harvard Library, which had heretofore given him access to all the books he wanted and to newspapers and periodicals from around the world. He was back to his garden tools, his plane, hammer, and saw.[1] But his languor was not lasting. In 1856 and 1857 he made successful tours to New York City. And the two years following that he went West, as far as St. Louis. He achieved a widespread reputation as an itinerant conversationalist. In the fall of 1857 he fulfilled his dream of establishing a permanent home in Concord. The people of Concord finally warmed up to the once-ridiculed eccentric and appointed him to be their superintendent of schools, a position that brought him little income but priceless rewards in honor and self-esteem. For the first time he felt that he was a recognized authority in education. Yet new-found success came in the context of a personal tragedy, the death of his daughter Elizabeth, and of a national one, the Civil War.

At first he deemed Walpole a pleasant retreat. "Tis refreshing," he said, "to yoke one's Idealism sometimes with this team of Tug-along-the ruts (of Realism), and so get practical wisdom out of it and sanity." Manual labor was a kind of therapy, as it had been in Concord in the mid-1840s. He supposed that the country air was good for the girls, especially for the frail Elizabeth and for Abby May. The Willis family, he thought, was full of good intentions and good will for the Alcotts. And he had his genealogical interests. When not in his garden he kept busy writing a history of the Bronson family, which he submitted to publisher Henry Bronson of Waterbury, Connecticut, who was compiling a history of that town and its people. He hoped to try his hand at writing again and to make a complete catalogue of his growing collection of books and manuscripts. Benjamin Marston Watson had asked him to build a summerhouse at the Watson estate in Plymouth, and Alcott looked forward to that pleasant task. Anna and Louisa, although they preferred lively Boston to the comparative dullness and drabness of Walpole, found some enjoyment performing in the Walpole Amateur Dramatic Company. Alcott liked watching his daughters perform and thought he detected in them a talent for acting.[2]

243

Alcott was instantly attracted to the summer minister of Walpole's Unitarian Church, Dr. Henry W. Bellows. Bellows, who was a leader in the American Unitarian Association and who served a parish in New York City during the winter months, was a native of Walpole. His ancestors had founded the nearby town of Bellows Falls, Vermont, in the middle of the eighteenth century. Alcott found Bellows to be "social, affable, and of a broader apprehension than is usual with the heads of the sect to which he belongs." Bellows was an interesting man and a generous man. When he left for New York in September, he loaned his piano to the musically talented Elizabeth.[3]

But by the fall of 1855 Walpole's charms had worn off. Bellows left. Anna returned to Syracuse, this time to work at Dr. Wilbur's "Asylum for Idiots." Louisa headed for Boston to spend the winter. Watson decided not to build the summerhouse after all. There was little to do on winter days but to read and reread his books and to lengthen his manuscript diaries. He spent hours writing, copying, and recopying. He wrote lengthy passages from Plato and Swedenborg into his manuscripts. The past—genealogy and autobiography—filled his thoughts. There were no new ideas, no attempts to synthesize old ideas. There was no stimulus for intellectual growth.[4]

Nor was there much to stimulate concern for reform. William Wells Brown came to preach abolition in early November, but Walpole lacked the drama and excitement of Vigilance Committees, attempts to rescue fugitive slaves, and provocative speeches by Garrison, Phillips, or Parker. The newspapers were filled with indignant gossip about Mary Gove Nichols's *Mary Lyndon*, a sensational novel espousing "free love." Alcott had met Mrs. Nichols in Lynn in 1842, when he nearly persuaded her to join Fruitlands, and he suspected that her book had more merit than the reviewers claimed. He did not read *Mary Lyndon*, but he did read similar ideas by Stephen Pearl Andrews, who advocated absolute individual freedom. Nichols and Andrews were publishing ideas once dear to Alcott, but in his lassitude in the fall of 1855, he had nothing to say about them but that they demanded "deeper consideration."[5]

Walpole's citizens politely supported a couple of Alcott conversations in December 1855, but Alcott was bored nevertheless. He wrote to Louisa that he was "all too dull and prosy to be very interesting to the livelier scion luxuriating in town, far away from my little chamber of reminiscences here." Dreams of a long conversational tour through New England kept his hopes alive, but there seemed to be no means to effect it. The indifference of Walpole people irritated him. Their hostility would have been easier to bear than their apathy. He felt as if he had retired to await death. Abby found the solitude of her sociable husband pathetic.[6]

The spring of 1856 brought some relief. In April bookseller J. B. Johnson arranged a series of conversations in Manchester, New Hampshire, which was successful enough to rekindle Alcott's belief that his conversations were the prototype of a new, nationwide cultural institution. From Manchester he traveled to Boston to visit Louisa and to read at the Athenaeum. With the help of avid conversers Caroline Healey Dall, Caroline Hildreth, and Dr. William

F. Channing, he arranged a series of three successful conversations on the spiritual effects of "Social Life." At the same time he managed a trip to Worcester to converse with a group gathered by H. G. O. Blake and another to Groveland to meet David Wasson's congregation. A visit with Emerson revived hopes of returning to Concord and of being buried there one day near his friend in the new cemetery at Sleepy Hollow. Eighty-eight dollars from his conversations helped him pay old Concord debts and to buy a new suit of clothes. He returned to Walpole and to his garden on May 13 full of encouragement.[7]

Prospects for a pleasant summer were interrupted by Elizabeth's dangerous illness. She had contracted scarlet fever from the Hall family nearby, whom Abby had nursed and comforted. For several days she lay near death, and although she recovered from the fever, her health remained precarious thereafter. The Alcotts refused to call for medical help, relying instead on home remedies and on the advice of Samuel Christian Hahnemann's works on homeopathy. Reflecting on his own battle with smallpox, Alcott liked Hahnemann's idea that disease was only a derangement of the body's "vital principles." He was sure, as was Hahnemann, that the natural healing mechanism of the body would restore the balance. Drastic remedies such as bleeding or blistering or the administration of laudanum would, they felt, only inhibit the healing process.[8]

The summer brought a renewed interest by Alcott in national politics. On May 22 the chivalrous southerner Preston Brooks had caned Massachusetts' Charles Sumner on the floor of the Senate in retaliation for Sumner's vicious verbal attacks on Brooks's cousin, Senator Andrew P. Butler. Sumner had been unremitting in his hostility toward slavery. He was particularly horrified at the violence of the proslavery gunmen who sacked Lawrence, Kansas, on May 21. News of the Sumner incident and the events in Kansas inflamed Northern opinion. Alcott hoped this example of "club rule" would arouse the North to forceful resistance to slavery and its expansion. In his opinion there was no escaping conflict. Dr. Bellows, back in Walpole for the summer, began organizing a Frémont Club to work for the free soil platform of John C. Frémont, the Republican presidential candidate. Alcott attended the organizational session and invited members to his home to discuss the coming conflict between slavery and freedom.[9]

Bellows also offered Alcott a chance to visit him in New York that fall, and he promised to arrange conversations. Alcott was elated. There would be no better chance to spread his message than in the nation's largest city and with the support of the influential Bellows. On September 13 Alcott started for New York by train, proud of being included in the *New York Tribune's* published list of traveling lecturers for the 1856 season. He stopped to converse in Fitchburg, Massachusetts, then went on to Worcester to see his longtime agents for conversation, H. G. O. Blake and Thomas Wentworth Higginson. Higginson, he discovered, had gone to Kansas, rifle in hand, to fight for free soil. In Hartford, Connecticut, he visited Henry Barnard, former Secretary of the Connecticut Board of Education, who was at work on a history of education in the United States. Barnard accepted a copy of *Record of a School* and promised to visit Walpole to hear more of Alcott's views on human culture. Alcott believed, and rightly so, that he deserved at least a paragraph in any broad study of American education.[10]

After a brief visit with his mother, his brother Ambrose, and several cousins at New Haven and Waterbury, Alcott called at Yale College. He was greeted suspiciously by Professors Nathaniel William Taylor, Benjamin Silliman, George Park Fisher, and Noah Porter. He found them condescending and generally unwilling to allow any hint of Plato to disturb their carefully guarded orthodoxy. Yet they did not close the door to him. Noah Porter agreed to arrange a series of conversations to be held on Alcott's return from New York. Alcott was more than pleased with the chance to "try the temper of Yale and orthodoxy." He also attended services at First Congregational Church in New Haven and found its minister, Leonard Bacon, to be affable and "truly patriotic," having spoken out openly for Frémont and freedom in Kansas.[11]

Alcott arrived in New York City on October 1 and took a room at Taylor's International Hotel on Broadway. He lost no time visiting friends and persons who struck his interest: Samuel Longfellow in Brooklyn, George Ripley and Charles Anderson Dana at the *Tribune* office, Dr. Bellows at his All Soul's Church, lecturer Edwin Hubbell Chapin, and the flamboyant literary genius Walt Whitman. Few persons had ever charmed, amazed, and overwhelmed Alcott as much as Whitman did. He was both intrigued and taken aback by Whitman's "brute power" and audacity," by his ostentatious non-conformity. In characterizing this self-styled representative poet of "young America," Alcott did some of his best writing. He described him in colorful detail down to his open-necked red flannel undershirt and coarse overalls, his cowhide boots and slouched hat. Alcott was amused rather than offended at Whitman's captivating egotism, finding him "incapable of omitting, or suffering anyone long to omit noting Walt Whitman, in discourse." Whitman greeted Alcott warmly, gave him a copy of *Leaves of Grass* for comments, and asked for information about Emerson, whom Whitman considered to be his master. Unabashed in the presence of the staid Alcott, Whitman lay on his couch with his arm propping up his head as he talked. He told Alcott, who doubtless guessed otherwise, that he had never been sick and had never sinned.[12]

Several of Alcott's former radical friends and followers had found their way to New York. He met the obstreperous comeouter William Chace of Providence and Edward Palmer, erstwhile advocate of a barter economy. Both of them, he found, had been "toned down" by life to "ordinary levels" and were somewhat apologetic to him for having made peace with society. He also visited Isaac Hecker, now a Roman Catholic priest, no longer seeking Utopia.[13]

On October 9 Alcott opened his first series of five conversations in Dr. Bellows's library. Bellows solemnly introduced him to the gathering as "Dr.

Alcott," the "father of transcendentalism" and the "Plato of our time." Alcott spoke each week until November 6 at Bellows's home and deemed the series successful, though he was paid only fifty dollars. It was a good introduction to the city. Further opportunities to talk and to socialize followed quickly. New Yorkers were far more accepting of him than they had been two years before. Samuel Longfellow, faithful as ever, sponsored several conversations, as did some of his parishioners. Mrs. Anne Lynch Botta, whom Alcott had known in Providence in the early 1840s, attended the Bellows conversations and invited Alcott to her evening parties and breakfasts. She had been holding such literary soirées since the mid-1840s and had attracted such illuminati as Margaret Fuller, Edgar Allen Poe, William H. Furness, Albert Brisbane, Christopher Cranch, George William Curtis, and even Charles Lane. Alcott found "very good company" at Mrs. Botta's parties, including Charles Loring Brace, founder of the Children's Aid Society, with whom Alcott went to visit an "Idiot Asylum" in Harlem.[14]

New York was full of popular faddists—phrenologists, spiritualists, proponents of water cures—and Alcott was fascinated by them, though he remained somewhat aloof and suspicious. Three times before he bad been analyzed by practicing phrenologists. He and Elizabeth Peabody had both gone to Dr. Silas Jones in Boston in November 1835, curious about the results but too cautious to give their names. Jones had measured Alcott's head and had written a lengthy statement telling what those measurements revealed about Alcott's character. Jones's conclusions were so general that they were bound to touch on the truth. He said that Alcott had the manner of a clergyman; that he was highly educated, with literary tastes; and that he liked harmony, honesty, and the country air. But the other two phrenologists, including one of the Fowler brothers, came up with conclusions that, according to Alcott, contradicted Jones and each other. Thus Alcott remained skeptical and suspected that he was the victim of quackery. Nevertheless, he was still intrigued, and in New York he called on the office of the Fowler brothers to get a chart of his character. Orson and Lorenzo Fowler had become the foremost practitioners of popular phrenology in the United States. Their phrenology was far removed from the reputable science of Spurzheim and Combe and had become little more than a faddish character reading, like palmistry or fortune telling. Despite his suspicions, Alcott gave way to his insecurities about himself and sought proof of his character by means that he knew, intellectually, were not trustworthy.[15]

Alcott also gave an ear to the popular spiritualists, those who claimed that they could communicate with the supernatural, particularly with the spirits of the deceased. Such ideas had grown apace since the alleged revelatory rappings of the Fox sisters of Hydesville, New York, in 1848. Alcott met once again with self-proclaimed medium Andrew Jackson Davis and heard Davis's associate, Thomas Lake Harris, speak at Dodsworth Hall. Harris, a former Universalist minister, had published three books in the mid-1850s that were supposedly dictated to him by the spirit. He believed that each person had a spiritual counterpart with whom supernatural union or affinity was possible. Alcott was curious but skeptical. In November and December he held several conversations with a group of spiritualists and found "much sympathy" with them. Indeed, his ideas about the spiritual nature of the soul and of the magnetic nature of spiritual forces were similar to those of the popular spiritualists. Yet in the end he rejected spiritualistic rituals and the faddish attempts to talk with the dead. Such superstition and fanaticism, he said, only paganized things truly spiritual and divine. He wondered at the credulity of the populace, which supported a rapidly growing number of spiritualistic journals and lecturers in the 1850s. There was a fine line between what Alcott considered superstitious and what he considered truly spiritual. He did not make clear where that line was nor why it should exist at all.[16]

Water cures also captured Alcott's interest. He found enthusiastic support for his own ideas about diet and health at Dr. Russell T. Trall's Hydropathic Medical College. Both patients and students at the College were respectful and admiring of the ideas of Sylvester Graham and William Alcott. Trall invited Alcott to converse with his students on health and temperance, and on October 25 Alcott left Taylor's hotel and moved to the College, paying his board and room by conversing. Success at Trall's establishment led to invitations to speak at two other water cures in the city. Patients began calling on Alcott for advice and even for private confession about their failure to live the pure life. Such recognition added to Alcott's certainty that his ideas about diet were correct. He did not hesitate to tell Trall that the diet at his water cure was inferior because it lacked a sufficient quantity of fruits and grains. Trall, an entrepreneur as well as a healer, was not offended and offered Alcott a chance to manage another of his water cures at Meriden, Connecticut, a few miles from Wolcott. Alcott was interested but discovered that the capital investment required of him was too great to warrant his acceptance.[17]

His trip to New York gave Alcott a chance to look more closely at the Raritan Bay community in nearby Perth Amboy, New Jersey. On October 11 he visited "Eagleswood," the school operated by the Welds for the Raritan Bay members. The Welds asked Alcott to give examples of his teaching methods and to speak to the group on worship. They encouraged the Alcotts to join. Abby wrote, hoping that membership at Raritan Bay would provide steady work and relieve the family from their embarrassing reliance on the good will of other people. But Alcott did not find the community "inviting." He found it to be a cooperative rather than a true community. Members shared only the school and the land surrounding it, and even the school was unstable. Theodore Weld feared that the whole enterprise would soon collapse because of the lack of education on the part of members. Weld also hinted that there were some members who would, for unspecified reasons, object to Alcott's becoming a member, although they would welcome his family. Alcott gave them no opportunity to snub him.[18]

Henry Thoreau was at Eagleswood surveying and lecturing when Alcott visited for the second time on November 1. Thoreau decided to join Alcott in his visits around New York. They went together to see the increasingly famous editor of the *Tribune*, Horace Greeley. They heard the energetic and dramatic Henry Ward Beecher speak before a full house at his Plymouth Church in Brooklyn. And they called on the colorful Walt Whitman. Alcott was immensely impressed with the power and magnetism of Beecher. He thought he spoke to the needs of the people better than any popular preacher he had heard. But Thoreau, who was never comfortable at a formal religious service, was not impressed and thought there was an element of paganism in Beecher's performance and in the apparent spell he cast over his faithful listeners. Thoreau was even more uncomfortable in the presence of Whitman. They went to see the poet on November 10 along with the enormous Mrs. Tyndale from Philadelphia, who, as Alcott described her, was "a solid Walrus of a woman, spread full many a rood abroad." Whitman awkwardly ushered them up two narrow flights of stairs to his disorderly attic study where, without asking his guests to sit, he plopped down on his couch and told them about his habit of riding the omnibus from morning to night. Alcott, concerned about how Thoreau and Whitman would get along, watched as the two stared at each other "like two beasts wondering what the other would do." Thoreau later wrote to H. G. O. Blake that he was in a quandary about Whitman. He liked his "sweet disposition" but was provoked by his "strong, coarse nature." Alcott and Thoreau did not stay long at Whitman's, for it was clear that Thoreau and Whitman had little to say to one another. They left the "voluminous Mrs. Tyndale" to speak alone with the "Savage Sovereign of the Flesh."[19]

On December 12 Whitman called on Alcott to talk about American people and institutions over dinner. Alcott listened patiently as his guest praised Whitman and praised Emerson and praised Whitman again. He expected great things of Whitman, if only his arrogance would not get in the way. It was strange that the straitlaced and orderly Alcott should have been attracted to the free-living Whitman, with his frequent use of coarse, earthy, sexual imagery. But Alcott admired Whitman's nonconformity, and he might secretly have wished that he could be as unrestrained and carefree. He had once said himself that "the Human Body is itself the richest and raciest Phrase Book." Whitman had the genius, which Alcott admired but did not have himself, to make full use in his writing of the "blood-warmth and flesh colours of nature."[20]

Near the end of his stay in New York, Alcott reflected on the free range he had enjoyed, the variety of opportunities for conversation, and the variety of people he had met. He had talked with Albert Brisbane about Fourierism and "free love." He had argued for chastity against Stephen Pearl Andrews, "the Frisky Free Lover, and Sire of Sodom, the frankest sinner I have seen as yet," who advocated an end to all legal restraints on love between sovereign individuals. The Women's Rights Convention of November 23 had elected Alcott a vice-president, and he had held lengthy discussions with women's rights advocates Lucy Stone, Dr. Elizabeth Blackwell, Emily Blackwell, and

Lucretia Mott. Dr. Bellows had invited him to a formal breakfast where he listened as Fanny Kemble and Henry Ward Beecher, both actors in their own way, compared notes. He had attended the theater to see the popular Laura Keene perform. He had even had to run to escape the amorous advances of a friend of Lucy Stone's, who acted in the name of free love. Heaven save us, he said, from those who practice promiscuity and call it virtue.[21]

New York was alive with talk about Kansas and slavery. Alcott did his part with a benefit conversation to support the Kansas free soilers. He was proud of his wife and daughters, who were busy in Walpole making clothing to send to Kansas. Abby even offered to go with the next group of emigrants to be a matron of a water cure, a hospital, or a school. Upon hearing of Frémont's defeat in the Presidential election, Alcott was dismayed. He concluded that "the people are not ripe for freer institutions, nor ready to pay the cost of the great boon of liberty they prate so wildly about, yet know so little how to prize and maintain." Yet he had not voted in the election, still unable to reconcile citizenship with the rights of the "sovereign and transcendent personality."[22]

On December 30, 1856, Alcott returned to Walpole after nearly a three-month absence. His greatcoat had been stolen and he looked pathetic, cold, and "transparent as an icicle" as he stepped off the train. His appearance justified all of Abby's fears about the "perils of the big city." But he felt ten years younger and full of hope. His sojourn had brought in only one hundred eighty dollars, but it had advertised his conversations as never before. He felt like a celebrity. His confidence in the meaning of his life's work was restored. "My profession brings me advantages," he said. "The title of Dr. seems no longer strange, nor, as things go, altogether insignificant or misapplied I may believe." His family was overjoyed. Louisa was ready to wear a placard on her back saying "Mr. Alcott's daughter." A young reporter for the *New York Times*, John Swinton, offered to transcribe Alcott's conversations; he would finally have his own Boswell. It had been a glorious year, and his journal for 1856 reflected his enthusiasm. It expanded to over thirteen hundred pages for the year compared to a meager three or four hundred for each year since 1851.[23]

The winter of 1857 was a busy one. There was a series of conversations in Manchester, New Hampshire; a trip to Boston to visit Louisa and Abby May; a few conversations with neighbors in Walpole; and another brief journey to New York in February. In New York Mr. and Mrs. Henry V. Poor, he the editor of the *American Railroad Journal* and she the sister of Frederic Hedge, sponsored a series of conversations, as did poet Alice Cary. He had intended to go on to Philadelphia, but the conversations promised by William Henry Furness did not materialize.[24]

Instead, he went to New Haven to visit his mother and brother again and to make his long-awaited assault on Yale College. On March 11 he began a series of six conversations arranged by lawyer Joseph Sheldon at the Young Men's Institute. Several Yale professors attended each session, as did thirty to forty students. The conversations found unexpected interest among the Yale students and transformed at least one of them, William Torrey Harris. Harris, then a junior, was in a period of his life he later described as "die Aufklärung," experimenting with all the popular fads—phrenology, water cures, spiritualism, diet, and dress reform. Alcott's conversations proved to be a turning point in his life. Alcott gave him a concept of the higher power of the soul able to transcend the limits of "mere sense experience." For Harris it was a beautiful glimpse of the infinite creative potential of the human soul. All this happened while college chaplain George Park Fisher was gravely warning his students against Alcott and the "new Philosophical Infidelity."[25]

At the end of March the tireless Alcott was back in Boston visiting friends and attending lectures. Then on March 31 he traveled to New Bedford, Massachusetts, to visit Thoreau's friend Daniel Ricketson at Brooklawn, the Ricketsons' country estate, For two and one half weeks he discussed people, literature, and nature with Ricketson, Thoreau, and Ellery Channing, and held a series of five conversations in New Bedford arranged by Unitarian minister John Weiss. Ricketson, who wrote pastoral poetry and modeled himself after English gentlemen, was impressed by this "modern Plato" whom he called "Father Alcott." He declared that Alcott had the noblest character of anyone he had ever met, and he wrote an appreciative notice of Alcott's conversations in the *New Bedford Mercury*.[26]

Alcott talked at length with Ricketson about moving back to Concord. He was more anxious than ever to return to that "center of fairer and finer influences." Frank Sanborn, who was teaching in Concord, suggested a plan for a new college there with Emerson, Thoreau, Hedge, Parker, Louis Agassiz, and Alcott as professors. Alcott, enthusiastic about this revival of the dreams of the early 1840s, hoped that Ricketson also would join the faculty. And Alcott's family was growing more and more restive at Walpole. The town's dullness was more oppressive than ever, and Abby especially was tired of living in obligation to her cousins. But the family failed to see the idyllic grandeur of Concord. They preferred returning to Boston to escape the comparative isolation and inactivity of small-town life. Alcott was painfully aware of his family's prejudice, and he hoped that Sanborn's proposed College would help his wife at least to overcome it.[27]

On May 9 Alcott went with Louisa to Concord to visit Emerson and to look for possible houses. He hoped to own his own home again, possibly near Emerson, possibly the Moore property next to Hillside, now Hawthorne's Wayside. In late May he was back in his garden in Walpole hoping for a move to Concord that fall. Elizabeth's health had the family worried again because she was still weak from her bout with scarlet fever the previous year. Alcott gave up conversation opportunities in order to be near her. He talked, played games and rode with her, and brought her fresh strawberries from the nearby hills. She got no better. Perplexity over the nature of her condition and fear for her life caused a loss of faith in homeopathy. In mid-July they asked Dr. Charles Windship, Abby's nephew, to examine her. He recommended convalescence at the sea coast. Accordingly, on August 1 Abby took her to

Boston and on to Swampscott and the ocean. Meanwhile, Alcott kept busy on a manuscript called "Initia Divina," although his worry over Elizabeth made concentration difficult. Her cyclical improvement and decline, along with conflicting doctors' reports, kept the family alternating between hope and despair for her survival. In late August she was worse again. Alcott hurriedly left for Swampscott to see her. They consulted more doctors, and their favorable reports allowed Alcott to leave Elizabeth and go to Providence to find means from his friends to buy a house in Concord. On September 5 he arrived in Concord determined to buy the property next to Hillside, "Orchard House," from John Moore for nine hundred forty-five dollars. He wrote to his daughters in Walpole asking them to give him one last chance to control the family fortunes and to redeem their opinion of his "good sense and discretion."[28]

The family relented, evidently convinced by Alcott's recent successes in New York. Alcott bought Orchard House with help from Emerson, who paid the five hundred dollar down payment and signed a note to secure the rest. Providence friends Thomas Davis and Joseph Barker agreed to contribute five hundred dollars between them over the next four years. On October 3 the family moved to Concord and occupied a rented house for the winter while awaiting needed repairs on Orchard House. Alcott managed to pay debts to Concord merchants outstanding since the 1840s.[29]

On November 11, Elizabeth's condition having stabilized, Alcott left for a tour of the West, hopeful that the financial panic would not hurt his chances for successful conversation. His aging mother, who had spent the summer with them, accompanied him as far as West Edmeston, New York, where she planned to live with Alcott's sister, Betsey Pardee. He followed the route of his successful 1853 tour—Syracuse, Rochester, Buffalo—conversing effectively in each place. In Buffalo, Emerson's friend, wealthy ex-Congressman Albert H. Tracy, introduced Alcott to ex-President Millard Fillmore. Alcott found Fillmore to be a genial man but disturbingly unappreciative of the abolitionists and too much "a devotee of constitutions." Fillmore and Tracy both attended Alcott's conversation on December 16, but ruined the evening by engaging in "debate."[30]

Alcott spent Christmas in Cleveland talking with his former pupil in Cheshire, Horace Hitchcock, who flattered Alcott by agreeing that there had never been a school like Alcott's Cheshire School before or since. But the season was "unpropitious" in Cleveland. Few people attended his conversations, and his nagging concern about Elizabeth kept him preoccupied. News from home was not encouraging, yet not alarming. The family tried to buoy his spirits by telling of the delightful time Anna, Louisa, and Abby May were having acting in plays with Frank Sanborn's scholars. Daniel Ricketson had visited, and Anna was sure that he was crazy and would hang himself one day.[31]

On January 4, 1858, Alcott hesitantly went on to Cincinnati, where conversations were planned by Ainsworth Spofford and by Moncure D.

Conway. Conway, a regular at Alcott's Harvard Divinity School conversations in the early 1850s, had just moved to Cincinnati to become minister of the Unitarian Church. The series of conversations went very well. Large numbers attended, despite the panic, and paid Alcott sixty dollars. Spofford provided Alcott with a full schedule of social engagements, introducing him to nearly every member of the literati in Cincinnati. Christopher Cranch was there and eagerly showed Alcott his *Dial* caricatures of Emerson, Alcott, and the "Orphic Sayings." Alcott was not offended, and found Cranch, his onetime companion at the Groton Convention, to be "good company." Alcott had hoped to extend his journey to St. Louis, but Elizabeth's condition had worsened, forcing him to hurry home, stopping briefly in Cleveland for conversations on three successive nights. The western trip had provided one hundred ninety dollars and the promise of great things in the future.[32]

Elizabeth was extremely weak when Alcott arrived in Concord on January 23. She was in pain; she knew that she was dying and had already divided her possessions among her sisters. Alcott talked openly with her about death, but he refused to admit that her condition was hopeless, even when Dr. Geist from Boston said as much, describing her disease as "atrophy consumption of the nerves with wasting of the flesh." He spent the next six weeks close to Elizabeth, occasionally spending the night sitting by her in her room. She died in the early morning of March 14. Alcott bore his grief by spending hour after hour superintending repairs on Orchard House board by board. His friends saw little of him. His journal entries became matter of fact, recording the daily progress of his house and the planting of his garden. The family moved to their new home in late May, but repairs on the delapidated seventeenth-century structure continued throughout the summer and fall. Alcott escaped only once to converse: a trip to Greenwood to talk with a group assembled by his friend J. J. Locke.[33]

On November 6 Alcott received a letter from William Torrey Harris asking him to visit St. Louis, where Harris had gone after leaving Yale, and to talk to a circle of friends he had found who liked to ruminate about the idealism of Hegel and Kant. Harris had first written to Alcott in November 1857, confessing his conversion to idealism at Alcott's hand, and his debt to Emerson and Thoreau. Elizabeth's illness had prevented Alcott from accepting Harris's invitation in 1857, but now he was ready to oblige Harris and banker Benjamin Wiley, who had asked him to visit Chicago.[34]

He left for the West on December 3 and headed directly for Chicago, stopping briefly in Syracuse, Buffalo, and Rochester to arrange conversations for his return trip. In Chicago he became the guest of Unitarian minister George Noyes, who had attended Alcott conversations at Harvard Divinity School in the early 1850s. Noyes had prompted the invitation through Wiley, his parishioner. Chicago impressed Alcott. He was sure it wold become one of the most important cities in the West. And it gave him moderate acceptance: three evenings with good attendance and fifty dollars. He hurried on to St.

Louis to meet Harris on December 28. For the next three weeks he talked at
length about Kant and transcendentalism with Harris, with Prussian refugee
and translator of Hegel Henry C. Brokmeyer, and with members of Harris's
philosophical class. Harris advertised Alcott as the greatest conversationalist
since Socrates, and his first public session on January 10 attracted between
fifty and sixty people. But few of these people actively participated in the
conversation, leaving Alcott to do all the talking and confirming his opinion
that a "commercial" city like St. Louis had little to offer. Its citizens, he
thought, supported only the "fatuities and superstitions" of popular
spiritualism or the "dangerous" opinions of the now staunch Catholic Orestes
Brownson. Alcott met both Brownson and the ubiquitous Andrew Jackson
Davis, who were lecturing in St. Louis at the time, but found satisfaction in
neither, believing them "hopelessly lost." And Alcott's public reception at
subsequent conversations was meager. Harris was disappointed, but
optimistically talked of forming a "Mississippi Club" of those interested in
contributing money to get Emerson, Thoreau, and Alcott to come in future
seasons.[35]

On January 18, 1859, Alcott started his homeward journey, stopping for
four conversations in Cincinnati and six in Cleveland. He found nothing in
Buffalo, Syracuse, or Albany, and when he arrived in Concord on February
19, he was tired and discouraged. The tour had been rough, tedious, and
largely unprofitable despite one hundred eighty-five dollars in receipts and
accolades from Noyes in Chicago and Spofford in Cincinnati. He was glad to
return to his books and his garden after the "privations and discomforts" of
the "slovenly West." The opportunities for conversations and the numbers of
people interested in his ideas were substantially fewer than he had hoped. An
"inhabitant of the mind," he declared, could never be a pioneer, a settler, or a
planter of the backwoods. Such "wild country" only served to drive the most
unflinching optimists to cynicism and despair. Yet he refused to abandon the
possibility of future westward excursions. There were some "earnest men and
women" whom he hoped to meet again. And he felt he was the kind of teacher
who could serve the needs of those few Western folk who could no longer
accept the "old answers." There was potential for him in the West, he
thought, if only he could avoid the mammoth gatherings of "frivolous and
stupid" people at Western lyceums and library associations.[36]

Alcott spent the early spring reading and working again on the manuscript
he hoped to publish, variously called "Initia Divina," "Tablets," and
"Leaves." He was interrupted on March 18 by a visit from his cousin and
lifelong friend William Alcott, who hoped to rectify the partial estrangement
between the two that had existed since the mid-1830s. They had had little
contact with each other since then, but now they talked at length about
education and reminisced, their differences over religious and philosophical
beliefs forgotten. William confessed that his life of writing and lecturing on
education and health was a failure. Bronson reassured him that he had been
one of the most useful people of the time. They parted friends again. Ten days

later, on March 29, William Alcott died unexpectedly at his home in Auburndale.[37]

The sadness of William Alcott's death was somewhat relieved on April 7 when Frank Sanborn, Secretary of the Concord School Committee, came to invite Alcott to be Superintendent of Schools. Alcott accepted with only brief hesitation. He immediately dropped the writing of "Leaves" and energetically began to plan his program for the district schools. He pored over the reports of the previous superintendent, Dr. Reynolds, and the reports of the Secretary of the Massachusetts Board of Education for 1857-58. And he began visiting each district school in turn. The job paid only one hundred dollars a year, but Alcott cared little about financial rewards. For the first time the town he loved so much was offering him appreciative recognition instead of scorn, ridicule, and the constant harping of bill collectors. More important, his appointment as superintendent meant acknowledgment as an authority in education, a status denied him since the failure of the Temple School. It was a kind of vindication, a sign to him that the dull and dense public was finally beginning to appreciate his true worth.[38]

Once again he had the opportunity to be in the classroom talking to children, preaching to them about the importance of thinking rather than rote memorization, and reading to them from his favorite stories and parables. As superintendent, he felt that he was in a position to effect important improvements in the Concord educational system. He would have a voice in book selection, in the purchase of materials, in curriculum development, in the evaluation of teachers, and in the examination of students. The old spark of reform flashed again as he envisioned the Concord schools as models of excellence for the rest of the nation to follow. Concord not only could exemplify the best in ideas and literature, but also could demonstrate how the relationship between a town and its schools measured the quality of community life. To help accomplish his mission he invited all the town's teachers to meet each month at Orchard House to discuss the problems of teaching and discipline with examples from the Cheshire and Temple Schools. Obviously impressed with Alcott's dedication and enthusiasm, the School Committee agreed to sponsor Sunday evening meetings with parents and children at the various schoolhouses to discuss "family culture."[39]

The first of these meetings with parents took place at Bateman's Pond School House on October 9. To Alcott's delight the whole neighborhood, parents and children, came to hear him tell of the importance of parents' maintaining a direct interest in their children's education. Alcott was committed to the idea of the neighborhood school. He believed that the school should be the focal point for the social life of every neighborhood, and he hoped that his Sunday evening sessions would strengthen that idea among the families involved. "We best describe a school in describing a neighborhood," he said. "And where the sentiment of a neighborhood is divided and feeble, there is not much to be said."[40]

He also wanted to impress on parents and teachers his idea of moral culture.

As always, he was more concerned about the morals and behavior of students than in recitations or the acquisition of knowledge. The chief agent in moral culture in the classroom, he still believed, was the personal example of the teacher.[41] A true teacher inspired the truth in others, he declared:

> A teacher is a choice person.... Cold sense, rigor, the stiff, the conventional; brute strength, any lack of delicacy, any selfish stains, are hostile to the art and spoil whatever they touch. An ingenuous, glowing soul, along with the kindliest, the mellowist gifts, are the aptitudes and skills for the task.... None can teach anything admirably who does not love it and find reward in it.[42]

Teaching was an "instinct of the heart," he told his parents and teachers. A good teacher necessarily was kind, sincere, and full of appreciation for the power of ideas. Education was already too much impoverished of ideas by the "materialism and prevailing atheism" of the times, he said. He insisted that the classroom be free of monotony and routine. To lessen the tedium he introduced singing, marching, dancing, and recreation periods. In his regular monthly visits to each district school he gave examples of his conversational technique, telling students and teachers that free expression cultivated thought rather than parrotry. He encouraged teachers to visit one another's classes to facilitate the exchange of ideas and methods. Most important, he stressed the goals and philosophy of education and inspired the young Concord teachers to discuss and think about that philosophy and those goals. For a short time at least, he developed a new excitement and enthusiasm for education and its potential among teachers, parents, and students.[43].

The inductive method, the cornerstone of Alcott's approach to teaching since the 1820s, was still important to him. But now he related it, as never before, concretely and directly to the neighborhood and community. The town, he said, was a microcosm of the world. Students could best learn about their complex world by first studying the simple and the known, the geography and history of the neighborhood and town. Learning by experience was best, he thought, so he advocated walking and observing in the manner of Henry Thoreau rather than studying the landscape from lifeless maps. "Good teaching makes the child an eye witness, he seeing, then telling what is seen, what is known; a dissolving of the text for a moment and a beholding in thought as in a glass."[44]

He hoped that Thoreau, "our resident Surveyor-General," would prepare an illustrated atlas of the Concord area as a student guide to the study of the community. Further, he proposed the preparation of a "Concord Book" to include an illustrated record of the history, geography, and antiquities of the town as well as the writings of Concord residents—Emerson, Thoreau, Hawthorne, Ellery Channing, perhaps even Alcott. He began collecting materials for the book in the spring of 1861, hoping to complete it by Christmas. In his prospective Concord Book Alcott included the early history of Concord drawn from Lemuel Shattuck's *History of the Town of Concord*

(1835), and of New England from Edward Johnson's *Wonder Working Providences* (1654). He collected biographical material about Concord's leading citizens, descriptions of significant events in the town's recent history, selections from the authors, and information about education in Concord—schools, lyceums, the town library.[45]

For Alcott the Concord Book was to be more than just a textbook for implementing the inductive method of teaching geography and history. It was also his means of cultivating and preserving the sense of community he believed so important. He envisioned a community centered in the schools, in the family, and in the neighborhood, interested in promoting a better quality of life by means of education, moral culture, and a faith in ideas. His community would also be rooted in the past, in the example of past leaders and people of "character." Concord would become Alcott's Fruitlands, or more accurately, his Wolcott. It might become the model of an ideal society, or if not that, it could preserve and foster the kinds of things he valued most about community life: sharing, concern for others, a common faith, a pride in the community and its traditions, and a commitment to improve—socially, personally, intellectually. The Concord Book symbolized his acceptance, at long last, by the people of Concord. Concord was finally giving him a context in which he could try to preserve those institutions and values which rapid change had threatened to destroy forever.

Unfortunately, the Concord Book was never finished. It did not survive the disruption of Civil War and the deaths of Thoreau in 1862 and Hawthorne in 1864. But the Concord Book did not exhaust Alcott's ideas for improving Concord schools. He purchased maps, globes, histories, new books such as Krummacher's *Parables* and Plutarch's *Lives*, copies of the Declaration of Independence and the United States Constitution for each school, and reference books for the teachers. He obtained sets of flash cards, called "Tablets," containing letters of the alphabet, numbers, sounds, words for spelling, and examples of punctuation. These "Tablets" were the creation of Boston school superintendent John D. Philbrick, who introduced them to the Boston public schools in February 1860. Alcott also encouraged his teachers to use the recently developed system of phonetic writing and reading, which he lauded as a great improvement over earlier methods of teaching reading. He instructed his teachers in the importance of teaching composition by means of letter writing and diary keeping. He encouraged the establishment of school newspapers to record students' ideas on sports, amusements, social customs, art, books, lectures, science, and politics. Newspapers, he felt, would be an excellent learning aid as well as a means of involving young people in the affairs of the community.[46]

Alcott put his ideas and a record of his reforms into annual school reports, the first of which was printed in April 1860. The reports gave him a precious opportunity to make his ideas more widely known and to effect greater interest in education among Concordians. He considered them to be "portraits" of the community. For the first time in twenty-five years his writing was well received. Citizens of Concord and educators outside Concord praised the school reports. Henry Barnard thought Alcott's report for 1859-60 the best school report he had ever seen and he advised making it into a book for general circulation to schools and teachers across the country. Alcott resolved to do just that with his report for 1860-61. He arranged to have one thousand copies of the sixty-seven page report printed. Four hundred fifty were given to families in Concord and two hundred fifty were given to Alcott for circulation to whomever he chose.[47]

On March 18, 1861, at the annual school exhibition, the town rejoiced with Alcott over two successful years of his superintendency. Alcott had planned and arranged these exhibitions to give students and teachers an opportunity to display their year's work. They had become a kind of community celebration of education, with songs, speeches, and ceremony. At this second exhibition Emerson spoke, Sanborn's actors performed, and Louisa wrote a song for the children to sing. Praises were heaped on Alcott; and when the school children presented him with a surprise gift of *Pilgrim's Progress* and Herbert's *Poems*, tears filled his eyes. Thoreau told Parker Pillsbury that Alcott, in April 1861 at least, was the most popular and successful man in Concord. Teachers, parents, and children now asked counsel of the man they had disdained to hire as a teacher only a few years before. Upon reading Alcott's school reports, Josiah Quincy, former pupil at the Temple School, wrote to Emerson that the reports only confirmed his belief that the Temple School had been the best thing attempted in modern times for a properly human culture. Superintendent John Philbrick found Alcott's school reports masterful and felt himself to be far short of the example Alcott provided of the true educator. Longtime friend William Russell added to the compliments by completing a sketch of Alcott to be included in Barnard's *History of Education*. The Concord Lyceum asked Alcott to speak, although he declined, feeling that lecturing did not show his true genius. Former Transcendental Club member Caleb Stetson invited him to lecture on education in Lexington, and George B. Emerson encouraged him to lecture on education throughout the state and to write essays on education for the *Atlantic Monthly*.[48]

Success drew Alcott away from his normal activities. His journals became day-to-day accounts of his school visits. There was little time for reading, writing, and conversation. He easily passed up an opportunity for another Western tour in the fall of 1860. More than ever before, he was interested in the affairs of the community, even to the point of attending and participating in town meetings. He felt that his family had genuine cause to be hopeful for the future.[49]

Alcott's vindication did not result from public enlightenment so much as from a change in his own approach. Now he was much more politic in his methods of instituting change. All reforms were accomplished in consultation with and by sanction of the school committee. He had made peace with the established authorities and they with him. All the hostile rhetoric against the state was gone. He was circumspect about the content of his school reports.

He engaged in no theological controversy. There were no references to his theories about diet and health, no attempt to impose on his readers his concept of the genesis of the unvierse. His prose in the reports was direct and readable, reminiscent of his early essays on education. And the transcendentalists were no longer feared as dangerous heretics. Concord was proud of Emerson, of Thoreau, and now of Alcott.

With Alcott a respected citizen, prospects for the Alcott family had brightened considerably. They had a home of their own, and longstanding debts were finally paid. Anna was married to John Bridge Pratt of Concord on May 23, 1860, her parents' thirtieth wedding anniversary. Samuel May came from Syracuse to perform the ceremony, and Emerson and Thoreau came to witness the "pleasing and impressive spectacle." Alcott was so moved that he had difficulty writing about it—and Alcott was rarely at a loss for words. Anna left Concord to live with her husband in Chelsea. She was pleased with the security and peace that John Pratt's steady job as a bookkeeper provided, for although she dearly loved her family, she was glad to escape the sometimes contentious atmosphere that resulted from poverty, trial, and disappointment. The *Atlantic Monthly* of March 1860 published Louisa's story "Love and Self Love," and she was beginning to capture some of the glory that her sister Elizabeth had predicted for her. Twenty-year-old Abby May went off to Syracuse in December 1860 to teach at Dr. Wilbur's Asylum, although she was more interested in art than in teaching. She had become accomplished enough in drawing that her father asked her to provide a sketch of Orchard House for his Concord Book.[50]

Alcott's success and the rising fortunes of his family were over-shadowed by the growing national tension over the slavery issue. On May 8, 1859, Connecticut-born John Brown, hero of the free soil cause in Kansas, spoke at the Concord Town Hall about his proposed assault on the slave power. Brown impressed and inspired Alcott and the "best people" of Concord with his "courage" and "religious earnestness." Alcott spoke with Brown afterward and was further convinced that the bearded zealot was a "disciple of the right" who was "superior to legal traditions" and willing to "strike a blow for freedom at any moment." Brown promised to take bold, courageous, maybe even foolish action against the evil of slavery. He captivated abolitionists like Alcott, who admired his driving, fearless energy and doubtless wished they had a little of it themselves even if it did border on madness. For Alcott had once said himself that "a little madness, a touch of it for once or twice, is quite worth having."[51]

Brown did not reveal his immediate plans to his Concord supporters, leaving them to wonder and imagine. On October 16 he fulfilled their expectations of him as the resolute, audacious hero by leading a desperate attack on the federal arsenal at Harpers Ferry, Virginia. He hoped to lead a spontaneous slave revolt, but few slaves came. Most of Brown's men were killed; he and the rest were captured, quickly tried for treason, convicted, and sentenced to be hanged.[52]

News of Brown's deed filled the antislavery Concordians with both joyful excitement and defiant indignation. Thoreau mounted the lecture platform in Brown's defense. Alcott considered the raid on Harpers Ferry a "bold stroke for justice." At first he expressed his willingness to march under Captain Thomas Wentworth Higginson to attempt a rescue of Brown. Sanborn suggested that Alcott go alone to plead Brown's case before Virginia's Governor Henry A. Wise and at the same time secretly ascertain the chances of a successful rescue. But in the end these plans came to nothing. Brown declared that he would not accept a rescue, and Alcott decided that Brown's martyrdom would do more good than years of agitation by the press to bring an end to slavery. On the day Brown was hanged, December 2, the Concordians held a public celebration of the hero's martyrdom. Church bells remained silent, signifying the town's sorrow. Alcott, Emerson, and Thoreau read from Brown's writings and from Scripture. The crowd sang a dirge written by Sanborn by the occasion. James Redpath, Brown's English friend, collected accounts of the Concord ceremony for a printed eulogy of Brown called *Echoes of Harpers Ferry*.[53]

In late December a United States Senate committee investigating the raid on Harpers Ferry summoned Frank Sanborn to testify. Sanborn was one of the so-called "secret six" who provided direct aid to help Brown implement his plans. Sanborn adamantly refused to testify. Instead, he fled to Canada to avoid the authorities, thus earning the rebuke of fellow conspirator Thomas Wentworth Higginson, who defiantly remained in Boston, daring federal officials to come and get him. Sanborn soon returned to Concord, having screwed up his courage and believing that he could not be forced to testify. On the night of April 4, 1860, officials sent by the Senate committee forcibly dragged him out of his house with the intention of whisking him off to Washington. But outraged Concordians, responding to the alarm as their minutemen ancestors had responded, flocked to Sanborn's rescue. The Massachusetts Supreme Court dismissed all charges against him and sent the Senate officials fleeing. Alcott, who joined the local vigilance committee to help protect his friend, called the incident the beginning of another American Revolution, "April 19th on the new calendar."[54]

On November 4, 1860, Alcott voted in a national election for the first time in his life, casting his ballot for Abraham Lincoln and the Republicans despite Thoreau's reminder that a "free man" should not descend into the pit of politics by voting. Alcott kept up with day-to-day newspaper accounts as Southern states, fearing the hostility of a Republican administration, began to secede from the union. By January 1861 Alcott was resigned to civil war. "The South is insanely in earnest," he said,

> and intent on pressing her interests at any cost: even to civil war and its frightful evils. I suppose the day must come, and the deadly conflict, to adjust the scales of Justice, and give freedom to the slaves, at the Nation's cost.

The possibility of a peaceful separation between North and South never crossed his mind. The seceding states were in league with Satan and in unjustified defiance of the United States government. It was clear to him that the Buchanan administration was duty bound to use force, if necessary, to put down the rebellion. Buchanan's vacillation was just further evidence of his complicity with the "slave power." He fully expected Lincoln and the Republicans to take positive action.[55]

Lincoln's hesitant decision to attempt to maintain federal authority over Fort Sumter, though hardly positive action against slavery, did bring the expected conflict. On April 14 Federal troops surrendered Fort Sumter to the Confederacy. Two days later Lincoln called for 75,000 militia. With intentional symbolism, forty Concord men under Captain Prescott left town for war on April 19, amid ceremony and with $4,400 contributed by Concord citizens. Alcott, his erstwhile commitment to nonresistance long since forgotten, celebrated the heightened spirit of community that the war brought to Concord. He rejoiced as townspeople worked together in the Town Hall sewing clothes for their company of militia. Like all of Concord, he was proud of the fighting men and wished he were younger so that he might also march away to do battle. He believed that the surprising unanimity of opinion by Concordians in support of the war effort reflected a smiliar unanimity throughout the North. This unanimity, Alcott felt, was a victory in itself.[56]

The excitement of war noticeably diminished interest by Concordians in their schools. Attendance became irregular. Superintendent Alcott faithfully continued his monthly visits to district schools, but the war absorbed his attention as well. He rejoiced when on August 30, 1861, General John C. Frémont declared martial law in Missouri and freed the slaves of anyone who resisted the United States. When Lincoln countermanded Frémont, Alcott chided the President for hindering the "march of freedom." To Alcott the war meant nothing less than a battle to free the slaves and to create a Republic founded on justice for all people.[57]

Amid the wartime excitement was the sad reality that Henry Thoreau was dying. He had been ill with consumption for over a year, and by the winter of 1862 he was failing rapidly. Alcott wrote a short essay about his friend for the April issue of the *Atlantic Monthly* called "The Forester." It served as a eulogy, but one that Thoreau saw before his death and liked. Alcott wrote: "We have been accustomed to consider him the salt of things so long that they must lose their savor without his to season them. And when he goes hence, then Pan is dead, and Nature ailing throughout." Thoreau died on May 6, 1862. All of Concord mourned the forty-four-year-old naturalist. Alcott arranged to have the school children attend the funeral. Emerson gave an address, Ellery Channing read some poetry, and Alcott solemnly read from Thoreau's works.[58]

News of the war and of governmental action became more favorable to Alcott's viewpoint in September 1862, when Lincoln issued his preliminary Emancipation Proclamation. It was at least one step in the right direction,

Alcott thought. On December 12 Louisa, anxious to take part in the crusade, left for Washington, D.C., to nurse the sick and wounded at the Union hospital in Georgetown. On January 1, 1863, Alcott did his part for the cause symbolically by attending the unveiling of a marble sculptured head of John Brown at the home of abolitionist and Brown supporter George Luther Stearns in Medford. Five days later he held a conversation on patriotism and national destiny at the home of George B. Emerson in Boston.[59]

On January 14 word came that Louisa was seriously ill, and Alcott left immediately for Georgetown to bring her home. He found her delirious with typhoid fever and her doctors hesitant to allow her to make the long journey back to Concord. While awaiting the doctors' decision, he went to the Senate to hear his old friend William Henry Channing, then Senate chaplain, and sat near President Lincoln, whom Alcott now respected for his "honest bearing." He wanted to meet Lincoln and to visit the sites of the capital city, but worry about Louisa's condition prevented further excursions. His week's stay amid the misery and suffering of the patients in the wards of the Georgetown hospital, along with Louisa's perilous condition, impressed on him the ugly reality of war. The crusade for liberty lost its glamor. Finally, on January 21, Louisa's doctors agreed to allow her to travel and, with the help of Dorothea Dix, Alcott put her on the train to Boston and Concord. For the next two months she lay bedridden in her upstairs room at Orchard House. As he had done with Elizabeth, Alcott sat up with her at night reading to her and talking.[60]

Meanwhile, he held a series of successful conversations at Temperance Hall in Boston on "Representative Men": the Concord authors, the abolitionists, the writers for the *Atlantic Monthly*, and the transcendentalists. The newly established *Boston Commonwealth*, edited by Frank Sanborn, printed transcripts of the conversations on the abolitionists and the transcendentalists in April and May. Sanborn also printed Louisa's account of her experiences in Georgetown, called "Hospital Sketches," for which she received immediate praise from Boston literary critics such as Edwin Whipple and even from the sometimes acerbic Henry James.[61]

The *Commonwealth* gave Alcott a long-awaited vehicle for his publications. With the favorable reception of his school reports, Alcott renewed his hope of publishing again from his manuscripts. He thought that he could overcome his past difficulties with the pen and that he had something new to offer the reading public. "Time ripens the substance of Life as the Seasons its fruits, and mellows them," he said hopefully. "The best apples fall the latest; they keep the longest, surviving the earliest ones, and the winter itself." Especially did he want to publish an essay on gardening. He had worked throughout the winter and spring of 1862 on a manuscript he called "The Countryman in his Garden," and he had talked to James T. Fields, publisher of the *Atlantic Monthly*, about printing it. Unfortunately, Fields refused, and Emerson, because of modesty, refused to allow Alcott to publish an adulatory essay on him called "The Rhapsodist." Again Alcott despaired of ever being able to write successfully. He blamed the "deplorable lack of early discipline in expression" for leaving him "lame" and with little to show for sixty-three years. But when Sanborn became editor of the *Commonwealth* in early 1863, Alcott found that at last he had a receptive, though not uncritical, publisher. Sanborn not only printed the transcripts of conversations, but also printed a few of Alcott's previously unpublished poems, and he agreed to publish "The Countryman in his Garden" in segments beginning in July 1863. This recognition renewed Alcott's hope to publish even more, and he began, in the summer of 1863, to copy furiously from his diaries with publication in mind.[62]

Alcott's enthusiasm for writing in 1863 did not lessen his interest in the war, although after seeing the hospital in Georgetown he was not quite so blind to its evils nor so sanguine about its results. He was especially interested in attempts to organize regiments of black soldiers. At long last, he thought, blacks were being recognized as having a stake in the matter. His friend, wealthy merchant George Luther Stearns, was instrumental in raising the black 54th Regiment. And Alcott signed a proposition by Massachusetts Governor John A. Andrew for the enlistment of 50,000 more black men. Abby worked to collect clothing for Harriet Tubman, who was distributing it to poor blacks. She ignored people who told her that she ought to work only for soldiers and let the "niggers" take care of themselves. Louisa considered going to South Carolina to teach the "freedmen" at Port Royal. Alcott celebrated the freeing of the slaves in a poem called "The Patriot," written for a Soldier's Fair to be held in Chicago.[63]

Alcott considered 1863 to have been a year of blessings. The family was in better financial shape than ever before. Louisa, though she had been dangerously ill, had regained her health. His writings were finding publishers. More and more he was recognized as an authority in education. A convention of Massachusetts teachers asked him to speak in November. The war was going better for the North after decisive victories at Gettysburg and Vicksburg, and the first steps toward ending slavery had been made. And he was now a grandfather. Anna's son, Frederick Alcott Pratt, was born on May 28. The year's only sadness was the death of Alcott's mother at age ninety in West Edmeston, New York, on August 27.[64]

By the spring of 1864 Alcott's self-confidence was at a new height, and his sense of mission was rekindled. Once again he thought of spreading knowledge and enlightenment to the cities and towns of New England. "Why should I be living here with an irresistible desire to promote the ends of morals and philanthropy, . . ." he said, "and not make the opportunity, if none is made for me." He presented his plan to be a traveling missionary of culture to his abolitionist friends George Luther Stearns and Wendell Phillips. They promised aid. Emerson suggested that the Massachusetts Board of Education appoint Alcott as its agent. Alcott feared the possible restraints and preferred to work privately, although had the Board agreed to the idea, he would have accepted. Stearns sent one hundred dollars to get the missionary enterprise started and suggested that Alcott begin in Washington and enlighten the leaders of the nation.[65]

Alcott's plan was in motion by mid-April. He told the story of his early education to students at a school in Newton. He addressed the children of the state Charity School in Tewkesbury. He visited the Worcester schools and addressed the Worcester teachers on the personal qualities necessary for effective teaching. The four hundred children of the reform school in Westboro heard him speak, as did the young women of the Framingham Normal School. By the end of June he had visited schools in Plymouth and Marblehead and had addressed the normal schools in Salem and Bridgewater. He talked of a possible series of lectures at Concord's Town Hall. In tones reminiscent of his radicalism of the 1830s and 1840s, he condemned the American Institute of Instruction and the National Teacher's Association for their failure to escape the "beaten tracks of usage and tradition" and for their inability to keep up with the "progressive spirit."[66]

In September, George Luther Stearns sent another hundred dollars to further Alcott's crusade, but opportunities were not forthcoming. Alcott remained in Concord, making his usual rounds of the local schools. Then in November he had another idea for spreading his ideas on human culture. He began organizing a series of Sunday evening lectures to be sponsored by the members of Theodore Parker's Twenty-Eighth Congregational Society, which had remained together under Parker's name despite his death in 1860. Alcott hoped to lecture along with Emerson, Higginson, Henry James, David Wasson, and Samuel Johnson. The series began on February 5, 1865, with Alcott's lecture on American religion. That same weekend Alcott spoke to two hundred fifty Boston primary school teachers on the "dignity and duty of their calling," and conversed at the Parker Fraternity rooms on education. On March 5 he lectured again on religious tendencies, and the next day he spoke to Governor Andrew about the need for a missionary of education to travel and speak throughout the state.[67]

The war was coming to a welcome end, and Alcott's renewed fervor for reform extended to thoughts of postwar America. He was dissatisfied with the nation's leadership. "Where is the great inclusive common sense, the commanding idealism to shape mind and institutions in this revolutionary period," he asked. "I fail to find these." The chaos of war promised, at least to the perpetually hopeful Alcott, a new order, a new nation. But the United States lacked a Plato, or a Christ, or even a Cromwell or a Washington to instill faith and to provide decisive leadership. In August 1864 Alcott met John C. Frémont at the home of George Luther Stearns, and found him to be a fit leader for revolution and reconstruction. He hoped that Frémont would succeed in his attempt to unseat Lincoln as the Republican candidate for President in the election of 1864. Lincoln was a good man, Alcott thought, but he agreed with Wendell Phillips that he was not an effective leader. Yet he voted for Lincoln in November after all, sure that a victory by George McClellan and the Democrats would bring "rebel rule" and the end of "free institutions."[68]

Stearns was talking about establishing a "Reform League," a nationwide network of people interested in improving the condition of the Freedmen, tied together by a telegraphic communications system. Alcott thought it an excellent idea and provided a list of people he thought would contribute effectively to the organization. The war had made Alcott, and the nation as a whole, more aware of the power of organization, leadership, and government to effect reform. He, like Americans generally, was slow to dismiss his faith in the individual; he still believed that true reform began with the individual and in the family. But he was much more willing to place hope for change in the hands of political leaders. The "revolution" he hoped would accompany the end of the war was in large part to be enacted by government.[69]

Lincoln's assassination in April 1865 had the same psychological effect on Alcott that it had on most Northerners. It made Lincoln a martyred hero. Whereas only a few months before Alcott had considered Lincoln lacking in leadership abilities, he now saw him as the fallen defender of justice and righteousness. His death was a national sacrifice that Alcott believed would help knit the nation together in a commitment to God and to the right. Alcott now saw the war, as did many of the transcendentalists, in theological terms, as an expiation of sins, an atonement, a purificiation, a blood sacrifice, which prepared the way for the nation's redemption. The loss of Lincoln was the last, the greatest sacrifice in this ritual. It was the ultimate symbol of national atonement and the herald of national redemption.[70]

But in the end hope for redemption lay in the hands of the national leaders of reconstruction policy, and unfortunately President Andrew Johnson did not live up to his calling. His policy, thought Alcott, meant only slavery for blacks under another name. If the nation allowed Johnson to have his way, it would be clear that the American people were still bent on keeping blacks under foot, and were unwilling to allow them to take the place in society that their courage had rightfully won.[71]

With all of his success, his reform zeal, and his hope for the nation, the occasion of his greatest joy was the printing of his essay on Emerson. In November 1864 Mary Elizabeth Stearns, wife of Alcott's abolitionist friend, offered to pay for the preparation of "The Rhapsodist" for private distribution. Alcott presented the book to Emerson as a surprise for his sixty-second birthday on May 25, 1865, and sent copies of it to a large number of friends, his and Emerson's. The essay was full of admiration and praise. It was Alcott's way of expressing his appreciation for the long years of Emerson's support, aid, and friendship. "I consider his genius the measure and present expansion of the American mind," Alcott said with much justice. Friends praised the book. Oliver Wendell Holmes, William Henry Channing, Parker Pillsbury, and Henry Wadsworth Longfellow all expressed pleasure in reading it. Most important, Emerson appreciated it, and no praise was more dear to Alcott than Emerson's, particularly in light of his earlier comment that Alcott's "whim of writing" was a "false instinct."[72]

Alcott was not reappointed as Superintendent of Schools for 1865-66. The town had failed to authorize the school committee to select and pay a superintendent. The desire to unseat Alcott did not reflect the sentiment of Concordians generally, but rather the machinations of a few of his enemies on the school committee. The reason for their opposition to him is not clear, but it may have resulted from the long-standing grievance against his unwillingness to attend church. But it made little difference to him now. He was absorbed in other interests. His renewed desire to write, lecture, and reform had caused him to give the schools much less of his time since 1863. His ambition to be a nationwide missionary of culture overshadowed any concern of his for the day-to-day problems of local schools. The family's condition continued to improve. Louisa published *Moods* on Christmas day, 1864, and money from it paid all family debts. The following summer she sailed for Europe as the nurse to a young invalid. A second grandson, John Sewall Pratt, was born on June 24, 1865. Abby found her journal, once a dismal reflection of poverty and misery, recording "serener skies" and gentler gales." William Torrey Harris wrote to Alcott in November 1865, urging him to visit St. Louis again and meet "the most magnificent philosophical society that ever was in the United States." Alcott was attracted but hesitated, seeking assurance of an adequate reception and at least some remuneration. "A scholar's time is precious," he said. He was not so desperate for recognition now and was more solicitous than ever before of outward comforts. He still feared that it was a dishonor to philosophy to consider in the least way material necessities, but he asked that Harris guarantee him two hundred dollars instead of the one hundred already pledged. George Luther Stearns predicted that, whereas Emerson had nearly finished his work, Alcott's best days were yet to come. Indeed, Alcott looked forward with bright prospects to a new field of activity. He wanted to extend his range as a missionary of culture and to spread the gospel of the "New Church."[73]

Notes

1. AJ 30 (1855): 293.

2. Ibid., pp. 325, 361, 369, 376-77; Alcott to Benjamin Marston Watson, August 12, 1855, from a copy in Alcott's hand in ibid., pp. 299-302; Alcott to Hiram Bronson, August 27, 1855, in A. Bronson Alcott, comp., "Letters, 1855-1859," at Houghton Library, 59M-305 (4).

3. AJ 30 (1855): 294, 296, 312, 395-96.

4. Ibid., pp. 415, 430-41, 433, 497, 505 ff.

5. Ibid., pp. 434-35, 439-40, 460; Madeleine B. Stern, *The Pantarch: A Biography of Stephen Pearl Andrews* (Austin: University of Texas Press, 1968), pp. 83-85.

6. Alcott to Louisa May Alcott, November 27, 1855, in Herrnstadt, ed., *Letters*, p. 190; AJ 30 (1855): 548-51; AJ 31 (1856): 272; Abby May Alcott to Samuel J. May, October 9, 1855, in "Family Letters, 1828-61."

7. AJ 31 (1856): 309-16, 319, 329, 330-32, 336, 341, 353-54, 357-58, 365-77; William F. Channing to Alcott, April 29, 1856, in "Letters 1855-59"; printed Prospectus of the conversation on "Social Life" in "Letters, 1855-59"; Alcott to Abby May Alcott, April 26, 1856, in A.

Bronson Alcott, comp., "Family Letters, 1856-1858," at Houghton Library 59M-305 (27).

8. Russel B. Nye, *Society and Culture in America, 1830-1860* (New York: Harper and Row, 1974), pp. 351-52; AJ 31 (1856): 424, 449-54.

9. AJ 31 (1856): 400, 413-16, 423, 651, 653.

10. Ibid., pp. 668, 854, 865, 871-72, 875, 895 ff.

11. Ibid., pp. 895 ff., 916, 929, 933; Alcott to Abby May Alcott, September 30, 1856, in "Family Letters, 1856-58."

12. AJ 31 (1856): 949-50, 952, 957, 959, 963-67.

13. Ibid., pp. 970, 972.

14. Ibid., pp. 995-96, 1012, 1013, 1031-32, 1063, 1065, 1091, 1111, 1182, 1223; Charles Lane to Alcott, February, 1846, in "Letters, 1836-1850."

15. AJ 8 (1835): 459-67; AJ 11 (1838): 185, 188, 295, 298; AJ 31 (1856): 999; Davies, *Phrenology: Fad and Science*, pp. 43-47.

16. AJ 31 (1856): 1017, 1059, 1122; Howard Kerr, *Mediums, and Spirit-Rappers, and Roaring Radicals: Spiritualism in American Literature, 1850-1900* (Urbana: University of Illinois Press, 1972), pp. 3-4, 16, 96-97; AJ 32 (1857): 141-42, 174.

17. AJ 31 (1856): 979-80, 1013-14, 1061, 1069, 1127-28; Alcott to Abby May Alcott, November 7, 1856, in "Family Letters, 1856-58," and November 13, 1856, in "Letters, 1855-59."

18. AJ 31 (1856): 1000-1008, 1023-29, 1061-62; Abby May Alcott to Alcott, October 23, 1856, in "Family Letters, 1856-58"; Alcott to Abby May Alcott, October 21, 1856, in "Letters, 1855-59."

19. AJ 31 (1856): 1060, 1063, 1094-97, 1098, 1101-3, 1105-6; Henry David Thoreau to H. G. O. Blake, November 19, 1856, in Sanborn, ed., *Familiar Letters*, pp. 340-41.

20. AJ 31 (1856): 1231-32; AJ 32 (1848): 208.

21. AJ 31 (1856): 1030, 1122, 1147-51, 1167-70, 1177-78, 1199-1200, 1234, 1275; Alcott to Abby May Alcott, February 18, 1857, in "Letters, 1855-59"; Stern, *The Pantarch*, pp. 82-83; AJ 32 (1857): 138.

22. Abby May Alcott to Alcott, October 9 and October 17, 1856, in "Family Letters, 1856-58"; AJ 31 (1856): 1029, 1061, 1077-78, 1081-82; Alcott to Abby May Alcott, November 15, 1856, in "Family Letters, 1856-58."

23. AJ 31 (1856): 1137, 1199, 1294; Abby May Alcott to Samuel J. May, January 26, 1857, in "Family Letters, 1828-61"; Abby May Alcott to Alcott, December 6, 1856, and Anna Alcott to Alcott, December 6, 1856, in "Family Letters, 1856-58"; AJ 32 (1857): 14; Abby May Alcott, "Diary," January 1 and 19, 1857; Alcott to Abby May Alcott, December 19, 1856, in "Family Letters, 1856-58."

24. AJ 32 (1857): 31, 59, 65-67, 113, 121, 129, 137, 149, 152, 155; Alcott to Abby May Alcott, February 26, 1857, in "Family Letters, 1856-58."

25. AJ 32 (1857): 191, 206, 208, 211, 215-16; Alcott to Abby May Alcott, March 13, 1857, in "Letters, 1855-59"; Sanborn and Harris, *A. Bronson Alcott*, 2: 544-52; Kurt F. Leidecker, *Yankee Teacher: The Life of William Torrey Harris* (New York: Philosophical Library, 1946), pp. 357-65.

26. AJ 32 (1857): 230, 232-33, 235, 241-42, 254-55, 261, 290; Daniel Ricketson to Henry Thoreau, November 3, 1858, and Daniel Ricketson, "Journal," April 18, 1857, printed in Anna and Walton Ricketson, eds., *Daniel Ricketson and His Friends* (Boston: Houghton, Mifflin and Co., 1902), pp. 83, 301-2.

27. AJ 32 (1857): 283, 411; Abby May Alcott to Alcott, December 14, 1856, and February 26, 1857, in "Family Letters, 1856-58."

28. AJ 32 (1857): 408-11, 447, 476-77, 544, 578, 582, 586, 620, 626, 638, 650, 666, 679, 710, 715-16, 722, 733-34, 735-36; Alcott to Anna, Louisa and May Alcott, September 9, 1857, in "Family Letters, 1856-58"; Abby May Alcott to Alcott family, August 18-19, 1857, in "Family Letters, 1856-58."

29. AJ 32 (1857): 747, 759-60, 763, 792-93; Abby May Alcott, "Diary," September 16-19, 1857.

30. AJ 32 (1857): 814, 825-27, 846, 848-49, 850-51, 853, 856-58, 859, 862-63; Alcott to Benjamin Marston Watson, October 10, 1857, in "Letters, 1855-59"; Abby May Alcott to Samuel J. May, November 3, 1857, in "Family Letters, 1828-61"; Alcott to Abby May Alcott, November 20,

December 8, and December 14, 1857, in "Letters, 1855-59"; Alcott to Anna Alcott, November 21, 1857, in "Family Letters, 1856-58"; Alcott to Abby May Alcott, November 26, and December 1, 1857, in "Family Letters, 1856-58."

31. AJ 32 (1857): 890-91, 900-901; Abby May Alcott to Alcott, December 5, 13, and 27, 1857, Anna Alcott to Alcott, December 21, 1857, Louisa May Alcott to Alcott, December 13, 1857, and Elizabeth Sewall Alcott to Alcott, December 13, 1857, in "Family Letters, 1856-58."

32. AJ 31 (1856): 1228; AJ 33 (1858): 13, 19, 20, 31, 35, 38, 55-57; AJ 32 (1857): 904; Anna Alcott to Alcott, January 9, 1858, in "Family Letters, 1856-58."

33. AJ 33 (1858): 65-68, 70, 95, 97-98, 115, 120, 125, 135 ff., 196, 232-35; Abby May Alcott to Samuel J. May, January 21, 1858, in "Family Letters, 1828-61"; Henry David Thoreau to Daniel Ricketson, June 30, 1858, in Sanborn, ed., *Familiar Letters*, p. 388; Abby May Alcott to Samuel J. May, May 9, 1858, in "Family Letters, 1856-58."

34. AJ 32 (1857): 867, 874; William Torrey Harris to Alcott, November 26, 1857, and October 30, 1858, in "Letters, 1855-59"; Alcott to William Torrey Harris, December 22, 1857, from a copy in Alcott's hand in "Letters, 1855-59"; AJ 33 (1858): 385, 422.

35. AJ 33 (1858): 434-48, 451-52, 454 ff., 462; Alcott to Abby May Alcott, December 11 and December 27, 1858, in "Letters, 1855-59"; AJ 34 (1859): 9-12, 13, 23, 25, 28-29, 33, 36; Henry A. Pochmann, *New England Transcendentalism and St. Louis Hegelianism* (Philadelphia: Carl Schurz Memorial Foundation, Inc., 1948), p. 8.

36. AJ 34 (1859): 37 ff., 51-52, 103-4, 147-50; Alcott to Abby May Alcott, January 21, 1859, in "Letters, 1855-59"; William Torrey Harris to Alcott, December 18, 1858, and George Noyes to Alcott, January 4, 1859, in "Letters, 1855-59"; Louisa May Alcott, "Diary," 1850-1885.

37. AJ 34 (1859): 153 ff., 175, 191, 197-201, 234-35, 239-42; William A. Alcott to Alcott, November 10, 1858, in "Letters, 1855-59."

38. AJ 34 (1859): 258, 280, 295, 302-3, 333 ff., Franklin Sanborn to Alcott, April 20, 1859, in "Letters, 1855-59."

39. AJ 34 (1859): 338-39, 364, 371, 389-90, 410-11, 558; A. Bronson Alcott, "Superintendent's Report," 1859-1860, in *Reports of the School Committee and Superintendent of Schools of the Town of Concord, Massachusetts* (Concord, 1861), pp. 11-15.

40. AJ 34 (1859): 323, 327, 561-62; Alcott, "Superintendent's Report," 1859-60, pp. 10-11, 26; A. Bronson Alcott, *Superintendent's Report of the Concord Schools to the School Committee for the Year 1860-1861* (Concord, 1861), pp. 35-37.

41. AJ 34 (1859): 540, 701-2.

42. Alcott, "Superintendent's Report," 1859-60, p. 17.

43. Ibid., pp. 8-9, 13; Alcott, *Superintendent's Report*, 1860-61, pp. 5-6, 8-10, 21-23; AJ 35 (1860): 17.

44. A. Bronson Alcott, comp., "The Concord Book," pp. 5-9, MS owned by the Concord Free Public Library; Alcott, "Superintendent's Report," 1859-60, pp. 10-11 and 1860-61, pp. 26-27; AJ 36 (1861): 264.

45. AJ 36 (1861): 149-50, 359-61; AJ 35 (1860): 385; Alcott, *Superintendent's Report,* 1860-61, pp. 16, 26; Alcott to May Alcott, April 12, [1861], in A. Bronson Alcott, comp., "Family Letters, 1859-1864," at Houghton Library, 59M-305 (28); Alcott, "The Concord Book," pp. 5-11 ff., 37 ff.; John C. Broderick, "Bronson Alcott's 'Concord Book,'" *New England Quarterly* 29, no. 3 (September 1956): 365-80.

46. Alcott, *Superintendent's Report*, 1860-61, pp. 30, 32; AJ 35 (1860): 97, 157, 159, 167; printed leaflet explaining Philbrick's "Tablets" is attached to AJ 35 (1860): 163.

47. AJ 35 (1860): 52, 385; AJ 36 (1861): 128, 237-38, 335-36; *Reports of the School Committee and the Superintendent of Schools of the Town of Concord, Massachusetts* (Concord, Mass., 1861), p. 4.

48. AJ 35 (1860): 110-13; AJ 36 (1861): 47-50, 119-22, 283-84, 317; Abby May Alcott, "Diary," March 18, 1861; Louisa May Alcott, "Diary," March [18], 1861, MS at Houghton Library, 59M-309 (1); Anna Alcott Pratt, "Diary, 1860-1861," pp. 77-80, MS at Houghton Library, 59M-311 (6); Henry David Thoreau to Parker Pillsbury, April 10, 1861, printed in Walter Harding and Carl Bode, eds., *The Correspondence of Henry David Thoreau* (New York: New York

University Press, 1958), p. 611; William Russell to Alcott, March 8, 1861, and John D. Philbrick to Alcott, April 9, 1861, in A. Bronson Alcott, comp., "Letters, 1860-1864," at Houghton Library, 59M-305 (5); Josiah Quincy to Alcott, April 26, 1861, at Houghton Library, 59M-312 (148); John D. Philbrick to Alcott, May 14, 1860, at Houghton Library, 59M-312 (135); AJ 37 (1862): 87-88, 134; Abby May Alcott to Samuel J. May, December 22, 1861, in "Family Letters, 1859-64."

49. Abby May Alcott to Samuel J. May, December 10, 1859, from a copy in Alcott's hand in "Autobiographical Materials"; AJ 35 (1860): 40, 95.

50. Abby May Alcott, "Diary," January 1, January 17, October 7, and December 30, 1860; AJ 35 (1860): 81, 173, 175-77, 371, 374; Anna Alcott Pratt, "Diary, 1860-61," pp. 2, 9-10; Anna Alcott to Samuel J. May, [between April 14 and May 23], 1860, in "Family Letters, 1859-64"; Elizabeth Sewall Alcott to Alcott, November 27, 1856, in "Family Letters, 1856-58"; Alcott to May Alcott, February 10 and April 12, 1861, in "Family Letters, 1859-64."

51. AJ 34 (1859): 311-15; AJ 36 (1851): 150; Stephen B. Oates, *To Purge This Land With Blood: A Biography of John Brown* (New York: Harper and Row, 1970), p. 269.

52. Oates, *John Brown* pp. 301 ff.

53. AJ 34 (1859): 583-89, 590-91, 599-600, 613-14, 633, 644-55, 689; Franklin B. Sanborn, *Recollections of Seventy Years*, 2 vols. (Boston: The Gorham Press, 1909), 1: 202; James Redpath, *Echoes of Harpers Ferry* (Boston: Thayer and Eldridge, 1860).

54. Oates, *John Brown*, pp. 314-16; Sanborn, *Recollections* 1: 188-89, 208 ff.; AJ 34 (1859): 715; AJ 35 (1860): 31, 33-34, 50, 93, 121-22, 133.

55. AJ 35 (1860): 345, 350; AJ 36 (1861): 21-22.

56. AJ 36 (1861): 371, 386, 396.

57. Ibid., pp. 451, 715-16; Alcott to Mrs. Anna Alcott, November 29, 1861, in "Family Letters, 1859-64."

58. AJ 37 (1862): 158, 195, 202, 253-54, 255-58, 295; A. Bronson Alcott, "The Forester," *Atlantic Monthly* 9 (April 1862): 443.

59. AJ 37 (1862): 349, 417, 419, 424; AJ 38 (1863): 406, 413-14.

60. AJ 38 (1863): 27-28, 30-34, 41, 44; Alcott to Anna Alcott Pratt, January 25, 27, 29, 30, and February 4, 1863, in "Family Letters, 1859-64"; Louisa May Alcott, "Diary, 1863-1867," MS at Houghton Library, 59M-309 (2).

61. AJ 38 (1863): 17, 60, 122, 139, 149, 154, 157.

62. AJ 36 (1861): 51-53, 487, 773; AJ 37 (1862) 5-6, 158, 195, 211, 235, 246, 248, 368; Alcott to Abby May Alcott, [July 31?, 1863], in "Family Letters, 1859-64"; James T. Fields to Alcott, September 23, 1862, at Houghton Library, 59M-312; AJ 38 (1863): 166, 190, 209.

63. AJ 38 (1863): 65, 115-16, 149-50, 222, 310, 311, 313; Alcott to W. A. Wellman, August 7, 1863, in "Letters, 1860-64"; Franklin Sanborn to Alcott, January 4, 1864, in "Letters, 1860-64"; Abby May Alcott to Samuel J. May, July 19, 1863, in "Family Letters, 1859-64."

64. AJ 39 (1864): 1; AJ 38 (1863): 76, 250, 393, 396-98, 399; Abby May Alcott to Samuel J. May, August 20 and September 10, 1863, in "Family Letters, 1859-64."

65. AJ 39 (1864): 67-68, 82-84, 89, 97-98, 100-101, 103; George L. and Mary Elizabeth Stearns to Alcott, April 11, 1864, in "Letters, 1860-64."

66. AJ 39 (1864): 105, 175, 190, 193, 195, 197-98, 207-9, 215, 218-19, 237, 291, 293; Alcott to Abby May Alcott, June 8, 1864, in "Family Letters, 1859-64."

67. AJ 39 (1864): 323, 407-8; AJ 40 (1865): 4, 7, 9, 14, 50, 53, 57, 59, 96, 103; Alcott to Daniel Ricketson, February 12, 1865, in A. Bronson Alcott, comp., "Letters, 1865-1866," at Houghton Library, 59M-305 (6).

68. AJ 39 (1864): 273-80, 283, 380; George Luther Stearns to Alcott, August 9 and September 11, 1864, in "Letters, 1860-64."

69. AJ 39 (1864): 410-12. For a full discussion of the impact of the Civil War on American consciousness about government and organization see George M. Frederickson, *The Inner Civil War* (New York: Harper and Row, 1965).

70. AJ 40 (1865): 156-57, 161, 170; Robert C. Albrecht, "The Theological Response of the Transcendentalists to the Civil War," in Brian F. Barbour, ed., *American Transcendentalism*

(Notre Dame, Ind.: University of Notre Dame Press, 1973), pp. 211-21.

71. AJ 40 (1865): 319, 349, 353; Alcott to Mary Elizabeth Stearns, October 22, 1865, owned by the Fruitlands Museum.

72. AJ 39 (1864): 394; AJ 40 (1865): 199-200, 203, 259, 262; Alcott to Mary Elizabeth Stearns, May 30, 31, and June 12, 1865, owned by the Fruitlands Museum; A. Bronson Alcott, *Emerson* (privately printed, 1865), p. 21; Oliver Wendell Holmes to Alcott, August 6, 1865, and Henry Wadsworth Longfellow to Alcott, February 11, 1866, at Houghton Library, 59M-312; William Henry Channing to Alcott, August 2, 1865, and Parker Pillsbury to Alcott, November 4, 1865, in "Letters, 1865-66"; Ralph Waldo Emerson, "Journal VA" (1862-63), p. 229, from a typescript owned by the Concord Free Public Library.

73. AJ 40 (1865): 72, 149, 219, 346-48; L. W. Bean to Alcott, April 14, 1865, in "Letters, 1865-66"; Louisa May Alcott, "Diary, 1850-85"; Abby May Alcott, "Diary," January 14 and December 31, 1865; William Torrey Harris to Alcott, November 14, 1865, in "Letters, 1865-66"; Alcott to William Torrey Harris, December 31, 1865, from a copy in Alcott's hand in "Letters, 1865-66"; Frank Preston Stearns, *The Life and Public Services of George Luther Stearns* (Philadelphia: J. B. Lippincott Co., 1907), p. 345.

10

The New Church, 1865–70

THE theology of the New Church became Alcott's urgent message to his contemporaries in the first few years after the Civil War. It reflected the renewed hopefulness about human nature and human culture that his newly found recognition and success had inspired. He had turned away from the harsh fatalism of his theories of race and temperament that had darkened his vision in the 1850s. In effect, he had battled fate and won, for he was well on his way toward overcoming the personal and family problems that had plagued him in the late 1840s and 1850s. In developing his theology Alcott was creating a new intellectual synthesis. This synthesis arose from the interaction between his own long-held ideas, as he was reshaping and restructuring them in the late 1850s and early 1860s under the broad concept of personalism, and two major movements in American thought, both of which had their greatest influence in the 1860s and 1870s: free religion and Hegelianism. The resultant theology—Alcott called it personal theism—became his ideological stance against the growing trends in American thought towards evolutionary naturalism, which seriously questioned human power and human free will. Fortified by this new theology, Alcott went West in 1869, and found long-sought acceptance. For Westerners were seeking a defense of idealism and spirituality against the bleak determinism of natural theology and Darwinism. Alcott provided just such a defense.

Throughout the 1840s and 1850s Alcott had struggled to find an organizational superstructure that would help resolve the tension in his thought between determinism and free will, while at the same time explaining his concept of the divinity of human nature, the relationship of human beings to God, and the always troublesome problem of evil. The organizing concept around which his thoughts began to coalesce was the idea of *personality*. He had used the word several times before, but it had no clear meaning to him until he read Plato's *Parmenides* in March 1859. Plato helped him distinguish *personality* from *individuality*. "Personality," said Alcott, "is that in which souls are *alike* essentially in virtue of being One, and as partaking of the same." God was the "Person," and personality was the God-like attribute in human beings. "Individuality," he went on, "is that wherein [souls] *differ* as partaking of the nature of things or in distinction from Persons, and are several, not one, unlike, impersonal, not the same." Thus human beings were "personal" to the extent that they shared a oneness with God and "individual" to the extent that they remained separate from God.[1]

Alcott easily applied his newly defined concept of personality to his idea of the lapse, which was his version of the doctrine of original sin or the fall from grace. Individuality, or separation from God, was the result of lapse or a "loss of Godhood." The material world was the ruins caused by lapsed humanity. Alcott saw the universe as an ascending and descending scale from matter to divinity to matter, a process activated by the force of personality, which, in essence, was the ability of divine creatures to choose oneness with God or separation from God. Human beings, he said, had the power to attain salvation (oneness with God or the Universal Spirit) or destruction (a lapse into matter) by the action of their will. "Though his [a human's] Will conspiring with the divine will, or spurning it, he multiplies in nature's forms, the qualities of good or evil in himself by his *Choices*, drawing his own portrait therein." To choose evil was a loss of freedom, a lapse from perfection. To follow the divine will was to attain the truly free will. His concept of the freedom of the will had finally solidified into a position similar to that of traditional Christian theology from St. Paul to St. Augustine to Martin Luther to Jonathan Edwards. Indeed, he had complemented his reading of Plato in March 1859 with the reading of the *Confessions* of St. Augustine.[2]

Alcott's theory of personality also encompassed the Platonic idea of the preexistence of souls. Human beings, said Alcott, existed as spiritual beings before the creation of the physical world. Indeed, these spiritual beings were responsible for the creation of the physical world through the action of their will. Human beings, he added, would again exist as spiritual beings after the end of the physical world. This was his concept of immortality and ultimate salvation, although he offered no eschatology, no explanation of how the end of the physical world would come about. The determining factor in a soul's immortality was its personality. "His [a human being's] Personality transcends his condition, and determines here and forever his circumstances in all modes of his Being and existence."[3]

Personality was that vital and creative aspect of human nature which Alcott had celebrated for years but had not named. It meant free will and "character." It was immanent and ecstatic, a "receiving and imparting of the Creative essence." God, Alcott believed, was present in all creatures. Thus all creatures had potential personality. But human life was characterized by the consciousness of personality, an awareness of the divinity within. The "brute" was a creature unconscious of its inner divinity and was unable to realize the potential of personality. This distinction betwen the brute and the creature conscious of personality clarified Alcott's role as teacher and converser. His mission was to awaken within human beings the consciousness of personality. Education, he said, was a "pentecost" to the human faculties.[4]

By systematizing his philosophy under the banner of personalism, Alcott finally clarified his concept of free will, his explanation of the problem of evil, and his view of the divinity of human nature. But he did not eliminate his paradoxical view of nature. Indeed, he only heightened the contradiction. On the one hand, he still appreciated the imagery, the symbolic beauty of the physical world, its power as a revelation of the spirit, and even its importance as an aid to attaining consciousness of personality. He lauded Emerson and Thoreau for their ability to capture that beautiful imagery. On the other hand, he reiterated his perplexing belief that the physical, objective world in all its forms—including the human body, the sea, the flowers and birds, the butterflies—was a result of poor human choices. It was, he said, a manifestation of the creative human mind that indicated a separation from the oneness of the spirit. Thus it represented decay, dissolution, the ruins of a fallen divinity. Alcott never attempted to reconcile the dichotomy.[5]

The usefulness of the concept of personality as a paradigm for explaining Alcott's entire philosophic system overrode any apparent contradictions. It even explained the kind of atmosphere that Alcott tried to capture in his conversations. It meant a sharing of the spiritual oneness common to all Persons. It was the sense of openness to one another's thoughts. It was culture. "Culture," he pointed out,

> translates the individual into the personal through the cordial sympathies and makes company and conversation possible. Individualism is brute, egotistic, inhuman, till admitted into the private sense whereby souls seem similar and partakers of a common Personality in the One.[6]

Friendship and social harmony resulted from drawing upon the divine essence, the personality. Conversation was a means of cultivating the personality, of making humans aware of their divine essence. In the same way, society, the community, the state, could share in the divine essence. They could become "personal" by cultivation and in turn become moral and responsive to the needs of all people.[7]

Alcott's personalism caused an illuminating conflict with Emerson. In *The Conduct of Life*, published in 1859, Emerson had evidenced a disturbing fatalism. "Providence," he said,

> has a wild, rough, incalculable road to its end, and it is of no use to try to whitewash its large, mixed instrumentalities, or to dress up that terrific benefactor in a clean shirt and white neckcloth of a student of divinity.[8]

It was the same kind of fatalism that Alcott had toyed with in the 1850s, with his ideas of race, temperament, and complexion. But now Alcott was disturbed and displeased with Emerson. Now he had renewed hope for, and renewed appreciation of the ability of humans to overcome external deterministic forces and to attain a divine life on earth. This was the larger meaning of his idea of personality. In most ways personalism was merely a new organizational framework for ideas he had held since the mid-1830s, but it also meant a strong reaction against fatalism. Alcott was now sure that a consciousness of the personality, the divinity within, could liberate human beings from "Fate." Fate was the abuse of the freedom God had given to his creatures; it was the transgression of moral laws. Freedom from fate was the freedom to obey the will of God.[9] "Only good men comprehend as God comprehends infinitely," he said,

> they being freed from the limitations of the senses, partaking of freedom, and liberated thereby from Fate, which is simply an abuse of it. God is free in virtue of using his freedom without abusing it; and goodness is simply the integrity of liberty.[10]

Alcott was unsuccessful in his attempt to convince Emerson of the truth of his doctrine of personality. Only Emerson's "liberating imagination," Alcott decided, saved him from fatalism.[11] Emerson's objection to Alcott's personalism echoed Orestes Brownson's criticism of Alcott in 1838. Emerson felt that the First Cause should be distinguished as superpersonal, lest the creation be made identical to the Creator. But Emerson appreciated what Alcott was saying:

> Alcott's true strength is in the emphasis he gives to partnership of power against the doctrine of Fate. There is no passive reception. The receiver, to receive, must play God also. God gives, but it is God, or it takes God also, to receive.[12]

To Alcott's discomfort, Emerson continued to conceive of the Godhead as impersonal, or rather, superpersonal, and to describe the "All," the Universal Spirit, as "Nature" or an impersonal force. He refused to agree to Alcott's optimistic dictum that human beings shared the power of God and thus could shape and manipulate those forces which Emerson increasingly saw as fatalistic and deterministic.[13]

When Alcott conversed on the Transcendental Club and the *Dial* in Boston in March 1863, he discussed the ideas of the 1830s in light of his newly developed concept of personality. He told his audience why he felt that transcendentalism failed to establish itself as a church. The transcendentalist, he said, talked of God or the Spirit in impersonal terms, as a universal law, or as universal right, or as universal truth. They talked of the sustenance each individual received from the Universal Spirit, he said, but they never emphasized the personality shared by all people. They failed to perceive the spiritual personality common to all people. But Alcott was wrong. True enough, Emerson and the transcendentalists did not fully share Alcott's belief in the creative divinity of human nature. True enough, they glorified the individual. But they clearly did recognize the bonds shared by all people in spiritual oneness. They just did not believe that physical union, a physical community, was necessary for individuals to share that oneness. Yet neither did Alcott in the 1830s. It was only later at Fruitlands, in his conversations, at Concord, and in his beautiful vision of the New Church, that Alcott began to advocate such physical unity. Only then did he begin to criticize the transcendentalists for their individuality and impersonality. "We have been Protestants," he said of himself and the transcendentalists,

> protesting against what was; have taken sides with the iconoclast, and been rather demolishing idols than planting new institutions. The time is coming when new institutions shall spring up, but hardly yet. We have been in pursuit of a Church; but the tendency of our teaching, a good deal, has been rather to favor individualism—to confirm the student or inquirer in what was peculiar to himself, more than to lead himself forth into what belongs to all mankind; I mean to say, into what I am better pleased to call the personality which all share in common.[14]

The New Church Alcott spoke of was an idea he derived from religious beliefs he had always held. He had deplored sectarianism, traditions, and rigid dogma. He had celebrated free thought, free expression and openness to new ideas in worship and theology. He had rejected institutionalized religion. The expression of his faith, especially during his years of trial and despair, had become a private matter. Thoughts of reforming the church, or of bringing about the "New Church" as he had called it, had been secondary since the universal reform conventions of the 1840s. He said little about the church in his public conversations except to reiterate his belief that the clergy, and organized religion in general, did not meet the needs of the time. He still adamantly refused to attend Sunday church services despite strong suggestions by the Reverend Grindall Reynolds of the Unitarian Church in Concord that it was the duty of each citizen, especially the Superintendent of Schools, to do so.[15]

He had first begun to outline his concept of the New Church privately in his journals. "But churches in the true sense we have none," he had said in 1856,

> the Sunday lecture breaking up the old congregations, while the new societies are but audiences for the time, and liable to be scattered at any moment. The true Church, to which these are transitional and introductory, will not be a crowd and an auditory, but a few men and women cordially related, and meeting from Sunday to Sunday, for the interchange of sentiment, inspiration, and social good will: for readings, conversations, sometimes in the great moments, of exhortation, prayer and praise; and with the advantages of pictures [,] statuary, and the suggestions of art. I think the services will be improvised in a good measure, embracing the claims of personal religion, the duties and rites of private life, the means and sacraments of discipline and culture.[16]

His new self-confidence as a purveyor of enlightenment and the apparent need of a war-torn nation for a renewal of faith, brought back his idea that a new church, the "true church," was forthcoming and that he might help to institute it.[17]

His revived vision of the New Church received impetus and sustenance from his interaction with the free religious movement. On February 28, 1865, the newly formed Free Congregational Society of Florence, Massachusetts, invited

Alcott to talk on religion. The Free Society had been founded in this small manufacturing town near Northampton by radical abolitionist and anti-sabbatarian Charles C. Burleigh. Its constitution affirmed freedom of conscience, freedom of inquiry and expression, and promised an end to any distinctions based on sex, race, or nationality. Alcott was impressed. Clearly, this was a congregation seeking a "more vital service" and a more "inspiring priesthood." He illustrated to them his idea of the true church: communal sharing, improvisation in worship, and a free pulpit filled with members of a traveling priesthood ever open to new ideas.[18]

The Free Society of Florence was impressed enough with Alcott's "profound and elevating doctrines" to ask him to join Charles Burleigh as their delegate to the National Conference of Unitarian Churches to be held in New York City in April. The National Conference was largely the work of Alcott's old friend and supporter, Henry W. Bellows. During the war Bellows had organized the United States Sanitary Commission, which was notably successful in aiding wounded soldiers by supplementing government-sponsored medical care. The energetic Bellows hoped that his organizational genius might bring about greater denominational unity among Unitarians, who until then had been only loosely bound together by the weak American Unitarian Association. He wanted the National Conference to represent all Unitarian churches and to affirm a basic statement of doctrine to which all Unitarians could adhere.[19]

The Conference met at Bellows's All Soul's Church in New York on April 5. Radical delegates—including Alcott, Burleigh, David Wasson, who would soon become minister of Boston's Twenty-Eighth Congregational Society, and Edward C. Towne of Medford, Massachusetts—had high hopes that all Unitarians would magnanimously affirm doctrinal freedom and repudiate sectarianism. They should have known better; the very nature of such a conference was sectarian and implied a delineation of doctrinal limits.[20]

Trouble began immediately. Bellows, despite his sympathy with transcendentalism and "liberalism," was conservative enough to demand a statement in the proposed constitution indicating that all Unitarians were disciples of "the Lord Jesus Christ." Several of the radicals, including Towne, objected to the phrase because it had sectarian implications that might limit "wider fellowship," that is, fellowship with non-Christians. Burleigh shocked and offended the majority of those present by arguing that Jesus was not the Messiah. As a result, Bellows declared him out of order, claiming that since his congregation was a free church it was not officially recognized. Debate was heated, but this was to be no Chardon Street Convention. The orderly Bellows had seen to it that discussion of even this vexing issue was limited to five minutes. Alcott sympathized with the radicals, not so much because he objected to the conservatives' statement about Jesus but because of the limitations on free debate and free expression. He cared little about constitutions, agreements, and resolutions. He believed that if all ideas were aired, the truth would somehow mysteriously rise to the surface.[21]

Among the radicals Alcott found his old friends William Henry Channing and Samuel Longfellow and three younger men who won his interest: Towne, Octavius Brooks Frothingham, and Sidney Morse. They all were talking of the need for a medium to express radical religious thought. Soon thereafter, two new periodicals appeared, which Alcott was pleased to see were dedicated to "free thought" and "progress": the shortlived *Friend of Progress*, edited by Frothingham, and the more successful *Radical*, edited by Morse. The *Radical* first appeared in September 1865, and Alcott immediately found it a "fit organ" for the "new faith." Morse advertised it as "a medium for the presentation of the best floating free thought of the time." And it was liberal and free enough to accept several of Alcott's poems and short essays for publication. Naturally, he wanted to see it become the "oracle of American thought."[22]

In early October 1866 the National Conference of Unitarian Churches met again in Syracuse, New York. Alcott did not attend, but he followed newspaper reports closely. The radicals, now led by Francis Ellingwood Abbot, minister of the Unitarian Society of Dover, New Hampshire, and formerly a teacher in Frank Sanborn's school in Concord, introduced a substitute preamble to the constitution affirming "perfect freedom of thought" and advocating "unity of spirit rather than uniformity of belief." Their position was deliberately vague in order to make Unitarianism a common bond for the widest possible variety of opinion. Indeed, they came close to rendering formal organization meaningless and useless. The conservatives, led by Bellows and by erstwhile theological rebels James Freeman Clarke and Frederic Henry Hedge, feared that removing the words "Lordship of Jesus" from the constitution would make Unitarianism no longer Christian. The conference voted down Abbot's amendment, leading Alcott to believe that Unitarianism was rapidly hardening into an episcopal hierarchy. Alcott believed that a new free church was needed, independent of the Unitarians. He hoped that the *Radical* would speak out in favor of such a free church and invite all thoughtful men and women outside existing sects to join on the "broadest grounds."[23]

Meanwhile, Alcott spoke out publicly himself on the New Church. At the Melodeon on May 6, 1866, he told his audience that the "Radical Church" was rooted in the soul of each human being and employed the sacred books of all races as its scripture. On February 5, 1867, Alcott attended a meeting of the friends of "free thought" at the home of Cyrus Bartol to discuss a new religious association. There he met, among others, Towne, Abbot, Frothingham, John Weiss, and the minister of the Unitarian Church in New Bedford, William J. Potter. They clearly had given up on any chance of peaceful union with the Unitarian Conference. Abbot, Potter, and Towne presented a constitution for a Free Religious Association. The group appointed a committee to arrange a public convention in Boston. Alcott left the meeting full of hope and excitement.[24]

The convention met at Horticultural Hall on May 30, 1867, with

Frothingham presiding. To symbolize their commitment to free expression, the members heard speeches by Universalist Henry Blanchard, Quaker Lucretia Mott, Spiritualist Robert Dale Owen, Unitarians Abbot, Wasson, and Higginson, and finally Ralph Waldo Emerson. Emerson, a guiding light to all those in attendance, was the first to pay his one dollar fee for membership in the new Free Religious Association.[25]

Alcott enthusiastically promised to helped spread the word by arranging conventions, lectures, and conversations to awaken and inform the "minds of the community." He discussed at length ways of promoting the "New Divinity" with Wasson, Towne, Weiss, and Emerson. With his own future in mind, he proposed that missionaries be sent across the country to preach free religion. He continued to speak on his version of the New Church—at Groveland, Northampton, Florence and Haverhill. He conversed at the Radical Club, formed in April 1867, which met at the home of John T. Sargent on Chestnut Street in Boston. He proposed that the Unitarian Church in Concord open itself to free thought by inviting a variety of speakers to share the pulpit from week to week, but the members' fear of "dissension" in the church thwarted the plan. Once again he raised the possibility of a school in Concord, this time to teach the "New Divinity," with himself, Emerson, Samuel Johnson, Weiss, and Wasson on the faculty. "Concord is the proper seat for an Academy of Philosophy, Literature and Religion," he said. "Here should be founded the Divinity School to which young men and women might resort, for the inspiration and insight which our colleges fail to cherish."[26]

The Radical Club inspired Alcott. There had been nothing so fresh, so exciting, he thought, since the time of the "transcendental aurora." It offered opportunities for the "widest discussion of all questions affecting human welfare." The Radical Club, along with the Free Religious Association and the *Radical*, would be the chief instrumentalities for the "free theology." Once again he felt a part of a revolutionary movement. As was the case in the 1830s and 1840s, his sense of participating in vital movements for reform reinforced his personal sense of mission. "It is in no sense of vain pretension," he said in the fall of 1867, "that I deem the experiences of my life and thought suited to meliorate and strengthen the character of a large class of my contemporaries." He saw himself as a pioneer in bringing the dream of "paradise and light" to the multitude. His new-found identity as a missionary of the New Church would justify to himself and to others his seemingly unprofitable days and years of improvident speculation.[27]

Early in the spring of 1868 Alcott was instrumental in the organization of a Radical Religious Association at Concord Hall in Boston's South End. He wrote the preamble to its constitution, asserting complete freedom of thought and expression and free fellowship with any sincere person, and "recognizing an Infinite Intelligence as pervading the Universe, but leaving all forms of its expression or conception to each persons' conscience or conviction." In May he was asked to address the first annual meeting of the Free Religious Association in Boston. He told the members that they were the fruit of forty years of transcendentalism. They had the unparalleled opportunity, he added, to speculate in the most transcendent way, to absorb all thought, all peoples, all races, all bibles. They should not, he warned, ignore any idea from any sect. Free religion would be a grand, inclusive faith, approaching Alcott's emotionally uplifting ideal of the spiritual oneness of all people. He further warned them of the danger of degenerating into a crusty series of conventions and annual meetings. They had to act, to express, and to promulgate the faith.[28]

Alcott further attempted to serve the cause of free religion by publishing his first major book in thirty years. *Tablets*, the edited version of the various speculative manuscripts he had worked on for two decades, reached the book stores in September 1868. It presented his ideas in the manner of oracular testimony rather than logical argument, covering his favorite topics such as conversation, friendship, the family, children, human culture, books, politics, the spirit, human nature, the origin of the universe, and religion. It had no dominant theme or systematic framework; it was rather a scattering of thoughts tied together, Alcott hoped, by a thread of spiritual truth. He wanted *Tablets* to be an organ of the new free thought. In it he advocated an openness to ideas from all over the world. All ideas, he claimed, were records of Revelation. The belief that the Bible of Christianity was the only inspired volume was patently false, he thought, "as if Truth were a geographical resident dwelling in our neighborhood only."[29]

As an additional means of spreading the new faith and providing a platform for the "priests of the free faith," Alcott proposed another series of weekly lectures, drawing on a wide range of ideas and persons and taking the place of the "narrow sectarianism" of regular Sunday church services. In October 1868 he and his friend J. J. Locke of Greenwood engaged Horticultural Hall and lined up Emerson, Weiss, Wasson, Abbot, and Potter as lecturers. The lectures were scheduled for twelve Sunday afternoons beginning on January 17, 1869. Samuel Johnson, Frothingham, Higginson, Wendell Phillips, Ednah Cheney, and Julia Ward Howe were added to the list of speakers. Alcott declined lecturing himself, feeling that he had done his part by conceiving the series, and that conversation was his best medium. On January 24 and 31 he held conversations on the "church of the future" at Horticultural Hall following the lectures. Conversation, he believed, was the chief instrumentality of the New Church anyway.[30]

Alcott was attracted to Free Religion because it seemed to be the most recent evidence of beneficent change and progress. To him it was a renewal and an extension of the transcendental enthusiasm. The Free Religionists, though perhaps not so messianic as Alcott, did believe that their ideas would bring progress and enlightenment and would help cultivate the best elements of human nature. They also battled Alcott's longtime nemesis, sectarianism. And they reinforced his rebellion against churchly tradition and dogma. They were committed to a universal faith, a faith common to all human beings and transcending denominational bounds.[31]

Free Religion also touched Alcott's uplifting faith in the free individual. The free religionists shared Alcott's belief in the basic goodness of human nature. All human beings, they believed, had in common basic spiritual and moral elements such as love, the power to forgive, piety, and faith. There was no need to fear free inquiry and free expression. Such freedom only helped to cultivate the spiritual qualities of human beings.[32]

Even more significant was the free religionists' effort to combine science and spirituality. They put tremendous emphasis on the scientific method, believing that human intelligence could resolve any conflict between science and religious faith. Observation, experiment, and reflection were the means of discovering all truth. Alcott was attracted to this empiricism because he too fancied himself a scientist. Faith in the power of human intelligence was the basis of his observations of the development of his children, his study of the human mind, the use of the inductive method in teaching, and his fascination with technological developments. His transcendentalism was a synthesis of the rational and the spiritual, and exploration of the interaction between internal human powers and the external world. He believed that Free Religion was further developing this synthesis, that it was the heir to transcendentalism.[33]

In February 1866 Alcott took his personalism and his increasingly enthusiastic faith in the New Church to St. Louis. There he found confirmation of his idealism but a challenge to his imprecise philosophic method in the rigid logic of the ideas of Georg Wilhelm Friedrich Hegel. William Torrey Harris greeted Alcott heartily on February 9. They had corresponded during the war but had not met since Alcott's ill-fated trip to St. Louis in 1859. Harris introduced him to the members of the Philosophical Society, which had been recently revived after a wartime interruption. The most prominent member was Henry C. Brokmeyer, the rough-hewn Prussian who had faithfully served as a Union officer during the war. Also present, though less influential than Harris and Brokmeyer, were George Holmes Howison, professor of mathematics at Washington University in St. Louis; Dr. J. H. Watters of the St. Louis Medical College; A. E. Kroeger, translator and staunch defender of the ideas of Johann Gottlieb Fichte; Judge J. Gabriel Woerner, legal scholar and author; and the young writer and social activist Denton Jacques Snider.[34]

The members of the Philosophical Society were all avid connoisseurs of German idealism, particularly that of Hegel. Hegelianism had reached the midwestern United States by way of New England scholarship and German immigrants. Brokmeyer had been introduced to Hegel by reading Frederic Henry Hedge's *Prose Writers of Germany*, published in 1847. By the early 1850s German immigrants Johann B. Stallo, August Willich, and Peter Kaufmann had brought Hegelianism to Cincinnati. The St. Louis group was familiar with the writings of the Cincinnatians, and particularly with Stallo's *General Principles of the Philosophy of Nature*. There was no organized philosophical club in Cincinnati, so Stallo and Willich became auxiliary members of the St. Louis Society.[35]

Hegel had believed that America was destined to be the next stage in the development of civilization, the next step in the progressive process of thesis, antithesis, and synthesis. Filled with the idea of progress, the American Hegelians had a faith that America would be concrete proof of Hegel's dialectial process at work. They shared with the transcendentalists a faith in the ability of human reason to perceive the spiritual world, the realm of *a priori* experience. They shared the same faith in individual expression. But Hegel offered them a logical process by which they could relate abstract ideas about the spirit or the Universal Mind to concrete events. They could demonstrate the creative action of ideas, thus avoiding the "mysticism" of the transcendentalists.[36]

The Hegelian dialectic was a process by which the mind of God was revealed to both God and to human beings in concrete experience. It was a formula for realizing the identity, the self-knowledge, of an individual, or an institution, or a civilization. The mind gained knowledge of everything by means of the interaction of opposites. Error revealed truth; good revealed evil; imperfection revealed perfection; and the external world revealed the internal self. Alcott was familiar with the general direction of all these ideas. They were central to the same philosophical questions he was asking. He had dealt with the problems of the progressive revelation of God through experience, and the knowledge of the internal self gained by knowledge of the external world. But Alcott lacked the rigorous logical process, the dialectic, which the St. Louis Hegelians found so attractive.[37]

Hegelianism was an optimistic philosophy. The Hegelians believed that out of every conflict and contradiction came resolution into a progressively better state. Like the transcendentalists, they had a positive, spiritual, teleological view of the process of change that confronted them in the nineteenth century. And they shared the transcendentalists' faith in the powerful, creative role of innate human powers. Hegelianism offered an attractive explanation of conflict and chaos to the young intellectuals of St. Louis, who had just experienced four years of Civil War. It gave expression to their hope that the frontier city of St. Louis might become the vanguard of progress.[38]

When Alcott became the guest of the St. Louis Philosophical Society in February 1866, he was not unfamiliar with Hegel. Although he had not read Hegel, he had read Stallo's explanation of Hegel's philosophy in *General Principles of the Philosophy of Nature.* During his 1859 visit to St. Louis he had heard Harris and his friends discuss Hegel at length. And Harris had rarely failed to mention Hegel in his correspondence with Alcott during the war. Indeed, Alcott's personalism contained elements similar to Hegelian ideas. Alcott's idea that "individuals" became "persons" when they found that common spiritual bond that united all persons suggested Hegel's idea that the self was best identified as a part of the community. But Alcott understood very little of the Hegelian dialectic. Between 1859 and 1866 he had made no attempt to formulate his theories in terms of Hegelian logic, despite Harris's efforts. Harris noted that as a metaphysician Alcott had not changed.[39]

No sooner did Alcott arrive in St. Louis than he met with Harris and the philosophers to unfold for them his theory of genesis. He had developed this idea during thirty years of speculation on the origin and nature of the universe, and had refined it by his reading of Plato and the Neoplatonists, particularly Plotinus. Souls, he told them, emanated from "pure being" or the "Person" though the agency of mind. These souls, having a creative mind and a free will, lapsed downward, creating matter. The material world, he claimed, was organized in a descending series of natural kingdoms that served as scaffolding for the soul in its ascent or descent according to its choices.[40] "Man is a soul," he explained,

> informed by divine ideas, and bodying forth their image. His mind is the unit and measure of things visible and invisible. In him stir the creatures potentially, and through his personal volitions are conceived and brought forth in matter whatsoever he sees, touches, and treads underfoot, the planet he spins.[41]

Many of the St. Louis Hegelians, particularly Brokmeyer, were unimpressed. Brokmeyer felt that Alcott's theories amounted to nothing but "infantile assininities" because they were attempts at what he believed was a logically impossible deduction from an unknown. He conceded that Alcott was "a sincere and earnest man, who has found the solutions to life's mysteries, propounded to him in the sacred places, unsatisfactory; and is striving to find and utter what his soul craves." But he disliked Alcott's "divining" as opposed to "reasoning," his oracular utterance of truth without logical argument to support it. On February 17 Alcott spoke again before the Society. Brokmeyer sat directly in front of him and made gratuitous comments about the "oracles" as Alcott was reading. The usually even-tempered Alcott was angered. He accused Brokmeyer of confounding the company by his "multiplicity of words." Denton Snider added that perhaps "only an Alcott can rightly interpret an Alcott," drawing laughter from the members present. Snider later said that he was ashamed of his behavior and admitted that he found Alcott's "poetic expression" in conversation "captivating." However, he and the other Hegelians continued to criticize Alcott for his lack of logical organization and structure. Alcott's logical deficiencies, they believed, made his ideas a string of detached observations that could be "luminous" but also could be "trivial."[42]

After the uncomfortable experience of February 17, Alcott concluded that his Western friends were seriously lacking in the courtesies of conversation. He told Abby that he had to "run the gantlet of their fierce logic and come out of the encounter as best I can." But he found their brash iconoclasm, their willingness to set aside customs, traditions, and authorities, refreshing. And despite Brokmeyer's cynicism, some Society members were awed by Alcott. Howison was overwhelmed to have a man as celebrated as Alcott visit his home. Unlike his experience in 1859, Alcott's public conversations were very successful. On the whole he was flattered by his reception and told Abby that he would have to leave soon to escape apotheosis.[43] Soon after Alcott left St. Louis on March 5, A. E. Kroeger wrote a letter to the Boston *Commonwealth* describing Alcott's visit as a "significant and hopeful event," a harbinger of closer ties between East and West. "It is at all times impressive," Kroeger added,

> to see a whole, clear-minded man, who, freed from the thraldom of tradition-worship, has brought harmony into himself, and to listen to utterances bearing the mark of earnest conviction.[44]

Harris invited Alcott to return the following fall. The members respectfully elected Alcott as an "auxiliary" of the Philosophical Society. And Harris and Kroeger maintained a regular correspondence with Alcott about their work and their proposed publications.[45]

On November 28, 1866, Alcott was off to St. Louis again with Harris's assurance of two hundred dollars for his services. He planned to stay two weeks, to hold four public conversations, and to have four meetings with the Philosophical Society. On December 2 he met with the Hegelians and managed to convince them, he thought, of his concept of personality. But he remained wary of them and wished they would not persist so much in the use of Hegelian terminology. He suspected, not without reason and justice, that his St. Louis friends were more concerned with the Hegelian process than with the meaning behind it. "They seem emulous rather of knowing than of being," he said, "and so far fall short of my ideal of excellence in which knowing and being are equally sought as complement and crown."[46]

But his stay was successful. His conversations were well attended, especially the one on New England authors. Curious Westerners flocked to hear of Eastern culture and Alcott's firsthand accounts of such literary lights as Emerson, Thoreau, Margaret Fuller, Lowell, and Longfellow. He visited St. Louis schools and spoke on education. At the Normal School he met its principal, Anna C. Brackett, a graduate of the Normal School in Framingham, Massachusetts, and the first woman to hold such a position in the United States. An authority on the ideas of Prussian educator Karl Rosencranz, she was interested in Alcott's educational ideas, attended his conversations, and wrote reports on them for the Boston *Commonwealth*. She said that Alcott's conversations were pleasurable and harmonious for the most part, although sometimes "intuition" and "logic" did not agree. A student of Hegelian logic herself, she noted the lack of order in Alcott's thoughts. "He glides over the subject as a swallow flies over a field," she said, "every now and then touching the subject, and then soaring again as fancy leads, again to stoop, and again to float away."[47]

Alcott did not return to St. Louis until the fall of 1870, but he maintained his close association with the Hegelians, particularly Harris. He served as a cultural communications link between East and West. His regular correspondence with Harris continued. Harris, Kroeger, and Anna Brackett visited Concord, and he arranged meetings for them with his New England friends. The energetic Harris, finding existing periodicals such as the *North American Review* and even the *Radical* not fully receptive to philosophy, founded a new journal devoted exclusively to speculative philosophy. The first edition of the *Journal of Speculative Philosophy* appeared in April 1867, and Harris offered to publish in it anything Alcott might offer. It became the organ of the American Hegelians and the most important philosophical journal in the United States for the next decade and more. Alcott was quick to send his short essay on "Genesis" to be published in the fall 1867 issue. He soon found the *Journal of Speculative Philosophy* the "fittest organ" for publishing his works and believed Harris the readiest of his contemporaries to comprehend and appreciate his speculations.[48]

Proud of his role as a liaison between East and West, Alcott eagerly sought to promote interaction. In April 1867 Thomas Davidson, then a professor of language and literature at the Collegiate Institute in London, Ontario, visited Alcott on the recommendation of Sidney Morse. The philosophically minded Davidson was disgruntled by pressures for religious conformity at his college and sought a more stimulating atmosphere. Alcott offered to introduce him to the "radicals" in St. Louis. He wrote to Harris about Davidson and sent Davidson's translation of Schelling to Harris for publication in the *Journal of Speculative Philosophy*. By November 1867 Davidson was in St. Louis, living with Harris and using his linguistic abilities to aid in the editing of the *Journal*. He promised Alcott, with whom he corresponded often thereafter, that he would translate Plotinus. Davidson preferred Greek philosophy to that of Hegel, but he was still interested in Harris and the St. Louis philosophers, and they in him. Alcott assured him that he was at "the very Court and Academy of Thought" in St. Louis.[49]

Harris remained unfaltering in his appreciation and praise of his spiritual mentor Alcott. When Alcott published *Tablets* in the fall of 1868, Harris wrote a lengthy critique of the book for the *Round Table*. After a systematic explanation of Alcott's philosophy, Harris concluded: "[Alcott's] whole life and utterances have been one unceasing effort toward the emancipation of spiritual self-consciousness." Naturally, Alcott believed Harris's critique the most learned and discriminating of any written about *Tablets*. He was sure that it would powerfully serve the interests of "pure idealism," and he hoped to included it as a preface to the second edition. Harris's systematic presentation of Alcott's ideas gave them an element of legitimacy that Alcott had seldom experienced. Harris welcomed Alcott as a recognized leader among American philosophers. Accordingly, Alcott's opinion of Harris grew ever higher throughout the late 1860s. No one, Alcott believed, matched Harris's metaphysical ability and his ability to comprehend the laws of method. He talked to Emerson and Hedge about using their influence to obtain a professorship for Harris at Harvard. Harris, Alcott exulted, was the herald of freedom and philosophy in both the East and the West.[50]

In the spring of 1869 Alcott renewed his recurrent dream of a "philosophical academy" in Concord. This time, Harris and Davidson would join the faculty. Harris's genius, he was sure, would enable the "forces of thought" to concentrate. And Concord still seemed the appropriate gathering place. In April 1870 Harris hinted that he might move to Concord, prompting Alcott to inquire about houses. Alcott offered to give his house, his grounds, and his library to the new school. But Harris decided not to come, and the dream remained unfulfilled for the present.[51]

As his relationship with Harris and his Hegelian friends became ever closer, Alcott began to try to understand Hegel and to apply Hegelian methods to his own ideas. Still preferring secondary treatments of Hegel's ideas, he read *The Secret of Hegel* by the Scottish philosopher J. H. Stirling. Stirling presented the Hegelian method as an "organon of the spirit" or a "mathematics of nature." Clearly Hegel was the "profoundest of modern thinkers," Alcott thought. Surely his ideas would counteract "material tendencies" in America and in Europe. Alcott began using logical paradigms in his writings—"if ... hence" constructions for example—which had never appeared before. He jotted thoughts into his diaries that resembled Hegel's such as "nothing is conceivable only through something" and "every 'nay' implies a secret affirmation of a 'yea'."[52] He talked of the need for a systematic presentation of his theory of personality. "What we need," he said,

is a *Calculus*, or *Organon*, serviceable alike to metaphysician and naturalist,—a *Dialogic* for resolving matter into Mind, body into spirit, organ into life, power into personality, many into one, the Soul in all souls, seen as the creative controlling energy, pulsating throughout nature inspiring, animating, organizing, immanent in all atoms, substance of all bodies, will in all wills.—Spirit, in short, present alike at centre and circumference of all things, Personality embodying all Persons in unbroken synthesis of Being.[53]

"To philosophize is to think methodically," he concluded.[54]

But by 1870 Alcott despaired of ever being able to master the dialectic. He finally resigned himself to his inability to write a systematic book, although he felt that he could imply systematic thinking in his books. He would leave it to logicians such as Harris to find the structure and system that he only hinted and suggested. "I find that I must content myself with the results," he decided, "without always comprehending the steps by which these are reached. Ideas are an Estate that one may possess without knowing their Genesis from the beginning." Alcott never had been nor ever would be constrained by logic or the burden of empirical evidence. Brokmeyer's criticism that Alcott was trying to deduce something from nothing was no problem to one like Alcott, who believed that human beings had a higher power of reason to do just that. Humans, possessors of divine personality, could intuit directly the answers to religious and philosophical questions. Alcott was a mystic, not a reasoner, said George Ripley in his *New York Tribune* critique of *Tablets*. "From the serene hights [sic] of intuition," said Ripley, "he utters the burdens of his soul."

Some of Alcott's readers and listeners, like Brokmeyer, scoffed at his divinations. An unsympathetic reviewer of *Tablets* in the *Nation* accused Alcott of "emptiness and affectation." The "village idiot," said the unidentified reviewer, could be "orphic" like Alcott just by saying the first thing that came into his head. Alcott's friend David Wasson remarked that the lack of framework, precision and proof in Alcott's thought made him the "Don Quixote of speculation." But Wasson appreciated Alcott's gift of intuitive reason, which made him superior to the Sancho Panzas who knew a windmill as only a windmill.[55] It was Emerson who most appreciated Alcott's intuitionism:

> The moral benefit of such a mind cannot be told. The world fades: men, reputations, politics shrivel: the interests, power, future of the soul beam a new dayspring. Faith becomes sight.[56]

Alcott respected the abilities of the logicians. He did not shrug off criticism of his intuitionism without careful consideration. But in the end he felt that his basic assumptions—a divine essence pervading the universe, the immortality of the soul, the divinity of the human soul—were ultimately matters of faith. Logical argument might help support and illustrate that faith, but they could not take its place. He suspected that those who rested their philosophical or religious case on logical paradigms or on empirical evidence were seeking only crutches to support them in their lack of faith. He agreed with Plotinus that only a faculty superior to both sense and reason, that is, an ecstatic intuition founded on the personality of the soul, could truly apprehend the infinite.[57]

On January 13, 1869, in a public conversation in Boston later published in the *Radical*, Alcott brought together his idea of personality, fortified as it was by interaction with the Hegelians, with his view of the new theology and the New Church. He called his theology "personal theism." "Religion is One, as the Personality of God is One," he said. "Faiths are many and individually diverse. We make progress only as we find that common basis and ground of agreement wherein all have their root." He told his audience that any true concept of God had to include all attributes common to human beings: "Must He not be present in idea, answering to the intellect; be felt also as a person, answering to our affections; have a will, distinguishing person from thing; be Spirit therefore, and Creator?" He outlined the central aspect of his idea of personality, the concept of free will. "The free will," he said, "is the Redeemer, the Christ within." It was the power to destroy or to save. Regeneration, he told them, resulted above all from the perception of personality achieved by the highest form of thought. "Sensuous" thought, he said, perceived God as a thing, an idol; "intellectual" thought perceived God only as an idea; but "spiritual" thought perceived God truly as a Person. Spiritual thought was the means of achieving a redeeming consciousness; it was the means of salvation.[58]

Alcott hoped that the free religious movement, with its strong challenge to sectarianism, would be the perfect vehicle for personal theism. All the creeds, traditions, dogmas, and doctrine that had separated people of different faiths for centuries would dissolve in the common faith in the personality. The New Church would be the external manifestation of Alcott's ideas, of his mission and his faith. It would be the lasting result of his long, lonely crusade to save humanity by making it conscious of its divine power.

Unfortunately, free religion failed to live up to Alcott's expectations. By mid-1869 his enthusiasm had turned to distrust. The members of the Radical Club failed to show eager acceptance of his personal theism. Instead, he detected hints of a belief in sheer materialism. In words similar to Emerson's distressing fatalism, Octavius Frothingham suggested that God was not a Person but rather a Force in nature, a Principle or an Influence. Alcott concluded that "if God is but Force, then free will is denied." Once he had lauded the Radical Club as an instrument of the New Church. Now he found it unsympathetic to his ideas. In October 1869 he began refusing its invitations.[59]

Further dissatisfaction followed. In November 1869 Alcott began a lengthy Western tour hoping to converse on his usual themes—New England authors, human culture—and to preach on Sundays in various towns on the New Church. On December 11 he arrived in Toledo, Ohio, having been asked by Francis Abbot to preach at his Independent Society. Since the beginnings of the free religious controversy Abbot had interested Alcott with his "liberality of spirit." Alcott had conversed with Abbot's friends in Dover, New Hampshire, and had considered Abbot to be among the most "spiritual" thinkers of the time. In 1868 Abbot had faced a storm of controversy in Dover. His Unitarian society had divided over his radicalism. He had founded an Independent Society as a result, but had resigned shortly afterward because of a bitter court battle over the use of the meeting house. The New Hampshire Supreme Court finally forbade Abbot from preaching in any Unitarian Church in the state unless all members agreed. In the wake of this furor, David R. Locke, the owner of the *Toledo Blade* and author of a nationally syndicated column under the pseudonym Petroleum V. Nasby, who sympathized with rational religion, had offered to sponsor a weekly journal of free religion if Abbot would accept the pulpit of the Unitarian Society in Toledo. Abbot had agreed on the condition that the Unitarian Society dissolve all connection with larger Unitarian organizations.[60]

Alcott preached to Abbot's new congregation on December 12, 1869, and the next day conversed with the Toledo version of the Radical Club. Such clubs and independent congregations, he discovered, were forming in many cities throughout New England, New York, and the Old Northwest as the split between Unitarianism and free religion widened. But he found this proliferation of free religion disturbing rather than hopeful. And he discovered that his impression of Francis Abbot was changing for the worse. He now felt that Abbot was inclined to rationalism instead of idealism and that he was more a "scholar" than a "thinker." Abbot upset Alcott by stating his dislike of any reliance on revelation or innate religious feeling as the grounds of religious thought. Only science, applied with rigorous logical methods, he said, could provide answers to religious questions. He would not accept the transcendentalists' belief in the ability of the "higher reason" to intuit religious truths.[61]

Alcott's criticism of Abbot extended to all the free religionists as he began to read the new *Free Religious Index*. The *Index* first appeared on January 1, 1870, edited by Abbot with Locke's financial aid. It quickly became the national organ for the free religious movement and attained a circulation of nearly five thousand. Its pages reflected a commitment to the scientific method and scholarship, and opposed the uncritical acceptance of dogma and tradition. Alcott still applauded free religion's free thinking and its battle against sectarianism. But he now feared its open skepticism of all ideas based on faith alone. It could not be the basis of the true church; it lacked a foundation in idealism. He now realized that the coming together of individuals to hear the free expression of every shade of opinion, such as at the Sunday lectures at Horticultural Hall, was not a church either. The true church, he felt, was made members drawn together by a common sympathy of thought and purpose. Free religion, he decided, was just a stepping stone from the old creeds to the New Church. It served to shatter traditions and superstitions, but he feared its proponents might overstep and "plunge into positivism or worse." In pleading for science," he complained, "they discredit religion in its divine sense."[62]

Alcott did not doubt that the free religionists were devout and earnest in their search for truth. Their journals, including the *Radical*, the *Index*, and the *Chicago Examiner* established by Edward C. Towne in 1870, had much to say that was good. But these people were "individualists," he felt. They had no core philosophy to offer. They failed to perceive the personality that bound all people together in a spiritual oneness.[63]

Indeed, free religion made clear to Alcott the dangers of his own transcendentalism. And he reacted in much the same way that the Unitarian establishment had reacted to the threat of transcendentalism in the 1830s, when Andrews Norton and his fellow conservatives had realized to their horror that the logic of their own ideas had contributed to the heresy. Free religion had built upon the same radical base established by transcendentalism: the attack on the external authority of Scripture and tradition, the impetus to social reform, the interest in the ideas of Europe and the Orient, and the great importance attached to human reason and the power of the individual. The affinity between free religion and transcendentalism was clear. However, Alcott and the transcendentalists assumed that their "higher reason," their intuitive spiritual faculties, would inevitably lead each person to the same conclusions about the existence of God and the assurance of immortality. Theodore Parker called it absolute religion; Alcott called it personal theism. They felt free to kick away authority and tradition while still retaining the fundamental elements of the faith. Free religionists, in questioning all authority, questioned even the higher reason. They went beyond the transcendentalists by challenging even the existence of God and the assurance of immortality. They were left with only a faith in the scientific method as the source for religious and philosophical truths.[64]

The free religionists shared the transcendentalists' faith in human progress. But their evidence for progress was the rapid development of science and technology, which was ever more apparent in the 1860s and 1870s. They expressed their idea of progress in terms of the science of Charles Darwin, whose *Origin of Species* had appeared in 1859, and the science of Herbert Spencer, whose *First Principles* appeared in 1862. It was a faith in the natural laws of evolutionary development, which guaranteed human progress. Empirical evidence, the scientific method, justified this assurance. It was not based on a mystical faith in the Unseen Spirit.[65]

Alcott was horrified at the direction free religion was taking. Evolutionary naturalism seemingly made God a deterministic force that acted above any human power. It left no room for free will, thought Alcott. It obscured the role of the individual human being. Free religion had accepted the transcendentalists' emphasis on human potential but had reduced it to the ability to understand natural laws through scientific investigation. It did not acknowledge the possibility of supernatural forces that might transcend natural laws either by the agency of humans partaking of the spirit or by the spirit itself. For Alcott remained convinced that nature and natural laws were only external manifestations of spiritual forces. To deify nature and natural laws was only a shallow and bleak materialism. Natural religion left out what Alcott considered most important: the absolute faith in the Unseen.[66]

The shocking tendencies of free religion led Alcott to a greater appreciation of orthodoxy. On one occasion at least during his Western tour of 1869-70, he discovered that he was the most "orthodox" of any of the people assembled. The often iconoclastic Alcott took on the role of the preserver of traditions. Reminiscent of Andrews Norton, he began to condemn as "idolators" those "pantheists" whose passions had led them to skepticism and indifference. "Idealize materialism rhetorically as you may, no matter by what fine names, by what sounding titles, show of method," he declared, "tis all brute animalism, dire demonism—man, mind, spirit omitted." He feared that New England was already far too much stained with the "so-called" thinking of Herbert Spencer and his "school of *knownothingarianism*."[67]

In his battle to defend idealism and faith from the inroads of naturalism, Alcott found strong allies in William Torrey Harris and the St. Louis Hegelians. Harris had already taken issue with Herbert Spencer in the first issue of the *Journal of Speculative Philosophy*. Alcott thought Harris's critique of Spencer a masterly defense of the ideal. Surely Harris was just the person to counter the ideas of Francis Abbot and the free religionists. Harris agreed with Alcott that the *Index*, the *Radical*, and the *Chicago Examiner* were organs for "individualists" who had no core philosophy. Alcott hoped that papers by Harris and Howison at the Boston Radical Club in the fall of 1870 would "enlarge the vision" of that group.[68]

Thus by 1869 and 1870 Alcott's mission encompassed not only the spreading of his gospel of the New Church and his personal theism, but also a battle against the mounting forces of skepticism and materialism. His growing public acceptance and acclaim in the late 1860s and 1870s testified to the growing cultural need for just such a defense of idealism, as well as reinforcement of traditional religious values. The Civil War and the unsettling theories of Charles Darwin had shaken the optimism and faith of many Americans. They responded well to the confident idealism and serene faith of this white-haired emissary from Concord.

With the publication of *Tablets* in September 1868, Alcott became more and more an object of public attention. Newspapers and periodicals all over the country reviewed the book. With the exception of that of the *Nation*, all reviews were favorable. He had written *Tablets* for "a few choice readers" and did not expect fame or popularity. Yet surprisingly, the first edition of one thousand copies sold quickly and the publishers, Roberts Brothers, were talking of a second edition. Even more encouraging was praise from readers such as Annie Preston of South Amherst, Massachusetts, who wrote to Alcott that *Tablets* fascinated her even though she did not quite understand his theory of genesis and lapse. Most reviewers were not unduly disturbed by Alcott's lack of logical argument. Indeed, they were taken by Alcott's confident testimony of idealism, his presentation of his thoughts as indisputable truth. The spirit, the atmosphere, created by the book charmed them.[69] The *Boston Daily Advertiser*, once Alcott's nemesis, remarked:

> His *Tablets* are like windows through which the busy worker, pausing for a minute in the rush and distraction of his thousand little cares and duties, may look out into great spaces and draw a deep full breath, may look far into the past, far forward into the future, and far up into the heavens.[70]

Reporters began appearing at the door of Orchard House asking for interviews and biographical information for newspaper and magazine articles. The *New York Tribune*, the *Springfield* (Mass.) *Republican*, the *Boston Daily Advertiser*, and the *Buffalo Courier* all published accounts of Alcott in 1868 and 1869. Of course, Alcott benefited not only from a greater public appreciation of his own work but also from the growing fame attached to Concord and Ralph Waldo Emerson. Many reporters and visitors found it easier to gain information and even access to Emerson through the hospitable Alcott than to approach the aloof Emerson directly. Added to this was Louisa's rising popularity. *Hospital Sketches* and *Moods* were both well received. In late 1867 she accepted the editorship of *Merry's Museum*, a children's magazine, thus becoming one of the few women in the United States to edit a periodical. Then in September 1868 Roberts Brothers published the first volume of a fictionalized account of her family called *Little Women*. It sold rapidly. An edition of fifteen hundred was gone in a little over a month, and by December nearly four editions had been sold. The immediate popularity of *Little Women* undoubtedly helped the sale of *Tablets*, which appeared at the same time.[71]

But Alcott did not receive attention merely as the father of the "Little Women" or the friend of Emerson. Searchers for truth and religious inspiration asked his advice as a reputable philosopher and theologian. He patiently and respectfully answered each request for information and guidance. In January 1869 the students of the Boston School for the Ministry asked him to give a series of conversations on immortality and personal theism, which he did gladly. Thereafter, several of these students and some from Harvard Divinity School made pilgrimages to Concord to talk with Alcott and seek his counsel. He did not hesitate to play Plato and Pythagoras for them.[72]

Louisa's income, especially from *Little Women*, finally stabilized the family's financial condition and made life at Orchard House comfortable. In April 1870 she and May sailed for Europe, this time not as servants to the wealthy but as self-sufficient world travelers. Abby, though she had been in poor health in the late 1860s and had nearly lost her sight in one eye, was by 1870 feeling better than she had for a long time. The presence of her grandchildren made life happier than ever for her. Alcott wrote his appreciation of his long-suffering and faithful wife: "What would I have been, and done, without her practical sense to balance my adventurous idealism."[73]

Success and security made Alcott's regular round of reading, writing, gardening, and occasional conversation much more enjoyable. He considered prepared another three books for publication. He planned to compile a record of his conversations held over thirty-five years, to revise *Conversations on the Gospels* and to edit selections from his Diary to be called *Concord Days*. Still a recognized authority on education, he was invited several times to speak to area teachers and even to the Massachusetts Association of Teachers. He commented smugly in his journal that the Concord schools had degenerated since he left the superintendency. Concordians would have retained him as superintendent, he reasoned, if only they had "cherished an interest as deep and productive in their children, as in their autumnal crops."[74]

Alcott avoided Western tours for nearly three years after his return from St. Louis in December 1866. Such excursions were costly and risky. His last one had left him thin, tired, and afflicted with rheumatism. But in the fall of 1869 he was in good health and anxious to travel once again and to spread his message of personal theism. Louisa gave him one hundred forty dollars for traveling expenses, which he expected to repay. Although he had few contacts and no guarantees of conversations, he resolved to make the effort and abide by the result. He hoped to meet with potential sponsors for conversations at the Women's Suffrage Convention to be held in Cleveland on November 24 and 25. With the support of Frank Sanborn, who was then writing for the *Springfield Republican*, he was chosen a convention delegate representing Hampton Country, Massachusetts (Springfield). At the Convention he did indeed encounter several Ohio people willing to organize conversations in their respective cities, including Rebecca D. Rickoff of Cleveland, Mary Hall of Toledo, and Louise Ely of Elyria.[751]

Mrs. Rickoff arranged a series of five successful conversations for Alcott in Cleveland in early December. Her husband Andrew, the Cleveland super-intendent of schools, gave Alcott a guided tour of the Cleveland schools. At each institution Alcott wanted to present his theories of education, but, since he was invariably introduced as the father of *Little Women*, he had to talk about Louisa instead. Wherever he went, he discovered, he rode in his daughter's "chariot of glory." Although he said nothing about it, he must have been concerned lest his audience be interested more in anecdotes about Louisa and Concord celebrities than about his message of idealism. Nevertheless, he was genuinely proud of Louisa and wrote to her telling of the enthusiasm and admiration for her in the West.[76]

But there was evidence that Alcott's reception was based on more than the curiosity of celebrity seekers. Superintendent Rickoff discussed education with him at length and asked him to address the Cleveland teachers on subjects more serious than Louisa's girlhood. After the five Cleveland conversations in early December, Mrs. Rickoff was able to find an audience for four more in early January 1870. The public paid to hear him talk not only on New England authors but also on human culture, conversation, and his theories of genesis and lapse. He found pulpits open to him on Sunday mornings where he could speak on the New Church. His Christmas season conversations in Elyria were successful, and his friends there, including Mrs. Ely, were quick to help him arrange sessions in Tiffin, Akron, and Sandusky. In Akron he conversed and lectured on the "Church of the future." In Sandusky he conversed, visited schools, and found a sympathetic friend in W. W. Farr, the Episcopal minister of Grace Church. Farr reminded him of William Henry Channing, and he had a faith that touched the heart in a way that Abbot and free religion could never do.[77]

At the end of January Alcott was in Detroit, where he conversed at the homes of Eliza Seaman Leggett and Frances Bagley. He visited schools and spoke on the New Church at the Reverend W. R. G. Mellen's congregation. From Detroit he wrote to Professor Moses Coit Tyler of the University of Michigan, who had met Louisa in Europe the previous summer. Tyler duly arranged conversations in Ann Arbor, invited Alcott to one of his University classes, and scheduled Alcott to lecture the student body.[78]

In Battle Creek, Michigan, Alcott found his ideas on the New Church favorable to Quakers, Adventists, Congregationalists, and comeouters alike, and an evening speech to the Spiritualists was met with "rapturous favor." The spiritualism in Battle Creek, he found, was "preternatural" and usurped the place of the truly spiritual. But he felt that it was "a kind of lay gospel for the otherwise unchurched multitude." It was a harbinger, he thought, of the "universal revival" then taking place.[79]

After two conversations in Kalamazoo, Michigan, Alcott left for Chicago, arriving there on February 18. The Reverend Robert Collyer, the blacksmith turned preacher who Alcott thought was the ablest speaker for the "liberal" faith East or West, gave Alcott the opportunity to speak at his Unitarian

Church. The next day the Reverend Robert Laird Collier opened his home for a conversation on New England authors. Chicago amazed Alcott by its size and rapidity of growth. Every time he left his hotel he had to ask his way back. "Heads stronger than mine," he said, "are dizzied and lost in this Jonah's Gourd of a city."[80]

Originally, Alcott had intended to go to Cincinnati and St. Louis, but news of Louisa's and May's intention to leave for Europe drew him home sooner than he had planned. On his way he stopped again in Detroit for a conversation at Mellen's church, and in Buffalo, where *Courier* editor Thomas Kean had arranged a successful and well-attended conversation at the Mansion House. After the conversation Kean praised Alcott in the *Courier*, calling him "the most fascinating conversationalist we have ever heard."[81]

Alcott completed his tour in early March at Syracuse, where he conversed at the former church of Samuel J. May, who had just retired. On March 9 he arrived in Maplewood, where he and Abby had spent the past two winters living with Anna and John. It had been by far his most successful Western excursion. His receipts totaled seven hundred twenty-two dollars. He was able to reimburse Louisa and to pay forty-two dollars toward the education of a young orphan, Delphine Delores Clement, whom he had met in Elyria. It was something of a miracle, he thought, that he should bring both money and popularity into his home. And even more impressive were the prospects for future tours. Louis T. Ives, a Detroit artist and a participant in conversations, proposed himself as a midwestern agent to arrange conversation and lecture tours for Alcott, Emerson, and other New England luminaries. Alcott was sure that parlor conversation would become annual affairs like the lecture circuit.[82]

By midsummer 1870 Alcott was talking of a trip to San Francisco, so that he might "belt the continent with talk" and create a blaze of light between Massachusetts and California. His daughters, though impressed with his ambition, discouraged his going. Louisa felt that he would be as out of place in San Francisco as "a saint in a barroom," and that he was too old for such ventures anyway. But the impact of his recent journey was significant enough to justify his exaggerated enthusiasm. Robert Laird Collier wrote from Chicago encouraging further tours and telling Alcott that in the future he was going to use the conversational method himself. Eliza Leggett told Alcott that Alcott-like conversations had continued in Detroit after his departure and had begun in Dubuque, Iowa. People in Dubuque had heard of Alcott through friends in St. Louis. For several years they had wanted Alcott to visit but had had no point of contact. Finally, in 1870 the Dubuque culture seekers were able to issue a formal invitation through Alcott's Detroit friend Frances Bagley. Mrs. Bagley was the sister of Mary Newbury Adams, indefatigable organizer of literary and philosophical clubs in Dubuque. Alcott accepted the invitation with pleasure.[83]

Public acceptance had finally come to Alcott. To be sure, the success of *Tablets* and of his conversational tour was partly the result of Louisa's popularity and of his Concord connections. But it was also clear that there was a market in the West for his idealism and his enthusiasm for human culture. He no longer despaired at the futility of "chasing after himself," nor feared that his now enormous series of journals was but "a poor excuse for not living." He told William Oldham, his old friend from Alcott House in England, that since Fruitlands his life had been rich and full of satisfaction. "It is true that I have not *planted a Paradise outside*, as I once dreamed of doing," he explained, "but rather cultivated the one already planted *inside*, and grown a little pleasant fruit, still good to taste and promising future crops of satisfactions." He would lay the seeds for these future crops in the West.[84]

Notes

1. AJ 32 (1857): 328-29; AJ 34 (1859): 157-59.
2. AJ 34 (1859): 163, 181-87.
3. Ibid., pp. 223, 225, 229, 230-31.
4. Ibid., pp. 493-94, 496-97; AJ 35 (1860): 78, 82.
5. AJ 34 (1859): 493-94; AJ 37 (1862): 397, 411, 415.
6. AJ 36 (1861): p. 58.
7. A. Bronson Alcott, "Friendship," *The Commonwealth* 2, no. 37 (May 13, 1864) and no. 38 (May 20, 1864); AJ 37 (1962): 397-403.
8. Ralph Waldo Emerson, *The Conduct of Life* (Boston: Houghton, Mifflin and Co., 1904), pp. 3-49; Rusk, *Emerson*, pp. 405-6.
9. AJ 33 (1858): 452; an unidentified newspaper clipping of Alcott's January 24, 1859, Cincinnati conversation on "Fate" is pasted into AJ 34 (1859): 56.
10. AJ 32 (1857): 367.
11. AJ 38 (1863): 93.
12. Emerson and Forbes, eds., *Journals of Emerson*, 9: 503.
13. AJ 40 (1865): 64, 196, 203; Alcott, *Emerson*, pp. 14, 18.
14. A. Bronson Alcott, "The Transcendental Club and the *Dial,*" *The Commonwealth* 1, no. 34 (April 24, 1863).
15. AJ 36, (1861): 187-88; AJ 39 (1864): 25-26.
16. AJ 31 (1856): 967-68.
17. AJ 40 (1865): 60, 62-63.
18. Ibid., pp. 85, 116, 118, 128; Stow Persons, *Free Religion: An American Faith* (New Haven, Conn.: Yale University Press, 1947), p. 16; a printed brochure on the Florence Free Congregational Society is pasted into AJ 40 (1865): 118; an unidentified newspaper clipping of Alcott's March 26, 1865, speech at Florence is pasted in AJ 40 (1865): 119.
19. AJ 40 (1865): 119 (newspaper clipping), 121, 128; Persons, *Free Religion*, pp. 12-14.
20. Persons, *Free Religion*, pp. 14-15; AJ 40 (1865): 130; Alcott to Abby May Alcott, April 8, 1865, in "Letters, 1865-66."
21. Persons, *Free Religion*, pp. 15-16; AJ 40 (1865): 141.
22. AJ 40 (1865): 141-42, 200; AJ 41 (1866): 86-87, 92, 110; Gohdes, *Periodicals of American Transcendentalism*, p. 214.
23. Persons, *Free Religion*, pp. 31-32, 38, 40; AJ 41 (1866): 260-62.
24. Persons, *Free Religion*, pp. 44-45; AJ 41 (1866): 139; AJ 42 (1867): 43-44, 103-4; George Willis Cooke, "The Free Religious Association," *New England Magazine*, n.s. 28, no. 4 (June 1903): 484-99; A. Bronson Alcott, "Modern Religion," *The Commonwealth* 5 (February 23, 1867).
25. Persons, *Free Religion*, pp. 45-50; AJ 42 (1867): 210.

26. AJ 42 (1867): 218-22, 224-26, 229-30, 250-52, 276-77, 280-81; AJ 45 (1870): 252.

27. AJ 42 (1867): 339-40, 347, 356, 405-6.

28. AJ 43 (1868): 39, 47, 117-18; printed notice of the "Principles" of the South End Religious Fellowship pasted in ibid., p. 87; "Remarks of A. B. Alcott," in *Proceedings of the First Annual Meeting of the Free Religious Association* (Boston: Adams and Co., 1868), pp. 77-78; A. Bronson Alcott, "Thought and Deed," in Free Religious Association, ed., *Freedom and Fellowship in Religion* (Boston: Roberts Brothers, 1875), pp. 408-9.

29. AJ 42 (1867): 230; A. Bronson Alcott, *Tablets* (Boston: Roberts Brothers, 1868), p. 143.

30. AJ 42 (1867): 10-11; AJ 43 (1868): 303-6, 459-60; AJ 44 (1869): 35-42, 73, 97-98, 290-92.

31. Persons, *Free Religion*, pp. 57, 60.

32. Ibid., pp. 57-60.

33. Ibid., p. 62.

34. AJ 41 (1866): 22, 24, 27, 29; William H. Goetzmann, ed., *The American Hegelians* (New York: Alfred A. Knopf, 1973), pp. 7-9; John Wright Buckham and George M. Stratton, *George Holmes Howison: Philosopher and Teacher* (Berkeley: University of California Press, 1934), p. 46; William Torrey Harris to Alcott, November 14, 1865, in "Letters, 1865-66."

35. Goetzmann, ed., *The American Hegelians*, pp. 5-6; Easton, *Hegel's First American Followers*, pp. 1-2.

36. Goetzmann, ed., *The American Hegelians*, pp. 10, 13.

37. Ibid., p. 14; cf. Georg Wilhelm Friedrich Hegel, *The Phenomenology of Mind* (1807) (New York: Harper and Row, 1965).

38. Goetzmann, ed., *The American Hegelians*, p. 15; Easton, *Hegel's First American Followers*, pp. 24-25; Pochmann, *New England Transcendentalism and St. Louis Hegelianism,* pp. 14-25.

39. Goetzmann, ed., *The American Hegelians*, p. 15; Charles H. Foster, ed., *Beyond Concord: Selected Writings of David Atwood Wasson* (Bloomington: Indiana University Press, 1965), pp. 13-14, 37; Sanborn and Harris, *A. Bronson Alcott*, 2: 553.

40. AJ 41 (1866): 30-31; AJ 29 (1854): 299-303; AJ 42 (1867): 5-6, 254; Alcott to Thomas Davidson, November 22, 1867, in A. Bronson Alcott, comp., "Letters, 1867," at Houghton Library, 59M-305 (7); Thomas Taylor, ed. and trans., *Select Works of Plotinus* (London: George Bell and Sons, 1895), pp. 46, 153, 157, 159, 253-54; Alcott, *Tablets*, p. 184; A. Bronson Alcott, "Pantheon," *Journal of Speculative Philosophy* 2, no. 1 (1868): 46-50; A. Bronson Alcott, "Genesis," *Journal of Speculative Philosophy* 1, no. 3 (1867): 165-68.

41. Alcott, *Tablets*, pp. 166-67.

42. Henry C. Brokmeyer, *A Mechanic's Diary*, ed. and published by E. C. Brokmeyer (Washington, D.C., 1910), pp. 230-32; Pochmann, *New England Transcendentalism and St. Louis Hegelianism*, pp. 36, 39-40, 44-45; Henry A. Pochmann, "Plato and Hegel Contend for the West," *The American-German Review* (August 1943), pp. 8-13; Denton J. Snider, *A Writer of Books in his Genesis* (St. Louis, Mo.: Sigma Publishing Co., 1910), pp. 334-39; AJ 41 (1866): 45-46.

43. AJ 41 (1866): 46; Buckham and Stratton, *George Holmes Howison*, p. 53; Alcott to Abby May Alcott, March 1, 1866, in "Letters, 1865-66."

44. A. E. Kroeger to the Editor of *The Commonwealth*, March 7, 1866, from a clipping in AJ 41 (1866): 88.

45. William Torrey Harris to Alcott, March 26, April 21, May 13, June 10, July 6, and August 9, 1866, and A. E. Kroeger to Alcott, April 26 and October 1, 1866, in "Letters, 1865-66"; AJ 41 (1866): 268.

46. AJ 41 (1866): 301-2, 304-6; William Torrey Harris to Alcott, October 2 and November 3, 1866, in "Letters, 1865-66."

47. AJ 41 (1866): 309-17; Goetzmann, ed., *The American Hegelians*, p. 278; Alcott to Abby May Alcott, December 3, 10, and 13, 1866, in "Letters, 1865-66"; A. E. [Anna C. Brackett], "Mr. Alcott and the Philosophers," *The Commonwealth* 5 (December 29, 1866, and January 11, 1867).

48. AJ 43 (1868): 143, 148, 151; AJ 41 (1866): 186-87; William Torrey Harris to Alcott, July 6, 1866, in "Letters, 1865-66"; Goetzmann, ed., *The American Hegelians*, p. 100; AJ 42 (1867):

463-64; William Torrey Harris to Alcott, May 20, 1867, in "Letters, 1867"; Alcott to William Torrey Harris, November 26, 1867, from a copy in Alcott's hand in "Letters, 1867."

49. AJ 42 (1867): 166, 335, 455-56; Sidney Morse to Alcott, April 22, 1867, Thomas Davidson to Alcott, April 28, June 9, November 30, 1867, and William Torrey Harris to Alcott, December 16, 1867, in "Letters, 1867"; Thomas Davidson to Alcott, February 19, 1868, in A. Bronson Alcott, comp., "Letters, 1868," at Houghton Library, 59M-305 (8); Alcott to William Torrey Harris, August 5, 1867, from a copy in Alcott's hand in "Letters, 1867"; Alcott to Thomas Davidson, November 22, 1867, in "Letters, 1867."

50. AJ 43 (1868): 355, 371; a clipping of Harris's *Round Table* critique is pasted into ibid., pp. 357-60; AJ 44 (1869): 471, 684; AJ 45 (1870): 474, 704; William Torrey Harris to Alcott, November 30, 1868, in "Letters, 1868"; Alcott to William Torrey Harris, September 22, November 4, and November 22, 1868, from copies in Alcott's hand in "Letters, 1868"; Alcott to William Torrey Harris, November 19, 1870, from a copy in Alcott's hand in A. Bronson Alcott, comp., "Letters, 1870," at Houghton Library, 59M-305 (10).

51. AJ 44 (1869): 397; AJ 45 (1870): 252, 255, 258, 360; William Torrey Harris to Alcott, April 20, and August 15, 1870, in "Letters, 1870"; Alcott to William Torrey Harris, June 6, 1869, from a copy in Alcott's hand in A. Bronson Alcott, comp., "Letters, 1869," at Houghton Library, 59M-305 (9).

52. AJ 41 (1866): 96-97, 167-68, 311; AJ 42 (1867): 76-77.

53. AJ 42 (1867): 242.

54. AJ 44 (1869): 126.

55. AJ 45 (1870), pp. 179, 457, 753-54; AJ 44 (1869): 133-40; clippings of George Ripley's review of *Tablets* in the *New York Tribune* and of David Wasson's review in *The Commonwealth* are pasted into A. Bronson Alcott, comp., "Autobiographical Collections," 8 (1868-1871): 30, 32; "Mr. Bronson Alcott's Essays," *The Nation* 7 (August 20, 1868): 151-52.

56. Emerson and Forbes, eds., *Journals of Emerson*, 10: 158.

57. AJ 44 (1869): 133-40; AJ 45 (1870): 179.

58. AJ 44 (1869): 25-26, 258; A. Bronson Alcott, "Personal Theism: A Conversation," *The Radical* 6 (July 1869): 22-33.

59. AJ 44 (1869): 430-33, 734; Persons, *Free Religion*, p. 69; Alcott to Sidney Morse, May 20, 1869, in "Letters, 1869."

60. AJ 44 (1869): 118, 123, 790, 793, 819-20, 831, 838; AJ 41 (1866): 323-24; AJ 43 (1868): 121, 181; Francis Abbot to Alcott, November 15, 1868, in "Letters, 1868"; Persons, *Free Religion*, pp. 84-85; Gohdes, *Periodicals of American Transcendentalism*, p. 234.

61. Persons, *Free Religion*, pp. 35, 37, 91; AJ 44 (1869): 842.

62 Persons, *Free Religion*, pp. 51, 88-89; Gohdes, *Periodicals of American Transcendentalism*, p. 235; AJ 45 (1870): 42-43, 166-68, 303-4.

63. Persons, *Free Religion*, p. 90; AJ 45 (1870): 648.

64. Persons, *Free Religon*, pp. 20-23, 35-37.

65. Ibid., p. 105.

66. AJ 44 (1869): 152, 432-33; AJ 45 (1870): 304.

67. AJ 45 (1870): 32, 106; AJ 42 (1867): 111; Alcott to William Torrey Harris, March 28, 1870, from a copy in Alcott's hand in "Letters, 1870"; AJ 44 (1869): 431, 433; Alcott to William Torrey Harris, September 2, 1869, from a copy in Alcott's hand in "Letters, 1869."

68. Alcott to William Torrey Harris, May 12, 1867, from a copy in Alcott's hand in "Letters, 1867"; William Torrey Harris, "Herbert Spencer," *Journal of Speculative Philosophy* 1 (1867): 6-9; AJ 45 (1870): 705; William Torrey Harris to Alcott, October 8, 1870, in "Letters, 1870"; Alcott to William Torrey Harris, October 3, 1870, from a copy in Alcott's hand in "Letters, 1870."

69. AJ 43 (1868): 172, 241-48, 257-58, 273-74, 281, 307, 343-44, 355-57, 437-39; Alcott pasted many of the reviews, favorable and unfavorable, into ibid. and "Autobiographical Collections," vol. 8; Annie A. Preston to Alcott, September 7 and October 31, 1868, in "Letters, 1868"; Annie Fields to Alcott, March 31, 1869, at Houghton Library, 59M-312.

70. A clipping of the *Boston Daily Advertiser* review is pasted into AJ 43 (1868): 439.

71. AJ 43 (1868): 194-96, 299, 467; Alcott, "Autobiographical Collections," 8: 72, 100, 163-64; AJ 44 (1869): 330, 563; AJ 42 (1867): 494; Louisa May Alcott, "Diary, 1850-1885."

72. AJ 43 (1868): 235; AJ 44 (1869): 51, 65, 327, 334-36, 438, 559, 723; Henri Batchelder to Alcott, February 25, 1867, John Savary to Alcott, May 9, 1867, and Alcott to Henri Batchelder, February 27, 1867, in "Letters, 1867"; Carrie K. Sherman to Alcott, November 13, 1868, and Alcott to Carrie K. Sherman, November 25, 1868, in "Letters, 1868"; James T. Lee to Alcott, March 17, 1869, David Cronyn to Alcott, August 9, 1869, J. N. Pardee to Alcott, October 11, 1869, and Alcott to James T. Lee, March 22, 1869, in "Letters, 1869."

73. Louisa May Alcott, "Diary, 1850-85"; Abby May Alcott, "Diary," December 31, 1866, January 13, February 27, March 27, and December 31, 1868; AJ 42 (1867): 56; AJ 41 (1866): 248. 258, 274-75; AJ 45 (1870): 675; AJ 43 (1868): 664.

74. AJ 43 (1868): 60-61, 277-78; AJ 42 (1867): 476; AJ 44 (1869): 245-46, 275, 471-73, 582, 689; AJ 41 (1866): 138; AJ 45 (1870): 350-31,365.

75. Louisa May Alcott, "Diary, 1863-67"; Abby May Alcott, "Diary," January 13, 1867; AJ 42, (1867), pp. 25, 39; A. Bronson Alcott, "Itinerary, 1869-1870, at the West," MS at Houghton Library 59M-308 (57); AJ 44 (1869), pp. 790-94, 801-6, 814-15; A. Bronson Alcott, "Western Evenings, An Itinerary, 1869-1870," MS at Houghton Library, 59M-306 (14).

76. AJ 44 (1869): 814-16, 818-19, 829-30.

77. AJ 44 (1869): 831, 836-39, 849-50, 859-63; Alcott, "Western Evenings, 1869-70"; AJ 45 (1870): 7, 9-10, 15, 17, 19-23, 25-32.

78. AJ 45 (1870): 45-46, 49, 51, 59-60, 63, 65-66, 70-72; Alcott to Moses Coit Tyler, February 1, 1870, and Moses Coit Tyler to Alcott, February 2, 1870, in "Letters, 1870."

79. AJ 45 (1870): 77-81; Alcott, "Western Evenings, 1869-70."

80. AJ 45 (1870): 85-90, 92-94, 104-10; Alcott, "Western Evenings, 1869-70."

81. AJ 45 (1870): 112-14, 131-34; Alcott to William Torrey Harris, December 17, 1869, and February 22, 1870, from copies in Alcott's hand in "Letters, 1869" and "Letters, 1870" respectively; a clipping of Thomas Kean's *Buffalo Courier* article is pasted into "Western Evenings, 1869-70."

82. AJ 45 (1870): 64, 73, 145-49, 154-58, 685-86; AJ 44 (1869): 849-50; Alcott, "Itinerary, 1869-70"; Alcott to William Torrey Harris, March 28, 1870, from a copy in Alcott's hand in "Letters, 1870."

83. AJ 45 (1870): 332-33, 433, 439-40; May Alcott to Alcott, June 20, 1870, Louisa May Alcott to the Alcott family, August 2 and September 20, 1870, from copies in Alcott's hand in A. Bronson Alcott, comp., "Letters Received from Louisa and May Abroad, 1870," at Houghton Library, 59M-305 (23); Robert Laird Collier to Alcott, July 14, 1870, at Houghton Library, 59M-312; Mary Newbury Adams to William Torrey Harris, November 27, 1870, and Mary Newbury Adams to Alcott, November 27, 1870, in "Letters, 1870"; Alcott to Mary Newbury Adams, December 1, 1870, in "Letters, 1870."

84. AJ 44 (1869): 394-95; Alcott to William Oldham, April 26, 1869, in "Letters, 1869."

11
Apostle to the West, 1870–77

THE West proved to be a fertile field for Alcott in the 1870s. Three highly successful tours took him to scores of cities throughout the Old Northwest and as far west as Fort Dodge, Iowa. It was a growing, changing, youthful America that Alcott found in his travels. But it was not a disorganized frontier. Even central Iowa had been settled for over a generation, and community institutions had taken firm root. Now the inhabitants sought education and culture; they sought ties with the Eastern literati. Colleges, universities, lyceums, library associations, philosophical and literary clubs were flourishing and proliferating in cities and towns no matter what their size. Westerners were receptive to Alcott because he provided them with culture, with a link to the East and, more important, with reaffirmation of traditional moral and religious values along with an affirmation of free thought and free expression. He seemed to manifest and personify the balance between freedom and authority that was such a problem in a changing, expanding America. Alcott referred to the midwest as his "Bishopric,"[1] and indeed to many people he was a priest, an apostle. For Alcott, as for many other Americans, the West took on a symbolic meaning. It meant progress, hope, and a realization of dreams for himself and his country.

When Alcott first went West in 1853, he carried with him the expectations and preconceptions of a person who had never traveled farther west than New York State. He anticipated finding an untamed wilderness containing scattered enclaves of excitingly energetic but certainly uncultured and undisciplined settlers. Instead, he found a surprising appreciation of Eastern ideas, such as those of Emerson, Parker, and Garrison, and even a surprising willingness to listen to his own conversations. He found the same receptivity during his second trip in 1857-58. "Eastern men of Culture take rank as magi," he said. "Starry Concord rays forth Auroras of Promise to multitudes." The West seemed friendly to the "darling designs of the widest scope," and therefore, he thought, was "truly American" in spirit and deed.[2]

But his 1859 tour changed his opinion. Western cities were less receptive to him. He worried that only the novelty of his conversations explained his earlier successes and that now the novelty had worn off. He was depressed as he peered out his train window on his way to St. Louis. The Illinois landscape appeared "slovenly" and "dismal," with its rude dwellings embedded in prairie mud. "The eye takes flight into the overspreading sky to get relief from the sameness," he complained. Even speech patterns seemed "flattened" and lacking in images for expression. He became concerned that even a generation's residence in the West might have detrimental effects. When he saw the Mississippi River upon his arrival in St. Louis, its promised grandeur escaped him. He could see no basis for its claim to be "father of waters." He felt he had little in common with the "wild life of the West," with its materialism and its "rough ways." It was as though he had been cast on the banks of the Mississippi by some accident, many centuries too soon. He decided that only Henry Thoreau, the "Old Explorer" who celebrated primitive untamed nature, could appreciate the West.[3] In the summer of 1865, the Civil War over and the miseries of his 1859 trip partially forgotten, Alcott began to change his mind. After all, the West had produced Abraham Lincoln, now the martyred hero. Lincoln was the precursor of the "future man," who would surely come from the West rather than from the East. New Englanders, thought Alcott, were "New Englishmen" and not true "Americans." This revitalized ideal of Western potential as well as his interest in the St. Louis philosophers finally convinced him to cast aside his reservations and to try the West again in the spring of 1866. As he headed toward St. Louis he found the landscape just as dismal as before and considered that the faces at the train stations matched the landscape. Yet the prairie had to have some value, he thought, in order to have produced the "native sense and humanity" of Lincoln. And the people, if Harris's friends were good examples, made up for their brusqueness and lack of courtesy by their candor and conviction. He now thought that Easterners could learn a great deal by visiting the West. "The possibilities of this wondrous West are infinite," he claimed," and the thoughts rise naturally out of all limitations into freest expression." His warm reception, his new friends, and his success had shed a new light on the "Great West." Despite his fatigue and illness at the end of the 1866 trip, he was ready to go again that fall. The communication he was maintaining between East and West, he felt, would help free the East from "superstition" and "convention."[4]

The tour of 1866-67 did not dim Alcott's vision of Western greatness, although his journey was tiring and not so successful as he had hoped. His visit to St. Louis confirmed his opinion that the genius of William Torrey Harris could lead to the development of an "American culture," presumably one unstained by European influences and welling up indigenously in the heart of America. How Harris's Hegelianism fitted into this image Alcott did not say. The tour also made Alcott ready to defend the West to those of his Eastern friends who were slow to believe that any good could come from any place west of the Berkshires. He said that those who had the "misfortune of being born with Cambridge eyeglasses" simply could not see so clearly as Westerners could. St. Louis, he thought, was stealing New England's crown. The West was now in the forefront of the popularization of philosophy. The *Journal of Speculative Philosophy* was now overshadowing New England's *Atlantic*

Monthly and *North American Review*. It seemed a silly pretense that a small group of Boston intellectuals should presume to review all of North America anyway. It was also clear to him that the West would be ever more receptive to his ideas than Boston had been or ever would be.[5] He wrote to Harris:

> I find it stimulating and invigorating, this eager and curious West. Unlike our East, which is mostly content with dainty nibble at my things, the western people like a bold bait, and bite hard and ask for more of that sort.[6]

Any thought of the hazards and inconvenience of travel, or the dislike of being away from home and family, dissipated with the success of the 1869-70 tour. Midwestern scenery still failed to impress Alcott, and the cities—Cleveland, Detroit, Chicago—were still "slovenly" despite their "Brute energy." But he cared less for landscape than for a "humane population." Westerners were youthful, vivacious, and hospitable to new ideas. An aging person seemed to become younger in their midst. The West epitomized all that was progressive, purposeful, and enterprising. "It is much to be present at the beginning of things," he exulted, "and share in the work of creation." He believed that he was destined to serve the West as Emerson had served the East. He ventured to criticize his fellow Concordians for their provincialism. Emerson had spurned the West, saying that he felt more at home with Eastern audiences. Alcott thought that such an attitude was only further evidence of Emerson's individualism and exclusiveness. "To him, the continents are but suburbs to his individualism," Alcott said of his friend. Emerson did not seek the personal oneness found in sharing with other people, Alcott thought. He preferred to remain separate, aloof and isolated in his Concord chambers. Thoreau, Hawthorne, and Ellery Channing, Alcott believed, were also victims of provincialism.[7] "Our Eastern scholars should go West," he declared,

> in order to divest themselves of their egotism and breathe the freer fresher air of that section of the country. A six month tour were of more worth and significance than a degree from Harvard or Yale.[8]

On October 26, 1870, Alcott left for the West with his enlarged concept of Western potential. He had no definite engagements, but went ahead on the strength of the previous year's acquaintances. His first stop was Connecticut, where he visited relatives in Wolcott and conversed in Waterbury under the sponsorship of wealthy manufacturer Frederick J. Kingsbury. The venerable editor E. Bronson Cooke admiringly reported the conversation of his famous distant relative in his *Waterbury American*. After a brief visit with his sister Betsey in West Edmeston, New York, Alcott went on to Syracuse, where he spoke from the Unitarian pulpit on Sunday School teaching and met the Syracuse Radical Club for conversation. He then stopped in Rochester, Buffalo, Cleveland, and Elyria to visit friends and to arrange conversations for his return trip.[9]

In Toledo, Ohio, he was once again the guest of Francis Abbot, despite their growing theological differences. He spoke to the Unitarian congregation on the ideal church and conversed twice, though not in his opinion successfully. The opera house rented for the occasion was too large for a parlor conversation, and those attending expected a lecture. His stay in Detroit was much more successful. With the help of Louis Ives, Frances Bagley, and Eliza Leggett, he held five conversations on "Ideals" and another on New England authors, and gave a Sunday lecture on children at W. R. G. Mellen's church.[10]

On November 28 Alcott was again in St. Louis talking with the Hegelians. Harris took time from his busy schedule as superintendent of schools and editor of the *Journal of Speculative Philosophy* to arrange four public conversations. Alcott talked on New England authors and on the meeting of East and West, the latter becoming ever more his theme. He spoke to the students at Anna Brackett's Normal School and visited the high school where Davidson and Snider taught. Letters from Maplewood told of the unexpected death of Anna's husband, John Pratt, but the family advised Alcott to complete his tour. Thus, after talking with Harris once again about a possible philosophical school in Concord, he went on to Bloomington, Illinois, where he encountered heavy rain and an "Egyptian mud from which there is no deliverance." Despite the weather he visited schools, conversed three times, and lectured at the Bloomington Normal School. He found that the Bloomington schools, and those of the West in general, were good, the teaching excellent, and the public willing to adopt improvements.[11]

Alcott's best reception was in Dubuque, Iowa, his next stop. He was welcomed on December 14 by Mary Newbury Adams and her husband, lawyer Austin Adams. Both of them had originally come to Iowa from Vermont and had been educated in the East. Alcott enjoyed his greatest success in the West among transplanted New Englanders like the Adamses. Mary Adams immediately struck Alcott as a fascinating, brilliant woman; she reminded him of Margaret Fuller. She had organized a "Ladies Club" for literary and philosophical conversation, and her husband had organized a men's club called the "Round Table" for the same purpose. For two weeks the Adamses led Alcott to all the centers of culture in Dubuque: the library, the Episcopal Institute, the Ladies Club, the Round Table, the Methodist Church, and the private homes of cultured friends of the Adamses. He was so busy and well entertained that even the sub-zero temperatures did not bother him. Mary Adams praised Alcott in an article in the *Dubuque Evening Journal*. His "ennobling personality" and "invigorating suggestion" were sure to make American homes centers for "refined and elevating influences."[12]

On January 2, 1871, still dreaming of his delightful experiences in Dubuque, Alcott went on to Davenport, Iowa. Judge John F. Dillon, a brother-in-law of Robert Laird Collier, had invited him, and George H. French, ex-mayor of Davenport, gave him lodging and a parlor for conversation. The Iowans continued to keep him busy. In a week he conversed five times, spoke to the children of the home for soldier's orphans, addressed the students of Griswold

College, visited city schools, and illustrated the ideal church for the members of the Unitarian Society. On January 9 he left for Chicago, where Collier had arranged conversations. His Chicago audiences were "mixed" and more interested in "excitement and sensations" than the polite and receptive Iowans. But seven conversations earned one hundred twelve dollars and sent him happily on to Jacksonville, Illinois.[13]

In Jacksonville he was astonished to find devoted students of Plato and an organized Plato Club. Such an interest in ideas did not seem to fit the dullness of the prairie landscape. The Jacksonville Plato Club had been organized in 1860 by Hiram K. Jones, a physician from Virginia. Jones interested Alcott more than any "mind" he had yet encountered in the West. Although he struck Alcott as more a student and an interpreter of idealists than an idealist himself, he was certainly a person with whom one could have "olympian communication." Alcott conversed with the Platonists at the home of Martha D. Wolcott, one of Jones's most zealous disciples. He eagerly outlined his theory of the descent of souls from the Universal to finite matter. The Club members listened with interest and understanding. There was neither the searching skepticism of the St. Louis Hegelians nor the wry indifference of Eastern audiences. Ten days of endless discussion with Plato Club members reminded him of the stimulating atmosphere of the Transcendental Club. At his last meeting with the Club on January 31, he enthusiastically told the members of his plan for a school of philosophy in Concord, clearly hoping that they would be a part of it. The next day he left for Quincy, Illinois, sure that the friendship begun in Jacksonville would endure and that he would return.[14]

Another group of Platonists held forth in Quincy. Their focal point was a woman's organization known as "Friends in Council." This club was founded in 1866 by Sarah Atwater Denman, feminist, tireless organizer of woman's suffrage conventions, and campaigner for improvements in higher education for women. She was a friend of Hiram K. Jones and the members of the Jacksonville Plato Club. The Friends in Council was one of the first women's clubs in the country and the prototype for similar organizations in Berlin, Wisconsin; Marquette, Michigan; Burlington and Rutland, Vermont; and Lawrence, Kansas. Mrs Denman and her wealthy husband, Matthew B. Denman, were Alcott's hosts and they also helped arrange conversations. Quincy, a city of thirty thousand inhabitants, was receptive to Alcott's discussion of New England authors. And the Friends in Council and the Quincy Literary Society enjoyed his discussion of personalism, genesis, and lapse. Nearly one hundred people attended his Literary Society conversation. These Westerners, Alcott thought, were able to engage in true conversation without the "impertinent criticism" that so often confounded him in the East.[15]

On February 10 Alcott returned to Chicago, where he spoke to the children of Charles William Wendte's congregation, dined with Robert Collyer, and met novelist Bret Harte. He conversed with the fifty families of the Riverside

Improvement Company, a homestead association that sold landscaped suburban lots to low-income families. Further invitations to speak awaited him, but growing concern about his family—his fatherless grandsons both had scarlet fever—caused him to decline. He headed East on February 16, stopping briefly in Kalamazoo, Ann Arbor, and Detroit, Michigan, to see friends and make future arrangements. He then rode the train through Canada to Buffalo, where he spoke on the ideal church to the Unitarian congregation of Abby's cousin Frederick Frothingham.[16]

After single conversations in Rochester and Syracuse, Alcott arrived in Concord on March 3. He had been away for four months. The tour had been his most successful yet. He had received an enthusiastic reception everywhere and a total of eight hundred seven dollars. Consequently, he overwhelmed his Concord friends with such a roseate picture of the West that it rendered Emerson, despite his hearty sympathy for Alcott's purposes, a bit skeptical.[17]

Writing projects and the demands of his family kept Alcott from making his planned westward excursion in the fall of 1871. He was busy with "Concord Days" and with a new edition of *Record of a School*. Publisher Thomas Niles of Roberts Brothers thought the *Record* would be a timely account of the "real Plumfield," corresponding to the fictional school described in Louisa's recently published *Little Men*. Alcott also hoped to publish notes of his conversations, a new edition of *Tablets*, and several short articles for the *Journal of Speculative Philosophy*.[18]

But he did not lose his enthusiasm for the West. "*Westernize* is a phrase meaning *progress*," he said. He shrugged off news of the disastrous Chicago fire of October 1871 with the assurance that the city would rise quickly from its ashes and exemplify the wonderful vigor and enterprise of the West. Contacts with Western friends continued. The effusive Mary Adams wisely warned Alcott not to compare her with Margaret Fuller. It was not his genius, but rather Emerson's, she said, to tell people what they are. Alcott's power, she maintained, was to tell people what they might become, to reveal to people their "unawakened being." Louis Ives of Detroit visited Concord to paint portraits of both Emerson and Alcott. William Torrey Harris wrote that his friend General H. N. Buford of Chicago was ecstatic about Alcott's success in the West. Sarah Denman visited Concord in August 1871, and offered to buy Hawthorne's Wayside as a summer residence in order to be closer to the influence of the Concordians. Frances Bagley also came and said that she would buy Wayside if Mrs. Denman did not.[19]

Alcott finally convinced the doubting Emerson that he should to go to Jacksonville, Quincy, and Dubuque, where he met Dr. Jones, Mrs. Denman, Mrs. Adams, and their friends. He was duly impressed, although Mary Adams noted that, unlike Alcott, Emerson preferred the hotel instead of her home, and that he did not stay in Dubuque long enough to allow the "free play of spirit." In May 1872 Mrs Adams visited Concord and proposed a fall tour for both Alcott and Emerson, to begin in Dubuque. Alcott's widespread contacts—Frances Bagley in Detroit, George French in Davenport, Sarah

Denman in Quincy, Dr. Jones in Jacksonville, Harris in St. Louis, Thomas
Kean in Buffalo, and Charles Mills in Syracuse—promised to make all the
arrangements. Alcott was enthusiastic; Emerson was not.[20]

Alcott's Western contacts kept alive his idea of establishing a philosophical
academy in Concord. In July 1871 he had a dream of a conversation with Dr.
Channing, in which Alcott proposed to his erstwhile mentor a summer school
for young men and women in "classic" Concord, away from the "paralyzing
atmosphere" of Cambridge. In the dream Channing agreed to the desirability
of such a plan. The dreamed of project became more real and concrete when
the Denmans and Bagleys suggested purchasing Wayside. Alcott's old house
could serve as a gathering place for Western participants in the Academy. Mrs.
Adams encouraged the idea; the Bagleys offered to supply money and
students. Alcott discussed the practical aspects of the school with Quincy,
Illinois, businessman Samuel H. Emery, who visited Concord in the summer
of 1872. Alcott suggested that Concordians should make their community
more attractive to visitors by establishing a good boarding house. The "New
Academy," he said, would inculcate the "New Divinity." Such an institution
would keep Concord abreast of the "advancing spirit of the time." And it
would symbolize the joining of hands east and west.[21]

In November 1872 Alcott was ready to pack his carpetbag and head West
once again. He was more certain than ever that his style of parlor conversation
was fast becoming an American institution. The affectionate appreciation by
his Western friends, who kept begging for his return, gratified him, especially
since he felt Bostonians were more and more considering him an "old story."
This tour promised to give him a chance to promote his "New Academy,"
which was fast becoming an obsession with him. The work that had kept him
in Concord the previous winter was finished. *Concord Days* had been
published on September 21, 1872, after a full winter and spring of
uninterrupted work. It was a book much like *Tablets*, but written in diary
form. Hence it better captured the atmosphere of spontaneity that Alcott
sought than did *Tablets*. Included in *Concord Days* were characterizations of
famous Concordians, remarks on Alcott's favorite authors, reports of past
conversations, and thoughts on the ideal church. But it contained much less of
the theory of genesis and lapse, which had confounded readers of *Tablets*.
Alcott spent more time talking concretely of people and things, with less airy
speculation. The reviews were good, and the book sold better than *Tablets*.
Alcott hoped that his Western tour would provide materials for a companion
volume to *Concord Days* to be called "Western Evenings." The new edition of
Record of a School was yet unfinished. Elizabeth Peabody was miffed at
Alcott's attempt to publish the *Record* again without consulting her. She
wanted to add a new introduction explaining that her views had been modified
by her acquaintance with the ideas of the German founder of kindergartens,
Friedrich Wilhelm August Froebel. Froebel's systematic, structured approach
to children's activities and to classroom discipline had led her to reject Alcott's
less methodical program, although she admitted that Alcott's ideas were

theoretically and psychologically correct. Alcott accepted her conversion to Froebel and generally agreed with Froebel's methods, but he wanted no such allusions in the introduction to the *Record*. At length Alcott agreed to include an appendix by Peabody, and the book was sent to the printers. But in the end Alcott and Louisa refused to publish it with any qualifying statements, much to Peabody's chagrin. She then refused to consent to the publication without the appendix, so nothing was done.[22]

The wrangle over *Record of a School* was forgotten as Alcott headed west on November 8, 1872. He stopped first in Syracuse to stay with Charlotte Wilkinson, daughter of Samuel J. May. May had died in July 1871 and Alcott had spoken at his funeral. Abby had been grief stricken at her brother's death, and Alcott greatly missed the man who had given his family more sympathy and direct aid than anyone except Emerson. During this visit to Syracuse Alcott spoke at May's former church, met the Radical Club for conversation, and addressed a temperance meeting at the Town Hall. He then left for Buffalo, where he and Thomas Kean arranged conversations for the return trip.[23]

He bypassed Cleveland, that "puritan city" which had given him a less-than-flattering reception during his last visit in 1870. In Detroit he called on Frances Bagley, whose husband, wealthy banker and manufacturer John T. Bagley, had just been elected governor of Michigan on the Republican ticket. Mrs. Bagley agreed to arrange conversations for the return trip. Moses Coit Tyler promised the same in Ann Arbor. On November 16 Alcott was in Dubuque with the Adamses. They had planned meetings with the Round Table and the Ladies Conversational Club and were arranging for Alcott to visit other cities in Iowa, using Dubuque as his base. They asked H. P. Ward, a friend and a member of the Dubuque Board of Education, to schedule an Alcott lecture at the high school. Alcott jumped at the chance to challenge the students to cultivate their minds as internal springs of ideas and to avoid rote memorization of facts. A steady stream of interested friends came to the Adams's home to hear Alcott describe his peddling experiences and the founding of Fruitlands. His audience was amused. He was now able to laugh at his own foibles, although he had not forgotten the serious meaning that Fruitlands had for him. Alcott was sure that his conversations had the effect, in Dubuque at least, of bringing people together into unexpected sympathy and of fostering a positive social culture. His Dubuque friends agreed, and they topped off their enthusiastic reception with a surprise party for him on November 29, his seventy-third birthday. The new walking stick they gave him fittingly symbolized Alcott's peripatetic ministry to the West.[24]

On December 3 Alcott was on his way to central Iowa. The influential Austin Adams had contacted his friends in Waterloo, Fort Dodge, Des Moines, and Iowa City. Before the year's end Alcott had conversed in each of these communities as well as in Marshalltown, Davenport, and Grinnell. In Des Moines lawyer Galusha Parsons introduced him to the members of the Iowa Supreme Court, many of whom subsequently attended his conversations. But the judges were not so gracious as their distinguished presence might have suggested. Parsons expressed annoyance at the "want of delicacy" in Alcott's practice of asking his audience for voluntary contributions rather than advertising a fixed admission price. Judge Chester C. Cole gladly crowded his parlors for a conversation and then proceeded to engage Alcott in a battle for center of attention. At Grinnell and Iowa City Alcott met antagonism toward his supposedly heretical religious opinions. His reception at Grinnell College was as cold as the minus twenty-three degree temperature. The opinions of these college officials, Alcott decided, were "less liberal than is befitting of this free western population." Some of Iowa City's orthodox were disturbed by Alcott's visit, but nevertheless he was able to speak at the Congregational Church, to converse at Irving Hall on the Iowa University campus, and to meet University President George Thacher and several members of the faculty. On the whole Iowa City was a hospitable place.[25]

Alcott spent New Year's Day at George French's in Davenport. The river town was less enthusiastic about him this time, but Alcott blamed the extreme cold, the holidays, and the lack of "New England spirit." For all of his celebrations of Westerners, he carefully noted that settlers from New England were largely responsible for the growth and progress evident in the West. The West might have been outstripping New England, but only the legacy of New England enabled it to do so. Alcott held only two conversations in Davenport and visited a high school across the Mississippi River in Moline, Illinois, before journeying to Mount Pleasant, Iowa, some sixty miles southwest of Davenport. He found this little village to be pleasant enough, but he could see no mountain. The people of Mount Pleasant, he found, had largely come from New England, thus explaining their receptivity to his message. Six hundred high school students gathered to hear him tell about Louisa. Another large group assembled for his January 13 conversation on New England authors. Interested citizens talked of forming a "Conversation Club," and the local newspaper was filled with paeans to the "best conversationalist in the country."[26]

In Burlington, Iowa, thirty miles east of Mount Pleasant, Alcott found a warm reception from former Concordian Ripley Bartlett, who promised to arrange conversations while Alcott was in Muscatine, fifty miles to the north. Several citizens had formally invited Alcott to Muscatine, but he found that arrangements had been in "incompetent hands" and that few people attended his conversation. He found it true in Muscatine, as in many Western cities, that frequent prayer meetings tended to diminish literary audiences. Fortunately, Bartlett had done his work well in Burlington. On January 21 over one hundred people came to hear him describe the essentials of character. The next day the children of the public schools gave him thunderous applause for his description of his youth and that of Louisa. Mrs. James W. Grimes, whose husband had been a United States Senator, offered a one thousand dollar scholarship for Alcott's proposed Academy in Concord.[27]

A similar reception awaited Alcott in Keokuk, Iowa, where he arrived on

January 27. The Reverend Edwin C. L. Browne offered his pulpit for an Alcott description of the ideal church. Three conversations were well-attended. Again he visited schools where he felt his message was doing even more good than it was in parlor conversations. On February 3 he was once again in Quincy, Illinois, meeting the Plato Club and the Friends in Council. Sarah Denman offered a scholarship for the Concord Academy, although she had decided not to buy Wayside.[28]

After a week with the appreciative people of Quincy, Alcott left for St. Louis. He had intended to be in St. Louis long before, but as he told Harris, the appetite for philosophy in Iowa was so strong that he found it difficult to get away on schedule. The craving was so great, he said, that he felt unable to meet the demand, and he hoped that younger devotees would follow in his footsteps to complete the work. In St. Louis he visited the high school, conversed on New England authors, and talked at length with Harris and Snider. But his visit was cut short by news from Concord that Anna was perilously ill with pneumonia. On February 14 he left for Concord, bypassing scheduled stops in Jacksonville, Galesburg, Bloomington, and Chicago, Illinois; Lansing, Jackson, Ann Arbor, and Detroit, Michigan; Cleveland, Toledo, Sandusky, and Medina, Ohio; and Buffalo, Rochester, Elmira, and Syracuse, New York. When he arrived in Concord on February 17, he found to his relief that Anna was out of danger. His trip had been successful. Receipts totaled five hundred fifty-eight dollars and would certainly have been greater had he not been called home so soon. He had had a delightful time. More and more he felt at home in the West and less so in the East.[29]

Alcott had every intention of going West again in the fall of 1873. His Western friends encouraged him. Supporters in Mount Pleasant, Iowa, wrote that the planned Conversation Club had indeed been formed, and that members had read from *Tablets* at the first meeting. Mary Adams assured him that his tours were the beginning of permanent educational institution. She reported that Iowa City had, like Mount Pleasant, formed a conversation club. Several of his Western acquaintances asked him to return. The Adamses offered to contact friends on the West Coast about prospective conversations. Martha Wolcott wrote of the reverence in which the Jacksonville Plato Club held him. Nothing, she said, could compensate for his not visiting them 1872-73. Despite all this encouragement, unforeseen circumstances interfered with Alcott's plans. Financial panic struck the United States in 1873, and the consequent depression made lecture tours risky. In November Ednah Cheney wrote from St. Louis, in the midst of her tour, that economic troubles would certainly hurt his chances. Mrs. Adams warned that lecturers were not doing well west of Chicago. Louisa's income was uncertain because the railroad stock in which she had invested suffered from the depression. Alcott wisely decided to postpone another trip until the economy improved.[30]

But there was much to keep Alcott busy. Soon after his return from the West in February 1873, he received a letter from the Reverend Samuel Orcutt, Congregational minister in Wolcott, Connecticut. Orcutt asked for brief biographical sketches of Alcott and his cousin William, to be included in a proposed "History of Wolcott." The book was to be published in connection with the Wolcott centennial celebration scheduled for September. Orcutt offered no financial remuneration, but that did not matter. Alcott beamed with joy at this coveted recognition by his home town. Immediately, he made plans to go to Wolcott in order to consult Orcutt about the history and the celebration. He contacted William Alcott's son, William Penn Alcott, to get further family information. In June he bundled up twenty years' worth of genealogical and autobiographical materials and hauled them with him to Connecticut. Orcutt was pleased, though doubtless overwhelmed by Alcott's enthusiasm. He talked with Alcott, drove him to the Alcott family homestead, arranged conversations, and asked Alcott to speak to his Sunday School about life in Wolcott in the early nineteenth century. Upon his return to Concord, Alcott eagerly wrote to his sister, brothers, nieces, and nephews about a family reunion in Wolcott at the time of the centennial celebration. He managed to persuade Ellery Channing to write a poem for the occasion. Frank Sanborn agreed to write the sketch of Alcott's life for Orcutt's "History." On September 8 Alcott was off to Wolcott to attend the celebration and to address the gathering on the social customs of his boyhood. His brother Chatfield and family joined him at the family reunion, and did his nephew Edward Gaylord and his niece Jennie Brown. Cousins Edward and Jennie had never met, although they were the children of Alcott's sisters, the twins Pamila and Pamela. Alcott, always sentimental about the importance of family ties, had engaged in extensive detective work to find Mrs. Brown, whose parents had died when she was a child, leaving her with no knowledge of her ancestry. For Alcott the celebration was a joyous occasion. He was an honored and respected man among his numerous relatives and in his home territory.[31]

Opportunities for local lectures and conversations also filled Alcott's time. In March and April 1873 the Harvard Divinity School students asked him to give a series of conversations. He presented his theory of genesis, expecting appreciative comments but getting only curious bewilderment. He decided that the students were unable to free themselves from the "senses and understanding." Other speaking opportunities came from the Women's Physiological Society, the New England Historical and Genealogical Society, and the students of Tufts College. He even presented one of the lectures in the now annual Horticultural Hall lecture series. In the spring of 1874 he helped organize a philosophical club, with membership by invitation only, for "select conversation on the highest themes." "Our Club," as it was called, designated Alcott, the eldest member, as its leader. Alcott hoped it would become the nucleus for his new academy. The club met in April, May, and June with discussions led by Alcott, Emerson, and Cyrus Bartol. But like the Town and Country Club, Our Club failed to attract lasting interest and soon dissolved.[32]

As always, Alcott welcomed any chance to share hs educational views with others. In June 1874 he spoke by invitation to the Worcester County

Association of Teachers on methods of teaching. Elizabeth Peabody, forgetting her spat with Alcott, asked him to visit a kindergarten in Cambridge to converse and tell stories to the children. Peabody had her disagreements with Alcott, but she never doubted his ability in the classroom. The new edition of *Record of a School* was finally published on February 25, 1874, adding to Alcott's hopes that he would be a lasting influence on education. Peabody had reconciled herself to the new edition and wrote to Alcott of her happiness that it was published at long last. She signed her letter "your old friend who has always kept the faith." The reviews of the *Record* were favorable, recommending the book as a source of inspiration to all educators, though not as a manual to be followed step by step. The controversy that had once accompanied the *Record* and the Temple School was no more.[33]

Public recognition became ever more common for Alcott. The new edition of Evart and George Duyckinck's *Cyclopedia of American Literature* contained a sketch of him. The *New York Independent* published transcripts of his conversations. Keningale Cook, an English writer and educational enthusiast, wrote to him for advice, praised *Record of a School*, and offered to be an agent to promote Alcott's ideas on education in England. Especially significant to Alcott was his election as an honorary member of Phi Beta Kappa at Harvard in June 1874. Such recognition was a gratifying compliment to a man who had had no formal university education.[34]

Despite the accolades and appreciation in the East, Alcott was certain that the West was his "fairest field." The West, he believed, was shaping the "Ideal Republic," while New England lived in the past. In September 1874 he began talking of another Western tour. He sent circulars to over seventy people advertising his coming. The tour, he hoped, would both promote the new academy and raise money for much-needed repairs on Orchard House. On October 1 he began what would be his longest trip to date.[35]

He went first to Connecticut, to visit relatives and to converse in Waterbury on his theory of genesis. He then headed directly for St. Louis, arriving there on October 8. Harris, Brokmeyer, and Snider met with him as before. But Alcott was still unable to respect Brokmeyer fully. All the Hegelians, but especially Brokmeyer, disturbed him by relying on reason as their sole authority and not valuing the emotions and the affections. "I defend the Heart," said Alcott, "and marry the head and heart in my philosophy." As always, Harris graciously arranged a series of public conversations that were well attended, and Alcott enjoyed opportunities to visit schools and to preach in the pulpit of an Independent congregation.[36]

On October 22 Alcott left for Jacksonville, Illinois. Dr. Jones and the Plato Club greeted him eagerly and arranged several private and public conversations. Between philosophical discussions Alcott visited the high school where William Torrey Harris's brother, David H. Harris, was superintendent, the Asylum for the Blind, the Jacksonville Female Institute, and the Asylum for the Deaf and Dumb. His ten-day stay was filled with Plato and plans for the new academy. Jones and his disciples still bothered Alcott a little by what he felt was their lack of "pure idealism." They would not accept his concept of lapse, believing instead that the lapse was predestined and independent of human choice. Thus he considered their interpretation to be narrow, and he detected a tendency on their part to avoid views differing from their own. Nevertheless, in all his travels he had not found a like familiarity with Plato. Dr. Jones and his friends carried the spirit of Plato into their lives as no one else he knew. Surely, they would make a substantial contribution to the founding of the new academy.[37]

In Quincy, his next stop, he stayed with the Denmans for a week and spoke several times to the Friends in Council. Frederick L. Hosmer invited him to speak on the ideal church to his Unitarian congregation and to an organization of city ministers. Samuel H. Emery, the merchant-philosopher, invited Alcott to meet his Plato Club. Alcott enjoyed doing so, of course, but he felt that Emery was too critical and dogmatic and lacking in true idealism. On November 10 Alcott headed for Iowa, where he spent the remainder of 1874 visiting Keokuk, Burlington, Mount Pleasant, Fairfield, Agency City, Oskaloosa, Des Moines, Humboldt, Fort Dodge, Iowa City, Davenport, and Dubuque. Furiously attempting to satisfy the craving for philosophy, he gave scores of conversations and lectures, spoke at Sunday services, visited schools, and socialized with friends old and new.[38]

Devoted followers in Mount Pleasant proudly introduced Alcott to their Conversational Club, of which he was the progenitor. The students of Iowa Wesleyan College heard him speak on the meaning of worship, and his hosts in Mount Pleasant, Mr. and Mrs. W. R. Cole, listened with fascination as he described Fruitlands. In Agency City, an old Indian post of seven hundred people five miles east of Ottumwa, he spoke to a Thanksgiving union meeting of the several churches in town, where he was introduced as "Brother Alcott." It was, he thought, a "primitive neighborhood." Friends in Fort Dodge had also founded a conversational organization since Alcott's last visit, which they had duly named the Alcott Club. In Humboldt, Alcott became good friends with S. H. Taft, the enterprising founder of the town and the president of Humboldt College. Taft combined an avid interest in culture with his more mundane interests in mills, farms, and railroads. Famous New Englanders fascinated Taft—he had named the streets of Humboldt after Emerson, Parker, Phillips, Garrison, and others—and he gladly organized conversations for Alcott and arranged for him to speak to his eighty college students. Alcott conversed in Iowa City with the help of Professor William G. Hammond. Hammond also permitted him to visit classes at Iowa University in Latin, law, physics, and physiology. Alcott knew very little about the subject material, but he willingly lectured the students on the proper methods of study.[39]

He spent the Christmas and New Year holidays in Dubuque, although Mrs. Adams's illness prevented his staying at her home and holding his usual large number of conversations with the receptive people of the city. On January 4 he was off to Rockford, Illinois, where he held one conversation, and to Beloit, Wisconsin, twenty miles from Rockford, where he met President

Aaron Lucius Chapin of Beloit College. Chapin was cordial, but did not care to have Alcott's ideas infect his student body. With the temperature dropping to near minus twenty, Alcott traveled to Broadhead, Wisconsin, and from there five miles into the country by sleigh to visit his elderly cousin Denison Alcott, a retired minister and a former member of the state legislature. Denison undoubtedly wondered what powerful force drove his equally ancient cousin so far from home in the middle of winter. But on January 9 Bronson battled the cold and wind again to make his way back to Rockford, where he lectured on the ideal church before five hundred members of an independent congregation and again before a crowd of one thousand gathered at Brown Hall.[40]

In Janesville, Wisconsin, he met Unitarian minister Jenkin Lloyd Jones, who agreed to write to friends in other parts of the state concerning Alcott's tour. Jones's efforts resulted in a trip to Monroe, where Alcott addressed the high school students and spoke on Concord authors at the Universalist church, and to Whitewater, where he conversed on methods of teaching, spoke on worship at the Universalist Church, and visited the public schools. He then returned to Janesville, where Jones sponsored conversations and introduced Alcott to the proponents of free religion and reform in Wisconsin. Alcott was impressed enough to subscribe to Jones's reform newspaper, the *Liberal Worker*.[41]

By the end of January Alcott had conversed and lectured in Baraboo and Whitewater again, visited schools in Madison and in Oshkosh, and called on his brother-in-law Ransom Gaylord, who had moved West after the death of his first wife, Pamila Alcott. On February 1 Alcott was in Milwaukee staying with the Congregational minister J. L. Dudley, who impressed him as a devout man of vigorous intellect, a Western version of Horace Bushnell. Dudley gladly permitted Alcott to address his congregation on the ideal church. Alcott, Dudley, and Alcott's friend and disciple Charles Mills of Syracuse engaged in lengthy discussions of the Trinity, of personalism, and of the need for mystery in religion. Mrs. Marion V. Dudley thought that Alcott and Mills were prophets of a new age. One hundred women of the Young Ladies College were equally fascinated when Alcott told them about Louisa's career.[42]

From Milwaukee Alcott returned to Madison, where Professor William F. Allen had arranged conversations and an address at the Young Ladies College. Had he found the right contacts Alcott no doubt would have attempted to find an audience at the University of Wisconsin. Inexplicably no such contacts appeared, and he rarely tried to sell his wares without introduction and sponsorship. But he was able to speak at the Congregational Church, and he closed his highly successful venture into "fresh and fertile" Wisconsin with a two-hour conversation on social life held at the state capitol. On February 9 he left for Chicago and called on Harris's friend General H. N. Buford, who had praised Alcott's conversations before and now promised to arrange more of them. Buford was a man of considerable influence. He spoke to Potter Palmer, owner of the famous Palmer House, and arranged for Alcott's room rate to be reduced by one dollar a night. Alcott also found the Palmer House open to his conversation on ideals. Buford's friends enabled Alcott to speak on New England authors before five hundred people at .the Philosophical Society of Chicago, where he drew a larger audience than any previous speaker in its lecture series. Wealthy socialite Kate Doggett, a member of the Philosophical Society, asked Alcott to converse with the seventy-five women of the Fortnightly Club, of which she was president. Charles William Wendte, a previous acquaintance of Alcott, asked him to speak to his congregation on worship.[43]

Alcott conversed several more times in Chicago, once in Evanston, Illinois, and twice in Bloomington, before falling victim to a heavy cold on March 1. He cut short other planned engagements and began his journey home. Yet his illness did not prevent his stopping on the way in Detroit, Cleveland, and Akron for conversations and Sunday lectures. Finally his cold made him unfit for meeting the public and was bordering on a dangerous illness, so he chose not to converse in Buffalo, Syracuse, or Albany. He arrived in Concord on April 1. His receipts totaled eight hundred dollars, and he felt that he could not have passed six months more pleasantly. And prospects were good for future tours. A wealthy Kenosha, Wisconsin, merchant, H. M. Simmons, offered to take charge of plans for Alcott's tours and to establish a lecture bureau. Such support promised a secure means to back his "ministry" and to ensure the spreading of the "new divinity" and the "new literature." Alcott's Eastern ideas would supplement the work of "bright and bold" Westerners like Dudley, Jones, and Wendte. There was a transplanted New England in the West, he told his Concord friends, a new New England that in many ways was a vast improvement over the old. The West would lead the East, he said. "Let it learn its mission and leap forward in its youthful might and hopefulness, without measuring its steps or checking its speed by our slower and cautious notions."[44]

Alcott was never precise in the expression his ideas and was even less so in explaining the purpose of his message to the West. To be sure, he considered his tours a ministry and the area encompassed by his travels his "bishoprick." But he never fully explained in his diary, though it may have been clear in his mind, just what good his ministry would do for the people he encountered. He talked endlessly about progress, about the "new literature," and about the "new divinity." But these vague concepts, although they were exhilarating and hopeful and evoked strong emotional commitment, lacked concrete definition and explanation. Even in his early years as a reformer at the Temple, at Fruitlands, and at abolitionist conventions, Alcott's concepts of "reform" and "progress" had consisted of emotion-laden phrases defying precise definition. His specific proposals for the classroom or for family life had encompassed only part of what he meant by reform and progress; they had only hinted at the larger meaning. Of course, in those early years he had had a clearer view of those things which inhibited progress: chattel slavery in the South, dullness and routine in the classroom, antagonism toward new ideas by those in power, formalism in the churches, and popular interest in material gain rather than spiritual enlightenment. The contrast he saw between his ideal of the potential of human nature and the obvious failings of individuals and institutions had been greater then. His heightened sense of what was wrong with American society had made him iconoclastic, rebellious, and an outspoken proponent of all sorts of specific reforms.

Alcott was a far different person when he addressed Westerners in the 1870s. There was no bitter rhetoric, no talk of an apocalyptic battle with the forces of evil. Indeed, when Alcott met former abolitionist Parker Pillsbury in Chicago in 1875, he was irritated at Pillsbury's continuing radicalism. Pillsbury was a "literalist," he said, and not an "idealist." Alcott engaged in few hostile attacks against ideas and institutions anymore. Rather, he confidently asserted the ideas he believed to be true and above debate. As a result, Westerners praised Alcott's suggestiveness, his charm, his inspiration, his serenity, his ability to uplift, and his ability to stimulate. He conveyed a profound assurance that he had discovered a paradise within.[45] One reporter summarized a common Western impression:

> The sweet, kindly and tender hearted iconoclasm of the man whose life seems to have been a continual benediction, appears like the only true doctrine, and one is led to believe that philosophy that results in such perfect living cannot be wholly bad or false.[46]

Thus his influence was as he had hoped: like the sun rather than like the wind—penetrating, healthful, but not destructive.[47]

One of Alcott's favorite topics, and probably the most popular of his conversations and lectures in Western cities, was New England authors. If nothing else, he provided a literary and philosophical link between East and West. However advanced the West was, it would benefit, he thought, from an acquaintance with the literature of the East. Emerson, Thoreau, Hawthorne, Ellery Channing, Fuller, Lowell, Longfellow, Holmes, Whittier, and Whitman offered much that transcended regional distinctions. He characterized his friends as skillfully as he had done in some of his best writing in *Concord Days*. He told of the Emerson who shunned publicity, loved the country, and preferred staying home. Thoreau, said Alcott, was "one of those Sledge hammer fellows who generally knocked one's ideas to pieces, and yet did it in such a humorous way that people used to like it so well that they would ask him to do it again." And Hawthorne was "the most diffident of men," Alcott claimed, "as coy as a maiden, he could only be won by some cunning artifice, his reserve was so habitual, his isolation so entire, the solitude so vast."[48]

One clear element of Alcott's message to the West was his theory of education. He jumped at every chance to visit schools, enter the classroom, and discuss with teachers his principles and methods. His Western friends were eager to listen. They heard him present all the ideas and techniques that he had developed in Cheshire, in Boston, and in Concord. But especially did Alcott stress the importance of a coherent philosophy of education. The development of thought, the cultivation of ideas, and the formation of character were, as always, his chief goals as an educator. Education for Alcott primarily meant moral culture. Such moral culture, he told his listeners, began in the home and extended to the whole community through the agency of the school. The purpose of education was the development of individual creativity and individual virtue, and its result was the cohesive, spiritually alive neighborhood and community.[49]

Occasionally, Alcott talked to his Western audiences about temperament, complexion, and race. He still held his peculiar views about the influence of hereditary characteristics on human development, which directly clashed with his faith in education and his belief in free will. Apparently, he did not see the contradiction and hence felt no call to reconcile it. "We are," he said, "with slight deviations, copies of our ancestors. Family traits descend from generation to generation overriding climate, callings, intermarriages, culture." But other ideas were more important and better remembered than his ideas on heredity. In every city or town that offered him a pulpit—and that was most of them—Alcott outlined his captivating vision of the New Church. Freedom and spontaneity in worship were his watchwords. Speaking would be conversational. Freshness, variety, and free expression would replace encrusted traditions and ceremonies. Inclusion of the Scriptures and the faith of all humanity would put an end to narrow and divisive sectarianism. Few things were more important to Alcott than making his Western friends aware of the true meaning of freedom of religion.[50]

The closest Alcott came to defining precisely his purpose in the West, and also the closest he came to bitter conflict like that of old, was in his attempt to spread idealism in the face of the growing influence of Darwinian naturalism. His discomfort with Francis Abbot and the free religionists arose from the rapidly growing naturalistic sentiment in the Radical Club, in the *Index*, and among ministers in "free" congregations. His friends Thomas Wentworth Higginson, John Weiss, Octavius B. Frothingham, and William J. Potter had all been tainted, he felt, by the "negations" of Huxley, Darwin, and Spencer. The Free Congregational Society of Florence, Massachusetts, which had first introduced him to free religion, now, he believed, lacked openness to idealism. The Society's new Cosmian Hall, at the dedication of which Alcott spoke in February 1874, was a model of design and construction for other churches, he thought, but unfortunately it now housed speakers with "shallow scientific notions" empty of spirituality.[51]

Nearly everywhere he went on his Western tours he encountered Darwinism. In Syracuse, Cleveland, Sandusky, Detroit, Chicago, St. Louis, Quincy, Fort Dodge, and Iowa City he battled clergymen, traveling lecturers, college professors, and attendants at his conversations who espoused various forms of Darwinism. Some gave a strictly scientific explanation of Darwin's theory of evolution. Others advocated a kind of religion based on a teleological Spencerian version of Darwinism. In all cases Alcott countered with his own idea of spiritual genesis. Alcott acknowledged that Darwin was a legitimate natural philosopher. But he felt that Darwin restricted his explorations and investigations to only one aspect of life: material nature. Darwin talked of process and ignored genesis. He ignored the true origins of life in the supernatural. Alcott's concept of genesis also involved a process, but one of descent instead of ascent. Lower animals and the inanimate external world, said Alcott, resulted from human descent from the Universal Spirit. The free will of souls to choose good or evil was the vital force determining the nature of the universe. Human beings did not, Alcott asserted, ascend from lower beings by the evolutionary process of natural selection. Rather, they pre-existed as souls, as spirit, prior to an evolutionary descent into nature. Alcott had stood Darwin's evolutionary theory on its head and added a supernatural teleology. It did seem to Alcott that Darwin and the Darwinians were raising the fundamental questions of the time. His own theory of genesis, he felt, led directly to equally fundamental answers to those questions. His job was to synthesize Darwinism and Platonism. "The Descent of souls, though common to Platonism and Christianity, finds its counterpart in the new doctrines of the Darwinians, and to correlate and interpret these appears to be the problem of the great thinkers of our time."[52]

Alcott's objection to Darwinism and the naturalistic determinism that resulted from it was that it robbed human beings of free will, of a choice in their own destiny. Naturalism, Alcott felt, left humans with no personality. It rendered them captives to impersonal forces, devoid of conscience and under the sway of fate. "The Forces must surrender to Ideas," he declared, "mechanism to intelligence, thus overbridging matter with Personality." All those who relied strictly on scientific investigation, he claimed, would lose the "mysteries of life." They would have no concept of that spiritual essence that lay beyond the grasp of reason, subject to intuition alone. "Science is shallow devoid of philosophy," he said, "and lifeless without religion." The free religionists who had turned to naturalism were just "critics of religion" and were not truly religious themselves. Darwinism produced a "lurking atheism," and those who accepted Darwinism could not escape the dreadful emptiness of that unbelief. "Any faith declaring a divorce from the supernatural, and seeking to prop itself upon *Nature* alone," said Alcott, "falls short of satisfying the deepest needs of humanity."[53]

In part at least, Alcott considered his mission to the West to be that of stemming the tide of materialism in its most recent form of Darwinian naturalism. There was plenty of evidence of a strong reaction against materialism in the West. Among the forces of hope and enlightenment Alcott counted the St. Louis philosophers, the various Plato clubs, the *Journal of Speculative Philosophy*, and the enthusiastic reception of his own conversations. Correspondence with Thomas M. Johnson, the young prosecuting attorney of Osceola, Missouri, confirmed Alcott's faith that there were budding idealists ready to gather about his banner. Johnson wrote of his avid interest in Plato and his desire to write something to further the cause of idealistic philosophy. Alcott's unconquerable optimism assured him that the present materialism was a temporary phenomenon that would cleanse the atmosphere and prepare the way for idealism. His own mission was to encourage that process.[54]

Alcott's battle against Darwinian naturalism only occasionally involved direct and hostile confrontation. Most often Alcott challenged by a positive statement of his idealism. He disliked debating or disputing with anyone. He simply proclaimed as truth his concept of personality. Personality, he told his Western listeners, was the spiritual aspect of human nature, embracing the ideas of freedom, will, responsibility, and creativity. Any theology that did not include the intuition of divine personality was, he believed, "shallow" and "inoperative." Only by means of intuition or "divination" could human beings free themselves from symbols and types—that is, material nature—and ascend to the world of the spirit.[55]

During his Western excursions Alcott discussed his personal theism again and again under the topic "immortality." Questions of life and death maintained the interest of his audience, thus providing a captivating motif for the presentation of his core philosophy. Death, he said, was merely a transition, a slight change of condition but not of essence. The unifying link between life and death was a consciousness of personality. Such consciousness of the union of the soul with the divine spirit was proof itself of immortality. But only through intuition did this consciousness come about. Only an immediate perception of the soul's spiritual identity gave assurance of immortality. Alcott supplemented his conversations by writing several articles on the subjects of personality, genesis and lapse, and immortality for the *Journal of Speculative Philosophy* in the early 1870s. Then, in 1877, he included many of these same ideas in his book *Table Talk*. He intended to spread the message of idealism as widely as possible with the pen as well as the spoken word.[56]

Westerners, at least those who were predisposed to agree with him, were enthusiastically receptive to Alcott's idealism. His audiences welcomed his reminders of the reality of spiritual things. They appreciated his "religious warmth" and the beauty of the ideal world he opened before them.[57] In large degree Alcott represented a resolution of tensions in American—especially Western—thought and culture. He personified a reconciliation between freedom and authority, between mobility and stability, and between desire for change and progress and respect for long-revered values and traditions. Change had confronted Alcott throughout his life. Now the focus of change was the growing, expanding West. And Alcott brought to the midst of it the means of coping with and understanding change that he had been developing for the past fifty years or more. Thus he spoke glowingly of freedom, change, growth, progress, creativity, and human potential, yet confidently asserted the spiritual and moral values that had sustained him in his long personal search. He inspired Westerners, and he did so less by the beauty of what he said and how he said it than by what he was and how he lived.

After the highly successful 1874-75 tour, Alcott hoped to make annual excursions. Yet family circumstances, particularly Abby's declining health, prevented his going West again until 1879. He was disappointed, but a better reception in the East made up in part for his loss. Upon his return to Concord in April 1875, he was greeted by the official letter from the Harvard chapter of Phi Beta Kappa announcing his election. On July 1 he attended Phi Beta Kappa Day ceremonies and proudly received his ribbon. With a smile he remembered the day in the 1830s when he had attended the same function as a relative unknown and a definite outsider. At that time he had hesitated entering the church for the exercises, but the noble Emerson had taken his arm and escorted him inside, assuring him that he was a member "by right of genius." Harvard was now officially honoring that genius.[58]

Eastern friends began to laud Alcott's stand against materialism. Cyrus Bartol felt that all human beings should feel indebted to Alcott for his concept of personality and his unfailing conviction that the soul was transcendent and immortal. Sheldon Clark, a young minister in Scituate, Massachusetts, praised Alcott. "We need the gospel of your word among us," Clark told Alcott, "to counteract the materialistic tendencies of modern thought." Opportunities to speak and converse in New England increased markedly over previous years. In April 1875 he followed James Freeman Clarke and Julia Ward Howe in a lecture series in Wayland, Massachusetts. On May 30, 1875, he spoke on worship to the Free Religious Society in Providence, remembering as he traveled there the "unbelievable quixotisms" and "outrageous extremes" he found and fostered in Providence in the 1840s.[59]

On June 6, 1875, Alcott began a series of surprisingly successful Sunday evening conversations in Concord. For the first time since his days as superintendent of schools, he felt like a living element of his chosen community. He regained the flash of hope that he could promote greater fellowship among his townspeople and thus realize the village ideal he talked about. Consequently, the topic of his first Concord conversation was "village influences." He expected to raise questions not normally approached in "dry and profitless" Sunday preaching, but he found Concordians still overly critical about matters of theology. Too many of them, he felt, believed that they dare not question what was spoken on Sunday mornings. Indeed, the Unitarian minister, Grindall Reynolds, at first refused to attend the conversations, though he later relented. Alcott intended not only to foster a community spirit but also to stimulate his audience to "new points of view." And his fellow Concordians appreciated his efforts. Interest increased from Sunday to Sunday, despite reservations about Alcott's religious fidelity and his continued refusal to attend church. Even the staid Judge Ebenezer Rockwood Hoar, who had never attended an Alcott conversation before, came to hear him talk of the meaning of friendship at Emerson's on August 1. Alcott thought that Hoar and Reynolds "swam less buoyantly in the stream" that night, but Hoar later agreed to hold one of the conversations at his home. The conversations went on for fifteen weeks as Alcott's neighbors even listened patiently to his discussion of genesis and lapse. Nothing pleased Alcott more than this local appreciation. It certainly was not just a token acknowledgement of a friend of the venerated Emerson, nor just curiósity about Louisa, who attended only one of the sessions. Frank Sanborn felt that the success of the Concord conversations proved that people were not attracted to Alcott because of the novelty of his ideas but rather because of the "steady and lucid emanation of high thought" that came from his lips.[60]

Other speaking engagements also kept him busy. The Unitarian church in Newburyport asked him to speak at the urging of its minister, Abby's nephew Joseph May. Sheldon Clark invited him to Scituate. And on December 13, 1875, he explained his distinction between personality and individualism to the Conference of Unitarian Ministers meeting in Boston. In 1876 and 1877 his opportunities continued. There were lectures before the New England Women's Club on transcendentalism and immortality, conversations in Cambridge with Harvard divinity students, addresses at the Boston Young Men's Christian Association, preaching at the Unitarian churches in Pembroke, Uxbridge, and Bolton, Massachusetts, and Peterboro, New Hampshire, conversations with the one hundred members of the "Home Club" in East Boston, an address to the seven hundred inmates of the Massachusetts State Prison in Charlestown, and a lecture at Samuel May's former church in Brooklyn, Connecticut. Recognition in education continued. The Massachusetts State Normal School in Worcester invited him to speak on April 6 and 7, 1876. And in January 1876 the St. Louis Society of Pedagogy acknowledged his educational efforts by electing him an honorary member.[61]

Piles of manuscripts awaited his attention and organization. He was considering a book called "Ideals" or "Tablets, part II" which would include revised material from his "Philosophemes" just published in the *Journal of Speculative Philosophy*. It would be discreditable, he felt, not to have something to say about the "great problems of life and destiny" after having lived so long. He finally decided to make from his manuscripts a book of sayings in paragraph form and to call it *Table Talk*. Scripture-like orphic sayings or philosophemes, he thought, came closest to an adequate presentation of his "deepest speculations." He was sure that his paragraphs were far better than his long essays. *Table Talk* was published in the spring of 1877, and it included, in a manner similar to *Tablets* and *Concord Days*, brief comments on all the topics he had conversed about for years: books, gardens, education and childhood, temperance, conversation, the new church, and village life. He added a full explanation of personalism, genesis, lapse, immortality, the intuitive method, and his plans to train idealistic ministers at his new academy in Concord. As George Ripley noted in his *New York Tribune* review of *Table Talk*, Alcott's words were like those of a seer. He left his thoughts to be received by the reader as he received them: by the light of spontaneous intuition. Ripley's conclusions were much like those of Western newspaper reporters who evaluated, or tried to evaluate, Alcott's conversations. "If he breathes an atmosphere too attenuated for the common purposes of life," said Ripley, "he lends a powerful aid to our aspirations after the highest, and supplies a refreshing cordial amidst the cares and perturbations of this working day world." Sidney Morse told his readers in the *Radical Review*, successor to the *Radical*, that *Table Talk* failed to express Alcott's thoughts as well as his conversations did, but that he nevertheless returned to the book in the quiet hours of the evening to find meanings that the busy day often obscured. Most reviews of *Table Talk*, like Ripley's and Morse's, were favorable. Only the *Atlantic Monthly* refused to praise it. And Alcott felt that the *Atlantic Monthly*, along with the *Nation*, had "lost the confidence of able scholars."[62]

Along with his speaking and writing, Alcott found a renewed interest in temperance, diet, and health, as a result of his contacts with the Christian Scientists. In January 1876 Mrs. Mary Baker Glover, soon to be Mrs. Eddy, gratuitously sent him her new book, *Science and Health* (1875), which was to become the ideological basis for the Christian Science movement. Alcott was fascinated with Mrs. Glover's claim that metaphysical means could cure bodily diseases. Her faith in the soul's power over the body reinforced Alcott's own long-held beliefs about health and regimen. On January 20, 1876, Alcott went to Lynn, Massachusetts, to meet Mrs. Glover and the Christian Science followers who gather at her home every two weeks to discuss "metaphysical healing." He found her to be one of the "fair saints," a Christian in the truest sense, an idealist. Resolving to acquaint the Christian Scientists with other aspects of idealism, he presented his "Philosophemes" to George Barry, Mrs. Glover's disciple, who came to Concord to dine on February 7. Shortly thereafter, Barry sued Mrs. Glover for payment of past services and left the movement, so he was hardly the one to spread Alcottian notions among the Christian Scientists. But Mrs. Glover gave Alcott another opportunity to share his ideas. On February 16 he held a formal conversation with the Christian Scientists in Lynn.[63]

Alcott did not become a Christian Scientist. He detected an element of fanaticism, even superstition, in the movement, albeit of a genial kind, and he could never become more than a strong sympathizer. Clearly Christian Science manifested the same intellectual trends that Alcott did: the defense of the spiritual and supernatural in an age of science and technology, and an attempted synthesis of science and religion, of the material and the spiritual. But it too much reminded Alcott of sectarianism. It hinted too strongly a threat to freedom of thought for Alcott to find peace within it. But his acquaintance with the Christian Scientists caused him to reflect more about health and regimen than he had done for many years. His own temperance and sobriety, he decided, were responsible for his long life and good health at age seventy-six. For fifty years he had avoided meat, although he had consented to eat some fish, eggs, milk, butter, and cheese, from which he had for many years abstained. "Health and genius," he still believed, "are but other names for originality of mind and body. Virtue and Temperance are the best physicians for all the ails of both."[64]

Some people considered Alcott an expert on health and regimen. Martin Luther Holbrook, editor of the *Herald of Health*, asked him for a recommended daily regimen for publication in his edited collection of essays by noted health experts. Alcott also received letters from individuals seeking advice about diet and health, such as S. H. Haskell of Newtonville, Massachusetts, who asked what to do about a forty-three-year-old body, presumably his own, broken down by "overtaxation of mind and harassing cares." Alcott's advice may not have been entirely reassuring to Haskell. He told him that diseases of the body arose in the soul and that only strict continence, sobriety, temperance in diet, exercise in the open air, and a "cheerful spirit" could restore health and sanity to body and mind. Alcott still believed, though he was less extreme about it than in the 1840s, that there was a direct connection between one's living habits and future salvation: "Sobriety in all pleasures is the open path to the purest satisfactions this life can give, as it is the gateway to future beatitude."[65]

Additional recognition came to Alcott after his return from the West in 1875 with his inclusion in *Johnson's New Universal Cyclopaedia*. The brief notice lauded Alcott's Western tours and proclaimed his conversational abilities as his chief distinction. But Alcott's contribution to transcendentalism also received attention with the publication of Octavius Frothingham's *Transcendentalism in New England*. Alcott enthusiastically greeted the news of Frothingham's proposed book in 1875, certain that it would encourage idealism while celebrating that select group of American geniuses who had "created a literature." The book came out in June 1876, and Frothingham sent Alcott a gift copy. In his history, Frothingham praised Alcott and gave him second place to Emerson as a representative of transcendentalism in New England. Alcott was a "mystic," said Forthingham, one who sought wisdom not by induction or deduction but by immediate insight. Although Alcott was guilty of pouring out his ideas in monotonous reiteration, that did not make those ideas any less profound and significant. Alcott did much good, Frothingham claimed, in awakening the spiritual powers of individuals by means of his public conversations. And his conversations had become a recognized institution in America. On the whole, it was a just and able criticism by a man sympathetic to transcendentalism but who had finally rejected it in favor of the rationalism of free religion. Alcott thanked Frothingham, especially for his generous assessment of Emerson's contribution, and told him he thought the book would provide a great service. But Alcott was disappointed. He felt that Frothingham presented only a "partial estimate" of his share in transcendentalism. Frothingham, he guessed, was "touched too deeply with Darwinism" to have done adequate justice to transcendentalism and idealism.[66]

Nevertheless, Frothingham's critique was belated appreciation and recognition for a seventy-six-year-old man who had outlived many of his contemporaries. As the decade of the 1870s proceeded, Alcott became ever more aware of his age and the absence of old friends. Samuel May had died in

1871, and William Russell in 1873. Charles Sumner, whom Alcott respected as embodying the national conscience, died in 1874. In 1876 Alcott noted the death of Orestes Brownson in Detroit, and remembered his early friendship with Brownson, which had ended because of what Alcott considered Brownson's "dogmatic temperament." Most distressing to Alcott was the obvious decline of Ralph Waldo Emerson. Even in 1872 Emerson was complaining of the rapid approach of old age. The trauma of a fire in July 1872, which nearly destroyed his home, compounded the problem. By 1874 Emerson was telling Alcott about his partial loss of memory and about the lack of that ready command of imagery which had been so much his strength as a lecturer and a writer. Alcott found it difficult to interest his friend in his Western missionary enterprise and his plans for the new academy. Emerson told him that his diary entries were becoming fewer and fewer, and shortly thereafter Alcott began increasing the size of the entries in his own diary in an apparent effort to convince himself that age was creeping up on him more slowly than it was on Emerson.[67]

Disturbing changes were taking place in Alcott's own household. In the summer of 1873 Abby suffered a severe stroke. She recovered, but never enough to resume the active, vigorous life she had always known. Yet she did not lose the spirit of reform or the desire to battle injustice. She helped pack clothing to send to Sallie Holly's school for freedmen in Virginia. And she vociferously supported the cause of women's suffrage. When the speaker's platform collapsed at the centennial celebration of the Battle of Concord Bridge on April 19, 1875, dropping honored guests ignominiously to the ground, Abby suggested that it happened because the women's suffrage plank was left out. She was proud of her daughters—of Louisa's success in writing, of May's in art, and of Anna's in her devotion to family—and she was proud of her husband, certain that he would one day find honor. "He had *enjoyed* much—*endured long*, and will be accepted I am sure," she said. "So much trust cannot be wholly betrayed—The world must acknowledge and honor him, for his efforts to improve it—and advance the best interest of Education, and Morality [,] Temperance and free religion."[68]

Louisa's success had made the family comfortable, and May was enjoying similar success in art. She had been in Europe twice for lengthy stays, in 1870-71 and again in 1873-74. In 1874 she made over two thousand dollars selling paintings and giving drawing lessons. On her father's seventy-sixth birthday she happily presented him with the deed to the Moore lot adjoining Orchard House, which she had purchased for five hundred dollars and which Alcott had long wanted to buy. Louisa was nearly drowned in a "sea of admiration" during her trip to New York City in the winter of 1875-76. She had pleased her father in 1873 by writing a brief but witty account of Fruitlands called *Transcendental Wild Oats*. Since the death of her husband, Anna had spent much of the time at Orchard House, helping with the housekeeping and finding security in the company of her parents. Alcott enjoyed having his grandsons near him, although he feared that he was often "the graver and less inviting party," which prevented him from getting the attention from them that he would have liked.[69]

In September 1876 May sailed for Europe, tired of Concord despite her horseback riding, art classes, art clubs, and parties. She had overcome strange "forebodings" and fear for her mother's health. Abby was particularly shaken by May's departure, but had stoically encouraged her to go in order to further her career. By April 1877 May was writing joyous letters home about her success. Her parents were delighted at the report that one of her paintings had been admitted to the National Exhibition in Paris.[70]

By mid-September 1877 Abby was feeble and languid, suffering from angina pectoris. Alcott canceled all engagements to be at her side, knowing that death would not be long in coming. On November 14 the family moved from Orchard House to the home that had once been Henry Thoreau's on Main Street. Anna had purchased it with Louisa's help in May. Alcott left Orchard House sadly, not sure that he would ever return to it and knowing that it would not be the same without his wife. The family urged May to remain in Europe, and her regular letters comforted her mother as she lay in an upstairs bedroom of the new Alcott home. On November 25 Abby died. Two days later she was buried near Elizabeth in the family plot at Sleepy Hollow.[71]

1. AJ 48 (1873): 465.

2. Alcott to Abby May Alcott, August 10, November 12, and November 29, 1853, in "Family Letters, 1850-55"; AJ 31 (1856): 1097; AJ 32 (1857): 863; Alcott to Abby May Alcott, December 14, 1857, in "Letters, 1855-59"; Alcott to William Torrey Harris, December 22, 1857, from a copy in Alcott's hand in "Letters, 1855-59."

3. AJ 33 (1858): 450, 462-64; AJ 34 (1859): 8, 36; AJ 36 (1861): 517.

4. AJ 40 (1865): 215; AJ 41 (1866): 22-23, 46-47, 61, 74, 111; Alcott to Abby May Alcott, February 20, and March 10, 1866, in "Letters, 1865-66."

5. AJ 41 (1866): 324; AJ 42 (1867): 193-94; AJ 44 (1869): 376, 760; Alcott to Abby May Alcott, December 10, 1866, in "Letters, 1865-66"; Alcott to William Torrey Harris, September 17, 1867, from a copy in Alcott's hand in "Letters, 1867"; Alcott to William Torrey Harris, January 19, 1868, from a copy in Alcott's hand in "Letters, 1868"; Alcott to William Torrey Harris, May 12, 1869, from a copy in Alcott's hand in "Letters, 1869."

6. Alcott to William Torrey Harris, December 17, 1869, from a copy in Alcott's hand in "Letters, 1869."

7. Alcott, "Western Evenings, 1869-70"; AJ 45 (1870): 446-48.

8. AJ 45 (1870): 450.

9. Ibid., pp. 649, 709-18, 725-27, 729-30; A. Bronson Alcott, "Western Evenings, An Itinerary, 1870-71," p. 27, MS at Houghton Library, 59M-306 (15).

10. AJ 45 (1870): 731-34, 735-40; Alcott to William Torrey Harris, November 19, 1870, from a copy in Alcott's hand in "Letters, 1870."

11. AJ 45 (1870): 744-54, 759-67, 770, 775-77, 779-81; Alcott, "Western Evenings, 1870-71," p. 58; Alcott to Abby May Alcott, December 16, 1870, in "Letters, 1870."

12. AJ 45 (1870): 782-84, 788 ff, 808, 813-15; Alcott to Abby May Alcott, December 16, 1870; William J. Peterson, *The Story of Iowa*, 4 vols. (New York: Lewis Historical Publishing Co.,

1952), 4: 671; a clipping of Mary Adams's article in the *Dubuque Evening Journal* for December 31, 1870, is in AJ 45 (1870): 816.

13. AJ 45 (1870): 815; AJ 46 (1871): 10-22, 26, 28-36, 40-42, 46, 50-52; Alcott to Mary Newbury Adams, January 2 and 7, 1871, in A. Bronson Alcott, comp., "Letters for 1871," at Houghton Library, 59M-305 (11).

14. AJ 46 (1871): 53-57, 75-76, 90, 106; Alcott, "Western evenings, 1870-71," pp. 140, 146, 197; Paul Russell Anderson, *Platonism in the Midwest* (New York: Temple University Publications, 1963), p. 6.

15. Anderson, *Platonism in the Midwest*, pp. 19, 125-26, 129, 133; AJ 46 (1871): 107-16, 120-29, 131-32, 138-40.

16. AJ 46 (1871): 140-42, 146-51, 156-65; Bessie Louise Pierce, *A History of Chicago*, 3 vols. (New York: Alfred A. Knopf, 1940), 2: 144.

17. AJ 46 (1871): 168, 176, 179-80, 185-87.

18. AJ 46 (1871): 236, 340-41, 371, 374, 380, 626-27, 682-83, 690; Alcott to William Torrey Harris, September 20, 1871, from a copy in Alcott's hand in "Letters, 1871"; Alcott to Franklin Sanborn, December 16, 1871, in "Letters, 1871."

19. AJ 46 (1871): 242, 372-73, 539-40, 542-43, 551, 604-5, 660-61, 755: Mary Newbury Adams to Alcott, June 23, 1871, and William Torrey Harris to Alcott, June 28, 1871, in "Letters, 1871."

20. AJ 46 (1871): 754-55; Mary Newbury Adams to Alcott, December 17, 1871, in "Letters, 1871"; AJ 47 (1872): 305-7.

21. AJ 46 (1871): 447-52, 542-44, 551; Mary Newbury Adams to Alcott, August 14, 1871, and Alcott to Mary Newbury Adams, September 8, 1871, in "Letters, 1871"; AJ 47 (1872): 196-98, 383-84, 568-71.

22. AJ 47 (1872): 211-12, 503-10, 520-21, 532-38, 560-61, 563-64, 591-92, 625, 633, 649-50; A. Bronson Alcott, "Western Evenings, an Itinerary, 1872-1873," pp. 4-5, MS at Houghton Library, 59M-306 (16); Alcott to William Torrey Harris, September 19, 1872, from a copy in Alcott's hand in A. Bronson Alcott, comp., "Letters for 1872," at Houghton Library, 59M-305 (12); AJ 48 (1873): 113; Elizabeth Palmer Peabody to Alcott, July 29, 1871, August 22 [1871?], August 30, [1871?], and undated, at Houghton Library, 59M-312; Louisa May Alcott to Mrs. Horace [Mary Peabody] Mann, [187?], in the Horace Mann Collection owned by the Massachusetts Historical Society; AJ 46 (1871): 462, 467-71, 575, 602, 665; Elizabeth Peabody to Alcott, [June 19-21, 1872?], in "Letters, 1872"; Alcott to William Torrey Harris, September 2, 1871, from a copy in Alcott's hand in "Letters, 1871."

23. AJ 47 (1872): 666, 670-73; AJ 46 (1871): 380, 394-96.

24. AJ 47 (1872): 674, 677-79, 692, 705-6, 712-13, 714, 718-22, 729, 732-34; an unidentified newspaper clipping on Alcott's Dubuque High School lecture is in ibid., pp. 707-8.

25. AJ 47 (1872): 755-57, 759 ff, 761, 766-68, 772, 777, 782-84, 791, 797-98; Mary Newbury Adams to Alcott, January 9, 1873, and William G. Hammond to Austin Adams, January 6, [1873], in A. Bronson Alcott, comp., "Letters for 1873," at Houghton Library, 59M-305 (13).

26. AJ 48 (1873): 7, 13, 15, 17-18, 20-25, 28; AJ 44 (1869): 861-63; Alcott," Western Evenings, 1869-70"; Alcott, "Western Evenings, 1872-73," p. 214; an unidentified clipping on Alcott's Mount Pleasant conversation is in AJ 48 (1873): 26-27.

27. AJ 48 (1873): pp. 29-32, 36-37, 41-45, 49; Several citizens of Muscatine, Iowa, to Alcott, January 11, [1873], in "Letters, 1872."

28. AJ 48 (1873): 50-52, 55-57, 65-68, 72, 74-76, 78, 80, 82-84.

29. Ibid., pp. 84, 97-98, 102, 105-8; Alcott to William Torrey Harris, January 20, 1873, from a copy in Alcott's hand in "Letters, 1873"; Alcott to Ellen Chandler, February 27, 1873, in A. Bronson Alcott, comp., "Letters; embracing Correspondence with Miss Ellen A. Chandler, 1867-1882," at Houghton Library, 59M-305 (30).

30. AJ 48 (1873): 116, 586, 903, 981, 999-1000, 1016; Mrs. C. T. Cole to Alcott, February 16 and November 17, [1873], Mary Newbury Adams to Alcott, March 7, April 6, July 28, and November 9, 1873, Mrs. C. Perry to Alcott, March 12, 1873, Martha D. Wolcott to Alcott, April 25, 1873, George S. Bowen to Alcott, November 2, 1873, [Frances Bagley] to Alcott, November 7, 1873, Ezra Prince to Alcott, November 9, 1873, and Ednah Dow Cheney to Alcott, November 11,

1873, in "Letters, 1873"; Alcott to Charles D. B. Mills, May 4, 1873, Alcott to Thomas R. Gould, October 1, 1873, and Alcott to Mrs. W. D. Gunning, November 22, 1873, in "Letters, 1873."

31. AJ 48 (1873): 146, 210-12, 316-17, 337-38, 345 ff., 389-90, 398, 401-7, 659-60, 678, 704, 715, 721-23, 735-37, 739-43,, 897; Samuel Orcutt to Alcott, March 11, 1873, and Alcott to William Penn Alcott, April 21, 1873, in "Letters, 1873."

32. AJ 48 (1873): 157, 183-85, 198, 216; Alcott to William Torrey Harris, April 14, 1873, from a copy in Alcott's hand in "Letters, 1873"; AJ 49 (1874): 8, 39, 77, 79, 236, 238-39, 256, 310-11, 390-91, 567, 627-28; AJ 51 (1875) (April-December): 112, 659; Alcott to Mary Newbury Adams, April 17, 1874, in A. Bronson Alcott, comp., "Letters for 1874," at Houghton Library, 59M-305 (14).

33. AJ 49 (1874): 180, 239, 240-43, 262, 280, 452, 631-35; "Recent Literature," *Atlantic Monthly*, 34 (July 1874): 115-16; Elizabeth Palmer Peabody to Alcott, [ca. March 1 and ca. March 7, 1874], in "Letters, 1874."

34. AJ 48 (1873): 220; Evart A. and George L. Duyckinck, eds., *Cyclopedia of American Literature,* 2 vols. (Philadelphia: William Rutter and Co., 1875), 2: 843-45; AJ 44 (1874: 67, 512, 733; Keningale Cook to Alcott, March 3 and May 19, 1873, in "Letters, 1873."

35. Alcott to J. H. Temple, October 21, 1873, in "Letters, 1873"; Alcott to Mary Newbury Adams, April 17, 1874, in "Letters, 1874"; AJ 49 (1874): 976, 981-84, 939-92; AJ 50 (1874-75): 15.

36. AJ 50 (1874-75): 25-26, 31-32, 36-37, 38-40, 43, 58-59, 65, 70, 75.

37. Ibid., pp. 75-82, 99-102, 104-14, 132, 135-36.

38. Ibid., pp. 137-51, 153, 156-62, 164-67.

39. Ibid., pp. 158-62, 166, 168-69, 183-94, 203-8.

40. Ibid., pp. 218-20, 249-51, 252-55, 259.

41. Ibid., pp. 263, 265-69, 271-73.

42. Ibid., pp. 275-79, 281-83, 286, 295-96, 299; Alcott to Louisa May Alcott, February 4, 1875, printed in Herrnstadt, ed., *Letters,* p. 646.

43. AJ 50 (1874-75): pp. 305-10, 311-16, 323-24; Alcott to Frances Bagley, January 21, 1875, owned by Houghton Library, bMS AM 1817 (46); William F. Allen to Alcott, February 1, 1875, [H. N. Buford] to Alcott, February 5, 1875, and Kate Doggett to Alcott, February 6, 1875, in A. Bronson Alcott, comp., "Letters, 1875," at Houghton Library, 59M-305 (15).

44. AJ 50 (1874-75): 328-30, 333, 335-45, 347-53, 355-59, 361-64, 365 ff., 378-79; AJ 51 (1875) (April-December): 5-10, 13.

45. AJ 48 (1873): 936; AJ 50 (1874-75): 340; A. E. M. Swain to Mary Newbury Adams, December 12, 1872, in "Letters, 1872"; unidentified newspaper clippings in AJ 46 (1871): 21, 27, in AJ 47 (1872): 764, in A. Bronson Alcott, comp., "Autobiographical Collections," 9 (1872-1877): 95-96, MS at Houghton Library, 59M-307 (8), and in Alcott, "Western Evenings, 1872-73"; Mary Newbury Adams to Abby May Alcott, December 30, 1870, in "Letters, 1870"; Alice French to Hubert H. Hoeltje, March 31, 1926, quoted in Hubert H. Hoeltje, "Some Iowa Lectures and Conversations of Amos Bronson Alcott," *Iowa Journal of History and Politics* 29 no. 21 (July 1931): 377.

46. From an unidentified newspaper clipping in AJ 50 (1874-75): 270.

47. AJ 47 (1872): 671.

48. From unidentified newspaper clippings in AJ 45 (1870): 741, and in AJ 46 (1871): 114-115; A. Bronson Alcott, *Concord Days* (Boston: Roberts Brothers, 1872), pp. 32, 194.

49. AJ 49 (1874): 80.

50. From unidentified newspaper clippings in AJ 45 (1870): 718, in AJ 46 (1871): 166, and in AJ 47 (1872): 301-2; AJ 48 (1873): 1129-32, 1136, 1146; AJ 49 (1874): 40.

51. AJ 46 (1871): 301; AJ 48 (1873): 1089; AJ 49 (1874): 216-18, 339-44, 600, 602-3, 663-64.

52. AJ 54 (1869): 800, 814; AJ 45 (1870): 27, 113; Alcott "Western Evenings, 1869-70"; AJ 46 (1871): 53, 111; AJ 47 (1872): 93-96, 322-24, 326; AJ 50 (1874-75): 47, 68, 197, 208; an unidentified clipping containing Alcott's remarks at the February, 1872 Radical Club meeting is in AJ 47 (1872), pp. 99-101; unidentified clippings of Alcott's conversations are in AJ 50 (1874-75): 48-50, 69, 331-32; Franklin B. Sanborn to Alcott, February 21, 1872, in "Letters, 1872."

53. AJ 46 (1871): 261-62, 416; AJ 47 (1872): 675-76; AJ 49 (1874): 224; AJ 53 (1877): 30, 200, 365, 680.

54. George Mills Harper, "Thomas Taylor in America" in Kathleen Raine and George Mills Harper, eds., *Thomas Taylor the Platonist: Selected Writings* (Princeton, N.J.: Princeton University Press, 1969), pp. 49-102; Anderson, *Platonism in the Midwest*, p. 53; AJ 49 (1874): 72, 377; Thomas M. Johnson to Alcott, July 10, 1874, in "Letters, 1874"; AJ 48 (1873); 1132; AJ 53 (1877): 522.

55. AJ 46 (1871): 710-12, 749-52, 764-66; AJ 49 (1874): 18, 577; A. Bronson Alcott, "Philosophemes," *Journal of Speculative Philosophy*, 8 no. 1 (January 1873): 46-48, and 9, no. 3 (July 1875): 245-63.

56. Unidentified clipping in AJ 47 (1872): 770-71; AJ 48 (1873): 131; AJ 49 (1874): 641-42; a printed circular listing Alcott's conversation topics for his Western tour of 1874-75 is in AJ 49 (1874): 983; unidentified clippings in AJ 50 (1874-75): 48-49, 62, 308-9; Martha D. Wolcott, "Report of Conversation," October 24, 1874, from a copy in Alcott's hand in AJ 50 (1874-75): 83-98; AJ 50 (1874-75): 201-2.

57. Unidentified clippings in Alcott, "Autobiographical Collections," 9: 95-96, 247-48, and in AJ 50 (1874-75): 334, 354.

58. AJ 53 (1877): 776; AJ 51 (April-December 1875): 23-24, 293-95; Alcott to F. E. Anderson, April 8, 1875, in "Letters, 1875."

59. Cyrus. A. Bartol, *Radical Problems* (Boston: Roberts Brothers, 1872), pp. 89-90; AJ 51 (April-December 1875): 88-89, 127-28, 188-90, 791; Sheldon C. Clark to Alcott, November 16, 1875, in "Letters, 1875."

60. AJ 61 (April-December 1875): 235-36, 253-54, 277-78, 286, 306-8, 325-26, 365-66, 419-22, 445-46, 489, 506, 536, 557-59; Franklin B. Sanborn, "Bronson Alcott at Home," *Springfield Republican* (October 6, 1875).

61. AJ 51 (April-December 1875): 345-51, 787-93, 803; AJ 52 (1876): 35, 75, 93-94, 128, 204-8, 223-25, 381, 486-91; AJ 53 (1877): 145-48, 196, 214-21, 441-48, 700-704, 884; William Deutsch to Alcott, January 24 and February 21, 1876, in A. Bronson Alcott, comp., "Letters for 1876," at Houghton Library, 59M-305 (16).

62. AJ 51 (April-December 1875): pp. 322, 477, 485; AJ 52 (1876): 415-16; A. Bronson Alcott, *Table Talk* (Boston: Roberts Brothers, 1877); a clipping of George Ripley's review of *Table Talk* is in AJ 53 (1877): 417-18; [Sidney Morse], "Chips from my Studio," *Radical Review 1* (November 1877): 622; a clipping of the *Atlantic Monthly* review is in AJ 53 (1877): 472; Alcott to William Torrey Harris, June 30, 1877, from a copy in Alcott's hand in A. Bronson Alcott, comp., "Letters for 1877," at Houghton Library, 59M-305 (17).

63. AJ 52 (1876): 45-46, 57-58, 105, 126; Alcott to Mary Baker Glover, January 17, 1876, in "Letters, 1876"; Edwin Franden Dakin, *Mrs. Eddy: The Biography of a Virginal Mind* (New York: C. Scribner's Sons, 1929), pp. 118-19.

64. AJ 52 (1876) pp. 86, 89, 91-92; AJ 54 (1878): 401-402; AJ 53 (1877): 747-48.

65. AJ 53 (1877): 743-49; S. H. Haskell to Alcott, December 11, 1876, and Alcott to S. H. Haskell, December 12, 1876, in "Letters, 1876"; Martin Luther Holbrook to Alcott, [ca. October 17, 1877], and Alcott to Martin Luther Holbrook, October 18, 1877, in "Letters, 1877."

66. Frederick A. P. Barnard and Arnold Guyot, eds., *Johnson's New Universal Cyclopaedia* (New York: A. J. Johnson and Co., 1875), 1: 87; AJ 51 (April-December 1875): 299-301; AJ 52 (1876): 267-70, 670; Octavius Brooks Frothingham, *Transcendentalism in New England* (New York: G. P. Putnam's Sons, 1876), pp. 249-53, 257-61, 282-83, 358; Alcott to Octavius B. Frothingham, May 14, 1876, in "Letters, 1876."

67. AJ 47 (1872): 21, 402; Rusk, *Emerson*, pp. 452-54; AJ 48 (1873): 662-64; AJ 49 (1874): 285-91, 949-52; AJ 51 (April-December 1875), pp. 91-93; AJ 52 (1876): 114, 239-40.

68. Abby May Alcott, "Diary," April 30, 1870, and November 21, 1875; AJ 48 (1873): 551-55, 567, 577; AJ 49 (1874): 543; Abby May Alcott to Louisa Bond, February 24, 1876, and Abby May Alcott, "Diary," April 19, 1875, from copies in Alcott's hand in "Autobiographical Materials."

69. AJ 51 (April-December 1875): 125, 755; AJ 48 (1873): 1164, 1168; AJ 52 (1876): 162; Louisa May Alcott, "Diary," 1850-85"; Alcott to L. M. Alcott, November 17, 1875, in "Letters, 1875."

70. AJ 52 (1876): 478, 510, 530, 533; Abby May Alcott, "Diary," September 10, 1876, from a copy in Alcott's hand in "Autobiographical Materials"; AJ 53 (1877): 119, 280.

71. AJ 53 (1877): 382, 715-16, 718-19, 730, 734-36, 821-22, 826, 851, 855; Alcott to Mary Newbury Adams, September 17, 1877, in "Letters, 1877"; Alcott to May Alcott, November 18 and 25, 1877, in A. Bronson Alcott, comp., ["Family Letters, 1877-1879"], at Houghton Library, 59M-305 (29); Abby May Alcott to May Alcott, November 11, 1877, owned by Houghton Library, bMS AM 1817 (45).

12

The Concord School of Philosophy, 1878-82

THE last five years of Alcott's active life reflected the extremes of sadness and joy. Death among family and friends loomed larger than ever before. Old age and grief seemed to go hand in hand. Yet these years brought Alcott his greatest success and achievement. Two more Western tours, the last of which was his longest and most rewarding, amazed his friends and impressed his audiences. In 1879 his new academy, the dream of forty years, became reality in the Concord School of Philosophy. The School symbolized his lifelong message and mission, and it rendered to him the ultimate recognition and the ultimate happiness and satisfaction.

Alcott dealt with his grief over his wife's death as he had dealt with grief, sorrow, and disappointment in the past: by writing furiously. He began by reading Abby's diaries and letters and copying from them for a memoir to be compiled by him and Louisa. Abby's bold and hurried hand writing told of the depth of her suffering and anxiety during the days of poverty and misapprehension. Such memories filled Alcott with "tearful admiration" and made him repentant of his incompetence and inability to relieve her burdens. Abby's forceful writing style impressed him as well. "Here is greatness," he said, "displayed in humble privacy and devotedness to duty day by day." Unfortunately, nothing was published fom the mass of manuscript material Alcott collected. He felt that he lacked the talent to write such a memoir. Louisa had hoped to do it, but her poor health and her sadness and grief prevented it.[1]

Months of reading and copying his wife's writings led Alcott to consider writing his autobiography. In October 1878 he began to copy his manuscripts and to compile his own biographical information as zealously as he had that of his wife. He felt that no one could write his biography as well as he could, if only because no one else would want to read the awesome bulk of material that he had collected since 1826. As he read through his diaries he worried about the egotism evident in them, but he concluded that a diary was a true self-portrait, that it showed the Person in relation to its surroundings, as reflected in one's special individualism. Hence, to omit the ego would be dishonest and not a true rendering of his character.[2]

Not until January 1880 did Alcott begin to compose the autobiography, and by then he had decided that an epic poem would best convey it. The result was a lengthy sketch of his early life in verse called *New Connecticut*. Originally he had intended to make it available only to friends and family, but its reception was so good that he permitted it to be published in 1881. *New Connecticut* concerned only Alcott's boyhood and years of peddling in the South. But it gave details of Alcott's life about which other information was scanty, and it provided an interesting sketch of life in a small New England town in the first two decades of the nineteenth century. More significantly, it reflected Alcott's conception of himself, his time, and the importance he attached to his life's work and to his character. And it was a much different picture from one he might have drawn in the 1830s, 1840s or 1850s. This autobiography said nothing about educational reform, civil disobedience, withdrawal from society, abolitionism, or religious radicalism. Rather, it was a romanticized account of the simple, virtuous life in a rural community. It portrayed the qualities that Alcott admired and that he felt his parents had given him: the love of books and learning, truthfulness, and "personal purity":

> Lovingly his mother did her lore impart;
> While with soft eyes he did her daily see,
> Flushed his young fancy, touched his tender heart,
> His conscience christened in his infancy.
> . . . .
> Plainly books have close kinship with his mind,
> And he that kinship will in kind repay;
> Some compensating errand he will find,
> On tables will a goodly volume lay.

He described his travels in the South, especially his visits to the elegant Virginia plantations, as a "school for manners." In short, *New Connecticut* was the product of a one-time radical turned genteel.[3]

Alcott did not disdain his early career as a reformer. He was proud of his contributions to education, his stand against slavery, even of his valiant efforts at Fruitlands. But by the late 1860s and 1870s, his commitment to radical change was gone. He viewed his comeouterism and his reform activities of the 1840s as "extravagances" and "extremes," the results of "a wild sense of individual license." He spoke of the need to seek unity of extremes and opposites. Antagonism, he said, was the product of "individualism" rather than the unifying personality.[4] When in 1873 his friend, *Radical* editor Sidney Morse, advocated an end to all political rule, Alcott spoke like a veteran who had been down that road before:

> Once, I might have accepted fully his [Morse's] doctrine of Individual Sovereignty, ignoring all interference from institutions [,] conventions and creeds of all kinds, as during the Fruitlands and non-taxpaying periods of my life. It was putting this logic to its ultimate consequences, and individual issues,—abolishing the social and political order altogether. . . . It left me an outcast and a vagabond. —The sincere victim of a half-truth seen in the light of an idea at last.[5]

"Individualism," he felt, had to be subdued and softened into a "nobler form of personal character." Instead of rebelling against the community, a "Person" would serve it in a way that would foster closer bonds of sympathy and fellowship.[6]

The key to reform, Alcott maintained, was in the home, in family life. And good in society, institutions, and national morality came from the home, from domestic influences. The family was the nursery of the state and the church. "Reform begins at the beginning," he said, "with parents personally, and at home. Every family is a little Seminary and world of its own: has its climate, characteristics, its manners and morals: each the reflex and image of its heads." Schemes for social reform were doomed to failure unless centered in the traditional family structure. Only there could "Paradise" be planted and piety and morality assured. He feared that Americans were fast losing those "virtues," "graces," and "accomplishments" that had always rendered homes humane. "Loose notions of authority," he claimed, were "demoralizing" the population.[7]

This change in Alcott's reform thought had less effect on substance than on tone, direction, and emphasis. He had always believed that the family was the key to reform, but to that he had added a militancy, an unbending commitment to destroy bad institutions, and to root out evil from society so that nothing would impede the family's development. Now there was no militancy. He largely accepted, and even defended, existing institutions as the guarantors of "civilization." Whereas he had once been unhesitating in his defiance of traditions and conventions, now, in June 1875, he refused to attend a Radical Club Sunday picnic in Waltham lest it offend good churchgoers.[8] His view of the family was now more defensive than offensive, guarding against the loss of supposed traditional virtues rather than presenting a hopeful idea of the potential within the family structure for positive change. Also, he had always understood the importance of authority. His classrooms had always been highly structured and disciplined. But in his years of radical reform he had taken this need for authority for granted and had emphasized instead the freedom, the scope for human creativity, that could be derived from the disciplined situation. He had felt that rules, forms, precedents, and procedures should never become ends in themselves, should never get in the way of learning. Now he was defensive about authority. He began to claim it as an end, as a bulwark against the loss of traditional values, manners, and forms of behavior.

The same tendency was evident in Alcott's changing attitudes toward politics and legislative reform. After the Civil War he continued to support the Radical Republicans, hoping that their program for reconstruction would help ameliorate the social, economic, and political condition of the freedmen. He considered Andrew Johnson's attempts to combat the policies of the Radicals to be disagraceful. When George Luther Stearns died in 1867, Alcott eulogized him as the courageous founder of Radical Republicanism, the one man who had made possible John Brown's "bold stroke for freedom" at Harpers Ferry. Alcott believed that black people would never be truly free until they were adequately represented in Congress. Frederick Douglass, he thought, would make an excellent Senator. When, in May 1865, William Lloyd Garrison called for the disbanding of the American Antislavery Society, Alcott joined Wendell Phillips and the majority of the members in opposition, believing that although slavery had ended, the Society still had the duty to work for the rights of black Americans. Alcott considered the speech he delivered in favor of Phillips's position the best public address he had ever given. It was the only occasion, he recalled, at which Garrison publicly accused him of partisanship. He continued to support Phillips's radical position on Reconstruction. In October 1867 he wrote an essay in the *Radical* praising Phillips for his stand against the "slave South" and his unflinching support of equality among the races.[9]

In 1871 Alcott supported Phillips's choice for governor of Massachusetts, General Benjamin F. Butler. Phillips's support of the Butler platform which advocated both temperance and labor reform, brought upon him the unending reproach of Boston's upper class. The *Nation*, the bulwark of "liberal reform" in America, charged that Butlerism meant a "transfer of power to the ignorant and poor." In December Alcott called on Phillips, many of whose former friends had deserted him because of the Butler affair, to encourage him and to pledge support for Phillips's attempt to fuse the temperance, women's rights, and labor movements into one great national party.[10]

Phillips had in fact become a militant supporter of the Massachusetts Labor Reform Party, which advocated such things as the overthrow of the profit-making system, the abolition of monopoly, an end to privilege, and the prohibition of the granting of public lands to speculative capitalists. Alcott too had become interested in labor reform. Never having had a stake in the capitalistic system, and having been a lifelong critic of those who hungered after material wealth, Alcott easily sympathized with the workers whose plight in the burgeoning factories of industrial America was worsening. He believed that a proper distribution of the products of labor would give each person an adequate living. Alcott was no economist or political scientist. The writings of Karl Marx and the other late nineteenth-century socialists were unfamiliar to him. He offered no plan of action for the redistribution of wealth. But he did understand that laborers were often the victims of circumstances created by the capitalists, and that the capitalists used these circumstances against the workers for profit. Alcott said these things at the convention of the Labor Reform League in Boston in January 1869. League representatives praised him for his remarks and invited him to speak again in May; he decided against it because he felt out of place as a lecturer for partisan causes. Problems of the growing cities also concerned him. In Boston he noted with disgust that tenements were being erected on land that the high tide would surely flood. He condemned the capitalists who callously pleaded their right to dispose of their property as they wished with no concern for the laboring poor who would fill up the squalid tenements and ignorantly consider the capitalists their benefactors. Labor reform was a pressing need, Alcott thought, and Phillips was an excellent choice to lead a labor party.[11]

Despite these remnants of his earlier radicalism, Alcott's main interests in the 1870s and 1880s were elsewhere—in philosophy, in the West, in summer schools. He lost touch with the issues, and thus lost the fervor for reform. Such was the case when the Liberal Republicans broke with the Grant Republicans in 1872 to nominate Horace Greeley and Charles Francis Adams. Alcott admitted that he knew very little about the Grant administration but said he would support Greeley and Adams because they were good men who would "honor their country." Liberal Republicanism was a reaction against the corruption of the Grant regime, but also a reaction against Radical Reconstruction policies. The Democrats also chose Greeley. Wendell Phillips refused to support the Liberals, and accused Greeley of being a "trimmer" who would unflinchingly sacrifice principles for success. The Liberals were ignorant and unconcerned about the problems of the laboring classes, thought Phillips, and their election would only bring former Southern rebels to power in Washington. However, Charles Sumner, whom Alcott respected as a statesman as much as he did Phillips, supported the Liberals. Sumner condemned Grantism on the floor of the Senate and accused the Grant Republicans of failing to carry through radical reconstruction policies. Phillips, Gerrit Smith, and several black leaders lashed out at Sumner for indulging in a vindictive, personal attack on Grant at the expense of political rights for blacks. Even Emerson believed that Sumner was wrong. But Alcott continued to support Sumner and the Liberals. He visited Sumner the day before he left for Europe for his health and told him that time would confirm the truthfulness of his course.[12]

Certainly Alcott was confused about his political allegiance. He was in anguish because the two men he considered the foremost leaders of the nation, Phillips and Sumner, did not agree. Part of his problem was that there was no real choice for Radical Republicans to make in 1872. Reconstruction was dying under the increasing nationwide demand for reconciliation between the sections. No party was willing to take a solid stand in favor of improving the condition of blacks. Yet Alcott's confusion resulted more from ignorance than anything else. He was naive about politics, had little knowledge of the true condition of blacks, and had no idea of the means necessary to help black people. When Rutherford B. Hayes became president in March 1877, Alcott considered it a red-letter day for the nation. He was glad to see a reconciliation of the sections and a settlement of Civil War questions. News of Hayes's appointment of Frederick Douglass as United States marshall of the District of Columbia, of Sallie Holly's work with the freedmen in Virginia, and of General George Armstrong's Hampton Institute for blacks, was enough to satisfy him that the needs of blacks were being served. Of the pressing social and economic needs of blacks, especially for land, capital, and education, Alcott had no conception. Without a doubt he would have supported programs to supply blacks with their needs, but he had no idea of how desperate the situation was. But he was perhaps no less naive than most Northerners by 1877, including the president himself, who was certain that reconciliation between North and South would assure the rights, safety, and interests of black people throughout the nation.[13]

Alcott began to judge politicians and governmental officials by their gentlemanly bearing rather than by their position on issues. In the summer of 1875 Senator George S. Boutwell, former governor of Massachusetts and secretary of the treasury under Grant, invited Alcott to his estate at Groton, Massachusetts. Boutwell had been a leading Radical Republican in the late 1860s. He had laid the legal groundwork for the impeachment of Andrew Johnson and had managed the Fifteenth Amendment through the House of Representatives. But Alcott said nothing about Boutwell's record. Rather, he was impressed with the senator because he managed his farm like a "true republican and gentleman" and he was a man of "republican manners." In December 1880 Alcott met president-elect James A. Garfield at Garfield's home in Mentor, Ohio. Again, issues meant much less than the former general's "noble presence," although Alcott did ask Garfield to do something about the "Mormon iniquity." He included Garfield among those he considered to be the "best men," those whom he hoped would come together to form a "pure" political party freed from partisan wrangling. In "cultivated communities," Alcott mused, there was a class of eminent thinkers of "superior character," the lords and gentlemen of the land, who made up a fellowship for the promotion of the public welfare. The public welfare included the manners and morals of the general populace. The "best men" would zealously guard these manners and morals, he thought, and protect the public from the encroachments of demagogues such as the irreverent apostle of agnosticism Robert G. Ingersoll and the crowds of "shallow and restless" persons who followed him.[14]

Throughout his life Alcott had manifested ideas and characteristics best described as "genteel." Stow Persons has defined gentility broadly as a belief in the importance of manners, character, integrity, intelligence, and especially in the significance of a cultivated elite in guiding the social and cultural life of the nation. Alcott's educational theories emphasized the need to develop character and to cultivate morality and manners in the young. His conversations addressed the same theme to the old. His fascination with clubs—the Transcendental Club, the Town and Country Club, "Our Club," the Plato Clubs of the West—was in part the result of his romanticized conception of the power of an intellectual elite to sway the ideas of the community at large.[15]

Alcott's gentility was especially reflected in his close association of culture and character with the tilling of the land, family life, and the development of individual talents and capacities through a "chosen task." "Human life is a very simple matter," he declared,

Breath, bread, health, a hearthstone, a fountain, fruit, a few garden seeds, and room to plant them in: a wife and children, a friend or two of either sex, conversation, neighbors, and a task, life-long, given from within—these are contentment, and a great estate.[16]

It was the countryman who best exemplified the "primary virtues," the keeping of his conscience and the care of his garden. "Omit the garden, treat the orchard as of secondary importance," he warned, "all falls fast into impiety and ruin."[17]

A major theme of Alcott's later writings was the cultivation of the land. *Tablets, Concord Days, Table Talk* and his essays in the *Commonwealth* were filled with quotations from and references to the pastoral poets and essayists: Virgil, Columella, Varro, Cowley. It was the garden and the orchard, he told his readers, that distinguished civilized human beings from the forester and the hunter. Only as country people could human beings find Paradise, the kind of paradise that Alcott supposed that his friend Benjamin Marston Watson had found at his Plymouth estate, where he cultivated his nurseries like an English country gentleman and still retained his interest in books and learning. Indeed, the garden had been Alcott's salvation after the Temple School and Fruitlands disasters. The garden became a vicarious form of regeneration for Alcott as he directed his reform energies from persons and institutions to the molding and reshaping of the land. Alcott believed that by overcoming the "brute force" in themselves and in nature, human beings could achieve victories over themselves and nature. The planting of orchards and gardens meant the taming of such brute force, thus a regeneration. Gardening was a mingling of mind and matter, the converting of the earth into something humane and civilized by means of ideas, by means of human genius. Gardening was an art, an expression of human creativity.[18]

Alcott also had a genteel fascination with cultivated elites. He was ever desirious of conversing with the "best people" of the community, much as he had done with the aristocratic plantation owners of Virginia in the 1820s. Generally, he associated the "best people" with such attributes as character, integrity, manners, virtue, benevolence, politeness, and openness to ideas—particularly his own. Never was he impressed with wealth or material adornment, although he could be swayed by titles and hereditary distinctions. He doted upon England's John Francis and Katherine Louisa, Viscount and Viscountess Amberley, when they appeared in Concord and Boston for a visit in the fall of 1867. He and Emerson arranged for a special meeting of the Radical Club for their benefit. Alcott bought a new black suit for the occasion and acted as Master of Ceremonies at Cyrus Bartol's parlors, with the Amberleys sitting one on each side of him and the room filled with "superior persons." A few days later Lady Katherine pleased Alcott and proved the association of titled nobility and culture by writing to him of her enjoyment of the "free discussion on speculative matters."[19]

But Alcott was at his most genteel when he considered the decay of manners in industrial America. "Manners are the man refined," he said, "and freed from the brute appetites and animal propensities which relate him to the beast." By the late 1870s he was concerned that manners had ceased to be the measure of a human being in popular circles. Young people had few examples to imitate. Family discipline was neglected. As a result, young people were indifferent to the amenities of polite society. When some Harvard students wearing "ridiculous gear" came to Concord to hear Oscar Wilde speak in January 1882, Alcott thought it an "assault on good manners," which the Harvard faculty should have forbidden or at least discouraged.[20]

Stow Persons has explained the decline of American gentility in the late nineteenth century as the result of a loss of power by the intellectual elite to the new industrial and financial elite. The erosion of genteel values, he claimed, was caused by the diffusion of those values into mass society. Persons included among the declining "gentry" Alcott, Emerson, Lowell, Hedge, Oliver Wendell Holmes, Sr., and the entire group of transcendentalists and literary figures of the nineteenth century.[21] In some ways Alcott's growing conservatism and defensive traditionalism were results of the gentry's loss of power and influence, particularly the declining influence of some of the values they held dear. But this paradigm does not fully explain Alcott's intellectual development during his last years. For Alcott, unlike Emerson and others of his intellectual counterparts, never had been in a position of power and influence. He had nothing to lose from the rise of an economic elite. If anything, his influence, as he perceived it, was greatest during his later years. He had no reason to feel disaffected or isolated or impotent, and he did not.

By the 1870s and 1880s, however, a good share of Alcott's characteristic optimism, especially his faith that change would always result in good or in progress, and that the individual, if freed from traditions and institutions, would always arrive at the good, had been shaken. His faith that change was an instrument of regeneration had made him a radical reformer, an apostle of individual freedom, an iconoclast. But at bottom Alcott had always held onto many traditional values and assumptions, as had his contemporaries among the transcendentalists and reformers. Among these values were an unquestioned belief in God as a transcendent and supernatural being; a code of moral behavior including integrity, decorum, politeness, hospitality, and benevolence; a certainty that the family was the core of society; and a strong belief in personal purity. Alcott had also assumed that an increase in individual freedom, and a furthering of social, economic, and political change, would only enhance these traditional values and provide room for their expression. Encrusted institutions and outworn authorities only prevented the inherent goodness in each individual—as defined in part by his traditional values—from being realized.

By the 1870s traditions and institutions were no longer the enemy. Rather, Alcott began to fear that rapid change and an excess of individual freedom were threatening, not enhancing, his basic assumptions about God, morality, decorum, and family life. Free thought in religion had led to skepticism and a questioning of the supernatural. Unrestrained individualism was threatening the bonds of neighborhood and community life. A breakdown of authority had led to affronts to good manners and decorum. Technology, once hailed by Alcott as a force for progress, was creating havoc. "Machinery," he said, "is fast replacing the poetry of farm and fireside; the sickle, the distaff, the chimney piece, the family institution, being fast superseded by prose powers; and with their sway, have come slavery, pusillanimity, dishonor." Rapidly growing cities brought overcrowding and misery. Alcott refused to ride Boston's horse cars because he feared being jostled into some lady's lap or having to endure the incivility of treading on some passenger's toes.[22]

The damage that industrial society could inflict upon traditional morality became even clearer to Alcott during his Western tour in the fall of 1879. He left Concord on October 24 on his way to Cincinnati. In order to visit several of his nieces and nephews, he decided to travel by way of Pennsylvania. It was in Bradford, in the midst of the oil country of northwestern Pennsylvania, that he found his niece Jennie Brown and nephew Charles Bailey, children of his sister Pamela.[23]

Bradford, Alcott discovered, was a filthy town of some five thousand "motley" people, mostly "dealers and speculators in oil." His nephew served these unpleasant people by operating several "card palaces," an occupation sure to rank low on Alcott's list of genteel "chosen tasks." Jennie managed a boarding house in nearby Cole Creek, where she took her uncle the day after his arrival in Bradford. Alcott feared for his life as he rode with Jennie in a rickety carriage over a muddy road along steep precipices past wells oozing oil, large oil tanks, and shaggy, blackened, half-cleared land. Cole Creek was an oil boom town created out of nothing seven months before. Now Alcott found rows of shops, boarding houses, inns, "houses of good and ill fame," and women and girls tramping the streets at all hours. He felt that he was present at the origin of civilization. He spent the night at Jennie's boarding house talking with the "rude and slovenly" boarders who told him that Cole Creek could easily vanish in another seven months and another city spring into existence just as quickly.[24]

The next day Alcott returned to Bradford by stagecoach through hub-deep mud. Bradford citizens urged him to speak at one of the local opera houses where Robert Ingersoll had spoken the week before to a crowd of one thousand at one dollar a ticket. Rarely did Alcott turn down an offer to speak, but this time he did, disdaining Bradford's "easy money" and loose morality. "Three opera houses for a population of 5000," he noted, "supposes a surplus of sinners to support them briskly, and scatter their money and morals profusely for the benefit of the borough." He was not at home in Pennsylvania, he discovered, and he quickly left for more familiar and congenial places in Ohio.[25]

As a result of his growing fear that traditional morality, propriety, and piety were being undermined in industrial America, Alcott diverted his attention from the problems of blacks and factory workers to questions of personal morality. He became more actively involved than ever in the temperance movement and in what David Pivar has called the "purity crusade."[26] More and more he looked to the power of governmental authority to help regulate behavior and morality.

He had always been concerned with temperance, chastity, and personal purity, but by the 1870s he had diverted nearly all of his reform energies toward those things. Always before he had felt that such matters of personal morality were necessarily the objects of individual reform, to be accomplished by education, moral suasion, and the reliance on the innate goodness in human nature to be expressed by the free individual. Now he was willing to call on the power of the state to force individuals to be pure. At a Concord town meeting in November 1867, Alcott voted to restrict the sale of intoxicating beverages. He did not favor prohibition. Rather, he preferred that innkeepers be elected town officials responsible for the revenue obtained from liquor sales. Such revenue, he proposed, could be used by the town to provide community centers for reading, games, and socializing. These social centers, he hoped, would in turn "check the spread of ignorance and idleness" and help to rehabilitate those who wasted their evenings with drink and idle talk at "groceries and eating houses where they corrupt one another." Much to Alcott's shame and disappointment, the town voted down the proposal to restrict the sale of alcohol. In disgust he declared that "rum and democracy have probably carried the state." By the 1870s Alcott was finding the prohibitionist ideas of Neal Dow agreeable and was himself advocating that temperance become a political issue and the platform of a political party.[27]

Another concern of Alcott's was sexual purity. The obvious increase in prostitution in the large cities made him aware of the threat to this fundamental standard of personal morality. His first extensive introduction to the growing problem came in Chicago in February 1871, when he met with the Society for the Promotion of Social Purity. Robert Collyer had organized the Society in 1866 as the Unity League. It sponsored educational campaigns to prevent prostitution and programs to extend aid and sympathy to the "fallen." The members worked to end the double standard; that is, they demanded that men be as pure as women. Education was the prime weapon against promiscuity and incontinence, but Alcott was sure that governmental power would have to aid in the fight. Communities, he declared, had to oversee the morals of their inhabitants. For it was more than just a matter of personal morality for Alcott. Sexual license was an attack on the family and the home. "Only as marriage is chaste and children conceived and begotten in purity," he said, "are families and states planted on safe foundation."[28]

In April 1874 the Moral Education Association of Boston, the president of which was Alcott's longtime friend Caroline Severance, invited Alcott to converse with them. The members of this group made it their business to try to eliminate all "social vice," and Alcott told them that the purification of the sexual relation would purify all of society. Thereafter, Alcott spoke regularly at Association meetings and was pleased at its valiant battle against "the torrent of corruption that infects the private morals of our community." In 1875 the Association asked him to be a member of the Advisory Board. The members thanked him for his open and unqualified support of their efforts in the face of warnings from some religious leaders such as Edward Everett Hale that publicizing the evils would only increase them. Alcott agreed with the Association that sexual morality was a matter affecting national, as well as individual, honor and stability. Therefore legislation was essential to promote the purity of the nation as well as that of its citizens. In 1878 Alcott was astounded and horrified at the "facts" provided by the self-styled moral policeman and censorship advocate Anthony Comstock in a speech at Boston's Park Street Church. Alcott did not say how he felt about censorship, but he did firmly believe that there were some things no one should read. And he did not hesitate to play the moral policeman himself. When a woman of "free love notoriety" appeared at a Moral Education Association meeting, apparently to debate the issues, Alcott took her aside and sternly warned her of her "errors and dangers."[29]

Alcott knew that one cure for vice was personal discipline. His years of strict regimen and abstinence from alcohol and meat were, he thought, partly responsible for his eighty years of good health. He claimed that a vegetable and fruit diet could both curb the sexual appetite and cure alcoholism. But he also knew that not everyone was as strong willed as he was. Therefore he called upon the government to shield the weak and unfortunate from temptation. He still retained his idealistic view of the state as a "personal polity," planted in the "common will" of its members and existing to ensure the security and liberty of each person within it. Once again he confronted the problem he had battled all his life: to balance the often conflicting concepts of liberty and security, of freedom and authority. He certainly believed that without virtue freedom could not exist. Those who did not practice moral uprightness and personal purity, he said, were enslaved. In order to preserve freedom, the state had to enforce behavioral codes. No community, he felt, was safe unless it maintained the "laws of social order."[30]

Fortunately, Alcott's community theory was not so narrow as to include only considerations of personal morality. It also encompassed the social problems with which he had become concerned, especially the problems of the laboring classes. The New England Labor League had disturbed him with what he considered its extreme radicalism. And he was one of the "conservative citizens" who were alarmed by the unsuspected strength of socialists and communists in the wake of the nationwide railroad strike in the summer of 1877. Yet Alcott was no friend of the business classes and no defender of capitalism. Instead, he portrayed the orderly ideal community. Led by its eminent thinkers, the ideal community, he believed, could ameliorate the problems of laborers without violence. It would furnish suitable employment for all its members, adequately compensate the labor of both the head and the hand, and enhance everyone's quality of life. "Man must have some recognized stake in society and affairs to knit him lovingly to his kind," he said, "or he is wont to revenge himself for wrongs real or imagined." The merchants and bankers controlled public affairs, he believed, because the poets, philosophers, and "common people" had not yet awakened to their roles in the ideal community. In a sense Alcott harked back to a romanticized youth in Wolcott and was seeking refuge from change in a community that no longer existed, if it ever had. Yet at the same time he prophesied the day when communities and governments, national and local, would begin to respond to social problems through legislation and planning.[31]

The change in Alcott's reform thought from individualism to an incipient collectivism demonstrated in one person's intellectual odyssey the change in American reform thought that led to the progressive movement of the late nineteenth and early twentieth centuries. This change was one of emphasis. Antebellum reformers stressed the transformation of individuals as the precondition of an improvement in society and institutions. Late nineteenth-century reformers looked to the power of government and institutions to recast themselves and individuals. The goals were largely the same: to produce morally pure, regenerated individuals, and to defend traditional moral and religious values in the face of rapid change.

Nothing better illustrated the curious combination of conservatism and radicalism, of the defense of tradition and the celebration of freedom, in Alcott the reformer, than his stand on women's rights. He was a lifelong supporter of increased civil and political rights for women and of their enlarged role in society—in the professions, in the arts, and in public affairs. In his early days of teaching in Connecticut, Boston, and Philadelphia, he was careful to treat the sexes equally. He allowed his female students to sit on the classroom juries he established to hear disciplinary problems, whereas only males were permitted to sit on their official counterparts. The disparity in opportunities for education for men and women was clear to him, and he sought to promote such opportunities for women. Among his initial interests in reform literature in the 1820s was Mary Wollstonecraft's *Rights of Women*. Accordingly, in his teaching he pledged to facilitate the "emancipation of the female mind" from "tyrant man," deploring the idea that a woman should think and believe only what her husband believed.[32]

Alcott's views about women were directly related to the liberating spirit of transcendentalism and reform in the 1830s and 1840s. He admired Elizabeth Peabody's "superior mind" and Margaret Fuller's "free and bold speculation." Frances Wright and Angelina Grimké impressed him by their outspoken stands on reform in an age that considered it improper for women to speak in public and before legislatures. Grimké's antislavery speech before the Massachusetts legislature in February 1838 prompted Alcott to write for the first time at length in his journal about women's rights. "Proud day was this for woman!" he declared, and added: "Heretofore, man has been slow to acknowledge the rights of woman; and in his measures, for the development and guidance of humanity, has failed to recognize her place, as coworker with him in the accomplishment of its mighty destinies." Without fail, he demanded that women be allowed to speak and particpate freely in the various Bible and Sabbath conventions of the 1840s.[33]

He welcomed women to his conversations and greatly relied on their contributions. He was sure that the exclusion of women from the Town and Country Club had led to its ruin. The judgments of women concerning the "essentials of Genius," he thought, were often more reliable than those of men. The company of sincere women, he said, was the type and spirit of "ideal society." He believed that women should be actively involved in the professions, in art, in science, in philosophy, in politics, and on the public platform.[34] He opposed all restrictions based on sex:

> Whatever woman can do, let her be free to do: we wish her to do it in her way, not in ours, and thus justify her art and capacity as a woman. She has shown herself equal to every position which she has chosen to fill, and if there are new positions awaiting her in the advancing culture and civilization, let her take those as they rise.[35]

Alcott's wife and daughters were all strong advocates of women's rights. Abby worked all her life for an increase in political power for women, an end to the subordination of women to men, and an enlarged role for women in society. In her most bitter moments she commented that women were but God's afterthought and of little account given their place in American society. But Abby was a forceful woman, unwilling to accept traditional roles and status, particularly for her daughters. She wanted them to think, feel, and live individually, to be something in themselves, not a mirror image of some man. Undoubtedly it was her example that led Louisa and May to professional careers in writing and art. Both Louisa and May were conscious of the threat to career and independence that marriage would mean. Louisa avoided it altogether, and May waited until she was in her late thirties and well established professionally before marrying a man nearly twenty years younger than she.[36] Anna accepted the traditional role of wife and mother but not without complaint. "Wise women" told her that the keeping of a house ought to be her greatest delight, but she refused to believe it. "Alas," she said wryly,

> owing to a father whose beloved head is forever in the clouds, & a dear mother whose love of books & early education prevented [her] from early learning to bake & scrub, I did not inherit that blessed disposition that riseth not above pots & pans, & I detest cooking above wash tubs & a scrubbing brush, as much as ever did the veriest blue stocking in the land.[37]

Abby took an active part in the women's rights movement, especially in the 1850s. In May 1853 she started a petition to the Massachusetts Constitutional Convention asking for an amendment to the constitution giving women the vote and equal rights with men. Lucy Stone and Wendell Phillips spoke in favor of the petition, but the Convention Suffrage Committee disregarded it. In later years Abby's health prevented her being outwardly active, but even in 1875 she was working for the vote, this time urging that women be allowed to vote on local tax bills. In September 1876 Anna, Louisa, and May, with Abby's moral support, sent a joint letter to the Concord town collector asking that a protest be read at the next town meeting. Women, they said, should not have to pay taxes without proper representation in government, especially in the year of the centennial of the Revolution. Alcott supported all of this and encouraged it. He recognized that women had to submit and endure the wrongs of society while men could often dodge and escape them. And his leaving Abby with nearly all the household chores in the style of the traditional American husband was ironic proof of his position. He supported Abby's efforts for women's rights and encouraged his daughters to pursue their professions. Indeed, his educational efforts led them to explore their creative potential and to realize their talents.[38]

In his later career Alcott himself became actively involved in the women's rights movement. Dr. Harriot Hunt, a frequent participant in his conversations, first asked him to attend a women's convention in Worcester in September 1851. He refused, saying that although the claims of the women were just, he felt that the debate and display of a convention was not properly feminine. But he lost these reservations after attending the Women's Rights Convention in New York City in November 1856. Lucy Stone presided ably and efficiently, he thought, and the conduct of the convention and the abilities demonstrated by the women in attendance impressed him. During the 1860s and 1870s Alcott was invited to many such conventions, as a delegate and as a speaker. He hoped to see women elected to high office. Elizabeth Cady Stanton, he believed, should have been elected to the Senate. In September 1867 Lucy Stone circulated an appeal to be signed by gentlemen of "national reputation" in support of the women's suffrage referendum then at issue in Kansas and also in support of the effort to remove the word *male* from the constitution of the state of New York. Alcott signed it gladly, although Emerson refused. In December 1877 his nemesis the *Atlantic Monthly* offended Alcott again when it failed to invite the magazine's female contributors to a celebration of John Greenleaf Whittier's birthday.[39]

But while Alcott supported women's rights and a greater freedom of action for women, he also idealized and sentimentalized them and placed them on an uncomfortably high moral pedestal. He associated everything "lovely, kind, pure, hallowed" with women. They were a higher moral force than men: "May it not be that on all subjects connected with character," he said," the intuitive *moral* discernment of women, is a purer guide to truth, than the more calculating temper of man?"[40]

In his early years as an educator and a theorist on child rearing, Alcott wrote extensively on the importance of the mother in the education, especially the moral education, of young children. The relationship between mother and child, he said, was a visible emblem of the goodness of God. It was the mother who had the chief responsibility to develop a child's affections; she would teach the child to love. Mothers had a "sacred duty" to be guardians of childhood.[41] "Thy sex," he wrote orphically in 1838,

is the emblem of unfailing love, and ever enduring constancy! O belie thou not thy nature. Be what thou wast designed to be. Be woman indeed. Be God's loveliest minister on earth.[42]

Alcott's idealized portrait of women did not alter with age and experience. As superintendent of schools in Concord he reported that women in his schools made the best teachers because they could lead and prompt with the heart and the affections. His defense of women's right to vote and hold office resulted from his certainty that they would purify and uplift politics. Their presence in government would surely bring about better laws and improve the morals of the country. "Certainly liberty is in danger of running into license," he warned, "while woman is excluded from exercising political as well as social restraint upon its excesses." The influence of women in local government, he felt, would reinforce a town's sense of community and social cohesion because these things were a natural part of femininity. Women would also stem the tide of vice and corruption. Their votes would provide bulwarks in defense of personal purity, temperance, chastity, and peace.[43] "Women are the natural and ordained promoters of pure morals and refined manners," he gushed:

And when good women associate to promote these, something effective must follow. Woman's power is greater than she has suspected, and it is a hopeful sign of our time that she is beginning to intimate, in ways hitherto deemed derogatory to her sex, that she has public responsibilities as well as private resting upon her, for the welfare of the community.[44]

"Women" was one of Alcott's favorite topics of conversation during his Western tours. The prototype for these conversations was a highly successful session held in Boston in December 1868, a transcript of which subsequently appeared in the *Radical*. It contained all the elements of his idealized conception of woman: their purity, their moral leadership, their "ideal" intellect, which subordinated logic and experience to intuition. This message he carried to all parts of the midwest in the 1870s. He found personifications of his ideal in young, brilliant women such as schoolteacher Ellen Chandler. He first met her in 1864 during a visit to the Framingham Normal School, where she was a student. For fifteen years beginning in 1867, he maintained a regular correspondence with her. She often visited Alcott in Concord and regularly accompanied him to meetings of the Radical Club. She was interested in education, in conversation, in the literature and ideas of transcendentalism, and, most important, in the ideas of Bronson Alcott. Alcott found vicarious youth in this vivacious and intelligent young woman, just as he had found it in Anna Thaxter in the 1830s and in Ednah Littlehale in the 1850s. His poem "Bright Visions of my Sprightlier Youthful Days," was addressed to her.[45]

Ellen Chandler wisely criticized Alcott for what she considered his overly flattering view of women, a view she felt to be not altogether helpful. Indeed, Alcott approached the stultifying "cult of true womanhood," especially with his belief that women were the foremost upholders of purity and virtue. This led him inevitably to expect only certain kinds of behavior from women and to narrow his definition of what an appropriate social role for women should be. For example, he felt that both Frances Wright and Elizabeth Peabody were overly masculine in their aggressive, forthright manner. He believed that men should be dominant in the family as the delegates of God on earth, and that the husband and wife had clearly defined and unalterable roles in the family. "A family is the Patrimonial Estate," he declared, "Man the Husbandryman and Woman the Housekeeper." He accepted the biological fallacy that men planted the "seed" in sexual union and that the woman merely provided a sanctuary for that seed. It was the male force, he thought, that was "initiative" and "generative". Despite his belief that women were the best teachers, he never considered a woman for the job of high school teacher in Concord. Instead, he believed that "a man of weight and character" was needed.[46]

Alcott's romanticized and sentimental view of women could well have caused him to resist their entrance into politics and the professions. The cult of true womanhood also included the "virtues" of submissiveness and domesticity. Even Emerson, who like Alcott celebrated the superior purity of women, opposed, at least for a time, the inclusion of women in politics lest their engaging in politicking and aggressive debate spoil them. But Alcott escaped the potential narrowness of his position. Instead, his ideas became liberating for women. His confidence that personal goodness could transform institutions allowed him to approve of an enlarged social role for women without fear of their consequent degradation. Even the value he placed on family life did not cause him to disapprove of those women who resisted domesticity, such as Elizabeth Peabody, Fredrika Bremer, and Louisa Alcott. His admiration for women such as Ellen Chandler, Anna Brackett, and Ednah Cheney rested not on their skills as wives and mothers but on their intellectual attainments and interests, their abilities as writers, speakers, and educators. In many ways Alcott regarded Ellen Chandler as a protégé, someone with many of the same characteristics and attributes that he prized most about himself. He had no difficulty identifying himself with women because he believed that the best people—the most gifted, the most moral—were androgynous, were combinations of masculine and feminine qualities. "The perfect Mind," he said, "is of both sexes, finely conjoined in disposition and sympathy."[47]

Alcott continued to support women's rights and to advocate for women an expanded social role despite the growing conservatism of his later years and his increasing tendency to emphasize the preservation of morality rather than the transformation of institutions and social relationships. The reason for this was the close association he made between women's rights and social purity and morality. Increased involvement by women in government, politics, and the professions, he believed, did not threaten but rather enhanced the stability of home, community, and traditional values. In his ideas about women, at least, Alcott had found what for him was a satisfactory resolution of the tension between freedom and authority.

He sought a similar resolution of tensions in his religious ideas. The ultimate measure of the substance and direction of Alcott's thought was his religious belief. For above all, transcendentalism was a religious movement. Alcott justified all of his reform efforts in religious terms. Much of his early social and political iconoclasm resulted from his religious radicalism. His separation of what he considered the essential elements of religion—a personal faith, a direct relationship with God—from the structure of organized religion and the social organization and traditions it supported, enabled him to reject institutions, customs, and social roles he considered ephemeral, and to support radical alternatives in society without fear of threatening the basic values he held dear. There was no danger, he had thought, to essential moral values, to the family, and to the community from an attack on organized religion. Indeed, he had felt that it would enhance morality and social cohesion to lift religious belief out of custom and tradition and into the light of the transcendent spirit that dwelt in each person regardless of dogma or creed.

However, free religion, which was largely an outgrowth of both the transcendentalist resistance to sectarian dogma and tradition, and its upholding of the power of the human mind to perceive religious truths directly, disturbed Alcott. As free religion drifted toward natural religion and even toward a denial of the supernatural and the mysteries, Alcott moved closer to orthodoxy, toward the trinitarianism of the Congregationalism and the Episcopalianism that had been his heritage in Connecticut.[48]

Alcott sought in orthodoxy the spiritual emphasis he felt was lacking in both Unitarianism and free religion. He still did not accept the forms, customs, and traditions of organized religion, but he did seek confirmation of his long-held and cherished belief in the supernatural transcendence of God and the supernatural working of the spirit within human beings. In the West he found ready acceptance of his ideas by Congregational churches. And by the 1870s he began to find that he was more "puritan" in faith than he had heretofore recognized.[49]

By the mid-1870s Alcott was finding sympathetic friends among the orthodox clergy. When Dr. J. L. Dudley, the Congregational minister in Milwaukee whom he had met and liked, accepted the pulpit of Boston's Twenty-eighth Congregational Society, Alcott was joyous. Dudley, he felt, would be the true spiritual successor in Boston to Theodore Parker and Dr. Channing. It was strange that he should consider a Congregational minister able to fill the shoes of a Unitarian and a transcendentalist, but he now felt that heterodoxy had lost its spiritual emphasis and could never replace Parker and Channing. An even more impressive representative of orthodoxy was Joseph Cook. In 1875 Cook, an Andover graduate and a Congregational minister, began his series of Monday noon lectures in Boston that were popular for twenty years thereafter and attracted some of the largest audiences in the city's history. Alcott first heard Cook in May 1876, and was immediately attracted by Cook's fervor and zeal. He saw in Cook the best hope for uniting all protestant denominations into a common faith. Each week thereafter Alcott faithfully attended the Cook lectures and pasted newspaper reports of the lectures into his journals.[50]

Cook spoke without reservation about a wide range of topics from theology to labor reform, from foreign countries to biology. His lectures were widely reported and reprinted in America and in England, reaching an estimated million readers weekly. He spoke for a "Christian" solution to the labor problems which anticipated the social gospel. He spoke out for morality and purity. He defended the orthodox doctrines of the Trinity, the Atonement, and original sin against the skepticism of free religion. And he asserted his unfailing belief in the supernatural origin of the universe in opposition to the "negations" of the Darwinists.[51]

Thus Cook touched those things that had concerned Alcott since the late 1860s. Cook was a conservative reformer much like what Alcott had become. He was committed to individual moral reform and was opposed to socialism, but advocated limited governmental efforts to ameliorate social problems. Alcott was impressed by Cook's counter to the Darwinists and Huxleyans that a life force existed beyond that of the mere chemical or physical. Cook used science and the scientific method to marshall evidence to support his theology, and Alcott, reflecting on his own lifelong effort to synthesize science and religion, was enthralled.[52]

What most attracted Alcott to Cook was the kind of revival spirit his lectures brought to Boston. They heralded a kind of religious awakening that could combat the atheism and skepticism that Alcott perceived to be growing apace. Alcott looked to just about any quarter for that kind of religious fervor. He even found virtue in popular evangelist Dwight L. Moody. Moody was "bigotted" and "over-biblical," Alcott thought, but at least he stirred the religious instincts. "Let the heart's affections be turned toward divine things," Alcott pleaded, "by any humane instrumentalities."[53]

It was not long before the free religionists and the liberal Unitarians began launching counterattacks at Cook. In March 1877 they began publicly confuting the doctrines of sin and atonement that Cook defended. Alcott was not completely sold on Cook's dogma, but he believed that, whatever its deficiencies, it was better than the "loose" doctrine of the liberals, which came close to denying the supernatural altogether. Cook's lectures, he thought, would deepen the piety of the churches and establish the supremacy of the spirit over pantheism, nihilism, and atheism.[54]

In April 1877 Cook, in an obvious effort to draw upon the respected wisdom of the Concord transcendentalists to support his arguments, used Alcott's method of discipline in the Temple School as an illustration of the Atonement. By asking the guilty party to strike him on the hand with the ferule, Cook said, Alcott was vicariously accepting the punishment of the offender much as Jesus atoned for the sins of fallen humanity. As Cook presented his illustration Alcott noted that the eyes of the audience all turned to him. He was proud of the acknowledgment, and he agreed with Cook's explanation, although in the 1830s Alcott had never associated his disciplinary practices with the

Atonement. Cook's example gave rise to a stir of theological debate in Boston over the nature of the Atonement. Washington Gladden, then minister of the North Congregational Church in Springfield, Massachusetts, and soon to be a leader of the social gospel movement, wrote a pamphlet attacking Cook on the Atonement and the Alcott example. Gladden believed that there had been no vicarious atonement in Alcott's school but rather direct punishment of a sensitive student who was forced to strike a revered teacher. Alcott, inattentive to the finer theological points at issue, accepted Cook's version because it "appealed to the heart" by revealing in an example the mercifulness of the Cross.[55]

In the same way Alcott found comfort in orthodoxy generally by accepting its tone and its spiritual emphasis but not every element of its doctrine. He even tried to blend his idea of personalism with the concept of the Trinity. The personality, he had said, was the divine element within each human being. Now he identified the Person as threefold, as embracing a "Trinity of Personal Attributes." The meaning of his idea of the personal trinity was imprecise, but it suggested that each person partook of the threefold attributes of the "Person of Persons," that is, will, conscience, and reason. Alcott had no trouble accepting the decidedly Platonic concept of the consubstantial Deity that had been a part of trinitiarian Christianity since the Council of Nicaea in 325. Where he continued to differ from the orthodox, of course, was in his application of the trinitarian formula to the divinity within human beings, something the orthodox could never accept. However, the representatives of Boston orthodoxy were so glad to find that a known heretic such as Alcott had finally begun talking of the Trinity and the Atonement that they opened their doors to him without considering the extent to which he still differed from them.[56]

Acceptance by the trinitarians was especially hearty during and after the lengthy series of Alcott conversations sponsored by Joseph and Georgiana Cook. These conversations began in December 1877 at the suggestion of Joseph Cook, who by this time was providing Alcott with a seat near him on the speaker's platform at his lectures and was referring to him as the "American Plato." For his part Alcott associated Cook with the inspiration of the early years of transcendentalism. "Nothing since the descent of the spirit in transcendental days," he told Mrs. Cook, "has inspired like hopes in the future of religious thought, and Christian fellowship." Persons of various shades of opinion—trinitarian, Unitarian, free religion—attended the Monday evening conversations, giving rise again to Alcott's recurrent hope that his message would serve to reconcile opposites and bring about a union of faiths in the true church. Attendance grew from session to session throughout the winter of 1878, as a surprisingly large number assembled at the Cook apartments in the Belleview Hotel to hear and discuss Alcott's views of immortality, the relationship between the purity of parents and purity of offspring, and the Concord authors. The newspapers reported Alcott's new orthodoxy. New-found trinitarian friends such as George Zabriskie Gray,

Dean of Cambridge's Episcopal Divinity School, asked to visit Alcott in Concord. The Reverend F. M. Grout, minister of the Congregational Church in Concord, attended the Cook conversations and lent Alcott his prized collection of books by Horace Bushnell. Episcopalian clergyman and newspaper correspondent Julius H. Ward visited Alcott and wrote a flattering article about him in the *Boston Sunday Herald.*[57]

In the fall of 1878 Alcott was named to the committee of arrangements for the Cook lectures, making him close to an official sponsor to orthodoxy. The students of Amherst College invited him to speak, which he did on December 6, 1878. They were glad to hear that Alcott was what he described as a "philosophical trinitarian," and Alcott felt that Amherst students were more dedicated to a serious religious life than were Unitarian counterparts at Harvard Divinity School. Professor William Seymour Tyler of Amherst subsequently wrote an article in the *Christian Union* about Alcott's visit, lauding Alcott's belief in the Trinity and the Atonement and his battles against materialism and skepticism. However, Tyler remained suspicious of Alcott's transcendentalism and wisely questioned how completely Alcott had returned to traditional beliefs. Alcott tried to reassure Tyler by confessing that he was now freed from Unitarianism and that transcendentalism was in harmony with orthodoxy.[58]

As Alcott more and more associated transcendentalism and his own "Christian theism" with orthodoxy, he began to seek ways to connect Emerson with the same ideas. Alcott chose to interpret Emerson's essay "The Sovereignty of Ethics," which was read to the Concord Fortnightly Club in May 1878, as indicating that Emerson was moving ever closer to Christian theism as Alcott perceived it. Alcott announced these conclusions to his audience at Cook's parlors. Joseph Cook assumed that Emerson had finally in his old age found the truth of traditional doctrine, and he proceeded to say so in his public lectures. Meanwhile, Alcott stated publicly his opinion that the theology of Dr. William Ellery Channing had been close to present-day trinitarianism. In saying this, Alcott was equating Channing's faith with his own concept of personal faith. He was blurring the differences between orthodoxy and Unitarianism and between Channing's Unitarianism and transcendentalism, while attempting to capture the strong influence that Channing had on transcendentalism. Thomas Wentworth Higginson and Cyrus Bartol immediately challenged Alcott's appraisal of Channing. They would admit no suggestion that Channing was in any way trinitarian.[59]

As a result of these statements by Alcott and by Cook, the question of Alcott's and Emerson's supposed conversion became a matter of public debate during 1879 and 1880, causing Alcott no end of bewilderment and some embarrassment. Rumors claimed that Emerson had officially joined the Congregational Church and had recanted the heresies of the past. In fact, Emerson was too feeble and confused much of the time to play an active role in any religious controversy. He finally authorized his son Edward to issue a public statement flatly denying any conversion. Indeed, he retained his elected position as vice president of the Free Religious Association. Alcott had stated his opinions about Emerson and Channing in the interests of sectarian harmony, hoping to find points of agreement whereby all the faithful might come together. But in doing so he had ignored or muddled important theological issues. He was nonplussed that anyone should care about such things anyway as long as everyone agreed in spirit. He thought the distinctions between orthodox and heterodox meaningless. The perplexing controversy about his and Emerson's orthodoxy, he decided at length, was unimportant and did not deserve comment by him or by Emerson.[60]

Nevertheless, Alcott agreed to explain his theological position publicly at Boston's Park Street Church on April 14, 1879. The church parlors were filled as Alcott submitted to questioning by a panel of trinitarian ministers including Grout of Concord, J. S. Withrow of the Park Street Church, and William F. Warren, president of Boston University. Alcott explained his philosophical concept of the Trinity, expressed his acceptance of the ideas of the Atonement and original sin, and vaguely stated his belief in the divinity of Jesus, the "uniqueness" of the Christian religion, and the "reality" of divine revelation. His confessions were enough to convince the tribunal that Alcott was indeed in line with traditional beliefs. Warren wrote to Alcott expressing his hearty approval.[61]

In September 1879 Alcott went with Cook to Andover Theological Seminary, where he once again faced ecclesiastical examination. Again the questioners found him acceptable, although the newspaper reporters noted the vagueness of Alcott's definition of the Trinity. By this time the *Free Religious Index* had chimed in by claiming that although Alcott had gone orthodox, he did not fully represent transcendentalism, and he did not prove that Emerson had surrendered to trinitarianism. The hostility of the *Index* was easily countered by the welcome Alcott received at Yale in October, when a pleased Yale president Noah Porter praised Alcott for his association with the Congregationalists and with Joseph Cook. For his part, Alcott was willing to be claimed as an orthodox, but he still had a lurking suspicion that his particular interpretations would not be acceptable to trinitarian churches in general. Indeed, the orthodox theologians were in a sense misled by Alcott. So anxious were they to claim a noted man as one of their own that they ignored the theological differences that still existed.[62] In part Alcott had planned it that way:

> If I succeed in weaving around the Orthodox faith, such philosophical attire as to clothe [it] in fairer forms, render [it] attractive alike to the affections and aspirations, while winning the assent of reason and conscience, I shall have wrought my miracle indeed.[63]

The wisest statement about Alcott's "orthodoxy" was that of Marion V. Dudley. Mrs. Dudley pointed out that Alcott's fundamental beliefs had not changed. He accepted the doctrine of the Trinity in a mystical and spiritual way, she said, but not in a theological way. Alcott still did not believe that

Jesus was the *only* son of God. Rather, she said, he continued to believe that there was a divinity within each human being. Alcott's overtures to trinitarianism just represented his effort to bring about unity and toleration among the various denominations.[64]

Alcott's conservatism, his growing concern with morality and purity, his gentility, his dabbling with orthodoxy to preserve traditional religious values, and especially his battle against materialism, naturalism, and Darwinism, all came to a focus in the institution that became the culmination of his career and his ultimate achievement: the Concord School of Philosophy.

His longtime dream of a Concord academy became a possibility in the winter of 1878, just as he was enduring the grief of Abby's death and the sense of loss he felt at having to leave his beloved Orchard House. In February Sarah Denman wrote from Quincy, Illinois, that she intended to visit Concord that summer and would try to persuade Dr. Hiram Jones to join her. A month later Jones wrote asking for accommodations for himself and several friends. In June Samuel H. Emery of Quincy arrived with the intention of settling permanently in Concord. Then in mid-July Mrs. Denman, Dr. and Mrs. Jones, and Martha Wolcott came and began two glorious weeks of philosophical discussions at various homes, with Alcott and interested Concordians. Dr. Jones gave readings from Plato and compared idealism and evolution. "Darwinism," Alcott exulted, "dissolves in the mists." Talk of the new academy became serious as Alcott noted that Concord had not shown such an interest in philosophical matters since the "first stirrings of transcendentalism." He pleaded with William Torrey Harris to visit Concord and add to the stimulus for philosophical studies that Jones and his group had begun. "We are a little proud just now of Ideas," he told Mary Adams, "and celebrate philosophy as never before since my residence in this little Athens." In September he told Charles Mills that the success of the Jones visit had all but assured the creation of a "Concord Summer Symposeum," and he reported to Martha Wolcott that "our Concord circle having once tested the nectar and ambrosia, asks eagerly for more.[65]

That fall and winter Alcott proposed his "Symposeum" to any group that would listen—to Harvard divinity students who visited him, to the students at Amherst College, to Emerson, Sanborn, and other likely supporters in Concord. He talked with George Howison, David Wasson, and Thomas Davidson about their becoming teachers at the summer school. On January 19, 1879, he and Sanborn drew up a prospectus to be sent to interested people around the country for their comment. Especially did they seek the advice of Harris and Jones. The school was to be called the "Concord Summer School of Philosophy and Literature." Both Harris and Jones responded favorably and agreed to be members of the faculty, although Harris could promise only a week because of his duties with the St. Louis schools.[66]

By March 1879 the approved prospectus was in the mail and in the newspapers. It advertised a five-week course of lectures beginning in Concord on July 15 at a cost of three dollars a week. The regular faculty included

Alcott, Harris, Jones, Wasson, and Ednah Cheney, with special lectures by Davidson, Howison, Sanborn, and Thomas Wentworth Higginson. Scores of requests for applications and further information began to flow in immediately from people in Massachusetts, Pennsylvania, New York, New Jersey, Michigan, Connecticut, Tennessee, Illinois, Kansas, Ohio, Wisconsin, Iowa, Minnesota, Missouri, Vermont, Kentucky, and Ontario, Canada. Students at Harvard, Andover, and Amherst expressed interest, as did professors from Johns Hopkins, Yale, and Northwestern Universities. Some of the Amherst students used proceeds obtained from Emerson's lecture there in March to finance their attendence. Alcott busily arranged room and board for prospective participants, carefully avoiding Concord's Middlesex Hotel because it served liquor. He meticulously prepared Orchard House and the grounds around it. Regular sessions were to be held there, and Samuel Emery was to live there for the summer.[67]

The School opened as scheduled on July 15, with Samuel Emery as official chairman and Alcott giving a welcoming speech to the fifty people that crowded into Orchard House. "The town swarms with budding philosophers," said Louisa, "& they roost on our steps like hens, waiting for corn." She was glad for something new in dull Concord, and although some people laughed, she was joyous that her father's dream had come true. However, the practical Louisa was concerned about the seeming irrelevance of "speculation." "Why discuss the unknowable," she wondered, "till our poor are fed & the wicked saved?"[68]

Young Florence Whiting, who attended this first year, noted that the School was conducted in deadly seriousness. Frivolity was clearly out of place. "The seats were hard and the air was hot," she remembered, "but a company such as met there were soaring above all such minor discomforts. Those of us who were not yet freed from these physical limitations, kept very quiet about it, and who knows how much good just that may have done for our youthful souls?" The session lasted the full five weeks. Ednah Cheney lectured on art. Harris applied Hegelian logic to matters of religious faith. Jones did the same with Platonism. David Wasson talked about the relationship of the individual to the state. And Alcott conversed on personal theism. These regular speakers were supplemented by Thomas Wentworth Higginson, who lectured on American literature, Harvard professor Benjamin Peirce, who held forth on the "Cosmogony of the Universe," and Thomas Davidson, who used the fascinating stereopticon to project pictures on a screen illustrating his lecture on Greek antiquities. Emerson lectured once—ironically, on memory—to a large audience at the Congregational Church, prompted by his daughter Ellen. Harrison Blake read selections from his master, Thoreau. Cyrus Bartol spoke on education, and Frank Sanborn on public charities.[69]

The School was successful beyond all expectations. Close to four hundred persons attended altogether, an average of forty per lecture. They came from all over the country, from as far away as San Francisco. Receipts totaled seven hundred thirty-three dollars, about equaling expenses. Prominent participants included Henry A. Beers of Yale; E. H. Russell, principal of the State Normal School in Worcester; John Steinfort Kidney, Episcopal minister from Faribault, Minnesota; President Daniel Coit Gilman of Johns Hopkins University; philosopher-manufacturer Rowland Hazard; and Alcott's Western friends—Mrs. Denman, Mrs. Wolcott, Judge Bryan of Akron, Ohio, and Rebecca Rickoff of Cleveland. The newspapers, which had given the School but scanty coverage at first, began to wake up to its evident importance and reported its successes.[70]

As it turned out, the most important participant in terms of the School's future success was the wealthy philanthropist Elizabeth Thompson of New York City. She offered to donate one thousand dollars for the purchase of Orchard House and its dedication to "philosophic culture." The fifty-eight-year-old widow so charmed Alcott that he wondered if there might not be an "affectionate sentiment" budding in his heart. He worried that such feelings might be dangerous to one as ancient as he. With promises of support such as that of Mrs. Thompson, and with the enthusiasm generated by success, plans for continuing the School in 1880 proceeded without delay. Alcott, Jones, Sanborn, and Emery talked of prospective faculty members, hoping to make the School more philosophical and less eclectic in the future. Alcott was overjoyed and not a little surprised at the School's accomplishments. He recognized the debt to his Western friends. Without them, he knew, the School would never have begun. His neighbors in Concord had always treated the enterprise with skepticism and expected it to fail, as had so many of Alcott's plans in the past.[71]

By the last session on August 16, 1879, the cultural meaning of the School was clear. It was to be a bulwark of idealism and Christianity against materialism, naturalism, and Darwinism. Without a doubt the surprising popularity of the School arose from the need of the participants and those interested in the School to defend long-held religious values and beliefs in the face of skepticism, materialism, and the disrupting effects of social and economic change. Joseph Cook lauded the School for its opposition to materialism and "pantheism," and for its belief in a "conscious personality." Newspaper reporters noted the extent to which Alcott had "given up his peculiar ideas of forty years ago." Now, they maintained, Alcott was strong believer in Christianity, and the School's purpose was to uphold Christian principles against the "assaults of agnosticism."[72] For Frank Sanborn, Alcott—and the School—symbolized solid principles standing in the face of the superfluous. "In a frivolous age he was earnest," said Sanborn,

> amid the self-seeking and the successful, he sought first the kingdom of heaven and its righteousness; amongst those who knelt before the shrine or the idol, he worshipped the divinity, standing erect and serene as becomes the priesthood.[73]

Alcott also viewed the School as just such a bulwark against atheism and materialism. Significantly, Alcott and his fellow planners agreed to exclude followers of positivistic, cosmic, or evolutionary philosophy from the list of speakers for the 1880 session.[74]

Alcott put all his efforts into plans for the 1880 program. In September 1879 he traveled with Sanborn and Elizabeth Peabody to Saratoga Springs, New York, for the meeting of the American Social Science Association, of which he was an honorary member. His interest was less in science than in wooing the School's benefactor, Elizabeth Thompson. For five days he cultivated his relationship with Mrs. Thompson, musing that an "unseen agency" must have thrown him into her presence. At his suggestion the Association elected both Elizabeth Thompson and Elizabeth Peabody as honorary members. Back in Concord, he discussed with Sanborn the possibility of a permanent winter school at Orchard House, with Harris, Jones, and Alcott as the faculty. In October Mrs. Thompson presented her check for one thousand dollars to Alcott and Sanborn, and the three of them agreed that the School should be incorporated. Shortly thereafter Alcott distributed printed circulars describing the proposed 1880 session and decided to go West himself to publicize the School. Harris finally decided to reside permanently in Concord, a move that Alcott felt assured the School's future success. Harris, he believed, was the only "true philosopher" in America, and his presence would be the School's chief attraction.[75]

On October 24, 1879, Alcott left for the West, making his way through the horrible Pennsylvania oil region. He had intended to visit St. Louis and other Mississippi River cities but got only as far as Ohio when he was driven home by overwork and concern for his health. In Columbus, Ohio, arrangements had been made by Frank Wakeley Gunsaulus, a young Congregationalist minister who had earlier impressed Alcott with his book *The Metamorphosis of a Creed*. Gunsaulus was a good friend of Joseph Cook and had sent the book to Alcott at Cook's suggestion. Gunsaulus arranged conversations and lectures at his church, at Ohio Wesleyan University in nearby Delaware, at Wellington, Ohio, and at Ohio State University. After a week of fast-paced activity in the Columbus area, Alcott went with the enthusiastic Gunsaulus to Cincinnati. During a lecture at the Farmer's College, Alcott nearly collapsed. His friends advised him to cut short his tour and return to Concord, which he did on November 25.[76]

Alcott arrived home just in time to hear that May had given birth to a daughter, Louisa May Nieriker, on November 8. May had surprised her family by marrying the youthful Swiss Ernest Nieriker on March 22, 1878. They had been married quickly at a London Registrar's Office and had gone to Paris, where Ernest worked as an inspector general for a mercantile house. May had pledged that their life would be "free from conventionalities," but she was glad that her husband was an ambitious businessman rather than an impractical philosopher. Alcott had sent his blessings and good wishes. He only feared that he would never see his daughter again and would never meet her husband. He had written to May about the School, and she had been pleased to hear of her father's happiness and excitement at its success. But the joy of a new granddaughter was shattered by the news that May had become dangerously ill. On December 31 Emerson came to the house and tearfully handed Louisa a telegram from Ernest telling of May's death two days before.[77]

For Alcott this was another winter of grief. Once again he found consolation in writing, this time a long poem dedicated to May called "Love's Morrow," and his autobiographical poem *New Connecticut*. Ernest had consented to May's deathbed wish that their child be given to Louisa for care. Thus the family could assuage its grief with the expectation that little Louisa May would soon arrive.[78]

Spring brought pleasant anticipations of the next session of the School of Philosophy. Mrs. Thompson's thousand dollars was applied to the building of a "Hillside Chapel" just behind Orchard House and on the hill where Alcott's prized grape arbor had stood for a dozen years. Originally, the money was for the purchase of Orchard House, but Alcott, still hoping to return there to live, resisted its sale. Beginning in March 1880 Alcott closely supervised the building of the Chapel, which would house the School in July. On June 3 the Chapel was finished, and that same day Harris arrived with his family to live in Orchard House. From now on Harris would put full effort into the School and would edit the *Journal of Speculative Philosophy* in Alcott's study.[79]

The School opened on Monday, July 12, with fifty persons in attendance. Dozens of newspaper reporters and journalists descended on the School. A horse barge ran daily from Main Street carrying students to the Chapel. The lectures were held in the mornings and evenings to avoid the oppressive afternoon heat. Inside the Chapel the "stern relentlessness of duty" was "rigidly enforced." Students sat on pine chairs and benches and confronted an interior decorated only by plaster busts of Plato and John Brown and a few flowers and evergreens. The participants again heard series of lectures and conversations by Alcott, Jones, and Harris. William Henry Channing joined the faculty, having come from his pulpit in England to attend the April centennial celebration in memory of his revered uncle's birthday. Channing, who was one of Alcott's closest and most steadfast friends over the years, agreed to support the School of Philosophy by lecturing on oriental mysticism. Denton J. Snider, St. Louis philosopher and teacher of literature, lectured on Shakespeare. Snider later considered his opportunity to speak at the School to be the great turning point in his career, leading to his success as a writer and speaker. Episcopal minister John Steinfort Kidney came from Minnesota to speak on "beauty." Poet John Albee presented his conception of "literary art." Julia Ward Howe, popular lecturer and author of the "Battle Hymn of the Republic," jammed the diminutive Chapel with one hundred fifty listeners for her lecture on "modern society." Elisha Mulford, Episcopal clergyman and author, spoke on the relationship of religion and philosophy to Christianity. Ednah Cheney, Cyrus Bartol, David Wasson, Frederic Hedge, Charles Mills, Andrew Peabody, Harrison Blake, and Frank Sanborn also lectured, as did Emerson, whose audience of three hundred at the Town Hall was the largest of the summer.[80]

Attendance at the 1880 session was a little larger than the previous year. As in 1879, participants were largely those with the leisure time as well as the interest necessary to attend: college professors and students, schoolteachers, writers, theologians, and some businessmen. When the School closed on August 14, the books showed a slight profit, and Alcott rejoiced that the future of the School was assured.[81]

But Alcott was disturbed that the "purely intellectual" aspects of philosophy had had an undue influence. This was especially true, he believed, because of Harris and Jones. They tended merely to interpret Hegel and Plato rather than to assert their own heartfelt faith in idealism. Their approach was too academic and cold. The spiritual and the ideal, he felt, had been obscured. Thus the proceedings had an "air of secondariness" about them. In his own conversations on mysticism and the mystics he illustrated his ideas on the intuitional method of attaining knowledge of the supernatural with references to St. John, Plotinus, Tauler, Eckart, Boehme, and Swedenborg. His purpose was to influence the participants to "divine the mysteries" themselves rather than to listen only to the "formularies" of the "foreign masters." As always, he taught by example. He expected that by his own actions he would excite his students to a living faith in the spiritual and the ideal. Unfortunately for Alcott, enthusiasm was greater for the more logical and structural approaches of Harris and Jones than for Alcott's unsystematic intuitionism. Alcott's ideas too often rested on leaps of faith that his hearers were not always willing or able to make. And the dynamism, the creativity, in Alcott's thought was gone. His theories had become settled. His questions had been answered. He was secure in his beliefs. It was not that he lacked the ability to inspire others. The reports of participants testified to his continued power to suggest and uplift. "A mystic among mystics," said journalist Ellen Mitchell, "he dwells in a serene but stimulating atmosphere, influencing others through his high discourse and moral purity even more than through his writings." As before, his audience was attracted to his wonderful certainty and serenity. But as his friend and supporter Sanborn reported, once participants had heard Alcott's initial statements about intuitionism, personalism, the lapse, immortality, and the preexistence of the soul, they lost interest. Subsequent conversations on the some topics were repetitious and predictable, and the audience diminished.[82]

Nevertheless, Alcott was cheered by the evaluation of the School in newspapers and periodicals. Reporters and journalists saw the School, as Alcott hoped they would see it, as an attempt to battle "rampant materialism"; as a school of Christian theism, free from sectarian squabbles yet full of religious conviction; as having demonstrated the power of ideas and aspiration; and as the latest phase of the constructive enthusiasm that transcendentalism had given to America. Even the *Nation*, which had never been friendly to Alcott's ideas and writings, praised the School as a "pleasing antedote to the sensationalism of the day."[83]

Some observers worried that the School could not last unless it included the exponents of modern scientific thought. Free religionist George Willis Cooke warned that "a dogmatic materialism cannot be cured by a dogmatic spiritualism." The attitude of the Concord School, said Cooke, was indeed dogmatic, at least concerning the relationship between science and religion. He accused the School of propagandism, of opposing free inquiry, and of being "merely a Joseph Cook effort to bolster up Christianity, without a scholarly regard for the truth." Such narrowmindedness, he said, made the School unable to attract "competent" people to the faculty. The outspoken Elizabeth Peabody immediately engaged in a newspaper debate with Cooke, denying that the School disdained science and challenging Cooke's statement about the lack of competence of the faculty. Cooke responded by reiterating his belief that the School had no appreciation of what scientific people were doing.[84]

Clearly, Cooke was right about the narrowness of the School, though not about the competence of the faculty. The School deliberately excluded advocates of Darwinism and Spencerianism. It defended traditional ideas and God and immortality in a way that struck at least one observer as a kind of religious revival. Cooke also charged that the School was not the latest form of transcendentalism because it lacked the spirit of openness to new ideas that had been evident in the Transcendental Club forty years before. Again, Cooke was correct. The School, much like Alcott himself in his later years, was not in the forefront of creative thought. It was defensive in its outlook and unwilling to look at all possible avenues to knowledge. Yet the School served a purpose in supplying philosophical support for religious absolutes in a way that churches could not. It was a forum for a modicum of the much-heralded free inquiry while providing security against the skepticism that free inquiry often produced. It supplied a prophetic challenge to those who would forget the spiritual element in human nature and in the universe. The Concord philosophers radiated a calm sense of security in an age of rapid change, the same sense of security that Alcott often gave to his listeners, who perceived in him a man who was absolutely certain that he had found the key to eternal truth.[85]

On September 19, 1880, Ernest Nieriker's seventeen-year-old sister Sophie arrived with little Louisa May. Alcott rejoiced. "She comes!" he wrote in large letters in his journal. He wanted to remain home with his new granddaughter, but he also felt that he should go West to converse and advertise the School. He hoped that William Henry Channing would accompany him. Surely the two of them would do unmatched service for "freedom" and "ideas." Unfortunately, Channing declined, feeling that he had to return to England and to his family. But Alcott, outfitted with a new black suit, started out on his own. He left Concord on October 12, 1880, just a month and a half short of his eighty-first birth-day.[86]

This was Alcott's last Western tour, the last visit of the Bishop to "All Soul's Diocese." It was also his longest and most successful trip. It lasted seven months, touched thirty-eight cities including nearly all of the places he had visited on earlier trips, and rewarded him with $1,254, more than ever before. Alcott maintained an exhausting schedule, often speaking three times a day. But this time there were no problems of health, and the tour proceeded safely and happily.[87]

He began at Northhampton, Massachusetts, where he spoke on methods of education to the teachers of the Deaf and Dumb Institution where Sanborn was chairman of the Board of Directors. Then he headed for Connecticut and a triumphal return to Cheshire. In 1878 he had been cheered by letters from Frances Street Higby of Austin, Texas, a former pupil at his Cheshire School. Mrs. Higby had told Alcott how she cherished his memory and how she had gathered her younger brothers and sisters and neighbor children around her and had tried to teach them as Alcott had taught her. She had invited him to converse in Austin, but he was unable to go. Now, at the town hall that stood on the site of the old Cheshire Centre District School, Alcott spoke as the dean of the successful Concord School of Philosophy and told the townspeople about the improvements he had made in his Cheshire School. He found a few people who remembered him from 1825 to 1827. But even they did not recall the difficulties the town had caused him then.[88]

After his usual visits to friends and relatives in Waterbury, New Haven, and Wolcott, and his effort to persuade Yale president Noah Porter to speak at the School of Philosophy, Alcott headed westward to Shelburne Falls, New York. Catherine B. Yale, a participant in the School of Philosophy, had arranged a series of conversations in Shelburne Falls with a club called "The Neighbors," of which she was president. The one hundred members of the club, she said, were uncertain and anxious about whether human beings had a kingdom of God within them or whether they were mere "wandering atoms" whose destiny only the environment could shape. Alcott solved this problem for "The Neighbors" and then began a fast-paced series of trips to several little towns in eastern and central New York. In West Edmeston he visited his sister Betsey and his mother's grave. In Rome he spoke at the Presbyterian Church and with the children of the kindergarten taught by Elizabeth Sherwood, another School of Philosophy participant. He addressed the students at Madison University in Hamilton and at Hamilton College in Clinton. Episcopal Bishop Francis D. Huntington, having been impressed by the "Christian hope" offered by the School of Philosophy, invited him to converse in Syracuse. In Oswego he spoke at the State Normal School and visited his nephew, the son of his brother Chatfield, who had died the previous year. On November 12 he was in Ithaca where his longtime friend Charles C. Shackford arranged for him to speak at Cornell University. The Ithaca *Journal* reported that Alcott held his audience spellbound for nearly two hours telling about the transcendentalists, Brook Farm, and Fruitlands. In Rochester he found reporters flocking to see him, and numerous articles on the "Concord Philosopher" appeared in the newspapers.[89]

Alcott took the train for Cleveland on December 9 after several conversations in Rochester, Albion, and Danville, New York, and after a brief delay because of snowstorms in Buffalo. Traveling still excited and interested him, especially because of the people he observed. "Next to a lunatic asylum," he said with utmost seriousness, "the rail car is the [best] school for the study of character." In Cleveland he spoke on immortality to the "Church of the Unity" and to a congregation of Disciples of Christ. Superintendent Rickoff again conducted him through the public schools, and friends of the Rickoffs arranged for his meeting with President-elect Garfield in Mentor. On December 16 he went to Oberlin, where Oberlin College president James H. Fairchild asked him to speak to the nine hundred students and faculty who attended a regular Thursday lecture series. After more conversations in Cleveland he spent Christmas with his cousins in nearby Medina and spoke at the Congregational and Methodist Churches.[90]

On January 1, 1881, Alcott was in Columbus, Ohio, with his young admirer Frank Gunsaulus. Gunsaulus had Alcott speak to his congregation and visit schools, and Gunsaulus's friend and disciple, J. R. Shannon, scheduled lectures and conversations in Piqua, Ohio. Shannon accompanied Alcott to Cincinnati, where Charles Wendte had arranged conversations at the YMCA and with the "Unity Club." From there Alcott went on to Indianapolis and met May Wright Sewall, another participant at the School of Philosophy, who sponsored conversations and school visitations. He then returned to Cincinnati to speak at Wendte's church. After a speech at Antioch College in Yellow Springs, Ohio, several conversations at the State Normal School in Terre Haute, Indiana, and more conversations in Indianapolis, he headed for Bloomington, Indiana, where he met William Torrey Harris, who was lecturing at Indiana University on educational psychology. Alcott also spoke to a large crowd at the University and supplemented Harris's lectures with an account of his own educational ideas to the teachers and students of the Bloomington city schools.[91]

Alcott also spoke at Wesleyan College in Bloomington, Wabash College in Crawfordsville, and to the eighty students at Purdue Agricultural University in Lafayette, before reaching Jacksonville, Illinois, and Dr. Jones's home on March 1. In the "City of Clubs," as he fittingly called it, Alcott met with the Plato Club, the Ministerial Club, and the Literary Club, and he talked at the Congregational Church, the high school, and the Female Academy. Then he headed toward friendly Iowa, stopping briefly in Peoria, Illinois, and at Knox College in Galesburg, Illinois, before arriving in Burlington on March 16. He conversed at and addressed the high school in Burlington, and did the same in Mount Pleasant, Des Moines, and Cedar Rapids. In Ames he spoke at Iowa State University. On April 1 he arrived in Dubuque, where Mary Adams received him as warmly as before.[92]

He stayed a week in Dubuque, visiting friends, speaking on immortality at the Congregational Church, and worrying that the Round Table was giving way to creeping "skepticism." On April 9 he left for Rockford, Illinois, where he spoke at the Congregational Church, visited schools and held two public conversations. He also addressed the students of Rockford College, on which occasion the youthful Jane Addams, then in her final year at the college, dutifully cleaned the clay from the cloth undershoes of this friend of her adored Ralph Waldo Emerson.[93]

From there Alcott's pace became fast and furious: Beloit College in Beloit, and Milwaukee, Wisconsin; Chicago, Batavia, Illinois; Evanston, Illinois, and Northwestern University; Lewistown, Illinois; Ypsilanti and Battle Creek, Michigan. The press of time forced him to turn down some invitaitons. In Battle Creek he called on black abolitionist Sojourner Truth. She was about three years older than Alcott, but he found her "bright and sparkling." He also spoke on temperance and health at Dr. John Harvey Kellogg's Sanitarium. Kellogg, who agreed with Alcott about the value of temperance and a meatless grain and fruit diet, later sent Alcott a copy of his *Cyclopedia of Health and Longevity* and asked him to review it.[94]

After a stop in Detroit and a short visit with Gunsaulus in Columbus, Alcott headed back to Concord, arriving there on May 14, in time to make plans for the School of Philosophy. He was sure that the success of his Western tour was enhanced by the rumor preceding him that he had been converted to orthodoxy. The School of Philosophy reaped the same benefit. Two Episcopal bishops and the Philadelphia *Episcopal Register* endorsed the School for its move toward a "true Christian philosophy." They made much of Alcott's Episcopal background. And Methodist minister Charles F. Deems wrote to Alcott that he was planning an "American Institute of Christian Philosophy" at Greenwood Lake, New York, modeled after the Concord School.[95]

The 1881 session of the Concord School of Philosophy began on July 11. Eighty people were present for Alcott's welcoming speech. Harris and Jones again provided the contrast between Hegelianism and Platonism. Alcott lectured on the "Philosophy of Life," a topic broad enough to allow him to explain his doctrines of genesis, lapse, personalism, and the preexistence of the soul. The "spontaneous overflow of enthusiasm," as Denton Snider described it, made this session, in Snider's opinion, the best of all, the culmination of Schools' efforts. Snider, John Kidney, Samuel Emery, John Albee, Rowland Hazard, Julia Ward Howe, Ednah Cheney, Cyrus Bartol, Frederic Hedge, Edwin D. Mead, Elisha Mulford, and Harrison Blake also lectured. During the first week in August the School celebrated the centennial of the publication of Immanuel Kant's *Critique of Pure Reason* with special lectures by Hamilton College professor John W. Mears, Michigan University professor George S. Norris, Yale College president Noah Porter, Kant expert John Watson, and Michigan University president John Bascom.[96]

Again most newspapers and journals lauded the School for its defense of "true morality," for its faith in "absolute truth and goodness," and for its inspiration. One reporter accused the philosophers of using "materialism" as a cant term and a red flag to frighten the crowd. The *Boston Transcript* covered the School glibly and brushed it aside as "harmless." But such negative response was exceptional. Alcott was ecstatic about the success of the session and was sorry to see the five-week program end despite the exhausting pace it had demanded of him.[97]

That fall he received invitations to go West again but resolved instead to stay at home and supervise the addition of a study to Anna's house, which he financed with the receipts from the previous winter's tour. He planned to read, write, spend time with his granddaughter, and to venture occasionally into Boston to visit his old haunts: the Athenaeum, the bookstores, and the publishing houses. *New Connecticut* was published, and he spent the early fall sending copies to friends and writing an addition to it called "Pedlar's Progress." In early September he was honored by having selections from his writings on child development read along with those of Charles Darwin at the American Social Science Association meeting in Saratoga Springs. On September 26 he read his poem on Garfield at the Concord memorial service for the President who had died a week before.[98]

In the fall and winter of 1881-82, Alcott, with Sanborn's editorial help, wrote a series of verses on his family and his most beloved and respected friends. Poetry, he felt, better captured his feelings for friends and loved ones than did his prose. Among those he celebrated and remembered in *Sonnets and Canzonets* were William Alcott, William Russell, Emerson, Thoreau, William H. Furness, Dr. Channing, Elizabeth Peabody, Lidian Emerson, Margaret Fuller, William Henry Channing, Harris, Sanborn, Benjamin Marston Watson, Ellery Channing, Hawthorne, Ednah Cheney, Ellen Chandler, Cyrus Bartol, Samuel J. May, Wendell Phillips, John Brown, Parker, and Garrison. He did not fail to notice as he wrote that many of these persons were dead, that he was nearly the last of his "circle." Emerson still lived, but he was the shadow without substance. He was largely oblivious to his friends, and Alcott hesitated to call on him.[99]

Sonnets and Canzonets went to press on February 20, 1882. A few copies were illustrated with photographs of the principals for distribution to close friends and family. Upon receiving his personalized copy, William Henry Channing thanked Alcott for keeping alive the memory of transcendentalism. Channing's letter read like an epitaph for the movement, which he felt had been a vital center of inspiration, illumination, and revival, an era of hopeful prophecy and ideal optimism. Transcendentalism, said Channing, was "the *heart* of Puritan New England in the hour of her *New Birth*." The mood for such epitaphs was set on April 27, 1882, when Ralph Waldo Emerson, the personification of transcendentalism, died quietly in his home. Alcott had visited his friend on April 22, only to find him confined to his bed with a severe cold that threatened to become pneumonia. Mrs. Emerson tried to reassure Alcott, but he feared the worst nonetheless. He saw Emerson for the last time on April 26, and Emerson was lucid enough to comment on Alcott's good health. "You have a good hold on life, and maintain it firmly," Emerson said. They shook hands affectionately, and Alcott left, certain that he would not see his friend alive again.[100]

Thousands attended the funeral services on April 30. Alcott read a sonnet. "I all alone," he mourned,

Alone am left by unrelenting fate
Vanished my loved ones all,—the good, the great,—
Why am I spared? Why left disconsolate?

He included these lines in a long poem called "Ion: A Monody," to be part of a new edition of his 1865 essay on Emerson. The School of Philosophy set aside July 22 as a memorial, and Alcott read his poem then. One reporter observed: "The old gentleman never seemed more truly the messenger between two worlds than while reading it."[101]

Emerson's death was a severe emotional blow to Alcott. That strain, as well as the heavy load of writing and traveling, had imperceptibly weakened him. He still hoped to live to be one hundred and was sure that his diet of fruits and grains would serve that end. But warnings of serious illness had come as early as March, when he was forced to leave his writings and take long walks to recover from what probably were spells of dizziness.[102]

Nevertheless, he remained as active as ever. He conversed in West Acton, Lowell, and Boston. He attended every meeting of the 1882 session of the School of Philosophy. As was his custom, he gave both the salutatory and valedictory addresses for the five-week session beginning on July 17, and he gave four conversations on personalism and immortality. He endeavored to explain concretely the relationship between his concept of personality and the doctrine of the Trinity. The personality was "inspiration," he said. It was the life of the spirit manifesting itself in all human faculties: in reason, conscience, and the affections. The personality was the immanent Godhead operating in its threefold aspects of soul, mind, and will. President James McCosh of Princeton University spoke at the School about Scottish philosophy on July 21. He had praised the School for its courageous opposition to skepticism, agnosticism, and materialism. He had appreciated Alcott's attempts to link traditional Christianity with philosophical idealism. But McCosh had worried that the strain of mysticism, the reliance on the "vague and unbounded" theories of Plato, the lack of rigorous logic in the School and in Alcott, would in the end lead to further skepticism.[103]

Alcott found himself extremely sensitive to the heat in the summer of 1882. The ninety-degree temperatures on Sunday August 6 kept him indoors and prevented his planned attendance at the Episcopal church. But the continued success of the School buoyed his spirits. He admitted that Jones, and especially Harris, provided the substance of the School, but he was content with the thought that he had contributed to the program a spark of inspiration and a breath of soul.[104]

After the School closed in mid-August, Alcott remained busy correcting proofs for a soon-to-be-published edition of the lectures given at the School that summer. He also spoke about Emerson to the New England Historical-Genealogical Society. In late September, along with his seventy-four-year-old sister Betsey Pardee, he visited Wolcott for the last time. In mid-October he was still trying to convince Harris of the importance of the mystical element in philosophy, the intuitional source of inspiration that could not be "Hegelized" or even "Platonized." At tea with Harris in his study at Orchard House on October 22, Alcott once again tried, without success he felt, to win Harris's assent to his idea of the lapse. Two days later he suffered a paralytic stroke. He never wrote again.[105]

Notes

1. AJ 54 (1878): 5-8, 372-73, 413, 415-17, 427-28, 526-27; Louisa May Alcott, "Diary, 1850-85."

2. AJ 54 (1878): 581, 595-96, 645, 652-54; AJ 55 (1879): 813-14.

3. AJ 56 (1880): 41, 45, 70; Alcott, *New Connecticut*, pp. 22, 51; Alcott to William Torrey Harris, March 30, 1880, from a copy in Alcott's hand in A. Bronson Alcott, comp., "Letters for 1880," at Houghton Library, 59M-305 (20).

4. An unidentified clipping of Alcott's May 29, 1867, speech to a Boston antislavery convention is in AJ 42 (1867): 209; AJ 44 (1869): 782; AJ 51 (April-December 1875): 127-28; AJ 53 (1877): 595-96; AJ 55 (1879): 654, 845; AJ 54 (1878): 76.

5. AJ 48 (1873): 1020.

6. AJ 47 (1872): 191; AJ 49 (1874): 142.

7. AJ 34 (1859): 575; Alcott to Charles W. [Felt?], October 5, 1875, in "Letters, 1875"; AJ 36 (1861): 252-58; AJ 49 (1874): 351; AJ 48 (1873): 290-91.

8. AJ 48 (1873): 1138-39; AJ 51 (April-December 1875): 251.

9. AJ 41 (1866): 234; AJ 42 (1867): 119-22, 295-96, 394-95; Thomas, *The Liberator*, pp. 431-34; Oscar Sherwin, *Prophet of Liberty: The Life and Times of Wendell Phillips* (New York: Bookman Associates, 1958), pp. 512-16, 532; AJ 43 (1868): 372; AJ 55 (1879): 302-3; A. Bronson Alcott, "Wendell Phillips," *The Radical* 3 (October 1867): 105-10.

10. AJ 46 (1871): 631-33, 789; Sherwin, *Prophet of Liberty*, pp. 586-93; John G. Sproat, *"The Best Men": Liberal Reformers in the Gilded Age* (New York: Oxford University Press, 1968), pp. 48-49.

11. Sherwin, *Prophet of Liberty*, pp. 596-97; AJ 44 (1869): 66, 386-89, 440; E. H. Heywood to Alcott, May 5, 1869, and Alcott to E. H. Heywood, May 7, 1869, in "Letters, 1869"; AJ 45 (1870): 481-82; AJ 47 (1872): 317-18.

12. AJ 47 (1872): 283-86, 431-34, 454-55, 459, 481, 656-59; Sproat, *"The Best Men"*, pp. 86-87; Sherwin, *Prophet of Liberty*, pp. 614-15; Stanley P. Hirshson, *Farewell to the Bloody Shirt* (Bloomington: University of Indiana Press, 1962), pp. 126-27; David Donald, *Charles Sumner and the Rights of Man* (New York: Alfred A. Knopf, 1970), pp. 548-53.

13. AJ 47 (1872): 431-34; Sproat, *"The Best Men"*, p. 86; Hirshson, *Farewell to the Bloody Shirt*, p. 35; AJ 53 (1877): 159-60, 193; AJ 55 (1879): 820-31.

14. George S. Boutwell to Alcott, July 5, 1875, at Houghton Library 59M-312; AJ 51 (1875) (April-December): 282, 317, 327-32, 712; Michael Les Benedict, *A Compromise of Principle* (New York: W. W. Norton and Co., Inc., 1974), pp. 35-36; AJ 47 (1872): 481; AJ 52 (1876): 367; AJ 57 (1880-81): 131-34; AJ 54 (1878): 195-98.

15. Stow Persons, *The Decline of American Gentility* (New York: Columbia University Press, 1973), p. 38; Frederick Ives Carpenter, "Bronson Alcott: Genteel Transcendentalist," *New England Quarterly* 13, no. 1 (March 1940): 34-48; David P. Edgell, "Bronson Alcott's 'Gentility,'" *New England Quarterly* 13, no. 4 (December 1940): 699-705; Frederick Ives Carpenter, "The Genteel Tradition: A Re-interpretation," *New England Quarterly* 15, no. 3 (September 1942): 427-43.

16. AJ 31 (1856): 393.

17. AJ 37 (1862): 116.

18. [A. Bronson Alcott], "The Countryman in his Garden and Orchard," *The Commonwealth*

(July 10, 17, 24, 31, August 7 and 14, 1863); Alcott, *Tablets*, pp. 5-56; AJ 35 (1860): 35; AJ 37 (1862): 21-23, 27.

19. AJ 42 (1867): 412, 423, 431, 433, 439-40, 451-52; Mary Thacher Higginson, ed., *Letters and Journals of Thomas Wentworth Higginson* (Boston: Houghton Mifflin Co., 1921), p. 227; Bertrand and Patricia Russell, eds., *The Amberley Papers*, 2 vols. (London, 1937), 2: 66, 74; Alcott to John T. Sargent, October 30, 1867, in "Letters, 1867"; Katherine Louisa Amberley to Alcott, November 19, [1867], at Houghton Library, 59M-312.

20. AJ 55 (1879): 818-20; AJ 59 (1882): 26.

21. Persons, *Decline of American Gentility*, pp. 102, 277, 279, 301-2.

22. Alcott, *Tablets*, p. 54; AJ 45 (1870): 480.

23. AJ 55 (1879): 671, 693-94, 706-8.

24. Ibid., pp. 708-15.

25. Ibid., pp. 716-19.

26. David J. Pivar, *Purity Crusade: Sexual Morality and Social Control, 1868-1900* (Westport, Conn.: Greenwood Press, Inc., 1973).

27. AJ 42 (1867): 427-30; AJ 44 (1869): 527; AJ 45 (1870): 594-95; AJ 52 (1876): 144, 564, 574.

28. Pivar, *Purity Crusade*, pp. 31-32, 57-58; AJ 44 (1869): 796; AJ 45 (1870): 483-85; AJ 46 (1871): 151; a printed prospectus of the Chicago Society for the Promotion of Social Purity is in AJ 46 (1871): 152-55.

29. AJ 49 (1874): 365-68, 529-30; AJ 51 (April-December 1875): 713; AJ 53 (1877): 283, 405; Alcott to Georgiana Davis, November 6, 1875, Georgiana Davis to Alcott, [November 1?], and November 23, 1875, in "Letters, 1875"; Pivar, *Purity Crusade*, p. 23; AJ 52 (1876): 330-31; an unidentified clipping of Alcott's address to the Moral Education Association on January 7, 1876, is in AJ 52 (1876): 27; AJ 54 (1878): 377, 388.

30. AJ 56 (1880): 226; Harriet P. Fowler to Alcott, January 30, 1880, and Alcott to [Harriet P. Fowler], March 30, 1880, in "Letters, 1880"; Alcott, *Table Talk*, pp. 53-54, 71-74.

31. AJ 54 (1878): 194-98; AJ 49 (1874): 227-29; AJ 53 (1877): 104, 568-69; Alcott, *Table Talk*, pp. 37, 47-48.

32. Sanborn and Harris, *A. Bronson Alcott*, 1: 80; "School Journal Number 3," p. 87, in AJ 1 (1826-27); AJ 2 (1827-28): 204; AJ 3 (1829): 76.

33. AJ 3 (1829): 32-34, 168-69; AJ 10 (1837): 54-55, 212-13, 434; Alcott to W. A. Alcott, August 20, 1829, in "Letters, 1828-34"; AJ 11 (1838): 142-43; "Bible Convention," *Boston Daily Advertiser*, March 30, 1842.

34. AJ 24 (January-March 1850): 346, 428, 442; AJ 26 (1851): 1229-31, 1283-84; AJ 28 (1853): 38.

35. AJ 41 (1866): 314.

36. Abby May Alcott, "Diary," August [26?], 1843; Abby May Alcott to Samuel J. May, November 3, 1847, and April 12, 1853, in "Family Letters, 1828-61."

37. Anna Alcott Pratt, "Diary, 1860-61," p. 19.

38. An unidentified clipping of the 1853 women's rights petition is in "Autobiographical Collections," vol. 6; AJ 28 (1853): 316; Sherwin, *Prophet of Liberty*, p. 226; Abby May Alcott to William Lloyd Garrison, May 16, 1875, owned by the Boston Public Library, MS A.1.2, v 38, p. 20(a); AJ 55 (1879): 579; AJ 52 (1876): 68; AJ 25 (March-December 1850): 54-55; Anna Alcott Pratt, Louisa May Alcott, and May Alcott to the Collector of the Town of Concord, September 8, 1876, owned by the Fruitlands Museum; Alcott to Louisa May Alcott, March 25, 1866, in "Letters, 1865-66."

39. AJ 26 (1851): 1097-98; AJ 31 (1856): 1147-50; AJ 42 (1867): 295-96, 335-36; AJ 43 (1868): 400; AJ 44 (1869): 339-41, 806-13; Paulina W. Davis to Alcott, October 11, 1869, Alcott to Elizabeth Cady Stanton, May 4, 1869, and Alcott to Julia Ward Howe, August 22, 1869, in "Letters, 1869"; Alcott, "Western Evenings, 1869-70"; AJ 48 (1873): 1121; AJ 58 (May-December 1881): 39-41; Elizabeth Cady Stanton to Alcott, April 19, [1869], at Houghton Library, 59M-312; Lucy Stone to Alcott, September 5, 1867, and Alcott to Lucy Stone, September 13, 1867, in "Letters, 1867"; AJ 53 (1877): 915.

40. AJ 2 (1827-28): 139; AJ 4 (1830): 74.

41. [A. Bronson Alcott], "Maternal Instruction," *Unitarian Advocate* 1, no. 4 (1828): 304-8; Alcott, "Observations on the Life of my First Child," 1: 285; [A. Bronson Alcott], "Maternal Influence," *American Annals of Education and Instruction* 3, no. 1 (January 1833): 16-24; Alcott, "Observations on the Life of my Second Child during her First Year," p. 321; AJ 8 (1835): 483; Alcott, "Researches on Childhood," pp. 40, 44.

42. Alcott, "Psyche: An Evangele," p. 31.

43. Alcott, *Superintendent's Report*, 1860-61, p. 6; AJ 44 (1869): 73; AJ 42 (1867): 336; AJ 45 (1870): 622; AJ 46 (1871): 139; Alcott, *Tablets*, pp. 89-90; Alcott to Julia Ward Howe, August 22, 1869, in "Letters, 1869"; Alcott to Anna C. Brackett, April 7, 1874, and Alcott to Mrs. Stone, April 11, 1874, in "Letters, 1874."

44. AJ 49 (1874): 530.

45. AJ 43 (1868): 448, 468; AJ 42 (1867): 291; A. Bronson Alcott, "Woman: A Conversation," *The Radical* 5, no. 2 (February 1869): 89-102; AJ 44 (1869), pp. 551, 556; Ellen Chandler to Alcott, March 13, April 5, 15, July 8, August 18, 1868, July 29, 1869, and January 19, 1873, in "Correspondence with Miss Chandler."

46. Ellen Chandler to Alcott, March 31, 1872, in "Correspondence with Miss Chandler"; AJ 47 (1872): 223-26; Barbara Welter, "The Cult of True Womanhood, 1820-1860," *American Quarterly* 18 (Summer 1966): 151-74; AJ 2 (1827-28): 107; AJ 3 (1829): 168; Alcott, "Psyche: An Evangele," p. 57; AJ 28 (1853): 153; Alcott, "Leaves from Diary, January, 1846"; AJ 35 (1860): 254.

47. Welter, "Cult of True Womanhood"; Rusk, *Emerson*, pp. 370, 440-41; AJ 26 (1851): 253; Alcott, "Woman," *The Radical* 5: 100; Alcott, *Report on the Concord Schools*, 1861-62, p. 21.

48. AJ 47 (1872): 795; AJ 48 (1873): 109-10.

49. AJ 49 (1874): 973-74; AJ 51 (April-December 1875): 669; AJ 50 (1874-75): 24; Alcott to Mary Newbury Adams, October 27, 1873, In "Letters, 1873."

50. AJ 50 (1874-75): 285, 296; AJ 53 (1877): 175-76; J. L. Dudley to Alcott, March 13, 1877, in "Letters, 1877"; Ahlstrom, *Religious History*, p. 791; Charles Howard Hopkins, *The Rise of the Social Gospel in American Protestantism, 1865-1915* (New Haven, Conn.: Yale University Press, 1967), p. 39; AJ 52 (1876): 314-15.

51. Henry F. May, *Protestant Churches and Industrial America* (New York: Octagon Books, Inc., 1963), pp. 164-66; Hopkins, *Rise of the Social Gospel*, pp. 40-42; Joseph Cook, *Orthodoxy* (Boston: Houghton, Mifflin and Co., 1880), pp. 169 ff., 257-59 ff; Joseph Cook, *Biology* (Boston: Houghton, Osgood and Co., 1880), p. 32; AJ 54 (1878); 147-48, 152, 634.

52. May, *Protestant Churches and Industrial America*, pp. 164-65; AJ 52 (1876): 604, 609, 697-98.

53. AJ 53 (1877): 63-64, 226-28.

54. Ibid., pp. 197-201, 315, 759-60; Cook, *Orthodoxy*, pp. 225 ff.

55. AJ 53 (1877): 272-74, 293, 295, 388-89: Hopkins, *Rise of the Social Gospel*, pp. 27-28; Washington Gladden, *Was Bronson Alcott's School a Type of God's Moral Government?* (Boston: Lockwood, Brooks and Co., 1877), pp. 3-11, 33-37.

56. AJ 46 (1871): 710-12; AJ 51 (April-December 1875): 135; AJ 54 (1878): 219-20, 227, 316; AJ 55 (1879): 367.

57. AJ 53 (1877): 691-93, 895, 907-10; Alcott to J. L. Dudley, January 19, 1877, in "Letters, 1877"; Alcott to Georgiana Hemmingway Cook, October 5, 1877, printed in Herrnstadt, ed., *Letters*, p. 699; AJ 54 (1878): 29-30, 96-97, 169-71, 261, 314-15, 362-63, 406; an unidentified clipping on Alcott's orthodoxy is in AJ 54 (1878): 82; a clipping of Ward's article is in AJ 54 (1878): 367 ff.

58. AJ 54 (1878): 590, 621, 659-61, 664, 667-68; AJ 55 (1879): 164-67; William S. Tyler, "Mr. Alcott at Amherst," *Christian Union* (April 30, 1879); William S. Tyler to Alcott, March 20, 1879, and Alcott to William S. Tyler, March 22, 1879, in A. Bronson Alcott, comp., "Letters for 1879" at Houghton Library, 59M-305 (19).

59. AJ 54 (1878): 323-24, 661, 684-86; Rusk, *Emerson*, p. 500; AJ 55 (1879): 81-85.

60. Rusk, *Emerson*, pp. 500-504; AJ 54 (1878): 407; AJ 55 (1879): pp. 154, 811-12: B. B. Marshall to Alcott, May 26, 1879, J. Merritt to Alcott, June 12, 1879, and Alcott to [Edgar S.

Shumway], December 10 and December 22, 1879, in "Letters, 1879."

61. AJ 55 (1879): 209, 217-20, 223; undidentified clipping on Alcott's Park Street Confession is in ibid., pp. 225-26; William F. Warren to Alcott, April 15, 1879, in "Letters, 1879."

62. AJ 55 (1879): 610-18, 625, 684; unidentified clippings of Alcott's Andover visit are in ibid., pp. 619-21.

63. AJ 55 (1879): 217-18.

64. Marion V. Dudley, "A. Bronson Alcott's Trinity," Janesville (Wisconsin) *Journal* (December 1879), from a clipping in AJ 55 (1879): 839-40.

65. AJ 54 (1878): 31, 87, 190, 230, 232, 429-30, 441-59; Sarah Denman to Alcott, February 6, 1878, Hiram K. Jones to Alcott, March 14, 1878, Mary Newbury Adams to Alcott, June 30, 1878, Martha D. Wolcott to Alcott, September 15, 1878, Alcott to Sarah Denman, August 17, 1878, Alcott to Mary Newbury Adams, August 21, 1878, Alcott to C. D. B. Mills, September 30, 1878, and Alcott to Martha D. Wolcott, November 10, 1878, in "Letters, 1878"; Alcott to William Torrey Harris, July 25, 1878, and August 15, 1878, from copies in Alcott's hand in "Letters, 1878."

66. AJ 54 (1878): 559, 663, 693; AJ 55 (1879): 35-36, 40, 55, 57; Hiram K. Jones to Alcott, February 2, 1879, in "Letters, 1879"; William Torrey Harris to Alcott, February 13, 1879, and Alcott to William Torrey Harris, January 26, 1879, from copies in Alcott's hand in "Letters, 1879."

67. AJ 55 (1879): 175-76, 180, 185, 266, 273; a printed prospectus for the 1879 session of the School of Philosophy is in ibid., p. 118; requests for information about the School are found in Alcott's bound collection of "Concord Summer School Correspondence," for 1879, at Houghton Library, 59M-305 (31).

68. AJ 55 (1879): 414-19; Louisa May Alcott, "Diary, 1879-1886," MS at Houghton Library, 59M-309 (3).

69. Florence Whiting Brown, *Alcott and the Concord School of Philosophy* (privately printed, 1926), pp. 6, 38-40; AJ 55 (1879): 419 ff, 426-31, 437, 454, 473-74, 485, 489, 505-6.

70. AJ 55 (1879): 488, 506, 517; numerous newspaper clippings about the School are in ibid., and in A. Bronson Alcott, comp., "Atuobiographical Collections" 10 (1878-79), at Houghton Library, 59M-307 (9); Sanborn, *Recollections*, 2: 485-514; Austin Warren, "The Concord School of Philosophy," *New England Quarterly* 2, no. 2 (April 1929): 199-233; Mary Newbury Adams to Alcott, August 23, 1879, in "Letters, 1879."

71. AJ 55 (1879): 493-94, 498, 500, 517-20, 536; clippings in "Autobiographical Collections," vol. 10; Elvira Kenyon to Alcott, August 11, 1879, A. T. Frizelle to Alcott, August 10, 1879, and John Steinfort Kidney to Alcott, August 21, 1879, in "Concord Summer School Correspondence," 1879.

72. Joseph Cook to Alcott, September 9, 1879, in "Letters, 1879"; unidentified clipping in "Autobiographical Collections," vol. 10.

73. Sanborn, *Recollections*, 2: 463-64.

74. Alcott to Robert D. Weeks, May 13, 1879, in "Letters, 1879"; AJ 55 (1879): 19; unidentified clipping in AJ 55 (1879): 527.

75. AJ 55 (1879): 575-90, 593, 598-600, 644, 647, 652-53; Alcott to William Torrey Harris, October 6, 1879, from a copy in Alcott's hand in "Letters, 1879."

76. AJ 55 (1879): 282-86, 671, 741-45, 747, 753-55, 758-59, 764-66, 771; Alcott to Frank Wakeley Gunsaulus, October 6, 1879, in "Letters, 1879."

77. AJ 55 (1879): 480, 863, 875-76; Louisa May Alcott, "Diary, 1850-85"; Louisa May Alcott, "Diary, 1879-86"; May Alcott Nieriker, "Diary, 1878-1879," MS owned by Houghton Library, bMS Am 1817 (58); May Alcott [Nieriker] to the Alcott family, March 11, 15, April 20, and October 8, 1878, from copies in Anna Alcott Pratt's hand in Anna Alcott Pratt, comp., "Extracts from May's Letters, 1878-1879," at Houghton Library, 59M-311 (17); AJ 54 (1878): 237-38, 271-72; May Alcott Nieriker to Alcott, August 17, 1879, from a copy in Alcott's hand in "Family Letters, 1877-79"; Alcott to May Alcott Nieriker, April 2, and June 8, 1878, in "Family Letters, 1877-79."

78. AJ 56 (1880); 5 ff., 16, 36; Louisa May Alcott, "Diary, 1879-86"; Louisa May Alcott,

"Diary, 1850-85."

79. AJ 55 (1879): 519-20, 808; AJ 56 (1880): 61, 170, 183, 188.

80. AJ 56 (1880): 247, 256, 282, 301, 309; Octavius B. Frothingham, *Memoir of William Henry Channing* (Boston: Houghton, Mifflin and Co., 1886), pp. 395-96; Hester M. Poole, "The Concord School of Philosophy," *Our Continent* 2, no. 17 (November 1882): 519-23; Ellen M. Mitchell, "Concord School of Philosophy," *Free Religious Index*, n.s., 1, no. 13 (September 23, 1880): 146-48; William Henry Channing to Alcott, January 1, 1880, in "Letters, 1880"; Denton J. Snider, *The St. Louis Movement* (St. Louis, Mo.: Sigma Publishing Co., 1920), pp. 263-64; unidentified clippings in AJ 56 (1880); 314-16, 335-36, 350-51, 356, 361-62, 364-65, 369.

81. George Willis Cooke, "The Concord School of Philosophy," *Christian Register* 59 (August 21 and 28, 1880); letters from many of the participants in the 1880 session of the School are bound in A. Bronson Alcott, comp., "Summer School Session," 1880, at Houghton Library, 59M-305 (32); clippings in AJ 56 (1880): 286-87, 365.

82. AJ 56 (1880): 379-80; a printed prospectus of the 1880 session is in "Autobiographical Collections," vol. 10; Snider, *St. Louis Movement*, p. 267; Mitchell, "Concord School of Philosophy," pp. 146-48; A. Bowman Blake, "Philosophy at Concord," *Appleton's Journal* 25 (1880): 63-69; Cooke, "Concord School of Philosophy"; Sanborn, *Recollections*, 2: 504-5.

83. Cooke, "Concord School of Philosophy"; Julius H. Ward, "The Concord School of Philosophy," *International Review* 9 (1880): 459-67; Blake, "Philosophy at Concord"; Poole, "Concord School of Philosophy"; Charles William Wendte, "Memories and Friendships," *Christian Register* (May 4, 1922), p. 423; George P. Lathrop, "Philosophy and Apples," *Atlantic Monthly* 46 (November 1880): 652-56; "The Grip of the Concord School," *Boston Sunday Herald* (July 25, 1880); clippings in AJ 56 (1880): 372-73, 396; "Philosophy at Concord," *The Nation* 31 (July 29, 1880): 74.

84. Unidentified clipping in AJ 56 (1880): 342; Cooke, "Concord School of Philosophy"; Elizabeth Peabody, "The Concord School," *Christian Register* 59 (September 1880); George Willis Cooke, "The Concord School Again," *Christian Register* 59 (September 1880).

85. Unidentified clipping in AJ 56 (1880): 373; Cooke, "Concord School of Philosophy"; W. S. Kennedy to Alcott, February 15, 1880, in "Letters, 1880."

86. AJ 56 (1880): 419, 451-52, 454-55, 457, 471, 476; Alcott to William Henry Channing, September 22, 1880, Alcott to Mary Newbury Adams, September 29, 1880, and William Henry Channing to Alcott, October 7, 1880, in "Letters, 1880."

87. AJ 56 (1880): 454; AJ 57 (1880-81): 327; AJ 57 (May-December 1881): 5, 10.

88. AJ 57 (1880-81): 7-8, 11, 14; unidentified clippings in ibid., pp. 12-13; Mrs T. C. Higby to Alcott, January 22 and February 10, 1878, in "Letters, 1878."

89. AJ 57 (1880-81): 15-16, 23-27, 28-31, 34, 37-39, 41, 44-48, 51-52, 57-63, 67-68, 73-74; Catherine B. Yale to Alcott, October 4, 1880, in "Letters, 1880"; Francis D. Huntington, "The 'Summer School' at Concord," *Boston Transcript* (August 26, 1880); AJ 55 (1879): 566-68; clipping from the Ithaca *Journal* is in AJ 57 (1880-81): 65.

90. AJ 57 (1880-81): 92-95, 99-106, 115, 117, 125-36, 141-42, 146, 150; James H. Fairchild to Alcott, December 10, 1880, in "Letters, 1880."

91. AJ 57 (1880-81): 151-52, 158, 167-71, 172-81, 186-87, 190, 195-205, 214-21.

92. Ibid., pp. 221-24, 233-45, 247-49, 259-65, 273-75, 279.

93. Ibid., pp. 281-85, 288-95; James Weber Linn, *Jane Addams: A Biography* (New York: D. Appleton-Century Co., 1935), p. 52.

94. George L. Collie and Robert K. Richardson, "A 'Conversation' of A. Bronson Alcott," *Wisconsin Magazine of History* 32, no. 1 (September 1948): 85-88; AJ 57 (1880-81): 296 ff., 318-23; Ella A. Giles to Alcott, April 25, 1881, John Harvey Kellogg to Alcott, September 9, 1881, and Alcott to [John Harvey Kellogg], September 19, 1881, in A. Bronson Alcott, comp., "Letters for 1881," at Houghton Library, 59M-305 (21); Alcott to Frank Sanborn, April 8, 1881, owned by the Fruitlands Museum; Richard W. Schwarz, "John Harvey Kellogg," *Dictionary of American Biography* supplement 3 (New York: Charles Scribner's Sons, 1973), pp. 409-11.

95. AJ 57 (1880-81): 324-26; AJ 58 (May-December 1881): 10; clipping of the *Episcopal Register* article is in AJ 58 (May-December 1881): 11-13; Charles F. Deems to Alcott, [December 22,

1881?], in "Letters, 1881."

96. AJ 58 (May-December 1881): pp. 99-100; unidentified clippings in ibid., pp. 113-15, 209-12 ff.; Raymond L. Bridgman, ed., *Concord Lectures on Philosophy* (Cambridge, Mass.: Moses King, 1883), pp. 9-12; Snider, *The St. Louis Movement*, pp. 307-8.

97. AJ 58 (May-December 1881). 135, 283; unidentified clippings in ibid., pp. 136-37, 268, 274; A. N. Alcott, "Some Impressions of the Concord School of Philosophy," *Free Religious Index* (September 22, 1881) 3: 135; K. A. S., "Concord Philosophy," Cincinnati *Commerical* (August 21, 1881); Stuart J. Reid, "A Summer Day at Concord, Massachusetts," *The Manchester Quarterly* (January 1882), pp. 1-13.

98. AJ 58 (May-December 1881): 24, 54, 287, 289, 291, 315, 327-28, 381, 399, 423; unidentified clippings in ibid., pp. 335, 389, 391-95, 401-2; several letters inviting Alcott to the West are in "Letters, 1881."

99. AJ 58 (May-December 1881): 465-66, 497, 505, 521-22; A. Bronson Alcott, *Sonnets and Canzonets* (Cambridge, Mass.: John Wilson and Son, 1882).

100. AJ 59 (1882): 57, 67, 89, 91-92; William Henry Channing to Alcott, September 24, 1882, in A. Bronson Alcott, comp., ["Letters for 1882"], at Houghton Library, 59M-305 (22).

101. AJ 59 (1882): 93-97; Rusk, *Emerson*, p. 508; Alcott, *Emerson*, p. 61; unidentified clipping in AJ 59 (1882): 285.

102. AJ 59 (1882): 55, 184.

103. Ibid., pp. 57, 146, 148, 234-36; unidentified clippings in ibid., p. 260; Bridgman, ed., *Concord Lectures on Philosophy*, pp. 13, 31-32, 109-10, 129-30, 148-49, 167-68: James McCosh, "The Concord School of Philosophy," *Princeton Review*, n.s. (January 1882): 49-71.

104. AJ 59 (1882): 326, 358, 394-96.

105. Ibid., pp. 409, 415-16, 434-39, 466, 475; Louisa May Alcott, "Diary, 1879-86."

Epilogue

ALCOTT lay near death in late October 1882. He was conscious but speechless and helpless. Louisa gave up her apartment in Boston to help care for him. In December he began to rally, although his speech remained indistinct. Sanborn and Harris came to talk about the School. Alcott laughed and tried to talk with them but was too tired to continue long. Friends sent gifts and advice. Dozens of callers appeared at the door but his weakness prevented their seeing him.[1]

A remarkable physical vitality kept him alive and brought unexpected improvement. By the summer of 1883 he had regained some use of his paralyzed right side and was able to walk alone with a crutch. The vacant stare and the confusion went away, although his memory and his speech were still imperfect. He was able to enjoy an occasional carriage ride, and he asked to attend the 1883 session of the School. But the doctors and his family forbade it fearing that the excitement might cause another attack.[2]

For the next five years Alcott led a dim and feeble life. He required constant care and attention from Anna, Louisa, and a succession of nurses. It saddened his daughters that his once-brilliant mind was relegated to checkers and idle chatter. Yet he remained serene and happy, without pain or suffering. Most of the days he spent in his chair, thumbing through his books and his manuscripts, aware of people and events but incapable of speculation or creative thought.[3]

The School of Philosophy continued each summer through 1887, symbolizing Alcott's continued life and expressing thoughts that he no longer had the power to evoke. William Torrey Harris continued to be the leading figure. His Hegelianism dominated the School, because Alcott's incapacity and Hiram Jones's departure limited the influence of transcendentalism and Platonism. In 1885 and 1886 the School turned less to philosophy and more toward literature, with entire summer sessions devoted to a study of Goethe and Dante. Alcott was able to attend a few times. He enjoyed the atmosphere and the attention he received as the dean, but he could not follow the discussions or participate in them. The School's opposition to naturalism and positivism mellowed after Alcott's illness. Indeed, John Fiske, popularizer of the social Darwinism of Herbert Spencer, became one of the best-received lecturers at the School. Significantly, William James gave three lectures on

366

philosophy. Other manuscripts include three volumes of Alcott's reflections about his travels in the West called "Western Evenings," two volumes of letters and diary entries copied for the memoir of Abby, five volumes of genealogical materials, the speculative "Tablets for 1849," the records of the Town and Country Club, two volumes of autographical materials including his attempts to write his biography in prose, and his extremely useful "Autobiographical Index." The Index, which he compiled in 1851, contains a brief summary of the events in each year of his life from 1800 to 1850 and is an especially valuable source for the years from 1841 to 1845.

Along with manuscripts in Alcott's own hand there are a large number of letters and diaries written by others, mainly the members of his family. Only a small portion of Abby's lifelong diary escaped Louisa's scissors, but fortunately the entries for the years from 1841 to 1845 were preserved and serve as a partial replacement for Alcott's missing journals in filling out the events of the Fruitlands period.

Aside from the Alcott-Pratt materials at Houghton Library, the most important source of Alcott manuscripts is the collection at the Fruitlands Museum, Harvard, Massachusetts, which contains several dozen letters both to and from Alcott and a few miscellaneous manuscripts. The Houghton Library also owns some forty items, mainly letters, not in the Alcott-Pratt Collection. A few Alcott-related letters are located at the Boston Public Library and the Massachusetts Historical Society. The Concord Free Public Library owns several relevant items, as well as a microfilm copy of Alcott's journals and letters.

Alcott's published works do not reflect the full force of his thought, intellect, and expressive ability—much of which he manifested orally through conversation—yet they remain valuable and inspiring. A complete list of his works, including his numerous short articles and poems, can be found in Shirley W. Dinwiddie and Richard L. Herrnstadt, "Amos Bronson Alcott: A Bibliography," *Bulletin of Bibliography* 21 (January-April, 1954): 64-67 and (May-August, 1954): 92-96. The most important of his works for an understanding of his ideas on education are "Primary Education: Account of the Method of Instruction in the Primary School No. 1, of Cheshire, Connecticut," *American Journal of Education* 3 (January-February 1828): 26-31, 86-94; "Elementary Instruction," *American Journal of Education*, 3 (June-July 1828); 369-74, 440-43; *Observations on the Principles and Methods of Infant Instruction* (Boston: Carter and Hendee, 1830); "Principles and Methods of Intellectual Instruction Exhibited in the Exercises of Young Children," *American Annals of Education and Instruction* 2 (January 1832): 52-56, (November 1832): 565-70, and (May 1833): 219-23; his three reports as superintendent of schools in Concord (1860-1862); and, of course, *Record of a School*, edited by Elizabeth Peabody, 1st ed. (Boston: James Munroe and Co., 1835), 2d ed. (Boston: Russell, Shattuck and Co., 1836), and 3d ed. (Boston: Roberts Brothers, 1874).

For an understanding of Alcott's early transcendentalism, the most significant of his published works include *The Doctrine and Discipline of Human Culture* (Boston: James Munroe and Co., 1836); *Conversations with Children on the Gospels*, 2 vols. (Boston: James Munroe and Co., 1836-37); and "Orphic Sayings," *The Dial*, 1 (July 1840): 85-98 and (January 1841): 351-61. The later development of his idealism as personalism or personal theism is evidenced in *Tablets* (Boston: Roberts Brothers, 1868); "Personal Theism: A Conversation," *The Radical* 6 (July 1869): 22-33; "Philosophemes," *Journal of Speculative Philosophy* 7 (January 1873): 46-48, ibid., 9 (January, April and July 1875): 1-16, 190-209, 245-63, and ibid., 15 (January 1881): 84-88; *Table Talk* (Boston: Roberts Brothers, 1877); and Raymond L. Bridgman, ed., *Concord Lectures on Philosophy* Cambridge, Mass.: Moses King, 1883).

Alcott did some of his best writing in characterizing his friends and comtemporaries, as exemplified in *Ralph Waldo Emerson: An Estimate of his Character and Genius* (Boston: Stanley and Usher, 1882); *Sonnets and Canzonets* (Cambridge, Mass.: John Wilson and Son, 1882); *Concord Days* (Boston: Roberts Brothers, 1872); and "The Transcendental Club and *The Dial*," *The Commonwealth* 1 (April 24, 1863). He described his own character in *New Connecticut: An Autobiographical Poem*, 1st ed. (Cambridge, Mass.: John Wilson and Son, 1881), and 2d ed. (Boston: Roberts Brothers, 1887).

The estimate of his contemporaries is an indispensable source for an understanding of Alcott. Most important is the high but not uncritical praise bestowed upon Alcott by his famous fellow Concordians Ralph Waldo Emerson and Henry David Thoreau. Emerson's trenchant comments are found mainly in *The Journals and Miscellaneous Notebooks of Ralph Waldo Emerson*, ed. William H. Gilman et al., 12 volumes completed (Cambridge, Mass.: Harvard University Press, 1960-1977); *The Journals of Ralph Waldo Emerson*, ed. Edward Waldo Emerson and Waldo Emerson Forbes, 10 vols. (Cambridge, Mass.: Riverside Press, 1909-14); *The Letters of Ralph Waldo Emerson*, ed. Ralph Rusk, 6 vols. (New York: Columbia University Press, 1939); *The Correspondence of Emerson and Carlyle*, ed. Joseph Slater (New York: Columbia University Press, 1964); and "Amos Bronson Alcott," *The New American Cyclopaedia*, ed. George Ripley and Charles A. Dana (New York: D. Appleton and Co., 1858), pp. 301-2. Thoreau's characterizations of Alcott are found in *The Writings of Henry David Thoreau*, edited by Bradford Torrey, 20 vols. (Boston: Houghton, Mifflin and Co., 1906); *The Correspondence of Henry David Thoreau*, edited by Walter Harding and Carl Bode (New York: New York University Press, 1958); and *The Familiar Letters of Henry David Thoreau*, edited by Franklin B. Sanborn (Boston: Houghton, Mifflin and Co., 1894).

Other significant comments by contemporaries are those of William Andrus Alcott, especially in "Biography of a Teacher," *American Annals of Education and Instruction* 2 (May 1832): 257-59, and *Recollections of Rambles at the South* (New York: Carlton and Phillips, 1854); Samuel J. May in *Memoir of Samuel J. May*, edited by Thomas J. Mumford (Boston: Roberts

Brothers, 1873); Thomas Wentworth Higginson in *Carlyle's Laugh and Other Surprises* (Boston: Houghton, Mifflin and Co., 1909) and *Contemporaries* (Boston: Houghton, Mifflin and Co., 1900); Denton J. Snider in *The St. Louis Movement* (St. Louis, Mo.: Sigma Publishing Co., 1920) and *A. Writer of Books in His Genesis* (St. Louis, Mo.: Sigma Publishing Co., 1910); Henry C. Brokmeyer in *A Mechanic's Diary*, edited by E. C. Brokmeyer (Washington D. C.: E. C. Brokmeyer, 1910); Fredrika Bremer in *Homes of the New World*, 2 vols. (New York: Harper and Brothers, 1868); and Daniel Ricketson in *Daniel Ricketson and His Friends*, edited by Anna and Walton Ricketson (Boston: Houghton, Mifflin and Co., 1902). Orestes Brownson's perceptive analysis of Alcott's transcendentalism is found in "Alcott on Human Culture," *Boston Quarterly Review* 1 (October 1838): 417-32. Ednah Dow Cheney added her estimate of her lifelong friend in *Reminiscences* (Boston: Lee and Shepard, 1902), *Louisa May Alcott: Her Life, Letters and Journals* (Boston: Little, Brown and Co., 1889), and "Reminiscences of Mr. Alcott's Conversations," *The Open Court* 2 (August 2 and 9, 1888): 1131-33, 1142-44. And Franklin Sanborn and William Torrey Harris confessed their indebtedness in the first biography of Alcott, *A. Bronson Alcott: His Life and Philosophy*, 2 vols. (Boston: Roberts Brothers, 1893).

The overwhelming opinion of Alcott's contemporaries was favorable to him, lauding his breadth of insight, his ability to inspire and uplift, and his power in conversation. But, lacking tangible evidence to support such conclusions, historians of American ideas and literature in the early twentieth century were slow to recognize his significance. Some ignored him. Others, such as Harold C. Goddard ("Transcendentalism" in William P. Trent et al., eds., *The Cambridge History of American Literature*, 4 vols., [New York: G. P. Putnam's Sons, 1917] 1: 337-39), Russell Blankenship (*American Literature as an Expression of the National Mind*, [New York: Henry Holt and Co., 1931], p. 314), and Barrett Wendell (*A Literary History of America* [New York: Charles Scribner's Sons, 1900], p. 339), brushed him aside as an impractical visionary who embodied the useless excesses of transcendentalism and offered nothing worthy of a scholar's attention. One unsympathetic journalist, Edgar Watson Howe, in *Ventures in Common Sense* (New York: Alfred A. Knopf, 1919), labeled Alcott a lazy, despotic, foolish nuisance who should not have been allowed to exist.

In 1927, however, Honoré Willsie Morrow attempted to resurrect Alcott's reputation by examining his educational theories. Her biography, *The Father of Little Women* (Boston: Little, Brown and Co., 1927), though sentimental and inaccurate, at least was based on the manuscripts and initiated a new interest in Alcott and his ideas. Shortly thereafter Austin Warren gave serious attention to the "Concord School of Philosophy" in the *New England Quarterly* 2 (April 1929): 199-233. Hubert Hoeltje provided a brief summary of Alcott's influences in Iowa in "Some Iowa Lectures and Conversations of Amos Bronson Alcott," *Iowa Journal of History and Politics* 29 (July 1931): 375-401. Later Hoeltje's interest extended to the friendship between Alcott and Emerson in *Sheltering Tree* (Durham, N. C.: Duke University Press, 1943). Arthur Christy used Alcott as a prime example of the influence of Oriental literature on American transcendentalism in *The Orient in American Transcendentalism* (New York: Columbia University Press, 1932).

Ten years after the appearance of Morrow's biography, Odell Shepard published his more scholarly *Pedlar's Progress: The Life of Bronson Alcott* (Boston: Little, Brown and Co., 1937). Shepard made extensive use of the manuscript materials and gave full consideration to Alcott's educational ideas, his transcendental philosophy, his reform efforts, and his broad significance in American culture. He failed, however, to provide a solid analysis of the intellectual transformation that made Alcott a transcendentalist. He gave only scanty discussion of Alcott's ideas and experiences after 1860. And he spent undue effort trying to convince his readers that the idealistic Alcott was as representative of America as Henry Ford and Thomas Edison. A better and certainly less effusive analysis of Alcott's educational ideas and practices was provided by Dorothy McCuskey in her excellent *Bronson Alcott: Teacher* (New York: The Macmillan Co., 1940). McCuskey's book superseded George Haefner's *Critical Estimate of the Educational Theories and Practices of A. Bronson Alcott* (New York: Columbia University Press, 1937), which is not based on the manuscript sources although it still offers some valuable insights.

Following the lead of Shepard, Haefner, and McCuskey, several scholars have pointed to Alcott's role as a pioneer educator and have chastised earlier historians of American education for ignoring him. Among them are Edmund G. Berry, "Bronson Alcott" Educational Reformer," *Queen's Quarterly* 52 (Spring 1945): 44-52; John B. Wilson, "Bronson Alcott, Platonist or Pestalozzian?" *School and Society* 81 (February 19, 1955): 49-53; Marjorie Stiem, "The Beginnings of Modern Education: Bronson Alcott," *Peabody Journal of Education* 38 (July 1960): 7-9; and Thomas P. Pietras, "Amos Bronson Alcott: A Transcendental Philosophy of Education," *Educational Theory* 21 (Winter 1971): 105-111. George Hochfield, in his excellent essay on transcendentalism that introduces *Selected Writings of the American Transcendentalists* (New York: New American Library, 1966), concluded that Alcott's educational experiments revealed the inner meaning of transcendentalism as surely as anything written or done during the period. Echoing McCuskey, Hochfield called Alcott the patron saint of American progressive education.

With a renewed appreciation for Alcott's educational contributions came an interest in his child-rearing practices. Sherman Paul examined the symbolic meaning of Alcott's interest in children in "Alcott's Search for the Child," *Boston Public Library Quarterly* 4 (April 1952): 88-96, and Barbara Garlitz placed Alcott in the larger cultural stream of the nineteenth-century celebration of childhood in "The Immortality Ode: Its Cultural Progeny," *Studies in English Literature* 6 (Autumn 1966): 639-49. But the best and most complete study of Alcott's ideas about child rearing and their cultural significance is Charles Strickland's "A Transcendentalist Father: The Child-

Rearing Practices of Bronson Alcott," *Perspectives in American History* 3 (1969): pp. 5-73.

Aside from Alcott's attempts at educational reform, the aspect of his career that has drawn the most attention from historians has been his effort to establish a New Eden at Fruitlands. Early interest in the Fruitlands utopia was sparked by Clara Endicott Sears, who not only published an account of the community consisting largely of previously unpublished documentary material (*Bronson Alcott's Fruitlands* [Boston, Houghton, Mifflin and Co., 1915]) but also preserved the dilapidated farmhouse that had served the Fruitlands family and turned it into a museum. This supplemented the only previous accounts: Louisa May Alcott's fictionalized "Transcendental Wild Oats" in the New York *Independent* (December 1873), Franklin Sanborn's *Bronson Alcott at Alcott House, England, and Fruitlands, New England* (Cedar Rapids, Iowa: The Torch Press, 1908), and a brief sketch by William Alfred Hinds in *American Communities and Cooperative Colonies*, 2d ed. (Chicago: Charles H. Kerr and Co., 1908). The first analytical treatment of Fruitlands was by Odell Shepard in *Pedlar's Progress*. Victor F. Calverton provided a lengthy critique of the community in *Where Angels Dared to Tread* (Indianapolis, Ind.: Bobbs-Merrill Co., 1941). More recent articles include David P. Edgell's "Charles Lane and Fruitlands," *New England Quarterly* 33 (September 1960): 374-77, and Aurele Durocher, "The Story of Fruitlands: Transcendental Wild Oats," *The Michigan Academician* 1 (Spring 1969): 37-45. The most searching recent analysis of the meaning of Fruitlands (although in chapter 7 the present biography takes issue with some of its major points) is Richard Francis, "Circumstances and Salvation: The Ideology of the Fruitlands Utopia," *American Quarterly* 25 (May 1973): 202-34.

Alcott's experiences in the West have received some, but by no means adequate, attention. The best treatment is in Henry Pochmann's *New England Transcendentalism and St. Louis Hegelianism* (Philadelphia: Carl Schurz Memorial Foundation, Inc., 1948), but it deals only with relations between Alcott and the Harris circle. Other efforts, including Hubert Hoeltje's article on Alcott's Iowa conversations, David Mead's "Some Ohio Conversations of Amos Bronson Alcott," *New England Quarterly* 22 (September 1949): 358-72, and *Yankee Eloquence in the Middle West* (East Lansing: Michigan State College Press, 1951), are largely descriptive and make little effort to analyze the cultural meaning of Alcott's Western tours.

The renewal of interest in Alcott following Shepard's work gave rise in the early 1940s to controversy over the question of Alcott's gentility. Frederic Ives Carpenter opened the battle with his "Bronson Alcott: Genteel Transcendentalist," *New England Quarterly* 13 (March 1940): 34-38. Reacting against Shepard, Carpenter blamed Alcott's failure as a thinker and writer on his genteel absolutism, which obviated the self-reliant pragmatism that made transcendentalism so attractive. David Edgell immediately challenged Carpenter in "Bronson Alcott's 'Gentility,'" *New England Quarterly* 13 (December 1940): pp. 699-705, claiming that Alcott was able to balance a concern for tradition with a radical challenge to society and institutions. Alcott's failure, said Edgell, was not his impracticality but his inadequacy of expression. Stow Persons added to Carpenter's description by including Alcott among the foremost examples of nineteenth-century gentility in *The Decline of American Gentility* (New York: Columbia University Press, 1973). But none of these works examines fully the intellectual changes that brought about Alcott's passionate concern for the preservation of values and cultural traditions, or the contradictions in Alcott's thought that made him both radical and genteel at the same time.

Other aspects of Alcott's career have received scant attention. Prior to the present biography no work has examined his connection with the free religious movement. Stow Persons, in *Free Religion: An American Faith* (New Haven, Conn.: Yale University Press, 1947), mentions him only once. No other historian has carefully dealt with Alcott's return to orthodoxy in the 1870s and 1880s. Nor has anyone else analyzed his relationship to reform movements and politics after 1860 and his reaction against evolutionary naturalism. No full treatment of the Concord School of Philosophy yet exists. Aside from contemporary accounts, only two brief articles have described the School: Austin Warren's "The Concord School of Philosophy," *New England Quarterly* 2 (April 1929): pp. 199-233, and Kurt F. Leidecker's "Amos Bronson Alcott and the Concord School of Philosophy," *The Personalist* 23 (July 1952): 242-56.

Among the works of a general nature that have aided in understanding the background and context of Alcott's ideas are Octavius Brooks Frothingham, *Transcendentalism in New England* (New York: G. P. Putnam's Sons, 1976); Paul F. Boller, Jr., *American Transcendentalism, 1830-1860: An Intellectual Inquiry* (New York: G. P. Putnam's Sons, 1974); William R. Hutchison, *The Transcendentalist Ministers* (New Haven, Conn.: Yale University Press, 1959); Clarence Gohdes, *The Periodicals of American Transcendentalism* (Durham, N. C.: Duke University Press, 1931); George Willis Cooke, *An Historical and Biographical Introduction to Accompany 'The Dial'*, 2 vols. (Cleveland, Ohio: Rowfant Club, 1902); Alice Felt Tyler, *Freedom's Ferment* (New York: Harper and Row, 1962); and F. O. Matthiessen, *American Renaissance* (New York: Oxford University Press, 1941). Four anthologies provide a valuable collection of transcendentalist writings and analyses of them: Perry Miller, ed., *The Transcendentalists* (Cambridge, Mass.: Harvard University Press, 1950), and *The American Transcendentalists: Their Prose and Poetry* (Garden City, N. Y.: Doubleday and Co:, 1957); George Hochfield, ed., *Selected Writings of the American Transcendentalists* (New York: New American Library, 1966); and Brian Barbour, ed., *American Transcendentalism: An Anthology of Criticism* (Notre Dame, Ind.: University of Notre Dame Press, 1973) Laurence Buell offers suggestive criticism in *Literary Transcendentalism: Style and Vision in the American Renaissance* (Ithaca, N. Y.: Cornell University Press, 1973), as well as an excellent discussion of Alcott's theory of conversation. Catherine Albanese's *Corresponding Motion:*

Transcendental Religion and the New America (Philadelphia: Temple University Press, 1977) is an illuminating study of the transcendental world view. The tireless work of Kenneth Walter Cameron, as reflected in collections such as *Concord Harvest*, 2 vols. (Hartford, Conn.: Transcendental Books, 1970) and *Emerson, Thoreau and Concord in Early Newspapers* (Hartford, Conn.: Transcendental Books, 1958), has preserved a large number of documents relating to transcendentalism. Joel Myerson has provided similar service in his studies of the transcendentalists such as "'In the Transcendental Emporium': Bronson Alcott's 'Orphic Sayings' in the *Dial*," *English Language Notes* 10 (September 1972): 31-38; "Bronson Alcott's 'Scripture for 1840,'" *Emerson Society Quarterly* 20 (4th Quarter 1974): 236-59; "Additions to Bronson Alcott's Bibliography: Letters and 'Orphic Sayings' in the *Plain Speaker*," *New England Quarterly* 49 (June 1976); 283-92; and "William Harry Harland's 'Bronson Alcott's English Friends,'" *Resources for American Literary Study* 13 (Spring 1978): 24-60.

Other general studies have provided background for the various segments of Alcott's career. Samuel Orcutt's *History of the Town of Wolcott (Connecticut) from 1731 to 1874* (Waterbury, Conn.: American Printing Co., 1874) is a rare source for information on Alcott's home town, and Richard J. Purcell's *Connecticut in Transition, 1775-1818* (Washington, D. C.: American Historical Association, 1918) gives the same for his home state. Sidney Ahlstrom's *Religious History of the American People* (New Haven, Conn.: Yale University Press, 1972) is excellent for the broad religious background out of which Alcott came. William H. Goetzmann's edition *The American Hegelians* (New York: Alfred A. Knopf, 1973) supplements Pochmann's work in understanding Alcott's relationship with the St. Louis group. Paul Russell Anderson's *Platonism in the Midwest* (New York: Temple University Publications, 1963) illustrates the context for Alcott's contacts with Hiram Jones and the Jacksonville Platonists. Several biographies help in appreciating Alcott's relations with his contemporaries. Especially useful are Ralph Rusk's *The Life of Ralph Waldo Emerson* (New York: Charles Scribner's Sons, 1949); Henry Seidel Canby's *Thoreau* (Boston: Houghton, Mifflin and Co., 1939); Louise Hall Tharp, *The Peabody Sisters of Salem* (Boston: Little, Brown and Co., 1950); and Kurt F. Leidecker, *Yankee Teacher: The Life of William Torrey Harris* (New York: Philosophical Library, 1946).

Index